Is economics a science? Donald McCloskey, a leading economist and historian, says Yes, of course. Yes, economics measures and predicts, but – like other sciences – it uses literary methods too. Economists use stories like geologists do, and metaphors like physicists do. The result is that the sciences, economics among them, must be read as "rhetoric," in the ancient and honorable sense of writing with intent.

McCloskey's books *The Rhetoric of Economics* (1985) and *If You're So Smart* (1990) have been widely discussed. In *Knowledge and Persuasion in Economics* he converses with his critics, suggesting that they too can gain from knowing their rhetoric. The humanistic and mathematical approaches to economics, says McCloskey, fit together in a new "interpretive" economics. Along the way he places economics within the sciences, examines the role of mathematics in the field, replies to critics from the left, right, and centre, and shows how economics can take again a leading place in the conversation of humankind. This highly readable book offers an insider's guide to the intersection of economics and philosophy.

Knowledge and persuasion in economics

Knowledge and persuasion in economics

Donald N. McCloskey

CAMBRIDGE
UNIVERSITY PRESS

Published by the Press Syndicate of the University of Cambridge
The Pitt Building, Trumpington Street, Cambridge CB2 1RP
40 West 20th Street, New York, NY 10011–4211, USA
10 Stamford Road, Oakleigh, Melbourne 3166, Australia

© Cambridge University Press 1994

First published 1994

Printed in Great Britain at the University Press, Cambridge

A catalogue record for this book is available from the British Library

Library of Congress cataloguing in publication data

McCloskey, Donald N.
Knowledge and persuasion in economics / Donald N. McCloskey.
   p.   cm.
Includes bibliographical references and index.
ISBN 0 521 43475 0 (hardback). – ISBN 0 521 43603 6 (paperback)
1. Economics. 2. Rhetoric. I. Title.
HB71. M378 1993
330 – dc 20   93–12078 CIP

ISBN 0 521 43475 0 hardback
ISBN 0 521 43603 6 paperback

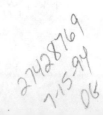

contents

List of figures and tables   *page* ix
Preface   xi
Acknowledgments   xvii

Part I   Exordium   1

1   A positivist youth   3
2   Kicking the dead horse   13

Part II   Narration   25

3   Economics in the human conversation   27
4   The rhetoric of this economics   38

Part III   Division   53

5   The Science word in economics   55
6   Three ways of reading economics to criticize itself   71
7   Popper and Lakatos: thin ways of reading economics   85
8   Thick readings: ethics, economics, sociology,
    and rhetoric   94

Part IV   Proof   109

9   The rise of a scientistic style   111
10   The rhetoric of mathematical formalism: existence
     theorems   127
11   General equilibrium and the rhetorical history
     of formalism   146
12   Blackboard Marxism   155
13   Formalists as poets and politicians   164

Part V   Refutation   179

14   The very idea of epistemology   181
15   The *tu quoque* argument and the claims
     of rationalism   199
16   Armchair philosophy of economics   215
17   Philosophy of science without epistemology:
     the Popperians   236
18   Reactionary modernism: the Rosenberg   247
19   Methodologists of economics, big M and small   265
20   Getting "rhetoric": Mark Blaug and the
     Eleatic Stranger   280
21   Anti-post-pre-metamodernism: the Coats/
     McPherson/Friedman   297
22   Splenetic rationalism, Austrian style   313
23   The economists of ideology: Heilbroner,
     Rossetti, and Mirowksi   324
24   Rhetoric as morally radical   340

Part VI   Peroration   365

25   The economy as a conversation   367
26   The consequences of rhetoric   379

     List of works cited   397
     Index   435

figures and tables

Figure

1 The *A*-Prime, *C*-Prime theorem   *page* 139

Tables

1 The rhetorical tetrad: the four devices   62
2 Persuasion is a quarter of employment   78
3 A Barnes table: the hermeneutics of the
   rhetorical program   286

preface

Economics in its modern and mathematical form has grown into a brilliantly successful science. Unquestionably, it has. Its arguments are for the most part true, and even when they are false they are interesting. Its facts are true and rich and astounding.

People who disbelieve this – which is to say, most intellectuals since about 1880 – have not read enough economics. They imagine that a smattering of Marx will do. The English professor who has neglected Adam Smith and John Stuart Mill, not to speak of Friedman, Galbraith, Samuelson, Hirschman, Heilbroner, Schelling, Coase, Becker, Fogel, Olson, Buchanan, Kirzner, or the other modern masters is missing a lot. He is missing, for example, the logic of unintended consequences. And he is missing the facts of modern economic growth. So I believe, as an economist and economic historian.

Yet the Methodology of economics, its declared theory about theory, is bizarre. Its declarations, if not its practices, lack good reasons. And so the good practices of economics lack rigorous defense. As C. S. Lewis the critic and taleteller put it, "Correct thinking will not make good men of bad ones; but a purely theoretical error may remove checks to evil and deprive good intentions of their natural support" (Lewis 1967, p. 72).

The theoretical error is of long standing. Since 1910 or so Europeans have been depriving themselves of support for good intentions in many places: literature, philosophy, architecture, psychology, painting, politics, and economics (Klamer 1991). The error separated fact and value, advocating a flight from natural language, in a word, "modernism."

"Modernism" had two obverse though connected kinds, joined by their rejection of tradition: "On or about December 1910," said Virginia Woolf in 1924, "human character changed" (Woolf 1924 [1967], p. 320). The one kind, usually called "literary modernism" and instanced by Woolf, Joyce, Picasso, and Stravinsky attacked Science with a big S. It entailed "dislocation of conventional syntax, radical breaches of decorum, disturbance of chronology and spatial order, ambiguity, polysemy, obscurity, mythopoeic allusion, primitivism" (Lodge 1981 [1991], p. 71; see also Kenner 1984 [1989], esp. pp. 34–35). The other, which may be called "architectural" modernism and instanced by Le Corbusier, Mondrian, Russell, and Paul A. Samuelson, worshipped Science with a big S. That is, it simplified conventional syntax, stressed Scientific decorum, elevated chronology and spatial order to mechanical rules, and fled from ambiguity, polysemy, obscurity, mythopoeic allusion, and primitivism.

The two sorts of modernisms were connected as recto and verso. They were formed out of the Truce of Modernism, which in its popular version left a mechanical notion of Science with one half of the culture and a romantic notion of Art with the other half. Both modernisms, as the economist Jack Amariglio has said, were obsessed with transcending time and space (Amariglio 1990, p. 18). Modernism is the elevation of being modern to the acme of creative work; it is the triumph of the avant-garde and the defeat of tradition.

Economics has been much influenced by the architectural sort of modernism. I say at once with a sincerity which has an autobiographical base that architectural modernism – its philosophical version being "positivism" – was a worthwhile and even a noble teaching, from which we, and I, have learned much. But by now we have been to the positivist school and can get back to work, without casting aside what was learned in school. Most economists do not understand that their Methodological theory was never coherent and has now become a bad old relic. They do not understand that in its popular form, unthinkingly applied, positivism conceals what economics does, especially from economists. An economist claiming that she endorses only "Pareto optimal" policies, benefiting everyone (desirable as such policies are when we can get them), has mislaid her wider work of moral philosophy. An economist claiming that he believes only econometrically certified results, exactly identified (satisfying as such results are when we can get them), has mislaid his wider work of quantitative persuasion. Economics after modernism needs a new way of talking about its work. It needs a place to stand from which to look back on its models of international trade and its elasticities of labor supply.

I advocate a "rhetorical turn," such as many other disciplines are taking (J. Nelson *et al.* 1987; Simons 1989, 1990), as part of the neo-pragmatic and meta-modern turning away from modernism. I spend some time here quarreling with the modernist though antique philosophy of science overlaid on economics. Economics fits poorly with the hypothetico-deductive model beloved of young men in the 1940s. In this respect economics is in good company: recent studies of science have found that the model does not fit biology, chemistry, or physics.

We need a new philosophy, or anti-philosophy, to understand economic science as she actually works. The form of anti-philosophy recommended here is the oldest one, "rhetoric." The word "rhetoric" has always had two definitions, the one Platonic and the other Aristotelian, the one mere flattery and cosmetics, the other all "the available means of [uncoerced] persuasion," as Aristotle put it. I use here the Aristotelian definition. Such a definition takes in all of wordcraft, from syllogism to elegant variation, and furnishes a place from which to look back on a scientific language.

As my colleague at Iowa, the historian Jeffrey Cox, puts the matter: we must of course as scholars and scientists ask of a new work what its argument is and what we think about it; but the critical step is to ask *what kind* of argument it is. Does it depend on a metaphor, called perhaps "the model"? Does it gain authority from its style? Does it shape history with a master narrative, suppressing other stories? What kind *is* it? Criticizing economics in the literary sense of "criticism" does not necessarily mean grading or demolishing. A criticism is a reading. Economists would do well to criticize their science by learning how to read it differently.

Other self-conscious readings of science are rhetoric under the skin. The history and sociology of science, and miscellaneous self-reflection of practitioners in structural engineering (Billington 1983), astrophysics (Chandrasekhar 1987), psychology (Mahoney 1976), biology (Levins and Lewontin 1985), design (Tufte 1990, Margolin 1989), and battle history (Keegan 1976, esp. ch. 1 on "the rhetoric of battle history"), to name a few, and reflections on practice itself (Schön, *The Reflective Practitioner* [1983], and before that Michael Polanyi, *Personal Knowledge* 1958 and John Dewey, *The Quest for Certainty* 1929), come to similar conclusions as does a rhetoric of X. The social constructionists in psychology such as Kenneth Gergen or the social epistemologists in philosophy such as Steve Fuller have likewise reinvented the rhetorical wisdom of the Greeks. Economic methodologists themselves, seeking something beyond Popper, have started to ask what kind of arguments economists actually use, and have been giving rhetorical answers.

Most economists seem to have reacted well to the rhetorical turn, understanding that it amounts merely to discussing candidly what we do, namely, persuade. We economists and calculators, if we attend to the departments of communications and literature, linguistics and social psychology, all specializing in persuasion as it is actually accomplished, acquire another way to watch our work. Economists will say: it is mutually advantageous exchange. Yet some economists, especially those who have tasted the Pierian spring of Anglo-American philosophy *circa* 1955, have had doubts, examined here in detail. The details exhibit the death of positivism, the end of ideology, the experiment with mathematics, and the place of rhetoric in the economy itself. In a nutshell, economists can become better by becoming rhetorically self-conscious.

The book originated in controversies about the rhetorical turn with economists and philosophers over the past decade, and especially in controversies about *The Rhetoric of Economics* (1985). The book is therefore controversial in tone. It occasionally uses dialogues, a neglected form of controversial reasoning which was good enough for Plato, Galileo, and Bishop Berkeley. They are named, as Plato's editors had it, for the antagonists.

And of course, as for example in the dialogues, the book "uses rhetoric." But I especially want my economist readers to understand the following point. In italics: *everyone, without exception, "uses rhetoric" in all their verbal or mathematical work, without exception.* Rhetoric is merely speech with designs on the reader. It is as I said "wordcraft." The alternative to rhetoric is catatonic silence, since even a soliloquy has an implied audience of the Prince himself. To repeat: everybody uses rhetoric.

Mathematics, for example, has been rightly described as a language. Therefore in human mouths a mathematics has designs on its readers. A mathematical proof uses rhetoric, which is to say the available means of persuasion in the case at hand. Ask any mathematician on the frontier. The proofs are multiple. A mathematician once collected 367 different ways of proving the Pythagorean Theorem, ranging in style from the clumsy and geometric proof by Pythagoras himself to the elegant and algebraic proof of about the same vintage from China (E. S. Loomis, cited in Tufte 1990, p. 84). The philosopher Imre Lakatos, in the course of showing that a mathematical proof is merely a remark in an ongoing conversation of proofs and refutations, noted that "Many working mathematicians are puzzled about what proofs are for if they do not prove [forever and infallibly and non-rhetorically, by God]. On the one hand they know from experience that proofs are fallible but on the other hand they know from their dogmatist indoctrination that *genuine* proofs must be infallible" (Lakatos 1976, p. 29n). The mathematicians Philip Davis and Reuben Hersh conclude that "the actual daily experience of mathematicians . . . shows that mathematical truth, like other kinds of truth, is fallible and corrigible" (Davis and Hersh 1981, p. 406). They "propose a different task for mathematical philosophy, not to seek indubitable truth, but to give an account of mathematical knowledge as it really is, . . . to . . . account for it as a part of human knowledge in general." They propose, that is, a rhetoric of mathematics (and use the very word in Davis and Hersh 1987).

The choice is not between rhetoric in the history and English departments and non-rhetoric in the math and physics departments. The choice is between being aware or not being aware of the effects of one's speech, whether verbal or mathematical. Let me say it again: *the people like Arjo Klamer, Roy Weintraub, and me who want to see economics as "rhetorical" are not advocating flowery speech or the abandonment of mathematics. We are advocating the study of how economists actually persuade each other and the world.*

I should note that my objections to the walking dead of architectural modernism and its philosophical theory, positivism, are not directly inspired by Continental philosophy, of which I am wholly and shamefully ignorant. But they are consistent with the attempts by English-writing philosophers like Richard Rorty, Stanley Rosen, Stephen Toulmin, and Alasdair MacIntyre to reintroduce the English readers of philosophy to the wider philosophical conversation, from which the English readers in their pride have absented themselves for the better part of a century.

The divisions of the book are the six parts of a speech in classical rhetoric: the Exordium (an appeal to ethos, that is, to the character worthy of belief), the Narration (presenting the facts of the case), the Division (presenting what is to be proven), the Proof (the argument, here by example), the Refutation (dealing with objections, here at length), and the swelling crescendo of the Peroration.

The book follows from *The Rhetoric of Economics* (1985) and *If You're So Smart: The Narrative of Economic Expertise* (1990). The first set economics beside poetry; the second beside fiction. This book sets economics beside philosophy. All three offer literary criticism as the model. This book does not report every single thing that I have ever thought about economic criticism. My thoughts keep stumbling forward, or backward, and I here simply record some of the stumbles. I do not have the wit to repeat without tedium what I said before. The three books – this one, *If You're So Smart*, and *The Rhetoric of Economics* – represent different modes of thinking: philosophical, narrative, and poetic. They are in a manner of speaking one big book (*mega biblion, mega kakon?*) reflecting on how economists argue.

acknowledgments

The chapters here have mostly appeared elsewhere, though it would be an unusually catholic reader who would have come across more than a couple, and all have been modified, some quite heavily. I thank the editors of *American Journal of Agricultural Economics, American Sociologist, Critical Review, Eastern Economic Journal, Economic Notes, Economics and Philosophy, Journal of Economic Psychology, Market Process, Politics and Society, Rethinking Marxism, Review of Radical Political Economy, Review of Social Economy, Ricerche Economiche* for permission to use fragments of essays that appeared first in their pages. Several chapters first appeared in another form in other Cambridge University Press books, namely, Neil de Marchi, ed., *The Popperian Legacy in Economics* (1988) and Arjo Klamer, D. N. McCloskey, and Robert Solow, eds., *The Consequences of Economic Rhetoric* (1988). An early draft of one chapter appeared in Neil de Marchi, ed., *Post-Popperian Methodology and Economics; Recovering Practice* (1992) and an early draft of another in Walter Fisher and Robert Goodman, eds., *Knowledge, Value, and Praxis* (forthcoming).

I have benefited since the beginning of my own rhetorical turn from the atmosphere of the University of Iowa, excellence in a democracy. The University of Iowa's Project on Rhetoric of Inquiry ("Poroi," which is Greek for "ways and means") has since 1980 brought hundreds of professors and others from across the state and the country to examine how the academy persuades. Many of the points I make are lifted unacknowledged from colleagues at Poroi.

I thank Roger Backhouse, Bruce Caldwell, Steve Fuller, Roy Weintraub, and the referees for Cambridge University Press for their comments on drafts, which as they can see have improved the book.

Stephen Ziliak of the University of Iowa and Jean Field of Cambridge University Press copyedited the manuscript with great care and insight. The reader should bless these people.

Arjo Klamer of George Washington University and I have written an elementary economics book together – the academic equivalent of marriage – and have collaborated heavily in thinking about the rhetoric of economics, joint thinking which shows here. A story: Seymour Harris was an economist at Harvard in the 1940s, a more useful man to economics than many who sneered at him for his mere editing of numerous books that mainly others wrote. A smart aleck was asked once whether he knew the books of Seymour Harris. Replied he smirkingly: "*Know* them? Do I *know* them? I *wrote* them." In this book chapters 3, 4, 24, 25, and part of 6 started as collaborations with Klamer and all the rest have benefited from his criticism. Does he know the book of D. N. McCloskey? *Know* it? He *wrote* it.

part I

Exordium

ex OR di um; L. "beginning" . . . The first part of a classical oration. It caught the audience's interest while introducing the subject.

Richard A Lanham, *A Handlist of Rhetorical Terms*, second edition, Berkeley and Los Angeles: University of California Press (1991), p. 49

chapter 1

A positivist youth

In 1964, when social engineering was in its prime, all the best people were positivists, or so a first-year graduate student in economics would naturally have believed. Among philosophers the doctrines of strict positivism were moribund. Philosophical positivism had had its day in the 1920s. One of the headings of Karl Popper's intellectual autobiography, *Unended Quest* (Popper 1974 [1976], pp. 87f) asks "Who Killed Logical Positivism?" He answers, "I fear that I must admit responsibility." I, said the Popper, / With my little chopper, / I killed logical positivism. His book of 1934, written when he was about thirty and translated into English twenty-five years later as *The Logic of Scientific Discovery* (Popper 1934 [1959]), was the knell. Popper quotes the Australian philosopher John Passmore as writing in 1967 that "Logical positivism, then, is dead, or as dead as a philosophical movement ever becomes" (Passmore 1967, p. 56). Even the broader doctrines of logical empiricism under which positivism sheltered had by 1964 been under attack for a long time. W. V. Quine's "Two Dogmas of Empiricism" had in 1951 undermined the distinction inherited from Kant between analytic and synthetic statements. Hilary Putnam dates the reign of positivism from 1930 to about 1960 (Putnam 1990, p. 105). Over in the philosophy department, then, no one earned prestige by declaring himself to be a positivist; not in 1964.

Over in the economics department, however, there was still prestige to be earned by sneering at the soft little qualitative people. No one in economics in 1964 had heard that positivism was dead. Positivism then was the philosophy of the hard-nosed against the soft-headed. The division of "soft" and "hard" was irresistible to a male 22-year-old in 1964. A new graduate student wanted to be hard, of course: that was why one studied economics rather than history or, perish the thought, English. Economists and other academics in the 1960s espoused a positivism notably cruder and more masculinist than the philosophical kind.

The crude version persists. An economist who uses "philosophical" as a cuss word ("That's rather philosophical, don't you think?") and does not regard philosophical argument as relevant to his business will not watch what is going on in the department of philosophy. Even mature economists therefore do not have an occasion to rethink their youthful positivism. Economists young and old still use the positivist way of arguing, against the advice of economists who have paid attention to the history of philosophy since 1955 (Caldwell 1982; Caldwell 1984, 1987; Backhouse 1985, 1988, 1992a). The non-philosophical economists talk about hypotheses, verifiability, observable implications, meaningful statements, science vs. pseudo-science, the unity of sciences, the emulation of physics, the fact/value split, prediction and control, hypothetico-deductive systems, axiomatization, and the formalization of languages. Logical positivism had charmed the young men in philosophy during the 1920s and 1930s. Long dead, it charmed the graduate student in economics of 1964. In zombie form, dead from the neck up, it still charms young men in many fields (the young women find it less attractive).

An article by Milton Friedman in 1953, interpreted as positivism and using the word "positive" throughout, is supposed to be the Torah of economic Method. Daniel Hammond (1990) and Abraham Hirsch and Neil de Marchi (1990) argue persuasively what I from personal acquaintance have long believed – that Friedman is no dogmatic positivist, but a practical arguer, intent on finding scientific agreement. Indeed, Friedman (unlike George Stigler, for example) can be claimed as an early exponent of a pragmatic and rhetorical and (I don't mind saying so) thoroughly American approach to economic discourse. He said recently that "the role of statistics is not to discover truth. The role of statistics is to resolve disagreements among people" (quoted in Hammond 1990, p. 167). In a letter of 1983 he said flatly that "logical positivism and the kind of positivism I favor are wholly different" (Friedman 1983, p. 3).

And yet positivistic sentences from Friedman's pen, contradicting Friedman's practice, provide the philosophy for economics. As the philosopher of economics Daniel Hausman observed, "Friedman's advice has rarely been followed, and to implement it would require that microeconomics be radically transformed. Yet, since Friedman presents his views in defense of theoretical 'business-as-usual' against critics of standard economics, one finds economists espousing Friedman's methodology, who would never dream of seriously acting on it" (Hausman 1992, p. 275). And the Methodologists – economists and philosophers who say they are interested in how economists explain – go over and over the Friedman text, Mishnah-style, seldom getting beyond the terms defined at the height of positivism's prestige. The history and appeal of positivism continues now to be hot news in economics, and was hotter in 1964.

The graduate student at the Harvard of 1964 was typical. I do not want to laugh too harshly at him: people forget that from Olympus we all look pretty funny. And I want to emphasize again that I do not regard positivism as a useless or silly movement. In its day it did good. In 1938 Terence Hutchison argued against the a priorism of the 1920s and 1930s; in 1953 Friedman argued against the refusal to examine facts of the 1940s and 1950s. But its day has passed; its values need scrutiny; it has become an oppressive rather than a liberating force in economics and has become (positively) Stalinist in econo-wannabe fields such as academic accounting and political science.

A young non-philosopher who declared himself to be a positivist in 1964 must be seen as declaring an allegiance vaguely understood. The young are good at vague allegiances (something to be borne in mind when teaching them) but are not so good at the details of doctrine. The young man was beginning in 1964 to stop thinking of himself as a socialist, yet even during his socialist phase had not read much of *Capital* (vol. I), or much else of the doctrine. On the positivist front he seems to have owned a copy of A. J. Ayer's, ed. *Logical Positivism* (1959), but internal evidence suggests that he didn't read it until later, and then never more than a couple of essays. (At the head of the essay by Otto Neurath the young man wrote in pencil: "This paper reeks of metaphysics," which is either a complaint by a naïve positivist against what he imagined was backsliding or an observation by a sophisticated anti-positivist that logical positivism requires metaphysics to live; probably the former.) Like everyone else, he had been charmed by Friedman's article. He thrilled especially to the part about leaves on trees not having to know that they "want" to face towards the sun, and wondered at Hendrick Houthakker's diffident lecture on the matter to the first-year students of price theory at Harvard. A year or so into graduate school, following the economist John R. Meyer, his mentor and a leading young scholar in econometrics and transportation economics, he read some of R. B. Braithwaite's book (1953), and fancied himself advanced about hypothetico-deductive systems in science.

At about the same time, having decided to study economic history, he read Carl Hempel's "The Function of General Laws in History" (1942) and concluded that storytelling could be reduced to model testing. Believing that hypothetico-deductive testing of models covered what was of value in human thought, he tried to force his work on British economic history into the plan. In the margin next to Braithwaite's positivist sneer at "a policy of deep breathing followed by free association" (p. 272) he wrote "*verstehen*," which he understood without inquiry to be the method over in the department of history.

His grasp of the doctrines of the new religion, then, was weak in book learning. Yet one did not need book learning in the mid 1960s to be a thoroughgoing positivist. The intellectual world then was positivist. To take back the earlier point about philosophy being utterly dead in the departments of philosophy, even in philosophy a version of it reigned: "much of the philosophy that succeeded it in the Anglo-American world, though it would disclaim the name, has been and remains thoroughly Positivist in spirit" (Barrett 1979, p. 49). A sense in which the wider world remained positivist was soon to be demonstrated in the Vietnam War: here were social engineers, committed to the observable and the verifiable, armed with falsifiable if loony hypotheses deduced from higher-order propositions and a wide protective belt of rationalization when the dominos did not fall, unencumbered by the value half of the fact/value split, seeking body counts from the gunboats on the Mekong. Positivistic thinking, a popular version of philosophical positivism, pervaded intellectual life from economics to art (see again Klamer 1991).

Amateur positivism fitted the trend of Western philosophy, or at any rate the trend as discerned by the logical positivists themselves, who were the best of the philosophical crop between 1920 and 1940 and were the writers of the books that young men bought and admired. The young man had when in high school in the 1950s browsed on the non-technical works of Bertrand Russell. He picked up Russell's scornful attitude towards the intellectual past, a convenient scorn for a young person to have. Logical positivism was seen by Russell and his fans as a culmination: glorious if muddled Greek beginnings; Christian fall back; then the ascent to Descartes, Hume, Kant, and Bertrand Russell.

Positivism therefore appealed in 1964 to a young man's desire to be up to date. And it was Scientific. A touching faith in what science could do seemed justified: Scientism. Science seemed then, as it still seems to people who do not know economic history, to have been the main engine of economic progress since 1700 (Rosenberg and Bird-zell 1986 and Mokyr 1990 decisively overturn the notion). The history of science had not yet established that the rational reconstructions of which philosophers talked had nothing to do with how science worked (Farley and Geison 1974; Shapin and Schaffer 1985). The philosophers of science had not begun to use Thomas Kuhn (*The Structure of Scientific Revolutions* [1962], of course, but more particularly the case studies in his articles collected in 1977) against Popper (Feyerabend 1975 [1978]; Laudan 1977). A sociology of science that scrutinized laboratory life was still a decade away (Latour and Woolgar 1979; Mulkay 1979). Someone trying to become an economic Scientist around 1964 was going to latch on to a theory of how to be scientific. How do I know what Scientific Economics is? Positivism tells what, in this little book.

Being Scientific means in English being different from the rest of society. Demarcating Science from other thinking was the main project of the positivist movement. The project of demarcation, when you come to think about it, is strange. Perhaps the mixing of the positivistic program of demarcation with the English definition of Science explains why positivism of a sort has stuck to the English-speaking world. English-speaking people even now worry a good deal about whether they are scientific or not – witness the ignorant sneers which non-scientists such as mathematicians and journalists in English-speaking countries direct at social "science." A graduate student in 1964 had a desire to be Scientific, in the English, honorific, lab-coated, hard-nosed, and masculine definition of the word (the desire of students has not changed, although then as now some of them have wise doubts: see Klamer and Colander 1990).

Importantly in 1964, as I have said, the economic scientists whom the graduate student took as models were positivists. I have mentioned the economist John Meyer, whose positivistic work with Alfred Conrad on the economics of slavery and on quantitative economic history had come out as papers a few years before. The graduate student had been a research assistant for Meyer, helping him put the papers with Conrad into *The Economics of Slavery and Other Studies in Econometric History* (Conrad and Meyer 1964), and later he worked on Meyer's projects on the economics of commuter buses and on a simulation model of Colombian transport, meeting there the first-rate engineers, civil and economic, that Meyer had gathered. All the economic historians and engineers he met were positivists, though all more sophisticated about it than the student. "Bliss was it in that dawn to be alive / But to be young [and positive] was very heaven!"

The student soon met his next hero, the economic historian Alexander Gerschenkron, who presided from Harvard over a piece of the new economic history. Gerschenkron, a learned and cagey teacher, a polyglot European and a fan of baseball, gave the young man another example of an admired scholar talking positivism (while doing something else; but the point here is the official doctrine, not the scientific behavior). Near the beginning of Gerschenkron's essay "Economic Backwardness in Historical Perspective" (1952 [1962a], p. 6, my italics]) he declared that "historical research consists essentially in application to *empirical material* of various *sets of empirically derived hypothetical generalizations* and in *testing the closeness of the resulting fit*, in the hope that in this way certain *uniformities*, certain typical situations, and certain *typical relationships among individual factors* in these situations can be ascertained." *Scientor gloriosus.* The sentence has a whiff of Bacon in it, but could pass for the usual positivism of the chair. And elsewhere Gerschenkron said repeatedly that the concept of relative backwardness is "an operationally usable concept" (Gerschenkron 1962b, p. 354).

Avant-gardism, hero worship, being scientific, and joining in the ceremonies of scientism, then, partly explained the student's youthful positivism. Its univocal certitude was half the rest. The longshoreman and sage Eric Hoffer wrote in *The True Believer* that "The effectiveness of a doctrine does not come from its meaning but from its certitude. No doctrine however profound and sublime will be effective unless it is presented as the embodiment of the one and only truth" (Hoffer 1951 [1963], pp. 83f). William James had made a similar point: "I read in an old letter – from a gifted friend who died too young – these words: 'In everything, in science, art, morals and religion, there must be one system that is right and *every* other wrong.' How characteristic of the enthusiasm of a certain stage of youth!" (James 1907 [1949], p. 240). Our fate seems to be to lurch from one dogma to the next, from one univocal certitude to another, because the youngsters like it.

The remaining charm of the dogma was efficiency. Even to a graduate student with a feeble grasp on scholarship it was clear that positivism saved effort. Positivism was economical in ways attractive to the young and impatient. Here was a Method of being an economic historian, for example, that required no tiresome involvement with "all the sources" (as students in the department of history put it so irritatingly). No. You needed merely to form an "observable implication" of your "higher-order hypothesis," then proceed to "test" it. Most of the facts of the matter could be ignored, since most could be construed, if you were dull enough, as not bearing on the hypothesis under test. No tacit knowledge was necessary, no sense of the landscape, no feel for the story.

A young historian of the British steel industry 1870–1914 therefore did not have to learn about what was going on from 1870 to 1914 in the British steel industry, or anywhere else. (He did in fact learn more than was required on positivistic grounds, because he was thrown into a company of historians at the London School of Economics while doing his research, and anyway had a non-positivistic father, also an academic, who from time to time would remark mildly to his technocratic son that one needed to know something in order to write about it.) Nothing could be simpler than the positivistic formula. In fact, nothing was. The proliferation of normal if unpersuasive science in economics has shown how simple it is.

The simplicity of positivism has great appeal to the young. To put the point harshly, positivism is a 3″ × 5″-card philosophy of science, which the young can read in a minute and understand in a day. Once it is understood they can apply it to everything. (For their simple-minded devotion to Method the young should be forgiven. They have few enough weapons against the old.)

Positivism from its beginnings tried to narrow the grounds on which scholars could converse down to the observable, to the numerical, to the non-tacit. Positivism commends intellectual narrowness. The word "positivism" was coined by Auguste Comte early in the nineteenth century, but by century's end the successes of science appeared to warrant another and more rigorous neopositivism. The physicist Ernst Mach, for example, attacked in the 1890s the idea of the electron, calling it a non-observable figment. His slogan was "the observable." A century later the economic slogans with which economists narrow their arguments are similarly unreasonable: "macroeconomics must always be re-expressed as microeconomics"; "no economics unless constrained maximization"; "ethical discussions are meaningless." Positivism is one of the great sloganeering movements, substituting intellectual bumper stickers for thought.

It is like that with movements that young intellectuals find attractive, as Hoffer said. The German classicist Ulrich von Wilamowitz-Moellendorff wrote thus of his own youthful fascination with the Method of his age: "Philology had [in 1870] the highest opinion of itself, because it taught method, and was the only perfect way of teaching it. Method, *via ac ratio*, was the watchword. It seemed the magic art, which opened all closed doors; it was all important; knowledge was a secondary consideration." He remarked fifty years on, "Gradually the unity of science [*Wissenschaft*, "inquiry" in the German] has dawned on me . . . Let each do what he can, . . . and not despise what he himself cannot do" (Wilamowitz-Moellendorff 1928 [1930], p. 115; cf. 1927 [1982], p. 136; *via ac ratio* is "method and theory," literally "the way and the reason," as for example in Cicero, *De Oratore*, I, 205).

The third-year graduate student's attitude towards *via ac ratio* in 1966 is best illustrated by the Churchillian motto he and his colleagues affixed over the doorway of the Economic History Workshop, in the attic of a building just off Harvard Square: "Give us the data and we will finish the job." It seemed clever at the time. Economists need not be concerned with the mundanities of *collecting* the data. (For this reason the student spurned the chance to take courses from Simon Kuznets, the great historical economist who had just come to Harvard from Johns Hopkins. Graduate students, being graduate students, have defective intellectual taste.) And there was of course nothing beyond the easily quantifiable, observable implications to be known from a phenomenon.

By way of contrast consider the eminent biologist, Barbara McClintock, who approached nature with the idea, as Evelyn Fox Keller puts it in her account of McClintock's career, that

> Organisms have a life and an order of their own that scientists can only begin to fathom . . . [McClintock said] "there's no such thing as a central dogma into which everything will fit." . . . The need to "listen to the material" follows from her sense of the order of things . . . [T]he complexity of nature exceeds our own imaginative possibilities . . . Her major criticism of contemporary research is based on what she sees as inadequate humility . . . [The usual] dichotomies of subject–object, mind–matter, feeling–reason, disorder–law . . . are directed towards a cosmic unity typically excluding or devouring one of the other pair.
>
> Keller 1985, pp. 162–163

Perhaps positivism is a male method. The style of empirical inquiry that spends six years on the aberrant pigmentation of a few kernels of corn is rare in economics. Yet no one is surprised to find it disproportionately among female economists: Margaret Reid of Iowa State and Chicago, for example, or Dorothy Brady of Pennsylvania and of the Women's Bureau at the Department of Labor, or Anna Jacobson Schwartz of New York University and the National Bureau of Economic Research; and latterly Francine Blau of Illinois or Claudia Goldin of Harvard. "The thing is dear to you for a period of time; you really [have] an affection for it," said McClintock (Keller 1985, p. 164). What is dear to male economists, by contrast, is the alleged model and the alleged test. "Testing hypotheses," after all, is easier than thinking; and it is a lot easier than making the phenomenon "dear to you for a period of time."

The men (I choose the word carefully) of the seventeenth century were the patriarchs of positivism (see Bordo 1987). The inventors of rationalism in the seventeenth century – Bacon, Descartes, Hobbes, Spinoza – had a paradoxically low opinion of the power of reasoning in human affairs. Ancient and medieval writers had more faith in the power of speech to move people towards the light. The men of the seventeenth century had seen words kill and sought therefore a way to disarm them. Their refuge was "crushing" proof and "compelling" demonstration, to "put Nature to the rack," as Bacon said so sweetly. They assigned everything else, as for example Hobbes did in his book on rhetoric, to mere ornament, suited only to arousing a feminine passion. We have inherited their low opinion of reasoning.

So the young man in 1967, aged twenty-five, now working on his dissertation, was a positivist. Einstein wrote to his friend Michele Angelo Besso about Mach's positivism: "I do not inveigh against Mach's little horse; but you know what I think about it. It cannot give birth to anything living; it can only exterminate harmful vermin" (May 13, 1917; Bernstein 1989, pp. 86f; later he called it "fairly dried-up petty-foggery" [quoted in Lakatos 1976, p. 93n]). That seems about right. Positivism was a reaction to German idealism. Harmful or not, idealism was exterminated in the English-speaking world for half a century. It is coming back as something more grown-up, as pragmatism or rhetoric or other projects after virtue, finding its reality in social discourse rather than in the transcendental spirit or in the datum seen clearly and distinctly by a lone observer.

In the meantime positivism *per se* did not give birth to anything living, at any rate in economics. Our theories of the economy are more numerous and interesting now than in 1955 or 1964 because more people have thought longer and more mathematically and more empirically about the economy, not because of positivism. They are more precise than they were before positivism, and claim to be more observable, at least by a narrow standard of observability. But our living understanding of the economy has not been much advanced by pretending to adhere strictly to a philosophical doctrine. In some brains the result of economic positivism was and is a first approximation to an intellectual lobotomy, as in our graduate student.

chapter 2

Kicking the dead horse

The graduate student became a "Chicago" economist at Harvard, influenced by John Meyer's approach to transportation economics and Peter Temin's pellucid course in economic history up the street at Massachusetts Institute of Technology. In the violent summer of 1968 he began twelve years' teaching at the University of Chicago.

Gradually his student positivism faded. Before Chicago he had spent a year in England working, as I have said, with English economic historians trained more traditionally. At Chicago he attended seminars with historians from the history department and could not shake off the impression that these people, though not following the positivism of economics, were intelligent. He served on committees and played poker with people from other departments in the Division of the Social Sciences. Even anthropologists, sociologists, geographers, and political scientists, it turned out, were not misled dolts. The experience of different ways of knowing made the formulas of positivism seem less convincing.

Such intellectual growth will come as a surprise to people who cannot think of the Chicago School of Economics as anything but the incarnation of evil (such people are surprisingly common, and surprisingly ready to organize necktie parties to give expression to their thoughts; it often develops that they do not know what they are talking about, namely, the Good Old Chicago School of such people as Frank Knight, T. W. Schultz, Margaret Reid, and Ronald Coase). The young professor's experience in dealing with necktie parties of non-Chicago economists increased his doubts that one way of arguing was all there was to scholarly life. His formulaic positivism faded, to be replaced by a confused tolerance when at length the

Method talk of other Chicago economists stopped sounding fresh. The replacement took ten years, because he was not an apt pupil and the environment in economics was hostile to doubt.

At Chicago the positivism was laid on thick, and conversations with the late George Stigler in particular were likely to be terminated by a positivist edict and a sneer. One conversation with Stigler was especially eye opening to an associate professor beginning at last in 1978 to doubt the epistemological claims of positivism. Stigler was holding forth in the bar of the faculty club on the merits of behaviorist theories of voting, in which people are said to vote according to their pocketbooks. His younger colleague, who had just read Brian Barry's devastating attack on such models (Barry 1970 [1978]) and for ten years had been teaching first-year graduate students about the small man in a large market (following Stigler's own exposition in *The Theory of Price*, 1966, appendix B, note 7, p. 342), remarked that people would be irrational to go to the polls in the first place. A single voter has as much to do with the outcome of an election as a single farmer in Hills, Iowa has to do with the price of soybeans. The voter therefore appeared to have shown by entering the voting booth that he was nuts (by an economistic definition of nuttiness), and it would be strange if he voted according to his pocketbook with strict rationality after he closed the curtain. The argument struck a nerve, and Stigler became as was his custom abusively positivistic, declaring loudly that all that mattered were the observable implications.

To the doubting positivist the procedure seemed to throw away some of the evidence we have. Strange: throw away some of the evidence and then proceed to examine the evidence. He noticed, too, that Stigler refused to talk any more about the matter, striding off irritated by the idiocy of the young. By 1978 Milton Friedman had left Chicago for the Hoover Institution at Stanford, Harry Johnson was dead, Robert Fogel was at Harvard, and T. W. Schultz was long retired. The ethics of conversation at Chicago was being governed by Stigler. The doubter, who was now tenured and had no reason to tolerate Stigler's abuse, wondered whether a Method that resulted in such an irrational end to conversation was all it was cracked up to be.

A conversation with Gary Becker a year or so later at the weekly luncheon of the Department disturbed the dogmatic slumber still further. The conversation took place at the cafeteria of the Episcopal Theological Seminary, bordering the Chicago campus. The Chicago economists were talking about the economics of capital punishment (all conversations at Chicago were about economics, which is why it was the best place to be a young economist in the 1970s). Becker was explaining a result from his colleague and student Isaac Erlich that on the evidence of a cross-section of states a single execution appeared to deter seven murderers. The now definitely apostate colleague (he was reading philosophy of science again, starting around 1975 with Popper and the Kuhn of *The Structure of Scientific Revolutions*) remarked that an execution was not the same as murder. He expressed it muddily, because his thinking on the matter was muddy at the time, and Becker may not have followed the point (he was somewhat more open-minded than Stigler on such matters). Execution, the apostate from positivism and utilitarianism meant, is an elevation of the State to life-and-death power, whereas a murder is an individual's act. The two are not morally comparable. It would be like deterring truancy by shooting the parents: shooting would no doubt work, probably in a ratio even higher than seven to one, but would not therefore be morally desirable. Becker got up, annoyed (again that conversation-rupturing feature of positivism). In a positivistic and utilitarian spirit he hustled off with his food tray muttering, "Seven to one! Seven to one!"

And so it went, now quickly. At about this time, as bell-bottom trousers went out of fashion, the former positivist picked up a copy of Feyerabend's *Against Method* (1975 [1978]) at the University of Chicago Bookstore, found Stephen Toulmin's book *The Uses of Argument* (1958) in a New Orleans secondhand shop, and finally in 1980 was asked by a professor in the English department, Wayne Booth, to give a talk on "The Rhetoric of Economics," whatever that was. The invitation probably came on the strength of a reputation for knowing a few more people outside economics than most economists at Chicago did and being marginally less inclined to sneer at non-economists than the rest of the department. The economist hurriedly read Booth's *Modern Dogma and the Rhetoric of Assent* (1974) and Michael Polanyi's *Personal Knowledge* (1962) in his mother-in-law's house in Vermont over Christmas 1979. He gave the lecture in the new year and wondered what he was talking about.

In the spring came the final break with Chicago's version of positivism (but not at all with Chicago economics, whose standing has little to do with positivism; for which see the careers of Knight, Schultz, and Coase). An otherwise excellent graduate student gave a thesis seminar consisting of "observable implications" which massively ignored evidence and reasoning that did not fit into a positivistic mold. Our associate professor, having by this time declared that he was going to leave Chicago, made himself a pain in the neck at the seminar, grilling the candidate and the faculty supervisor on why they did not want to look at all the evidence. It dawned on the ex-positivist that the purpose of a 3″ × 5″-card Methodology (with a big-M, claiming Truth) was after all to make science cheaper, ending arguments before learning anything and restricting empirical studies to the simple bits. Cheap science, an economist would naturally suppose, could not be very good.

Later the other arguments against positivism became important. The thirtysomething professor moved in 1980 to the University of Iowa (just in time for an agricultural depression) and started there with other faculty an interdisciplinary seminar on argument. Argument in general, though attached to a work in a particular field, turns out to be a good subject for bringing people from different fields together, since you can always find professors who want to learn about it elsewhere. The learning is a way to reflect on one's own arguments.

The format imitated conferences in historical economics and workshops in Chicago, and Iowa's famed Writers' Workshop. A faculty member would submit a draft paper, distributed in advance in order to minimize filibustering (the speaker had five minutes to set the scene), and then all the participants, from eventually thirty different departments of the university, worked for two hours offering suggestions for improving it. It was the sort of thing, rare in academic life, that Michael Oakeshott called an "unrehearsed intellectual adventure."

A professor of English cannot help a mathematician on the details of his proof; but he can note the form and the citations, and ask the mathematician to reflect on the role of symmetry and authority in mathematics. The law professor cannot comment with much persuasiveness on the technical details of an economic argument (too often she nonetheless tries), but she can draw attention to its implied audience, and the ethical effects of making such an audience. The background of the seminar, meeting fortnightly all year round from 1980 on, was classical rhetoric, the core of Western education. The Iowans invented what the political scientist and co-leader of the group, John Nelson, dubbed "the rhetoric of inquiry" (J. Nelson *et al.* 1987). The Project on Rhetoric of Inquiry continues, bigger, with book series from Wisconsin and Chicago and with space and a tiny budget, puzzling the coasties and frightening the pigeons.

The Project on Rhetoric of Inquiry ("Poroi," recall, means "ways and means") was an education in intellectual tolerance – not Dr. Feelgood tolerance, live and let live by staying disengaged; more like the tolerance of married people, who must engage but also must keep from sneering at each other. It is the tolerance of a democracy. No wonder it flourishes in democratic Iowa, a state with politics that to a former resident of Massachusetts and Chicago looked in 1980 startlingly civil. Besides a bit of literary criticism and communication studies and philosophical disputation the new Iowan learned in the seminar to think about the rhetorical commitments of democracy.

In the seminar a number of other arguments against positivism came clear. Positivism recommends phenomenalism, that is, looking at the outside of things, behaviorism. One argument against behaviorism is Hannah Arendt's: "The trouble with behaviorism is not that it is false but that it is becoming true." The argument that struck home first, though, is that in a social science, after all, behaviorism is silly, because it throws away the evidence of introspection.

Positivism recommends prediction, that is, judging every theory by its ability to foretell the future. But historical sciences such as paleontology or history itself do not predict.

Positivism recommends parsimony, that is, the merit of simple theories over complex theories. But any theory, however simple on the surface, involves an unbounded set of side conditions for it to apply in any historical case. God finds nothing complicated. We do. What looks parsimonious in 1955 is parsimony only relative to a conceptual scheme. Parsimony is rhetorical, not timeless.

And positivism recommends the unity of science, such as the reduction of all of biology to physics. But the unity of science, nice as it sounds, is pie in the sky, achievable only at the Second Coming. For the present we need to deal with varied conversations.

Finally, positivism, claiming to be independent of culture and history, suited in the end only the culture and history of Mitteleuropa around 1910, Wittgenstein's Vienna. The philosopher Gustav Bergmann, a junior member of the Vienna Circle who lived in Iowa City three houses down the street from the reformed positivist, had brought Vienna to the University of Iowa in the 1930s. Positivism has suited poorly the liberal democracies of the late twentieth century, least of all the mature democracy of Middle America.

In the 1930s positivism had claimed on the contrary to be the very sword and buckler against totalitarianism. The Demarcation Criterion was taken to demarcate civilization from the darkness.

The economist Terence Hutchison, at one time among the most learned students of the discipline, expressed the idea in 1938:

> The most sinister phenomenon of recent decades for the true scientist, and indeed to Western civilization as a whole, may be said to be the growth of Pseudo-Sciences no longer confined to hole-in-corner cranks . . . [Testability is] the only principle or distinction practically adoptable which will keep science separate from pseudo-science.
>
> Hutchison 1938 (1960), pp. 10–11.

Such a rhetoric has been popular since then, with parallels in many fields. Fascism arose, somehow, from Hegel and Nietzsche and even from the anti-fascist Croce. In America it arose, somehow, from the pragmatists in philosophy (Peirce, James, Dewey) or the regionalists in painting (Missouri's Thomas Hart Benton, for example, or Iowa's Grant Wood), both disdained by the European avant-garde. The historian Peter Novick, in his astonishing book on the rhetoric of history in the United States, *That Noble Dream: The "Objectivity Question" and the American Historical Profession* (1988), observes that "as early as 1923 Bertrand Russell [McC: consider the source] had made a connection between the pragmatic theory of truth and rigged trials in the Soviet Union [McC: in 1937, as a matter of fact, the American pragmatist John Dewey chaired a retrial of Trotsky; see Spitzer 1990]. In a 1935 discussion of the ancestry of fascism he made it clear that doubts about the existence of objective truth figured prominently in that genealogy" (Novick 1988, p. 289).

In 1938 Hutchison was attacking of course the pseudoscience of racism. Lately the philosopher of science Alexander Rosenberg has seconded Hutchison's identification of positivism with antifascism (Rosenberg 1992, p. 33). What the latter-day positivists have failed to notice is that the pseudoscience of racism was itself a product of early (neo-)positivism. The political analysis of Hutchison and his genera-tion, echoed in rearguard actions by neo-neopositivists nowadays, was always weak on the evidence, but especially so because the positivists themselves, most prominently the brilliant British statis-tician Karl Pearson, devised the pseudosciences of which Hutchison speaks – eugenics, for example, and racial anthropology, the positive sciences of the extermination camps. Listen to Pearson in the neopositivist bible, *The Grammar of Science* (2nd edn. 1990):

> From a bad stock can come only bad offspring . . . [H]is offspring will still be born with the old taint . . . What we need is a check to the fertility of the inferior stocks, and this can only arise with new social habits and new conceptions of the social and the antisocial in

conduct . . . Now this conclusion of Weismann's [*Essays on Heredity and Kindred Biological Problems,* trans. 1889] – if it be valid, and all we can say at present in that the arguments in favour of it are remarkably strong – radically affects our judgment on the moral conduct of the individual, and on the duties of the state and society towards their degenerate members . . . The "philosophical" method can never lead to a real theory of morals. Strange as it may seem, the laboratory experiments of a biologist may have greater weight than all the theories of the state from Plato to Hegel!

Pearson 1990, pp. 26–28

And later, "It is a false view of human solidarity, which regrets that a capable and stalwart race of white men should advocate replacing a dark-skinned tribe which can neither utilise its land for the full benefit of mankind nor contribute its quota to the common stock of human knowledge" (p. 369). On grounds of cost and benefit he draws back a little from the implications: "This sentence must not be taken to justify a brutalising destruction of human life . . . The anti-social effects of such a mode of accelerating the survival of the fittest may go far to destroy the preponderating fitness of the survivor" (p. 369n). And yet, and yet: "At the same time, there is cause for human satisfaction in the replacement of the aborigines throughout America and Australia by white races of far higher civilisation."

Stephen Jay Gould notes that Pearson's inaugural paper in his new journal *Annals of Eugenics* (1925), an attack on Jewish migration to Britain, met the highest scientific standards of the day, alas (Gould 1984, p. 296). Most scientists were racists, as were most other people before the end. The racist narrative was of course common among educated people from the 1880s to the 1940s. The economist Alfred Marshall, for example, explaining David Ricardo's method (so unEnglish in its abstraction, thought he, Ricardo's ancestors being Sephardic Jews), noted that "Nearly every branch of the Semitic race has had some special genius for dealing with abstraction" (Marshall 1920, p. 761n, appendix B, 5).

Commonplace though they were, it is a mistake to think of such remarks as unscientific or pseudoscientific, that is, as something we can avoid merely by Being Scientific – factual or logical as against metaphorical and narrative. Karl Pearson and Alfred Marshall were among the handful of leading scientists of their generation. Science does not protect us from all nonsense, only some. Science is human speech, too. If we do not realize that science uses metaphors and tells stories now as it did in 1900 and 1938 we are going to do worse than make fools of ourselves. In 1933 the leading British journal of science,

Nature, approved of a new law which "will command the appreciative attention of all who are interested in the controlled and deliberate improvement of human stock" (Mackenzie 1981, p. 44). What new law? That just instituted by the Nazis in Germany to sterilize those suffering from congenital feeblemindedness, manic depressive insanity, schizophrenia, hereditary epilepsy, hereditary St. Vitus' dance, hereditary blindness and deafness, hereditary bodily malformation, and habitual alcoholism.

A day at Auschwitz does not put one in mind of the learned discourses of Hegel or of Nietzsche, least of all the down-to-earth pragmatism of Dewey or James. It puts one in mind of factories and laboratories and record-keeping, the measuring of boiled skulls and the testing of human tolerance for freezing water, gloriously positive science. I am not claiming that positivists are fascists or that science leads to totalitarianism (the eugenicists in Britain, for example, for the most part edged away from Nazi racial theories in the 1930s; Mackenzie 1981, p. 45). I am claiming merely that positivists or the other believers in a religion of Science cannot in all fairness make such charges against everyone they disagree with, as they have a notable tendency to do. It is their commonest rhetorical turn. The trick of charging that anyone who does not agree with a particularly narrow version of French rationalism or British empiricism is an "irrationalist" (Stove 1982) and is therefore in cahoots with Hitler and Mussolini needs to be dropped: it sticks to the bringers of the charge.

It has arisen again in the case of Paul de Man, a Belgian professor of literature at Yale who annoyed cultural conservatives and was therefore vilified after his death by the many profound students of literature at *The New York Times*. De Man in his youth had flirted briefly with fascist ideas of culture in one or two newspaper columns among hundreds he wrote at the height of Hitler's European prestige. The truth about Nazism and the Holocaust is that they came from Western civilization, from its best as from its worst, from academic positivism itself as much as from irrationalism (cf. Bakan 1967, p. 166). The point is one of the proper obsessions of the literary critic George Steiner. In *Language and Silence* he quotes a Jewish victim of the camps noting in wonder that the Germans were highly educated, a people of the book. Steiner comments, "That the book might well be Goethe or Rilke remains a truth so vital yet outrageous that we try to spit it out" (1967 [1982], p. 162). A startlingly high percentage of the officers in the SS had advanced degrees in the humanities. And it was not difficult to find scientists to run experiments in working people to death.

The same is true of the left, with the additional point that the theory of Stalinism was literally old-style positivism, the centralizing rationalism of early nineteenth-century intellectuals, on which the mid-twentieth century paid the interest, compounded. The positivists have long been accustomed to shouting angrily that open discourse leads to totalitarianism. Perhaps their anger assuages a wordless guilt.

Positivism, in other words, claims noisily to contribute to freedom. The apostate from positivism living in hilly Iowa did not observe such results. The observation was sharpened by the atmosphere in some departments at Iowa in the 1980s: during the university's most creative decades, from 1920 to 1940 (when it invented among other things the writer's workshop, the master of arts in performance, the public-opinion survey, the field of speech pathology, the pencil-and-paper test of schoolchildren), it was an important locus for positivism, by way of Bergmann among others, and the old conviction lingered. The memory seemed to make deans and professors more not less intolerant in propping up the ideas they had learned as boys. A few of the deans and professors resembled the sometime chief rabbi of the British Empire, one Hertz, of whom it was said he never used reasoning until he had exhausted violence. The violence with which economists outside the main stream are excluded from the conversation is a less local example (though in economics the National Science Foundation has in fact been tolerant, to its cost). Similarly, a physicist who works on the paranormal (works on it, not believes in it) is instantly ostracized from science (Collins and Pinch 1982). And chemists who have the nerve to call their novel reaction "cold fusion" are crucified by the physicists (Mallove 1991).

A case can be made in fact that positivism is a denial of human freedom, a step beyond freedom and dignity. It is a subordination of individuals to the rare systematic genius. Totalitarianism of the left, I repeat, has its positivistic origins as the science of historical materialism, presented as a plan for history by a few systematic geniuses. Totalitarianism of the right, again, has origins in this or that self-described genius' plan for a racial purity based on Science.

John Ruskin, the nineteenth-century critic of architecture (I do not recommend his views on economics), noted that the search for a crystalline Ideal has been an incubus on classical and Renaissance, and now one may say modernist, architecture. He attacked the tyranny of the lonely genius, seeking by contemplation in his warm room a system to impose upon us all. Of the Renaissance he wrote:

> its main mistake . . . was the unwholesome demand for perfection at any cost . . . Men like Verrocchio and Ghiberti [consider Marx or

Samuelson] were not to be had every day . . . Their strength was
great enough to enable them to join science with invention, method
with emotion, finish with fire . . . Europe saw in them only the
method and the finish. This was new to the minds of men, and they
pursued it to the neglect of everything else. "This," they cried, "we
must have in our work henceforward:" and they were obeyed. The
lower workman secured method and finish, and lost, in exchange
for them, his soul.

> Ruskin 1851–1853 (1890), vol. III, pp. 17–18

Ruskin's argument fits positivism in economics and elsewhere,
which seeks an all-embracing, testable Theory apart from the practical skills of the statesman, of the craftsman, or of the economic
scientist. An "interpretive economics," as Arjo Klamer, Metin Cosgel, and Don Lavoie began to call it at the end of the 1980s, would
turn the other way, as economists already do in practical work (see
Lavoie 1990a, 1990b; Cosgel and Klamer 1990). It is in Ruskin's terms
"Gothic economics," an end to searching for a grail of a unified field
theory, an awakening from Descartes' Dream. As Ruskin said again,

it requires a strong effort of common sense to shake ourselves quit
of all that we have been taught for the last two centuries, and wake
to the perception of a truth . . . : that great art . . . does not say the
same thing over and over again . . . [T]he Gothic spirit . . . not only
dared, but delighted in, the infringement of every servile principle.

> Ruskin 1851–1853 (1890), vol. II, pp. 174, 176

The Gothic spirit is seen in the best works of applied economics,
work from the economic historian Robert Fogel, say, or the agricultural economist Theodore Schultz, work from the financial economist
Robert Shiller or the statistical economist Edward Leamer. It is not
seen in the routine science of the field, servile to the undoubted
genius of Paul Samuelson, Kenneth Arrow, and Lawrence Klein.

Positivism depends on the young man's willingness to enslave
himself to a 3″ × 5″ card, and evokes a corresponding intolerance. A
few years before his death A. J. Ayer, the importer of a simplified
form of Vienna positivism into the English-speaking world, gave a
speech at the University of York on the subject, astonishingly, of
tolerance (it was a series, not his own choice of topic). He of course
used religion as the example of intolerance, as suiting the condition
of the West that positivism helped cure. At the reception after the
talk Ayer was asked if he had been tolerant of non-positivists in the
1930s. He did not seem startled by the question: "No," he said, "I
was not tolerant."

Toleration is not the strong point of positivism. The philosopher

Clark Glymour amused many of his colleagues by beginning his *Theory and Evidence* (1980) with the following *jeu d'esprit*, an example of the openness to ideas in positivist circles: "If it is true that there are but two kinds of people in the world – the logical positivists and the god-damned English professors – then I suppose I am a logical positivist" (Glymour 1980, p. ix). That most English-speaking philosophers find this funny is a measure of how far they have strayed from the love of truth. Another and more tolerant philosopher, Stanley Rosen, noted that "the typical practitioner of analytic philosophy" succumbs "to the temptation of confusing irony for a refutation of opposing views" (Rosen 1980, p. xiii). Hilary Putnam, himself a distinguished analytic philosopher, noted that the way to tell a philosopher with analytic training is to note the sneering tone: his "analytic past shows up in this: when he rejects a philosophical controversy . . . his rejection is expressed in a Carnapian tone of voice – he *scorns* the controversy" (Putnam 1990, p. 20). The Iowa economist, reawakening around 1983 to the humanities, would reply to Glymour: "If there are but two kinds of scholars, and one loftily scornful towards what can be learned from the other, then I suppose I am a god-damned English professor."

Many older economists whom the apostate positivist admired talked in positivist terms – Friedman, Fogel, Schultz, Samuelson, Armen Alchian, Harold Demsetz. All that can be concluded is that it is possible to be a good economist and a poor philosopher. A naïve positivism seems to have given the economists of its generation the strength to carry on. No one should object if a mistaken philosophy makes an economist courageous in collecting facts and bold in thinking thoughts about the economy. The English professors are willing to be more tolerant of the positivists than they were of others.

If some good economists espouse positivism the question arises how economics would be different without it. That remains to be seen, though one thing is clear: economics without positivism would be more, not less, rigorous and scientific, because it would face up to more arguments. An economist without the 3" × 5" card, for example, would take questionnaires more seriously. Nowadays a confused argument that people sometimes, shockingly, do not tell the whole truth suffices to kill questionnaires in economics. An interpretive economist, further, would be more serious about analyzing his introspection. Now the introspection comes in by the back door. He would recognize his metaphors and his stories. Now he calls them models and time series and fancies himself superior to the humanists. He would reassess his devotion to allegedly value-free hypotheses, without abandoning the distinction of fact from value in its modest uses.

Now the values run the wizard's show from behind the curtain. He would be less enamored of utilitarianism. Now utilitarianism seems to most economists to be the same as thinking. He would look at all the evidence. Now his positivism allows him to narrow the evidence to certain mismeasured numbers and certain misspecified techniques. Economics would become less rigidly childish in its method.

The failure of a childish modernism in philosophy, psychology, linguistics, architecture, and economics to achieve its promise does not say it was a bad idea to try. And it certainly does not say that we should abandon fact and logic, plane and cube, and surrender now to the Celtic curve and the irrational. We all cherish what has been learned from the Bauhaus or the Vienna Circle or the running of rats. It says merely that we should now turn back to the work at hand equipped with all the resources of fact, logic, metaphor, and story.

And so the economist went from a thin and positivistic youth to a plump and tolerant middle age. It is the usual progression in body and mind. The Italian Shelley, Giacomo Leopardi, wrote that "it is a bad sign for a man to remain scornful and scrupulous beyond his early youth. Those who do lack either the intelligence or experience necessary for knowing the world; or else they are the kind of fools who scorn others out of excessive self-esteem" (Leopardi 1845 [1984], xxxiii, p. 73).

One might reverse the old calumny on socialism: anyone who is not a scrupulous positivist before age N has no brain; anyone who is still a positivist after age N has no heart. But that is not right. The brain / heart dichotomy is itself a piece of positivism (and, while we're at it, sexism), dividing up the world into what we know and what we feel, science and passion. Positivism is a young man's passion about what he feels positively and what he knows Scientifically. If "youth" could be defined, most charitably I must say, to last until N = the late 30s, our interpretive economist just about made it.

part II

Narration

Narration (L. *narratio*). The second part of a six-part classical oration. It gives the audience the history of the problem.

Lanham, *A Handlist of Rhetorical Terms* (1991), p. 110

chapter 3

Economics in the human conversation

"As civilized human beings," wrote the political philosopher Michael Oakeshott in 1959, "we are the inheritors, neither of an inquiry about ourselves and the world, nor of an accumulating body of information, but of a conversation begun in the primeval forests and extended and made more articulate in the course of centuries" (Oakeshott 1959 [1991], p. 490).

In economics in the late 1980s a conversation about the conversation began. It might be interpreted as just carrying on an old conversation about how economists know (if they do), a methodological conversation started a century and a half ago by John Stuart Mill. The new remark in the conversation of economics was simply that economists use arguments beyond syllogism and measurement, a remark being made at about the same time in dozens of other fields from physics to linguistics. The point of making it was not, say, to undercut the math in economics, as non-mathematicians sometimes wish they could. The point was merely to note that all economists, mathematical or not, use analogies, appeals to authority, and other rhetorical devices, using them as thoroughly as poets and preachers, though with less understanding of why. So the recent conversation about conversation can be interpreted as more of the old stuff, an inward and philosophical affair (as in Blaug 1980; Klant 1984; de Marchi and Blaug 1991).

The new conversation might also be interpreted as arising from the battle of schools, additional looking inward. Disagreements among economists are commonly exaggerated, even by economists themselves. If they think that economics is the only field with long-lasting disagreements they should look at medicine, classics, or paleontology. Yet it is true that the field had become by 1980 more warlike than fifteen years before. Everyone knows about the battle then between Keynesians and monetarists. The other battles – Marxist vs. neoclassical, classical vs. Bayesian, Austrian vs. statist, Chicago vs. the rest of the world – have been more academic, if no less vicious. By 1980 no economist could announce with a straight face that the business cycle was dead, science regnant, justice done. He wondered, what's going on here? In answer the new conversation about the conversation noted merely that the weapons wielded were figures of speech, not strict logic alone; that the older alliance had required stories to keep it together; and that other alliances would require stories of their own.

These interpretations are fine. They go some way towards explaining, internally, why economists have begun a conversation about their conversation. But another interpretation is that the economists have started overhearing other conversations, becoming at last aware of the din outside. After a long and useful isolation, economists have begun to recivilize themselves.

Outsiders are surprised at how far economics since the 1940s has wandered away from the human conversation. The main, neoclassical conversationalists will listen to what is said among a few statisticians and a few electrical engineers; they listen intently to mathematics, when they can catch its drift, hoping to achieve the Parisian accents of Nicholas Bourbaki; they listen to the blare of the newspapers, or at least to the financial pages. But beyond these there is not much listening going on. Economists are deaf to history or philosophy; most of them yawn at geography or psychology; they do not take seriously anthropology or sociology; although they want to speak to law and political science, they do not want to listen. They ignore remoter conversations altogether, and ignore too their own past conversations. The suggestion that the study of literature or communication or even the nonliterary arts might also speak to them would be regarded by many economists as lunacy.

The deaf isolation is a pity, for both outsider and insider. Economics is such a splendid science, such a beautiful model for social thinking, that it is a pity that most non-economists, irritated by the cultural barbarism of its practitioners, write economics off as politically slanted rubbish. They lose a chance to think clearly about economic growth or social justice. The isolation is a pity for economists, too. The conversations outside economics are so varied, so close to life as it is lived, that the economist who writes them off as emotion or nonscience or pictures at an exhibition will lose much. She will lose in fact the same thing the outsiders lose: a chance to think clearly about economic growth or social justice. Much can be gained on both sides from breaking the isolation.

The conversation about conversation has helped break it. Economists have begun to see that their talk is rhetorical – "rhetorical," as I have stressed, in the Aristotelian sense of honest argument directed at an audience. Realizing at last that economics uses more arguments than axiom-and-theorem and data-and-regress, they have begun to listen more intently to arguments elsewhere.

Vogue words like rhetoric, hermeneutics, sociology of knowledge, interpretation, pluralism, pragmatism, and postmodernism may be heard a little these days among the few economists who read the *New York Review of Books*. But the impetus to listen to outsiders comes mainly from non-literary lives:

Frustrated Scientist: I came to economics thinking it would be a Science, like my high-school chemistry. My teachers said so. I liked chemistry because it was more conclusive than the tedious discussions in history or English. As I moved beyond textbook verities in economics, though, I grew discouraged. Seldom is a result replicated (Dewald *et al.* 1986). The classical statistical procedures are violated daily (Tullock 1959; Ohta and Griliches 1976; Denton 1985; McCloskey 1985c). Empirical tests in economics are indecisive, predictions uncertain. I find now that economic seminars have as much inconclusive discussion as history or English did. Controversies in economics seem never to be decided. They just stop, at mutual exhaustion, or move on to some new fashion proclaimed as a "tool." The tools become unusable in a few years. So what is the economic conversation really about? What sort of "knowledge" does it produce? It doesn't look a bit like the Science I signed up for (Mayer 1980).

Once-Positivist Philosopher: My interest in economics is mainly philosophical. I expected economics to be a fulfillment for the social sciences of the positivist program: objective, operational, quantitative, hypothetico-deductive, a chapter in a scientific philosophy, an entry in the international encyclopedia of unified science. The expectation formed in graduate school has been painfully disappointed. I share in part the disappointments of my friend here, the Frustrated Scientist. But after Popper, Toulmin, Kuhn, Lakatos, and Feyerabend (not to speak of Rorty, the wild French and Germans, and the new British sociologists of science) I'm less sure that the Science/Non-Science demarcation is worth much. The search for a demarcation criterion seems to have run out of steam. I grow cynical. Adherence to "knowledge" in economics, then, must be a matter of sheer taste or sheer power, right? Or are there other ways of reestablishing standards, once the old rules, which did not provide standards, though loudly claiming to provide the only ones, go by the board?

Political Economist: You miss the point, which is not to understand history but to change it. In this also there is something wrong with the conversation. It seemed to me in my youth that economics was a tool for social engineering and social betterment. I came to Washington in 1968 filled with enthusiasm for cost-benefit analysis in the Department of Defense and fine tuning in the Federal Reserve System. But I left ten years later depressed. I saw the social engineers propose a dozen different designs for the same bridge. After a while there was a finished bridge, but it went to Nowhere. At last the whole thing fell to pieces in a light wind out of Saudi Arabia. I get no credit here for quick insight, but at least by now I know what the question is: why doesn't social policy work? Sure, sure: the politicians and bureaucrats don't carry it out. But there's something wrong, too, with our conversation as economists if we can't advise them, and each other, in more persuasive ways.

Sophisticated Academic Researcher: Don't give yourself airs. I myself know, roughly, how to write a paper that will get published and keep my salary up. You've been listening to social and scientific visionaries. What's important is to change the way economists argue. I see changes coming in statistical procedures, for example, that will alter the conversation radically. Microcomputers have made simulations possible for the masses. The cheapening of computation has made algorithms more respectable relative to existence theorems. The academic philosophy or public policy doesn't matter: what matters is the next turn in the argument. The old way of arguing will have to move over.

Economic Journalist: The ivory tower speaks. And no one listens. Look: what matters to most people is what comes down from the tower as newsworthy ideas. I once viewed economists either as social weather forecasters or as spokespeople for special interests. So my stories had one of two lines: either the economist is Herr Doctor Professor delivering the genuine Scientific Word or he is just another cheap lobbyist. But I have become aware that such categories do not contain the whole story. Like everybody else the economists try to manipulate the press, but to what end is seldom clear (R. Solow 1981, p. 17). Economists seem to be passionately attached to ideas that can't predict, that can't be proven, that can't be made clear, and that don't even reliably serve the self-interests of the economists advocating them. What's the talk among economists for? Is it just "communicating results" as the rhetoric of Science would imply? I ask again the journalist's question: What's going on here?

There are plenty of others: the Sophomore Student, a wise fool ("Why does economics have to be so far from common sense?"); the Worried Forecaster ("A non-commonsensical science should be able to predict better"); the Rational Expector ("It's common sense that economic science *can't* predict the future"); the Irritated Eleemosynary Executive ("If this stuff isn't predictive science, beyond common sense, what am I giving all this dough for?"). All these too have contributed to the unease. It is the unease that comes in a conversation before people change the subject.

Presumably economic knowledge is manufactured in the 15,000 or so articles catalogued annually in the *Index of Economics Articles*. Economics is a field of articles rather than of books, although less so than physics, its model beloved from afar (very far). Most of the articles present a fact or two, suggest an easy tool. Probably most of the articles, as is said to be the case in the physical and biological sciences, turn out in the long run to be mistaken or, most commonly, irrelevant. Only a few have influence.

The articles pose the puzzle of what constitutes economic Knowledge, the puzzle of publication. Even the most influential articles are puzzling. In Gary Becker's article on "A Theory of the Allocation of Time" (1965) the Knowledge is presented in the rhetoric of the hypothetico-deductive model of science ("little systematic testing of the theory has been attempted . . . The theory has many interesting . . . implications about empirical phenomena"), but it looks more like a metaphor, an analogy between budgets of income and budgets of hours. In Robert Lucas' article on "Some International Evidence on Output-Inflation Tradeoffs" (1973) the Knowledge is presented in the rhetoric of the Empirical Finding, but looks more like a reading of history, one of many possible readings permitted by the data. One wonders whether economists could agree on what constituted the remarkableness of these remarks in the scientific conversation. And for more routine articles the puzzle is more puzzling. T. F. Cooley and S. F. LeRoy have showed that prior convictions about monetarism as against Keynesianism have large effects on the *econometric* results of the normal science they studied (1981). What would be the point of publishing one's prior convictions dressed up as "findings"?

Or consider another literature of economics, the textbook, and another forum, the classroom. These pose the puzzle of teaching. The textbooks are usually written in the same fiercely scientistic rhetoric as the articles. But when the professor faces the class she must compromise with human speech. An economist cannot teach successfully with axiom and finding. Those who try to do so get low ratings, except from the math majors, who miss the main point anyway. The students do not learn how to reason economically. If axiom and finding constitute economic Knowledge why is it so disastrously dull and ineffective to rely on them exclusively in the classroom? Important knowledge is interesting. Professors of economics say they want to teach students how to think like economists. But the professors, in love with Being Scientific, do not reveal to their students the pragmatics of the trade. Such is the puzzle of teaching.

Or consider the academic seminars or coffee rooms, away from the students, the puzzle of scientific doubt. Economists will often express doubt that a properly scientific finding in economics is true: "Sure, his *t*-statistics are fine, but I just don't believe it." Such doubt plays a role in other sciences, too. The failure to agree is not scandalously unscientific, though economists think so, and mope around the faculty club depressed by the unScientific character of their field. Economists have no rhetoric beyond the grunt of disbelief for articulating most doubt, and have a rhetoric of assent that in its imprecision would embarrass a fashion reporter for *Vogue:* "deep," "interesting," "rigorous." When they discuss hiring another economist they have no way of talking rationally about the work, and can only sneer or emote, which opens the door to intellectual and political thuggery. The rhetorical situation is demoralizing. An economist asked why he goes on writing normal science he himself considers unpersuasive will say with unethical cynicism, "I don't really *believe* it: I do it just for fun.'

There is an opposite puzzle, too, of scientific dogma. Economists march to and fro under different banners, raising huzzahs for different candidates for the Nobel Prize. Party loyalty provides a career. The young upwardly mobile indoctrinated economist (a

YUMIE) always votes at his party's call and never thinks of thinking for himself at all. Yet the existence of schools fits poorly with the received theory of science. The theory most economists espouse says that "findings" will "falsify" the "observable hypothesis derived from higher-order hypotheses" and then of course everyone will change his mind. But nobody changes his mind. The number of economists who have abandoned a hypothesis and have admitted so in public is close to zero. But that turns out to be true also of the Science that economists think they are emulating.

The economists, I would suggest, may be looking in the wrong direction; or, to put it better, listening to the wrong words. The notion of Knowledge has long been influenced by a metaphor of seeing. The metaphor has a long history of mischief. Since Descartes and the New Scientists of the seventeenth century we have spoken habitually of the known as "seen" (Rorty 1979; though the primacy of seeing over mere hearing or opinion is clear, evident, apparent, conspicuous in ancient Greek). I see what you mean. Seeing is believing. Scientific reflection is said to be a mirror of nature, to replace the mirrors distorted by men's idols. As Bacon wrote in 1620: "the minds of men are strangely possessed and beset, so that there is no true or even surface left to reflect the genuine ray of things" (Bacon 1620 [1965], p. 317).

This reflecting the genuine ray of things, however, seems lonely and pallid. It does not appear promising as a foundation for thought. As "hermeneutics" (that is, text-understanding) puts it, the seeing metaphor is specific to a culture and language, not written in the heavens. Thus "seeing" = "knowing" = "loving" in biblical Hebrew. The lonely and anti-social character of "seeing" shows in the Attic Greek distinction between verbs of eye-witnessing or ear-witnessing (that is, verbs of actually knowing) as against lower-status verbs of saying or merely socially, humanly, temporarily believing. The one took a participle in indirect speech, the other, like the Latin and later Greek usage, an infinitive. The grammatical distinction in Greek between witnessing and merely believing, between Knowing and knowing, first exploited by Plato, has persisted in philosophy.

A student can by himself *see* with his mind's eye the proof of the irrationality of the square root of 2. But if another person is to believe the proof, after all, there must be communication, some speech. There must be a sender/encoder sending a message to a receiver/decoder. It is not enough to point wordlessly at the sheer message, mirrored from nature. The rhetoric of experiment in the seventeenth century tried to enact mere wordless seeing. But it is a false rhetoric. The positivist model of scholarship cuts out the sender and the receiver as irrelevant to Knowledge. The Knowledge claimed is asocial, solipsistic (Latin *solus ipse*: oneself alone), as Descartes demanded. Yet Knowledge without human speech is merely an ideal type in the mind of God, or of the godlike mathematician inarticulate at his desk. Real knowledge entails communication.

To put it another way, the better metaphors for communication and for knowledge are speaking and listening in a group, not seeing by oneself. One really sees the painting *Work* by Ford Maddox Brown in the City Art Gallery of Manchester by conversing, literally or figuratively, with others, among them Brown himself through his elaborate seeing notes displayed below the picture; or with Victorian notions of the character revealed in the faces; or with historians of art; or with the person standing there beside.

Listen to Rom Harré, a student of science, speaking in the style of Oakeshott and his "conversation of mankind": "All our actions. . . are creating a kind of conversation, an endless conversation into which individuals enter, make their contribution to the common discourse, and eventually fall silent, though some may go on contributing to the conversations of mankind long after they are dead, by writing books" (quoted in J. Miller 1983, p. 159). Or Alasdair MacIntyre, a philosopher: "Conversation is so all-pervasive a feature of the human world that it tends to escape philosophical attention. Yet remove conversation from human life and what would it be? . . . For conversation, understood widely enough, is the form of human transactions in general" (MacIntyre 1981, p. 197).

The way things are communicated does matter in economics. The mere idea that "people are paid what they are worth," for example, can be uttered in various languages, resulting in different economics. Uttered in the language of historical relations and moral indignation it is a statement in classical Marxism, comforting to would-be commissars. Uttered in the language of evolution and competition it is a statement in social Darwinism, comforting to the country club. Uttered in the language of continuous mathematics it becomes the "marginal productivity" discussed by economics since 1900, carrying with it a rich set of images about "production functions" and "amounts" of labor. Uttered again in the language of discrete mathematics it becomes a branch of a new Marxist economics in the 1960s or the linear programming of the 1950s. Uttered in the language of production management, and embodied in a good novel, it becomes a fashion among American businesspeople (Goldratt and

Cox 1986). These all contain one might say "the same basic idea" (all ideas are "basic" when one is making such a point). And so it may be the same, crudely speaking. But the way of speaking modifies the idea, reversing for instance its political uses. "Marginal productivity" can justify a stony *laissez faire*; "to each according to his need" can justify a revolutionary slaughter. A disorder in communication, I am suggesting, explains the unhappy mood of economics (cf. Klamer and Leonard 1993). The problem is not in private seeing but in social communicating, for knowledge is social.

The analogy I have been using of "sender" and "receiver," though, which is what springs to mind when people start talking about "communication problems," oversimplifies the situation, making it sound like a job for the repairman. In most communication the message is not a preformed slug, a mere telephone number to be read out by a computer at Directory Inquiries (once named "Information"). Commonly the message is changed by the demands of the communication – which is to say, the presence and character of the audience, the attitudes of audience and speaker to each other, the language spoken in common, the style of the customary medium, the history of earlier and similar talk, the practical purpose to be achieved from the communication. They do not always "distort" it (the metaphor of distortion assumes again that the preformed slug sits there ready to be found). Saying "Too high a tax rate will bring in less revenue" to an audience of students in a price-theory course makes merely a routine point about supply and demand; saying the same thing to an audience of voters in 1980 makes the Reagan Revolution. The demands of communication change the message. Commonly, in other words, there is no "it" to be communicated without communication.

We need some other theory of scientific communication for economics. The sender / receiver metaphor, though an improvement on the metaphor of merely "seeing" the message without transmission, suggests that anything aside from the message slug is noise. The theory needs to be richer than a signal / noise ratio. The use of a certain kind of mathematical language in describing, say, the reward for labor will send along its own substantive message. What's sent is not mere prettiness (although prettiness communicates, too).

The other theory is rhetoric. Rhetoric is not what is left over after logic and evidence have done their work (so John Davis [1990b] and Peter Munz [1990]). It is the whole art of argument, from syllogism to sneer. Nor is rhetoric an ornament added on after the substance has been written. The very distinction between form and substance is a modern myth, useful as myths sometimes are, but not to be elevated to a plan for the universe.

The point of talking about this "rhetoric" is to make available to economists again another river of our civilization, descending as most do from the mountains of Greece. It is the river navigated by the sophist Protagoras of Abdera and the philosopher Aristotle of Stagirus concerning orations, persuasion, poetry, symbolism, story-telling, and literature in general. It is the thinking of lawyers and of . literary intellectuals.

If economists were to consider the matter they would probably view themselves as paddlers on the mathematical river of Pythagoras or the philosophical river of Plato or the scientific one of Aristotle. (Although while I am on the subject it might be noted that they in fact spend more time than they realize on the historical river of Thucydides.) Anyway, the economists would do better than at present if they listened even to the Greeks they honor. Keynes and Edgeworth and Mill among economic intellectuals had the advantage that they could read the classical languages with ease, and did.

The lines of argument invented by Plato and refined by Descartes, Kant, Frege, and Russell, however, once dominant in the conversation, have recently come to seem unpersuasive. They are being replaced by rhetorical appeals from Aristotle, Cicero, and Quintilian. The new rhetoric has been attended to by an audience of philosophers (Toulmin 1958; Rosen 1980; Madison 1982; A. O. Rorty 1983; Walton 1985), rhetoricians (Scott 1967; Lyne and McGee 1987), teachers of writing and literature (Lanham, 1976, 1991, 1992), academic lawyers (Perelman and Olbrechts-Tyteca 1958; J. B. White 1984, 1985a, 1985b), anthropologists (Rosaldo 1987; Geertz 1988; Clifford and Marcus 1986), theologians (Ball 1985; Klemm 1987), literary critics (Fish 1980; Booth 1974; Burke 1950 [1969]; Richards 1936), political scientists (J. Nelson 1983; Boynton 1989, 1990), planners (Throgmorton 1993), sociologists (Brown 1977, 1987, 1989; Hunter 1990), psychologists (Gergen and Gergen 1980; Billig 1987), students of management (Czarníawska-Joerges 1992, 1993), general historians (H. White 1973; Megill and McCloskey 1987), historians of science (Finocchiaro 1980; Bazerman 1988; Pera and Shea 1991; Gal 1992; Feldhay 1992), and even mathematicians (P. J. Davis and Hersh 1981). These people have noticed that scientists and scholars use analogies, tell stories, adopt a persona.

Economists should join the conversation. The new conversation encompasses the logic of inquiry (which does not yield good science) with a rhetoric of inquiry. Rhetoric in the broad definition given to it here, as the art of argument, already includes what is presently called "logic." The logic is often a routine and minor part, even in regions of the conversation allegedly dominated by it, such as high theory in economics. The poet and classicist A. E. Housman noted of textual criticism that "accuracy is a duty, not a virtue"; in mathematics, too, logic is a duty, not a virtue. The mathematical idea is the virtue.

But in any event the old talk about the context of justification, the criteria for Truth, the logic of explanation, and the rational reconstruction of research programs is to be expanded into talk about genres, arguments, metaphors, implied authors, and domains of discourse. The point is to figure out why some arguments work in economics and others do not, by reentering the human conversation.

chapter 4

The rhetoric of this economics

In the opening scene of the movie *The Graduate* a Mr. McGuire puts an avuncular arm around the Dustin Hoffman character and says, "I just want to say one word to you. Just one word." Yes, sir? "Are you listening?" Yes, I am. "Plastics." [Pause] Exactly how do you mean it? "There's a great future in plastics. Think about it. Will you think about it?" Yes, I will. "Enough said: that's a deal."

So nowadays the avuncular word to the wise is "rhetoric." There's a great future in rhetoric. Furthermore, unlike plastics, rhetoric has also had a great past, the twenty centuries during which it was the educator of the young and the theory of speech in the West – as the classicist Werner Jaeger called it, "the first humanism," the "rhetorical paideia." The three and a half centuries of modernity since Bacon and Descartes have been in this respect an interlude. "We are still bemused," notes Richard Lanham the historian of rhetoric, "by the 300 years of Great Newtonian Simplification which made 'rhetoric' a dirty word, but we are beginning to outgrow it" (forthcoming, ch. 2, p. 27; cf. Lanham 1992). British empiricism and French rationalism have had a long and glorious run. The revival of rhetoric has been explicit since the 1960s in the study of literature and speech. But a sense of how to do things with words has spread now to other inquiries, to philosophers ruminating on speech acts or linguists on the pragmatics of conversation.

Rhetoric in the late twentieth century has had to be reinvented in ignorance of its past. Yet the mathematician who reflects on the standard of proof in topology or the economist who notes that the Federal Reserve Board is a speaker with intent or the political scientist who wonders amidst his regression equations if politics should after all be reduced to public opinion polls (Barry 1965; J. Nelson 1983) are practicing rhetoric. When they reflect on their reflections they are practicing, to say just three words to you again – are you listening? – the "rhetoric of inquiry."

When Kenneth Arrow was asked by George Feiwel what criteria he uses to judge competing theories in economics he answered:

> Persuasiveness. Does it correspond to our understanding of the economic world? I think it foolish to say that we rely on hard empirical evidence completely. A very important part of it is just our perception of the economic world. If you find a new concept, the question is, does it illuminate your perception? Do you feel you understand what is going on in everyday life? Of course, whether it fits empirical and other tests is also important.
>
> Feiwel 1987, p. 242

Surprisingly the passage is quoted by Mark Blaug as demonstrating that Arrow is a Lakatosian (Blaug 1991, p. 505). Its prose meaning, though, is that Arrow, like us all, is a rhetorician. He seeks persuasion, through introspection, through a sense of the social world, and through fully identified best linear unbiased econometric tests, too.

The very word "rhetoric," though, makes it hard for moderns to understand what they are talking about. Like "anarchism" taken to be bomb-throwing or "pragmatism" taken to be unprincipled horse trading, rhetoric is a noble word fallen on bad times.

Rhetoric has since the beginning been defined in two ways, as I have said, one narrow and the other broad. The narrow definition is Plato's, made popular in the nineteenth century by the Romantic elevation of sincerity to the chief virtue. "Rhetoric" in the Platonic definition is cosmetic, hiding a disease under paint rather than providing a cure. Journalists use the cosmetic definition in their news stories and philosophers use it in their seminars. When the newspapers want to speak of obscuring blather and thirty-second spots on flag burning they write "Senate Campaign Mired in Rhetoric." The philosophy seminar uses the word "rhetoric" to characterize the meretricious ornament obscuring the clear and distinct idea. Thus even W. V. Quine, in an untutored entry for "Rhetoric" in his personal dictionary of philosophy, calls it "the rallying point for advertisers, trial lawyers, politicians, and debating teams" (Quine 1987, p. 183), without noticing that even in such a sneering and Platonic definition it is the rallying point also for philosophers.

In Plato's language "rhetoric" is associated especially with democratic institutions, such as assemblies or law courts, disdained by men of taste. "You attempt to refute me," says Socrates in the *Gorgias*, "in a rhetorical fashion, as they understand refuting in the law courts . . . But this sort of refutation is quite useless for getting at the truth." Or in the *Phaedrus*, "he who is to be a competent rhetorician need have nothing at all to do, they say, with truth in considering things which are just or good, or men who are so, whether by nature or by education. For in the courts, they say, nobody cares for truth about these matters, but for what is convincing" (*Gorgias*, 471e and *Phaedrus* 272d). Compare *Gorgias* 473e-474a: "Polus, I am not one of your statesmen. . . The many I dismiss" (cf. 471e; 502e on rhetoric as mere flattery); and *Phaedrus*, 260a, 275e, 277e, 267a-b, 261c-d, 262c, among other places where Plato expresses his contempt for law courts and democratic assemblies as against those who know. The attack on rhetoric has more than a little anti-democratic coloring.

If rhetoric is defined thus as ornament it is easily left to the "god-damned English professors" or advertising flacks. The setting aside began with Peter Ramus in the sixteenth century, who disastrously reaffirmed the Platonic separation of mere ornament from deep philosophy. As Lanham notes, "If you separate the discipline of discourse into essence and ornament, into philosophy and rhetoric, and make each a separate discipline, it makes them easier to think about. Thus begins modern inquiry's long history of looking for its lost keys not where it lost them but under the lamppost, where they are easier to find" (ch. 7, pp. 6–7). Another professor of English has warned against sneering at the "mere" rhetoric: we must "ward off the sensation that words are nothing but words when they are actually among our most substantial collective realities" (Petrey 1990, p. 37). Our politics, for example, is a set of speech acts and speeches about speech acts, and is easily corrupted by bad rhetoric. "We are only men," wrote Montaigne, "and we only hold one to the other by our word." (I:9).

The other, broad definition of rhetoric is Aristotle's, in *The Rhetoric*, I. II. 1 (to quote the Kennedy translation), "an ability, in each [particular case], to see the available means of persuasion." Of course the Greeks, ever talkers and fighters, distinguished sharply between persuasion (*peitho*) and violence (*bia*), an opposition finely discussed by Kirby (1990). Their literature is filled with speeches of persuasion weighing against the violent alternative. King Priam of Troy, prostrate before Achilles, pleads eloquently for the body of his son, linking in his final words the instruments of persuasion and of violence: "I put my lips to the hands of the man who has killed my children" (Homer, *Iliad* XXIV, line 506). The Athenians at the height of success in the Peloponnesian War sneer at "a great mass of words that nobody would believe," mere rhetoric. They tell the Melians, their victims, that as a matter of realism in foreign policy – compare the rhetoric of Henry Kissinger and the 1960s movement to "realism" in international relations – "the standard of justice depends on the equality of power to compel" (Thucydides, V, 89). The Athenians proceed to kill all the men and sell the women and children into slavery, an abandonment of sweet persuasion they live to regret.

All that moves without violence, then, is persuasion, *peitho*, the realm of rhetoric, unforced agreement, mutually advantageous intellectual exchange. It would therefore include logic and fact as much as metaphor and story. "Logic," as logicians have been making steadily clearer in the century past, is not an unargued realm. Logic can be Aristotelian, scholastic, first-order predicate, deontic, modal, relevant, multivalued, informal, intensional, counterfactual, epistemic, paraconsistent, relevant entailment, fuzzy, and so on and so forth through the various ways that people can formalize what they are saying. The linguist and logician James D. McCawley says that "only through arrogance or ignorance do logicians palm off any single full system of logic as unchallengeable" (McCawley 1990, p. 378). Likewise "fact" is not to be determined merely by kicking stones or knocking tables. That a fact is a fact relative only to a conceptual scheme is no longer controversial, if it ever was. Kant knew it; so should we. Studies of science over the past few decades have shown repeatedly that facts are constructed by words.

There is nothing shameful in this logic and fact of scientific rhetoric. As Niels Bohr said, "It is wrong to think that the task of physics is to find out how nature is. Physics concerns what we can say about nature . . . We are suspended in language . . . The word 'reality' is also a word, a word which we must learn to use correctly" (Moore 1966 [1985], p. 406; but not all people are gifted at every part of argument; Bohr, gifted at metaphor, could not follow the plots of his beloved movie westerns, and would bring someone along to whisper explanations in his ear). And Heisenberg: "Natural science does not simply describe and explain nature; it is part of the interplay between nature and ourselves: it describes nature as exposed to our method of questioning" (1959, quoted in Berger 1985, p. 176). That is to say, appeals to experimental finding are as much a part of a broad-church definition of rhetoric as are appeals to the good character of the speaker. Mill's logic of strict implication is as much rhetoric as is the anaphora of Whitman's poetry. Wittgenstein says, "Uttering a word is like striking a note on the keyboard of the imagination" (1945 [1958], p. 4). In this definition a science as much as a literature has a "rhetoric."

When economists look at something, say childcare, they think of markets. "Childcare" – which to other people looks like a piece of social control, or a set of buildings, or a problem in social work – looks to economists like a stock certificate traded on the New York exchange. By this choice of metaphor they are driven to identify a demand curve, a supply curve, and a price. If the economists are of the mainstream, neoclassical kind they will see "rational" behavior in such a market; if they are Marxist or institutionalist or Austrian economists they will see somewhat differently. But in any case the seeing will seem to them to make ordinary sense, to be the way things really truly are.

A rhetorician, however, notes that the "market" is "just" a figure of speech. Yet a serious rhetorician, or a serious philosopher of science, will not add the "just," because metaphor is a serious figure of argument. Noting the metaphors is not merely another way of saying that economics is approximate and unperfected. Economists believe that metaphor comes from the fuzzy, humanistic side of the modernist world. A model in economics comes to be called a metaphor, in this way of thinking, if "the statement can be tested only approximately" (thus David Gordon 1991). But the inverse square law of gravitational attraction is also a metaphor; so is Einstein's generalization. It is well known that the Romantics assigned metaphor to the realm of art, distinguishing an imaginative from a scientific faculty, as though different organs of the brain. The literary critic Francis McGrath has argued that the distinction cannot be sustained (McGrath 1985). Boyle's Law shares metaphor with Shakespeare's 73rd sonnet: metaphor, McGrath argues, is as fundamental to science as to art.

Models are metaphors, that is all. So in other fields: "the mechanistic, . . . the organismic, the marketplace, the dramaturgical, and the rule-following metaphors have all played a significant role in psychological research of the past decades" (Gergen 1986, p. 146). "The market" is a commonplace, a *locus communis*, a *topos* – a place where economists work. The rhetorician's metaphor here is locational. In the rhetorical way of talking since the Greeks the metaphor of a "conversation" is a *topos* for the language game across the playing fields of economics (Klamer and Leonard 1993 explore metaphors in economics more thoroughly, with reference to the now-large philosophical literature; and see McCloskey 1985a).

The conversational figure of speech suggests the Similarity Argument: that the economic conversation shares many features with other conversations differently placed. Any scientific conversation has much in common with, say, poetic conversation, as is demonstrable in detail beyond rational patience. The linguist Solomon Marcus listed fully fifty-two alleged differences between scientific and poetic communication (rational vs. emotional; explicable vs. ineffable; and so forth), and after much thought rejected them all as crudities (Marcus 1974). He noted that there is as much variation within scientific and poetic communication as between them.

The attempts to distinguish the artistic and scientific uses of metaphor presume that the categories of European thought around 1860 cut the universe at its joints. The English professor Richard Lanham argues at length that "nothing but confusion has ever come from the effort to fix the poetry–prose boundary" (Lanham 1974, p. 65). Attempts to distinguish art and science do not seem to work, though from the best workers. Thomas Kuhn, for example, noting truly that "we have only begun to discover the benefits of seeing science and art as one" (1977, p. 343), nonetheless attempts a distinction. He argues that beauty in science (a differential equation with startlingly simple solutions, say) is an input into the solution of a technical problem, whereas in art the solution of a technical problem (contrapposto in representing a standing figure, say) is an input into the beauty. But at different levels of the art and science different work will be done. An economic scientist will work like an artist at a technical problem to achieve beauty; but then the beauty at another level will work to solve a technical problem. One might stand better amazed, as a physicist famously did of mathematics, about the unreasonable effectiveness of aesthetic standards in science. The physicist Tullio Regge remarked to Primo Levi, the chemist and writer, "I liked the sentence in which you say that the periodic table is poetry, and besides it even rhymes" (Levi and Regge 1992, p. 9). Levi responded, "The expression is paradoxical, but the rhymes are actually there . . . To discern or create a symmetry, 'put something in its proper place,' is a mental adventure common to the poet and the scientist" (pp. 9–10).

The one distinction between art and science of which Kuhn half persuades me is that art continues to converse with dead artists. Physicists, notoriously, do not work in the past of their discipline. And yet: biologists are still conversing with Darwin, economists with Adam Smith. Even this most persuasive demarcation seems fuzzy and useless. One can ask of the cleverest of demarcation criteria, so what? In many of the activities of artists and scientists you can see and use the overlap. What is the corresponding usefulness of demarcating science from art?

Logic, for example, is by no means the sole preserve of calculators. The English Metaphysical poets of the seventeenth century were addicted to logical forms, forms that were viewed as figures of speech by writers still educated in rhetoric. John Donne's "Song" (1633) begins with a *reductio ad absurdum* ("Go and catch a falling star, / Get with child a mandrake's root / . . . And find / What wind / Serves to advance an honest mind"), turns then to an inferential argument ("Ride ten thousand days and nights . . . And swear / No where / Lives a woman true and fair"), and finishes with what an economist would call an assessment of a low prior probability ("If thou find'st one, let me know; / . . . Yet do not; I would not go, / Though at next door we might meet. / . . . Yet she / Will be / False, ere I come, to two or three").

Marvell's "To His Coy Mistress" (1681) is the type of an argumentative poem. The argument is of course economic: had we but world enough and time, my Lady, I could court you as your value warrants, to satiation; but time is scarce, and life especially; the rate of time discount (as the modern economist would say) is therefore positive; and the optimal consumption plan is therefore to seize the day. Marvell makes his appeal relentlessly and smirkingly: he plays with a convention of rational choice and mocks it, as language games have a tendency to do with themselves. (Irony for this reason is called by the literary critic Kenneth Burke the "trope of tropes".) The economist plays no less within a convention when drawing on inference ($N =$ ten thousand days and nights) or time discount ($t =$ Deserts of vast Eternity), or when making little jokes to other economists about "islands" in the labor market or how the data have been "massaged." The flatfooted among economists and poets lack this sense of irony about arguments. They pen lines like "The coefficient is significant at the .00000001 level" or "I think that I shall never see / A poem lovely as a tree."

Similarity is not identity. Economics may be like poetry in this or that important respect, but plainly it is not the same. At another level, the likenesses between stocks and childcare will allow the topos of The Market to work, but there are differences, too, that will figure sometimes. At still another level, academic poets have different conversations from greeting-card poets. And all poets differ in other ways from economists, however poetic the economists may be.

Economics, for example, is *not* poetry just to the degree that a piece of economics invites what the critic Louise Rosenblatt called an "efferent" reading (from Latin *effero*, "take away") as against an aesthetic reading (1978, pp. 25-28). That is, one expects to "take away" something useful from an article on the New Jersey income-maintenance experiment. The article is not read for itself (though recall Marcus' experiment and take care: some economics is read for the aesthetic pleasure, and could hardly give any other). As Oakeshott put it (1959 [1991], p. 525), " poetic utterance . . . is not the 'expression' of an experience, it *is* the experience and the only one there is" in the voice of poetry.

It is sometimes argued therefore that economics and other sciences, though using metaphors, use them in a different way from poets. The philosopher of science Cristina Bicchieri, for example, in a penetrating comment on my "poetics" of economics, argues that "A good literary metaphor should be surprising and unexpected . . . Scientific metaphors, on the contrary, *are to be overused*" (1988, p. 113, my italics; compare Oakeshott 1959 [1991], p. 528: the poet's "metaphors have no settled value; they have only the value he succeeds in giving them").

Well, yes and no. The economist A. C. Harberger tells the story of a cocktail party at his house in the early 1960s, when Gary Becker, a brilliant student at Chicago, was working on the dissertation that became *Human Capital: A Theoretical and Empirical Analysis, with Special Reference to Education* (1964). The party was well along, but Gary as usual was sober and serious, and always, always talking economics. He came up to Harberger and remarked out of the blue, soft drink in hand, "You know, Al, *children are just like consumer durables*." It was a poetic moment, unexpected certainly to Harberger (who in fact was an expert on consumer durables, but had no idea that procreation might fit the category). True, as Bicchieri says, Becker intended the metaphor "to be overused," which is to say, to become part of the dead metaphors of the field; and it has. But at the moment of creation – like a poem once alive that becomes a cliché – it was anything but dead.

And on the literary side Bicchieri and other philosophers who want to give scientific metaphors a special "cognitive" goal quite separate from poetry are overstating the strangeness of poetry. They are adopting without realizing it a romantic literary criticism that puts the poet outside the routines of conversation, the poem being "the spontaneous overflow of powerful feeling," taking its origin from "emotion recollected in tranquillity." But of course poets, even Wordsworth, in fact talk largely about poetry, quoting each other's metaphors. The coin of poetic tradition is well worn. Some good poems contain clichés like "the coin of poetic tradition is well worn." What makes the poem work as "the activity of being delighted in the entertainment of its own contemplative images" (Oakeshott 1959 [1991], p. 527) is what is done with the clichés (like what I did just now with the cliché of worn coins, or in this sentence with the convention of not referring to one's own clichés in academic prose, or in this clause with that of not engaging in tiresome reflexivity, or in the last clause with that of not disabling the reader's vexation by admitting that it is "tiresome," and so forth). But good science is like that, too. Good science like good poetry can take utterly routine metaphors and, as Harberger is fond of saying, "make them sing." Periods of classicism, in which a poet or scientist seeks originality within settled metaphors, are not non-poetic or non-scientific. Think of Alexander Pope or Lord Kelvin.

Still, to be less provocative, take a conversation more obviously similar to economics, one which is wholly efferent (maybe), economic journalism. Thinking about its metaphors and contrasting them to economics itself still proves useful. Economic journalism is written sometimes by journalists with no academic pretensions, such as Leonard Silk, Robert Samuelson, John Greenwald, Louis Rukeyser, and David Warsh, but also by academic economists gifted in this way, such as Milton Friedman, J. K. Galbraith, and Lester Thurow, or academics-turned-journalists like Peter Passell. The common reader is liable to think that such writings are academic economics "translated" into plain English, in the style of popular science. Without prejudice, they are not. (Which is not to say that economic journalism is easy or that it is inferior to seminar talk: anyone who could imitate the books by the financial journalist who writes under the pseudonym "Adam Smith," for example, would be justly rich; few academic economists are.)

The journalistic conversation runs on particular dramatic conventions, hinging on evil, suspense, and individuality. William Blundell, a feature writer for *The Wall Street Journal*, gives as "the major commandment" for newspaper reporting: "For Pete's sake, make it interesting. Tell me a *story*" (Blundell 1988, p. xii), and uses the old gag about the ideal *Reader's Digest* piece to make the point: "How I Had Carnal Relations with a Bear for the FBI and Found God." In the storied talk that market people use to dignify their work a market is "excited" or "depressed," overrun with bulls or bears, slit with cutthroat competition. "How I Had Business Relations with IBM for the S.E.C. and Found Competitiveness." Businesspeople are portrayed in a story by

Samuel Smiles or Louis Rukeyser as pioneers whose courage and creativity extends the frontiers of what is economically possible; or they are portrayed in a story from Lincoln Steffens or Robert Kuttner as the tyrants who oppress the powerless. The "story" is just that: a piece in a newspaper. The black hat appears in it as a foreign country underselling "our" products or "beating us" in productivity. We and they are the heroes and villains, in pervasive sporting and military metaphors. Personalizing images are common, as in the talk of the street.

A masterful example is *The Zero-Sum Solution* (1985), by Lester Thurow, a fine economist and dean of the business school at Massachusetts Institute of Technology. The book is sporting. "To play a competitive game is not to be a winner – every competitive game has its losers – it is only to be given a chance to win . . . Free market battles can be lost as well as won, and the United States is losing them on world markets" (Thurow 1985, p. 59). One chapter is entitled "Constructing an Efficient Team." Throughout there is talk about America "competing", and "beating" the rest of the world with a "world-class economy." A later book is called *Head to Head*. Thurow complains that more people don't appreciate his favorite metaphor: "For a society which loves team sports . . . it is surprising that Americans won't recognize the same reality in the far more important international economic game" (1985, p. 107). Note that my "reality" is your "metaphor." In more aggressive moods Thurow slips from sweatpants into combat fatigues: "American firms will occasionally be defeated at home and will have no compensating foreign victories" (Thurow 1985, p. 105). Foreign trade is viewed as the economic equivalent of war.

Three metaphors govern Thurow's story: this metaphor of the international zero sum "game"; a metaphor of the domestic "problem"; and a metaphor of "we". *We* have a domestic *problem* of productivity that leads to a loss in the international *game*. Thurow has spent a long time interpreting the world with these linked metaphors. The we-problem-game metaphors are not the usual ones in economics. Anti-economists since the beginning have favored the metaphor of exchange as a zero-sum game. But the subject is the exchange of goods and services. If exchange is a "game" it might better be seen as one in which everyone wins, like aerobic dancing. No problem. Trade in the mainstream economic view is not zero sum. To be sure, from the factory floor it looks like zero sum, which gives Thurow's metaphor the appearance of common sense. To a businessperson "fighting" Japanese competition in making automobiles, her loss is indeed Toyota's gain. But the competitive metaphor looks at only one side of the trade, the selling side. Economists see around and underneath the economy. Underneath it all (as the economists say, in their favorite metaphor) Jim Bourbon of Iowa trades with Tatsuro Saki of Tokyo. A Toyota sold by Japan pays for 2,000 tons of soybeans sold by the United States. But at the same time a Japanese and an American consumer are gaining soybeans and an auto. One kid gets the other kid's pet frog in exchange for giving up his jackknife. Both kids are better off. If we look on nations in the way we look on kids making such exchanges we can see that both nations win a little something.

Trade and development are in the economic metaphor positive sum, not zero sum. The economic metaphor suggests a different attitude towards trade than that of Friedrich List, the German theorist of the German customs union in the early nineteenth century, or Henry Carey, the nineteenth-century American theorist of protection, or Lester Thurow and other recent Jeremiahs of American decline.

Talking in such a rhetorically self-conscious way about a piece of economic journalism is not just a rhetorical trick for attacking it. The point is that all conversations are rhetorical, as I have said, that none can claim to be the Archimedean point from which others can be levered once and for all. The neoclassical economists who would disagree with Thurow, such as his colleague at Massachusetts Institute of Technology, Paul Krugman, use metaphors, too, of humans as calculating machines and rational choosers. The neoclassicals say that the human situation is rational choice, the maximization of an objective function subject to constraints. Their metaphor is less thrilling perhaps than the economy as a struggle between good and evil or as the final round of the National Basketball Association playoffs; but it is no less metaphorical on that count. The rational-choice model is the master metaphor of mainstream economics, enticing one to think "as if" people really made decisions in this way. The metaphor has disciplined the conversation among neoclassical economists – the discipline is: if you don't use it, I won't listen – and has produced much good. To it we owe insights into subjects ranging from the consumption function in the twentieth century to the enclosure movement in the eighteenth. Yet, to repeat, it is a metaphor.

The neoclassicals (I am one of them) are very fond of their metaphor of people as calculating machines. What is problematical is the "positive" and "objective" status they ascribe to it. It was not always so. Ambiguity and contention surrounded the triumph of calculating choice as the definition of economics, as did the triumph of the computer analogy in psychology, and it was by no means always regarded as an innocent analytic technique. More than a century ago William Stanley Jevons found the calculating machine persuasive on the non-positivist grounds that it fitted with Bentham's calculus of pleasure and pain; Vilfredo Pareto, too, credited it in the early years of this century with psychological significance.

The neoclassical conversation about the logic of choice, despite the centripetal force of a mathematics teachable to all, has itself tended to break into smaller groups. The new classical macroeconomist has enchanted many young economists, with their lust for certitude. The neo-Keynesian, once himself lusty, holds back, finding solace in tales of Akerlof and sayings of Sen (Klamer 1983b, 1984). The other heirs of Adam Smith diverge more sharply from the faith. Even when educated in neoclassical economics, for example, the Marxist economist will object to the neoclassical reduction of the social to the individual; the Austrian economist will object on the other hand to the aggregation of the individual in the social. The Marxist prefers a conversation about the class basis of work; the Austrian prefers a conversation about the ineffable individuality of the entrepreneur. The mutual overlap of these conversations is large by the standard of their overlap with non-economic conversations – you can get any economist to talk to you about the entry of new firms into ecological niches, for example, or the adequacies of a monetary theory of inflation – but the lack of overlap is large, too, by the standard of what it should be.

Speaking of conversations being more or less similar yet having different notions of how to persuade will make a monist angry. A good monist-detection device is to say to him "Truth is plural" and watch the color of his nose. The monist, though, has had his way for too long in the modern world, traveling about from conversation to conversation instructing people in the law. "Intelligence," he says, "must be measured in a single number and be used to stream school children." "The writing of history is solely a matter of gathering pre-existing facts from archives." "Economics must not use questionnaires, because any behaviorist knows that these might be falsely answered." "Economics will only be a real Science when it uses experiments such as a withered branch of psychology once depended on."

The new pluralist and pragmatic and hermeneutic and rhetorical conversation about the conversation "weaves a web of significance," in Clifford Geertz's phrase, around the talk of economists. The new conversation in economics is only imitating what the economists themselves actually do with their stories and metaphors when they talk about the Federal Reserve Board and the trade deficit with Japan. As the great applied economist Sir Alec Cairncross put it,

> When it comes to action, economic theory is only one input among many. It has to be combined with a grasp of political and administrative feasibility and above all has to take advantage of experience and observation, not rely wholly on logic. As has often been remarked, logic can be a way of going wrong with confidence.
>
> Cairncross 1992, p. 20.

Economics, then, might be well advised to step down from the pedestal on which like the woman of the 1950s it fondly imagines it stands. A conversation in modern economics differs from economic journalism but is similar, differs from fiction but is similar, differs from poetry but is similar, differs from mathematics but is similar, differs from philosophy but is similar. There is no hierarchy here, no monist philosopher king reaching into conversations to spoil their tone. I recommend a rhetorically sophisticated culture for economists, in which, as Richard Rorty says, "neither the priests nor the physicists nor the poets nor the Party were thought of as more 'rational,' or more 'scientific' or 'deeper' than one another. No particular portion of culture would be singled out as exemplifying (or signally failing to exemplify) the condition to which the rest aspired." Or as the linguist James D. McCawley puts it, "no particular tradition has a right to speak for humanity as a whole . . . or for 'Reason' as divorced from all the diverse reasoning individuals and traditions of reasoning" (1990, p. 380). The present attitude, at least among those who have not yet felt the doubts of the Frustrated Scientist and the others, is ignorance about the variety of economics and of similar conversations, an ignorance breeding contempt.

Consider as a down-to-earth example the public conversation in the early 1990s about the budget crisis. The budget crisis was and is a real thing, because Gramm–Rudman–Hollings made it so. But as President Bush would have said it was also a word thing. The words make the crisis, too.

Consider the word "crisis." An illness comes to a crisis, and passes, or else the patient dies. The very word puts a medical spin on the story. The Washington doctors could not agree on a treatment for the crisis and so the American economy was wheeled off to the morgue. Sad case. Or the word "summit." It calls up motorcades and chandeliers and peace in our time, the vain hope that the bosses will "hammer out" an agreement. Did the budget summit at Edwards Air Force Base in the fall of 1990 succeed or fail? Sad tale.

The point of such reflections is not the usual one of noting that politicians are full of hot air. Of course they are. What else is new? Cicero, Lincoln, and Newt Gingrich are full of hot air, on budget crises as on other matters. But so are we all full of hot air, we economists and journalists and plain folk beyond Washington's Beltway. Hot air is what humans breathe. The words of the budget crisis are not mere rhetoric, because there is nothing mere about wordcraft. The choice of plot, to take a piece of wordcraft, is crucial for how the budget story turned out. Representative Gingrich and Senator Kennedy, in fictional unity of purpose, imposed on the events a plot of counterrevolution against the Reagan years, for better or for worse. The story rallied the cadre from the right or left, with real political consequences.

The middle-of-the-road plot for the story also had consequences. It narrated the budget crisis as a disgraceful failure of politics, showing once again the wretched lack of responsibility in Congress and the White House. (By the way, the consequences of the middle-of-the-roader's way of telling the story are not all good. The tyrant's first rhetorical move, after all, is to discredit democratic politics as messy and irresponsible.)

In other words, rhetoric is speech with an audience. All speech that intends to persuade is rhetorical, from higher math to lower advertising. In 1991 the Republican rhetoric of the budget crisis intended to persuade an audience of "middle-income" taxpayers, the victims of the bubble in tax rates, sturdy yeomen, it turns out, who were the top 5 percent of incomes. The same wealthy audience was supposed to be persuaded by the Democratic rhetoric, because the audience of the top 5 percent is the politically influential one. The Democratic rhetoric in 1991 and in the election campaign of 1992 was to propose taxing the very (very) rich in order to save the "middle class." "Don't tax him; don't tax me; / Tax that fellow eating brie." It turns out that there aren't enough brie eaters to solve the budget crisis.

But wait a minute. The expert economists offer us a way out of the rhetoric, don't they? The public and politicians indulge in wordcraft, but don't the experts just give us the plain facts and logic?

No, they don't. Experts want to persuade audiences, too, and therefore exercise wordcraft, in no dishonorable sense. Their rhetorics agree on some points. For instance, economists agree that the "crisis" is self-imposed, a weapon wielded by the economist-turned-senator, Phil Gramm, trying to get the mule's attention. But the economic experts disagree on whether the "underlying problem" of the deficit is serious or not. Their disagreements spring not from idiocy or bad faith but from rhetorical choices, often made unconsciously.

Suppose the economist uses a metaphor of the United States as a mere portion of a world economy, in the same way as Iowa is a portion of the upper Midwest. He will therefore not believe the story of the deficit causing a higher interest rate in the United States. The interest rate, he will say, is a result of the whole world's demand for funds. Quit worrying about the little piece of it called the US federal deficit. Or suppose the economist uses a story of a slippery slope to socialism. In that story a loosening of the federal budget leads to B-1 bombers and subsidies to farm owners in the top 5 percent of incomes.

The expertise shows in the rhetoric, though many of the experts don't recognize their own rhetoric. An economist is a poet / But doesn't know it. He is a novelist, too, and lives happily ever after. He is a philosopher, but does not know himself. Is the budget in crisis? It depends on your wordcraft, that Greek word to the wise, "rhetoric."

part III

Division

Division . . . the third part . . . It set forth points . . . agreed on by both sides . . . and points to be contested.

Lanham, *A Handlist of Rhetorical Terms* (1991), p. 60

chapter 5

The Science word in economics

Economists, however, are neurotic about "science." They think that knowing, really knowing, means following something called "scientific Method." They think that if you don't know it that way then you don't know much.

For all their quarrelsomeness, economists know a lot. Some of it is obvious, the common sense of adults, such as that many things are scarce and that therefore we can't have everything. The postulate of scarcity is what makes economics hard to teach to young adults, who believe they live among the blessed.

But a good deal of economics is not so obvious, even to the middle aged. The sociologist Randall Collins wrote an illuminating book subtitled *An Introduction to Non-Obvious Sociology* (1982). His job would have been easier in economics, not because economists are superior to sociologists but because the economists have loved since the beginning all things counter, original, spare, strange. There is a genre in economics of Everything You Thought You Knew About the Economy That Is In Fact Wrong (North and Miller 1983; and Smith 1776 [1981]). Even more than other social scientists the economists love to dumbfound the bourgeoisie.

Did you think during the Oil Crisis of 1973 that the Oregon Plan, selling gasoline by license-plate number, would cut queues at service stations? Think again: it had no effect on the queues, because the queues needed to be long enough to ration out the existing supplies (which were low at the controlled price). Do you think that it is a good idea to restrict American imports of Japanese autos, thereby saving jobs in Detroit? Think again: the price of American and Japanese autos has been increased $1,000 each by the "voluntary" restrictions, costing American auto buyers some hundreds of thousands of dollars a year in higher price for each job saved at $25,000 a year (and, incidentally, sharply increasing the profits of Japanese auto companies). Do you think that unions are the main reason that wages have risen in the United States? Think again: 10 percentage points out of the 900 percentage points that wages have risen since the Civil War can be explained by unions. Do you think that Americans are rich because of abundant natural resources? Think again: no more than a few percent of the income of a modern economy is attributable to the original and indestructible properties of the soil (witness that same Japan).

As sociologists and political scientists and geographers can also claim for themselves, for all the ignorant scepticism in the newspapers about the standing of social science, we economists know a lot. We know for a fact that slavery was profitable. We know for a logic that first-price sealed-bid common-value auctions have a winner's curse. Economics, to use the magic word, is a science.

Most Methodological articles in economics concern themselves with the question, is economics a Science? The question should be retired. It was meaningful only in a brief period in the middle of the twentieth century, and now it merely serves to show that the person asking it has not read anything in science studies since 1955 and does not believe that biology, evolution, and geology are sciences.

The Science word capitalized, as it will be here when used in its magical sense, is potent (the literal magic in economic Science is explored in McCloskey 1991c and 1992a). We English speakers over the past century and a half have used "science" in a peculiar way, as in British academic usage – arts and Sciences, the "arts" of literature and philosophy as against the "Sciences" of chemistry and geology. A historical geologist in English is a Scientist; a political historian is not. The usage would puzzle an Italian mother boasting of her studious son, *mio scienziato*, my learned one. She does not mean that he is a physicist. Italian uses the science word to mean simply "systematic inquiry" (as does French, Spanish, German, Dutch, Icelandic, Swedish, Norwegian, Polish, Hindi, Hebrew, Hungarian, Finnish, Turkish, Korean, and Tamil). Only English, and only the English of the past century, has made physical and biological science (definition 5b in the old *Oxford English Dictionary*) into, as the *Supplement* and the *New Oxford English Dictionary* describe it, "the dominant sense in ordinary use." The first citation is from the *Dublin Review* of 1867: "We shall . . . use the word 'science' in the sense which Englishmen so commonly give to it; as expressing physical and experimental science, to the exclusion of theological and meta-physical."

The Italian half of the *Cambridge Italian Dictionary* warns of English "scientific" that *nell'uso comune non si referisce ai principi filosofici classici*: that is, in the common English use, by contrast with Italian, the science word excludes knowledge earned beyond the laboratory. In other tongues the word means "something more systematic than casual journalism." The pre-nineteenth-century and non-English sense is found for instance in Johnson: "Of Fort George I shall not attempt to give any account. I cannot delineate it *scientifically*, and a *loose and popular description* is of use only when the imagination is to be amused" (Johnson 1775 [1984], p. 50; my italics). In 1828 Macaulay uses the word freely in combinations similar to other languages: political science, experimental sciences (among them the science of government), moral sciences (Macaulay 1828 [1881], pp. 390, 410). Similarly John Stuart Mill writing in 1836 on the "science of political economy" refers to "moral or mental sciences," of which political economy is a part, and in the next paragraph uses "reasoners" and "inquirers" as though synonymous with (a word he does not use, because a later coinage) "scientists" (Mill 1836 [1844, 1877], p. 55; Mill later distinguishes "art" from science; by "art" he means applications of the abstractions of science, not the fine arts). And John Ruskin in *The Stones of Venice* (1851–53 [1890]) warns that "the principal danger is with the sciences of words and methods; and it was exactly into those sciences that the whole energy of men during the Renaissance period was thrown" (vol. III, p. 58).

By 1882 Matthew Arnold is struggling against the new speciali-zation of the word, and against Thomas Huxley: "all learning is scientific which is systematically laid out and followed up to its original sources, and . . . a genuine humanism is scientific" (Arnold 1885 [1949], p. 411), applying the word "science" to the study of classical antiquity and, two decades before, to chairs of Celtic literature at Oxford and Cambridge. A little after Arnold's tug-of-war with Huxley over the word the English economist Alfred Marshall, in arguing for the scientific proposition that both supply and demand determine price, being two blades of a pair of scissors, says that to say that one or another other blade dominates in a particular case "is to be excused only so long as it claims to be merely a popular and not a strictly scientific account of what happened" (compare Johnson above; Marshall 1895 [1961], p. 348 [Bk. V, iii, 7]). As against the older usage stands Lord Kelvin, sneering in 1883 at the non-measurable, which is left out of sense 5b: "When you cannot measure it, when you cannot express it in numbers, your knowledge is of a meagre and unsatisfactory kind. It may be the beginning of knowledge, but you have scarcely in your thoughts advanced to the state of *science*" (1883, his italics). Huxley and Kelvin won the quarrel over the definition.

English speakers over the past century have been in love with the project of demarcating this Science from the rest of the culture, declaring the demarcation problem to be the central problem of epistemology. In their view the set of correlated dichotomies popular among recent English speakers occurs naturally, like the ocean. The world, they think, comes in paired and correlated flavors of hard/ soft, objective/subjective, thing/word, fact/opinion, is/ought, male/ female, model/story, Science/humanities. But to sneer in this way at social "science" or, still more vulgar, library "science" and food "science" as unScientific is to use childish verbal categories. They are accidents of British academic politics around 1880, not properties of the heavenly spheres.

The tension between the English and the other uses of the word can be seen in the English translations of Freud, which have resulted in a misunderstanding of the Freudian project. Freud, as José Brunner has persuasively argued (1992), was not fleeing science for the humanities. On the contrary, he was trying to make use of as many as-if ways of looking at the mind as possible, to bring the humanities into the empire of science in aid of understanding and therapy. The project was inclusive, not reductionist. Bruno Bettelheim has noted the peculiar scientification that came from translating plain German *"das Es"* as *"the Id"*; Brunner focuses on the mistranslation of *"Geisteswissenschaft,"* which means "humanities," not, as invariably given in James Strachey's translation of Freud, "mental sciences" (a translation that the philosopher Alexander Rosenberg unwisely insists on in a recent book, 1992, p. 49). The Strachey translation misunderstands therefore the founding purpose of the International Psychoanalytical Association, "to foster and to further the science [*Wissenschaft* = 'inquiry'] of psycho-analysis founded by Freud, both as pure psychology and in its applications to medicine and the mental sciences [*Geisteswissenschaft*]" (Brunner 1992, p. 26). Freud's ventures into myth and anthropology for materials with which to improve his science take on a different color.

Economics has acquired since the Second World War the trappings of the dominant sense in ordinary use: numbers, models, and above all a tough mathematization that evokes envious squeals from other social scientists. Modernists in English long ago appropriated the word "science" for their purposes, erecting a positivist scientism and a priesthood to go with it. The word "science" has since become a cudgel with which to assail the arguments that the modernists do not wish to hear. Economists get into the National Academy of Science because they are armed to the teeth in the English-speaking manner with the weapons of Science. Political scientists, if mathematicians can prevent it, do not get in, because the mere name of science is not enough.

The weapons of Science are in daily use around the culture. The standard sneer, as I say, is to attack the appropriation of "science" in social science, judging economics or anthropology as failing to measure up to a formula for Science. Science must enumerate: that excludes political philosophy as true Science. Science must be mathematical: that excludes most of anthropology. Science must test hypotheses: that lets out history. Science must experiment: that excludes every social science except parts of psychology and tiny bits of economics, archeology, and sociology. Science must be about the physical world: that excludes everything but the modern, English-speaking definition of the word.

The Science weapon, backed by the English use of the science word, has consequences. A good deal of money has been spent by the National Science Foundation since the 1950s in examining periodic stars and subatomic particles. A good deal of money has been spent by the National Institutes of Health in examining genes and cells. The postwar expenditure on Big Science has been justified on the grounds that these are the core scientific activities and that such activities account for modern economic growth and modern improvements in health. It needs to be more widely known that the grounds are false, scientifically speaking. A sociologist of science could attest that the triumph of the physicists in chemistry and biology is a postwar accident. An economic historian, as I have mentioned, could attest that science had little to do with economic growth until the twentieth century, and even now is modest beside the big factors of peace, literacy, shop-floor ingenuity, and sound economic policies (Jones 1981, 1988; Mokyr 1990). An historian of public health could attest that most of the fall in the death rate since the eighteenth century occurred before medical science could save more people than it killed (Floud, Wachter, and Gregory 1989). Yet little is spent on testing such hypotheses in history or in economics. The National Science Foundation's budget for economics (about $11 million a year) would not pay the light bill for high-energy physics.

So our English usage puts physical and biological scientists in command. The grounds are verbal, as must be the case in a human world or in a science run by humans, *homo loquans*. We cannot avoid using words, though we can use them poorly or well. The people who sneer about social "science" being unScientific are scientifically naïve. People who scrutinize the hard facts about things in science come to the conclusion that the facts are constructed by artful words. The conclusion has become a cliché among scientists. To name three who make the point: Michael Polanyi (crystallography) does so in *Personal Knowledge* (1962); Ludwik Fleck (bacteriology) in *Genesis and Development of a Scientific Fact* (1935 [1979]); and Steven Weinberg (theoretical physics) in "Beautiful Theories" (1983). In economic science the very statistics are grounded in values, though no less scientific on that account.

The evidence that words make science is by now overwhelming (Kuhn 1977; Feyerabend 1975 [1978]; Rorty 1979; Finocchiaro 1980; Barnes and Edge 1982; Madison 1982; D. Bloor 1983; Pickering 1984; H. M. Collins 1985, 1990; Mulkay 1985; Pinch 1986; Fuller 1988, 1989). And except for government funding and a few other matters of persuading the electorate to go on paying for it, the demarcation of Science from non-Science, when you think of it, is lacking in point.

The pointless provinciality, an English-speaking one, is to think of science and literature as Two Cultures. The Two Cultures are not natural territories, though department chairs and college deans behave sometimes like border guards in the East Germany of old, erecting barbed wire and shooting people trying to cross it. A dean of research at a large state university gave a speech some years ago in which she described the humanities as what is left over after the (physical and biological) sciences and then after them the social sciences have expended their eloquence. The humanities in her mind are a residuum for the mystical and the ineffable. I have a friend, a remarkable economic scientist, the brother even of a distinguished English professor, who, when he learned that I was reading books about literature, asked me amiably whether I had become, as he put it, a "mystic."

The dean and my friend were being good natured, using the categories that appeared in 1955 to cut the universe at its joints. They good-naturedly tolerate the ineffable and the mystic, though of course one must carefully demarcate such things from Science. It is the 5 o'clock view of Art: until 5 o'clock we labor at Science; afterwards we play at Art. The bad-natured remarks muttered from each side are worse: that if we mention "metaphors" we are committed to an arty irrationalism; that if we mention "logic" we are committed to a scientific autism.

One wants to shake both sides and say, get serious. The better definition of "science" is broader and more serious and less English, as for instance in de Felice and Duro, *Dizionario della Lingua e della Civiltà Italiana Contemporanea* (1985): "science: . . . the speculative, agreed-upon inquiry which recognizes and distinguishes, defines and interprets reality and its various aspects and parts, on the basis of theoretical principles, models, and methods rigorously cohering." The contrast is not with the humanities but with, say, bad journalism or the untutored opinion of the street. Nothing is said about using calculus or test tubes. The "rigor" can come from any argument that coheres, that, as Arnold said, is systematically laid out and followed up to its original sources. And so the speakers of German have their *Altertumswissenschaft*, the "science" of olden times, Greek and Roman classics; and *klassische Wissenschaft*, similarly, what English speakers call the humanities.

In non-English worlds of language it is perhaps more evident that the sciences, such as chemistry, history, or economics, require "humanistic" methods, right in the middle of their sciences. They are sciences, not Sciences. As Niles Eldredge (the co-originator with S. J. Gould of the notion in evolution of "punctuated equilibrium") put it: "something more is afoot than the straightforward objective evaluation of a set of postulates about the nature of things – the standard, if distorted, view of scientific behavior" (Eldredge 1985 [1989], p. 16). The Sciences, big S, are figments of the British philosophical imagination. The real argumentative work gets done by small-s sciences. Newton used logic and metaphors. Darwin used facts and stories. And likewise the arts and humanities require fact and logic, right in the middle. Leonardo, the artist-scientist, used stories and logic (as a colleague of mine at Iowa in engineering, Enzo Macagno, is showing in his work on Leonardo's drawings of water, chaos theory before the name). Galileo, the scientist-artist, was "an excellent draftsman" and "loved and understood 'with perfect taste' all the 'arts subordinated to design' . . . He was originally inclined to study painting rather than mathematics" (Panofsky 1954, quoted in Tufte 1990, p. 19). Goethe wrote a scientific (*wissenschaftlich*) treatise on colors and his notion of a prototype for all animals was useful to Darwin. The definition of a "string quartet" at the Institute for Advanced Study is "three mathematicians and a physicist." Science is artistic and literary, requiring metaphors and stories in its daily work, and literature is precise and scientific.

Like other arts and sciences, to put it another way, economics as a science uses the whole "rhetorical tetrad" – the facts, logics,

Table 1. *The rhetorical tetrad: the four devices*

		Axis of particularity:	
FACT	STORY (metonymy)	closeness, particularity	Empirical British
from induction	from understanding	↑	
		↓	
LOGIC	METAPHOR	similarity, generality	Logical French
from deduction	from abduction		

impersonal ⟵——Axis of——⟶ personal
            impersonality

        The Modernist
        dichotomy
        (*c.* 1955):

scientific	*humanistic*
male	female
numbers	words
precise	intuitive
hard	soft
Truth	opinion
objective	subjective
cognition	feeling
Science	Arts
business	pleasure

metaphors, and stories necessary for completed human reasoning (see table 1).

Each of the four ways of reasoning has its activity: induction to fact, deduction by logic, understanding a story, and abduction, as C. S. Peirce named it long ago, to judge a metaphor. The four divide in various ways. Fact and logic are usually taken to be impersonal, which is to say uncontroversial; story and metaphor are taken to be personal. The division reflects the rhetorical situation, not God's truth. Many facts are more personal than some metaphors. Along the other axis, logic and metaphor appeal to similarity, fact and story to closeness, mere contiguity. A logic or metaphor will apply if one accepts the similarity of, say, ordinary reasoning to first-order predicate logic or of wolves to men. "Men are wolves" asserts a similarity between the realm of men and the realm of wolves. By contrast, facts and stories depend on association, not similarity. We speak of a story "hanging together," which is to say that its episodes are naturally close to each other. A story is one damned thing after another, not a comparison of one realm of discourse to another. The linguist Roman Jakobson plausibly divided all thinking along such lines, into metaphorical thinking, which draws on similarity, and metonymic thinking, which draws on contiguity or association (Jakobson and Halle 1956 [1988]). In economic language (which Jakobson and Halle use, p. 58), metaphors concern substitutability, metonymies concern complementarity. A set of supply-and-demand curves on a blackboard is a substitute, a map, for a market. The prediction of next month's unemployment is complementary with this month's figure. The one is modeling, the other history.

Fragments of the tetrad are not enough for full thinking. The allegedly scientific half of the tetrad, the fact and logic, falls short of an adequate economic science, or even a science of rocks and stars. The allegedly humanistic half falls short of an adequate art of economics, or even a criticism of form and color. Cutting the other way, a science that is wholly metonymic, like the worst history, or wholly metaphoric, like the worst economics, exhibits the aphasia that Jakobson studied in brain-damaged patients, "the fixation on one of these poles to the exclusion of the other" (p. 59). Scientists and scholars and artists had better be factual and logical. They had also better be literary – able to frame good models and tell true histories about the first three minutes of the universe or the last three months of the economy (Hesse 1963; McCloskey 1990a). They had better be able to tell factual stories and spin logical metaphors. A scientist with half of the culture is half a scientist.

The idea that Fact and Logic are by themselves enough for science puts one in mind of the rural Midwestern expression, "a few bricks short of a load." The program over the past fifty years of narrowing down our arguments in the name of rationality was a few bricks short of a load. The experiment in getting along with fewer than all the resources of human reasoning was worth trying and had plenty of good results. But it has done its work. To admit now that metaphor and story matter also in human reasoning does not entail becoming less rational and less reasonable. On the contrary, as I have said, it entails becoming more rational and more reasonable, because it brings more of what persuades serious people under the scrutiny of reason.

As the historian of science Maurice Finocchiaro put it, "the exclusive reliance on the formal logic of reasoning has the irrationalistic tendency of leaving most of the human sciences and of human affairs in the realm of the arbitrary and capricious" (Finocchiaro 1980, p. 274). Bertrand Russell, the master of modernism in philosophy, is a case in point (see Booth 1974, ch. 2). Santayana describes Russell during the First World War exploiting his retentive memory without the check of comprehensive reason: "This information, though accurate, was necessarily partial, and brought forward in a partisan argument; he couldn't know, he refused to consider everything; so that his judgments, nominally based on that partial information, were really inspired by passionate prejudice and were always unfair and sometimes mad. He would say, for instance, that the bishops supported the war because they had money invested in munition works" (1947 [1987], p. 441). Modernism, the ugly if fruitful experiment of the past seventy years, most ugly in positivism, was rigorous about a tiny part of reasoning and unreasonable about the rest.

Modernists in philosophy or architecture or economics cannot reason with most of their opponents; on most matters they can only shout and sneer. They would say: you are an unScientific fool if you do not believe that in building downtown Dallas the form should follow the function; you are an ignorant knave if you do not believe that political science during the 1980s should be reduced to secondhand econometrics. Umberto Eco notes the outcome of the avant-garde of modernism, 1910 to the present: "The avant-garde destroys, defaces the past . . . Then . . . destroys the figure, cancels it, arrives at the abstract . . . In architecture and the visual arts, it will be the curtain wall, the building as stele, pure parallelepiped, minimal art; in literature, the destruction of the flow of discourse, the Burroughs-like collage, silence, the white page; in music, the passage from atonality to noise to absolute silence" (Eco 1985, p. 66; cf. Klamer 1991).

Resistance to reason is dogma. It is unoriginal and uncontroversial to point out that Science is the modern dogma, and that after the sea of religious faith receded another religion flooded in: Scientism. Scientists in the English sense are of course ordained priests. Winners of the Nobel prize are granted a cardinal's hat, and in exceptional cases are canonized, to intervene for us with God. As the psychologist David Bakan puts it, the word "unscientific . . . [is] used almost synonymously with blasphemous" (Bakan 1967, p. 158). The Science-faith is practiced on college campuses, the cathedrals of modernism. When confronted with Scientists, the economists, historians, and most embarrassingly of all the political scientists live in dread of Scientific sneers, from one holier than thou. Scientific ayatollahs from physics and mathematics, assisted by anti-intellectuals in the media, have gotten into the habit recently of mounting jihads against other disciplines, or at the least a diverting heresy trial now and then.

You know the ranking in science itself: physics, math, chemistry, biology, geology, engineering. A physicist in 1945 sneered at the chemist who made the astounding chemical trigger for the atomic bomb: "You're a wonderful chemist, George – that is, a good third-rate physicist." In 1989 the notion that Science is whatever most closely approximates the higher-status parts of physics showed plain in the fury of the physicists in New Haven and Berkeley against the chemists in Utah ("Utah!" one could hear the coasties exclaiming) who had the temerity to claim to have made fusion in a test tube. I wonder if physicists realize that we bystanders prayed nightly in another faith that the low-status chemists would turn out to be right, liberating us from the arrogance of high-energy physics. (Economics, I've noted, thinks of itself as the physics of the social sciences. Richard Palmer, a physicist, testified after a conference involving both fields that "I used to think that physicists were the most arrogant people in the world. The economists were, if anything, more arrogant" [Pool 1989, p. 700]).

It is not merely funny. Science and Religion serve similar functions (Robert Nelson 1991), some good but some very bad indeed. An eminent anthropologist was asked by the anti-creationist side in the Arkansas case a while ago if he would testify. The lawyer argued something like this: "As a cultural anthropologist you are an expert in both religion and science, since you study one and practice the other. Therefore you would be an excellent witness testifying that creation 'science' is not Science and that Science is not a religion." The anthropologist thought about it for a while and then declined. He knew that on the witness stand he would have to admit that he could see no great difference between religion and Science, and surely not between Bible-belt Christianity and the Science-myth we have created in the newspapers and public assemblies over the past century (cf. Shweder 1986, p. 190, describing the debate between Haldane and Lunn; Shweder is not the anthropologist in the story).

The tone of religious reverence with which science is approached in the modern world is well illustrated in the service industries of Science, staffed by deans, journalists, publishers, foundation executives, and grant administrators. You would expect the service people to have the most cynically secular view of science. After all, the deacons and prayer boys know the priests without their vestments. They know the unguarded remarks and the petty jealousies and the rejected research proposals, and they know these from the outside, unindoctrinated in the special topics of the science.

Yet the service people adhere devoutly to the religion of our culture. When a conference was organized in 1986 at Wellesley College to discuss the "rhetoric of economics" the organizers expected the journalists invited from *Newsweek*, *The New York Times*, and *The Boston Globe* to be the most canny of the guests. After all, rhetoric is their business. But surprisingly the journalists were the most naïve about rhetoric, most likely to believe that words were "mere" and that the world was "reality," to be read like a thermometer. They could not grasp why the 3" × 5"-card definition of scientific method in scientism was inadequate. The working economic scientists had no problems understanding it (though the methodologists among them had some); but the working journalists were uncomprehending (Warsh 1988).

The rhetoric of journalism, especially science journalism, itself bears examination. William Blundell, a reporter for *The Wall Street Journal*, wrote, I have mentioned, a 1988 book *The Art and Craft of Feature Writing*. The book amounts to a rhetoric for reporters, explaining how to shape a story that appeals to ethos, pathos, and logos. "Before flying out the door," he writes, for example, "a reporter should consider the range of his story, its central message, the approach that appears to best fit the tale, and even the tone he should take as storyteller" (Blundell 1988, p. 23). The book has hundreds of such tips for effective rhetoric, which is what makes it a good book. But Blundell draws back, as journalists do, from the implications of his rhetoric. A few pages after the advice to emplot the story before examining it he avows that "Events, not preconceptions, should shape all stories in the end" (p. 27). It is the core faith of the journalist that "most of the time . . . he spends on the snowy summit of Mount Objectivity" (p. 13) – though Blundell makes gentle fun of the faith, too. He is like a Catholic who on Sunday morning believes fervently in the doctrine of the eucharist but by the end of the Bears game that afternoon does not *really* believe that the communion wine is in essence the blood of our Savior, and from Monday to Saturday, in truth, finds it all slightly amusing.

Non-normal science or a criticism of science puzzles most science journalists. Anti-clericalism is not their gift. A couple of exceptions among journalists, William Broad and Nicholas Wade, quote in their *Betrayers of the Truth: Fraud and Deceit in the Halls of Science* (1982) the more usual attitude, of June Goodfield, for example, explaining why science needs no external criticism: "Of all the professions science is the most critical. There are full-time critics of music, art, poetry and literature, but there are none of science, for scientists fulfil this role themselves" (Broad and Wade 1982, p. 61). You bet.

When the scientists and their allies in journalism tire of celebrating scientific orthodoxy they turn to exposing "scientific fraud," and here Broad and Wade are more typical. The exposure of fraud is the other side of piety: rooting out heresy. As David Goodstein, a physicist and administrator at the California Institute of Technology, put it, "the public's perception of what scientists do and why they do it is distorted by myths, . . . with the consequence that normal and even essential forms of behavior by scientists can be viewed as sinister" (Goodstein 1991, p. 505), instancing Newton's "little fixes" of his calculation of the speed of sound and Millikan's "mistakes discarded without comment" in his oil-drop experiment. Even quite sophisticated journalists don't get it. They reckon that the scientists must be doing something more serious than the mere writing and arguing and other acts of rhetoric that the journalists commit daily. Of Cyril Burt (the British psychologist who was accused posthumously of faking his data on ability in twins) Broad and Wade conclude, "He used the scientific method as a purely rhetorical tool to force the acceptance of his own dogmatic ideas" (Broad and Wade 1982, p. 211) – unlike true scientists, you see, who would never use a "purely rhetorical tool" or have "dogmatic ideas." Science journalists know how to cover astounding new findings or shocking new frauds, but not how to cover the middle ground of hardworking confusion seeking the light that constitutes 95 percent of science, and journalism. They know how to celebrate the dogma or burn the heretics, but not how to see rhetoric in daily action.

The service people of science forget that the only certitude is that yesterday's timeless orthodoxy in science will become tomorrow's laughingstock: a strictly Newtonian universe, for example, or a Lamarckian theory of inheritance, or a geology such as I was taught in 1963 by rearguard geologists at Harvard resisting plate tectonics with every atom of their being. The career of William Thompson, Lord Kelvin (1824–1907), contains the lesson. He campaigned against Darwinian evolution from its inception, on the grounds that the sun would have already burned out during the immensities of time required – unless, he sneered on the eve of the discovery of nuclear energy, some other form of energy is discovered. The blunder was not isolated. Kelvin often articulated the fatuities of a Science that regards itself as nearly complete.

In the dogma of Scientism it is today's credo, in substance or method or Nobel laureates, that is timelessly True. The service people protect orthodoxy with a fierce devotion. The evidence about cold fusion, writes Eugene Mallove, suggests something peculiar is there, perhaps a new branch of science, but "So thick has been the disparagement of Fleischmann and Pons and all their followers, that the mud stuck. It became 'socially unacceptable' in the science journalism community to give too much weight to any of the cold fusion rumblings . . . [W]ith good reason [the science journalists] feared ridicule if they pursued the continuing strange scientific reports. The power vacuum was filled with the opposition view-point" (Mallove 1991, pp. 270–271).

The service sector is forced into this conservative position partly by worries about its own status and partly by its other customers, the attending and reading and in any case paying public. The public has a magical view of science. Either it's heap good medicine, this science, or it's just a charlatan's trick. The on/off attitude accounts for the genre of Fads and Fallacies in the Name of Science and the careers of some professional magicians devoted to unmasking non-conventional science (the magicians, oddly, do not examine the magic in conventional laboratories; you would think they would want some controls). The average person, educated or not, views science as a simple on/off, true/false, real/phony matter. He understands science with the theory called "Baconian" (though it is plainer in *The Adventures of Sherlock Holmes* than it is in *The New Organon*). Darwin, for example, facing a public of Baconians, had to pretend from the first sentence of the *The Origin of Species* that he was following the established rite (Darwin 1859 (1968), p. 65; cf. J. A. Campbell 1987): "it occurred to me, in 1837, that something might perhaps be made out on this question by patiently accumulating and reflecting on all sorts of facts . . . After five years' work I allowed myself to speculate on the subject." He claimed too in his published *Autobiography* that "I worked on true Baconian principles, and without any theory collected facts on a wholesale scale" (quoted in J. A. Campbell 1987). But we know from his notebooks, not intended for publication, that he was telling a fib. It is the usual hypocrisy of official religions.

A 3" × 5"-card version of Karl Popper's thinking has replaced such Baconianism as the official religion among the Scientistic nowadays, but it is still dichotomizing and dogmatic, still invoked as ritual whether or not the scientist in fact governs her scientific life by the creed. We need a new anti-clericalism against the Church of Science. Voltaire, Hume, Gibbon, Tom Paine: where are you when we need you?

The economist George Shackle, in words still redolent of the Science/humanities dichotomy, said:

> I think there are two kinds of economics. One of them aims at precision, rigour, tidiness and the formulation of principles which will be permanently valid: an economic science. The other is, if you like, rhetorical. This word is often used disparagingly, but that is a modern unscholarly abuse. The rhetorician employs reason and appeals to logic, but he is a user of language in its fuller compass, where words are fingers touching the keyboard of a hearer's mind [recall Wittgenstein]. I do not believe that human affairs can be exhibited as the infallible and invariable working of a closed and permanent system.
>
> Shackle 1983, p. 116.

What is right in his remark is that we need a rhetoric of economic science. What is wrong is the implication that in getting it we must abandon science (small s) and its useful approximation of invariability. Abandon Science (big S), by all means, with all its churchy pretense, and note the close parallels between economic science and orthodox religion (again, R. H. Nelson 1991). Do not leave the Church in sole possession of the Word. We can have a good science without making it into a substitute for religion. The new history, sociology, and rhetoric of science can supply the offset to a Scientism grown hypocritical and arrogant, in the way that the old history, sociology, and rhetoric of religion a century ago put the other clerisy in it place.

Contrary to the century-long and especially English-speaking program to demarcate Science from the rest of the culture the actual science is after all a matter of arguing. The ancient categories of argument are going to apply. As Jacob Bronowksi said, and lived, "it is the business of each of us to try to remake that one universal language," which is to say, the conversation of humankind, "which alone can unite art and science, and layman and scientist, in a common understanding" (Bronowski 1951 [1960], p. 17). It is not a matter of choosing irrationality over rationality, or doing science on the job and art on vacation. To swing back against rationality is to adopt the same dichotomy of modernism, if only from the other side.

The symbiotic relationship between rationalism and its dichotomous opposite, irrationalism, is captured in this fact of geography: that the Rand Corporation, the bastion of rationalism, is located in Santa Monica, the bastion of irrationalism. Or in this fact of show business: that Gordon Liddy and Timothy Leary, the obverse and reverse of the modernist coin, are fast friends and appear together on the college lecture circuit. Robert Benchley noted once that the world is divided into two sorts of people: those who divide the world into two sorts of people and those who don't. I recommend don't, but the dichotomies of modernism are hard to get out of people's minds.

Economics can do better than taking sides between thought and feeling, between the Sciences and the Humanities. "You want a system that will combine both things," wrote William James, "the scientific loyalty to facts and willingness to take account of them, the spirit of adaption and accommodation, in short, but also the old confidence in human values and the resultant spontaneity, whether of the religious or the romantic type" (1907 [1949], p. 20). He viewed his Pragmatism as a step beyond the quarrels of tough- and tender-minded, realists and idealists, empiricists and rationalists, scientists and humanists: "I have all along been offering it expressly as a mediator between tough-mindedness and tender-mindedness" (James 1907 [1949], p. 269). The economists, if they only knew it, have such a pragmatic and rhetorical science in their grasp. Since Adam Smith the economists have been both analyzing action and analyzing behavior, understanding the reasonableness of what people do down in the ruck of the market and seeing them also "from the eighth floor," as a sociologist once put it. To do economics otherwise than in this scientific way is to be a few bricks short of a load.

chapter 6

Three ways of reading economics to criticize itself

It is early days yet for an interpretive and humanistic economics, straddling the dichotomies of modernism. But an economics brought back into the conversation of humankind has already a few things to whisper across the disciplinary walls, economic knowledge reappearing as self-knowledge (the genre was invented by Hirschman 1981, 1984).

First: if you're so smart

Economics should apply to itself. At one level the application is well advanced. Economics is a particularly thoroughgoing example of rationality, turning back on itself in, for example, the conflict between Austrian and neoclassical views of market equilibrium. Jack Amariglio (1990b) has argued that modernist economics, like modernist everything else, contained a contradiction, what Paul Wendt calls in a comment on Amariglio "the immanence thesis," that "postmodernism is immanent in modernist economics" (Wendt 1990, p. 47). In essentials the contradiction is of longer standing, though sharpened in modernism. It has been called "the aporia [indecision] of the Enlightenment". The philosopher Stanley Rosen describes it as "a conflict between mathematics and Newtonian science on the one hand and the desire for individual and political freedom on the other . . . The understanding is in essence the formulation of and obedience to rules. Since there are no rules for the following of rules . . . the understanding must be a spontaneous 'project' . . . of freedom . . ., Kant's unstable attempt to ground reason in spontaneity" (Rosen 1987, pp. 3, 4, 8). In a sentence: being unreasonably rational will eventually enslave us to rules (compare Ruskin on the Renaissance). As Amariglio puts it, "the desire to know Man, to control him for purposes of efficiency and utility through this increased knowledge, produces the notorious exercises of power in the modern age" (Amariglio 1990, p. 21).

Amariglio is right. Modern economics has in part deconstructed itself, especially as Amariglio points out in the treatment of uncertainty. Uncertainty concerns prediction. If economics is a good imitation of (some high-status branches of) physics, a capital-S Science in the definition offered by philosophers around 1955, then it should predict. Paradox, aporia, indecision: if economics is Scientific, then we can predict; but a predictable future is a freedomless nightmare. Thus Robert Lucas and the other developers of rational expectations pointed out that a predictable economy is not one in which government policy can work.

The philosophical prestige of prediction (as against post-diction, history; or against other virtues that a science can have) probably arises from a still dominant but "discredited empiricist conception of science" (Brush 1989, p. 1127). The economist's response to the empiricist conception of science is the American question: if you're so smart, oh predictor of human events, why ain't you rich? The American question cuts deeper than most intellectuals and experts care to admit. The test of riches is perfectly fair if the expertise claims to deliver actual riches, in gold or in glory. The American question embarrasses anyone claiming *profitable* expertise who cannot show a profit, the historian second-guessing generals or the critic propounding a formula for art. He who is so smart claims a Faustian knowledge, "Whose deepness doth entice such forward wits / To practice more than heavenly power permits."

Take it as an axiom of human behavior that people pick up $20 bills left on the sidewalk. This Axiom of Modest Greed involves no close calculation of advantage or large willingness to take a risk. The average person sees a quarter on the sidewalk and will try to put his foot over it, inconspicuously (experimentation has shown that Manhattanites will stoop for a quarter but not for a dime); he sees a $20 bill and jumps for it. The axiom is not controversial. All economists subscribe to it, whether or not they "believe in the market" (as the shorthand test for ideology goes).

Yet the Axiom of Modest Greed has a distressing outcome, a dismal commonplace of adult life, a sad little Twenty-Dollar-Bill Theorem:

Theorem: If the Axiom of Modest Greed applies, then today there exists no sidewalk in the neighborhood of your house on which a $20 bill remains.

Proof: By contradiction, if there had been a $20 bill lying there at time $T - N$, then according to the axiom someone would have picked it up before T, that is, before today. *Quod erat demonstrandum.*

From such delicate reasoning it is a short step to common sense. If a man offers advice on how to find a $20 bill on the sidewalk, for which he asks merely a nominal fee, the prudent adult declines the offer. If there really were a $20 bill lying there the confidence man would pick it up himself. "A tout," said Damon Runyan, who knew the score, "is a guy who goes around a race track giving out tips on the races, if he can find anybody who will listen to his tips, especially suckers, and a tout is nearly always broke. If he is not broke, he is by no means a tout, but a handicapper, and is respected by one and all."

The payment need not be monetary if money is not what the seer desires. Prestige in the local saloon would be cheaply acquired if the American question did not also cast doubt on predictions of sporting events. But it does. The lineaments of the sporting future apparent to the average guy will be reflected in the sporting odds. Only fresh details give profits above average measured in money or prestige. Fresh details are hard to come by. Information, like steel and haircuts, is costly to produce. Predictions are hard, especially about the future.

An economist looking at the business world is like a critic looking at the art world. Economists and other human scientists can reflect intelligently on present conditions and can tell useful stories about the past. These produce wisdom, which permits broad, conditional "predictions." Some are obvious; some require an economist; but in equilibrium, after the $20 bills have been picked up, none is a machine for achieving fame or riches. The study of the human sciences can produce wisdom, routine predictions. It cannot produce profitable prediction and godlike control.

No one can be embarrassed by the American question who retains a proper modesty about what observation and recording and story-telling can do. We can observe the history of economies or the history of painting, and in retrospect tell a story about how security of commercial property or the analysis of vanishing points made for good things. An expert such as an economist is an expert on the past, and about the future that can be known without divine and profitable possession. Human scientists and critics of human arts, in other words, write history, not prophecy. Economics teaches this, the limit on social engineering. It teaches that we can be wise and good but not profitably foresighted in detail, even if we are economists.

Second: economist, perform thy trade

So that's one thing economics can tell itself and other disciplines when it gets back into the conversation, that economics and other social engineering are not magic. Another thing it can tell is that the non-magical disciplines must trade. The only magic is wisdom, which can be achieved only by intellectual trade.

Academic life is thoroughly departmental. We know that some-day the departments of the academy will be organized in some way differently. Yet most universities are organized to prevent the future from happening. The departments keep the gates like three-headed dogs, and the deans are too busy filling in forms and fending off law suits to perform the Sybil's office. Many of the new departments of the intellect will come from between the disciplines, as did biochemistry and biophysics, comparative literature and social science history – but not if departmental specialists can prevent it.

Specialization is an economic idea. But it is misused by academic planners, and even by some economists when they become academic planners, to justify what could be described in economic terms as autarchic protectionism. The key economic point is this: *speciali-zation itself is not good*. In fact, Adam Smith himself was eloquent on the damage that specialization does to the human spirit: "The man whose whole life is spent in performing a few simple operations . . . has no occasion to exert his understanding . . . He . . . generally becomes as stupid and ignorant as it is possible for a human creature to become" (Smith 1776 [1981], V, i, f, p. 782). What is good is specialization *and then trade*. As Smith also observed, "Consumption is the sole end and purpose of all production; and the interest of the producer ought to be attended to, only so far as it may be necessary for promoting that of the consumer" (IV, viii, p. 660). There is no point in a shoe producer piling up shoes in the back yard unless he is going to sell them some day in order to consume the fruits of other people's specialization.

The trade in intellectual life is precisely the use of other people's work for one's own: it is what goes on in interdisciplinary activity, if the activity is something more than polite acknowledgment of the other's expertise, insulated carefully from disturbing one's own. If we actually read each other's work and let it affect our own, then we are well and truly following the economic model of free trade. If on the other hand we do not crack a book outside our subdiscipline, then we are following the economic model of old Albania, an autarchy of ox carts and mouldy wheat. Even Albania has given up the autarchic dogma. Modern academic life has whole departments of ox carts.

The classicist Sally Humphreys puts it well. The ruling picture of science is wrong, she says:

> It is not obvious that a conception of scientific theories as fitting together into a single, consistent model of the cosmos, temporarily divided up to facilitate discovery by a rational division of labour, has much function either heuristically or as a mechanism for reducing error. It tends to produce rivalry and dogmatism in disciplines that see themselves as offering competing solutions to the same problems (for example, anthropology and psychology); a view of scientific disciplines as neighbouring cultures, each with its own pattern of selective attention to partly overlapping aspects of the environment, might generate a more fruitful critical dialogue.
>
> Humphreys 1992, p. 20.

Specialization without trade, adumbrated in the sixteenth century by Peter Ramus and later by Bacon, beloved nowadays by academic administrators bereft of administrative ideas, resulted as Richard Lanham puts it in our "table-of-contents curriculum." It arose from "the Ramist separation of rhetoric from thought, of one discipline from another, and of both from any implicit indwelling value" (Lanham, forthcoming, ch. 7, p. 26).

Jacob Viner, the great economist, sneered at the result in characteristically economic terms: "The growth in the accumulation of data . . . seems steadily to be cutting down the number of those who would sacrifice even an inch of depth for a mile of breadth" (1950 [1991], p. 393). And the philosopher of economics Daniel Hausman writes, "Economics is a diverse enterprise, and there is no reason why it should become less diverse . . . . There is absolutely no [philosophical] reason why all economists should employ the same styles and strategies of theorizing" (1992, p. 255; italics omitted). Amen.

The argument is not against specialization but against the failure at last to trade. It will be sweet work for psychologists, say, to talk long and hard about Observable Behavior, temporarily setting aside arguments from introspection. There is nothing hostile to systematic work in the argument. No one would wish to stop systematic specialization. The problem comes when the narrow, temporary agreement hardens into a Methodological dogma for all time. Then the shoes start piling up unsold in the back yard. If the psychologists throw introspection into a non-scientific outer darkness forever and ever on merely epistemological grounds they start falling into absurdities. The psychologist Jerome Bruner, speaking of psychology in the late 1930s, noted that "For reasons that now seem bizarre, you *had* to convert contested issues into rat terms in order to enter the 'in' debates" (Bruner 1983, p. 29; see David Bakan's defense of introspection, Bakan 1967, ch. 9). Two strictly behaviorist psychologists make love. One says to other, "*You* enjoyed that. Did I?"

Specialization without trade is a few bricks short of a load. As the anthropologist Roy D'Andrade put it: "One cannot expect to improve upon Freud by observing less about human beings than he did" (D'Andrade 1986, p. 39). Economics again: we will do better with fewer arguments ruled out. The economic recommendation contradicts the philosophically inspired ruling-out by economists such as George Stigler and Murray Rothbard. Considering that other scholars read different books and lead different lives it would be economically remarkable, a violation of economic principles, if nothing could be learned from trading with them. Learning entails less sneering by physicists at chemists or by economists at sociologists or by mathematicians at statisticians. The notion that something can be learned from trading with others merely applies the economics of intellectual life. Just as differences in tastes or endowments are grounds for trade, disagreements about the causes of crime or the nature of capitalism are grounds for serious conversation, even with economists.

Third: talk is not cheap

A third way of using economics to criticize itself is to calculate the importance of persuasive talk within the economy itself, the profitable word-trade among merchants and bankers. Economists view talk as cheap and culture as insignificant. Yet humans are talking animals, and the animals talk a great deal in their marketplaces. Of course the economist does not have to pay attention to everything that happens in an economy. That farmers chew tobacco or paint traditional designs on their barns while dealing in corn does not necessarily have to appear in the econometrics. What would have to appear is a large expenditure, since expenditure is the economist's measuring rod.

For example, two economic historians, John Wallis and Douglass North, have argued that transaction costs – that is, expenditures to negotiate and enforce contracts – rose from a quarter of national income in 1870 to over half of national income in 1970 (Wallis and

North 1986, table 3.13). Their measurement is a model of how to make such calculations, and suggestive of the importance of talk in the economy. It is not precisely the measurement wanted here. Transaction costs include, for example, "protective services," such as police and prisons, which "talk" only in an extended sense. Literal talk is special – in particular it is cheap, as police and prisons are not – in a way that makes it analytically separate from the rest of transaction costs.

Information is one part of the talk; issuing orders is another. The conveying of information and orders is well understood by economics: much of game theory is concerned one way or another with information; and production theory might be construed as the theory of one mind issuing orders.

Persuasion is the third part of economic talk. It is not well understood. But it is startlingly big. Take the categories of employment and make an educated guess as to the percentage of the time in each category spent on persuasion (the calculation could be improved with more factual and economic detail; for instance, the workers could be weighted by salaries; the marginal product of persuasion could be considered in more detail; the occupational categories could be subdivided: I intend here only to raise the scientific issue, not to settle it). The preliminary result is notable, shown in table 2. Weighted sums yield 28.2 million out of 115 million civilian employment, or about a quarter of the labor force, devoted to persuasion.

The result can be confirmed in other measures. Wallis and North measure 50 percent of national income as transaction costs, negotiation costs being part of these. Similarly, over half of American workers are white-collar. Some do not talk for a living, but in an extended sense many do, as for that matter do many blue-collar workers and especially pink-collar workers. And of the talkers a good percentage are persuaders. The secretary shepherding a document through the company bureaucracy is often called on to exercise sweet talk and veiled threats. Or notice the persuasion exercised the next time you buy a suit. Specialty clothing stores charge more than discount stores not staffed with rhetoricians. The differential pays for the persuasion: "It's you, my dear" or "The fish tie makes a statement." As Smith says (1762–63 [1982], p. 352, spelling modernized here and later), "every one is practising oratory . . . [and therefore] they acquire a certain dexterity and address in managing their affairs, or in other words in managing of men; and this is altogether the practise of every man in the most ordinary affairs . . .,

Table 2. *Persuasion is a quarter of employment: guesses about the share of marginal product attributable to persuasion in selected occupations in the United States in 1988*

100%	75%	50%	25%
	Executive administrative, and managerial **(14.2 million)**		Natural scientists (0.395 million)
	Construction trades, supervisors (0.617m.)	Health assessment and treatment (2.15m.)	
	Teachers **(4.77m.)**		
Social, recreational, and religious workers (1.05m.)	Counselors (0.206m.)	Social scientists and urban planners (0.343m.)	
	Clerical supervisors (0.174m.)		
Actors and directors (0.100m.)		Teachers' aides (0.423m.)	
Lawyers and judges (0.757m.)	Editors and reporters (0.117m.)	Authors and technical writers (0.140m.)	Legal assistants (0.203m.)
Public relations specialists (0.260m.)	Sales occupations, *less* cashiers **(11.4m.)**	Adjusters and investigators (0.949m.)	
		Police and detectives (0.755m.)	

Source: US Bureau of the Census, *Statistical Abstract of the United States 1990* (110th edn.), GPO: Washington, D.C., 1990, Series 645.

the constant employment or trade of every man . . .." Not constant, perhaps, but in Smith's time a substantial percentage and in modern times fully 25 percent.

The same point can be made from the other side of the national accounts, the product side. The more obviously talkie parts of production amount to a third of the total, and much of these must have been persuasion rather than information or command. Out of an American domestic product of $2,360 billion in 1981 (note the change of year; there is nothing special about this year or that; *Statistical Abstract*, series 701, p. 424) the sum of wholesale and retail trade ($353 billion by itself), paper and allied products ($22.2 billion, producing memoranda for the circular file), legal services ($23.4 billion), educational services ($17.0 billion), social services ($10.7 billion), perhaps two-thirds of government and governmental enterprises ($224 billion), and perhaps half each of finance, insurance, and real estate ($162 billion), of hotels ($8.15 billion), and of air transport ($7.20 billion) amounts to $828 billion, or about 35 percent of national product. Adjust it down if you will. The figure squares with the income side. Persuasion is about a quarter of national product and national income.

Is the persuasive talk then "empty," mere comforting chatter with no further economic significance? If that is all it is then the economy would be engaging in an expensive activity to no purpose. A quarter of national income is a lot to pay for economically functionless placebos. The fact would not square with economics. The business people circling LaGuardia on a rainy Monday night could have stayed at home. The crisis meeting in the plant cafeteria between the managers and the workers would lack point. Wasteful motion, or empty words, sit poorly with conventional economics. By shutting up we could pick up a $20 bill (or more exactly a $1,500,000,000,000 bill). That cannot be. A quarter of our working time in the marketplace is spent in persuasive converse. The conversational metaphor acknowledges the fact.

What is "critical" in the non-academic sense about the fact and the metaphor of a conversational economy, a third way of using economics to criticize itself, is that economics as presently constituted does not acknowledge the fact (if it is a fact: I repeat that the calculation would need much elaboration to be scientifically persuasive). The conversation of the economy is taken as irrelevant to economic science. As Don Lavoie puts it, "economists seem to agree that the scientific discourse of economics should dissociate itself from the everyday discourse of the economy" (Lavoie 1990d, p. 170). He observes dryly, "Economists are not so clear why they think this" (p. 169).

The economy, one might say from the statistics, "rests" on persuasive talk. Yet economists are not required, I have said, to pay attention even to everything the economy "rests" on. It also rests, for example, on engineering, but in speaking of the economics of bridges and other social overhead capital an economist does not need to know about the equilibrium equations for three-dimensional rigid bodies.

In the present case, when economists can reduce some transaction to a *silent* physical action, they can properly ignore the talk, at least in its effects on the equilibrium price. Adam Smith, to continue the quotation from *Lectures on Jurisprudence*, said that persuasion, "being the constant employment or trade of every man, in the same manner as the artisans invent simple methods of doing their work, so will each one here endeavour to do this work in the simplest manner. That is bartering, by which they address themselves to the self interest of the person and seldom fail immediately to gain their end."

Of course, a sociologist would point out that the institutions of a bartering grocery store "rest" on all manner of talk, such as the giving of orders to the junior grocery clerk to spend the next hour fronting the stock in aisles 6 through 8. The anthropologist reminds economists that "behind" their market lies a culture, which is another talking matter. But given the culture and the institutions (a big given, I admit), and confining attention to the immediate result, if the clerk does not like the assignment he can silently walk, exercising his option of what Albert Hirschman calls "exit" (Hirschman 1970). He is not a slave. Likewise, a man who tries to haggle with his local grocery store about the price of a quart of milk is wasting his breath and wasting the grocer's time. If he thinks he can get a better price down the street, he can walk. If the grocer thinks the next customer will pay the price, he can ignore the haggler. The talk in such cases is not essential for the economics.

Walk or talk. To put it another way, that many transactions involve talk may be interesting but need not be a criticism of economics. The physical walking may still set tight limits on what can be charged. People bargain over houses and automobiles, talking a lot, yet no one will be talked into selling a four-bedroom apartment overlooking Central Park for $3.57 or into buying a '77 Chevy with a little rust and 220,000 miles for $500,000. The customer will walk away from such offers. What matters is the size of the "gold points" within which silent trade confines the price. If the gold points are narrow, the talking does not change the deal. If they are wide, however, it may well change it.

A case of wide gold points, by definition, is pure bargaining. Two people meet in the middle of the Sahara, alone. One person has plenty of water but no food; the other plenty of food but no water. At what price will the deal take place? Obviously, it depends on the bargaining skills of the two. Economists have not made much progress in understanding situations of pure bargaining. Game theory for all its wonders has not gotten far on the matter (F. Fisher 1989, esp. p. 122). Perhaps, I am suggesting, the theoretical impasse arises because bargaining is talk, all the way down. As the food owner in the Saharan encounter, Arjo claims forcefully that he has a physical ailment requiring an unusual amount of both water and food. Don detects a ruse, and offers little water in exchange for his pound of food. Arjo weeps affectingly; Don's heart softens, and he hands over half his water. Or he laughs sardonically and portions out to Arjo a tiny swig in exchange for most of his food. It depends on talk.

This unsatisfactory conclusion relates to a basic feature of speech, that it can apparently be trumped, cheaply, in a way that sweaty physical action cannot. Suppose you devised a rule that would predict the bargaining speech of lonely owners of water in the middle of the Sahara. Would this permit you to extract the water at a low price? No. As economists have pointed out repeatedly, if one person is predictable, the other can exploit the predictability, which will suggest to the exploited one that he had better randomize. If you're so smart about bargaining, why ain't you rich?

A limit on calculability is a feature of any speaking. If anyone could get their way by shouting, for example, then everyone would shout, as at a cocktail party, arriving by the end of the party hoarse but without having gotten their way. The philosopher H. P. Grice affixed an economic tag to the trumping of speech conventions, "exploitation." The linguist Stephen Levinson puts his finger on the limits of formalization when language is involved:

> [T]here is a fundamental way in which a full account of the communicative power of language can never be reduced to a set of conventions for the use of language. The reason is that wherever some convention or expectation about the use of language arises, there will also therewith arise the possibility of the non-conventional exploitation of that convention or expectation. It follows that a purely . . . rule-based account of natural language usage can never be complete.
>
> Levinson 1983, p. 112

A joke among linguists makes the point (the story is said to be true). A pompous linguist was giving a seminar in which he claimed that while there were languages in which two negatives made a positive (as in Received Standard English: "I did not see nobody" = "I saw somebody") or two negatives made a negative (standard Italian: *Non ho visto nessuno* = "I did not see anybody"), there are no languages in which two positives made a negative. To which a smart aleck in the front row replied with a sneer: "Yeah, yeah." Any rule of language can be trumped cheaply for effect.

The game theorist Joseph Farrell has made a similar point in a paper of his called "Meaning and Credibility in Cheap-Talk Games" (1988). What I call "trumping" he calls "neologism," and finds that games are sensitive to its use. "We could conclude that we have no satisfactory positive theory in a one-shot game [a conclusion which may explain the unpopularity of the paper with referees] . . . Games should be taken in context, especially when analyzing the effects of communication. Language that could not survive in equilibrium if the world were nothing but a particular game, can nevertheless affect the outcome of the game" (Farrell 1988, p. 19).

Economists specialize in knowing about costs and benefits. But someone – maybe even a specialized economist – might want to learn about the speech by which people construct their stories of the cost and benefit. Maybe some useful economics can be done, or the existing economics modified. Adam Smith, as usual, put the issue well. The division of labor is the "consequence of a certain propensity . . . to truck, barter, and exchange . . . [W]hether this propensity be one of those original principles in human nature, of which no further account can be given; or whether, as seems more probable, it be the necessary consequence of the faculties of reason *and speech*" he could not pause to consider (1776 [1981], I, ii, p. 25, my italics). *The Wealth of Nations* does not again mention the faculty of speech in a foundational role, though Smith, who began his career as a teacher of rhetoric, did remark frequently on how business people and politicians talked together. Half of his foundational formula, the faculty of reason, became in time the characteristic obsession of economists. Smith himself did not much pursue it. Economic Man, whether speaking or seeking, is not a Smithian character. It was later economists, especially Paul Samuelson, who reduced economics to the reasoning of a constrained maximizer, Seeking Man.

By contrast, Speaking Man has never figured much in economics, even among institutionalist economists. A man acts, by and for himself. That is what utility functions or institutions or social classes or property rights are about. No need to speak. Walk rather than talk. Smith would have disagreed. Towards the end of *The Theory of Moral Sentiments* (1790 [1982], VII, iv, 24, p. 336) he dug behind the faculty of speech (which led to the propensity to exchange, which led to the division of labor, which led to the wealth of nations). He connected it to persuasion, which is to say, speech meant to influence others: "The desire of being believed, the desire of persuading, of leading and directing other people, seems to be one of the strongest of all our natural desires. It is, perhaps, the instinct on which is founded the faculty of speech [Smith was the sort of writer who would have been well aware that he was using the same phrase here as he used in *The Wealth of Nations*], the characteristical faculty of human nature" (1790 [1982], VII, iv, 25, p. 336). Compare his *Lectures on Jurisprudence*, in the passage quoted: "Men always endeavour to persuade others . . . [and] in this manner every one is practising oratory through the whole of his life."

Economists have come to recognize over the past couple of decades that transaction costs are high – that an employee can indulge in opportunistic behavior, shirking on the job; that a sharecropper can malinger and the landowner can cheat; that governments cannot be bound to their undertakings, since they decide the bounds themselves. The talk that makes for friendship, contracts, or political culture is not cheap and dispensable. It is expensive, and essential to the work of a complex society.

In other words, economists might explore the economics of talk. Their theory concerns walking, but the economy does a great deal of talking. No English professor or sociologist would doubt the fact. An economics confined to the Faculty of Reason, and ignoring the Faculty of Speech, creates paradoxes, as in the theory of rational expectations or the theory of games. The Faculty of Speech deserves some analytic attention, even from economists.

The three propositions in metaeconomics, then, are: the Theorem of Intellectual Modesty, the Maxim of Intellectual Exchange, and the Paradox of Persuasion. It would be nice if specialized economists would think about them and then report back to the rest of us.

Incidentally, anything that smacks of reflexive criticism these days is liable to be tagged as "deconstruction" or some other foul-smelling French concoction, and then related to fascism, communism, and the decline of the West. But observe that the critical arguments here are plain old English-speaking, Scottish-invented economics, with a dash of American pragmatism and a half cup of ancient rhetoric. The American question and the Principle of Toleration and the Statistics of Persuasion are not French.

The way to inaugurate the intellectual trade and intellectual modesty and verbal sophistication that will I hope characterize the world after positivism and modernism is to focus on rhetoric, to ask: what kind of argument is this? Does it apply to itself? Does it use a metaphor of specialization or of silent trade? What is the story of Modest Greed or of Meeting in the Sahara through which it is argued? Rhetoric is an anti-epistemological epistemology that breaks down the barriers to trade between disciplines. It undercuts the claim to a hard self-sufficiency in economics. "There is no point in assigning degrees of 'objectivity' or 'hardness' to such disciplines," as Richard Rorty says. "For the presence of unforced agreement in all of them gives us everything in the way of 'objective truth' which one could possibly want: namely, intersubjective agreement" (Rorty 1987, p. 42). We can be wise if we trade intellectually. But we cannot be social engineers hovering over society like a new priesthood, for if we were so smart we would be rich, and in this manner would practice persuasive oratory through the whole of our lives.

chapter 7

Popper and Lakatos: thin ways of reading economics

The outsider makes the same complaint about philosophers as he does about economists, saying, "These writers thin down the question so." And so they both do. The economist thins the question of the good society right down to matters of price and marginal cost. The philosopher thins the good argument right down to matters of *modus tollens* and infinite regress. Precision comes from the conversational thinness, as does academic employment and other good. But even after such achievements we should not be surprised if outsiders want to get back to the main and fatter point.

Consider the favorite philosopher of economic Methodologists, Karl Popper. He is the favorite among scientists, too, because he flatters the scientists and they return the favor. Science in Popper's view is filled with romantic heroes falsifying the conventional view. The trouble with using Karl Popper's thinking for a history or methodology or criticism of economic thought is not mainly some flaw in its technique, though the philosopher Daniel Hausman among others has made the pervasiveness of the flaw clear (Hausman 1988; cf. Klant 1984). The main problem, even in this richest of rationalist philosophies, is its thinness. Rich as Popper's thinking is, supplemented by Lakatos, elaborated and applied with wonderful ingenuity by their followers during the 1970s and 1980s, it looks thin beside the actual conversation of science. A conversation begun in the primeval forest, extended and made more articulate in the course of centuries, is probably not going to fit easily into a few lines of philosophy. Or rather, since the issue is empirical, it might be that a philosophy could describe well what goes on in the conversation of science; but it hasn't. One can imagine a world perhaps in which the growth of knowledge was interestingly philosophizable. But it doesn't seem to be our world (compare Rorty 1982, p. xiv).

An economic Methodology "based" (that hopeful word) on philosophy, especially on philosophy as construed among English-speakers around 1955, is too thin to work. Such a remark is not to be taken as anti-intellectual, anti-rational, anti-philosophical, or even anti-analytic-philosophical. Thinking is good, even when thin, and so is thinking about thinking. No one wants to abandon first-order predicate logic, even though it might not be a complete model for sound thinking. Nor is the remark to be taken as one of those sneers at methodology, the sort that grace the exordia of Methodological papers by Paul Samuelson or George Stigler. Thinking about thinking about thinking is good, too.

The trouble is not so much badness as thinness. As Richard McKeon the Chicago Aristotelian put it in 1955, the dichotomies of modernism are "taken together or separately, implausible or at least impoverished as theory" (McKeon 1955 [1987], p. 70). Even those of us who from time to time make use of philosophy of science complain about its impoverished thinness. The economist E. Roy Weintraub, for example, who has experimented with Popperian and Lakatosian analyses of actual economic texts, complains rightly that Popper reduces the thick conversation of empirical work down to falsifying and Lakatos to a novel "fact." Weintraub notes in *General Equilibrium Analysis: Studies in Appraisal* (1985) that his case study "raises several other problems that rest uneasily in a Lakatosian bed" (p. 142). In *Stabilizing Dynamics: Constructing Economic Knowledge* (1991b) he has moved to a thicker and more literary approach to the study of economic writing, though the writing is mathematical.

In fact part of Lakatos himself, the early Lakatos of *Proofs and Refutations* (first drafted in 1961, at age thirty-nine), can be called in to testify against the thin, mechanical system of the somewhat later Lakatos (who wrote his main Methodological paper in 1968–1969 at age forty-six [Lakatos 1978, ch. 1]). His first book, rarely mentioned by the conventional Methodologists, is more playful and tentative and open to other disciplines than Neil de Marchi or Mark Blaug or most of the other Lakatosians in economics.

Thicker. Certainly this is how Paul Feyerabend reads his friend (Feyerabend's *Against Method* [1975 (1978)] was planned before Lakatos' death in 1974 as half of a dialogue, and warmly dedicated to Lakatos' memory). Lakatos is filled with playfulness, if a trifle grim; for instance: "The old rationalist dream of a mechanical, semi-mechanical or at least fast-acting Method for showing up falsehood, unprovenness, meaningless rubbish or even irrational choice has to be given up. It takes a long time to appraise a research program: Minerva's owl flies at dusk" (de Marchi and Blaug 1991, p. 25, from Lakatos 1978, p. 149; cf. Lakatos 1978, p. 87; the essay was written by Lakatos in 1970). It would be hard from this to justify rationalist "assessments" of a science actively in the making. Neil de Marchi, as the chief advocate of a Lakatosian line in economic Methodology, quotes these sentences in the introduction to his collection edited in 1991 with Mark Blaug. He lets it lie, without noting that it might undermine his interpretation of the master (it is hard to argue that economics is at dusk; more like 9.00 a.m.). The mechanical rationalism ascribed to Lakatos is I think contrary to the spirit revealed in *Proofs and Refutations* (from his Ph.D. thesis written under Richard Braithwaite at Cambridge; the very title of the book is a play on Popper's *Conjectures and Refutations*).

The fissures in Lakatos are notorious among sophisticated students of his work, such as Wade Hands (1991c, p. 94): "Either Lakatos changed his mind between (and sometimes within) works, or he simply held more than one view simultaneously." In the first essay in the de Marchi and Blaug collection Jeremy Shearmur defends the young Lakatos against his more naïve fans, and against his older self, the older self who came to espouse merely "a positivistic adaption of Popper" under the banner of novel facts (Shearmur 1991, p. 40). "In economics," Shearmur asserts, what we seek is "often . . . precisely the problem-solving abilities of a theory in the sense of its ability to furnish an explanation . . . of phenomena that are already well known to us." That fits the Lakatos$_1$ of *Proofs and Refutations* and many *obiter dicta* scattered later, but not the rationalism of Lakatos$_2$.

Even Lakatos' later and rationalist work was an extended complaint about the lack of thickness in Popper's model for science, as Popper's was a complaint about earlier and still thinner philosophies. The hard core of the rationalist philosophy, and the thinnest of theories, is: the Truth Will Out. It is a commitment necessary for working scientists if they are not to become as cynical as many economic scientists have become. But it is non-operational, because it can be tested only at the Second Coming. For students of science in the here and now it is naïve to think that power, analogy, upbringing, story, prestige, style, interest, and passion cannot block science for years, decades, centuries.

The naïve view is that science is rational in a rationalist sense, that is, non-rhetorical and non-sociological, understandable in our rationalist terms now, not at dusk. The history and sociology and rhetoric of science says it isn't so. A case in point in economics is the theory of the entrepreneur. Many neoclassicals like me are beginning to realize that the Austrian economists have been right about the entrepreneur and equilibrium for a century (cf. Blaug 1991, p. 508; Kirzner 1989; Lavoie 1990b; Wu 1989). A lot of good it has done the Austrians. Who knows if it will ever be adopted?

The rationalist program has been applied to economics and has failed. True, Mark Blaug and J. J. Klant, to name distinguished economic Methodologists of the old school, accept Lakatos' program, the "rational [which is to say, philosophical] reconstruction of research programs," as what methodology should do. But even they strain at its limits when applying the program to real work in economics. Lawrence Boland, a highly original Popperian, in fact comes close to advocating an economic literary criticism (e.g. 1982, pp. 116–117). In an unPopperian way he stresses the limitations of, say, Blaug's program of "methodological appraisal," arguing that the program should be "to establish a clear understanding of what neoclassical economics is rather than to determine what some philosophers think it should be" (Boland 1982, p. 48). Even the small, hard core of Popperians and Lakatosians find that rational reconstruction of economics does not work without modification.

Most students of the matter are harsher in their judgments. Wade Hands has for some years been demolishing the claims of the Popperian–Lakatosian project to philosophical coherence (Hands 1985, 1988, 1990, 1991a). He writes in his book summarizing the situation after a quarter century of trying to make Popper and Lakatos work: "There simply are *not* convincing arguments that by strictly following a falsificationist Methodology or by restricting our attention to research programs that consistently and correctly predict novel facts we will necessarily be guaranteed that our theories will produce economic knowledge" (Hands 1993, p. 149).

One contributor after another to the de Marchi and Blaug volume assessing the Lakatosian assessment (though not the editors themselves and Roger Backhouse) concluded also on empirical grounds that it has failed – failed to solve the Duhem–Quine dilemma (Kim 1991, p. 128), failed to capture the insights from game theory (Bianchi and Moulin 1991, p. 195), failed to account for the decline of process analysis in econometrics (Morgan 1991, p. 271), failed to apply to stabilizing dynamics (Weintraub 1991a, p. 288), failed to explain the anxiety of econometricians to nest their hypotheses about equilibrium unemployment (Cross 1991, pp. 319, 320), failed to predict the sociology of rational expectations (Maddock 1991, pp. 353–354), failed to grasp the anthropology of new classical macroeconomics (Hoover 1991, p. 385), failed to allow for critical work such as Sraffa's (Steedman 1991, p. 448), failed to encourage a practical subjectivism that reflects our human viewpoint (Lavoie 1991; Caldwell 1991, p. 487), and failed to fit the history, sociology, and rhetoric of science (H. M. Collins 1991a).

In his "Afterword" to the volume Blaug expresses vexation at the "jaundiced reaction to Lakatos" by all but two participants in the conference (Roger Backhouse and Vernon Smith are the two; possibly it is four, if Smith's coauthors Kevin McCabe and Stephen Rassenti agree with Smith's enthusiasm). And the thirty were not an untruncated sample. Blaug writes: "I was personally taken aback by what can only be described as a generally dismissive, if not hostile, reaction to Lakatos' MSRP" (de Marchi and Blaug, 1991, p. 500). Lakatos' work is treated by de Marchi as the Five Books of Moses, whose "hints" (pp. 9, 12, 19) are to be elaborated by the faithful; he, too, is scandalized and depressed by the spreading blasphemy.

The Methodology (big M) of Scientific Research Programs (MSRP), its most favorably disposed students have concluded, is too thin to cover economics. By a Popperian test almost the whole of conventional philosophy of science has been falsified. We have seen how its Lakatosian version has fared within economics. Though working scientists will occasionally use a philosophy for a rhetorical purpose, no one in science seems actually to have carried out a Baconian program or a Machian program or a Bridgemanian program, much less a Popperian or Lakatosian program. The project of rational reconstruction that the Popperian–Lakatosian philosophers and economists worked on earnestly and intelligently for twenty-five years has failed, though many isolated ideas of Popper and Lakatos are permanent gains. It is helpful to have available the rhetoric of "research program," "hard core," "negative heuristic," "excess content," and the like, as long as it does not harden into a dogma. But the core of the program – which asserts, to repeat, that science can be studied best by imagining it as rational progress in a narrow definition of rationality – is mistaken.

Look at how scientists and scholars read. If you listen with expert knowledge to the remarks in a scientific or scholarly conversation, reading the articles in *Mind* or *The Physical Review* or *The Journal of Political Economy*, you will know that most of them are erroneous, irrelevant, or trivial. You will often be impressed by the technical competence displayed, but if you know the field well you will know that most of the articles are normal science and that normal science will be superseded. It is so at least in the tiny subfields of economics and history in which I am expert. Michael Polanyi, an important chemist, said the same thing is true about chemistry: most of what Linus Pauling did was wrong or irrelevant, though Pauling was the best chemist of the twentieth century.

The scientific and scholarly writers are not charlatans or fools in writing these erroneous articles. They are trying, as well as they can. If nonetheless most of their efforts did not in fact fail, the advance of science and scholarship would be lightning fast. Each paper would be epoch-making. But it is not, the hucksters to the contrary. The average article in economics is read by fewer than half a dozen people. The economists appear to agree that most papers are not "worth reading." (Of course, one cannot tell which paper will be the new Muth or Solow, so it is optimal to read more.)

So pulling down the journals and studying them in any field, if done with expert knowledge and a couple of years' perspective, will suggest that the field is less than rational. Only in long retrospect, at dusk, do we learn what are the Important Articles. Viewed a century on the field will look highly progressive, moving from triumph to triumph, eminently rationally reconstructible. But the rational reconstruction is too easy. It is Whig history, company history. The difficult history is to connect the two ways of looking at the field, before and after, to see how articles are afterwards selected by sociology and rhetoric for classic status. Looking only at the successes in retrospect does not satisfy the scientific standard announced by the Methodologists as applicable to economics. It is too easy, like playing tennis with the net down (as Mark Blaug likes to put it) and does not satisfy.

The thinness of the philosophy comes from the thinness of the question it asks. The question in a rational reconstruction of a piece of science is: does the discourse fit, say, a Lakatosian model? What is its hard core, the protective belt, a typical negative heuristic? Can it be made to lie down on the bed, with suitable trimming at head and feet?

The question will strike the outsider as odd. A study that verifies or falsifies the fit of such a simple notion as sophisticated falsificationism to a part of economics does not ask many questions. The question it does ask – is Lakatos' model applicable here? – would not strike a working scientist as interesting. At the end of the day you are led to ask what has been accomplished.

Consider Roy Weintraub's earlier work, the imitation of Lakatos just mentioned (1985) and his elegant paper, "The NeoWalrasian Research Program is Empirically Progressive" (1988b). All right (as Weintraub himself would probably say now), suppose that by the Lakatosian definition the neoWalrasian program is empirically progressive. (Arthur Diamond 1988 persuasively demurs; and see chapter 11 below). But what follows? What has been accomplished? We are now persuaded that neoclassical economics can be rationally reconstructed to correspond with a pattern adumbrated by a certain philosopher. Well, so what?

The question is pragmatic, in no vulgar sense. It will be satisfactory if the cash value of the Lakatosian categories shows up merely in their value for further thinking: for setting economics in context, for making economists more self-aware, for telling persuasive stories about the history of economics, for understanding why economists go on as they do. Among professional intellectuals these should count as good reasons. There is no vulgar demand here for "better economic predictions" from the philosophy, or some market test.

Whether there is any practical payoff or not, professional intellectuals can reasonably require that ideas have at least intellectual consequences. If you explain that the orbit of the moon arises from the "orbital character" of the moon you have a handsome turn of phrase, applicable to other moons as well, but not rich in consequences, and not answering human questions. If on the other hand you explain that the orbit has to do with $F = ma$ the consequences are many, answering questions that people hadn't thought to ask: Why is a moon like an apple? Where did the moon come from and where is it going? How do you get to the moon from here?

The Lakatosian character of some piece of economics, like the orbital character of the moon, has no intellectual consequences. It does not answer a question that an economist, or even a non-Lakatosian philosopher, would be interested in asking.

The question it does ask is one of the nature-of questions that Popper and Lakatos claimed to spurn. Problem situations, not natures, they said, are the proper subject of science. Popper and Lakatos emphasized repeatedly that new questions – in other words continuity in the conversation – characterize progressive science. One is led to ask of the program of applying Popperian or Lakatosian or other philosophical ideas to the history of economic thought: is it empirically progressive? What is the problem of which Lakatos' Methodology of Scientific Research Programs is a progressive solution?

But answer came there none. It is considered important for

economics to be adjudged "empirically progressive" (in Lakatos' sense), just as a little earlier the talk of economists was abuzz with the importance of Popperian falsifiability (thus Blaug 1980); and before that of Bridgemanian operationality (Samuelson 1947); and before that of Millsian methodicalness; and before that of Baconian inferentiality. But it solves no problem. Around 1980 the task of the Lakatosian Methodologist or historian of thought was to check this out, this Lakatosian virtue in economic science. Yet Lakatos might alternatively have called a science "Scientific" or "free of false consciousness" instead of "progressive"; and these would amount in the end merely to "Lakatos-beloved" (compare Plato's *Euthyphro*, 10e–11b). Why would we care that economics would be beloved of Imre Lakatos? It seems Pickwickian.

We might indeed care about economics being "empirically pro-gressive" if "progressiveness" in Lakatos' sense were shown histori-cally to correspond to progress. But the assertion is doubtful, and is explicitly denied by both Popper and Lakatos. They do not pretend to give persuasive histories of how science actually did progress. Theirs is rational not historical reconstruction. To repeat, if their appeal rested on a claimed fit to science they would be in serious trouble with present-day historians and sociologists of science, not to speak of Michael Polanyi, Stephen Toulmin, and Paul Feyerabend. Lakatos' key requirement that a "progressive" (i.e. Lakatos-beloved) research program implies "novel facts" has resulted in, as Wade Hands puts it, "novel fact hunts . . . Since there are now so many definitions of novel facts in the literature, these papers can become mired in semantic debates which provide little insight into either economics or philosophy" (Hands 1991a, p. 70).

To take another possibility, we might care about Lakatos-belovedness if a "progressive" scientific research program could be shown to lead to Truth. But it is reliably reported that there is a problem with Truth. The problem is not with lowercase truth, which gives answers to questions arising now in human conversations, requiring no access to the mind of God: on a Fahrenheit scale what is the temperature in Iowa City this afternoon? On a historical scale what is the quality of the President's decisions in domestic affairs? You and I can answer such questions, improving our answers in shared discourse.

The problem comes when trying to vault into a higher realm, asking whether such and such a Methodology will lead ultimately to the end of the conversation, to the final Truth about economics or philosophy. It is the question asked by Plato and reiterated by Bacon and Descartes. The sophist Protagoras, who had a more modest program, said that man (literally, "a person": the Greek is *anthropos*, which means *Mensch*, that is, person, not *anêr*, male person, *Mann*) is the measure of all things. The modest program of the sophists was not pleasing to Plato, Descartes, and Bacon:

> For it is a false assertion that the sense of man is the measure of all things. On the contrary, all perceptions as well as of the sense as of the mind are according to the measure of the individual and not according to the measure of the universe. And the human under-standing is like a false mirror, which, receiving rays irregularly, distorts and discolours the nature of things by mingling its own nature with it.
>
> Bacon 1620 [1965], XVI

The "measure of the universe," however, cannot be taken direct; it can only be taken from the sublunary mirrors we have. Questions such as "What will economics look like once it is finished?" cannot be answered on this side of the Last Judgment. The physicist Wolfgang Pauli used somewhere an economic metaphor to scold physicists for anticipating the physics that would arise once judgment was ended, claiming "credits for the future." As Jacob Bronowski said about the positivists (he was praising Popper as a post-positivist), "Their eyes were always fixed (somewhere on the horizon) on a finished scien-tific system, and their analysis was always colored by the ideal relation between the parts that would be found on the day when the system was finished" (Bronowski 1977, p. 80).

Economists, with their witticisms about lunches not being free, should have no trouble seeing that little can be hoped for prescience in such matters. The problem is that it is pre-science, knowing before knowing (McCloskey 1990a, chapters 8 and 9; and chapter 6 here). Of Lakatos' proposal to justify a piece of science by how much Truth it produces, Wade Hands again makes the relevant point, with charac-teristic acerbity (Hands 1991a, p. 67): "However recurrent such pleas have been in the history of philosophy it is doubtful whether such a justification will soon be upon us."

chapter 8

Thick readings: ethics, economics, sociology, and rhetoric

If Methodology – Popperian, Lakatosian, or whatever – is not a guide to the history of thought or a guide to the completion of science, one may ask, what *is* it a guide to? What, really, is the philosophy of economic science about?

The answer appears to be that it is about morality for scientists. In this the philosophers commit no sin. Popper and company are not so much concerned to tell a persuasive story or lead a march to Truth as to persuade scientists to be good. Listen to these phrases from Blaug's Popperian book of 1980, The *Methodology of Economics*: "what is wrong is that economists do not practice what they preach" (p. xiii); "Feyerabend's book amounts to replacing the philosophy of science by the philosophy of flower power" (p. 44); "the scientific community is the paradigm case of the open society" (p. 46); "much of [modern economics] is like playing tennis with the net down: instead of attempting to refute testable predictions, modern economists all too frequently are satisfied to . . . [replace] falsification, which is difficult, with verification, which is easy" (p. 256); "What methodology can do is to . . . [set] standards that will help us to discriminate between wheat and chaff . . . [T]he ultimate question we can and indeed must pose about any research program is the one made familiar by Popper: what events, if they materialized, would lead us to reject that program? A program that cannot meet that question has fallen short of the highest standards that scientific knowledge can attain" (p. 264). Blaug's rhetoric is that of the moralist, not the describer or the reconstructor.

The sneering and name calling and bad-guy identifying and horrified viewing with alarm that characterizes Methodological discourse fits a program of goodness. The modern embarrassment about moral talk to the contrary, pursuing a program of goodness is a good idea, in science or elsewhere. Programs of goodness are the basis of moral sentiments, which is to say, the approval and disapproval that hold societies together as much or more than self-interest does, as Adam Smith said in his other book.

We berate and banish the criminal, the bad man. The Rules of the Game give us a way of classifying scientists as citizens or as thought-criminals. If Blaug and other Methodological conservatives can tag a descendant of Nietzsche as an "irrationalist," they can shut him up, or at any rate protect innocent students from his words. If they can identify Freudians and Marxists as aliens they can get them deported from the open society. (By the way, an unhappy side effect of such a policy strictly enforced would be the deportation of most economists forthwith, pleading from the back of the truck their falsificationist credentials.)

I repeat: there is nothing wrong with moral programs in general. They are in fact essential for scholarship. Implementing them would revolutionize economics. Michael Polanyi, who was a distinguished crystallographer, said in 1946, "we see now that this [scientific] judgement has a moral aspect to it . . ., a matter of conscience . . . Scientific conscience cannot be satisfied by the fulfillment of any rules, since all rules are subject to its own interpretation" (Polanyi 1946 [1964], p. 39). Rom Harré has made the same point, following Polanyi, and I agree:

> [W]e . . . owe to Polanyi one of the first clear statements of the position from which all epistemology must from henceforth take its start: there are no sure foundations for knowledge to be discerned in some basis of a final and incorrigible truth . . . Neither falsehood nor truth is an attainable epistemic ideal. [Epistemic ideals] are proper only for the moral exhortation and castigation of a community of seekers after trustworthy knowledge.
>
> Harré 1986, p. 19

"Moral exhortation and castigation" is not in Harré's view mere blather. On the contrary:

> When philosophers carry on their discussions of science in terms of the official or strict system they are not describing either the cognitive or the material practices of the scientific community, even in ideal form. They are describing a rhetoric and an associated set of narrative conventions for presenting a story in which rival teams of scientists appear as heroes or villains . . . Seeking the truth is a hopeless epistemic project, but trying to live a life of virtue within

> the framework of a rule is a possible moral ambition ... The
> concepts of the moral system appear in the rhetorical glosses on that
> [scientific] life.
>
> Harré 1990, pp. 95–96; also 1986, p. 89

That's right: note the way he uses the word "rhetoric." As Rorty has
argued, the better definition of "rationality" is not Method but
morality, "something like 'sane' or 'reasonable' . . . It names a set of
moral virtues: tolerance, respect for the opinions of those around
one, willingness to listen, reliance on persuasion rather than force"
(Rorty 1987, p. 40). And thus too Stephen Toulmin: "Men demonstrate their rationality, not by ordering their concepts and beliefs in
tidy formal structures, but by their preparedness to respond to novel
situations with open minds" (Toulmin 1972, p. vii). Such a definition
would cast the "rational reconstruction of research programs" into
another and moral light.

Deborah Redman has recently brought the message to economics:

> Science, rationality, objectivity can no more be captured, legislated,
> or demarcated than can the concepts of freedom or democracy
> because their existence hangs on both professional training and on
> an attitude that itself is bound up with freedom and democracy . . ..
> If we really want to know what we can do to advance science, we
> can guarantee that this attitude, scientific rationalism – tolerance,
> honesty, commitment to the advance of science above personal
> advance and to the freedom to exercise criticism, a willingness to
> listen and to learn from others, and so on – is not violated and
> becomes entrenched as a tradition.
>
> Redman 1991, pp. 168–172, quoted in Weintraub 1992, p. 183

I would quarrel only with her attribution of such virtues to what goes
by the name of scientific rationalism. Roy Weintraub comments on
this passage: "We do a thorough job training our students in the
technical methods, . . . but how much time is spent socializing our
new members to the ethical standards that we want to define our
community enterprise?" (Weintraub 1992, p. 183).

Conservative Methodologists, who talk morally but deny that they
need to know moral philosophy, will take such remarks as insults.
Their moral philosophy is that of modernism, the chocolate-ice-
cream theory, namely, that opinions about morality are mere preferences, like an uncriticizable preference for chocolate ice cream. Blaug
and the others would therefore be unhappy to be called moralists, for
they regard themselves as Scientists, and in keeping with modernist
ideas of morality they think that "there are long established, well-
tried methods for reconciling different methodological judgements.

There are no such methods for reconciling different normative value judgements – other than political elections and shooting it out at the barricades" (Blaug 1980, pp. 132–133). As Blaug's master Schumpeter put it, "We may, indeed, prefer the world of modern dictatorial socialism to the world of Adam Smith, or vice versa, but any such preference comes within the same category of subjective evaluation as does, to plagiarize Sombart, a man's preference for blondes over brunettes" (Schumpeter 1954, p. 330). Or Lionel Robbins: "If we disagree about ends it is a case of thy blood against mine – or live and let live, according to the importance of the difference, or the relative strength of our opponents . . . If we disagree about the morality of the taking of interest . . ., then there is no room for argument" (Robbins 1932, p. 134). The theory is "emotivism," "the doctrine that all evaluative judgments and more specifically all moral judgments are *nothing but* expressions of preference" (MacIntyre 1981, p. 11, his italics). Emotivism is of course self-contradictory: the sneer at evaluation applies to the evaluation of evaluation.

Undergraduates and many of their professors become uneasy and start giggling when a moral question arises. The agreement to disagree that ended the wars of religion in Europe can be traced in their unease, and in their stock remarks expressing it: "That's just a matter of opinion"; "Religion should not be mentioned in polite conversation"; "In questions of morality, it is thy blood or mine"; "The only methods for reconciling different normative value judgements are political elections or shooting it out at the barricades." The high-brow doubt of the Vienna Circle that moral statements were meaningful has this low-brow trace. According to modernist theory, therefore, to be caught making moral statements is to be caught in meaningless burbling. As I have said, the chocolate-ice-cream theory of morality is part of the Modernist Truce of 1900: Science is business, 9.00 to 5.00, Art is pleasure, after 5:00; meaning is for worktime, morals for Sunday.

The unrecognized moral purpose of Methodology explains the strength of feeling against John Dewey, Milton Friedman, Richard Rorty, and other harmless pragmatists. Moral and political purposes are not always denied by advocates of the received view. Sometimes they admit a moral purpose – though never stopping to argue it with care, since they do not believe that "argument" and "morality" and for that matter "care" have anything to do with each other. Recall Hutchison warning in 1938 about "the most sinister phenomenon of recent decades for the true scientist," and the urgent necessity to adopt positivism to "keep science separate from pseudo-science." An admirable desire to defend liberal values against the barbarians feeds Methodology.

The unargued, chocolate-ice-cream moral and political message in positivism and its offshoots explains perhaps the fascination with the Demarcation Problem. The main reason for demarcation seems to be that astrologers and parapsychologists are thought to be bad people, touchie-feelies from Santa Monica perhaps. It is taken as given that such intellectual criminals, violators of the rules of the game, are not to be tolerated in the open society. The appeal of Methodology, to repeat, is moral and political. Yet because the Methodologists do not take moral and political thinking seriously their implicit thinking about the subject is childish and bad. They make childish and bad remarks like: we may, indeed, prefer the world of modern dictatorial socialism to the world of Adam Smith, but any such preference comes within the same category as a man's preference for blondes over brunettes.

If the Methodologists scrutinized their moral and political fears, I would say, their opinions would take a less frantic and ill-reasoned form. As the economic methodologist Bruce Caldwell notes wisely, "The fear of anarchy [by which he means "chaos," the war of all against all], or of a totalitarian response to anarchy, cannot be based on a correct perception of science as it is currently practiced in free societies" (Caldwell 1988, p. 237). To solve the German Problem between the Wars, or the Slavic Problem after them, some rigid rules might have made sense, the more rigid the better – the better to defend a conversation from the state. I have been told by two distinguished economists, one from Hungary and the other from Poland, that they turned to mathematical economics of a rigidly abstract sort in the 1950s precisely to avoid political interference. When the Party man in charge of the scientist's soul detected some deviation the scientist could pull out a sheaf of algebra and ask mildly, "Yes, comrade: perhaps I have made a political mistake; please show it to me." But this obscurantist ploy is not so sweet in an open, plural, and pragmatic society. The appeal to the character of Scientist in such a place more often supports authoritarianism, in the Department of Defense or the National Aeronautics and Space Administration. In a democracy, especially after the fall of fascism and now communism, the barbarians against which philosophical Methodology should be fighting are mainly inside the gates.

It would be good to see the defenders of the fact/value split scrutinize their moral agenda. They will find enlightenment in the long conversation among philosophers and poets about values. If they knew that their Methodologies were about good values they could start their program of enlightenment with the Old Testament and the *Gorgias* and work forward. They would become learned and, more important, civilized.

The psychological literature on moral development, for example, is worth reading by economic Methodologists. Consider its feminist development. Conferences on Methodology in economics and elsewhere have notably few women participants. *In a Different Voice: Psychological Theory and Women's Development* (1982) by Carol Gilligan quotes Janet Lever's study of the games of boys and girls – "[B]oys were seen quarreling all the time, but not once was a game terminated because of a quarrel" – and explains that "it seemed that the boys enjoyed the legal debates as much as they did the game itself, and even marginal players of lesser size or skill participated equally in these recurrent squabbles. In contrast, the eruption of disputes among girls tended to end the game" (Gilligan 1982, p. 9). The parallel with Methodological disputes is suggestive. Gilligan reports on Piaget's observation of "boys becoming through childhood increasingly fascinated with the legal elaboration of rules . . ., a fascination that, he notes, does not hold for girls" (p. 10). The girls stressed community, conversation, solidarity, and other non-rule values, the values of what Richard Rorty identifies in himself, taking a kind suggestion of Clark Glymour's, as the values of "the new fuzzies" (Rorty 1987, p. 41). One is not surprised when Deborah Redman speaks of "a willingness to listen and to learn from others," a scientific value not featured much in the Methodological ruminations of men.

The good that lies behind Methodological thinking is the goodness of community, solidarity, openness to ideas, educated public opinion, and a better conversation of humanity. By their moral fervor the Methodologists reveal their values. The values are fine, though adopted uncritically, and not much different from those of the terrible fuzzies they fear and despise.

The word for it is *Sprachethik*, speech morality, the ethics of conversation. That the word comes from a hive of Marxist fuzzies in Frankfurt-am-Main should not be alarming, for it is liberalism incarnate: Don't lie; pay attention; don't sneer; cooperate; don't shout; let other people talk; be open-minded; explain yourself when asked; don't resort to violence or conspiracy in aid of your ideas. These are the rules adopted by the act of joining a good conversation (see Jon Wisman's useful discussion of Habermas and economics [Wisman 1990]). Early Socratic dialogue – reported/composed, though, by a man who wished to end conversation – is the model for Western intellectual life. An American philosopher put the point well. What is crucial, writes Amélie Oksenberg Rorty, is "our ability to engage in continuous conversation, testing one another, discovering our hidden presuppositions, changing our minds because we have listened to the voices of our fellows. Lunatics also change their minds, but their minds change with the tides of the moon and not because they have listened, really listened, to their friends' questions and objection" (A. O. Rorty 1983, p. 562). Good science is not good Method; it is good conversation in the laboratory and in the conference hall.

The modernist Methodologists such as Blaug or Backhouse have not thought much about the claims of *Sprachethik* – tolerance, for example. When Backhouse wants to criticize Sheila Dow for advocating mere tolerance he puts it this way: of course "economists should accept that the visions on which they base their theories differ, and should not judge other schools' theories against the standards according to which they judge their own" (Backhouse 1992b, p. 73). Hey, man: you have your vision, school, paradigm, or religion, I have mine. But this is not what tolerance can mean among intellectuals. It must mean, as Dow says, "openness to a range of methods, disciplines, and influences, accepting that no theory can be regarded as true in any absolute sense" (quoted by Backhouse, 1992b, p. 72). That is, one participates in a conversation, testing one's notions by mutual criticism, listening, really listening, to other remarks. Conversation does not consist of monologues in series. It has proven difficult to convey this notion to the Methodologists.

We know when conversations are going well among our own intellectual friends. Most economists would agree, for example, that the conversation about international trade since 1950 has been going through a bad patch, relieved only temporarily by a burst of creativity around 1970 on the financial side. They would agree, too, that economic history improved radically after 1958 and has flourished ever since, with a setback of jealous, angry talk around 1972 from which it has at length recovered. Working economists do not need the advice of a philosopher – least of all an economist in philosopher's clothing – to know when things are going well or badly in their field.

It is a crucial point about the conversational view of intellectual life that conversations overlap. You are almost as sure about neighboring conversations as about your own, which is what research panels, editorial boards, and tenure committees depend on. If good conversation is maintained in one part of the conversation of humanity the overlap provides standards for others. The overlap of the overlap spreads good standards, such as care in reading earlier work (and bad habits, too, such as the mechanical use of statistical significance). This market – not the central planning proposed in the official Methodologies – gives the only promise worth having that the economy of intellect will continue to run as well as can be expected.

The market and morality join in science as in society. Jerry Evensky has written with discernment on the matter. He is correct that "this heightened self-consciousness compels McCloskey to make the ethical dimension of [the market] metaphor explicit" (1992, p. 62) and that "ethics lies at the heart of the master metaphor in classical liberal thought" (p. 63). I have become gradually persuaded that an Inquiry into the Nature and Causes of the Wealth of Nations requires a Theory of Moral Sentiments (McCloskey 1992c).

The argument replies to certain monists, who insist that other people stick to what they call "standards." They exempt their own conversation from such rhetorical scrutiny. The alleged "standards" of philosophical empiric*ism* (as distinct from empiric*al* work, which no reasonable person speaks against) have persuaded some scientists to spurn whole classes of evidence: economists, I have noted, have spurned surveys, psychologists the evidence of their own minds, and policymakers the moral reasoning necessary for the making of policy. It is hard to take the claim of such philosophically and uncritically imposed "standards" seriously. The real standards, after all, reside where they should, on the lips of men and women of science conversing together.

The Methodologists, then, accept the *Sprachethik* of the fuzzies even as they attack what they think it is. So also, and more directly, Bruce Caldwell, Husain Sarkar, and other pluralists accept the *Sprachethik*. As human conversationalists they can hardly avoid doing so. The Methodologists are drawn thus into the "cultural sensitivity" of which Arjo Klamer speaks (1988a), though the Methodologists do not like it and will not admit it and grow cross when it is mentioned. While having a culture-bound conversation about whether knowledge is culture-bound they insist that conversation is not culture-bound. They think they can find some day an Archimedean point with which to lever the world of conversation into a world in which conversations have been ended and *The Republic* has been made real. They do not want serious rhetoric, but rules of perfect Knowledge for all time. They are not embarrassed by the failure of 2,500 years in the epistemological conversation to find it.

The question is how to converse about this culture-bound conversation of humanity. We know how to make the conversations lie down on the guest beds of philosophers, but agree that the result is unhelpful. Science doesn't fit well on a bed of science-is-*modustollens* or science-is-positive-heuristics. It has to be trimmed to fit.

Happily, as I have argued, there exists alternative thinking about how to do the thinking, thick and rich, called the humanities. The humanistic tradition of the West can be used to understand the scientific tradition. What historians and Methodologists of economic thought do anyway, without knowing it, is literary criticism. As Vivienne Brown says, "inevitably, historiographic debates within economics will become increasingly susceptible to wider postmodern influences in philosophy and literary theory" (V. Brown, 1993, p. 65). I would add only, ". . . and *premodern* influences in philosophy and literary theory." Sophisticated "criticism" is merely understanding how the texts of economists have their effect, as one criticizes poetry. "Criticism" in this sense is neither "assault" nor "ranking." It is not a murder trial or a beauty contest – it is not, as Northrop Frye put the point, "the odious comparison of greatness," a "pseudo-dialectics, or false rhetoric," "an anxiety neurosis prompted by a moral censor" which has "made the word critic a synonym for an educated shrew" (Frye 1957, pp. 24–27). The usual philosophical "criticism" encourages shrewishness: thin, bad-tempered, superficially judgmental. By the standards of good literary criticism a philosophical criticism – Lakatosian, say – seems thin and harshly normative, unattractive stuff. The literary model can lead to a better way of examining the conversations of economists. (I have noted that Lakatos' Ph.D. thesis was in fact a rhetorical criticism of the history of a proof in topology.) To put it more positively, as Paul Goodman does, science is language, and "the wisest method of exploring language is to analyze how it operates in actual concrete situations, rather than deciding beforehand what 'language' is. This is similar to the literary analysis of particular works" (P. Goodman 1971 (1972), p. 226). Philip Mirowski, who in *More Heat Than Light* (1989) has shown the way, concludes of another economist looking for something beyond Methodology that "Weintraub's linguistic turn . . . [is] the breaking of a deadlock in the Lakatosian tradition, the transcendence of the incoherent notions of rationality by means of research into the way linguistic and mathematical practice structures our history" (p. 292). That seems right. It could research even how Lakatos' passionate and intelligent rhetoric, however misleading as theology, has structured the recent history of economics and its philosophy.

The merits of a rhetorical criticism show up when placed side-by-side with some other alternatives to philosophical criticism. They are all at least as thick as the thin little philosophies of science. For example, the history of economic thought can be written as biography. The late George Stigler attacked this tradition persuasively, though doubtless it will survive even his pen (Stigler 1976). The biographical approach is certainly thick: one can know all about Ricardo's business dealings and Keynes' love affairs yet still have more questions to ask. The biography may be irrelevant to matters of import, as Stigler argued, but there is at least nothing thin about it. This probably explains its vitality in the face of much lofty Methodological sneering.

Another thick alternative is the Whiggish theory, practiced by Schumpeter, Stigler, Mark Blaug, and Roger Backhouse, that the progress of science can be viewed as successive approximations to the right answers. Eventually we'll get it right. In the meantime we can look on the history of the field as a dawning of enlightenment. It is history of science as examination question: quick, Ricardo: would it matter to your argument if labor were only 93 percent of costs? If 80 percent? Quick, Malthus: how would you draw your theory in the wage-population plane? Most history of thought by most economists takes this line, and has done great service. Though more useful for enriching economic thinking, the Whiggish approach is not so thick as the biographical. As with slow students disfiguring their examinations, one runs out of patience with the errors of the past. Still, it is not to be disdained. The current crop of young economists who have never read Keynes or Marshall, not to speak of Ricardo or Smith, and like most ignorant people do not care that they are ignorant, would be better scientists after a dose of Whiggish history of economic thought.

Another thick alternative to philosophical criticism was again advocated by the polymorphous Stigler. It is to turn economics on itself, and view the history of the field as itself a consequence of economic forces. Here again, as America's leading vulgar Marxist, Stigler showed a characteristic openness to leftwing thought. The program is as rich as is empirical economics itself (Diamond 1984, 1987, 1988; Levy 1992). It amounts to a narrow version of the next and better alternative to philosophical criticism.

The better alternative is sociology of science, advocated for economics prominently by A. W. Coats, although he wishes it would fit conveniently into the thinking of Richard Whitley (Coats 1984; cf. Mäki 1992 and Coats' comment). It is attractively thick. There is little limit to what one can ask about the sociology of the economics profession in England around 1900 or the sociology of journal editing around 1995. Furthermore, it is relevant to what we wish to know: if knowledge is social, as it is, then the growth of knowledge will be a social growth.

I should like to argue at the end, however, that the thickest parts of the so-called Strong Program in the Sociology of Science, the British and vigorous branch of sociology of science (about which Coats is nervous), overlap with a specifically rhetorical criticism. Sociology and rhetoric are one (cf. Amariglio 1990b, p. 230).

An illuminating example of the Strong Program is a book by Harry Collins, *Changing Order: Replication and Induction in Scientific Practice* (1985). It is about physics; the strong program has not had much of a trial in economics yet (though see Ashmore, Mulkay, and Pinch 1989 on health economics). Collins, a sociologist at the Science Research Centre at the University of Bath, calls his approach "sociological," which is fair enough: science is social, Collins is a sociologist, and sociological phenomenology has played a part in his thinking. But it is not sociological in the sense of the pioneering sociologists of science, such as Robert Merton or Joseph Ben David. Collins does not for example collect biographical data on the scientists, though he could have done so with less trouble. He did not because the scientists are not his subjects.

His subjects are controversies, debates, words, argumentative ploys – that is, the rhetoric of science. The quantified gossip that constitutes sociology of science in the Mertonian or Stiglerian vein is missing. Collins has elsewhere done Mertonian tasks (Collins and Pinch 1982). What interests Collins in *Changing Order* is not the resumés of his people but the course of the debate among them. He is providing what the American social psychologist Donald Campbell calls for, "an internalist sociology of scientific belief change" (D. T. Campbell 1986, p. 116). Collins speaks repeatedly of the "argumentative strategy" of this or that scientific remark. He never attributes a move in the argument to party or passion. Towards the end of the book he rejects the usual social correlates in favor of a definition of his subject that focuses attention on debate:

> The set of allies and enemies in the core of a controversy are not necessarily bound to each other by social ties or membership of common institutions . . . If these enemies interact, it is likely to be only in the context of the particular passing debate. This set of persons does not necessarily act like a 'group'. They are bound only by their close, if differing, interests in the controversy's outcome.
>
> Collins 1985, p. 142

Collins treats the debate among physicists about gravity waves, for example, as just that: as a debate, showing how one or another rhetorical move led to the result. For instance at its turning point the chief proponent of gravity waves, Joseph Weber, "in accepting . . . electrostatic calibration . . . accepted constraint on his freedom to interpret results" (Collins 1985, p. 105). Collins notes that Weber did not have to accept the calibration (which itself, by the way, is a rhetorical turn common to many fields, namely, the selection of a quantitative standard; see McCloskey 1985a, ch. 8, on economics and linguistics). It was a rhetorical choice. But having made it Weber was constrained by rules of debate, rules that can themselves be studied and partially understood, and that have in fact been studied and partially understood since the Greeks.

The varied rules of human debate, not godlike Tests, decide the outcome. "It is control on interpretation which breaks the circle of the experimenters' regress [Collins' phrase for Duhem's Dilemma that the side conditions of a test may be explaining the result], not the 'test of a test' itself" (Collins 1985, p. 106; for economics see the impressive list of side conditions in Cross 1982, p. 324). That is to say, it is rhetorical considerations, the workings of a human conversation, not mechanical applications of rules within a closed system, that ends a scientific debate (Galison 1987). Scientists do not commit a crime when they argue beyond the constricted realm of formal logic. Says Collins: "Scientists do not act dishonourably when they engage in the debates . . . ; there is nothing else for them to do if a debate is ever to be settled and if new knowledge is ever to emerge from the dispute" (Collins 1985, p. 143). It is not the logic of inquiry that allows scientific progress, but the rhetoric of inquiry (compare Collins, p. 153 n5).

I am asserting that Collins and other observers of scientific controversy contribute unawares to the rhetorical tradition (as in Mendelsohn 1987). Listen to another leader of the British sociologists of science, Michael Mulkay, describing the themes of one of his books, and ask if it could not be said of a rhetorical criticism of Demosthenes or Lincoln:

> my chapters . . . investigate and describe certain recurrent forms of scientific discourse which occur in connection with technical debate . . . [t]hey examine the relationship between participants' and analysts' discourse; between participants' and analysts' interpretative practices . . . [T]hey explore the difference between monologue and dialogue.
>
> Mulkay 1985, p. 7

Rhetorical criticism is the thickest approach (an application to the history of economic thought is Emmett 1992). It draws on a tradition from the Sicilian sophists to the present, running parallel to philosophy, though spurned by philosophers in most ages, "the art of probing what men believe they ought to believe, rather than proving what is true according to abstract methods . . . , of discovering good reasons, finding what really warrants assent, . . . of discovering warrantable beliefs and improving those beliefs in shared discourse" (Booth 1974, pp. xiii, xiv).

The rhetorical concern, in short, is how we really do convince each other, not "what is true according to abstract methods." Abstract Methods are necessary for the unlimited conversation of Ultimate Truth. Rhetoric is necessary for courts of law and conferences of science, places in which the bell rings and a decision must somehow be made. How they really do convince each other in the here and now is the main concern of the scientists; they could care less what is true at the Second Coming according to abstract Methods; they want to persuade, to bring a particular debate to a conclusion.

In aid of understanding this rhetoric of the science, Arjo Klamer (1990a), John Swales (1993), Willie Henderson and Ann Hewings (1987), and Mead and Henderson (1983) among others have studied the rhetoric of economics textbooks. Henderson, who first saw the metaphors in economics, has recently done a detailed reading of style in Edgeworth's *Mathematical Psychics*, noting its "lack of a consistently defined audience" (Henderson 1993, p. 220). Keith Tribe has attempted a Marxist rhetoric of economic discourse (1978). Axel Leijonhufvud likewise uses the notion of "ideology," which is the beginning of a rhetorical analysis, to see a path between excessive optimism and excessive pessimism about the market (1985). Brian Loasby offers a rhetorical analysis of Marshall's economics:

> Marshall consistently emphasised biological analogies, but there was simply no "biological mathematics" adequate for his purpose; and so evolution had to be explained in terms of static equilibrium. The use of a strictly timeless theory by one who was so conscious of the importance of time represents a heroic – and highly successful – use of abstraction; but only by the use of all Marshall's care and subtlety could it be made to appear convincing.
>
> Loasby 1971, p. 871

Yuval Yonay has described the "trial of strength," following Bruno Latour's vocabulary, in "The Struggle over the Soul of Economics, 1918–1945" in terms of characteristic appeals to authority of one kind or another: for example, the authority of other sciences or of the past of economics (Yonay 1991). In Yonay's account, which is sociology on the verge of rhetoric, neoclassicals of the sort I have called the "Good Old Chicago School" struggled with weapons of rhetoric against institutionalists like Wesley Clair Mitchell and George Soule (in the end, Yonay notes, both schools were out-argued by Samuelsonian mathematization). Scientists in all fields, psychology and economics as much as physics and biology, talk incessantly about rhetorical matters. They talk as though engaged in a debate at the Oxford Union or a case at law or an important business judgment. The scientific conversation is not governed by rules convenient for a 3″ × 5″ card. It is a thick and complex and rhetorical matter, a practice, not a theory.

One can ask with the novelist and English professor David Lodge, "Is it possible, or useful, to bring the whole battery of modern formalism and structuralism to bear on a single text, and what is gained by doing so? Does it enrich our reading by uncovering depths and nuances of meaning we might not otherwise have brought to consciousness? . . . Or does it merely encourage a pointless and self-indulgent academicism, by which the same information is shuffled from one set of categories to another?" (Lodge 1981 [1991], pp. 17–18). One could ask the same questions of economics. Lodge is right to warn that they cannot be answered in the abstract: "these questions will not be settled until we have a significant corpus of synthetic or pluralistic readings of narrative [read 'economic'] texts of various types" (p. 23). Economics is beginning to get such readings.

part IV

Proof

Proof . . . the fourth part . . . in which the pros and cons of the argument were brought out.

Lanham, *A Handlist of Rhetorical Terms* (1991), pp. 121–122

chapter 9

The rise of a scientistic style

The sociology or philosophy of science that economists bring to bear in thinking about their work, particularly their scientific work, and especially their scientific work in journals does not persuade. It is no more persuasive than their uninstructed literary criticism. To pick two, the cynical and the idealistic extremes, a journal is not a place of raw political power; nor is it a place where scientific hypotheses are subjected to decisive test.

A journal is where economists persuade. They persuade in beautiful figures of mathematics or of words or of statistics. The vocabulary and grammar of literary criticism can be used to think about their persuasion (Charles Bazerman has pioneered such studies in physics [1988] and has recently applied similar methods to Adam Smith [1993]; in biology Mulkay [1985] and Myers [1990] have done such work; and in economics Henderson [1982, 1993], Dudley-Evans [1993], and joint work with Hewings [Hewings and Henderson 1987, Henderson and Hewings 1987] and Dudley-Evans [Dudley-Evans and Henderson 1987, Dudley-Evans and Henderson 1990]). One can begin with the most obviously "literary" of what economic scientists do, their style. Style is character in prose and science depends on character, the ethos or persona that makes a scientist believable. Mary K. Farmer has pointed out, for example, that the tone in the New Home Economics or in the New Classical Macroeconomics "of doing what all economists agree we should be doing, but doing it more wholeheartedly" (Farmer 1992, p. 107) is a stylistic argument from authority, the authority of the tribe, Our Crowd.

Economic science has a problem with its style, which leads to an underlying insincerity about what the persona is trying to be. Wittgenstein wrote, and felt passionately:

> Lying to oneself about oneself, deceiving yourself about the pretense in your own state of will, must have a harmful influence on [one's] style, for the result will be that you cannot tell what is genuine in the style and what is false . . . If you are unwilling to know who you are, your writing is a form of deceit.
>
> Quoted in Monk 1990 (1991), pp. 366–367

The implied author of economic writings

Start with the data, viewed as an economist would, without literary thinking. Take, for example, agricultural economics. In the August 1989 issue of the *American Journal of Agricultural Economics* there are twenty-four articles. Of these, fifteen follow the received outline of formal model followed by a serious empirical implementation, especially regression analysis. Four of the twenty-four have no formal model yet engage in serious empirical inquiry (all four of these also use regression analysis). One other is a review article. Only two of the twenty-four have a formal model without any gesture at empirical implementation and only two others have a formal model with merely illustrative implementation, directed at the new method proposed rather than a problem in the world. Twenty out of the twenty-four, in other words, are empirical.

The high ratio of articles with serious empirical work to articles with a merely theoretical purpose is typical of the applied fields, such as labor economics or economic history. It is well above the ratio in the so-called general-interest (and higher status) journals of economics. Wassily Leontief calculated in 1982 that over 50 percent of the articles in the general journals of economics and sociology were theoretical (Leontief 1982). The figure in comparable journals in physics and chemistry was 10 percent. In economics the theorists are five times more common.

Compare the 1989 issue with the *Journal of Farm Economics* (as it was called before 1968) in 1929, sixty years before. Viewed superficially, the ten articles in the January issue of 1929 hardly overlap at all in type with those of 1989. Only one article is a formal modeling and simulation of behavior, another a piece of empirical accounting. There are five articles offering policy assessments and proposals, with an accounting framework. There is one outlook piece, one institutional description, and one extended appeal for more fact-collecting. Only the four non-modeling articles out of the twenty-four in 1989 look much like any of the articles sixty years before.

The differences, however, are more apparent than real. Most of the 1929 articles, for example, use quantitative thinking. It is false to say that the style of argument in economics has become more quantitative over the past sixty years. Counting, as I have noted before, has been the ethos of the economists and calculators since the beginnings in political arithmetic three centuries ago. What is plain in 1929 is something hidden in 1989, though there to be seen if you look hard enough: namely, that economics depends for much of its arguments on accounting (see Andvig 1991; Klamer and McCloskey 1992). Accounting is the master metaphor of economics (of all economics, not only of the neoclassical school), determining most of its quantitative findings. The economist makes an accounting decision, for example, to value family labor on farms at market prices. The decision alters radically how we view the efficiency of family farming. He makes an accounting decision to view future interest on the national debt as offset by future taxes. He makes an accounting decision to include savings in national income. And so forth, in all parts of economics.

The most striking change in method down at the practical level is that the empirical work in 1989 uses the statistical technique of regression analysis, nearly to the exclusion of any other technique. This is peculiar. When economists make policy arguments they use accounting, as I just said, together with simulation – all the way from back-of-the-envelope calculations of elasticities to formal simulations on computers. But when they seek the facts of the world they pretend that only the "experiments" performed by history and suitable to regression analysis are appropriate. I once had a graduate student who thought that the very word "empirical" meant "regression analysis on someone else's data." Regression analysis seems to have a tighter hold on the empirical imagination in agricultural economics than it has in other applied fields, perhaps because of the agronomical origins of the statistics. The British statistician R. A. Fisher, who devised and named most of the statistics, was employed at an agricultural experiment station. Regression analysis works markedly less well on non-experimental data and its devices of statistical significance are mostly irrelevant to what an economist wishes to know (Goldberger 1991, p. 240), but such statistical news has not gotten out to most economists.

Regression analysis, though, as much as agricultural and other applied economists love, honor, and obey it, is a detail of method. A deeper look at the articles in 1929 and 1989 shows them to be more similar than the listing of non-overlapping types suggests. Agricultural economics is still concerned at bottom with how farmers behave and whether their behavior is good for them or for anybody else, quantitatively speaking. Likewise in other applied fields.

A similar comparison can be made between the harvest in 1929 and 1989 of the *American Economic Review*, one of the "general interest journals." In 1929, of the twenty-two full articles, ten were theoretical (including accounting and statistical theory) and ten were institutional or historical (the history itself was of course strictly institutional, not statistical). In 1989 the ratio of theory, defined as explorations of models without serious tests against the world, is not much different: sixteen out of thirty-nine (issues 1, 4, and 5 only; compare Leontief's 50 percent over a longer modern span).

Only two of the articles in the *Review* of 1929 would seem modern to a modern reader: an impassioned theoretical and empirical defense of monetarism by Arthur Burns (Milton Friedman was an undergraduate student of his at the time) and a thorough statistical study by one H. La Rue Frain about the uniformity of wages from firm to firm. These combine theory and statistics in the manner of the twenty-two out of thirty-nine articles in the *Review* sixty years later that one would call "empirical." The same social role in the economics of the 1920s was played by institutional and historical articles. It is false to say, in short, that economics has become "more theoretical" since the 1920s, unless "theory" is narrowed to mean "certain techniques in optimal control theory borrowed from electrical engineering."

So economics has not become more quantitative or more theoretical since the 1920s. Economics is still social accounting, though it confuses itself by thinking always in terms of regression analysis; and it is still highly theoretical in its prestige branches, though the theory is expressed now in mathematics.

Yet the implied author of the articles, to use the literary idea, did change in the sixty years. A good literary word is that ethos, which is merely Greek for "character." It has meant in the 2,500-year history of rhetoric the character that a speaker claims in his speech. The modern term is the "implied author." The big change, in brief, was the rise of the ethos, persona, implied author of the Scientist. The theoretical articles of the 1920s took the philosopher as their model; the empirical articles took the historian, that is, as we say in English, "the scholar." By contrast, the implied author of the recent theoretical article is the mathematician, with his theorems and proofs; the implied author of the recent empirical article is a bench scientist, with his controlled experiments (in the guise of regressions) and his applications to policy. In English, and only in English: the Scientist.

An author creates from his opening first lines an implied author more or less different from his literal self. Dante the character in *The Divine Comedy* was more pious than the literal Dante Alighieri, and found himself, as the real Dante did not, in the middle of his life's road in a dark forest where the direct path was lost.

Consider the implied authors created by these opening lines in the *American Economic Review* of March 1989:

> Two decades of research have failed to produce professional con-sensus on the contribution of federal government civil rights activity to the economic progress of black Americans
>
> Heckman and Payner 1989, p. 138

The implied authors here are policy-oriented, precise (the ugly if accurate nominal phrase "federal government civil rights activity"), aware of the longer trends in scholarship, scholarly (with a Latinate vocabulary), dignified yet decisive, men who will succeed where others have "failed."
Or:

> After a period of intensive study of optimal indirect taxation, there has been a renewed interest in recent years in the problem of optimal income taxation, with particular emphasis on capital income taxation and economic growth.
>
> Howitt and Sinn 1989, p. 106

Here the implied authors are modest (contrast the ringing "Two decades of research have failed" or the unconscious arrogance of the next item, "Consider the . . . setting"), concerned to fill gaps rather than assault once more the great questions of the age, academic rather than political ("renewed interest," as there might be renewed interest in the satellites of Jupiter), but again Latinate in vocabulary, anonymous, American academic writers.
Or:

> Consider the following stylized setting
>
> Lewis and Sappington 1989, p. 69

These are mathematical, uninterested in facts, followers of a certain fashion, pretending to be direct but staying firmly in the lecture room, unaware of how funny the first sentence sounds to most economists. "Stylized" in economics means "I have not checked this in the world or even in the library, and am relying on the imaginary world that I and a few of my friends like to talk about, but never mind."

Or finally:

> There is good reason to think that the market for single-family
> homes ought to be less efficient than are capital markets
>
> Case and Shiller 1989, p. 125

These are candid, direct, practical, better writers than "After a period
of intensive study," interested in explaining an empirical phenomenon, up-to-date in financial theory.

The reader has to be an economist for the sentences to have exactly
such effects in establishing ethos, just as the listener must have been
a fourth-century Athenian for Demosthenes' appeals to have had
their effects. The writers of course need not be aware of every effect
their writing has on the audience, any more than poets need be.

As we have seen, however, the claim of Scientist in our culture is
usually accompanied by a faith in the religion of the times, Scientism, and by its theology, Positivism. The most notable difference in
ethical appeal between 1929 and 1989 is philosophical. The push for
"testable hypotheses," for example, is palpable. Just below the
surface in 1989 lies a commitment to a model of Scientific Method
current in philosophical circles around 1955, with all its weaknesses
and some of its strengths.

The rise of the scientistic ethos is most apparent in the past thirty
years. Comparing the *Journal of Finance* in 1960 and 1989 and the
Journal of Financial Economics in 1975 and 1990, one finds increases in
the number of joint authors (by 1989–1990 multiple authorships were
in the majority, as they were in the *American Economic Review*), in
mathematical complexity within the text, in mathematical appen-
dixes, and in references, and a very large increase in statistical
analysis of data; and decreases in the number of non-academic
authors (from 40 percent to nil). All these are characteristics of a
maturing Scientific field. The percentage of wholly theoretical articles
in the *Journal of Financial Economics* declined, though not below the
50 percent characteristic of the leading general journals.

Tony Dudley-Evans and Willie Henderson have given a longer
perspective on the rise of the scientific ethos. One of the four articles
from the British *Economic Journal* they studied intensively for style
was "Taxation Through Monopoly" by C. F. Bastable, 1891. The
article "strikes one immediately as having been written for a highly
educated reader [the implied reader] who happens also to be
interested in economic matters" (Dudley-Evans and Henderson 1987,
p. 7). And Bastable, they note, "frequently uses 'and,' 'but' and
'again' in initial position" (an ornament in modern English). Again,

he uses in initial position "elegant adverbial phrases," such as "So much is this the case" or "Alike in classical and medieval times" (p. 8). Alike in his scientific and his journalistic work, "Bastable based his writing not upon shared technical knowledge but on a shared understanding of an educated culture more widely defined" (p. 15). But the implied author of recent economics does not presume to be educated in the culture more widely defined.

The style of Scientism in economics

To get further in the literary analysis of the scientific article we need to get down into the words (as Backhouse, Dudley-Evans, and Henderson 1993 have argued). The journals became more professional in part by encouraging the growth of a technical vocabulary, fleeing the common culture. No elaborate test is necessary. The implied reader of an economics journal has changed to support the claim of Scientific standing for the implied author. The percentage of terms that a non-professional reader could understand has fallen steadily in economic journals since the 1920s.

It might be called the "blub-blub" effect, the "blub-blubs" being the words that only people socialized within the community of economics can understand. An interesting example of the rhetorical use of implied readers and authors is an essay in historical economics by Stephen Nicholas in 1982 in the *Economic History Review*. The implied (and actual) readers of the *Review* are not technically trained economists. Most of Nicholas' article is lucid prose accessible to such a readership. But suddenly, when he is trying to undermine the neoclassical measure of productivity change, the implied reader changes. By the mere statement of the "assumptions" said to underlie the measure he intends to sow doubt in the minds of all the historians and many of the economists reading. Listen as he undertakes to "explain" the calculation: "it is assumed [note the style borrowed suddenly from mathematics, after a long time in the persona of the historian] that the economic unit is a profit maximizer, subject to a linear homogeneous production function and operating in perfectly competitive product and factor markets. Given these limiting assumptions, the marginal productivity theory of distribution equates marginal products to factor rewards. It follows by Euler's theorem . . . " etc., etc. (Nicholas 1982, p. 86).

To most of his readers he might as well have written "*it is assumed that* the blub-blub *is a* blub *maximizer,* blub-blub blub-blub-blub and blub *in perfectly* blub *and* blub blub. *Given these limiting assumptions,*

the blub blub blub blub blub blub blub. *It follows* by blub blub . . . "
The audience that can understand the argument is the audience of
people who already understand it, leaving one to ask why the
argument was necessary. The people who do not understand it will
gain only the impression that "limiting assumptions" are somehow
involved. The apparent form of the passage is explanation; its actual
and intended effect in the pages of the *Economic History Review* is to
terrify the onlookers, convincing them that the "neoclassical" analysis makes all manner of strange assumptions (it does not, but that is
not the point here).

A non-economist could pick up the *American Economic Review* or
the *Economic Journal* in the 1920s and read it – not without effort and
not without boredom, of course. One must not exaggerate the user
friendliness of the older journals. Economics in the 1920s was already
a long-running conversation, with speech habits as specialized as
those of professional diplomats or professional burglars. Yet the style
of, say, Keynes' journalistic article of 1924, "Foreign Investment and
National Advantage" in *The Nation and Athenaeum* (35: 584–587) was
not far from that in his academic writing. In 1923 Virginia Woolf
remarked to her diary that "Maynard is grown very gross & stout . . .
[b]ut his eyes are remarkable, & as I truly said when he gave me some
pages of his new book [*A Tract on Monetary Reform*] to read, the
process of mind there displayed is as far ahead of me as Shakespeare's" (Woolf 1923[1980], p. 266). It would be hard to imagine a
literary friend of Robert Lucas being able to read even a page of his
latest book, much less to assess the quality of mind displayed there.
The speech community has of course changed, becoming more
specialized.

John Kenneth Galbraith explains the point of such obscurity in a
novel of his, in the words of a fictional distinguished woman
professor at the University of Cambridge (namely, the non-fictional
Joan Robinson):

> Never forget, dear boy, that academic distinction in economics is
> not to be had from giving a clear account of how the world works.
> Keynes knew that; had he made his General Theory completely
> comprehensible, it would have been ignored. Economists value
> most the colleague whom they most struggle to understand. The
> pride they feel in eventually succeeding leads to admiration for the
> man who set them so difficult a task
>
> Galbraith 1990, p. 50

St. Augustine, as the literary critic Gerald Bruns has noted, also
viewed the obscurity of the Bible as having "a pragmatic function

in the art of winning over an alienated and even contemptuous audience" (Bruns 1984, p. 157). The contrived obscurity is not nice but not rare in science and religion. Bruns quotes Augustine (who might as well be justifying the obscurities of a mathematical economist proving the obvious): "I do not doubt that this situation was provided by God to conquer pride by work and to combat disdain in our minds, to which those things which are easily discovered seem frequently to be worthless." Another English professor has noted the gain in converts to the faith. "Self-flattery and ritual mystification," says Richard Lanham, "make effective recruiting posters" (Lanham 1974, p. 72), in deconstruction and in freshwater macroeconomics, equally. He was speaking of the mummeries of the sociologist Talcott Parsons, attractively difficult for the young, but he might as well have been talking about game theory or general equilibrium analysis.

Yet jargon is not merely obscuring, to be rooted out. The advice of the English professors is similar to that of the economists in matters of policy: "Jargons, like other styles, respond to situations. To prevent them, we must change the situation" (Lanham 1974, p. 77). "When you call a style bad, or exaggerated, much less mad, you ought to make sure you understand the situation it responds to" (Lanham 1974, p. 58). Jargon is an argument in a word, and sometimes, though not always, it is more concise than ordinary language. (Economists put a lot of store on arguments being "concise"; it is one of the intellectual values they have adopted from mathematicians.) In macroeconomics, for example, the recent jargon of "constant subjective discount rate," "instantaneous subutility function," "perfect foresight," "private agent," "time-inconsistency problem" contains economics in the words – mainly the rediscovery of Keynes' insight that expectations run the show.

Much economic jargon, though, hides a five-cent thought in a five-dollar word. The tip-off is a Latinate choice of words. Thus "the integrative consequences of growing structural differentiation" means in ordinary English "the need for others that someone feels when he buys rather than bakes his bread." And "current period responses" means "what people do now"; "complex lagged effects" means "the many things they do later." "Interim variation" means "change," "monitored back" means "told." The "time-inconsistency problem" is the economics of changing one's mind. The "principal/agent problem" is the economics of what hirelings do. "Geographical and cultural factors function to spatially confine growth to specific regions for long periods of time" means in ordinary English "it's a good bet that once a place gets poor it will stay poor." And an extreme example of Latinate blather: "Thus, it is suggested, a deeper understanding of the conditions affecting the speed and ultimate extent of an innovation's diffusion is to be obtained only by explicitly analyzing the specific choice of technique problem which its advent would have presented to objectively dissimilar members of the relevant (historical) population of potential adopters."

The successful article in a journal will have an implied reader the actual reader can play – or, still better, can aspire to – and an implied author that the actual reader can tolerate. Writing of all kinds and scientific writing, too, is a little drama in which the writer chooses the roles. For example, Meriel and Thomas Bloor note that an economist making claims widely relevant for economics is so to speak a "house guest" intruding on other economists' space (Bloor and Bloor 1993, p. 158). They find that what the linguist George Lakoff called "hedging" – words and phrases like "probably" or "it is suggested that" or "tends to" – becomes most prominent when the writer is in the guest role. When she is on her home ground she is more emphatic. A good example of what the Bloors are talking about is the attempted intrusion of Ronald Coase's famous paper in 1937, "The Nature of the Firm." As an unknown house guest he had to establish an ethos worth believing. Late in the paper he generalizes in gray-beard style (he drafted the paper at age twenty-one): "Other things being equal, therefore, a firm will tend to be larger: (a) the less the costs of organizing" and so forth. The "other things being equal," "therefore," and "tend" are careful and conventional assurances in the contract between reader and economic Scientist. When claiming the ethos of Scientist the young Coase was especially fond of "tend to," the phrase becoming virtual anaphora on p. 46 (Coase 1937 [1988a]), repeated in all six of the complete sentences on the page and once in the footnotes. The politeness of "tend to" is forced on a young man, even so bold a young man as Coase.

The pre-print, which comes closer to the candor of seminar speech, is taking the place of the journal article, and appears to be affecting the style of the papers finally published. As the journals expand, becoming thereby more democratic, the elite withdraws into a system of pre-prints. The xeroxed copy of Joseph Farrell's "Meaning and Credibility in Cheap-Talk Games," mentioned earlier, announces its pre-publication history on its title page: "[first drafted] December 1983/ Current version: July 8, 1988 . . . Forthcoming in *Mathematical Models in Economics*, M. Dempster, editor, Oxford University Press." It circulated among the cognoscenti for five years and was already well known (though not approved: the conventional footnote of acknowledgment has a bitter twist – as such footnotes and prefaces occasionally do: "Thanks are due to Joel Sobel and Bob Gibbons, who encouraged me *when editors, referees, and colleagues did not*" (Farrell 1988, p. 1n [my italics]). The style of the pre-print is "lower" (as classical rhetoric said: there is no blame in the word) than that of articles submitted in the first instance for official publication in a journal. One can be more adventuresome in a community of pre-prints: the author is his own editor.

An article that does not follow the stylistic precepts of the modern journal article will often be said to "read like a speech," seen as an affront to decorum (the classical virtues of style were four: purity, clarity, ornament, and decorum; but the greatest of these was decorum). Henderson and Hewings (1988) speak of "the deletion of the actor" in economic prose, which creates "gaps" of abstraction in the texts: nominalization and a passive voice without an agent, making a phrase such as "the customers raised the price" into "a rise in price occurred when the demand curve was raised."

Yet in an actual spoken seminar the audience will resent the article style. In speaking the author must use the lower style, the result being "the talk" (as it is called revealingly in mathematics, statistics, and the physical and biological sciences). An article in the elaborate Asiatic style (the classical term) will be "available" beforehand but will be presented on site autobiographically and colloquially. As Arjo Klamer puts it, the square rhetoric of the formal paper is undercut, even treated ironically, by the rounded talk at the presentation (Klamer 1990c, p. 32 n12).

The point of view in economic writing

So the economists arguing formally in their journals in the role of Scientists are literary artists, using words to tell a persuasive story. Scientific talk has a surface rhetoric of plain candor, telling the story as it really happened. But "telling the story as it really happened" evades the responsibility to examine the point of view.

Realist fiction does this habitually – which shows another use for the literary analogy, to note that realist "fiction" in science can also evade declaring a point of view. The sociologist Michael Mulkay notes in the epistolary arguments of biologists a Rule 11: "Use the personal format of a letter . . . but withdraw from the text yourself as often as possible so that the other party continually finds himself engaged in an unequal dialogue with the experiments, data, observations and facts" (Mulkay 1985, p. 66). The evasion is similar in history: "the plot of a historical narrative is always an embarrass-ment and has to be presented as 'found' in the events rather than put there by narrative techniques" (J. H. White, 1973, 20). In science more generally, as Heinz Kretzenbacher has argued, the suppression of the I is connected to taboos against open narration and metaphor (Kretzenbacher 1992).

In the modern novel the suppression of the authorial I has resulted in a technique peculiar to literature, "represented speech and thought." Grammarians call it "unheralded indirect speech," the French *style indirect libre*. Any page or two of Jane Austen serves, as in *Persuasion*: "Sir Walter had taken a very good house in Camden-place, a lofty dignified situation, such as becomes a man of conse-quence" (1818 [1965], p. 107), Sir Walter's words ("dignified . . . a man of consequence") in Austen's mouth; "Could Anne wonder that her father and sister were happy? She might not wonder, but she must sigh that her father should feel no degradation in his change" (p. 108), Anne's words ("sigh . . . no degradation") in Austen's mouth.

The parallel suppression of the I in science might be called "represented Reality" or "unheralded assertion" or *"style indirect inévitable."* The scientists says: it is not I the scientist who make these assertions but reality itself (Nature's words in the scientist's mouth). Scientists pretend that Nature speaks directly, thereby effacing the evidence that they the scientists are responsible for the assertions. It's just there. The result is similar in fiction: "We (as readers) cannot question the reliability of third-person narrators . . . Any first-person narrative, on the other hand, may prove unreliable" (Martin 1986, p. 142). Thus Huck Finn, a narrator in the first person, misapprehends the Duke and we the readers know he does. The scientist, unlike Huck, avoids being questioned for his reliability by disappearing into a third-person narrative of What Really Happened. As Robert Solow wrote on the matter:

> Personality is eliminated from journal articles because it's felt to be "unscientific." An author is proposing a hypothesis, testing a hypothesis, proving a theorem, not persuading the reader that this is a better way of thinking about X than that. Writing would be better if more of us saw economics as a way of organizing thoughts and perceptions about economic life rather than as a poor imitation of physics.
>
> R. Solow 1981

The implied author of such stuff is not especially attractive. In such a style, as Richard Lanham would put it (Lanham 1974, p. 47), what is the "agreement struck between writer and reader"? Economists write with a remote and arrogant implied author more than do many other scholars or scientists, as visitors from other fields note. Tony Dudley-Evans, a visitor from applied linguistics, has argued persuasively that the rhetoric of controversy in economics arises from mixed genres (Dudley-Evans 1993). The face-saving and face-scratching of spoken genres entered the written world of the Friedman v. Rest-of-the-World debate on monetarism. He finds for example that the "academic sneer" identified by Klamer, Colander, and me was especially prevalent in the replies of James Tobin. One can find such rhetoric everywhere in economic controversy. In it the opponent is so obviously misled that it is incredible he got a B.A. in the subject. G. R. Davies' article in the *Journal of Political Economy* ("The Quantity Theory and Recent Statistical Studies," 1989) uses phrases such as "obviously," "it is evident," "doubtless," "merely," "easily seen," "needs no discussion," "we may expect" some 42 times in 8 pages. Perhaps the personality would better be eliminated. It survives in the unhappy and unexamined conventions of a scientistic style.

Vivienne Brown's analysis of the style of Adam Smith's two books is a model of what can be learned from a literary approach (V. Brown 1993). She notes that *The Theory of Moral Sentiments* has what the Russian literary theorist Bakhtin called a "dialogic" character, "in which the moral agent engages in an inner dialogue represented by the metaphor of the impartial spectator" (V. Brown 1993, p. 79). By comparison, *The Wealth of Nations* is closer to the "empiricist monologue" (a term popular among British sociologists of science). But she argues in a forthcoming book that even *The Wealth of Nations* is not entirely "scientific," which is to say disinterested and non-dialogic, and can even be taken, surprisingly, to criticize economic growth. This much can be read through a style, even a scientistic one.

Arrangement in the scientific paper

Style is only one of the three main parts of classical rhetoric. Arrangement is another. Arrangement has become formulaic. People sneer at Adam Smith's use of "casual empiricism," scattered throughout the argument. But the alternative is to cram all the empiricism into the last section of the paper, as a "test" which allegedly ends the conversation, giving over the earlier sections to unrestrained but coercive speculation. The arrangement of the scientific article was invented by Isaac Newton, a not altogether sweet fellow, as a device for crushing his scientific opponents (Bazerman

1988, ch. 4). An official arrangement has spread to the social sciences from physics and biology. The arrangement draws on the rhetorical style of the laboratory experiment, though without its rhetorical conclusiveness. (It is notable that the more prestigious the economic journal and therefore on average the more self-confident the authors the less formulaic is the writing.) An economics article is thought to be more scientific if it has a section entitled "Data" or "Results," as one finds in articles on chemistry. A good deal of economic prose implies that the proper arrangement of an empirical essay is Introduction, Outline of the Rest of the Article, The Theory, The (Linear) Model, The Results, Suggestions for Future Research (since nothing ever works), and (again) Summary.

"Boilerplate" is a good, industrial word for the received arrangement. Excessive introduction and summarizing is one sort of boilerplate; another is redoing for a large number of repetitive cases what can be done just as well with a single well-chosen one. Econometric chatter copied out of the textbook, rederivations of the necessary conditions for consumer equilibrium, and repetition of hackneyed formulations of the theory are all pieces of boilerplate ready to bolster the scientific standing of the economist, at least in the eyes of a naïve implied reader. A model of efficient capital markets will be "explained" by writing for the thousandth time "P_t given I_t, where I_t is all the information." The boilerplate establishes ethos cheaply–just as it does in other contexts, such as the slabs of prefabricated prose about project evaluation slotted into engineering reports on a Third World dam.

The old and new theories of scientific writing

The third main part of classical rhetoric is Invention, that is, the framing of arguments worth listening to. It is said to be the business of economic theory and of empirical economics. The theory of writing in the scientific article is that Invention is all there is. Either the novelty of invention is wrong or it is right. If it is wrong, it is to be contradicted by friendly criticism. If it is right, it is to be transcribed into the list of "references" that add a patina of scholarship to the next article. The style or arrangement is supposed to be unimportant. "They are *merely* matters of style or arrangement. Content is what matters."

Not so. For one thing, as I argued earlier, in both the ancient and the modern sense, invention arises from the metaphors and stories with which economists make their world. For another, the content is not separable from the style and arrangement. The rhetorical form of a scientific article establishes the ethos of the author and his relation to the reader in a way that makes an economic argument. "Our author," the reader thinks to himself, "is worth listening to: look how skillfully she uses the language and the mathematics."

The history of science has shown repeatedly in recent decades that mere rhetoric, even by the vulgar and narrow definition of the word, plays a bigger part in science than one might think. The history of ideas contains wide turns caused by mere ornamental decorum. · Galileo's *Dialogo* persuaded people that the earth went around the sun, but not because it was a Copernican tract (there were others) or because it contained much new evidence (it did not) but because it was a masterpiece of Italian prose (and of rhetoric in other ways: see Finocchiaro 1980; cf. Gal 1992). Charles Lyell, the Galileo of geology, was "a great writer, and much of his enormous success reflects his verbal skills" (Gould 1987, p. 107). Darwin's good English, Poincaré's good French, and Heisenberg's good German were no small contributors to their influences on biology, mathematics, and physics.

Keynes hypnotized three generations of economists and politicians with his graceful fluency in English. He is acknowledged as the best writer of English that economics has seen, though an economist winces to hear literary folk discussing his style (Graves and Hodge 1943 [1961], pp. 332–340; or Virginia Woolf, on *The Economic Consequences of the Peace*: "a book that influences the world without being in the least a work of art: a work of morality, I suppose," 1923 [1980], vol. II, p. 33).

The division of modern culture into a scientific and a literary branch has had a strange effect on the style of economics. Nowadays good writing arouses a suspicion among economists that the writer is not a Scientist. It is similar to the suspicion aroused in classicists when one of their genus uses statistics to make an argument. The worst prose is held up as the ideal, as John Muth's was by Robert Lucas and Thomas Sargent (both of whom write better than Muth). They said of Muth's justly famous but wretchedly written article inventing rational expectations that it was "one of the most carefully and compactly written papers of recent vintage" (Lucas and Sargent 1981, p. xvii; cf. McCloskey 1985a, ch. 6). The virtues commended are those of Scientism, compactness especially being the virtue of the modern journal article, following the Gaussian habits of mathematics (Gauss was called "The Fox" because he had, so to speak, a bushy tail with which he erased his tracks as he went). Discursiveness of most sorts (except mathematical proofs) has been reduced in pursuit of a

Scientific ethos. As Axel Leijonhufvud says, "editors [nowadays] require authors to be formally quite precise in what they are saying but do not give them much room to explain what they are *talking* about" (1991).

"Style versus content" is a rhetorical commonplace of our culture, most common since the seventeenth century, but dating back to Plato. Its assumption that one can split content from expression is mistaken. The two are yolk and white in a scrambled egg. Economically speaking the production function for thinking cannot be written as the sum of two subfunctions, one producing "results" and the other "writing them up." The function is not separable.

Richard Lanham argues that one must look at and through a style of writing. "Only attention to the stylistic surface yields the meaning it adumbrates – a meaning not beneath but on it" (Lanham 1974, p. 53). He gives an example of a pilot radioing back to his ship, "Sighted sub, sank same," a message about himself as much as about the action (Lanham 1974, p. 40). The form tells in what spirit an economic argument is to be taken. As we say, it sets the tone. As Lanham puts it, "A mass society now reenacts the aristocratic Renaissance discovery that man's nature is artifice" (Lanham 1974, p. 130). Style is substance. "Any writing course in America today should aim at an acute self-consciousness about style" (1974, p. 13).

There you have it: style and other literary matters can be seen on the surface of economic scholarship, and reveal something of the character hidden behind the ethos. As Lanham puts the issue, by looking at scientific prose we see *through* it. Wittgenstein identified "deceit" as the effect of bad rhetoric on style. An economist uses a rhetoric, good or bad. The most scientistic articles in economics use one. The choice is not whether to write "rhetorically" or not, since the most sober writing in science must be rhetorical. The choice is whether to have a rhetoric we acknowledge, without deceit, or not.

chapter 10

The rhetoric of mathematical formalism: existence theorems

The main figure of economic rhetoric has become the conspicuous use of mathematics. The rise of a scientistic style in economics has been accompanied by the rise of mathematical formalism. In 1972 Benjamin Ward identified a "formalist revolution" beginning in the 1940s (Ward 1972, p. 40). Philip Mirowski has recently dated what he calls "the second rupture" in mathematical rhetoric to the 1930s, attributable he argues to a belief by young physicists and other scientists that economic problems urgently needed their skills (1991b, p. 151; compare the similar entry of physicists into biology after the Second World War). In 1986 Herbert Grubel and Lawrence Boland surveyed the results. From 1951 to 1978 the number of pages containing a mathematical expression without empirical use rose in the *American Economic Review* from 2.2 percent to 44 percent (Grubel and Boland, 1986, p. 42; cf. Debreu 1991, p. 1). The rise was matched in other high-prestige journals, accelerated by the birth of journals devoted entirely to such products. (The products have not pleased the customers. Grubel and Boland sampled several hundred economists of various types and found that over two-thirds believed that excessive space in the journals is devoted to purely theoretical articles [1986, p. 433]).

It would course be idiotic to object to the mere existence of mathematics in economics. No one wants to return to the time, not distant, in which economists mixed up the movement of an entire curve and a movement along it. Look for example at the presidential address of Harry A. Millis to the American Economic Association (delivered in December, 1934), especially pages 4–5 on marginal productivity and the labor problem. Because he did not understand the notion of a mathematical function Millis misunderstood Hicks' *Theory of Wages.*

Economics made progress without mathematics, but has made faster progress with it. Mathematics has brought transparency to many hundreds of economic arguments. The ideas of economics – the metaphor of the production function, the story of economic growth, the logic of competition, the facts of labor-force participation – would rapidly become muddled without mathematical expression. Most economists and I agree with Léon Walras, who wrote in 1900, "As for those economists who do not know any mathematics, who do not even know what is meant by mathematics and yet have taken the stand that mathematics cannot possibly serve to elucidate economic principles, let them go their way repeating that 'human liberty will *never* allow itself to be cast into equations' or that 'mathematics ignores frictions which are *everything* in social science'" (Walras 1874/1900 [1954], p. 47).

But economists know that a qualitative argument for something does not automatically fix its optimal quantity. When America has market power in some exportable, and takes a selfish view, the economist can assert qualitatively that some tariff would improve on free trade. But an argument for the existence of an optimal tariff does not automatically tell how large the tariff should be, quantitatively speaking. Likewise, if some industries are monopolized, then forcing other industries to price exactly at marginal cost may be a bad idea, as a matter of qualitative, logical, on-off, what-might-possibly-happen truth. But the scientific question is quantitative. How far from competitive is the economy? What closeness to marginal cost would trigger the second best? (See the classic article by Paul David and Albert Fishlow making this point in 1961, simulation before the computer made it fashionable.) How much marginal cost pricing can the economy stand?

In other words, economists do not need more existence theorems about the role of mathematics in economics – "there does not exist a mathematical economics that can take account of human liberty" or "there does not exist a rigorous economic argument unless it is expressed in Bourbaki-style mathematics." Grubel and Boland put it economically: "Is the quantity of mathematics applied to the production of [economic] knowledge and human capital [of students] efficient?" (1986, p. 421). To answer the quantitative question about the role of mathematical formalism in economics we need a quantitative standard.

Comparison provides the quantitative standard. On several

grounds, physics is a good standard for comparison. For one thing, economists share some human qualities with physicists. Economists like to think of themselves as the physicists of the social sciences, and in a few ways they are. Like physicists, and unlike, say, historians, economists are frankly competitive, in love with conferences and conflict. They are hedgehogs, not foxes; they know one big thing ($F = ma$; $e = mc^2$; $P = MC$; $MV = PT$) not a large number of little things (cf. Khalil 1992, who wisely adds a third category, "owl"). They like to colonize other fields, in the way biology was colonized after the war by physicists ashamed of making bombs. And economists, as we have seen, are approximately as arrogant as physicists are.

For another, economists admire physicists and judge themselves, as do most people in our culture, to be intellectually inferior to them. Like the philologist in the centuries of Scaliger, Erasmus, Bentley, and Housman the physicist today is at the top. Physicists have the most prestige among intellectual workers, and are able therefore to persuade government to give them expensive toys. The first-rate economists imagine themselves to be good third-rate physicists. Comparisons with sociology, say, would not be to the point, since economists, without knowing any sociologists, imagine sociologists to be inferior to economists. The standard of comparison should be a field economists look ignorantly up to rather than one they look ignorantly down upon.

Most economists, then, would accept physics as a standard for the use of mathematics. The empirical result of applying it is this: physics is less mathematical than modern economics.

The proposition sounds crazy. The average economist knows a lot less mathematics than the average physicist, as is apparent from the courses both take in college. Walk the aisles of the college bookstore and open some of the upper-division undergraduate books in physics (or for that matter in the much-despised civil engineering). It makes the hair stand on end. Even the mathematically more sophisticated economists know less math than comparable physicists, if by "knowing math" one means "knowing about Bessel functions" or "knowing six ways to solve an ordinary differential equation" or even "knowing a lot about the theory of groups."

The proposition, however, does not say that economics uses more math; it says that economics is "more mathematical." In the economics department the spirit of the math department reigns. The spirit is different over in the physics department. The physicist Richard Feynman introduced a few simple theorems in matrix algebra into his notoriously difficult freshman class at the California Institute of Technology with evident embarrassment (1963, vol. I, 22-1): "What is mathematics doing in a physics lecture?" He answered by distinguishing the physicist's results from the mathematician's proofs: "Mathematicians are mainly interested in how various mathematical facts are demonstrated . . . They are not so interested in the result of what they prove." Feynman's rhetorical question – why math? – startles an economist. In most first-year graduate programs in economics it would be rather "What else but mathematics should be in an economics lecture?" The anthropologist Sharon Traweek reports that "theoretical physicists may be chastised by their peers for being 'too mathematical'" (1988, p. 79), a charge that would not be rhetorically effective in economics. In physics the familiar spirit is Archimedes the experimenter. But in economics, as in mathematics, it is theorem-proving Euclid who paces the halls.

Economists know little about how physics operates as a field, and the physicists in turn are amazed at the math-department character of economics. The new Santa Fe Institute, which brings the two groups together for the betterment of economics, has made the cultural differences plain. In 1989 *Science* described the physical scientists there as "flabbergasted to discover how mathematically rigorous theoretical economists are. Physics is generally considered to be the most mathematical of all the sciences, but modern economics has it beat" (Pool 1989, p. 701). The physicists do not, actually, feel "beaten," since unlike economists they do not regard mathematical rigor as something to be admired. To the seminar question asked by an economist, "Where are your proofs?", the physicist replies, "You can whip up theorems, but I leave that to the mathematicians" (Pool 1989, p. 701). A physicist at the Santa Fe Institute solved a problem overnight with a computer simulation, approximately, while the economist found an exact analytic solution. Who is the more mathematical?

Economists think that science involves axiomatic proofs of theorems and then econometric tests of the QED (*quod erat demonstrandum*, not quantum electrodynamics), which therefore will test the axioms. As Paul Feyerabend remarks, "It is to be admitted that some sciences going through a period of stagnation now present their results in axiomatic form, or try to reduce them to correlation hypotheses. This does not remove the stagnation, but makes the sciences more similar to what philosophers of science think science is" (Feyerabend 1978, p. 205). In truth the physicists could care less about mathematical proofs and very little about correlation hypotheses. Even the theoreticians in physics spend much of their time reading the physical equivalent of agricultural economics or economic history. Pure pencil-and-paper guys are common enough in physics departments, but they do not set its intellectual agenda. Physics is finding driven. Economics, like mathematics in the heyday of Nicholas Bourbaki, is proof driven. Ask your local physicist what he thinks about proofs. He'll say, "Well, I prefer to depend on an existence proof about existence proofs: if the mathematicians tell me they exist, fine; I reckon they know. But it ain't physics."

The economists, to put it another way, have adopted the intellectual values of the math department – not the values of the departments of physics or electrical engineering or biochemistry they admire from afar. The mathematical economist Gerard Debreu, in an address to the American Economic Assocation, notes that the mathematical economist "belongs to the group of applied mathematicians, whose values he espouses" (1991, p. 4); and he speaks of "the values imprinted on an economist by his study of mathematics" (p. 5). Debreu realizes that physicists do not share these values: unlike economics, "physics did not surrender to the embrace of mathematics and to its inherent compulsion toward mathematical rigor," but on the contrary occasionally was led "to violate knowingly the canons of mathematical deduction" (p. 2). But economists, says Debreu, do not have enough experimental data, and therefore must rely on deductive methods. A similar remark was made by Philip Anderson, the distinguished physicist who (with Kenneth Arrow) brought the Santa Fe Institute together, explaining the differences in attitudes towards mathematics on the part of economics and physics by reference to "the differences in the amount of data available to the two fields" (Pool 1989, p. 701).

As an economic historian I can attest that Debreu and Anderson are mistaken, as they would probably agree if they looked into the matter. Economists are drenched in data, as hard as may be, and recently even experimental data. And unless astrophysics and geology are to be accounted non-sciences because they do not experiment much, observational data are data, too, what we mainly can hope to have in paleontology or history or economics. Wassily Leontief attributes the tradition of fact-boredom in economics to the long and lazy era in which economics could advance on the basis of facts available to any alert person and, when these were exhausted, on the basis of easily acquired government statistics (1982, p. 104). His argument seems plausible. In any event, the old era is past. The new economic historians have revolutionized what even a lazy economist can extract by way of data (Sutch 1991; McCloskey 1976).

The manuscripts of the American Census of Production after 1840, for example, have provided stunning quantities of data. The word "data" anyway shows the real problem: it means in Latin "things given." The better, less mathematical, and more scientific word would be *capta*, "things seized" in long, cold nights at the telescope or long, dry days in the archive. The data are not "available" to physics: they are seized, with great difficulty. An astrophysicist studying neutron stars has thin and puzzling data, but she examines them closely, and lusts to have more. A theoretical economist, by contrast, fabricates some "stylized facts" out of his head and then devotes the rest of his career to axiom and proof.

No one would make the absurd claim, of course, that axiom and proof have no place in economic reasoning. They do, and should, though economists might be more sensitive to Alfred Marshall's remark long ago that "the function then of analysis and deduction in economics is not to forge a few long chains of reasoning, but to forge rightly many short chains and single connecting links" (Marshall 1920, p. 773). We had better know that assumption A leads to conclusion C, although it would be a poor economics that only knew this. True though it is that a science is axiomatized only on its death bed – but it is after all the owl of Minerva, the mathematizers would reply, that takes wing at dusk – no one should spurn knowing $A \rightarrow C$.

But at the heart of axiom and proof as practiced in economics is a rhetorical problem, a failure to ask how large is large. As the mathematical economist William Brock put it in 1988:

> We remark, parenthetically, that when studying the natural science literature in this area it is important for the economics reader, especially the economic theorist brought up on the tradition of abstract general equilibrium theory, to realize that many natural scientists are not impressed by mathematical arguments showing that "anything can happen" in a system loosely disciplined by general axioms. Just showing existence of logical possibilities is not enough for such skeptics. The parameters of the system needed to get the erratic behavior must conform to parameter values established by empirical studies or the behavior must actually be documented in nature.
>
> Brock 1988, p. 2 of typescript

The problem, to put it formally, is that economists have fallen in love with existence theorems, the beloved also of the math department. (They are not the beloved of the physics department.) Faced with a can of beans on a desert island the economist proves that there must exist a can opener, somewhere.

The most famous of these theorems is of course the Arrow-Debreu proof of the existence of competitive equilibrium, though I intend the word "existence theorem" to apply to all the qualitative theorems with which economists wile away the hours between 8.00 a.m. and quitting time. The problem of formalism in economics extends beyond the admitted vacuities of general equilibrium theory. It reaches down to the way the average economist sets up a problem, as a theorem rather than a simulation. When the chemist Linus Pauling, age ninety-one, sets to work in the morning he is reported to carry a calculator; an equivalently eminent economist carries a pencil alone or perhaps a piece of chalk, the better to prove theorems.

But general equilibrium is a leading case, and is often though wrongly taken as the core of economics. Significantly, what are commonly regarded as the first formal proofs of the existence of a competitive equilibrium, advanced during the 1920s and 1930s, were devised by professional mathematicians, John von Neumann and Abraham Wald. From everywhere outside of economics except the department of mathematics the proofs of existence of competitive equilibrium will seem strange. The proofs do not claim to show that an actual existing economy is in equilibrium, or that the equilibrium of an existing economy is desirable. The blackboard problem thus solved derives more or less vaguely from Adam Smith's assertion that capitalism is self-regulating and good. But the proofs of existence do not prove or disprove Smith's assertion. They show that certain equations describing a certain blackboard economy have a solution, but they do not give the actual solution to the blackboard problem, much less to an extant economy. Indeed, the problem is framed in such general terms that no specific solution even to the toy economy on the blackboard could reasonably be expected. The general statement that people buy less of something when its price goes up cannot yield specific answers, such as $4,598 billion. The proofs state that somewhere in the mathematical universe there exists a solution. Lord knows what it is; we humans only know that it exists.

Incidentally, I am speaking of neoclassical economics; but anti-neoclassicals should not therefore rejoice. They do the same thing. In Marxian economics, for example, the general statement that commodities are made with commodities cannot be expected to yield specific answers to any question worth asking. The various impossibility theorems that make institutional economists happy ("But after all the economy is obviously not competitive, and so all that neoclassical rhetoric is rubbish") are equally vacuous, equally in love with Kant's synthetic a priori, equally unlike the procedures of physics or any other science.

The usual way the quest for existence is justified is to say that, after all, we had better know that solutions exist before we go looking for them. Ask an economist why she's so interested in existence theorems and this is the reply you will get. Of course, the economist giving it does not then go out into the world and look for parameterized and empirical solutions, ever. Nobody's perfect. The reply anyway sounds reasonable to someone who has never studied another science, coming to economics from the department of mathematics: if you can't actually find the solution, nonetheless you can know that what you're endlessly looking for exists.

Judging again from physics, however, the reply is not reasonable, and is not the procedure in science. Mathematicians believe it is, but the physicists do not agree. Physicists have happily used the Schrödinger equation since 1926 without knowing whether it has solutions in general. The N-body problem in Newtonian physics, which mathematicians have been working on for three centuries, does not possess extant solutions in general. Yet astronomers can tell you with sufficient accuracy for most of the questions they ask where the moon will be next year (though in the long run its orbit is in fact instable). For that matter, poets can write particular *terza rima* poems without knowing whether the form has in general a solution possessing optimal properties. Whether a solution under assumption A exists in general is irrelevant if the physical or economic or poetic question has to do with particular finite cases covering assumptions A' or A'' or A''' merely close to A. For that question you need approximations and simulations and empirically relevant parameters, not existence theorems.

The way the mathematical rhetoric has been transformed into economic rhetoric has been to define the economic problem as dealing with a certain kind of (easily manipulable) mathematics and then to run the field as though math-department questions were in fact important for the science. It is a search under the lamppost because the light there is so good, as the drunk explained after losing his keys in the dark.

The notions of "equilibrium" and "maximization" in economics have been subject to such a mathematizing treatment, as historians of economic thought have noted with alarm (Weintraub 1991a, 1991b; Mirowski 1990). Many economists have claimed that Adam Smith's question *is* the mathematical one of existence. The move is doubtful as intellectual history. Smith used the phrase "the invisible hand" only once in each of the two books published in his lifetime (1776 [1981], IV, ii, p. 456 and 1790 [1982], IV, i, 10, p. 184) and it is not until the coming of mathematical values in economics that the matter of existence was considered to be important.

But what is more unhappy is that a proof of existence leaves every concrete question unresolved, while enticing some of the best minds in the business into perfecting the proofs (I note that the same diversion of talent occurred in the ruminations on ordinal utility from 1910 to 1950 and now is occurring on a bigger scale in game theory). With certain assumptions about preferences and technology one can write down equations that can be shown to have somewhere out there a solution and sometimes, more to the point, even a stable solution, insensitive to trembling hands. Naturally the result, which is about the equations, not about the economy, depends on the assumptions. The modernist task has been to vary the assumptions and see what happens.

Unsurprisingly, under some assumptions the equilibrium does exist and under others it does not; under some assumptions the equilibrium is efficient and under others it is not. Well, so what? Sometimes it rains and sometimes it does not. In some universes the moon is made of green cheese and in others it is not. None of the theorems and countertheorems of general equilibrium theory has been surprising in a qualitative sense, or else they are not believed, and their assumptions are perturbed until the lack of surprise is reinstated. *But the qualitative sense is the only sense they have.* They are not quantitative theorems. They are mathematics without numbers, of great and proper interest inside the department of mathematics, but of little interest to quantitative intellectuals. Among mathematicians an error however small is not to be overlooked (an intellectual value that Bishop Berkeley threw in the face of the early users of the calculus (Davis and Hersh 1981, p. 243). In physics and engineering and economics a small error *is* to be overlooked.

The problem is that the general theorem of Arrow and Debreu or any of the other qualitative theorems do not, strictly speaking, relate to anything an economist would actually want to know. We already know for example that if the world is not perfect then the outcomes of the world cannot be expected to be perfect. We know it by being adults. But economists arguing over the federal budget next year or the stability of capitalism forever want to know *how big* a particular badness or offsetting goodness will be. Will the distribution of income be radically changed by the outlawing of interest? Will free trade with Mexico raise American national income much? It is useless to be told that if there is not a complete market in every commodity down to and including chewing gum then there is no presumption that capitalism will work perfectly efficiently. Yet that is a typical piece of information from the mathematical front lines. It does not provide the economic scientist with a quantitative scale against which to judge the significance of the necessary deviations from completeness. It is social mathematics, not social physics. Chewing gum or all investment goods: no matter for the proof.

Practical people, including most economists, understand Adam Smith's optimism about the economy as asserting something like this: economies that are approximately competitive are approximately efficient, if approximate externalities and approximate monopolies and approximate ignorance do not significantly intervene; and anyway they are approximately progressive in a way that the static assertion does not pretend to deal with, even approximately. The claim has analogies to the theorems of general equilibrium (similarly fuzzy but relevant claims are made in other parts of economics). But except on the knife edge of exact results, where a set of measure zero lives, the theorems are not rigorously relevant (cf. Cowen 1990).

If we are going to be rigorous we should be rigorous, not rigorous about the proof and extremely sloppy about its range of application. William Milberg of the New School for Social Research (1988, 1991) and Hans Lind of the University of Stockholm (1992) have in a series of papers documented the lack of rigor in the opening and closing paragraphs of theoretical papers. Lind has exhibited the rhetoric of evasion in the work of one Swedish economist, a specialist in international trade theory. The Swedish economist does not fall below the usual standard, explored by Milberg in other fields of economics: great rigor in the middle; utter laxity on the ends. The argument put forward, in its middle parts so very precise, is usually vague to the point of scandal in its beginning parts – about why the assumptions A' or A'' are to be preferred to the old A. The new assumptions are said to be "more realistic" or "less restrictive" or something else obscure and untried. After a middle passage through pointless precision the argument again becomes fuzzy, at the end, where the "policy implications" are brought forward. More intellectual scandal. Because of the tangency of curves on a blackboard we are to adopt a policy of free trade. Because of a lack of tangency we are to overthrow capitalism.

The theorems are exact results, containing no definition of the neighborhood in which they are approximately correct. They choose the wrong rhetoric. They are fine for math but useless for science. For science we need quantitative simulation, not qualitative theorems.

Richard Lanham has pointed out that the ancient practice of *declamatio*, that is, the rehearsal of rhetorical techniques, the mock court of law schools, is precisely simulation. The rhetoric of science and life speaks of "trying out" this or that notion. It is useless, on the contrary, to prove by analysis that there exists an ideal speech at law or an ideal design of a bridge. Simulation tells us what we want to know: what works, how well. And simulation by computer becomes cheaper every few years by another order of magnitude. "Just as the rhetorical practice of declamation put dramatic rehearsal at the center of classical thought," Lanham notes, "the computer has put modeling at the center of ours" (Lanham, forthcoming, ch. 4, p. 14). The technique of simulation suits the postmodern economist, or the pre-modern, Gothic economist – anything but the modernist in love with existence theorems. The ancient prestige of analytic solutions and existence theorems, one might predict, will fade as the cost of computation falls. It is already happening in some branches of pure mathematics. The Greek idea of mathematics may be under a sentence of death by electronics.

The exact existence theorems are perhaps worth having, though why exactly they are worth having needs to be argued more rigorously than it has been so far – a matter of rhetorical or philosophical, not mathematical, rigor, but rigor all the same. The philosopher Gary Madison said, "the trouble with this kind of [philosophically unsophisticated] call for intellectual rigour is that it is not rigorous enough. On the one hand it naïvely accepts positivistic myths as to what natural science is . . . On the other hand, it does not raise any critical questions as to what the object of economics is or ought to be" (Madison 1990, pp. 35–36). Mathematical economics has not been sufficiently rigorous about its arguments – the way mathematical physics has been forced to be. As it was put by Wittgenstein, who was rigorous about the place of mathematics in our intellectual culture, "Confusions in these matters are entirely the result of treating mathematics as a kind of natural science. And this is connected with the fact that mathematics has detached itself from natural science; for, as long as it is done in immediate connection with physics, it is clear that *it* isn't a natural science" (quoted in Monk 1990 [1991], p. 326).

To put it rigorously, the procedure of modern economics is too much a search through the hyperspace of conceivable assumptions. In the second of his *Three Essays on the State of Economic Science* (1957) Tjalling Koopmans (trained as a physicist in the 1930s) argued for precisely such a program of research, referring to a "card file" of logical results connecting a sequence of assumptions A, A', A'', $A''', \ldots, A^N$ to the corresponding conclusions C, C', C'', and so forth. He specifically wished to separate blackboard economics from empirical economics, "for the protection of both. It recommends the postulational method as the principal instrument by which this separation is secured" (Koopmans 1957, p. viii). Economists should have a theoretical branch and an empirical branch (which he thought was going to result in an imitation of physics). The theoretical branch should devote itself to "a sequence of models" (p. 147 and throughout).

Koopmans' program has been widely accepted. In 1984, for example, Frank Hahn thought he was answering the objection that anything can happen in general theorizing by saying: "It is true that often many things can be the case in a general theory but not that anything can be. Everyone who knows the textbooks can confirm that" (Hahn 1984, p. 6). What he means is that the textbooks line up the sequence of assumptions $A, A', A'', \ldots$ with the conclusions C, $C', C'', \ldots$ True enough. That's nice. But of course it is not an answer to the objection that in economic theorizing, contrary to its declared love of rigor, in fact anything goes: choose A', A'', A''', as you will, like a gentleman preferring blondes to brunettes. I conjecture the following important

Metatheorem on Hyperspaces of Assumptions

For each and every set of assumptions A implying a conclusion C and for each alternative conclusion C' arbitrarily far from C (for example, disjoint with C), there exists an alternative set of assumptions A' arbitrarily close to the original assumption A, such that A' implies C' (see figure 1).

I have not been able to devise a proof, but you can whip one up; anyway, as an empirical scientist, I leave that to the mathematicians. The empirical evidence is overwhelming. Any experienced economist knows of examples. Name a conclusion, C, in recent (but not last year's) formal economics – say, that rational expectation obviates government policy or that interaction in many different markets makes for closer collusion of oligopolists. Observe that by now there have appeared numerous proofs that alternative assumptions A' or A'', which for most purposes look awfully close to the original A, result in C' or C'', disjoint with C – conclusions such as that government policy outwits rational expectations or that the oligopolists are nonetheless unable to achieve collusion (on the latter see F. Fisher 1989, p. 122). We have discovered empirically in economics over the past forty years that blackboard proofs that $A \rightarrow C$ are *not*

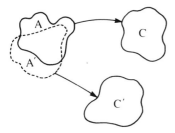

fig. 1 The A-prime, C-prime theorem

robust, cannot in principle be robust, because there always exists A' $\rightarrow C'$, A close to A', where C' is the negation of C.

Richard Feynman told of a game he used to play in graduate school at Princeton with the mathematicians. He offered to tell them at once, on the spot, whether any theorem they could explain to him was true or false. He listened closely to the set of assumptions A that the math students reported to him, and to the conclusion, C, making them express their topological theorem in terms he could understand, such as the cutting up of an imaginary orange. But then he merely guessed randomly at its truth or falsehood, without any attempt to think up a proof validly connecting the assumptions, A, to the conclusion, C. In the instances in which he guessed right, the game ended and the mathematicians went away impressed by Feynman's mathematical insight. If he guessed wrong, he ran the A-prime-C-prime exercise, and being a very bright boy he could always do so. If he called a true theorem false, for example, the mathematicians would exclaim "Ha! We got him . . . It's So-and-so's [true] theorem of immeasurable measure!" (Feynman 1985, p. 85). But then Feynman would exploit the fact that in order to explain the theorem the mathematicians had had to make particular assumptions, A, about, say, the imaginary orange. Under alternative assumptions A-prime, which Feynman was sure to find with a few moments of reflection, the theorem was false, as Feynman could assert without fear of contradiction. The mathematicians had assumed perhaps an infinitely divisible orange, whereas Feynman (if he wanted to reverse the result) claimed after the fact that *he* had been assuming one made of actual atoms. "So I always won." If you are as smart as Richard Feynman you can always win such a game. But it isn't physics, or even interesting mathematics. It's the game economists have been playing with growing unease for the past fifty years.

So have other departments, though not physics and engineering. A computer scientist has complained about the way the subject is taught in universities, a triumph of math-department values over those of electrical engineering:

> While programmers would certainly like . . . to be able to prove mathematically that their programs are bug-free, experience has shown this to be impossible in any practical sense. Real-world programs are too large ever to be proved "correct" and too ill-specified, in that the requirements for a large program are rarely completely understood in advance . . . Nearly every useful program has bugs, and nearly every program simple enough to be bug-free is likely to be of very little practical utility. In general, this doesn't matter, because big programs with occasional small bugs have proved to be so useful in the real world . . . One cannot fault a mathematician for seeing a computer program as a mathematical object. After all, mathematicians see everything as a mathematical object, and rightly so . . . However, none of this implies that a mathematical perspective is necessarily the most useful one for the practicing programmer.
>
> Borenstein 1992, pp. B3–4

The problem, to repeat, is a rhetorical one. The prestige of mathematical argument led economists to believe, contrary to their discipline, that they could get something intellectually for nothing, proving or disproving great social truths by writing on a blackboard. Programs of research since the 1940s that focused on existence theorems have for a time been rhetorically successful, until the economists have realized once again that after all nothing has been concluded, that A' $\rightarrow C'$ and $A'' \rightarrow C''$ and so forth without limit, as everyone who has read the textbooks can confirm.

The pattern has been repeated in most parts of economics. Besides the general equilibrium program itself, one can mention among others the $2 \times 2 \times 2$ program of international trade, the theory of international finance, and the rational expectations revolution in macroeconomics. The economists responsible for these excellent ideas have wandered off into discussions of whether or not an equilibrium exists for this or that "setting" and what its character might be, qualitatively speaking. They have rarely asked in ways that would persuade other economists how large the effects were. They have not asked how large is large. Eventually they have gotten bored with the formal tool of the day and have walked off to develop a new one. Terence Hutchison instances the rises and falls of growth theory and welfare economics: "In both cases, after decades of ingenious manipulation, efforts petered out with the level of abstraction almost as far-fetched as it had been, 'optimistically' [he refers to Joan Robinson's dictum that one must be patient and optimistic with simplifications], from the start, with any significant real-world relevance as far away as ever" (1992, p. 36). The Tin Lizzie of growth theory has been cranked up again, and can be expected to sputter to a halt in the mud of A', A'', A''', . . . once more, around 1997. Hutchison quotes Ward's complaint twenty years before that the formalization tends "to proliferate beyond the ability of anyone to vouch for its connection with the real world" (Ward 1972, p. 39). Nothing about the real world of economics has been concluded except that $A \rightarrow C$ and $A' \rightarrow C'$ and $A'' \rightarrow C''$ . . . . The orange is assumed to be discrete or infinitely divisible or something else. So?

Game theory is beginning (for the third time in its brief history) to bore economists; evolutionary theory stands enticingly ready to fuel careers and then to be abandoned in its turn. The economists, though they talk about Science quite a lot, and sneer at lawyers and sociologists, have not taken the rhetoric of science seriously, and have retreated from the library and laboratory to the blackboard. Research in many fields of economics (though not all) does not cumulate. It circles.

The problem was brought into focus by the philosopher Allan Gibbard and the mathematical economist Hal Varian some time ago. "Much of economic theorizing," they noted (without intent to damn it), "consists not . . . of forming explicit hypotheses about situations and testing them, but of investigating economic models" (Gibbard and Varian 1979, p. 676). That's right. Economic literature is largely speculative, an apparently inconclusive exploration, as I say, of the hyperspace of assumptions A, A', A'', . . . In defending the excess of speculation over testing in economics Gibbard and Varian use a phrase heard a lot in the hallways: "When we vary the assumptions of a model in this way to see how the conclusions change, we might say we are *examining the robustness of the model*" (same page, my italics). But it doesn't work out that way and their rhetoric shows they realize it does not: notice the diffident phrasing, "we might say." Economists commonly defend their chief activity by saying that running through every conceivable model will show the crucial assumptions. Ha.

The economists have embarked on a fishing expedition in the hyperspace of possible worlds. The trouble is that they have not caught any fish with the theoretical line. The activity works as science only when it gets actual numbers to fish in. But economic speculation does not use actual numbers. It makes qualitative arguments, such as existence theorems. Paul Samuelson, who founded the present paradigm in economics, spent much of his book of marvels in 1947 trying to derive *qualitative* theorems; his rhetoric of positivism not withstanding, he did not show the way to empirical work. Maybe for all his astounding excellences Samuelson in this respect set economics off in the wrong rhetorical direction.

What economics needs, say Gibbard and Varian with much justice, is a quantitative rhetoric, telling how large is large:

> When a model is applied to a situation as an approximation, an aspiration level epsilon is set for the degree of approximation of the conclusions. What is hypothesized is this: there is a delta such that (i) the assumptions of the applied model are true to a degree of approximation delta, and (ii) in any possible situation to which the model could be applied, if the assumption of that applied model were true to degree of approximation delta, its conclusions would be true to degree epsilon.
>
> Gibbard and Varian 1979, pp. 671–672

That sounds good. Yet they realize that the degree of approximation of this desirable, physical, engineering rhetoric to economics is poor. In the next sentence they concede that "Of course . . . few if any of the degrees of approximation involved are characterized numerically" (p. 672). But wasn't that the point? If the literature of economics consists largely of qualitative explorations of possible models, what indeed is its point? Don't we already know that there exists an unbounded number of solutions to an unbounded number of equations? That *A*-prime implies *C*-prime? Where, one might ask, will it end?

Gibbard and Varian are uneasily aware of how crushing their remark is. They conclude lamely "but the pattern of explanation is, we think, the one we have given" (same page). Well, be quantitative. Within what neighborhood of radius epsilon does economic theory, high-brow or low, approximate the quantitative procedures that are routine in physics, applied math, engineering, labor economics, or quantitative economic history?

Varying the assumptions of economic models with no rhetorical plan in mind – because "it's interesting to see what happens" when assumption A is replaced by assumption A-prime – is not science but mathematics. It is the search through the hyperspace, A-prime-C-prime economics. As Benjamin Ward observed sourly, "The lesson of economics is that it is not always enough that . . . practitioners are in substantial agreement as to the properties of acceptable puzzles and their solution to insure that a science is seriously engaged in the attempt to understand the relevant natural phenomena" (1972, p. 255).

Around 1980 a young man getting his Ph.D. at an important department of economics was interviewed for a job at another important department. He had written a thesis weakening one of the assumptions in Arrow's Impossibility Theorem. The economists interviewing him in a hotel room at O'Hare Airport listened to his spiel and then asked him encouragingly what the scientific uses of such a result might be. Why, they inquired politely, should we care if you have found an A-prime to substitute for the A? It was late in a tiring day and the youth waxed wroth: "What! Don't you understand? I have *weakened* an assumption in *Arrow's Impossibility Theorem*!" Oh. Yes. I see. Here was someone from the math department in spirit. (The department in the story did not hire him, but in most departments of economics he would have been a leading candidate.)

Scientists think differently. When the economic historian Robert Fogel varies an assumption he thereby plans to strengthen his economic case by biasing the empirical findings against himself. When Richard Feynman cut the safety seals of the Challenger space shuttle with a kitchen knife he also had an *a fortiori* plan in mind. But the most prestigious research method in modern economics, imitated at all levels of mathematical competence in the field from Debreu to the local undergraduate, has no such rhetorical plan. Economics does A-prime-C-prime scholarship, in the spirit of the math department.

The rhetorical problem is that economists have taken over the intellectual values of the wrong subject. It is not that the values or the subject are intrinsically bad. No reasonable person would object to such values flourishing within the department of mathematics. Splendid. Some of our best friends are mathematicians. Capital. The problem comes when the economists abandon an economic question in favor of a mathematical one, and then forget to come back to the department of economics. As A. J. Oswald put it with an empiricist's frustration, "Economics is in an equilibrium in which large numbers of researchers treat the subject as if it were a kind of mathematical philosophy" (Oswald 1991, p. 78). Questions of existence or questions that ring the changes on the mathematical object itself might be of interest to mathematics, regardless of how remote from an economy. Unless they can be shown to settle a dispute in economic science, however, they are not of interest to economics.

The problem lies in the sort of mathematics used, which is to say the extent of the formality, not its existence. Physicists and engineers routinely state the bounds within which their assertions hold approximately true and then they tell how true. As Gibbard and Varian put it, the applied mathematicians seek accuracy of "aspiration level epsilon." When Richard Courant, a mathematician of some repute, brought a bit of applied mathematics into his elementary but difficult calculus book, he emphasized the principle involved, so foreign to the analysis he had been expositing for 300 pages: "We wish to direct special attention to the fundamental fact that the meaning of an approximate calculation is not precise unless it is supplemented by an estimate of the errors occurring, i.e. unless it is accompanied by definite knowledge of the degree of accuracy attained" (Courant 1937, p. 342). The rhetoric is scientific, not mathematical.

Listen to page 3 of one of the leading textbooks in engineering mechanics:

> In mechanics models or idealizations are used in order to simplify application of the theory . . . A particle has a mass but a size *that can be neglected*. For example, the size of the earth is *insignificant compared to the size of its orbit* . . . Rigid Body: . . . In most cases, the *actual* deformations occurring in structures . . . are *relatively small* . . . Concentrated Force: . . . We can represent the effect of the loading by a concentrated force, providing the area . . . is *small compared to the overall size of the body*.

> Hibbeler, 1989, p. 3; my italics, except, characteristically, on the "small" in the last line, which is Hibbeler's.

Such rhetoric of magnitudes is foreign in economics and would be revolutionary on page 3 of a leading text in microeconomics. Their colleagues in physics, chemistry, and engineering and their elementary students even in economics are surprised that in what economists regard as their chief scientific work they do not talk about magnitudes at all. They talk about the existence of unique solutions, not the magnitude of the approximations. As Richard Palmer, a physicist involved in the Santa Fe Institute's attempt to instruct economists in science, put it: "while these ingredients might reasonably be expected to lead to many possible economic states or equilibria, it is not clear whether or not they do so in practice. The situation is somewhat obscured by the tendency in economics to look only for unique solutions, and to reject or modify models that do not provide them" (Palmer 1988, p. 179).

Of course, when economists come to advise on policy or to reconstruct past economies the bounds of error must be stated, and often are, with wonderful skill. Empirical simulation runs policy and history, and should. Economists practice *declamatio*, trying out in the computer or the board room this or that way of saying it.

At the blackboard, where they spend most of their time, however, academic economists routinely forget to say how large is large. They have taken over unawares the intellectual ideals of that admirable, excellent department where existence is all important and magnitude is irrelevant. The economists are in love with the wrong mathematics, the pure rather than the applied.

chapter 11

General equilibrium and the rhetorical history of formalism

It is not fair, however, to blame the department of mathematics for the economist's love of existence theorems. In fact, it is not fair to blame the mathematical economists themselves. Even non-mathematical economists have always loved existence theorems. Economists would have had to reinvent the calculus for their own lovely marginal analysis if it had not already been invented; likewise they would have had to reinvent fixed-point lemmas, the better to prove existence theorems. As Michio Morishima noted dryly, "students who have read works on social choice or Arrow and Hahn's monumental book *General Competitive Analysis* (1971) are likely to be surprised at the remarkable resemblance between such works and Spinoza's *Ethica Ordine Geometrico Demonstrata*" (Morishima 1984, p. 51).

It is not a matter of the use of modern mathematical notation. A mathematical spirit pervades the works of David Ricardo, who used no mathematics. Schumpeter called the spirit the Ricardian Vice, applying blackboard propositions untested to the world (Schumpeter 1954, p. 473). The Ricardian Vice has little or nothing to do with the use of *mathematical* formalism. The rhetoric of formalism, whether in words or statistics or mathematics, engenders the false hope that the blackboard will suffice. The physiocrats, a century before mathematics first came to economics, were attempting to solve great social questions by manipulating definitions. The Stockholm School around 1925 believed that manipulating the definitions of saving and investment could solve the macro-economy (Andvig 1991). Many of the wholly verbal Austrian economists are as much in love with their own sort of formalism, and hostile to the notion that science might have to come off the blackboard, as is the most math-besotted graduate of Berkeley or Minnesota (cf. chapter 22 below). The older sort of Marxian economists are, too; and so are the younger, trying to prove on a blackboard that power is worth paying attention to (for which see the next chapter). System and certitude are what people want. They want, as Francis Bacon promised in sounding the bell that gathered the wits, that "the mind itself be from the very outset not left to take its own course, but guided at every step, and the business be done as if by machinery" (Bacon 1620 [1965], p. 327).

Among the oldest questions in economics, after all, is a theorem about whether, as Bernard Mandeville put it in the early eighteenth century, private vice can be a public benefit: "Thus every Part was full of Vice, / Yet the whole Mass a Paradise," the central irony on which economics is built. Are social systems automatically virtuous as well as automatically stable? No numbers are expected in the answer, which is a tip-off that social philosophy, not social physics, is in question. It is to be answered at the blackboard or the lecture podium, not in the world of measurement. A modern student of this Hobbes Problem is the non-mathematical but eminent economist James Buchanan; and another the philosopher Robert Nozick; and another the lawyer and judge Richard Posner; and scores of lesser lights, none of whom can be accused of making a fetish out of mathematics.

The non-mathematical existence theorems are peculiar in the same way as are the mathematical ones. Why would it matter for an economic science that a knife-edge existence theorem could be proven? Unless it concerns the relevant quantitative questions – *how* full of vice, *how* paradisiacal – the theorems of Hobbes, Mandeville, Arrow, Debreu, Buchanan, Nozick, and Posner will not answer a question about the world. The problem, again, is not the presence of logic or mathematics – plainly, systematic imagination will often need them. The problem, as one can see clearly in the non-mathematical cases, is the quantitative extent to which economics depends on the rhetoric of existence theorems.

In August 1986 the British mathematical economist Frank Hahn published a long review in the *Times Literary Supplement* on the works of the American mathematical economist and Nobel laureate, Kenneth Arrow. The main points of Hahn's review are uncontroversial among thoughtful economists. In a different context they were well expressed, for example, by Herbert Stein: "1. Economists do not know very much. 2. Other people, including the politicians who make economic policy, know even less . . . These beliefs do not provide a platform from which to make strong pronouncements about economics or economic policy" (Stein 1986, p. xi).

The one, minor point of disagreement between Hahn and me is the Claim. The Claim is that the program initiated around 1950 of axiomatizing economics and bringing it to "testing" has been successful and should be continued. The Claim justifies blackboard economics, and economics with math department values, rummages through *A, A', A''*. Economics, says the Claimist, is "like physics. Physics, you know, has advanced on the basis of formal theories subject to test . . . or is it electrical engineering I'm thinking of? I forget. Anyway, so should we. Look at all the theorems we have proven since 1950."

I claim that the Claim is false; Hahn claims that it is true. He has on his side the weight of modern opinion down to roughly 1970, and behind it Plato, Descartes, and Russell. I have on my side the recent experience of economics, and another, parallel tradition, ancient in its own right, from Protagoras, Aristotle, Cicero, and others.

The publishing of Arrow's collected works is indeed, as Hahn said, "an excellent occasion for reflection on these matters." Arrow's achievement was translating into mathematical, $A \rightarrow C$ form the economic ideas of certain philosophers of the 1770s and 1780s (Adam Smith's Theorem on Exchange; Adam Smith's Theorem on Economies of Scale; Condorcet's Theorem on Social Choice; Bernoulli's Theorem on Expected Utility). It is quite wonderful economics of a Ricardian sort. Almost any economist, including me, would trade in a flash all his own work for any three of Arrow's articles. Whether in fifty years it will be viewed as more significant than, say, new methods of observation and their fruits is hard to know. One might hazard a guess that national income analysis (mere empirical slogging) and the broadening of economics to law, history, politics, and sociology (more of the same) may prove in the end to be more important to the science. But Arrow's is sweet stuff.

What is objectionable – and I think I speak here for most of the economics profession, many of whom would meet even Hahn's standards for inclusion in the conversation – is handing over the word "truth" and "demonstration" to Arrow's (and especially Hahn's) favorite form of argument. I don't believe Arrow himself would want to do so: he has long been a vigorous and articulate supporter of historical study in economics (Arrow 1986). The opposite view is associated more particularly with Frank Hahn and certain other mathematical economists. I must presume in this to speak for the non-mathematical economists because many of them have been browbeaten by the philosophically bankrupt notion that reasoning = formal logic = mathematics (never mind the small difficulties created by lying Cretans, *Philosophical Investigations*, and the mathematics of Gödel, Turing, and Church). The non-mathematicians have been browbeaten into accepting an obsolete theory of knowledge which sharply devalues their own.

The modernist mathematician's impulse will be to reply, "But mine *is* knowledge. What are you suggesting? That we deliver ourselves over to Imprecision and Contradiction?" No. I do not accept that this is the choice. One does not embrace unreason by arguing that a certain narrow form of argument fashionable at a certain stage in the history of mathematics does not make it as the only reasonable grounds for action. One could save a lot of time, of course, by eliminating from economic knowledge anything that could not be conveniently formulated as, say, a set-theoretic problem (and once in a great while solved). But such a definition of economic reasoning is unreasonably narrow:

> First come I, named mathematic,
> Which in Greek means learning (Attic).
> I am master of this college:
> Other things aren't eco-knowledge.

One is reminded of the way teachers of elementary logic (the Britisher Susan Stebbing, for example, or the American Irving Copi) have since the 1940s defended the equation: [first-order predicate] logic = all true reasoning. They do so by attacking all other forms of reasoning as "fallacies" (Stebbing 1939, ch. 9; 1943, p. 161; Copi, 5th edn., 1978, p. 87; and Monroe Beardsley 1956, attacking in pp. 63–70 "The Argument from Analogy" as though analogy had no place in proper argument, and citing at the end, of course, Stebbing 1939 and Copi 1978; Finocchiaro 1980, p. 333 gets it right). But in defending their turf they themselves commit the fallacy of circular reasoning (*petitio principii*). Define "true" or "correct" or "sound" or, as Hahn puts it (1986), "all we have now of honest and powerful thinking on the subject" as obeying the rules laid down by your friendly local (first-order predicate) logician. It is then a deduction, a trivial one, that truth, correctness, and soundness are identical to first-order predicate logic.

The identification of mathematical economics with eco-knowledge is bad for both. Hahn's identification of eco-knowledge with a subspeciality of mathematical economics called general equilibrium theory is very naughty indeed. Shame on Hahn, who is a serious man, who reads Jane Austen with care and who recognizes the rhetoric of economics, to use his phrase, as a "Grammar of Argument." He knows better than he lets on what the blackboard has accomplished, and in fact has noted that one cannot deny "that there is something scandalous in the spectacle of so many people refining the analysis of economic states which they have no reason to suppose will ever, or have ever, come about" (Hahn 1984, p. 88). The Claim that general equilibrium has afforded "that precise formulation which would allow [Adam Smith's arguments] to be evaluated and their range of applicability discussed" will seem unreasonable to many economists. It is similarly unreasonable to say that "the case for modern economics" rests on the achievements of one who "has only concerned himself with establishing what it is that can be claimed as true if certain assumptions are made," when the "assumptions" are formal only, the product of the blackboard rather than of the library or of the world. Against his own better instincts Hahn the Claimist claims that A-prime-C-prime *is* eco-knowledge.

No one, to repeat, would object to knowing that this or that assumption about convexity will yield this or that result. Such knowledge has a certain humble utility. Mathematical economists should be (like mathematical physicists) the useful dentists of the field, or perhaps the dental hygienists. What is objectionable is the folding of all of economics into a few pallid results in general equilibrium theory.

Yet among some economic philosophers, mathematical economists, and teachers of first-year graduate price theory the Claim rules. A mistaken vision of physics floats in the lecture hall. Economics is not such a field, to be reduced to a Schödinger equation. But neither, to tell the truth, is physics. The much-beloved notion that economics is "social physics" is mistaken, at least about the Claimist parts of economics. The Claim uses the alleged rhetoric of physics, saying that the program of the Claim is the formalization (preparatory to "testing") said to characterize physics. Notoriously, however, things in economics have not worked out that way.

I do not have in mind here the outsider's objection that econometrics is sometimes doubtful or that economists sometimes make errors in prediction: sure, of course; what isn't and who doesn't? The outsiders have a mistaken notion of Science, which bears no relation to, say, geology or biology. I have in mind rather the entire lack of connection between the research program of mathematical economics (whose practitioners are nonetheless careful to bow politely towards econometricians) and the research program of the rest of economics. The dance between theorists and experimentalists in physics does not happen in economics. At any rate it does not happen if "theorist" is defined according to Hahn (if it is defined the other way, to mean "thinkers in economics," the dance is long and lovely).

Philip Mirowski has shown that general equilibrium theory has misappropriated the physics analogy since its birth. He documents the ignorant cunning with which Walras evaded the complaints by physicists that he had misunderstood physics (Mirowski 1989; Mirowski and Cook 1990). Mirowski concludes that his finding damns all of neoclassical economics. But the conclusion is valid only if "neoclassical economics" is taken to consist of the numerous rewritings of Walras. Mirowski's argument does, however, cast in doubt the Claim that Arrow–Debreu provides that precise formulation which would allow Adam Smith's arguments to be evaluated and their range of applicability discussed.

The progress of the Claim can be detected in a point of nomenclature, the appropriation of the word "economic theory" by mathematical economists. The rhetoric, well displayed in Hahn's writing, is not so bad as the Department of War becoming the Department of Defense – at least not if Hahn, Stein, Friedman, and others can keep the social engineers away from the levers of power. But it has plenty of bad consequences.

The first consequence of the unjustified identification of economic theory with mathematical economics and general equilibrium theory is an erroneous history of economic thought. Arrow–Debreu is viewed as a capstone. So it may be, but only of a modest outbuilding in the wide estates of economics. Even in a formal sense Arrow–Debreu cannot be credited with "proving" or "demonstrating" the existence and stability of competitive equilibrium. Arrow and Debreu were far from the first to have "demonstrated . . . the logical possibility of the truth of Smith's claims," unless one takes over the words "proof" and "demonstrate" and "logical possibility" (and for that matter "Smith's claims") to mean Whatever I Want Them to Mean, again begging the question.

For most purposes, to take one of several points at which the deed could be said to have been done, F. Y. Edgeworth accomplished more than a century ago all that mattered by way of proof (see any intermediate book in microeconomics). "Arrow's First Theorem," as Hahn names it, says that offer curves cross on the contract curve. (It is of course a violation of the customs of theorem-naming to call this old proposition "Arrow's," not to speak of "Debreu's" – another example of how mistaken history arises from an excess of enthusiasm for recent formalisms.) The mathematical economist will say of Edgeworth's Proof, "But it holds merely for $N = 2$ and under other restrictive conditions." Most economists will answer, "That's good enough for me." On most days they are willing to believe that arbitrary N will give similar results, within the infinitesimal limits anyway of its exact applicability. The mathematical economist will say, "It is not a proof; it is mere handwaving." To which the answer is: "You are wrong. It is a proof, though limited like any other. After all, you yourself admit – indeed, emphasize – that the Arrow–Debreu 'proof,' which meets the fashion in proofmaking of mathematics around 1910, has its own handwaving, albeit more refined."

Even as a matter of formal demonstration, then, the Claim of success for postwar mathematical economics is dubious. But who says that formal demonstration is very important for economics? The formal demonstration leaves economics as a branch of philosophy (this is the truth among much that is mistaken in Rosenberg 1992). Philosophy is a good thing if kept in its place. In Hahn it pretends to an influence it does not have in actual economic science.

The assertion for example that Arrow-and-Debreu theory had "considerable influence, particularly on the planned economies, and on cost benefit analysis and project evaluation" must be true chez Hahn, since Hahn does not say things he does not believe, but it is not true elsewhere. General equilibrium as a metaphor is worth having, alongside others, with which as Randall Kroszner (1990) argues it need not be consistent. The persuasive arguments for workaday economists with the world on their minds are mainly those in Edgeworth or in Mill or even in Smith, not in *The Journal of Economic Theory*.

The worst consequence of the overblown Claim for mathematical economics is that it is liable to result in the demathematization of economics. If the Claim is taken seriously – and Frank Hahn saying it over and over again has already had this result – it is liable to result finally in a reaction to mathematics *tout court*, which most economists, including me, would regard as a disaster for the science. The reaction will come on that unhappy day when the Claim is recognized as nonsense.

For surely it is nonsense to claim that the only way to learn whether perfect markets tend to perfect efficiency is to translate into a particular branch of mathematics and proceed. As the mathematician Paul Halmos put it,

If you think that your paper is vacuous,
Use the first-order functional calculus.
It then becomes logic,
And, as if by magic,
The obvious is hailed as miraculous.

Halmos 1985, p. 216

Admittedly, that such nonsense is widely believed is one argument in its favor; but the point is that its popularity is not decisive.

In the penultimate sentence of his review Hahn declares, as I have noted, that "The theory which Arrow and his coevals and successors have built is all we have of honest and powerful thinking on the subject." The referent of "the subject" appears to be something like "what is in fact in the economy and what might be." Looked at in the light of day this is a bizarre assertion – that abstract general equilibrium theory, pure blackboard economics, A-prime-C-prime, is "all we have." What about the science of economics?

An instance of the way the Arrow–Debreu point has been used ideologically to bypass the science occurs in a book by the economic historian William Kennedy (1987). Arguing for a failure of British capitalism in the late nineteenth century, and wishing to find some way to show it without an onerous trip to the library, Kennedy quotes Hahn, appealing to the prestige of abstract theory in economics. Hahn has argued throughout his career that the assumptions for capitalism to work without intervention are "unrealistic." Why then spend so much time on the blackboard? For the precise purpose, says Hahn, of "showing" the unrealism. Hahn declares, and Kennedy repeats, that "This negative role of Arrow–Debreu equilibrium I consider almost to be sufficient justification for it, since practical men and ill-trained theorists everywhere in the world do not understand what they are claiming to be the case when they claim a beneficent and coherent role for the invisible hand" (Hahn 1973, pp. 14–15; quoted in Kennedy 1987, p. 11; observe incidentally the finely Cantabrigian conflation of lofty sneering in the style of Keynes with the notion that "good training" on the blackboard – at Cambridge it need hardly be said, since training at Cambridge is training as such – is the life experience necessary for rebuking practical men and Margaret Thatcher).

Kennedy, remarkably, proceeds then to draw empirical conclusions about the world from Arrow–Debreu and Arrow–Hahn. As I have noted, this is impossible if synthetic a priori is impossible, and for the same reasons. The theorems give some necessary and sufficient conditions for exact efficiency. But they do not tell how far from

exactly satisfied the conditions must be to yield *approximate* efficiency. Since this is the problem, the Arrow, Debreu, and Hahn
theorems are irrelevant, except under the lamppost.

Kennedy appeals to such mathematics to sustain his view that
imperfections were widespread enough in the capitalism of 1890 to
matter – which is of course an empirical question, not a blackboard
question. He calls on the authority of another mathematical economist, Stanley Reiter (who, like Arrow, incidentally, has a longstand-
ing interest in economic history – he invented the word "cliometrics"
– and would probably be similarly alarmed to see his arguments used
this way). Reiter, says Kennedy, proved that "Externalities, indivisi-
bilities and economies of scale . . . destroy the informational compactness that lies at the heart of the competitive process" (Kennedy
1987, p. 13). This is quite (indeed, trivially) true in the world of exact
results in which mathematical economics has so far operated, as one
can see from the vocabulary of "compactness." But it may or may not
be true in a world of approximate results, which is the world in
which we live. It would be like saying that the area of a field is not
equal to the width times the breadth if the sides are not exactly
straight and square. Well, yes, that is mathematically true. It is true in
the third digit of accuracy, perhaps, and in some contexts the third
digit will be the important one. But for most farming purposes the
approximation for a field approximately rectangular will be just fine.

I am not claiming here that Kennedy is empirically wrong about
Victorian Britain, merely that the blackboard propositions from the
world of *A*-prime-*C*-prime do not, as Kennedy appears to believe,
prove an empirical case. Kennedy is not egregious among economists. Most of them believe as he does, to repeat, that great social
questions can be answered by staring at a blackboard. That's what
general equilibrium and many other formal programs in economics
have promised to us then and now. The promise is contrary to
economics. Scientific insight is not to be had so cheaply.

chapter 12

Blackboard Marxism

The left wing of economics has been largely shut out of the conversation by a rhetoric, especially an American rhetoric, that does not admit that an economics under the spell of Marx is "serious work." The rhetoric is strange: the serious empirical work of the Marxist Paul Sweezy (1938; Baran and Sweezy 1966) is slighted by comparison with the blackboard economics of the anti-Marxist Paul Samuelson, the one "not serious" though about the economic world, the other "serious" though about A-prime-C-prime. It's not fair. Often enough the Marxists are better A-primers, too, having their own tradition of A-priming, the attempt to produce facts about the world from the sheer logic of production of commodities by commodities. In the Cambridge capital controversy of the 1960s the Marxist A-primers under the leadership of Joan Robinson and Geoffrey Harcourt annihilated the forces of Massachusetts Institute of Technology neoclassicism.

It did the Marxists little good. Since then some of the American Marxists (and a stray Norwegian or two) appear to have decided that if you can't beat them you should join them. The new analytic Marxists have produced an impressive literature doing MIT neoclassical economics as well or better than the MIT neoclassicals. The plan is to argue in terms that the neoclassicals appreciate, as in Stephen Marglin's *Growth, Distribution, and Prices* (1984). Rhetorically speaking the plan is admirable. We are not going to make progress in economics until we discover how to talk to each other.

An important example of the new work is an essay by Samuel Bowles and Herbert Gintis, "Contested Exchange: New Microfoundations of the Political Economy of Capitalism" (1990). Its rhetoric blends that of neoclassicism and Marxism, as in the title: "exchange" but "contested"; "microfoundations" but "political economy of capitalism." It is in many ways an extraordinary work, with the same admirable plan as Marglin's to find a common rhetoric between Marx and Marshall where people can argue fruitfully. Substantively I agree that Marx attacked the classical economic model for being, as Bowles and Gintis put it, "devoid of human agency and untouched by either memory or anticipation" – untouched by memory and desire, stirring dull roots with spring rain. Marx in this account was trying to bring stories back into a synchronic economics.

But the Bowles and Gintis essay illustrates the grip that formalization has on modern economics, and that is its relevance here. The essay is filled with mathematics and numbered propositions. A tiny stylistic example is the use of labels "*A*" and "*B*" assigned throughout to the boss and the workers. The essay, in the style of formalization, imposes a burden of translation for no reader's gain. The gain to the authors is an air of precision and generality: "*A* may use the threat of sanction to cause *B* to act in *A*'s interest, and the converse is not true. First, *A* may dismiss *B*, reducing *B*'s present value to *z*. Hence *A* can apply sanctions to *B*. Second, *A* can use sanctions to elicit a preferred level of effort from *B*, and thus further *A*'s interests." And so forth. What this means is: "The boss can threaten the workers but the workers can't threaten him. The boss can threaten to fire the workers – who want to keep the job because they can loaf some. In this way the boss can cut down the loafing a little." The *A-B* writing is not meant to be clear. Like most of modern economics, it is meant to participate in a rhetoric of formalism, elevating the implied author above the implied reader.

The new theory of Contested Exchange may be summarized in a phrase as saying that much of the economy operates face-to-face. The theory makes sense to an economist of the Good Old Chicago School (the school of price theory, that is, before formalization took hold), or to anyone else who has noticed how much businesspeople talk to each other. The Bowles and Gintis essay and the program of formalization in Marxism is a new name for some old ways of thinking, expressed in a formalist rhetoric.

William James spoke ruefully of his Pragmatism that he expected it to "run through the classic stages of a theory's career. First, you know, a new theory is attacked as absurd; then it is admitted as true, but obvious and insignificant; finally it is seen to be so important that its adversaries claim that they themselves discovered it" (1907 (1949), p. 198). The theory of Contested Exchange can be run rapidly through each of James' stages.

The objection is that the Bowles and Gintis argument is old and simple. To use James' stages, the theory of Contested Exchange should be attacked at the outset as absurd, because it is a case of blackboard economics and blackboard economics gets more absurd each year. Yet the theory is admittedly true. But it is obvious, because it merely rewrites the conventional notion of transaction costs in the language of conflict; and it is insignificant because the blackboard propositions in the essay are not confronted with the world. And finally the theory is so important that the Good Old Chicago School discovered it decades before Bowles and Gintis. The essay in short is a formalized version of Chicago School arguments of the 1950s and 1960s.

Bowles and Gintis are saying that in the face-to-face parts of the economy the more powerful person can exploit another person, within the limits imposed by the ability to move. Under capitalism, man exploits man (under socialism it's the other way around). Marriage is perhaps the most important case, though Bowles and Gintis think that the workplace is. A marriage makes it difficult to move away from abuse and neglect and exploitation. The exit option, as Albert Hirschman puts it, is not always easy to take. One does not often help a battered wife by saying to her, "It's a free country: why don't you exit?" She feels trapped, and to the extent she feels that way, or is legally placed in such a position, her husband can beat her.

To use the natural metaphor, transaction costs put walls around institutions, the way transportation costs put walls around an island. In a nutshell, the Contested-Exchange model of Bowles and Gintis is the story of what happens inside the walls. Calling exchanges with transaction costs "contested" gives it a Marxoid tone, but otherwise (as Bowles and Gintis admit) their story is the old and Chicago one of transaction costs.

The wall metaphor is how economists of whatever school would explain the argument to outsiders. They would explain it to themselves with an analogy to international finance. The cost of getting into and out of a job or a marriage or a country is like the cost of getting gold into and out of New York. At some differential between the price in Hong Kong and the price in New York the gold will flow from New York to Hong Kong; at the opposite differential it will flow in the opposite direction. The two differentials are of course the "gold points." At the gold points "the market works." That is, you won't find gold selling in New York for a price higher or lower than what it costs to bring some gold from Hong Kong. The New York price is limited by competition from Hong Kong, in the usual economistic way.

But inside the gold points the market doesn't "work." This means merely that strictly inside the range of prices set by the gold points a speculator would not find it worthwhile to send gold from one place to another. Within the gold points something besides arbitrage between Hong Kong and New York determines the price. Outside the gold points the prices are determined by international competition; inside the gold points they are determined by something else – in the case of gold, by the domestic as against international supply and demand (which amounts to the gold points between one vault in New York and another).

It is apparent from the analogy with gold points that whether or not the market "works" depends on how closely one is examining it. The market is like a post-impressionist painting. If one steps back and squints, then the gold points fade to insignificance, and there is effectively one world price for gold. The same is true for labor, if one squints more. When one gets close enough to any market, on the other hand, the brush strokes appear.

The close view is no more real than the far view. It may be more or less convenient for this or that human purpose to take a close view or a far view. That is all. Saying about a painting by Seurat that it is "really" just a bunch of dots is not ordinarily an intelligent comment, which is to say that it is not ordinarily useful. Likewise, to say that the market for loans or labor, as Bowles and Gintis say, are really "non-clearing" is to use words in a strange way. It would be like saying that the market for bricks is non-clearing because there are gold points (that is, brick points) between Iowa City and Cedar Rapids. The extent of non-clearingness depends on what we want to do with the notion of clearing, or how we want to think about the economy of Eastern Iowa. It is a matter of how far we wish to stand from the painting.

Bowles and Gintis go to a good deal of trouble to "prove" that "employment rents . . . will exist in a competitive equilibrium of a contested exchange." As an existence theorem, a mere statement of possibility, the proposition does not need the rhetoric of proof. If there are gold points, then within the limits of the gold points the price differentials caused by bargaining or law or violence can of course help or hurt one of the parties. Within the gold points one person can exploit another.

Economists admit it is true, but judge it, as in James' second stage, obvious and insignificant. They do not need to be told of walls and gold points again in the abstract, and most especially they do not need to be told about them in the labor market. Adam Smith noted a long time ago that "After all that has been said of the levity and inconstancy of human nature, it appears evident from experience that a man is of all sort of luggage the most difficult to be transported" (Smith 1776 [1981], pp. 92-93). Therefore the gold points in the market for labor are for some purposes, on a close view, large. "In the one case the advantages of the employment rise above, in the other they fall below the common level" (Smith 1776, p. 132). Therefore the competition with other laborers does not fix the wage to many digits of accuracy.

To repeat, within the gold points there is power. Economists have always thought so. In particular the Good Old Chicago School has always thought so. Bowles and Gintis speak of an "employment rent," that is, what a worker can get away with once he has the job. It is the prize for getting employed in a good job, that is, one with high rents. The prize justifies the investment in unemployment, the better to compete for it. Good Old Chicago School economists like A. C. Harberger and Larry Sjaastad have been making the same point for decades, using it to explain high unemployment in Latin American cities.

Bowles and Gintis revive Marx's focus on how the boss extracts labor from labor power, that is, how the boss gets the workers to work. Gary Becker has written on the subject recently, Oliver Williamson earlier, but in any case it is the main subject of Chicago's property-rights economics. Bowles and Gintis assert that the neoclassical model requires an actor "who obligingly declines to pursue his interest in any relationship plagued by agency problems." The phrase "the agency problem" has since the 1970s been a concern of the Chicago Graduate School of Business, which has carried on the traditions of the Good Old School after their demise in the Social Science Building.

A straw man named "Walrasian general equilibrium" plays a large role in the Bowles and Gintis essay, but again a Good Old Chicago School economist must object. It is strange to identify the straw man with actual men of Chicago such as James Buchanan, Milton Friedman, Armen Alchian, and Harold Demsetz. Chicago long resisted the desiccated charms of general equilibrium. To be sure, the skeleton Walrasian model beloved by blackboard economists does in fact rely on a "critical assumption that conflicts of interest . . . are resolved in contracts which are either voluntarily observed or are enforceable at no cost to the exchanging parties." But the Good Old Chicago School has been exploring the consequences of relaxing this assumption, in a case-by-case, empirical way, since about 1960 (Coase 1960, 1992). The Good Old Chicago School has in fact a lively awareness that politics precedes property and that society precedes politics. It puts great emphasis, for example, on the issue of education in economic growth.

But the most important doctrinal flaw in the Bowles and Gintis essay, to repeat, is that Contested Exchange is merely the negotiation within the gold points that Chicago economists such as Ronald Coase and Armen Alchian first emphasized. It is therefore strange to attribute to Alchian and Co. such a notion as that there exists "a costless means by which [the boss] can enforce a specific level of effort." A major task of the Good Old Chicago School has been to look into the enforcement of effort, as in the studies of sharecropping by S. N. S. Cheung (1969) and J. D. Reid, Jr. (1973). The Chicago work has its own narrowness, but in both the new Marxist and the Good Old Chicago School the task is to find a rational explanation.

Chicago called it "transaction costs," a colorless phrase, admittedly. But the Chicago phrase invites someone to measure it. That's the second problem with the essay, following on the doctrinal flaw: Bowles and Gintis do not direct our attention to measurement. It is the usual problem with existence theorems as a rhetoric of economics.

Milton Friedman is fond of asking people "How do you know?" How do you know, factually speaking? As a first-month assistant professor in 1968 I was retailing back to Friedman at a cocktail party his very own argument that professional baseball was a monopoly. "How do you know?" said he. Jeepers, I dunno: Milton told me so. In the Good Old Chicago School of Milton Friedman, Margaret Reid, Arcadius Kahan, Robert Fogel, Theodore Schultz, Gale Johnson, Mary Jean Bowman, Leland Yeager, Gordon Tullock, Lester Telser, James Buchanan, Harold Demsetz, Armen Alchian, and George Tolley, to name a few, you had to know what you were talking about, factually.

The Bowles and Gintis essay is packed with a quantifying rhetoric, as is common in economic theorizing, but to use a Jamesian phrase the rhetoric has no cash value. It uses quantitative words in non-quantified contexts, hypothetical quantification. Thus the sketch of the argument for "new microfoundations for political economy" features prominently words like "extensive," "reality," "fundamentally." How extensive? Real by what standard? How fundamental?

How do you know? Bowles and Gintis are not entitled to say how far capitalism deviates from some ideal unless they have taken its measure. And the measure is the only intellectually interesting issue. The blackboard will not reveal the secrets of the world.

The question, to use a technical word, is whether any of the theorems numbered One to Nine in their essay have oomph. Oomph is what we seek in social theorizing – not propositions that stay up on the blackboard, but propositions that get down to work in the world. About halfway through the essay Bowles and Gintis say "we have not shown that the exercise of this power is socially consequential." A critical reader will mutter, "Yes, that's right," and hope that now he will get served some evidence of oomph. But in the style of blackboard economics the authors continue claiming that thus-and-such an assumption or conclusion is "insupportable" or "important" without saying how they know.

The only way the essay can advance its case against capitalism is empirically. In explaining technological change, for example, we need to know how important is the motive of control over the workforce, as against the efficiency of new technology. How much oomph has (say) the class struggle got when set beside the desire for greater efficiency? How do you know? The questions are not unanswerable, or somehow biased against the left. William Lazonick and other historical economists influenced by Marx have tried to answer them empirically, and elsewhere so have Bowles and Gintis.

The essay tries to show that the traditional bad guy – the boss or the banker – always has the whip hand. In the world, of course, sometimes he does and sometimes he doesn't. It depends. It can't be settled at the blackboard; if one tries, the outcome will be obvious. Bowles and Gintis spend section 5 making Mark Twain's point, that "A banker is a fellow who lends you his umbrella when the sun is shining and wants it back the minute it begins to rain." The evidence needs to be examined. As Bowles and Gintis say in another connection, "the choice of emphasis cannot be determined by methodological fiat." Yes. It is not much of an argument, for instance, to call the worker's side "the long side" (an idiosyncratic usage, by the way) and then declare without evidence that the long side is always the loser. Borrowers can and sometimes do exploit lenders. Workers can and sometimes do tear up the "shoes" (*sabots*) holding rails in place.

Thus in another essay by Bowles and Gintis, circulating in draft, "Power and Wealth in a Capitalistic Economy" (on the same theme and with many of the same arguments), the Walrasian model is attacked in terms such as "sufficiently subject . . . even approximately valid . . . severely compromises," all quantitative (p. 3). A few pages later Bowles and Gintis sneer at the "untenable" character of free enforceability of contract, "failing egregiously." Wait à minute. These are empirical assertions. One can't settle them on the blackboard. The standard by which the Bowles-and-Gintis New Assumptions are better than the Old is not articulated. To get from the blackboard to the world you have to show that the effects are large. Bowles and Gintis do not, and neither do most other academic economists.

Proposition 3, for example, called "Divide and Rule," says that Contested Exchange (= transaction costs) may result in racial discrimination. Again: yes. Within the gold points we are in a world of power. The scientific issue is what the oomph of such power is. How fuzzy is the picture, and what degree of fuzziness will do for the purposes at hand? Should our view be close or far? If the gold points are small, then the power will be small, at least if you stand back and squint.

The capitalist writer on discrimination that Bowles and Gintis attack is Milton Friedman. Friedman argued a long time ago that discrimination might be eroded by the pursuit of profit. Even he had some small start on answering his own question, "How do you know?", since his family had been employed as sweated labor in the New York garment trade, and he knew also about antisemitism in the less competitive industry that his progenitors' sweat got him into. His students, such as Gary Becker, and Gary's students, such as William Landes, have given a great deal of attention to the oomph in discrimination. They have explored empirically, for example, the possibility that after all the bosses will go on discriminating, in the teeth of lost profits. They have measured the profits and examined the consequences. As Milton would say, it is an empirical matter. On this issue between Marxists and capitalists the worst capitalists have done the best empirical work.

But it is of course unfair to complain in this way about the affection that Bowles and Gintis show for the blackboard. It is by no means always true that the best capitalists do the best work. For one thing, Bowles and Gintis have shown elsewhere that they are more willing than most economists to go to the library. For another, everyone does it. Economists are covered with blackboard chalk.

The blackboard rhetoric requires its theorems to be qualitative, that is to say, that they not depend on quantities. Since 1947 we in economics have been on a wild goose chase to find theorems provable by mathematical means that will miraculously give us a purchase on the world, without having to venture out into it. Such a project had to be tried, I suppose, in view of human optimism, but unhappily the chase has not captured a single goose. Maybe a stray feather or two, but no complete animal.

I and most other Good Old Chicago economists think that the chase has been a diversion of talent, and that we should now get back to serious scientific work. A still older Chicago economist, Thorstein Veblen, once described sports as having "the advantage that they provide a politely blameless outlet for energies that might otherwise not readily be diverted from some useful end." As he said of British shooting and polo, so one might say of formalism since the 1940s, the neoclassical, Marxist, institutionalist, Austrian attempts to extract Truth from a piece of chalk. The rhetorical prestige of formality has given a politely blameless outlet for energies that might otherwise not readily be diverted from a useful end.

chapter 13

Formalists as poets and politicians

The classic definition of economics is Marshall's: "the study of mankind in the ordinary business of life" (Marshall 1920, p. 1). The literary critic Northrop Frye would have extended the definition to theory, and Marshall would not have objected: "The fundamental job of the imagination in ordinary life . . . is to produce, out of the society we have to live in, a vision of the society we want to live in" (Frye 1964, p. 140). Mathematical economics, and indeed theory generally, should be viewed as poetry in this act of the imagination.

Poets therefore are not mere luxuries in science or life. We need their vision. We do not, however, need large numbers of third-rate visions any more than we need large numbers of third-rate poems. In empirical work by contrast the third rate is often useful, something on which one can build. In theoretical work the third rate is perfectly useless, even bad for one's soul, like Joyce Kilmer's parlor poetry. I think that I shall never see / A science free of theoree. / But if the blackboards never pall / I'll never see a fact at all.

Theorists in economics, then, are nothing like scientists. They are bards, imaginaries, mathematicians, poets of consistency. One of them, Brock again, speaks of his work explicitly in such a rhetoric: "chaos theory unfetters our imagination . . . [L]ike much of abstract economic theory, it may give us a hint of how to formulate better empirical models even though the guidance is still rather limited" (Brock 1989, p. 443).

Still rather limited, after all these years. Fine as poets are, their values should not run the science. Just as the rhetoric of poets elevates memorable speaking to the only artistic virtue, the rhetoric of existence theorems elevates consistency to the only intellectual virtue – not merely the most important or the one necessary, but the only one. "A foolish consistency," said Emerson, "is the hobgoblin of little minds, adored by little statesmen and philosophers and divines." And adored by little and many not so little mathematicians. The singleminded pursuit of consistency, which is the mathematician's memorable speech, is the math department's delight (the beloved also of the logic section of the department of philosophy, and admired here and there all over the academy).

In economics it is too often a foolish consistency, not scientific. Paul Feyerabend argues, as have many other recent students of science, that "the idea of science ['rationally reconstructed'] that proceeds by logically rigorous argumentation is nothing but a dream" (Feyerabend 1987, p. 10). Rhetoric, not rhetoric's part called logic, is the life of science. Alan Turing, the British mathematician, had a good-natured debate in 1939 with Ludwig Wittgenstein, the philosopher (who was trained, not incidentally, as an aeronautical engineer and school teacher):

> *Wittgenstein*: The question is: Why are people afraid of contradictions? It is easy to understand why they should be afraid of contradictions in orders, descriptions, etc., *outside* mathematics. The question is: Why should they be afraid of contradictions inside mathematics? Turing says, "Because something may go wrong with the application." But nothing need go wrong. And if something does go wrong – if the bridge breaks down – then your mistake was of the kind of using a wrong natural law . . .
> *Turing*: You cannot be confident about applying your calculus until you know that there is no hidden contradiction in it.
> *Wittgenstein*: There seems to be an enormous mistake there . . . Suppose I convince Rhees of the paradox of the Liar, and he says, "I lie, therefore I do not lie, therefore I lie and I do not lie, therefore we have a contradiction, therefore 2 × 2 = 369." [Wittgenstein here refers to the proposition in some forms of logic that an accepted contradiction allows one formally to prove any false proposition whatever; see Debreu's appeal to it below.] Well, we should not call this "multiplication," that is all . . .
> *Turing*: Although you do not know that the bridge will fall if there are no contradictions, yet it is almost certain that if there are contradictions it will go wrong somewhere.
> *Wittgenstein*: But nothing has ever gone wrong that way yet . . .

Andrew Hodges, a mathematical physicist and the biographer of Turing, writes of this exchange:

> But Alan would not be convinced. For any pure mathematician, it would remain the beauty of the subject, that argue as one might

about its meaning, the system stood serene, self-consistent, self-contained. Dear love of mathematics! Safe, secure world in which nothing could go wrong, no trouble arise, no bridges collapse! So different from the world of 1939.

Hodges 1983, p. 154; cf. Monk 1990 [1991], p. 418

The mathematician's mad pursuit of consistency is aesthetic, not practical. The mathematical economist Gerard Debreu relies on the usual arguments in his defense of consistency-loving. He says that by contrast with physics, which he admits, as we have seen, cares little for mathematical values – and considering, he claims, that economics is "denied a sufficiently secure experimental base" – "economic theory has had to adhere to the rules of logical discourse and must renounce the facility of internal inconsistency" (Debreu 1991, p. 2). That is, we have to stay at the blackboard, and be rigorous there by the standards of the math department, because we poor economists have so little information about the world. Would that we were physicists and had all those data! But sadly it is not to be, and we are condemned to the blackboard. Debreu then, to clinch the argument, echoes unaware Turing vs. Wittgenstein: "A deductive structure that tolerates a contradiction does so under the penalty of being useless, since any statement can be derived flawlessly and immediately from that contradiction" (Debreu 1991, p. 2).

Debreu's argument is inconsistent with experience and is lacking in rigor. It is an old one, the standard justification in economics for staying at the blackboard. In 1924 Raymond Bye used it: "in the absence of the possibility of laboratory experimentation the economist is justified in approaching his subject matter by [reasoning from sound premises], and the carefully sifted results arrived at by generations of keen thinkers checking each others' results is not likely to be wholly useless" (Bye 1924, p. 285; Yonay 1991 discovered the remark). Finely put: keen thinkers, not wholly useless. But Bye continued: "The difficulty with deduction is that it . . . is a qualitative rather than a quantitative analysis" (Bye, same place). Yes.

Consistency is *not* the chief scientific virtue. If a deductive structure that tolerates a contradiction is useless, then calculus for the first two centuries of its existence was useless. Debreu himself admits that much of modern physical theory would fall into the same putatively useless class. And much of economics before G. Debreu and his colleagues came over from the Math Department to slay Inconsistency was according to his criterion similarly useless.

The notion that "if not consistency, then chaos" is not admitted even by all logicians, and is rejected by many at the frontiers of research. For the logicians Anderson and Belnap, reports James McCawley, "a contradiction causes only some hell to break loose" (McCawley 1981, p. xi). In other words, consistency is not to be spurned, but it is not the master virtue, except in the math department. Ray Monk, who is a mathematical physicist, points the moral in his biography of Wittgenstein: "You can set up a game and discover that two rules can, in certain cases, contradict one another. So what?" He quotes Wittgenstein's answer: "What do we do in such a case? Very simple – introduce a new rule and the conflict is resolved" (Monk 1990 [1991], p. 307). Paul Feyerabend asks, "What is the force behind [the] argument that makes a giant-killer out of a mere logician? . . . [C]ontradictions in science are not handled according to the naive rules of formal logic – which is a criticism of logic, not of science" (Feyerabend 1978, p. 211).

Thomas Mayer, in his readable and persuasive book, *Truth and Precision in Economics* (1993), presents the evidence for the economic point that "there is a trade-off between rigour and relevance. I certainly agree that one should be as rigorous as one can be [as Mayer has shown during a distinguished career as a monetary economist]; I just oppose trying to be as rigorous as one can *not* be" (p. 7). Like Henry Woo (1986) and Benjamin Ward (1972), Mayer is the little boy observing the emperor has no clothes. But this little boy is especially detailed and convincing in his sartorial analysis. Mayer describes, for instance, the modern fascination with rigorous econometrics to the exclusion of serious inference from data as "driving a Mercedes down a cow-track" (p. 132). He is equally devastating on the pretensions of highbrow economic "theorists," which is to say, poets who have learned a good deal of mathematics.

The values of the poet assist science but do not constitute it. We have seen the value of comparing artistic and scientific production. But as was said, similarity is not the same as identity. The poets offer us intriguing possibilities, "a vision of the society we want to live in," essential to science. But the adoption of mathematical values has made much economics into sheer poetry, the cultivation of metaphor and logic for their own sakes. Whatever may be the merits of aesthetic standards in pure mathematics (and there are doubters even there; Kline 1980, p. 352), the extreme aestheticization of science is bad.

The main argument that economists nowadays appear to have in favor of an argument is that it is "deep" or "elegant" or "rigorous" as against "*ad hoc*." The reason economists have such an airy and non-rigorous vocabulary of persuasion is that they are not aware they are persuading and that unlike physicists they have studied too much in the math department, acquiring there a love of consistency, foolish as most love is. One of the lovers, Debreu again, wonders at the foolishness and gives the same account of its origin (Debreu 1991, p. 5): "Essential to an attempt at a fuller explanation are the values imprinted on an economist by his study of mathematics . . . The very choice of questions to which he tries to find answers is influenced by his mathematical background" – for instance, the question of existence on which Debreu has spent his career. Economics is a science, using poetry and mathematics as all sciences do, but it is not a branch of poetry or mathematics.

For a real science the engineer's vulgar and ugly and *ad hoc* criterion is what matters: does the project work? The same criterion applies to the project of aping math-department values in economics. Quantitatively speaking, has the formalism of economics worked, resulting in good science? After forty years of rigorous trial it is fair to ask what has been learned.

It is not relevant to claim in answer simply the number of theorems or papers, as Debreu does in celebrating with mathematical economists "the cumulative process in which they are participating" (1991, p. 3). The mathematician Stanislaw Ulam calculated that in the mid 1970s some 200,000 theorems were being proven annually in pure mathematics (1976, p. 288). The National Science Foundation reckons that some 2,000,000 articles are published each year in science, from 20,000 journals. Not all of these matter. What ideas that matter have come out of the formalization of economics? What has the "cumulative process" of mathematical economics cumulated to?

In the mid 1960s one could stand back from the program of formalization in economics and remark wisely that economics needed to invest a little in searching the hyperspace of assumptions, because perhaps in a few decades one of the theorems would become empirically relevant. We should indulge the mathematical economists for a while, said the sage voices of toleration in 1965. After all, they never failed to note, non-Euclidean geometry was useless at its birth, but turned out to be just what Einstein needed; and Hilbert spaces, merely abstract, turned out to be concrete enough for quantum mechanics.

By now, a quarter century on, there are three practical problems with continued indulgence towards A-prime-C-prime work. First, it is no longer the mid 1960s. It is decades later, and we have yet to see the payoff. In the meantime the empirical parts of economics have taught us how economies work, which we will always know. Likewise, lowbrow theorizing, with the help of a little and very useful mathematics, has taught us possibilities we would not have thought of, without time wasted on math-department formalities. But the high-brow research, to repeat, has not paid off.

In game theory, for example, the proliferation of solution concepts and the anything-goes conclusion of the so-called Folk Theorem (no one is willing to claim it, so devastating is it to the pretensions of the the field) show that the promise of an intellectual free lunch has not paid off. We have discovered again (as with utility theory and linear programming and rational expectations and various other advances) that the blackboard deconstructs itself. As von Neumann and Morgenstern put it at the beginning of game theory:

> Our knowledge of the relevant facts of economics is incomparably smaller than that commanded in physics at the time when the mathematization of the subject was achieved . . . It was backed by several millenia of systematic, scientific, astronomical observations, culminating in an observer of unparalleled caliber, Tycho de Brahe. Nothing of the sort has occurred in economic science. It would have been absurd in physics to expect Kepler and Newton without Tycho, – and there is no reason to hope for an easier development in economics . . . It is due to the combination of the above mentioned circumstances that mathematical economics has not achieved much.
>
> von Neumann and Morgenstern 1947, p. 4

They were speaking of the past, but were unintentionally prophetic about the very field of mathematical speculation that they were inventing.

Any economist knows this, though many are reluctant to say so. Mark Blaug said it well:

> Despite the enormous intellectual resources that have been invested in the endless elaboration of GE [general equilibrium] theory – with and without money, with and without increasing returns, and the rest – it is extremely questionable, to say the least, whether these efforts have thrown any light at all on the way economic systems function in practice. Worse still, it has fostered an attitude to economics as a purely intellectual game in which we model economic processes that bear a vague resemblance to real-world processes and then comfort ourselves that their constant technical improvement will one day bear surprising fruit in generating substantive hypotheses about economic behavior.
>
> Blaug 1991, p. 509

Wassily Leontief has like many economists of his generation had the unpleasant experience of seeing a program of formalism that he initiated run wild into foolishness; but unlike some of his fellows he has stood up to be counted for science (Leontief 1982). Many of the new economists "entered the field after specializing in pure or applied mathematics," without "the harsh discipline of systematic fact-finding, traditionally imposed on and accepted by their colleagues in the natural and historical sciences" (Leontief 1982, p. 104). The result has been journals "filled with mathematical formulas leading the reader from sets of more or less plausible but entirely arbitrary assumptions [that is, A, A', A'', A''', . . .] to precisely stated but irrelevant theoretical conclusions [C', C'', C'', C''', . . .]."

Mischio Morishima is another disaffected creator of vacuous formalisms. He wrote in 1984 of the general equilibrium model,

> Economic theorists randomly modify those parts of the original model which they themselves happen to consider inapplicable, each develops a model which emphasizes and exaggerates his own modifications with no sense of proportion, and they have ended up with a whole pile of models which are even more difficult to deal with than the original.
>
> Morishima 1984, p. 58

A whole pile of models does require additional random modifications. It is true, as Morishima says, that "there should be no limit to the mathematics used in specialist writings" (1984, p. 64). It would be foolish to claim that some kind of mathematics not now in general use in economics is irrelevant, a priori. How would one know such a thing? It is Methodology of the worst sort. My criticism, and Morishima's, of the rhetoric of formalism in economics is not against mathematics or against any other kind of speech, a priori. The criticism is a posteriori: "as any economist knows, if any means whatsoever are used excessively their marginal productivity will decline . . . [M]athematics has been overused . . . from the greater injection of mathematics into a fixed quantity of material" (Morishima 1984, p. 64). He tells then a story of the fate of a traditional Japanese mathematics, called *wasan*, that never established contact with practical applications, and was reduced to the condition of flower arranging: a pretty skill, useless for science (pp. 65-66).

The second problem with continued indulgence towards *A*-prime-*C*-prime is that the average economist comes therefore to the anti-scholarly conclusion that being a social physicist means never having to read anything older than the last round of xerox preprints of *A*-priming and *C*-priming. Economists have been trained to be bad scholars: the extant macroeconomist who proudly announces that he has never read *The General Theory of Employment, Interest and Money* (I am not making this up) or the extant microeconomist who has no idea that price theory might be more than fourth-rate applied math. So they repeatedly reinvent the wheel. The claim that once-useless theorems will become useful later is not plausible if in fact no one remembers them. The low standards of scholarship in economics ensure that no one will. Monopolistic competition, for example, keeps getting reinvented. Likewise some economist reinvents every few years the point that pure bargaining, being language (which always can be cheaply trumped by itself, as I noted earlier), has no solution. There is no purpose in piling up theorems said to be useful only in the long run if their half-life in the consciousness of economists is six months. More exactly, to recur to the quantitative theme, the number of them we presently produce seems grossly non-optimal. To judge by Leontief's calculation mentioned earlier, that theoretical articles were five times as common in sociology and economics as they were in physics and chemistry, they might be estimated to be non-optimal by a factor of five.

The third practical problem with continuing to tolerate the large scale of formalization in economics is political: it is that a dominant coalition of the formalizers is not itself tolerant of science. As it is put by Maurice Allais, another of the Nobel laureates in economics who have spoken out against a formalism that they themselves invented, "A new Scholastic totalitarianism has arisen based on abstract and a priorist conceptions, detached from reality" (Allais 1989, p. 13). Scholastic, not scholarly. It is an open secret that the Scholastics want economics to become a branch of the math department. Many of them were first socialized in departments of mathematics and have never quite made the transition to curiosity about the world. "One cannot be a good physicist or economist," says Allais plaintively, "simply because one has some ability and skill in mathematics" (Allais 1989, p. 13).

The Scholastics acquire allies for their project of remaking their new department in the image of the old from certain misled denizens of real scientific fields, including the scientific parts of economics, by dazzling them with the math. No one objects, because mathematical intelligence, which shows early, is taken as an index of intelligence generally (falsely, of course: the kinds of intelligence that a good economist needs, in the opinion of some of the best, are not well measured by mathematical ability at nineteen). The Scholastics exaggerate the intellectual qualities of their students in letters of recommendation, and are believed by their readers because of the premium economists place on being "smart." (Being wise or, still less valuable, being factually correct are viewed as inessential, slack variables, no constraint on science.) The Scholastics block appointments of real scientists in favor of more *A*-primers. The scholastic *A*-primers have thereby achieved hegemony: "the methods used to maintain intellectual discipline in this country's most influential departments," wrote Leontief, "can occasionally remind one of those employed by the Marines to maintain discipline on Parris Island" (1982, p. 107). One economics department after another since the 1950s has been impressed by the formalists and marched off to a Parris Island of hyperspace searching.

The oldsters like Samuelson and Solow and Arrow were traumatized in their youth by the idiotic opposition to all mathematics. Continuing to fight in the 1990s the battles won in the 1950s, they have offered no resistance to the *A*-priming of the field. Indeed, they hired and promoted the *A*-primers, and cannot bring themselves to see them for what they are: clever lads (women are rare in these circles) who never learned to give a damn about the economic world. It is a Buddenbrooks dynamic common among scholars. Though the first generation was educated in economics (Samuelson, for example, was in the 1930s an undergraduate at Chicago) their students and especially their students' students have little taste for scholarship or science. The first generation, coming in that bright dawn from one way of looking at the world to another, had therefore at their disposal two ways. They could toggle between the two ways, and still can. Their intellectual grandchildren have one and only one, blessed be its name. The best of the first mathematical generation has reached down to protect the worst of the third, "an interest group," as Grubel and Boland put it, "that attempts to generate economic rents for its members" (1986, p. 421; 40 percent of their sample of economists agreed).

The result is that few graduate programs teach economics, especially to first-year students. Partly, as I have suggested, this is because of the vocabulary we use. The leading middle-aged economists laugh when Gary Becker of the University of Chicago, the most imaginative economist of his generation, is described as a "theorist," which he certainly is; and the leading young economists, the third generation of *A*-primers after the founders, do not even see the humor in using the word "theorist" to describe someone lacking a good undergraduate degree in mathematics.

First-year graduate programs follow the terminological confusion. If you do not know anything about any actual economy, the argument goes, perhaps you had better be assigned to the "theory" sequence, that is, the introductory courses that all graduate students must take in the first year. "Theory" will at least be your comparative advantage. As Grubel and Boland put it, "non-mathematical economists have opportunities for employment in private industry . . . This leaves mathematical economists with relatively more incentive to seek rents in the academic environment than other types of economists" (1986, p. 422). Whether attributable to comparative advantage in rent-seeking or merely static allocative efficiency, dynamically speaking the success of this rhetoric of specialization has had dismal effects. The first experience that graduate students have with their science consists of existence-theorem-proving and hyperspace-searching taught by *A*-primers. The students who stay come to believe (until experience drives the madness out) that economics is about a certain mathematical object called an "economy." They have no incentive to learn about the actual world's economy.

Arjo Klamer and David Colander asked graduate students whether having a thorough knowledge of the economy was very important for academic success in economics (Klamer and Colander 1990, p. 18). Two-thirds, 68 percent, said that such knowledge was unimportant. What, then, was the number who said that knowledge of the economy was "very important"? 3.4 percent. Student physicists, not to speak of biologists and chemists and historians, would probably give different answers to a similar question: is it important for a student of chemistry to have a thorough knowledge of chemical phenomena? Is it important for a student of history to have a thorough knowledge of history? Even the *A*-primers among older economists, it is reported, were made uncomfortable by the 3.4 percent. But they were not uncomfortable enough to allow serious proposals for reform to come out of a committee of the American Economic Association.

The economics students have little incentive to learn about economic theory itself beyond the theory embodied in certain mathematical articles of recent vintage (only 10 percent in the Klamer–Colander survey said it was very important to have a knowledge of the literature of economics: note again the failure of graduate programs to transmit scholarly values and see Colander and Brenner 1992 for suggestions on how to do it). The usual graduate program takes intelligent young people and makes them into idiot savants. If they do not somehow educate themselves, which many surprisingly do (teaching Economics 1 is educational), they become practitioners who do not understand economics – academic economists, say, who do not grasp opportunity cost and cannot think about entry; or advisors to business and government who do not know the history of their portion of the economy.

Such ignorance is commonly defended by saying that the students certainly did acquire in their education a lot of "tools." But the tool kit turns out to be filled mainly with bits of mathematics that in five years will become unfashionable again (in favor of other "tools," as happened in the history of linear programming or of 1960s-style growth theory or of 1980s-style game theory). Broken automatic drills and defective power jigsaws have crowded out the hammers and nails. Nothing is more sad than to behold the 35-year old economist who realizes suddenly that his "tools" have become in the past few years obsolete and that he has still not learned how to be an economic scientist and scholar. The waste of talent is enough to make an economist weep (Piero Mini calls it "tool-making for the sake of tool-making" [Mini 1974, p. 12]).

The problem of a training in technique that does not deal with life, and is therefore ill-adapted to life after age thirty-five, appears to be widespread. Look at modern art, School of Manhattan, or modernist architecture 1920 to 1980, from Bauhaus to our house. In a recent essay the critic John Aldridge attacks what is known in English departments as "the workshop writer," that is, the product of one of the numerous programs that teach writing in imitation of the University of Iowa's original Workshop. His description of "that odd species of bloodless fiction so cherished by the editors of *The New Yorker*" would fit most graduate programs in economics. With "academic economists" substituted for "writers," and similarly throughout, Aldridge's portrait reads:

> [W]hat finally counts . . . is not the quality of the work produced but the continued existence and promotion of academic economists. Any question raised about quality would surely be considered a form of treason or self-sabotage . . . [I]t is entirely possible for a young academic economist to be graduated from one of these programs in almost total ignorance of the traditions of his craft and, for that matter, with only superficial knowledge of the economy . . . [O]ften the promise they show is the variety most young people show up to the age of about twenty-five, while other qualities more essential to the continued productivity of academic economists are not so immediately detectable . . . [T]hese academic economists are

not only estranged from their culture but seem to have no impressions of, or relation to it, at all. In fact, they show no symptoms of having vital social and intellectual interests of any kind or any sense of belonging to an economic tradition . . . [A]ny of their books and articles might conceivably have been written by almost any one of them.

Aldridge 1990, pp. 31, 32, 33, 37

The benefits of formalization in economics, I claim, have been meagre by the physics or the engineering standard. A standard favored by the mathematical economists themselves is that of once promised and then boldly claimed accomplishments. Morishima notes that

propositions congealed into the form of "theorems" are not more than conclusions from assumed hypotheses, but create the illusion of being scientific discoveries. Mathematical economists construct a mountain as is were from these sorts of quasi-scientific (or pseudo-scientific) pieces, and worship as gods those who have contributed to making the mountain a high one.

Morishima 1984, p. 70

I repeat that the mathematical economists should not take all the blame for constructing such useless mountains of "results." The blame for elevating the mathematical economists to successful academic politicians must be shared with the electorate. American voters in real elections are always complaining about "dirty campaigning," but no politician has yet been punished for engaging in it. American economists complain about the pointless math-department formalism in economics, but then worship those who can do it, often as "smart."

One of the smarter of these gods and politicians, Gerard Debreu, again, in his address on accepting the Nobel prize for economics in 1983, claimed that "The benefits of the axiomatization of economic theory have been numerous" (Debreu 1984, p. 275), and then enumerates them. His main practical claim is that "Making the assumptions of a theory entirely explicit permits a sounder judgment about the extent to which it applies to a particular situation" (same page). No, it does not, if the theorist provides no standard by which an assumption A of convexity and the assumption A' of informational asymmetry can be judged as near or far from the particular situation S. Without such a quantitative standard it will be shown in six months that another set of assumptions, A'', empirically indistinguishable from A but qualitatively distinct, leads to opposite conclusions, C''. Without quantitative standards for judging the distances between S, A, and A'' the judgment on the realism of assumptions is an unargued intuition. The goal of the mathematics was to get away from unargued intuition.

Debreu is most convincing when he offers emotional reasons for wishing to axiomatize and then prove existence theorems: it leads to "deeper" understanding ("deep" is a conversation stopper in economics, as deep as saying that a woman's dress is "elegant"); it "fulfills an intellectual need of many contemporary economic theorists, who therefore seek it for its own sake"; "simplicity and generality" are "major attributes of an effective theory"; "their aesthetic appeal suffices to make them desirable ends in themselves for the designer of a theory." Debreu's is a dress-designer's notion of science. As Einstein the physicist said, elegance is for tailors.

In the first edition of his textbook, *Economics* (1948), Paul Samuelson was refreshingly down to earth. "The test of a theory's goodness is its usefulness in illuminating observational reality. Its logical elegance and fine-spun beauty are irrelevant" (quoted in Klamer 1990a, p. 134). But an economist who asks what illumination of observational reality we have gotten since 1948 from Samuelson's program of formalization must conclude that it has been slight, and shockingly so in comparison to the accomplishments promised long ago (the full catalogue is examined in Henry Woo's impressive book, *What's Wrong with Formalization in Economics?* [1986]). Arthur Diamond has performed a rigorous analysis of the claim that Debreu's work in particular has illuminated observational reality (a claim Debreu makes on his own behalf in Debreu 1991, p. 5): a sample of eighty-eight papers citing Debreu's work contained no use of his theory in confronting the facts of the world (Diamond 1988). So much for the payoff in explanation or understanding. We have learned more in economics from our continuing traditions of political arithmetic and economic philosophy. Human capital, the economics of law and society, historical economics, and the statistics of economic growth have come from economists who trade with someone besides the math department.

This is not, I repeat, to set *The Journal of Economic Theory* below its proper value (Grubel and Boland find that its value is in any event self-sustaining: 91 percent of the citations in it are to articles of a similar character [1986, p. 431]; contrast the use of empirical studies in theoretical physics). Surely we should have people doing some sort of mathematical job, finding out how much can be wrung from this or that convenient assumption, though judging from physics we should assign to the task a fifth of the present number. We are all very thankful to Smith and Marx and Keynes for having inspired those fine theorems by Hahn and Arrow and Samuelson. But we should not be thankful for the reduction of "theory" to a rump of mathematics.

Science, as Polanyi says, comes down to an inbred morality, because it is easy to defect:

> Though his income, his influence, in fact his whole standing in the world will depend throughout his career on the amount of credit he can gain in the eyes of scientific opinion, he must not aim primarily at this credit, but only at satisfying the standards of science . . . The quickest impression on the scientific world may be made not by publishing the whole truth and nothing but the truth, but rather by serving up an interesting and plausible story composed of parts of the truth with a little straight invention admixed to it. Such a composition, if judiciously guarded by interspersed ambiguities, will be extremely difficult to controvert, and in a field in which experiments are laborious or intrinsically difficult to reproduce may stand for years unchallenged. A considerable reputation may be built up and a very comfortable university post be gained . . .
>
> Polanyi 1946 (1964), pp. 53-54

An economist cannot read this passage without a wave of embarrassment. Most of economic scholarship is frankly careerist, first-derivative economics following the curve of what's hot as closely as the first few terms of a Taylor's expansion will permit. Parts of the truth and a little straight invention go a long way in a field detached from empirical tests that bite.

One of the Nobel laureates who has spoken out told me that he had been "practically excommunicated" for complaining about the empty formalism in modern economics. The excommunicates might consider forming a new religion, called perhaps "economic science." It would be empirical to the point of actually observing economic facts, mathematically sophisticated without adopting the intellectual values of the math department, curious about practical applications, aware of its ideological burden, and open to criticism. The proposal, I concede, is utopian.

In other ways, however, I stand foursquare with Frank Hahn: "[A]ll these 'certainties' and all the 'schools' which they spawn," he wrote, "are a sure sign of our ignorance . . . [I]t is obvious to me that we do not possess much certain knowledge about the economic world and that our best chance of gaining more is to try in all sorts of directions and by all sorts of means. This will not be furthered by strident commitments of faith" (Hahn 1984, pp. 7-8). We need a catholic rhetoric that encourages neoclassicals, Marxists, institutionalists, Austrians, and the other students of mankind in the ordinary business of life to gain more persuasive knowledge.

And I stand, too, with Léon Walras, he of general equilibrium a century ago. He attacked then (preface to edition of 1900 in Walras 1874/1900 [1954], p. 48) "the idea, so bourgeois in its narrowness, of dividing education into two separate compartments: one turning out calculators with no knowledge whatsoever of sociology, philosophy, history, or economics; and the other cultivated men of letters devoid of any notion of mathematics. The twentieth century, which is not far off, will feel the need, even in France, of entrusting the social sciences to men of general culture who are accustomed to thinking both inductively and deductively and who are familiar with reason as well as experience." The twenty-first century hurries near. We may hope by then, after a century of experiment in rhetorical compartmentalization, that Walras' vision of an undivided economics may be fulfilled, even in the United States.

part V

Refutation

The fifth part of a six-part classical oration . . . answered the opponent's arguments.

Lanham, *A Handlist of Rhetorical Terms* (1991), p. 130

chapter 14

The very idea of epistemology

"The last decade," Roger Backhouse noted grimly in 1992, "has seen an explosion of interest in the rhetoric of economics" (Backhouse 1992b, p. 65). I am asked sometimes how the reaction has been to the rhetorical turn. Occasionally I get news secondhand of apoplexy, often bearing signs that the sufferer has not read what he is apoplectic about. "Klamer, McCloskey, and the rest want economics to become rhetorical." (It already is.) "They think that economics is merely rhetoric, and not a Science." (No, rhetoric is not mere; and science is rhetorical; economics is such a science.) "I see absolutely nothing in what I have read of the rhetoric literature, that affects my practice in any way." (Uh, huh. Those who have missed the point often show it in the solecism of "the rhetoric literature"). As it was put once by the churchman and rhetorician Richard Whately (*Elements of Rhetoric,* 1828 and seven editions down to 1847), "I have ascertained that a very large proportion of those who join in the outcry against my works, confess, or even boast, that they have never read them" (1834, p. 284).

But in a bulky correspondence no one has actually written to me in this way (one man stormed out of a seminar I was giving on the utter uselessness of statistical significance, but that's about it for apoplexy openly expressed). For the rest the news is good. Judging by reviews and correspondence, the reaction has been calm from philosophers outside of economics (Hollis 1985 for example), from economists without analytic-philosophical leanings (Brennan 1984; Samuels 1984; Pen 1984, p. 160; Heilbroner 1986 [1988]; Coates 1986; Palmer 1986–1987; Klamer 1986c; F. Black 1986; Hahn 1987; Tribe 1986; Gay 1987; Kregel 1987; Bornemann 1987; Bonello 1987; Ruccio 1987;

Niggle 1988; Goodwin 1988; Winston 1988; Summers 1991), and from many humanists, journalists, and social scientists round and about (Kuttner 1985; Rhoads 1987; Webly 1987; Graziano 1987; Romano 1987; Warsh 1993; Ryan 1991). They seem to get the point reasonably quickly, at least for their own purposes, and take it away with satisfaction. Yes, they all say, we agree that economics is argument; yes, we would do better to pay attention to all the arguments.

The reaction has been similarly calm from most of the methodologists of economics: Bruce Caldwell, Neil de Marchi, D. Wade Hands, Daniel Hausman, Michael McPherson, Uskali Mäki, and Steven Rappaport, for example. Though not conceding every point, they have tried to understand. Not unnaturally they would like the rhetorical work to fit into the old conversation of Methodology. They push it and pull it to make it fit – without success, I think, but at least they are doing recognizably intellectual work.

The work they think they are doing is Epistemology, the philosophy of Knowing. A philosopher and an economist, Daniel Hausman and Michael McPherson, the joint editors of a journal they founded, *Economics and Philosophy*, wrote in 1987 a piece called "Standards" reflecting on their experience with the first few years of the journal. Their main surprise was what made the referees bad tempered. The bad temper, they noted, was not between economists and philosophers, as one might have anticipated in a journal spanning two different fields, but between different schools inside economics or philosophy.

The numerous cases of good temper and good understanding from the referees exhibited as they put it "McCloskey-ish" scholarly standards, "partly tacit and much more flexible" than the received Methodology (Hausman and McPherson 1987, p. 6). By this they appeared to mean that referees did not apply mechanically a 3" × 5" card of Methodological rules to the submitted papers. Hausman and McPherson nonetheless concluded, though not offering an argument, that "the exercise of informed judgment, guided by broad and evolving principles of assessment" still rests on "implicit or explicit epistemological principles" (p. 6). In short: the McCloskey-ish view of what happens and what should happen in science is accurate and even nice, but still must somehow, ultimately, in the end, in the last analysis "rest" on Epistemology.

Such a scripting of the McCloskey-ish position highlights the anti-positivism in the first few chapters of *The Rhetoric of Economics*, expanded in this book. The other seven chapters of *The Rhetoric* and the whole of the second book on the subject, *If You're So Smart* and the works by Klamer, Henderson, Hewings, Dudley-Evans, Milberg, Rossetti, and others in the literary analysis of economic texts, are usually treated by economic Methodologists philosophically if at all, because they do not know what to say about literary analyses of economic texts. The literary analysis is the main point of what has gone on since 1983, but no student of philosophy has gotten beyond chapter 3.

The early chapters of *The Rhetoric of Economics*, beating as the present book also does the dead horse of positivism, are conventionally methodological (even if they attack Methodology), which must explain why Methodologists feel comfortable in them. But I find the chapters a trifle tedious. For instance: how many times must we go over the Methodological issues of the 1950s, such as Friedman's article? Milton Friedman himself did not take it all that seriously, judging from his practice. In explaining why he did not write on methodology after his 1953 paper, he said, "I came to the conclusion that there was essentially no relationship between what people said about methodology and what they did in their actual scientific work" (Friedman 1983, p. 1).

By contrast, literary criticism, Talmudic commentary, Biblical exegesis, and rhetoric have illuminated every text of our civilization from Moses and Homer down to Jane Austen and the commercials for Coca Cola. As chapters 4 through 10 of *The Rhetoric of Economics* show, with all the chapters of *If You're So Smart*, and chapters 3, 4, 6, and 8 through 13 of this book, when we use math or metaphors we are talking. Now that's interesting. (Incidentally, those who do literary criticism, Talmudic commentary, Biblical criticism, and the rest do not find the proposition all that interesting; unlike economists, they find it obvious. For them of course it is. What the "new economic criticism" in literary studies finds interesting are verbal ways of thinking about the economy, such as chapter 6 above or chapter 25 below, and the conversation with the left wing of economics, such as chapters 12, 23, and 24.)

But Hausman and McPherson agree with me that "modernist ritual," "narrowly rule-bound" (p. 6), is dead; and that after all "there just isn't much choice in this interdisciplinary setting but to think hard about the arguments before you" (p. 5). I suppose that is what good scholars have always done. People of sense do not spend much time worrying about whether a work has proper Scientific Methodology. We agree that methodologists should inform economists that being narrowly rule-bound is out of fashion, and that when it was in fashion it was childish. As the philosopher William Barrett has put it,

"The worship of technique is in fact more childish than the worship of machines. You have only to find the right method, the definite procedure, and all problems in life must inevitably yield before it" (Barrett 1979, p. 25). Hypothetico-deductive procedure is the *via ac ratio* of modern economics, yet no problem has yielded to it. Name the economic argument in two centuries of the discipline that has been rejected by deducing the observable implications from higher-order hypotheses and proceeding to test. Something else must be going on.

Hausman, McPherson, and I agree, too, that there does exist, as they put it, a "middle ground" between day-to-day, small-m method (for instance: use statistical significance when the problem is a sampling problem) and glorious, humanity-making *Sprachethik* (for instance: do not sneer at arguments merely because the person making them is a friend of Milton Friedman's). The middle ground is called Methodology.

Hausman and McPherson appear to say that I do not believe in the existence of Methodology. But my own experience as an editor, like their's, suggests that "standards for judging papers . . . seem to derive in important measure from *theories of knowledge* . . . that carry normative implications" (p. 5, my italics). Methodology (big M) exists all right.

The question is whether it should. Hausman and McPherson do not in their piece argue the point, but leave the impression that they think Methodology in economics and its big brother Epistemology in philosophy are desirable. They are speaking contrary to their experience. Their experience as editors suggests the opposite normative conclusion: Methodology and Epistemology spoil conversations; let's get rid of them.

John Davis elegantly summarizes my position on Methodology vs. methodology: "Quite simply, there is no definitive format for this on-going scholarly discussion – no Methodology of economics, that is – there is only this sustained verbal and written interaction which defies abstract characterization, because it is inherent in the unavoidably concrete relationships obtaining between economists" (J.B. Davis 1990a, p. 83). Or perhaps one might say that it defies timeless abstract characterization, though philosophers in every age have tried. The historian of geology Henry Frankel, in the course of analysis of how the exponents of continental drift had won the argument by 1967, uses "methodology" unselfconsciously in the sense that scientists actual use it, namely, as the low-level decisions about what is to count in argument: "if problem solutions are at odds with a successful methodology, proponents must show why they have not followed the methodological convention" (Frankel 1987, p. 238). The closure of the debate (the word Frankel uses throughout) depended on rhetorical conventions, not on middle-level philosophies of science.

Consider the observation by Hausman and McPherson that the ill-temper and misunderstanding occur *inside* fields, not between different fields. We all have this experience. If a classicist invites me, an ignoramus on things Horatian, to think such and such about Horace's use of arithmetical structure in his first three books of odes I have no trouble being flexible in mind and open in spirit (more so, actually, than classicists themselves are on the matter, since they flee in horror from anything that looks mathematical). But when she asks me to think such and such about the Roman economy, and ventures an economic thought of her own, I start closing up, since I am supposed to know something about economics: "What's this nonsense, anyway? My Lord: if that's so I'm out of a job." If you have nothing in your brain or pocketbook about Horace you are, as we say, "open-minded." It is interference with established modes of thought, not a new thought on an entirely different subject, that generates academic noise. The closer the broadcasting bands are the greater is the interference.

Now what is the problem here? Are these "established modes of thought" equivalent to the modest, desirable small-m method, the rules of getting regressions right and making demand curves slope down? As Hausman and McPherson argue, no. On small-m matters no one gets agitated. A paper violating some small-m rule of method is easily fixed: as they note, "it is usually possible for the author of an otherwise worthy paper to spruce up his or her argument suitably" (p. 3). Get your R^2 higher here, fix up the entry argument there. No blood pressures rise.

On the other hand, do the established modes of thought make people cross because they disagree about some lofty matter of *Sprachethik*, some high-level point about the morality of scholarship? No again, although economists and philosophers, as I have said, should pay more attention to the morality of scholarly dispute – it is not only classical scholarship in the age of Bentley that is disfigured by "the extraordinary spectacle of men of learning and genius, of authority and divinity, brawling . . . , and calling each other names for all the world like bookies on a racecourse or washerwomen in a back street. For this vehemence of temper and virulence of language were . . .unhappily characteristic of the profession as a whole"

(Woolf 1925 [1953], p. 198; for a recent instance in economic Methodology see Hutchison 1992).

What then causes malicious misunderstanding among scholars, the Nasty Referee Reports? The cause is not lowly method or lofty *Sprachethik*. It is middle-brow Methodology. Like nations and religions, the schools in economics and in philosophy maintain their solidarity and their definitions of barbarians by means of Methodological talk. Such-and-such is "serious Scientific work," namely, the way we Hellenes talk; the rest is barbaric, bar-bar-bar.

Such sneering is alleged to give us "standards." Having standards is obviously good if worked out in good conversation within the field, as I have argued in detail in all my work, methodological (chapters 8 and 9 of *The Rhetoric of Economics*; chapters 3 and 11 in *If You're So Smart*) and scientific. Alexander Rosenberg has claimed that McCloskey "holds that there are no such transdisciplinary standards" (Rosenberg 1992, p. 237). That is certainly wrong: I hold that there are standards of courtesy, accuracy in quotation, relevance of statistical test, honesty in the handling of factual data, depth of scholarship in modern epistemology, and the like that should apply to many, many disciplines and that I have tried personally to apply in my own work, failing miserably in many respects. No one, and certainly not I, would believe that "anything goes" *in argument* (for example, Paul Feyerabend does not: see Feyerabend 1978, pp. 39–40 and 1987, p. 283), which is to say that burbling or grenades would not fit all argumentative situations (burbling would fit talking to one's infant grandson and grenades would fit disputing with a German soldier about a hill in Italy, but neither would fit the scientific seminar). The alleged standards, which are supposed to bring order to the seminars, are in practice used as conversation-truncating sneers. In the writings of Methodologists any old violation of the *Sprachethik* is permitted. Anything goes. Likewise, in a Chicago seminar you can shut someone up by sneering use of a Methodological rule about the unrealism of assumptions. In a Berkeley seminar you can shut someone up by sneering use of a Methodological rule of the opposite character. Thus it often is with the rhetoric of law and order, of which the "standards" argument in Methodology makes undisciplined use. It ends as an excuse for much order and very little law.

An Austrian economist who uses econometrics or a Marxist who uses continuous production functions or a fresh-water rational expector who uses macro arguments without micro foundations will simply be ostracized by the rules of middle-brow Methodology. "It's not serious work." These are Methodological convictions. They are not genuine scientific standards. They are excuses for not listening to some alleged barbarian. They are not the modest, concrete rules of method ("a *t*-statistic assumes the error is like a drawing from an urn") or the grand, moral rules of *Sprachethik* ("really, you should stop sneering ignorantly at Hegelians or Post-Keynesians and try reading what they have to say, on the plausible assumption that they like you are serious and honest scholars"). The Methodological convictions are something in between, neither rules of technique nor rules of morality. My empirical observation, and Hausman and McPherson's, is that they cause mainly mischief.

As Jerry Evensky has noted with acuity, McCloskey's attitude towards Methodology is similar to Adam Smith's attitude towards Mercantilism (Evensky 1992). Both Methodology and Mercantilism are attempts to blockade entry and acquire rents for the few already in possession. They sloganize about the public good, but violate it cynically, the better to stay in charge. To which I say, drawing on my radical youth, "So take your slogan / And kindly stow it. / If this is our land, / Why you'd hardly know it. / Let's join together / And overthrow it. / This land is *not* for you and me."

Of course, any conversation that is not going to ramble pointlessly must adhere to temporary agreements about what is relevant. A seriously considered limitation of the argument is always a good idea. Narrowness, to look at it the other way, is not always a bad idea. (Some economists at this stage will trot out again an argument that narrowness is on the contrary always good. When one queries some autistic speciality in economics hostile to every intellectual value except those imported unexamined from the department of mathematics, they will ask, "Don't you believe in the division of labor? Shouldn't I be allowed to *specialize* in arguments from micro foundations of overlapping generations?" Such economists are invited to reflect on the second part of chapter 6 above and to step back for a moment and think.)

But so is a serious considered expansion or extension or complete change of the argument, always a good idea. Serious consideration is what is good, a piece of *Sprachethik*. What I wonder about is the notion, asserted repeatedly in philosophy since Plato but seldom argued, that some temporary and practical narrowing of the conversation should be made permanent because it satisfies an Epistemology forever true. I therefore cannot make out what Hausman and McPherson are arguing when they say that scholarly "standards . . . are [not] a mere ratification of whatever practices turn out to be effectively persuasive" (p. 6). Like John Austin or Richard Rorty or Rom Harré or Stephen Toulmin or Alasdair MacIntyre, I cannot see why they view "effective persuasion" as "mere," to be spurned. Effective persuasion is what makes for free communities, from the Institute for Advanced Study at Princeton to the Ocean Waves Square Dancing Club at Iowa City. It seems good enough to me. It had better be good enough, because it's all we've got.

Effective persuasion would of course be spurnable if there were something better, some big-T Truth, big-K Knowledge. But I reckon there isn't, at least short of the Second Coming. Justified true belief, which is the traditional formula of "Knowledge" in analytic philosophy (for example, Rosenberg 1992, p. 110), is an admirable ideal. We would all be in favor of it, if we could get it in a finite conversation about something controversial. We would also be in favor of rock candy mountains and whiskey springs, if we could get them.

It has been known from the beginning that the first and third parts – the justified-in-others' eyes and the belief-in-our-own-eyes – we can achieve by conversing seriously. That is how Socrates appears to have understood his method of the "elenchus," the cross-examination (taken from the law courts; in Homeric Greek it meant "shaming"). The late Gregory Vlastos argued in his last book that for Socrates himself, though not for his star pupil after his encounter in middle age with the certitudes of mathematics, "'knowledge' does not entail certainty. It may therefore be used to mean simply justifiable belief – justifiable, in Socrates' view, by the highly fallible method of elenctic argument" (Vlastos 1991, p. 114). The justification of belief is the time-constrained conversation in the law court or the assembly. If people are not made to justify their assertions, and do not believe them, the conversation will of course be a poor one. (As some of the conversation of epistemology is, on these grounds.)

But the ancient and unresolved technical problem is that there is no route aside from human persuasion to knowing whether the middle part of the definition applies: True. The True part is not in others' eyes or in our's, sincerely expressed, but in God's, expressed however God chooses to express it. It is an ideal of a conversation with no time constraints, which is perhaps why Plato the leisured aristocrat found it so lovely beside the vulgarity of law courts and democratic assemblies. Vlastos notes that "Since Socrates does expect to discover truth by this method, he must be making an exceedingly bold assumption which he never states and, if he had stated it, would have been in no position to defend," since Socrates, unlike Plato, was no epistemologist. The assumption is what Vlastos calls elsewhere

Proposition A, the "tremendous assumption," that "his interlocutors always carry truth somewhere or other in their belief system" (1991, pp. 113–114 and 114 n32). A tremendous assumption it is, epistemologically speaking, an assumption in fact of the desired conclusion about getting Truth. It says that in a serious conversation we will stumble onto God's way of looking at things, because God has placed it in the soul of every man, waiting for an elenchus to uncover it. As epistemology this Proposition A merely begs the question – though of course for purposes of getting small-t truth it is the assumption of any civilized conversation, namely, that we can find small-t truth, as true as the limited resources of human argument can achieve, by justifying our beliefs. One justifies one's beliefs in a constrained time, required to come to a practical conclusion. But epistemology has not yet solved its self-imposed problem – its only problem – of getting outside civilized yet constrained conversation to decide what to believe on God's grounds, grounds with infinite time to discuss them, grounds other than what is persuasive to people inside the finite conversations of humankind.

Wittgenstein's rhetorical notion of a language game intended, among other purposes, to diagnose (not to trivialize or mock) the problem of believing there must be Knowledge of a thing if there is a word for it. The Truth is a Platonic idea, as Wittgenstein shows in considering whether mathematical objects exist before discovery, as the North Pole does: "Suppose someone were to say: chess only had to be *discovered*, it was always there! Or: the *pure* game of chess was always there; we only made the material game alloyed with matter" (Wittgenstein 1932–1934 [1974], p. 374). Imre Lakatos took up the notion of mathematical conjectures in his rhetorical dialogue on Euler's theorem on polyhedra, *Proofs and Refutations* (1976). He laughs at the interlocutors Lambda and Theta, conventional epistemologists scandalized by substitution of attainable conversation for ultimate (if unattainable) Truth (Lakatos 1976, pp. 53–54):

> *Lambda*: I still trust that the light of absolute certainty will flash up when refutations peter out!
> *Kappa*: But will they? What if God created polyhedra so that all true universal statements about them – formulated in human language – are infinitely long? . . . Truth is only for God.
> *Theta* [aside]: A religious sceptic is the worst enemy of science!
> *Sigma*: Let's not overdramatise! After all, only a narrow penumbra of vagueness is at stake. It is simply that, as I said before, *not all propositions are true or false*. There is a third class which I would now call "*more or less rigorous*."
> *Theta* [aside]: Three-valued logic – the end of critical rationality!

Sigma: . . . and we state their domain of validity with a rigour that is more or less adequate.
Alpha: Adequate for what?
Sigma: Adequate for the solution of the problem which we want to solve.
Theta [*aside*]: Pragmatism! Has everybody lost interest in *truth*?
Kappa: Or adequate for the *Zeitgeist*! "Sufficient unto the day is the rigour thereof."
Theta: Historicism! [*Faints.*]

A modern and also unresolved technical problem with the project of justifying true belief is the Gettier Paradox, offered in a brief paper in 1963 by Edmund L. Gettier, "Is Justified True Belief Knowledge?" An economic version of one of his examples would go as follows. Suppose an economist believes that inflation is always and everywhere a monetary phenomenon. Suppose it is True, in the sense that at the Second Coming of Christ, when all is revealed, it will be judged true. And suppose that here and now the economist justifies the belief by a series of closed-economy studies of inflation. By the standards of an economics that does not grasp the truth that we live in a big world, not in a set of nations cut off from each other (the cut-off world is the one in which monetarists such as Milton Friedman and Anna Jacobson Schwartz and in fact most other American economists have on the whole believed they live), the belief is therefore justified. It is believed, justified, and True. But it would be strange to say that the economist holding the belief has Knowledge, because after all we do not in fact live in the closed-economy world that her calculations posit. Something is wrong with justified true belief as a definition of Knowledge. To bring it down to economic earth, something is wrong with assigning Truth to *A Monetary History of the United States, 1867–1960* (1967), although it was a masterful remark in the scientific conversation, true (small t) in many ways, if on the whole untrue as history and as economics.

The Gettier Paradox seems to have pushed philosophers in a rhetorical direction, requiring them to think about speech communities. (My colleague at Iowa, Payanot Butchvarov, for example, has done so in a brilliant recent paper on skepticism. He argues that a skeptic's position is impossible in the social world of philosophical discussion, instancing a woman who wrote to Bertrand Russell claiming to be a strict solipsist, who believed only in her own existence, and wondering why there were not more like her.) In any event the agreed technical definition has turned out, once again, to be far from agreed. As John Passmore puts it, "Gettier's miniscule article generated some hundreds of replies, a clear sign that the old issues are by no means dead but also indicating just how many philosophers sit, with their typewriters ready, to comment on a new twist to an old controversy" (Passmore 1985, p. 14). Passmore does not report a resolution of the paradox. As I said, epistemology has not solved its self-imposed problem, in 2,500 years of trying.

But ancient and modern technicalities aside, the main mischief arises from the very idea of epistemology, the idea that there is an intellectual free lunch out there waiting to be seized that will allow us to decide whether such-and-such is True for all time. I would rather quietly drop the whole matter and get back to economic history or rhetorical analysis. As Milton Friedman wrote in 1984, "To me the word 'truth' [read Truth] has too much metaphysical baggage attached to it to be serviceable in a methodological discussion of positive science" (1984, p. 3).

The insistence that every issue is philosophical is one of the rare faults of philosophers, parallel to the economist's fault of economism. It amounts to insisting that we should never get off the subjects proposed by Plato (just as some economists, me for instance, insist that we should never get off the subjects proposed by Adam Smith). That Plato emphatically wished to change the subject away from rhetoric has long been a disability in trying to reintroduce rhetoric. But I'm saying that his subject comes from arbitrary definition, not from a rational argument we are obliged to accept.

The crux, then, is that nothing can provide the "Knowledge" defined by epistemology. This "Knowledge" – as distinct from the effective persuasions by which we run our lives, the small-k knowledge – is "whatever it is that is in the mind of God" or "what we will know at the end of history" or "what we will never, ever come to disbelieve." It is hopelessly non-operational, defended by drawing credits on the future. In replying recently to some of my doubts on epistemology Hausman admits that "The failed efforts of philosophers to provide contentful context-free accounts of notions such as confirmation or scientific explanation do indeed suggest that substantive norms will be context-specific" (Hausman 1992, p. 266). Good: at least one philosopher of economics has understood at last the main discovery of linguistic philosophy and linguistics itself since 1955, namely, that words occur in contexts. But then Hausman draws credits on the future: "Just how methodological rules should depend on features of the context of inquiry remains a vital epistemological question" (p. 266). Back to the Epistemological rock pile, condemned to hard labor until the Second Coming. As Hilary

Putnam put it, "the enterprises of providing a foundation for Being and Knowledge – a successful description of the Furniture of the World or a successful description of the Canons of Justification – are enterprises that have disastrously failed" (Putnam 1990, p. 19). Or William Rozeboom: "No harm will be done, I suppose, by retaining a special name for true beliefs at the theoretical limit of absolute conviction and perfect infallibility so long as we appreciate that this ideal is never instantiated, but such sentimentality must not be allowed to impede development of conceptual resources for mastering the panorama of partial certainties which are more literally relevant to the real world" (Rozeboom 1967 [1993], pp. 183–184). That's what the real epistemologists think, as contrasted with the epistemologists imagined in controversies over economic method.

Small-k knowledge, on the other hand, is merely the scene that we construct, after much social instruction from our mothers and friendly local policemen in order to get across the street without getting run over. Big-K Knowledge is something altogether more grand. As used by philosophers – in their rhetoric as actually performed – it means "what is Really, Truly True, according to what is in the mind of God himself, and is so forever and ever, amen, relative to no merely human culture, not to speak of European and male, True Knowledge, justified True belief, a rock on which we can found a scientific church, and most particularly launch assaults on the standing of anyone disagreeing with our conveniently brief rules of Method, and by the way prop up the financial condition of dull-normal scientists and the more narrow among professional philosophers."

The philosophers will sometimes put forward a more modest formula, such as: Proposition P ("It is raining outside") is true knowledge if and only if it *is* raining outside. The formula is of course circular, since the project of epistemology is just to find out how we know whether or not it is raining outside. "The way we Know how it is True that it is raining outside is . . ."; and then the vampire of Platonism rises from its coffin once again and starts snapping at necks.

Or they will say, "it is not true that all invocations of epistemology are bound up with the notion of truth, for not all epistemologies are realist. The instrumentalist wants only predictively useful hypotheses" (Hausman 1992, p. 267). To which I reply, first, that the most widespread and the most mischievous epistemologies are indeed realist, in the sense (among the many senses of that valuable but therefore overexploited word) that Hausman appears to have in mind; and, second, that the instrumentalist formula is nonetheless a formula. Why did it seem so plausible to Austrian and American analytic philosophers from 1910 to 1970, and so implausible to everyone else, that the business of getting along in a speech community such as that of science would be reducible to a 3" × 5" card?

The 3" × 5"-card definitions of knowledge and science don't work. As the wise Arthur puts it in Paul Feyerabend's *Three Dialogues on Knowledge*:

> *Jack*: Some things are knowledge, others are not – do you agree to that?
> *Arthur*: Sure. But I don't believe you can draw the line once and for all, and with the help of a simple formula . . . Knowledge is a complex matter, it is different in different areas and so the best answer to "What is knowledge?" is a list . . . The idea that knowledge and, for that matter, science can be captured in a simple formula is a chimaera.

Feyerabend 1991, pp. 19–20

The project of demarcating statements once and for all into what is Knowledge and what is Mere Superstition seems likely on past form to lead to absurdities, such as the demarcation of elements into earth, air, fire, and water. The categories have present use, mainly the use of letting some of our less intellectually secure philosophers and their students attack certain thinkers (for instance: Virgil, Jesus, Dante, Hegel, Darwin, Marx, Freud) for being uselessly non-Scientific.

It is well to bear in mind that the categories have only present use. In the seventeenth century, as Jorge Luis Borges tells it (1952 [1964], p. 103), one John Wilkins categorized metals into artificial (brass), recremental (filings), and natural (gold). Borges tells of a Chinese *Celestial Emporium of Benevolent Knowledge* that categorized animals as (a) those that belong to the emperor, (b) embalmed ones, (c) those that are trained, (d) suckling pigs, (e) mermaids, and so on and so forth, through (n) those that resemble flies at a distance. What is absurd about the categories is only that their arbitrariness is so distant from ours. The attempts to hurdle to a Knowledge that will only be demarcated from error at the Last Judgment are similarly futile. As Borges puts it, "obviously there is no classification of the universe that is not arbitrary and conjectural. The reason is very simple: we do not know what the universe is" (Borges 1952 [1964], p. 104). God does. We don't. Recall Niels Bohr, quoted in chapter 4: "Physics concerns what we can say about nature." Better stick to saying useful things about our sublunary life, about how we can effectively persuade each other for here and now. Rhetoric is man's project; Epistemology is God's.

In a penetrating discussion of how Rorty's hermeneutics relates to the rhetoric of economics John Davis notes that philosophical economists assume that the context of discovery is to be demarcated from the context of justification (1990c, p. 75). Wherever a theory came from (at this juncture the philosophers will usually mention toilet training) – that is, however it was discovered – it has to be justified separately. For example, an economist may discover that the market for wheat is perfectly competitive by being a farm girl or by political conviction or by love of beautiful diagrams. But the context of justification, the philosophers aver, is different: there she must prove it. The historical reason that a scientific proposition comes to be believed, say the philosophers, is irrelevant to whether it is scientifically acceptable.

But if science studies over the past quarter century had to be summarized in one philosophically relevant statement it would be: the demarcation between contexts of discovery and justification is wrong (in economics, see Wible 1990, who makes a useful demarcation of justificationism and, later, non-justificationism, in the study of science). Davis (1990c, p. 78) quotes Rorty (1979, p. 170) on the matter: "we understand knowledge when we understand the social justification of belief." The test of "accurate representation" is no test at all, considering, as studies of science from Kuhn's on Copernicus (1957) to Shapin and Schaffer on Boyle (1985) have shown, that standards of representation are socially justified beliefs.

Unhappily, John Davis, after his lucid analysis of how my thinking relates to Rorty's, falls back on an unanalyzed notion of "justification." The results of a rhetoric of science, says he, must be "coextensive" with the justification of the science (J.B. Davis 1990a, p. 84). But it can't be done if Justification has a capital J. Small-j justification is exactly coextensive with the rhetoric of, say, proving a market in steel to be competitive. There is no big J available to mortals.

The philosopher of science Peter Winch (who is unread or misread by the Methodologists in economics) wrote in 1958 that "to understand the activities of an individual scientific investigator we must take account of . . . first, his relation to the phenomena which he investigates; second, his relation to his fellow-scientists . . . [W]riters on scientific 'methodology' too often concentrate on the first and overlook the importance of the second" (Winch 1958 [1990], pp. 84–85). A reasonable philosophy would admit that human fictions aimed at fellow scientists have their scientific use, as in American pragmatism or in Hans Vaihinger's "as-if" philosophy (trans. 1924; lovers of Friedman's old article take special note). We humans must deal in fictions of our own making. Whether or not they correspond to God's Own Universe is something we cannot know. Three umpires are bragging to each other at the bar. The first, a relaxed relativist, says, "I call's 'em as I sees 'em." The second, a realist with insight into the mind of God, says, "I calls 'em as they ARE!" The third, unruffled, a pragmatist: "They ain't nothin' 'til I calls 'em."

The leap to "objectivity," free from our merely human "bias," is nice to imagine but appears to be impossible, short of encounters with God or other superior beings. (A history teacher parodied a bit of sophomore examsmanship so: "History, as we know, is always bias, because human beings have to be studied by other human beings, not by independent observers of another species.") Hausman and McPherson, like other people trained well in philosophy, want to keep the long vigil for an Epistemological Principle that will permit us to distinguish once and for all between Truth and Falsehood. Yet in human time we can do no better than what is "effectively persuasive" in a court of law or a court of scientific opinion or indeed, to get self-referential about it, a court of philosophical argumentation.

Hausman and McPherson are puzzled that the main bad temper in their referees is about epistemology, the middle-brow philosophizing, not about morality or technique. The bad temper comes from modernism. Modernists think they know a thing or two about what God will reveal concerning progressive research programs and neoclassical economics at the Second Coming; and they become correspondingly irritated when some fool gets it wrong. As Mark Blaug's writing illustrates, they do not believe that moral premises are arguable, or that any worthwhile talking can take place about them. Shoutable, yes; arguable, no. The moral model that most people use nowadays is utilitarian, or economistic. Moral judgments in such a model are sheer tastes; combined with circumstances (for example, behind a prenatal veil) they can say something; otherwise they are "just opinions" in more or less the same sense as our sophomore students mean the phrase ("Heh, man: you can't mark me off on that: it's just an *opinion* that Mozart was a better composer than the drummer for the Broken Heads.")

Unhappily, we do not know enough about God's plan to tell

whether the Knowledge/Opinion category of the twentieth century will last until the end of time. We had better not be dogmatic today. The experience of Hausman and McPherson as editors argues for a richer, rhetorical theory of how people argue than the one provided by epistemology of the pre-1955 sort, which revolves around "statements" like "The cat is on the mat." The recent exceptions in philosophy I can think of are philosophers arguing in implicitly or explicitly rhetorical terms, such as, above all, Ludwig Wittgenstein, but more recently Gary B. Madison, *Understanding: A Phenomenological-Pragmatic Analysis* (1982), Keith Lehrer and Carl Wagner, *Rational Consensus in Science and Society* (1981), Douglas Walton, *Arguer's Position: A Pragmatic Study of "Ad Hominem" Attack, Criticism, Refutation, and Fallacy* (1985), Martin Warner, *Philosophical Finesse: Studies in the Art of Rational Persuasion* (1989), and Carlin Romano, "The Illegality of Philosophy" (1989). The highly rhetorical theory of "speech acts" developed by the philosophers J. L. Austin and John Searle, for example, points out (as the English professor Sandy Petrey puts it in his lucid book, *Speech Acts and Literary Theory* [1990]), "When we state something, it's rare indeed for us to have no effect beyond producing the statement . . . [The point is] the daunting difficulty of coming up with a situation in which to *say* 'The cat is on the mat' is not also to *do* something with, to, for, despite, or against someone else at the same time . . . When we tell the truth, we do so many other things at the same time that it's foolish to venerate the truth as if it alone were consequential" (Petrey 1990, pp. 28, 30–31, 32). Truth-telling in economic science is a thick and rich affair. As Arjo Klamer puts it, rhetoric "stimulates one to see beyond epistemology (the points of departure in conventional methodology), and to watch the behavior of economists more directly" (Klamer 1990c, p. 22).

Janet Seiz has well summarized what bothers some critics of "the rhetoric approach," namely,

> It is one thing to investigate which arguments economists have found persuasive at particular times, and why – to study, as does the Strong Program in the sociology of science, "how scientists choose what to believe," without judging those choices. It is another matter altogether to offer *assessments* of how far scientists' beliefs are "really warranted." Klamer and McCloskey, critics complain, are not being clear about whether they are pursuing only the first task, or also the second (which is the standard concern of methodologists).
>
> Seiz 1990, p. 157, her italics

Yes, these are two things; but one person can do both, as a literary critic sometimes does. The conventional Methodologists would have less trouble understanding if they would recognize the metaphor of literary criticism that Klamer and I and some others are applying to economics. A literary critic can study the affective stylistics of *Paradise Lost* and yet can also assess the poem.

Knowing how the poem works does not debar one from assessing its merits and demerits, though literary critics such as Stanley Fish are less eager to award stars to literary works than are Methodologists like Mark Blaug to award stars to scientific works. It might even be claimed that knowing how it works would be relevant for erecting standards of assessment. The tyro in criticism will assess without a knowledge of technique. He thinks that the only question a criticism can ask is whether the poem belongs on the reading list of "great" works (for example Posner 1988, which presumes among hundreds of similar embarrassments to award Jane Austen the title of "immensely distinguished moralist"; cf. McCloskey 1991c). But literary criticism is not reducible to the awarding of stars like those in tonight's TV schedule. An example in literary practice in no way unusual of literary practice is James Longenbach's treatment of Wallace Stevens' "The Idea of Order at Key West." He discusses its history and rhetoric for nine pages before venturing by the way, with no sense that assessment is the main point of the discussion, the judgment that it was "arguably [Stevens'] finest poem to date"; no other stars are awarded for a poem about which non-professionals like me are inclined to gush mindlessly (Longenbach 1991, p. 165). The amateurs, lovers indeed, want to proceed to the star-awarding ceremony without knowing how movies or poems or pieces of economic science are made. Such Methodological praising and sneering, three stars or two thumbs down, imports unexamined a standard from the outside with no respect for the conversation within economics or, often enough, within philosophy either; and often with no plausible claim to knowing how economics works on the ground. A movie critic who does not know, say, the 180° rule or the definition of "best boy" is like a philosopher or Methodologist of economics who does not know the use of metonymy in economics or the definition of statistical inconsistency.

The assessments to which philosophical, unlike literary, critics are so unhealthily eager to move therefore get made and defended on irrelevant grounds. It is an old tradition in economic Methodology. John Neville Keynes, in his "The Scope and Method of Political Economy," first published in 1891, indulges in a startling *non sequitur* in defense of Methodology, one used since by every Methodologist: "It is . . . true, as the Austrian economist Menger has remarked, that sciences have been created and revolutionized by those who have not stopped to analyse their own method of enquiry. *Still their success must be attributed to their having employed the right method"* (Keynes 1891 (1984), p. 72; p. 5 in first edition; my italics). What? Pray tell: why? What argument says that a rational reconstruction, admitted to be poor sociology and naïve rhetoric of science, will give us useful advice on how to run our sciences now and forever after? The elder Keynes was missing the point, a Mengerian and Austrian point in fact, of unintended consequences and the unpredictability of future science.

Ill-defended as it has been, I must make clear, the older and philosophical approach does not therefore have zero marginal product. It too contains arguments, which in some rhetorics may responsibly persuade. I have no objection to using them, and have done so here. Applied to economics they are sometimes just right: it is well worth knowing that the Stockholm School's approach to macroeconomics was not operational (though a rhetorical analysis would see that it was so because it drew on the rhetoric of accounting [Andvig 1991]); it is well worth knowing that consumer theory can be expressed as hypothetico-deductive models (though a rhetorical analysis would see that it was so expressed because of the prestige of axiomatic mathematics). Philosophy is dependent on rhetoric, so it should be no news that this or that philosophical argument about economics can somewhat illuminate the field. But, to apply the rhetoric, the narrow and old-fashioned Epistemology favored by a certain school in the philosophy of science casts a feeble light, and needs other lamps besides.

chapter 15

The *tu quoque* argument and the claims of rationalism

One of the editorial tasks undertaken by Hausman and McPherson in *Economics and Philosophy* was a little symposium on *The Rhetoric of Economics* (in April 1988). Two of the participants, Uskali Mäki and Steven Rappaport, were conventional Methodologists, trained as analytic philosophers.

Least contentious was Uskali Mäki's suggestion that Arjo Klamer and I combine one version of "realism" with rhetoric. Mäki's piece is introduced with a rhetoric of sharp revision – Klamer and I are said to hold "erroneous" beliefs, and the first sentence announces a "critical tone." But in fact I agree with most of the points he makes, wondering why he would think I would disagree with them; and furthermore I admire his style and good sense. There is not much on which we disagree.

Mäki follows by instinct, as does Rappaport, the "Hippocratic Oath for Pluralists" proposed by Wayne Booth:

> II. I will *try* to publish nothing about any book or article until I have *understood* it, which is to say, until I have reason to think that I can give an account of it that the author himself will recognize as just. Any attempt at overstanding [*sic*] will follow this initial act of attempted respect . . . Paraphrasing Coleridge: Before I damn a critic's errors, I will try to reconstruct his enterprise as if it were my own.
>
> Booth 1979, p. 351, his italics

If I try to do the same I come to the following understanding of Mäki's argument. McCloskey, says he, talks as though a description of economic science could be *true*. (For instance, McCloskey says that

199

Milton Friedman's description is false.) This is labeled in Mäki's paper "proposition number 6." So McCloskey must be committed to truth. So McCloskey might as well accept realism, the talk of true and false.

He is applying to me the Philosopher's Friend, the rhetorical device of catching someone being committed to X at the very moment of arguing against X. Here X = Truth and the Real. Fair enough. Call it the Philosopher's *tu quoque*, "you also." It is the standard and indeed the sole argument by philosophers against what they imagine "relativism" to be. Even the admirable Hilary Putnam relies on it. "What relativist really thinks," he asks indignantly, "that relativism is only *true-for-my-subculture?*" (Putnam 1990, p. 106; the answer, Professor Putnam, is: all of them, and consistently). Philosophers believe that the Philosopher's *tu quoque* is decisive. (It is not, because it is not valid: as Richard Rorty and others have noted, "The world is out there, but descriptions of the world are not" [Rorty 1989, p. 5], which is to say that the argument equivocates between realism in ontology and realism in epistemology; but for the moment set this aside.) You, oh relativist, in asserting the truth of relativism must acknowledge a standard of truth. Gotcha.

All such reasonings must confront, however, another *tu quoque*: that you, oh philosopher, are in turn arguing rhetorically. Gotcha yourself. The argument is the Rhetorician's *Tu Quoque*. A philosopher is committed to rhetorical thinking at the very moment of arguing against rhetoric and for a narrowing in thought. It is the serious point behind Cicero's witticism in De Oratore (I, 11, 47) that Plato was the best rhetorician when making merry of rhetoric. Bacon, Descartes, and Hobbes turned against their rhetorical educations, but inconsistently (cf. A.O. Rorty 1983; and France 1972, ch. 2). As the rhetorician of science Henry Krips observes about Boyle's *New Experiments Physico-Mechanical* (in 1660, after decades of rhetoric against rhetoric),

> On the one hand, a text cannot be rhetorical if it is to conform to the collective scientific norm which favours proper method (say, reason and evidence) and disavows rhetoric. On the other hand, the text must be rhetorical if it is to fulfill its essential function of persuading readers who do not have at their disposal the evidence needed to justify the text's knowledge claims.
>
> Krips 1992, p. 10

I would only amend Krips' formulation by saying that reason and evidence should be construed as parts of rhetoric.

The French sociologist of science Bruno Latour puts the Rhetorician's *Tu Quoque* as follows:

> Those who accuse relativists of being self-contradictory . . .can save their breath for a better occasion. I explicitly put my own account [of French science] in the same category as those accounts I have studied without asking for any privilege. This approach seems self-defeating only to those who believe that the fate of an interpretation is tied to the existence of a safe metalinguistic level. Since this belief is precisely what I deny, the reception of my argument exemplifies my point: no metalinguistic level is required to analyze, argue, explain, decide, or tell stories. Everything depends on what sort of actions I take to convince others. This reflexive position is the only one that is not self-contradictory.
>
> Latour 1984 (1988), p. 266

This non-self-contradictory position is mine, too, and Wittgenstein's, Rorty's, Feyerabend's, and that of modern sociologists of knowledge. There does not exist a safe metalinguistic level. The only non-self-contradictory way to deal with this unfortunate fact is to stop making arguments – such as the Philosopher's *Tu Quoque* – that unconsciously depend on the existence of a safe metalinguistic level.

The game of three-line *tu quoque*, of course, popular though it is among philosophers, is a trifle silly. A good example of how silly it can get is a *tu quoque* cooked up by Daniel Hausman and Alexander Rosenberg to show that my strictures on economic prediction (see chapter 6 above) are self-refuting. As usual in the practices of philosophers their *tu quoque* depends on an equivocation. I argue above and elsewhere that a prediction of say the stock market or the interest rate – call it P_0 – that entails an opportunity for profit is impossible, or else the predictor would be rich. But this, Hausman and Rosenberg point out with the gotcha rhetoric that customarily accompanies the turn, *is a prediction*. Rosenberg can barely contain his glee: "What is this but an economic prediction, deduced from economic theory, just what McCloskey tells us is impossible!" (Rosenberg 1992, p. 54; cf. Hands 1987, p. 235). But of course the prediction is P_1, a "deduction that does not offer opportunities for profit," not P_0, a deduction that *does* offer opportunities for profit. No one got rich by writing for *The American Scholar*. The P_1 in question has not made me rich. Nor would a wise "prediction" (to use the word, if one insists on forcing everything into positivism's meagre verbal categories) that free trade with Mexico is good for the economic health of the country. Nor would a wise prediction that philosophers are not going to show us how to achieve Truth, or for that matter much of truth, by engaging in three-line games of equivocation.

It is surprising that the critics of postmodernism, pragmatism, rhetoric, and the like are so confident they have grasped the writings they disdain. Can they really think that, say, Rorty – the same applies to Feyerabend, Derrida, and other bogeymen in the conservative night – is such a dunce as a philosopher that he can't handle the sort of *tu quoques* that Munz, Hausman, Rosenberg, Coats, Blaug, or Backhouse are able devise after a few minutes of light thinking? The hypothesis does not seem plausible on its face: Rorty, eminent philosopher, well-known as an analyst, full professor at Princeton, university professor at Virginia, first of the McCarthur Fellows, scourge of his profession, president of the Association, etc., etc., falls prey to the simplest claim of circularity devised by an economist-philosopher on holiday.

Even facing the bowling of mere economist/rhetoricians the Methodologists miss the ball. Roger Backhouse, for example, claims to have adduced (1992b) "very serious, arguably fatal, objections" concerning the rhetorical program in economics. They turn out to be three-line *tu quoques*, incompetently handled. In a long paper Backhouse does not answer any of the sixty or so arguments, empirical and logical, that I and others have made in a growing literature. That's not good batting: ten overs, sixty balls faced, no runs. The cricketing term is "stonewalling." Hit the ball, man.

William James was annoyed by such a mentality, that supposes it has an answer as easy as the *tu quoque* to every serious argument: "Scholasticism still opposes to such changes [in thinking] the method of confutation by single decisive reasons [*sic*], showing that the new view involves self-contradiction, or traverses some fundamental principle. This is like stopping a river by planting a stick in the middle of its bed" (James 1907 [1949], p. 373). The method is trivially easy, even for an economist, and is far from the deep philosophical point that its users think it is.

Such a *tu quoque* is not a rejection of Mäki, whose practical reasoning, as I say, I accept. It is merely a rejection of the widespread notion that we can leap to a higher realm of Truth, big-T, by an argument outside of human rhetoric. Rhetorically and philosophically speaking, the ploy of arguing the "self-contradiction of relativism" is in fact a draw (cf. Mahoney 1976, p. 141, referring to W. W. Bartley III, *The Retreat to Commitment* (1962 [1984]), which also uses the phrase *tu quoque*). In his reply to my reply in the same issue of the journal (p. 168) Mäki agrees: "There seems to be a valid *tu quoque* against an anti-realist rhetorician, and another also against an anti-rhetorical realist. Therefore, I argued, rhetoric and realism had better be combined." Precisely.

Here is how I would do it. "Realism" in Mäki's sense seems to mean that the world exists independent of our perceptions of it. The crucial word is "our." If "our perceptions" are taken to mean "the perceptions of a Cartesian ego," then I reject realism as nonoperational, something that philosophers should abandon as a waste of their time. The Cartesian ego can never get behind his subjectivity to know if he is exempt from illusion. It is the problem of the solipsist wondering why there are not more members of the Solipsism Club. Is she a brain floating in a vat? Notoriously, after three and a half centuries of quarreling on the very point, philosophers do not know. And one Cartesian ego has nothing to say to another. A solipsistic theory of knowledge perplexes science and the conversations of humankind (the Cartesian perplexities of economics are traced in Mini 1974).

But if "*our* perceptions" are taken to mean "the perceptions about which we speak to each other, testing by conversation their mutual reasonableness and freedom from illusion," then I am a realist, and so is every working scientist. In such a definition the philosophers themselves have operational work to do, along with the scientists. They can examine the conversation of science, as Mäki does in all his methodological work: he properly constrains his philosophy by what economists in fact seem to think, in order to bring order to their thinking (a brief example is Mäki 1991). The work is operational because it deals with what we know together (what I shall call in chapters 21 and 24 below "the conjective"), a subject about which we can usefully debate.

Perhaps the words "true" and "real" might better be replaced with Nelson Goodman's word "right," which is social, not solipsistic. "The truth alone," as Goodman, no amateur in epistemology, puts it, "would be too little, for some right versions are not true – being either false [thus models] or neither true nor false – and even for true versions rightness may matter more" (1978, p. 19). To use an example of J. L. Austin's which I used in *The Rhetoric of Economics*, someone may state that "France is hexagonal." Is it true or false? Well . . .it's not true or false, though a statement. It's right or wrong, for this or that human purpose, from this or that choice of human perspective.

If worlds are merely "right" in a human conversation and not "True" then perhaps it is not so obvious that my world and Mäki's are different. It would seem pointless for an astronomer not to believe that there is a dark side of the moon or an economist not to believe in the law of demand. A round moon sits in the sky (*Guardate la luna!*) and a downward-sloping demand for bread governs Brooklyn. For purposes of argument, as we say, it would be lunacy to disagree. Realism is a social – that is, rhetorical – necessity for science. As Rom Harré puts it, "To publish abroad a discovery couched in the rhetoric of science is to let it be known that the presumed fact can safely be used in debate, in practical projects, and so on. Knowledge claims are tacitly prefixed with a performative of trust" (Harré 1986, p. 90; cf. Gilbert Harman's notion that authoritative statements are ones that we accept on behalf of some group, since "learning about the world is a cooperative enterprise" [Harman 1986, p. 51]).

Anyway, I agree with Mäki. He helped change my mind about surrendering the words "true," "real," "standards," and "foundations," among others, to the pleasures of the philosophers. I welcome Mäki's invitation to reclaim the words. The philosophers in English-speaking countries have too long made a living by taking such words hostage and demanding ransom from the rest of us. Generally (though not in Mäki's case) the purpose has been to silence the revolt against philosophical hegemony by accusing the doubters of an opposing "irrationalism" or "idealism" or "relativism" as nutty as the philosopher can imagine, though undocumented from the texts. It's time to stop this false rhetoric. I myself, for example, believe that economics is a report on the real, that reason will reveal its truths, and that empirical work is essential for economic science. Modernism in economics claims to believe the same things, but in practice it has undermined them all.

Truth to tell, the modernist philosophers have given the word "truth" a merely psychological value. Since "is true" is a timeless predicate (MacIntyre 1988, p. 71) and we are not now at the end of time, when we will Know the Truth, the phrase can only have such a psychological value. It performs for the modernist the speech act of affirming sincerely: "I am *really, truly* persuaded of this, when I call it True." The modernist uses "truth" to register an emotion about the subject, which is probably why he becomes so ill-tempered when called on to defend it. The registering of emotions, remember, is how the modernist characterizes aesthetic and moral judgments. "Good" and "beautiful," he says, merely register favorable emotions. The reply to the modernist and his ranting about Truth, in short, is: *tu quoque*.

My only objection to Mäki's invitation to realism is that I wonder whether we can accomplish much on such a high level of abstraction. Kant said so, to be sure, but does it really matter in the way you treat the dog or read the essay whether you believe in Hume's or Protagoras's definition of the real? Wouldn't your small-m methods in caring for the dog and reading Coase's "The Problem of Social Cost" matter more? I would prefer to "bracket" the matter of realism, that is, to set it aside, as the phenomenologists did and the hermeneuticists do now. William Barrett explains: "bracketing . . . is not identical with the epistemological doubt whether the object really exists; and it is not the postponement of this question for a later answer. It seeks to bypass this question altogether in order to find its way into a more fruitful field of philosophizing" (Barrett 1979, p. 129; cf. Madison 1990, p. 37).

In his reply to the reply Mäki writes that "comprehensive realism implies an obligation to study empirically economists' own views about the issue of realism and to take those views seriously" (Mäki 1988b, p. 168). He is claiming that his melding of realism and rhetoric is in fact concrete, that it offers concrete proposals of research into "a theory of economists . . . as rhetorical agents" (p. 169). I can agree that such a study would be a more fruitful way of philosophizing. I have proposed and practiced it. The research would probably discover that economists are not realists in a philosophical sense. Is economics a report on the Real? "No," says the average economist, demoralized by the evident failure of positivism. Why indulge, then? "It's fun; and I earn a good salary doing it," which is realism all right, though in a non-philosophical sense.

In the same symposium Steven Rappaport followed, like Mäki, the Hippocratic oath for Pluralists. He took the trouble of reading some in the immense and distinguished rhetorical tradition. If I was allowed a single sentence of advice for the Methodological critics of rhetorical criticism it would be this: emulate Rappaport and Jane Rossetti and a few others and learn what you are talking about.

Nonetheless Rappaport shows his philosophical training. His argument draws a distinction between "evidential" and "non-evidential" rhetorical devices, a distinction continued without further justification in his vexed reply to my reply. The "non-evidential" rhetorical device – for instance the sneer – is not "analyzable into a set of premises and a conclusion." "Evidential" devices are.

The category "non-evidential" does violence to the arguments people actually, seriously make. Notice Rappaport's use of the popular figure of philosophical reasoning that says, "I cannot judge your proposition unless I can 'analyze' it into the form of a valid syllogism with correct premises." It is not obviously, utterly, without question a good idea. The philosopher will say of an argument by analogy, for example, "It is helpful [above all the philosopher, like the man from the government, wishes to be helpful] to recast the argument so that it is logically valid. For in that case, all questions about its *soundness* can focus on the truth of the premises." The problem is that in the process the philosopher is free to supply the missing major or minor premise, and since these are unlimited in number he can choose one that makes the resulting argument sound or silly, as he wishes. As we have seen, it is the usual way that philosophers deal with "fallacies" or other arguments that their methods do not treat: drag the argument under the lamppost, deforming it along the way. We should worry that most of human reasoning has to be treated so abusively.

Maurice Finocchiaro notes that professors of logic seldom give real-life examples of the "fallacies" they skewer, and when they do they are often deforming legitimate arguments. Of the "fallacy," the "non-evidential" argument in Rappaport's terms, of affirming the consequent (such as, in economics: "Excess money growth implies inflation; we witness inflation; therefore excess money growth must have taken place") Finocchiaro remarks: "to show that the actual argument is a fallacy, the logician has to argue that it is deductive. This will usually be a difficult . . . task, since most such arguments are inductive" (Finocchiaro 1980, p. 336).

Frans H. van Eemeren and Rob Grootendorst have pointed out a rhetorical contradiction in such a method (1983, pp. 179ff). They observe that when the missing premise is supplied by a philosopher in a hostile way it entails a contradiction at the level of pragmatic rules necessary for speech to be possible at all. In particular, it entails the supposition that the speaker of the incomplete argument follows the principle of cooperation in speech (namely, that the argument can be made complete, and is intended to be made easily complete) yet violates grossly what has been called by Paul Grice "the Maxim of Quality" (namely, that the argument is meant to be true). It violates it because it requires, to be complete, a patently untrue premise, the one indeed supplied by the hostile philosopher. Van Eemeren and Grootendorst are merely illustrating for a special case the discovery in modern linguistics that the context of language is as important to its outcome as is its syntax and semantics. (The linguistic philosophy in which most philosophers are trained does not acknowledge advances in linguistics later than 1890, or 1790.) In 1964, in a neglected paper, the philosopher Arnold Levison made the modern point that formal validity is not trumps: "Why should we say that an argument is bad simply because we cannot plausibly represent it as a formally valid argument? It would seem fairer to say that the claim that any good argument must be formally valid fails when the attempt to represent it as such weakens instead of strengthening its cogency as an argument" (Levison 1964, p. 555).

Paul Feyerabend gives as an example, again in the words of the divine Arthur:

> *Bruce*: Socrates' arguments, therefore, do not refute relativism. They refute a Platonic version of relativism where statements are not tied to utterances but exist independently of speech so that a new statement may turn the preceding performance into a farce . . .
> *Arthur*: . . . In a way logicians and the philosophers who follow their lead are very superficial. They see a statement, such as Protagoras' statement [viz., A human is the measure of all things]. They interpret the statement in a simple-minded way and they trium- phantly refute it! But this procedure would have killed science long ago.

> Feyerabend 1991, p. 41

The linguist and logician James McCawley makes the same elemen- tary but often overlooked point that logical validity is not the same as factual truth:

> Reason [i.e. formal logic] does not establish that a conclusion is true, but at most that it involves no errors beyond those that one is already committed to. Since coercive arguments, even when they are valid in the technical sense, are usually directed at people who do not already share all the relevant commitments of the arguer, their success often depends on the arguer's prowess at bullying as much as on the deftness with which he marshalls uncontroversial principles of inference.

> McCawley 1990, p. 379

So *any* proposition can be reformed into a syllogism if sufficient pragmatic context is allowed. Any speech act can be reduced to syllogism. For instance: sneering at people undermines their auth- ority; people with less authority are less persuasive; and so on to the conclusion that the argument sneered at is overturned. Therefore Rappaport's distinction between "evidential" and "non-evidential" does not hold.

What after all is this "non-evidential" thing? Rappaport slips metaphor into the category, as an argument banned from "evidential" conversation. Banning such a common way of arguing as metaphor – "abduction" as Peirce called it, such as modeling in physics – signals a radically conservative move. Rappaport wants to define "evidential devices" as the devices reducible to syllogism, in a broad sense (as he makes clearer in his reply to my reply). The broad sense is "a group of statements one of which is a conclusion and the rest supporting reason" (Rappaport 1988b, p. 171). But then he wants further to keep out of the category of "evidential" most of the pragmatic content of speech – for instance, the tone of voice with which a French bureaucrat rebuffs one's application and the metaphors of dirt and idiocy and alienness that the bureaucrat will use.

A nice example of the salience of context is a parlor trick by the historians of science Steven Shapin and Simon Schaffer (authors of *Leviathan and the Air-Pump* [1985], which has a closely related if more grand theme). One of them will take a British Sunday newspaper with the Saturday football results and read *the first half* of a result, "Tottenham Hotspurs nil, . . ." The other will then announce, without the result being finished, whether it was a home win, away draw, or whatever else figures in the football pools. The trick depends on the tone of voice in which the first half of a result is announced. It turns out that British radio announcers have, consciously or not, adopted a convention about reading the results on Sunday when the players of the pools are checking their predictions. The intonation of the first half tells all the form-checker needs to know; in the way of reliable speech, the finishing of the result is redundant. The tone is evidential and to experienced form-checkers it is evident.

Reducing argument to syllogism, even in Rappaport's extended sense, is quite strange, at least after what has transpired in philosophy since 1955 – and after what happened earlier in American pragmatic philosophy and in economic philosophy, as in the works of Frank Knight. (Daniel Hammond [1991] argues on textual evidence that my notions on method are similar to Frank Knight's, an observation I agree with. I should read more Knight, as we all should.)

Rappaport says that "non-evidential devices" are not arguments (the assertion here may be a definition, not an argument, but I cannot tell for sure). J. L. Austin would reply (Austin 1962 [1975], p. 54) that "the truth of a statement may be connected importantly with the truth of another without it being the case that the one entails the other in the sole sort of sense preferred by obsessional logicians."

Richard McKeon, turning over the similar distinction between "cognitive" and "non-cognitive" matters, wrote that philosophers:

> assume . . . that the scientific use of language is cognitive, and that poetic and practical uses are non-cognitive inasmuchas they are emotive or persuasive. This is a reasonable enough distinction, but its theoretic scope and practical utility are limited . . . [I]t translates the numerous aspects of language employed in the development of scientific knowledge, proof, and expression into problems of proof and verification.
>
> McKeon 1955 (1987), pp. 68–69

Rappaport's arguments for giving up philosophical thinking about metaphor and pragmatic context are not strong. He claims that "a sensible goal of economic methodology is best served by adopting the epistemological conception" (Rappaport 1988b, p. 171, his italics). By this he means that "evidential" statements are how "the theories of economists acquire whatever credibility they have" (p. 171). So a philosophical and narrow definition of what constitutes argument is to be imposed on economists. (If it is not narrow it merges with the rhetorical approach, which examines all the arguments.) Where have we heard that claim before? From the philosophy of science long ago.

In other words, Rappaport simply does not want to deal philosophically with certain matters, namely, those that van Eemeren and Grootendorst note are covered by the Maxim of Quality. When an economist refers glancingly to a "market" in love he is making an argument, the "supporting reasons" for which have to be generously supplied. Since Rappaport does not want to deal with pragmatic context, his own argument (interpreted ungenerously, I admit) is driven to *non sequitur*: "irony often occurs where no argument is present. This makes irony a non-evidential rhetorical device . . ." Well, I suppose so, though remember what Stanley Rosen said about the role of irony in analytic philosophy. But wait a minute. Ordinary statements about the world – "It is raining," say – also occur in contexts without an argument in view. Does that make them non-evidential? Something has gone wrong with the criterion dividing evidential from non-evidential devices. It is identical with what has gone wrong with each criterion for demarcating Science from non-Science: people, including scientists, don't actually talk that way.

To be sure, if we stick with Rappaport's "evidential" devices then a narrow and philosophically obsolete epistemology will suffice to deal with science. But the argument is achieved by definition. Define "evidential" to mean those few devices of argument that old-fashioned logicians insist are the only ones worthy of attention.

Rappaport twice uses the phrase "arguments (in the logicians' sense)", showing his awareness that the definition is a radically narrowing one (in his re-reply he concedes that the word "logician" may be a bad choice). Induction would be disallowed: no arguments (in the logicians' sense) have been found to justify it. And certainly there is no justification in logic for abduction, the choice of a metaphor of progress or of foundationalism. That leaves a great deal of science and almost all of philosophy out in the cold.

I cannot imagine Rappaport wants to go this way. It would leave what he calls "epistemological methodologists" in charge merely of the housekeeping task of making sure conclusions follow from premises (in the logician's sense). Here, then, is what is wrong with Rappaport's claim that epistemology pursues truth while rhetoric pursues mere persuasion (cf. Martin Hollis 1985, in a comment on my work). If you *define* "truth" to be such-and-such a narrow construct, ignoring all the weighty objections to British empiricism and the project of epistemology since Plato, and if you ignore even the history of epistemology since 1955, then of course there will be no difficulty in showing that rhetoric does not pursue truth. This is why I would rather write Rappaport's ideal as big-T Truth, to keep in view that Truth is some special, narrow definition, pleasing to certain philosophers of science. It borrows prestige from the ordinary meaning of truth (small t), which scientists employ to say that the metaphor of a production function or of a macroeconomic equilibrium is "true."

In his re-reply Rappaport depends on an equivocation, as philosophers have depended with regularity since Plato, between Truth, big T, and truth, small t. They often bury the equivocation in other terminology – in Rappaport's case "evidential" or "epistemological." Alexander Rosenberg uses another word to prevent himself from realizing that he is talking in circles, "probative." The pragmatic result is the same: circularity. Rosenberg says, "economists allow themselves to be swayed by factors that lack probative force . . . But probative merit is not an explanation for the persuasive power of the economists' . . . ploys" (Rosenberg 1992, p. 40). Something is "probative" if it is big-T True. And how would you ascertain that, Professor? It is notable how frequently analytic philosophers, those experts in making definitions, get themselves going both ways with a definition.

I follow, as William James recommended, the scholastic adage that whenever you meet a contradiction you should make a distinction. He wrote: "What hardens the heart of every one I approach with the view of truth sketched in my last lecture is that typical idol of the tribe the notion of the Truth" (1907 [1949], p. 239), the "rationalistic notion of 'the Truth' with a big T" (p. 242). Truth, small t, is human made, for which reason James called the wider approach within which pragmatism fitted "Humanism" (1907 [1949], p. 242), "the doctrine that to an unascertainable extent our truths are man-made products, too." Compare the opening sentence of one of Richard Rorty's books: "About two hundred years ago, the idea that truth was made rather than found began to take hold of the imagination of Europe" (1989, p. 3). It is true.

When I say "true" I mean of course small t, the truth made rather than found. When philosophers like Rappaport, Hollis, Hausman, or Rosenberg commend the pursuit of Truth as a goal for science (without asking the scientists) they mean big T, found in God's mind. If they meant small t there would be no problem: it is a matter of the practical rhetoric of experiments, for example, to decide whether gravity waves are true (small t) or not. The scientists have problems with deciding about gravity waves as much as they do with business cycles, but the problems are rhetorical, not philosophical. Certain philosophers of science have created for themselves a set of problems for which their epistemological theories have signally failed to provide answers.

Once again I am moved to claim back the word "truth" from the philosophers. It is probably hopeless to try, against all the Popperian philosophers of science and philosopher-economists whose lives have been built on beard-stroking wisdom about Truth, equivocal with truth. But otherwise the philosophers and their friends are going to get away with rhetorical murder, as did Plato on this same point. Rhetoric is not hostile to truth. The "relation between persuasiveness and truth" is not "incidental," as Rappaport says. The relation is close, *as close as we poor humans are going to get*. What is persuasive to a citizenry of the intellect is what is true, for now. That's if you want to keep the word "truth" in sight, recognizing that big-T "Truth" is unattainable anyway.

Warren Samuels has generalized the point, calling it the "X:x problem," thus: "inasmuch as our only knowledge [small k] of X is x, how do we know that x is representative of X?" (Samuels 1990a, p. 3). Better stick to x, which we know, instead of trying for X, which we can never Know. This is not of course a solution to the insoluble, self-imposed puzzle of epistemology about Truth. As Richard Rorty puts it, "there is nothing to be said about either truth [he means Truth] or rationality [Rationality] apart from descriptions of the familiar procedures of justification [truth small t] which a given society – *ours* – uses in one or another area of inquiry" (Rorty 1987, p. 42). Putnam on this point agrees with Rorty: "metaphysical versions of 'realism' go beyond realism with a small 'r' into certain characteristic kinds of philosophical fantasy . . . There is nothing wrong at all with holding on to our realism with a small 'r' and jettisoning the big 'R' Realism of the philosophers" (Putnam 1990, pp. 26, 28).

If the philosophers Rappaport and Hollis and the rest have some other way of identifying Truth, a non-trivial Truth for all time, which answers the rhetorician's *tu quoque* and the Gettier example and the other puzzles, they should step forward immediately and tell the rest of us. "If the anti-pragmatists have any other meaning, let them for heaven's sake reveal it, let them grant us access to it!" (James 1907 [1949], p. 250). It would be news for the ages. If thou find'st one, let me know; / Such a pilgrimage were sweet. / Yet do not; I would not go, / Though at next door we might meet. / Though it were True when you met it / And last until you bet it / Yet it / Counterfeit / Truth, ere I come, to two or three.

The social construction of economics or other sciences is not dread Relativism. The Johnsonians among philosophers need not commence kicking rocks and pounding tables to show that the world is more than socially constructed. The world is still there. But we are still constructing it. It is like fishing. The fish are there by God's command, but humans make the nets. To catch fish we need both. It is pointless to argue that the socially defined and net-caught but sea-dwelling and corporeal fish are "really" social or "really" objective. They had better be both, or we are not going to eat fish on Friday.

Nelson Goodman writes:

> The scientist who supposes [under the spell of philosophers] that he is single-mindedly dedicated to the search for truth deceives himself. He is unconcerned with the trivial truths he could grind out endlessly . . . He seeks system, simplicity, scope; and when satisfied on these scores he tailors truth to fit . . . He as much decrees as discovers the laws he sets forth, as much designs as discerns the patterns he delineates. Truth, moreover, pertains solely to what is said, and literal truth solely to what is said literally. We have seen, though, that worlds are made not only by what is said literally but also by what is said metaphorically . . .

Goodman 1978, p. 18

Nothing in what Goodman says denies experience. It just says that experience is in part made, too, and that we are the artificers, individually and socially, in our imaginations and our institutions. The philosopher John Searle, for example, distinguishes "brute facts" from "institutional facts." Sandy Petrey, explaining the distinction in the context of J. L. Austin's example of scoring a goal in a soccer game, puts it this way: "When a ball scores a goal, the brute fact of the momentum imparted to it by a foot is of a different order from the institutional fact that it changes the relative standing of the two sides in the game" (Petrey 1990, p. 61).

"We receive in short the block of marble," wrote James, "but we carve the statue ourselves" (James 1907 [1949], p. 247). And similarly, "Does the river make its banks, or do the banks make the river? Does a man walk with his right leg or with his left leg more essentially?" (pp. 250-251). Truth is partly social, and the parts are intermingled by their makers. "You can't weed out the human contribution" to what we know (p. 254), which is to say, that "it is therefore only the smallest and recentest fraction of . . . reality that comes to us without the human touch, and that fraction has immediately to become humanized . . . When we talk of reality 'independent' of human thinking, then, it seems a thing very hard to find" (p. 248). "Altho' the stubborn fact remains that there *is* a sensible flux, *what is true of it* seems from first to last to be largely a matter of our own creation" (p. 255).

Thus Wallace Stevens, listening at Key West to a woman singing on the beach:

> She was the single artificer of the world
> In which she sang. And when she sang, the sea,
> Whatever self it had, became the self
> That was her song, for she was the maker . . .
>
> Ramon Fernandez, tell me, if you know,
> Why, when the singing ended and we turned
> Toward the town, tell why the glassy lights,
> The lights in the fishing boats at anchor there,
> As the night descended, tilting in the air,
> Mastered the night and portioned out the sea . . .
>
> Oh! Blessed rage for order, pale Ramon,
> The maker's rage to order words of the sea,
> Words of the fragrant portals, dimly starred,
> And of ourselves and of our origins,
> In ghostlier demarcations, keener sounds.
>
> "The Idea of Order at Key West," 11. 38-41, 45-50, 53-57 in Stevens
> 1972, pp. 97-99; by permission

We are the makers of order at Key West and in economics. It is our human rage for order, whatever self the sea or the economy has. That does not mean that our songs are arbitrary, aimless, capricious, inconsistent, fascistic, authoritarian, nihilistic, flower-power, subjective, emotional, illogical, non-cognitive, non-evidential, non-probative, non-epistemic, anti-empirical, irrationalist, or any other of the words that philosophers have used to insult the pragmatists and rhetoricians and poets since 399 BC. The insults better describe the philosophers who hurl them.

Rappaport claims that epistemology can provide "standards" for warranted belief in economics. There's that word again, and again with no rational backing. I believe his claim is unwarranted, illogical, non-cognitive. He offers no empirical evidence for it, of the sort offered for the opposite claim in the later chapters of *The Rhetoric of Economics* and in *If You're So Smart* and in the earlier chapters here. No one, not even philosophers like Rappaport or Rosenberg, would argue that the rules of first-order predicate logic and other house-keeping would *suffice* for good science. If so we could hand science over to HAL the computer. Well, then, are the logical rules necessary? No, as the history of science suggests; I recommend the philosophers read it. Are the logician's criteria at least goods, desiderata, along with others? Of course. A fully articulated syllogistic argument is persuasive sometimes, though not the only persuasive argument, and in actual science rare. Science is a human activity, as recent studies of science have discovered. Therefore what is at stake in science is what persuades human scientists, not God's plan for Reality or Logic.

On a rhetorical examination, then, Rappaport follows a long philosophical tradition, by begging the question. Put logically his syllogism goes like this. We want good arguments. Good arguments are defined (by Rappaport) to be "evidential." Evidential arguments are defined (by Rappaport) as what certain philosophers of science like to talk about. Therefore, to get good arguments the philosophers should continue talking as they have, epistemologically, around1955. I am not in all circumstances against begging the question. In certain fundamentals it may prove necessary and virtuous. But that is a rhetorical excuse for a philosophical argument, *tu quoque*, and I am not sure Rappaport and the other philosophical conservatives would want the help.

chapter 16

Armchair philosophy of economics

As William James said of his Pragmatism, so one can say of Rhetoric: we find the rhetorical movement spoken of, sometimes with respect, sometimes with contumely, seldom with clear understanding. The Methodologists in the last chapter spoke of it with respect and with considerable if not complete understanding. Yet, as Warren Samuels has remarked, "there has been an uneasy tension in economics and in other disciplines between the advocates and practitioners of the traditional study of methodology and those who advocate the study of economics as the practice of discourse or rhetoric" (Samuels 1990a, p. 4). From certain Methodologists of economics, represented especially here by Alexander Rosenberg and secondarily by Daniel Hausman (cf. Vaubel 1988; Blaug 1987; and a few others), the reaction to a rhetorical turn has been a contumelious fury, as may be gauged by Rosenberg's titles: "Economics is Too Important to Be Left to the Rhetoricians" (1988a) and "Rhetoric is Not Important Enough for Economists to Bother About" (1988b). Not all of them, but a subset of the conventional Methodologists act like members of the American Medical Association facing a nursing practice act.

Samuels wrote in 1984 (now I think he would take a somewhat different view): "The study of economics as rhetoric . . . is no substitute for the appraisal of economics as knowledge" (Samuels 1984, p. 208). The earnest phrase on the lips of Methodologists is "We need a basis for appraising (assessing, evaluating, demarcating) scientific ideas." The phrase is of course perfectly correct if the word "we" refers to the very scientists. Of course *they* need such a basis. They find it in the rhetoric of their disciplines, that is to say, the decisions, historically contingent but supported by various appeals to the authority of other disciplines (such as, in economics, a misunderstanding of physics), about what counts as argument. On-going science is a rhetorical convention, socially constructed and factually constrained.

But the "we" refers to "outsiders to the science." The outsiders have no standing to speak as scientists. They have no formula by which they can test from the outside whether or not a science is good as science. The scientists decide that. A philosopher cannot "appraise" as science the conversation of a science from the easy chair. Quite properly the outsiders can criticize the non-scientific consequences of the science, speaking as citizens paying for it or as social philosophers worrying about it. They can note as moral philosophers the moral failures within the rhetorical practice of the science (such as the common moral failure in science of enforcing by bad rhetoric a centralist view on every scientific question). Outsiders can evaluate physicists who lie about their oil-drop experiments or economists who ignore the distributional consequences of their policy recommendations. And if the scientists were making elementary errors of logic or fact the outsiders as logicians or statisticians might occasionally have something useful to say, although one would suppose that in most cases the scientists themselves would have taken care of it (and in what we in the West call "science" the instances would be rare). The outsiders may have some advantage in commentary under any of these three headings, since the scientists themselves may be too close to see. What it means to have a science, however, is that an earnest, critical conversation is going on among the scientists. Those competent to make remarks *in the science* are the scientists, not lightly trained philosophers of science.

Edmund Wilson put it well, asked in an interview to detail his tastes in music and painting: "I have preferences in music and painting, of course, but there wouldn't be any point in enumerating, for example, my favorite painters . . . [I]it would be like announcing in public that I like shad but don't like lobster. In order to talk critically about an art, you have to have some inside knowledge of it . . . " (Wilson 1965, p. 580). Having nonetheless indulged the interviewer he concluded: "Well, I guess that's enough. When people get to talking about subjects that they don't really know inside out, you are likely to get a combination of banalities, naïvetés and what I love to have my critics call 'gross errors,' and I expect I've been guilty of all of them" (p. 596). Such diffidence has much to recommend it.

The project of epistemology since Plato has supposed that there is something worthwhile to be be said about Truth *by non-practitioners of the particular truth-finding rhetorics*, namely, by philosophers. When the Methodologist says that he is anxious to "evaluate" or "assess" economics, he means "with respect to Truth." I say that *outside* evaluators have not come up with anything useful to say about Truth in 2,500 years of trying and that truth, small t, is mainly the business of scientists themselves.

Rosenberg writes: "In order to assess economics, we need a yardstick, we need a litmus test, we need some set of standards and criteria for what science is" (Rosenberg 1987, p. 216). Note the bossy tone: we need, assess, a litmus test, what science is. He does not here or elsewhere defend the bossiness, a defense that would require ethical and historical reflection he would regard as on a lower level than philosophy. Bossiness is the furniture of his intellectual home and he cannot imagine remodeling. Neil de Marchi put his finger on what is wrong with bossy "assessment": "Popper and Blaug fear that without their particular regulative ideals the tower of scientific achievement would come crashing down. I would expect that, if they are so concerned about the negative consequences of lapses from the ideal, they might be more seriously interested in understanding practice" (1992, p. 9). Yes. He continues in a footnote: "Blaug (1980) is replete with case studies, . . . but it is clear that he is less interested in understanding the practice than in showing how far it has deviated from Popperian ideal science" (de Marchi 1992, p. 13n7).

The long search for a litmus test for cognitive status assessing science as Science, Rosenberg admits in 1992, has failed (Rosenberg 1992, p. xiii). Daniel Hausman in his recent book agrees: he records throughout the "disappointment at finding no simple rules for doing science" (Hausman 1992, p. 318). Mary Hesse summed it up a while ago (Hesse 1980, p. x), and since then it has become more plain: "every set of metaphysical or regulative principles that have been suggested as necessary for science in the past has either been violated by subsequent acceptable science, or the principles concerned are such that we can see how plausible developments in our science would in fact violate them in the future." We cannot distinguish astronomy from astrology by any 3" × 5"-card test (the faith in simple tests led some eminent scientists a while ago to fake their data in an attempt to discredit a French statistical astrologer, at which fakery they were embarrassingly caught).

Nonetheless Rosenberg and other conventional Methodologists of economic science want to keep up the search. They believe that it is important to establish once and for all the Scientific status, if any, of economics. Like Rappaport, Hausman, and other philosophers,

Rosenberg's master issue is the "cognitive status of economic theory" (Rosenberg 1992, p. xii). The supreme status is Scientist. The word "cognitive" is one of the master terms, since it can be defined to force whatever character of argument the philosopher pleases. The second is "status," as though being a Scientist were to be included in an aristocracy of Knowers, the circle of Socrates. The third is "theory."

Rosenberg claims earnestly that determining the scientific status of economic theory is crucial for the good of humankind. He asserts that "the answers [to the question of scientific status] can have significant ramifications for public policy," and that he is serving "the needs of practical policy makers" (Rosenberg 1992, p. xii; cf. p. 31). In complaining about Roy Weintraub he insists that a "policy-relevant" economics must be able to predict in the sense Rosenberg means it (p. 111). Rosenberg's standing to make such pronouncements is at least uncertain. He and the other economic philosophers give no sign of knowing about economic policy concretely. As we shall see, in fact, their definition of economic science incapacitates them for reading the economics applied to economic policy.

On the other hand, the economic rhetoricians know a thing or two about policy economics. Arjo Klamer, for example, has a side career as a journalist in Holland and has written a book about the formation of public policy there. Even I as an economic historian have a modest claim to knowing something about at least modern economic growth (McCloskey, 1993, for example). I was trained at Harvard as a transportation economist and worked part-time for two years as one. My book on price theory is filled with policy analysis (1985b). My rhetorical works frequently deal with matters of policy (thus McCloskey 1990a). Against such evidence Rosenberg claims wildly that I am "thoroughly committed to a policy-irrelevant economics" (Rosenberg 1992, p. 52, repeated from his review of *The Rhetoric of Economics*). The charge would be true if it were also true of Milton Friedman and James Buchanan and Armen Alchian, from whom I learned my attitude towards public policy. The attitude, backed by hundreds of empirical studies of past policy, is that we economists can offer wise constitutional advice but are not very good at detailed social engineering; we are good at rules but bad at authority. Rosenberg does not appear to know that such an attitude is widely shared by economists with better claims than I have to a serious interest in economic policy. Herbert Stein is no ivory-tower economist. Yet recall his credo quoted earlier: "1. Economists do not know very much. 2. Other people, including the politicians who make economic policy, know even less . . . These beliefs do not provide a platform from which to make strong pronouncements about economics or economic policy" (Stein 1986, p. xi). My sentiments exactly.

It is difficult therefore to take seriously Rosenberg's talk of "scientific status" as an important matter for policy, unargued and contrary to the evidence as it is. In any event such talk is on several grounds unfortunate. For one thing, as we have seen, the talk is provincial. It elevates a meaning of "Science" common to English-speaking culture in the middle of the twentieth century to Universal Truth. Sense 5b in the *Oxford English Dictionary* does not cut the universe at its joints.

For another, the status talk is nasty and undemocratic. It echoes the violent world of the seventeenth century and the insolence of science in its adolescence. Who says that Science even in a pointlessly narrowed definition is all we have of expertise and that everything else is mere emoting? Modernists. We are supposed to have gotten over the emotivism of logical positivism some decades ago. Two categories, Science and Blather, are not enough to hold a world of reason.

The most unfortunate feature of the status talk, however, is that it does not help with any concrete question, scientific or policy-making. Does knowing that economics is or is not a Science by some definition of the word pleasing to English-speaking philosophers in 1955 help us decide anything about its findings? No. (This *contra* Rosenberg 1992, p. 111.) There are findings in economics of the least Scientific sort – such as that markets work pretty well compared with some of the alternatives, a proposition protected from falsification by a wide protective belt – that we know to be true better than we know some findings in the most Scientific of fields – for example, that cold fusion is wrong. Rhetoric, sociology of science, theoretical econometrics, and seminar-room practice all help an economist to see her field and criticize its findings fruitfully. No such help comes from knowing that economics fits the definition of Science in English around 1955, remembered fondly now by Alexander Rosenberg, Daniel Hausman, Neil de Marchi, and Mark Blaug.

One wonders what is supposed to result from "according the status of Science," as it is usually put in such discussions. Higher salaries for Scientists, perhaps, or the ability to shut people up. Certain scientists and their friends, such as mathematicians, seem to have this in mind.

But even if one wants for some better reason, whatever it may be, to decide on the "status" of economics as a science the philosophers of economics such as Rosenberg and Hausman make a methodological mistake. I construe "methodology" here (with a small m) as "low-level tips for doing worthwhile science." Tip: when studying science it is a good idea to look at the science.

Hausman puts it well, and it is his credo, a fine one for a pioneer in applied philosophy (he notes that it is also the credo of a rhetoric of economics):

> The sort of empirical methodological inquiry exemplified here embodies this vision of philosophy. People acquire knowledge, and, to find out, one must study what they do . . . To find out how people have learned and to find out which methods have been successful in which circumstances, one must study what has been done and how well it has worked. In so far as McCloskey is only insisting that those interested in economic methodology must study how economists argue, I fully agree.

> Hausman 1992, pp. 265-266

The mistake is that the conventional Methodologists such as Rosenberg or Hausman do not look at the whole of economics. They have not examined what economists do on the job. Instead they have listened to the Methodological credos of economists (especially the credos of my fellow Chicagoans Friedman, Becker, and Stigler). Or they have studied the most highbrow parts of economics, such as abstract general equilibrium theory. Neither corresponds to what economists do on the job for most of their days.

Hausman's book *The Inexact and Separate Science of Economics* (1992) is a case in point. Unsurprisingly in a book like his or mine, two-thirds of the 728 items in its bibliography are philosophy or economic methodology, not economics itself (in this book the share of economics mentioned, only 13 percent, is even smaller than in his; in *The Rhetoric of Economics* it was about 22 percent; in *If You're So Smart* about 43 percent). But of the 230 or so pieces of actual economic science mentioned in Hausman's bibliography, 79 percent are theory and only 21 percent empirical work. By contrast in the leading journals some half of the articles are empirical and in the less prestigious journals more than half are empirical (in physics and chemistry Leontief found the empirical to be 90 percent of the whole, but I speak of economics as it is, not how it should be). In this book the share of empirical citations in all citations to economics about the economy – distinguished from works about economics as a field – is 55 percent; in *The Rhetoric* it was 59 percent; in *If You're So Smart* 87 percent. Further, Hausman's bibliography contains half again more citations to experimental economics – a tiny field but philosophically attractive because it was self-consciously designed to fit the definition of Science according to philosophers in 1955 – than to all other empirical studies. Hausman's book, fine as it is in some dimensions, is typical of philosophical Methodology in discussing ten times more theory than non-experimental empiricism. Hausman's book of 1981, subtitled *An Essay in the Philosophy of Economics*, cites naturally a great deal of capital theory and very few empirical studies, since capital theory is its subject. But it would be a strange view of economics that took its most arcane theoretical portion as typical of the whole. It's the philosophers' empirical mistake.

The theory of the theory class contrasts with the bibliography in the de Marchi and Blaug book (1991), whose percentage of theory as against empirical work (setting aside as before the method and philosophy) approaches that in the leading journals. The contributors to the volume, unlike the editors themselves, were not under the spell of "testing theory." Nor was Thomas Mayer in his recent book, *Truth versus Precision in Economics* (1993). Of the 146 pieces of economics mentioned in his "References," about 62 percent are empirical, 38 percent theoretical – in a book attacking the presumption of the theorists. The conventional Methodologists fix their gaze on theory: in Blaug's 1980 book subtitled *How Economists Explain* two-thirds of the citations to economics are theoretical. Rosenberg opens his *Microeconomic Laws: A Philosophical Analysis* by declaring that "in my view the current task of the philosophy of science is to acquire an understanding of the actual practice of science. This involves a close examination of the particular sciences" (Rosenberg 1976, p. ix). Exactly what is wanted. His bibliography (pp. 229-231) mentions nineteen items that might be called economics, putatively studying the economy (again, distinct from works about economics itself). All are theoretical. His latest book (1992) mentions thirty. All but one are theoretical, and the one that takes the theory to the world (Solow's paper on technological change) is cited only for purposes of sneering at my analysis of it (Rosenberg 1992, p. 38). Rosenberg's "close examination of the particular sciences," Blaug's inquiry into "how economists explain," and Hausman's "empirical methodological inquiry," in other words, do the empirical work incorrectly.

The object they have chosen to study is the wrong one. Hausman and the other philosophers view their task as to "assess" economic theory. It is bold of them to presume to assess something they are not learned in (Blaug has standing to do so; the others do not). You would think they would be more comfortable with merely observing, as critics who first learn how a poem works, before evaluation. But what I wish to draw particular attention to here is that they always in their assessments use the word "theory." They therefore miss most of economic science. The trouble is that they take the one for the other, the part for the whole. Conventional philosophy of science depends on a synecdoche of high-level theory for all of science. Explaining phenomena is not what is at stake in the philosopher's notion of "theory."

Rosenberg chides me for naïvely supposing that the "theory" of evolution is meant to explain the history of life on Earth (Rosenberg 1992, pp. 46-47; he assaults me for using dinosaur bones as a synecdoche for all the data). Says Rosenberg, the Theory (another big-T word) is not about merely terrestial evolution; it is true (read True) "everywhere and always, here and across the galaxy" (p. 47). That most actual scientists using the theory of evolution would not care whether it applies also in the Andromeda galaxy does not disturb the philosophers in their reflections on cognitive, evidential, predictive, and epistemological matters. They are after Truth, broad gauge, forever and ever. Who cares what scientists actually do?

It is little wonder, to be perfectly fair, that the philosophers imagining economics from their easy chairs make the mistake of identifying the science with the theory. The economists themselves talk as though "theory" mattered more to them than it does in practice (although come to think of it they might be talking in this way because of a philosophy course in college). Some years ago an experiment was performed in the rankings of economics journals by prestige. A high percentage of the sampled economists claimed to be familiar with two fictitious journals inserted in the list. They then attributed to the fictitious journal whose name contained the word "theory" a higher rank of dignity than the one which seemed to be about the world.

The very title of the de Marchi and Blaug volume, chosen by the two economist-editors, is *Appraising Economic Theories,* as though it were not scientific propositions that mattered but higher-level theories. The editors were following the hypothetico-deductive dogma of positivism. Their contributors had more empirical sense. Many of the essays in the volume, as the heavy citation of empirical work would suggest, were factual studies of how empirical and theoretical economics proceeds. They concluded uniformly, as I have noted earlier, that economics does not proceed in a Lakatosian or Popperian or other theory-testing fashion. Christopher Gilbert remarked in an elegant paper in the book that theory testing is "the modern myth of economics" (C.C. Gilbert 1991, p. 139; cf. Boland 1982), a point made decisively by Edward Leamer in his pathbreaking book of 1978, *Specification Searches: Ad Hoc Inferences with Nonexperimental Data.*

The philosophical Methodologists buy into a hypothetico-deductive notion that Science is about "higher-order propositions" (the mistake goes back at least to John Stuart Mills' distinction between science and art, both words used in their Romantic, early nineteenth-century definitions). But as Thomas Kuhn showed, and as other history and sociology of science has shown repeatedly, "in scientific practice, as seen through the journal literature, the scientist often seems rather to be struggling with facts, trying to force them into conformity with a theory he does not doubt" (Kuhn 1977, p. 193). Something is wrong with a philosophy of science that focuses on the moment of encompassing doubt. Probably the wrongness comes from the overwhelming importance of early twentieth-century physics in the ruminations of present-day philosophers of science. Look into their journals, *Philosophy of Science* or the *British Journal for the Philosophy of Science*, and you will be struck by the number of articles on quantum mechanics. The rest of science – biology, notoriously, but also chemistry, geology, and the like – is given short shrift. A Popperian philosopher of science's test of Scientific Status will miss most of the science.

It is particularly mistaken to focus on general equilibrium as the Theory of scientific economics, as do many methodologists and even many economists when thinking about methodology (here one might fault the choice of subject though not the notable penetration of Hausman [1981] or Weintraub [1985, 1991b]; I believe that at least Weintraub would not disagree). Defining neoclassical economics as abstract general equilibrium theory, such as the stuff so ill-advisedly taught to first-year graduate students, allows non-mainstream economists to attack neoclassical economics with ease (Mirowski 1990). *Of course* a field that claimed Arrow-Debreu as its central theory would be non-science, as indeed Rosenberg (not Hausman) argues. $A \rightarrow C$ and $A' \rightarrow C'$ is not science but mathematics.

But as we have seen, abstract general equilibrium theory was probably not an important scientific development in twentieth-century economics. Time will tell. But without denying its beauty and difficulty and the smartness of its developers, abstract general equilibrium theory seems for the most part, like chess, to have been a waste of talent. Wastes of talent are common even in progressive sciences. Ask the hundreds of chemists and physicists who did research some years ago on heavy water (which turned out to be merely dirty water) if their time was well spent. Most science, in fact, is in retrospect wasted, which is what makes it so easy to propose "rational reconstructions" of the few durable bits. (This by the way is another methodological mistake in conventional philosophy of science, as the Strong Programme in the sociology of science emphasizes: rational reconstruction does not give an account of failure, which is 95 percent of what scientists do.) In any case, the successful bits of science in economics since the War appear to have been the notions of property rights, uncertainty and risk, macroeconomics, historical economics, Beckerish uses of maximization, signaling, game theory, the identification problem, productivity change, rational expectations, and the like. These, unlike abstract general equilibrium, have been used to explain phenomena.

Norman Clark of the Science Policy Research Unit of the University of Sussex has pointed out to me that even in engineering the useful knowledge is more likely to be craft based than science based. Young's modulus for various steel alloys and girder cross sections is known, but in fact the strength of girders is best estimated on the basis of practice, not theory. The structural engineers use the history of their craft as much as the math to build bridges and buildings, which is to say that they trust what has worked in the past – not blindly, but in a wise and prudent way. The engineer David Billington notes that "the primary uncertainties in reinforced concrete behavior have never been removed by mathematical analysis, however rigorously consistent . . . Stresses in concrete, . . . are mere guesses – even when computed following the most rigorous formulations of theoretical mechanics" (Billington 1983 [1985], pp. 215-217). One can hope that the fall in computation cost will make closer simulation possible, but the problem at present is still widespread. The materials engineer J. E. Gordon speaks in similar terms: "The difficulty with so many problems in materials science has been that the algebra and arithmetic, though theoretically soluble, are too laborious to be done by traditional methods" (J.E. Gordon 1976, p. 113). In consequence, "as far as metals are concerned it does seem rather as if most of the possible important improvements have already been made by traditional and empirical methods and that the role of dislocation theory has been to explain the reasons for the improvements afterwards" (p. 221).

Economics has a similar craft tradition, with its own ruling heuristics, overlooked by Methodologists. I really do think they have "overlooked" it, since they seem to believe most earnestly that the scraps of mathematics they study are What Economists Do. They are encouraged in this by the lamentable fact, already noted, that half of what is published in the leading journals is theory of one sort or another. But that means that at a minimum the philosophers have missed half of economics. Weighted by lasting value, more like 90 percent. An economist knows how to do a believable and useful analysis of the market for hogs, but not because he knows Arrow-Debreu or the other pieces of what passes for neoclassical theory in the pages of Methodologists and of the less scientific textbooks of graduate "theory." As economists discover shortly after graduate school, little of what they learned in their first-year course is applicable to the world. What they learn by teaching Economics 1 to freshmen is the economics they actually apply. Scientific status, as is true in many fields, has little connection with scientific practice. The science lies in the 90 percent practice of accounting and low-brow theory, not in the 10 percent of grand if hollow and fashion-ridden theorizing. How does an economist know that natural resources make a trivial contribution to the wealth of a nation? Because some growth theory drenched in math-department rhetoric tells him so? No: because he believes marginal productivity has some rough validity and he knows from the national accounts that the share of land in national income is a few percent. Kenneth Arrow, he of Arrow–Debreu, recently questioned the notion that undergraduate education gets its justification from the undergraduates who go on to research. Because he noted a blackboard tangency? No: because the accounting shows, of course, that a mere 1 percent of undergraduates become researchers.

Rosenberg has concluded that economics is a branch of (not very) applied math (Rosenberg 1983, 1986a, 1987, and 1992). He comes to the conclusion by observing that the High Theory in economics is not progressive, and so the field must not be Science. "Economics *doesn't* show the kind of secular cumulative progress in practical application that is one of the ultimate characteristics of physics or chemistry or certain parts of biology [explicatory note: not evolutionary biology]. We can't predict actual economic choices, individual choices, any better than Léon Walras could, or much better than Adam Smith could" (Rosenberg 1987, p. 217, his italics).

He is mistaken, as one might have anticipated from his defective empirical methods. An economic historian can agree with Rosenberg that many economists show little interest in explaining phenomena. Some economists carry amulets for warding off scientific work:

"stylized facts," "robustness of theory," "ad hoccery," "implicit theorizing," "theoretical vs. applied," "reasonable assumption," "my story," "Professor Smart's model," "what's hot this month." So there is certainly something in Rosenberg's claim that parts of economics are not empirical science ("science," small s, in the non-English sense, namely, systematic inquiry into phenomena). But the non-scientific attitudes are especially prevalent in the theoretical parts of economics – especially the highbrow parts that many economists and most philosophers mistakenly suppose to be the essence of the field. It is not going to be hard to prove that economics is mathematical instead of scientific if one takes, as Rosenberg does, Abraham Wald, a mathematician and junior member of the Vienna Circle, proving Arrow–Debreu before its time, as a representative economist. He admits that in "econometrics, agricultural economics, certain parts of macroeconomics, applied economics" there seems to be some point to it all (Rosenberg 1987, p. 218). But there is not in "what I take to be the core of economics, the theory of general equilibrium" (Rosenberg 1987, p. 218). He doesn't realize that taking general equilibrium as the core of economics is to eliminate progress in the field by definition.

Most of economics on the lips of actual economists, however, is empirical and cumulative. For example, economic history is. We know startlingly more about the economic past than we knew thirty years ago, and can offer believable explanations for a good deal of it (see the 500-page bibliography down to 1980 by McCloskey and Hersh 1991). We know that income per head has increased since the eighteenth century by a factor of twelve. We know that capital accumulation does not explain much of it. We know that slave prices in the American South reflected the productivity of slaves. We know that American economic growth accelerated in the 1840s. These are scientific findings, not maunderings on the blackboard. Other scientific parts of economics include modern (or indeed old-fashioned) labor economics (Divine and Kiefer 1991), urban economics, public finance, and agricultural economics (Randall 1990, pp. 263-264). Industrial organization was scientific, at least until its recent dive into game theory (it appears lately to be coming up for air). Experimental economics, though running itself on principles provided by antique philosophies of science, has at least provided honest employment for people who would otherwise spend their lives at a blackboard. The philosophers are misled – as, I repeat, many economists themselves are – by the large place and high prestige of blackboard theorizing in economics.

Rosenberg believes with many other philosophers of science that we must distinguish The Theory of economics from its mere applications and then set aside the applications, as not relevant to a "cognitive status" as Science. He thinks that philosophy should reflect chiefly on the testing of The Theory – the underlying hypothesis of close calculation by consumers and producers, say. But as we have seen this is unpersuasive. In empirical work on science why should philosophy confine itself to the lofty heights when the science goes on in the valleys? If God lies in the details, study the details. Rosenberg insulates his own theory of economics from refutation, in other words, by ignoring most of the data.

Rosenberg regards close study of the history or sociology of science as unnecessary for the philosophy of science. He says impudently that McCloskey "misreads the history of science" (1992c, p. 54, not supported by argument or citation), but gives no evidence that he has put himself in jeopardy for similar misreadings. Conventional philosophers of science like Rosenberg simply do not study the history, sociology, and rhetoric of science, a large literature now a quarter-century and more old. They read only other philosophers discussing quantum mechanics. They take as an ostensive definition of Science a tiny bit of physics, spurning studies of geology or biology or history (Rosenberg is also a philosopher of biology, but his study of it is as remote from the laboratory as his study of economics is from economic history). They do not study even the whole of physics very closely.

The scholarship of the philosophers can be tested with three names: Fleck, Polanyi, and Kuhn (cf. Pickering 1992, p. 3). Fleck before the Second World War (1935 [1979]), Polanyi after it (1946, 1962, 1966), and Kuhn in the 1950s and 1960s remade science studies. The three were trained as scientists; the first two were internationally known in their sciences; Kuhn, trained as a particle physicist, was internationally known as a historian. As Feyerabend observes, "Fleck, Polanyi and then Kuhn were (after a long time) the first thinkers to compare . . . school philosophy with its alleged object – science – and to show its illusionary character. This did not improve matters. Philosophers did not return to history" (Feyerabend 1987, p. 282), mainly because they stoutly ignored Fleck, Polanyi, and Kuhn. It is the main failing of the philosophers: they do not want to know how science works. No facts, please: we're philosophers.

For example, Hausman's long bibliography in his 1992 book and the bibliographies in his earlier works, contain no reference to the Strong Programme sociologists and historians who have done the most important studies of science in the past twenty years, such as Ashmore, Barnes, Bloor, Collins, Edge, Galison, Gaston, Geison, Knorr-Cetina, Latour, Mulkay, Pickering, Pinch, Schaffer, Shapin, Shedvin, Traweek, and Woolgar, to mention a few. References to the history or sociology of science of any sort, even of economic science, and even of a conservative and Mertonian kind, such as Richard Whitley's are surprisingly rare. As Feyerabend's theory about the philosophers would have predicted, Hausman does accord glancing mention to Kuhn's *The Structure of Scientific Revolutions* (1962 [1970] overlooking his best and rhetorical work *The Essential Tension* (1977), but does not mention Fleck or Polanyi.

The undervaluation of Polanyi and the ignorance of Fleck is characteristic of Methodologists (they cannot overlook Kuhn, but never use him seriously). Rosenberg, characteristically, does not treat in his recent book anything beyond odd bits of economic theory, biological theory, and philosophy of science. The name index to de Marchi and Blaug's 1991 collection evaluating Lakatos in economics does not mention Fleck. Polanyi is mentioned twice (in papers by Kevin Hoover and Don Lavoie) but spelled "Polyanyi" in the index; he is not mentioned in the end-of-book Bibliography; nor is Fleck, nor Kuhn's books other than *The Structure of Scientific Revolutions*. The bibliography, over forty pages long, contains three citations to the work of the seventeen historians and sociologists of science just mentioned, one Knorr-Cetina and two Latours (one with Woolgar), but the index reveals that these are all in E. Roy Weintraub's paper (the mention of Knorr-Cetina in de Marchi's introduction is merely to announce that Knorr-Cetina's paper, with one by Harry Collins, is to appear in the journal *The History of Political Economy*, papers too unorthodox, it would seem, for the book).

The bibliographies of the individual chapters are strikingly uniform, confined so far as meta-science is concerned to a few works within the apostolic succession Popper–Lakatos. Uskali Mäki makes a similar complaint about the "dependence on very popular and easily accessible sources in the general philosophy of science – figures like Karl Popper, Imre Lakatos, and T. S. Kuhn" (Mäki 1987, p. 220). Philosophically naïve scientists consider themselves up to speed in science studies if they can number the triad; that philosophers of economics also think so is less understandable. Popper–Lakatos, with some puzzled remarks on Kuhn, appears to be the limit of what the senior Methodologists such as Rosenberg, Hausman, Coats, de Marchi, and Blaug teach to their students. The exceptions are the bibliographies attached to papers by E. Roy Weintraub, Don

Lavoie, and Harry Collins, themselves major contributors to the anti-positivist tide. Otherwise the bibliographies and index omit the history of science, the sociology of science, the history of ideas, the intellectual life of the West, and indeed philosophy itself beyond a tiny group of self-absorbed students of Popper. Such limited reading reminds one of the joke on the old Johnny Carson show: *everything* you need to know about science or philosophy or intellectual life, *everything*, is contained right here in this sheaf of articles by Popper (12 citations), Lakatos (8), Agassi, Koertge, Musgrave, Watkins, Worrall, and Zahar (3 each on average; mentions of other philosophers of science are rare).

And yet Hausman maintains that he practices an "empirically oriented philosophy of science," asserting boldly that "philosophers of science know a great deal about science" (Hausman 1992, p. 318). It is not clear how they came to know this great deal. Hausman has done useful empirical work on the economic literature of general equilibrium and now of experimental economics and overlapping-generations models. Still, it seems a slender base on which to erect theories about the field, especially in view of Hausman's indifference to non-philosophical readings of economics. The more reasonable attitude is reflected in the concluding sentence of Gilbert's thorough survey in the de Marchi and Blaug volume of the econometrics of consumer demand and of permanent income: "But in view of my opening remarks on diversity, I would be wise to avoid concluding that this comparison of two closely related areas can encapsulate the whole of economic methodology" (C.L. Gilbert 1991, p. 162). Alexander Rosenberg's empirical work is slight and he does not appear to understand economic science on the ground, as one can see by the tangle he gets into when talking about rational expectations (Rosenberg 1992, p. 148). In attacking Weintraub, who is an economist (trained as a mathematician) who has troubled to examine the actual practices of economists, Rosenberg posits "some fact out there to be discovered by the philosophy of science" (Rosenberg 1992, p. 110). The problem is that the discovery procedure does not involve moving outside a tiny circle of cronies. It is astronomy without the telescope, history without the library.

The English professors who have studied science have done a better job of getting to the phenomena than the philosophers of science sneering at them from the easy chair (Bazerman 1988; N. Katherine Hayles 1984, 1990, 1991;Gross 1990a, 1990b). The Methodologists consider that they are viewing economics "from the perspective of natural science" (Backhouse 1992b, p. 74). They are not: they are viewing it from the perspective of what an aging coterie of Popperian philosophers of science claim is the perspective of science. It is the rhetoricians of science who are viewing economics from the perspective of science, since they have troubled to read in science and in science studies outside the Popperian canon, and many of them are the very scientists in question (Stephen Jay Gould, for example, or Richard Lewontin). The main epistemological puzzle in the philosophy of science is not how scientists know but rather how the philosophers of science know, considering that they will not consult the history, sociology, and rhetoric of science, are not themselves scientists, and do not read in the bulk of the sciences they presume to assess.

Rosenberg argues that economics is merely social mathematics. It is in his view unprogressive empirically. The argument requires some empirical standard of progressiveness in Theory, a standard that can be calibrated only by going to the data. He reveals his standards in his assertions, but does not back them with empirical observations on how science works and does not apply them consistently to economic science as a whole. He has jiggered the data to produce a non-Scientific economics every time. Little wonder that he has such a low opinion of the field.

For example, Rosenberg speaks of meteorology as a case of an improving "theory," contrasting it with the allegedly stagnant theory of economics. Now it is certainly true that forecasts of snow in Syracuse, New York, are better than two decades ago. But the improvement involves no theoretical advance, as meteorologists would be the first to say. The calculations in the American or the European forecasting model are more elaborate and helpful than earlier models, but as theory are admitted by the meteorologists to be simple applications of physics; they entail no improvement of Theory in the highbrow sense. The models say merely that the temperature, pressure, and humidity in one cell of the atmosphere with certain coordinates of latitude, longitude, and elevation will have an effect in the next hour on the temperature, pressure, and humidity in neighboring cells. Yet they are important scientific propositions, made possible by the fall in computation costs. The new models are computation-intensive uses of accepted theory of the type of Leontief's input-output tables, not advances in Theory. Advance in science is not the same thing as advance in Theory.

When Rosenberg says that economic theory does not advance he means that economists still think people maximize and that the invisible hand can be felt, just as they did in the eighteenth century.

It would be like saying that physics has not advanced since Newton because for many problems we still think in terms of $F = ma$. Observe again Rosenberg's universalist ambitions for Theory. Only at a lofty level would one say, as he does, that advances in economics consist merely of "the reiteration of the same old theory" (Rosenberg 1992, p. 52). Down at the level where economic science actually gets done the centuries since Smith have seen big advances, to which Rosenberg's unempirical Method blinds him.

As George Stigler said, "A useful general rule, which is a good part of a scientific theory, has two properties. First, it ought to be more or less true. Second, it ought to apply to a fairly large number of possible events. Most of the anguish that people have with scientific theories arises because these two properties are moderately incompatible" (Stigler 1987, pp. 5-6). Rosenberg has no anguish: he opts for universal rules over true rules, and is therefore able to show that economics has little truth. The economic theory of supply and demand, to take an important case, has improved strikingly since the eighteenth century – first in a clear separation of demand and supply (*c.* 1776), then in a mathematical formulation of it, then a formalization of demand as utility functions with other implications (*c.* 1870), then consumer and producer surplus, then systematic recognition of the *ceteris paribus* variables such as income or substitute commodities (*c.* 1935), then welfare economics, then an elaboration of cost curves, then a recognition of externalities, then a formalization of the production function (*c.* 1955) and its dual, then random error, then econometric specification, then fitting of production functions, then habit formation, then measures of technical change (*c.* 1957), then an inclusion of property rights (*c.* 1960), then rational expectations (*c.* 1961), then truncated samples, and so forth. If that's not a progressive research program, neither is astronomy or evolutionary biology (O'Brien 1976 makes a similar point). You cannot decide on whether a research program is progressive without reading intensively in its history and knowing what it is now on the ground.

I am not advocating Baconian methods in the philosophy of science. One must see the behavior of scientists with a conceptual scheme, a Kantian filter, just as the scientists themselves must see their phenomena. Therefore observing economic scientists is not as straightforward as the Baconians say. I do advocate, though, a little regard for the data and for those who have studied them.

Take the matter of "prediction." Rosenberg is scornful of economic prediction, and at one level so am I. But our choices of levels are not the same, and so we see different sorts of success and failure. I believe, as explained in chapter 6 above and at greater length in *If You're So Smart*, that economic predictions entailing profitable opportunities for the economist must deeply contradict the very science. Of course at some level economists can predict, and quite well. A famine strikes Ireland. If prices are controlled, a black market will develop. If black-marketeers are shot, supplies will fall. Queues will rise in length to extract the difference between the controlled price and the demand price at the supply forthcoming. And so forth. Economics is filled with such predictions, all of them correct, many of them startling: if the rich subsidize the buying of bread by paying half of its market price on behalf of the poor, the poor will not be helped at all (thus the history of Medicare and Medicaid in the United States).

Even Rosenberg's narrow criterion of prediction, philosophically bankrupt though it long has been, is satisfied in economics, if you look at the actual economics instead of the Theory. No reputable economist thinks that macro-prediction is the main purpose of economics, any more than geophysicists think that earthquake prediction is the main purpose of geophysics. But covered-interest parity, among hundreds of such instances, is a precise prediction, which works. Purchasing power parity is an only somewhat less precise prediction, which works (properly understood). And any microeconomist can make predictions such as: places with lots of wood pulp – Finland, say, which I have never visited – will have paper towels in the men's room instead of those wretched electric dryers. At some levels, and important ones, we economists can predict well, thank you.

But falsificationists like Rosenberg and Terence Hutchison do not see the difference in levels. Either economics can predict everything the Methodologists believe without economic criticism it should – interest rates, say, or the business cycle, both of which would make the scientist rich beyond the dreams of avarice – or else economics is no good. Either physics can predict both the position and the velocity of a subatomic particle or it is no good. The tradition of British empiricism says that "facts" are units of observation, requiring one merely to open ones eyes. No need to think about the level at which one is going to see the data; no need to worry about whether we are looking at the post-impressionist painting with a telescope or a microscope. So Rosenberg and Hutchison cannot see that economics and physics, though comical failures observed at one level, and absurd as predictors, are at another level spectacular successes, brilliant predictors.

The issue of the level at which economics is to be assessed does not occur to philosophers like Rosenberg and Hutchison. Viewed at one level, I say, physics is a comical failure. We ask physics to tell us why bodies fall to earth and it answers, "Don't ask *why*. I shall give you an answer of *how*, namely, $F = ma$." Chemistry, too, is a failure if the level at which it is supposed to work is not chosen cannily, by the chemists themselves. We ask chemistry to change lead into gold and it answers: "Sorry: no can do, and anyway we call such matters 'physics.' But look here at how I can tell you what air is made of." Physics and chemistry are not successes absolutely, in God's eyes, but only relative to a human conceptual scheme, a scheme devised by the Protagorian human who is the measure of all things, and who congratulates exact descriptions of acceleration due to mass, say, or of the constituents of air. The sciences are successes in their own terms, viewed as speech communities, more or less useful to other people. The physicists and chemists tell us in what terms they are to be evaluated, and so of course they can tell the story as a splendid, unbroken, heroic success. What use is the physics of the Big Bang? Don't ask, because over here I have a result in the physics of surfaces that you can actually use for testing metal fatigue in airplanes. What use is general equilibrium? Don't ask, because over here I have some economic accounting that you can actually use to make sensible policies for pollution rights. It's a matter of the level.

Rosenberg takes a conservative position in favor of prediction as the touchstone for Science. If we have learned one thing from the experiment with positivism and its various offspring over the past fifty years it is, as the anthropologist Roy D'Andrade put it, "being able to predict or explain particular events is not a good test of whether a science has found out something, since particular events have idiosyncratic boundary conditions . . .For example, it would be silly to say that physical sciences are a failure because they cannot predict when some bridge is going to fall down or explain why the earth has only one moon" (D'Andrade 1986, p. 28). It depends on the level one chooses.

And it depends on what you want to know. Rosenberg appears to be unusual among philosophers of science in adhering to prediction as the *sine qua non* of Science. Most of the others have come to realize that some sciences, and many parts even of physics, will want to know things other than the times of solar eclipses and the onset of severe recessions. The social sciences, for example, will sometimes wish to interpret a human meaning. D'Andrade said of Rosenberg, who "rejects the possibility of any kind of science that deals with meaning," "this kind of Draconian solution would simply leave most human phenomena unstudied" (D'Andrade 1986, pp. 36-37). Rosenberg was in 1986 untroubled in reply: "since this is the kind of knowledge we seek, and we are not likely to succeed in providing any, there is not much potential for knowledge in social science" (1986, p. 340). This is the kind of knowledge *we* seek? Not "we," thank you very much. The kind of knowledge that I and most of my economist colleagues seek is not predictive in Rosenberg's narrow sense. Nor is it predictive in paleontology or in plate tectonics, though making the world cohere. I realize the fact is irritating to philosophers of science, but lamentably nothing can be done about it.

Even Rosenberg has had doubts recently, for which he is to be commended (it is one of his intellectual virtues that he changes his mind). He writes in 1992:

> There is something a bit simplistic about demanding [his very word earlier in the book] that the summum bonum of science is everywhere and always [his very words four pages earlier to describe what an honest-to-goodness Theory is] predictive success. It is particularly vexing for philosophers of science that we do not even yet really understand what predictive success is, at least with the kind of exactness we should like.
>
> Rosenberg 1992, p. 51

As I said. There is nothing wrong with prediction as one of numerous merits that a science might have. Rosenberg is forever saying that "McCloskey . . . den[ies] that economics has or needs any predictive pretensions" (Rosenberg 1992, p. 80). I would never say such a silly thing. (As I have noted, philosophers who claim to be experts in analysis of language will often stumble when analyzing actual language; they might take a course or two from "the god-damned English professors".) Of course economists make predictions – such as that the Federal budget will rise $N next year or that abolishing the capital gains tax will increase investment by $M billion in the next five years or that food, which is self-testing, will not be advertised like automobiles, which are not. If the predictions do not violate the elementary requirement that a college professor cannot expect to outguess the market on average, then no one should make merry of the predictors. There is nothing wrong with predictions as one of the tests of whether economics is a worthwhile discourse. But prediction is not the *summum bonum*, as Rosenberg put it so well, not the one final demarcation. In such a 3″ × 5″-card role it simply does not work. Hilary Putnam would agree with D'Andrade and others: "we have many more cognitive interests than prediction, and, correspondingly, many more kinds of justification than are included in this narrow notion of 'evidence'" (Putnam 1990, p. 276).

In short, Rosenberg's practice of Methodology, though typical of the philosophers who have lived through an empirical revolution in science studies over the past quarter century without bothering to read it, is empirically unsophisticated and does not work. We have learned that the similar speculations without an empirical base by Popper, Lakatos, and lesser figures were on the whole mistaken. You are not going to be able to understand a science if you do not get down into its laboratories and papers at a workaday level. As Paul Feyerabend put it, if you get down to the workaday level you will then "no longer think of a theory" the way Rosenberg and the other conventionally Popperian philosophers of science do, "as a well-defined entity that says exactly what difficulties will make it disappear; you will think of it as a vague promise whose meaning is constantly being changed and refined by the difficulties one decides to accept" (Feyerabend 1991, p. 41).

Theories like supply and demand or thermodynamics are constructed by argument. Until they are dead and finished they are under construction, being argued. The point is hard for rationalists to grasp: as William James said, "for rationalism reality is ready-made and complete from all eternity, while for pragmatism it is still in the making" (James 1907 [1949], p. 257). But a sophisticated rationalist like Imre Lakatos grasps the point: "It takes a long time to appraise a research programme." In the meantime the scientists are arguing. The dialogic and rhetorical practices of science, exhibited by the form of Plato's dialogues though denied by their content, are "very much alive today, . . . not in . . . 'backward subjects' but in the most respected and the most quickly developing disciplines like mathematics and high energy physics" (Feyerabend 1991, p. 11). Or in the actual dialogues of economic science.

chapter 17

Philosophy of science without epistemology: the Popperians

If the philosophy of economics fails to persuade empirically, is it at least persuasive as modern philosophy? I can only judge from the outside in a rough and statistical way, since I am able to judge the arguments themselves only in the rare cases in which I as a non-philosopher have thought about them. But the data suggest that philosophy of economics ignores the conversation of philosophers, too, in favor of a tiny group of specialists in a safely narrow field, the school descended from Popper (though of course amending the master in this or that detail). The philosophers of economics favor a particular school in the philosophy of science; and the particular school in philosophy of science does not keep up with epistemology generally. It would be as though rhetoricians of economics did not read Wayne Booth or Stanley Fish, not to speak of Aristotle on rhetoric. Or as if historical economists did not read economics or history, but merely their fellow historical economists.

The data is again bibliographical, though a reading of the texts of the philosophers of science gives the same impression, if in a less (I am embarrassed to use the word) objective form. Daniel Hausman, for example, wrote a long "Introduction" to his anthology, *The Philosophy of Economics* (1984) and a long "Appendix: An Introduction to the Philosophy of Science" for his *The Inexact and Separate Science of Economics* (1992), about a hundred pages altogether. Much of it is Popperian or anti-Popperian: "contemporary philosophy of science is in large part a reaction against the views of Karl Popper or of the logical positivists" (Hausman 1984, p. 5). I would argue that on the contrary a philosophy of science *should* be – and in non-Methodological, non-Popperian circles is in fact – a case in point of the relationship between truth, language, and reality. The conventional Methodologists slip into such epistemological talk, as we have seen, when attacking deviations from the canon of Popper and Lakatos or philosophy of science at the University of Pittsburgh; so they would presumably accept the relevance of knowing something about epistemology.

Here is one way to use the standard empirically. John Passmore, well known as a learned and catholic philosopher, wrote in 1985 a supplement to his masterful *One-Hundred Years of Philosophy* called *Recent Philosophers*. The last two chapters of five in the book are devoted to a survey of the philosophical thinking that Passmore judges most important on "the relationship between truth, language and reality" (1985, p. 63), within which philosophy of science would stand (he explicitly eschews detailed commentary on the philosophy of science as a subfield, but that is not the point of my comparison).

Compare Passmore's view of the relevant philosophy with Hausman's. Passmore's chapter 4 is devoted to Donald Davidson and Michael Dummett. Davidson is cited incidentally once in each of Hausman's essays; Dummett is not mentioned. Passmore's chapter 5 devotes its thirty-four pages to eight other recent epistemologists. He discusses Karl Popper and Imre Lakatos for four and a half pages. They are of course discussed fully in the Hausman essays, and so by the other philosophers of economics and more generally by the Popperian school in the philosophy of science, everywhere. Passmore discusses Hilary Putnam for twelve pages. Putnam is cited once in Hausman 1992 – "see also Putnam 1962" – and on the same point in the same incidental way once in Hausman 1992. Passmore discusses Nelson Goodman for five pages. Goodman is cited once in Hausman 1984, incidentally to the main argument, in a footnote; and in Hausman 1992 twice, but solely on the Popperian matter of lawlike statements, not on Goodman's radical epistemology of "rightness" and "versions." (Putnam himself refers to Goodman's *Fact, Fiction and Forecast* as "one of the few books that every serious student of philosophy in our time *has* to have read" [Putnam 1990, p. 303]; none of the philosophers of economics give evidence of agreeing.) Passmore discusses Mary Hesse for four pages. Hesse is footnoted as an example among several of Bayesian approaches in Hausman 1984, but not as an student of analogy in science; and similarly in Hausman 1992, with again no mention of her epistemology. Passmore discusses Richard Rorty for four pages. Rorty is not mentioned in Hausman 1984; nor is he mentioned in the appendix in 1992, though one footnote in the text mentions him, among others.

Passmore discusses Daniel Dennett for three pages. Dennett is not mentioned in either Hausman book. Hausman is not referring to recent epistemologists when he claims the authority of Epistemology.

A similar test can be performed against the contents of Louis P. Pojman's *The Theory of Knowledge: Classical and Contemporary Readings* (1993), which is the first comprehensive reader in epistemology since Nagel and Brandt in 1965. Pojman's selection is purposely conventional. The fifty-five items reproduced in the book and the 101 other readings mentioned in the ten end-section bibliographies constitute a large and unbiased sample of the conversation in epistemology: $N = 156$. But the 500 items in Hausman's bibliography to *The Inexact and Separate Science of Economics* (1992) that are philosophical in character overlap with the Pojman selection in only nine cases: Kant in 1781, Mill in 1879 (a later version of a book Hausman cites), Ayer in 1936, Reichenbach in 1938, Quine in 1953, Chisholm in 1957, Quine again in 1969, Harman in 1973, Jeffrey in 1983 (with overlaps in two authors, Kitcher and Rescher, that do not exactly match). The median date of the nine, as one might have anticipated, is about 1955. In sum, Hausman is not conversant with modern epistemology, though claiming epistemology as backing for his philosophy of economics.

Likewise, Alexander Rosenberg's recent philosophy of economics (1992) mentions Popper and Lakatos in many places, and not always to agree; but it mentions the other recent epistemologists in one instance only, Nelson Goodman (1955: no other, and especially not N. Goodman 1978), merely incidentally, and as an ally of Hempel. The one overlap of Rosenberg's bibliography with the Pojman selection is Quine's "Two Dogmas of Empiricism" from 1953. The bibliography in the de Marchi and Blaug volume (1991), unsurprisingly, contains no references to the Passmore philosophers except Rorty (in papers by the demurrers from the conventional view, Weintraub and Mirowski, with a mention in the introductory essay) and none to the Pojman philosophers. After all, the authors are economists, not philosophers; it is enough that they stay in touch with the conversation of economics itself. And yet an economist such as Piero Mini, in his *Philosophy and Economics* (1974), ranges across philosophy and literature, though not in a way fashionable in the best circles: Archimedes, Arendt, Aristotle, Arnold (Thurman), Babbage, Bacon, Beard, Beethoven, Bentham (five subheadings and *passim*), Berkeley, Bober, Bronfenbrenner is how his index of Names begins. His scholarship would embarrass the conventional Popperian philosophers of economics.

Jeremy Shearmur says that "methodological appraisal and the study of sociology and the rhetoric of science are not necessarily enemies, but, rather, may complement one another" (Shearmur 1991, p. 47). True enough. But in order to complement one another they are going to have to trade. The English professor Richard Lanham notes that "mixing the Philosophers and the Rhetoricians is very hard. In fact, . . . you can't really mix them. You have to oscillate between them. Build a literary structure which holds these two opposite worlds in dynamic interchange" (Lanham, forthcoming, ch. 10, p. 2). Trade, conversation, the agora, and the assembly should be the models for a new discourse. The sociologists and rhetoricians are in daily converse. The historians of science converse incessantly with students of technology. Some philosophers, even some philosophers concerned especially with science (Max Black and Nelson Goodman, for example), read in literary and art criticism. Literature and science flourishes as a field in many departments of English.

But the Methodologists of economics have chosen to ignore all this and go on talking to a handful of other Popperian philosophers of science settled comfortably in their armchairs, the cobwebs of 1955 gathering about them, as in the books by Rosenberg, Hausman, de Marchi, and Blaug. The lack of exercise and varied conversation has been bad for their health. They would do better to take the air, walking over to the library to read a little sociology and rhetoric and history and philosophy. They will be astounded at the world beyond the armchair.

Epistemological incompetence among Popperian philosphers of science appears to be not uncommon, judging at least by a paper by one of its exponents, Peter Munz. *The Rhetoric of the Human Sciences* (J. Nelson *et al.*1987) made an early statement of the general case for a rhetoric of inquiry, applied by specialists to mathematics, literature, economics, political science, paleoanthropology, Darwinian evolution, theology, philosophy, law, history, psychology, sociology, communications, women's studies, and anthropology. It is the flagship of the series on The Rhetoric of the Human Sciences from the University of Wisconsin Press (and called by its friends The Red Book), stirring some controversy when it first came out (two similar collections were edited by Herbert Simons in 1989 and 1990: the three volumes might be read as one big book, the first wave of the rhetoric of science; there are now book series at many publishers on the subject, such as those edited from Iowa at Wisconsin and Chicago university presses).

Munz, in the January 1990 issue of the *Journal of the History of Ideas*, gave it a long review (with Brian Vickers' new book, *In Defense of Rhetoric* [1988]), to which Vickers and I were asked to reply. Munz did not grasp the point of *The Rhetoric of the Human Sciences* (nor for that matter the point of *In Defense of Rhetoric*), which is that intellectual historians among others need an art of argument.

According to Munz, rhetoric is what is left over when rational argument is finished, being merely "the power to persuade when more rational methods fail" (Munz 1990). "[W]e rely on rhetoric when there is no or little evidence for a statement . . . The heart of the matter is that when a statement can be shown to be true, no rhetoric is required to persuade people to give their assent." Rhetoric is said to concern "a number of irrational, psychologically effective devices." The Munz definition leaves rational persuasion as something outside of rhetoric. "There is one great exception where persuasion takes place without rhetoric," namely, "reasonable or rational evidence."

But the point of *The Rhetoric of the Human Sciences* is that reasonable evidence goes beyond a formula of certitude. On the contrary, what is reasonable is the whole art of argument, more rich and precise than, say, falsificationism or evolutionary epistemology. Anything but the whole art of argument is too thin for a satisfactory account of what happens in science, as argued by modern philosophers concerned with epistemology, such as Wittgenstein, Austin, Goodman, Putnam, Davidson, Hesse, Rorty. We need a way of examining how scientists do actually argue. Scientists use reliably attested facts and first-order predicate logic, to be sure; but they also, and rationally, use metaphors (they call them models) and stories (they call them histories).

To say, as Munz and Karl Popper do, that science is what survives scientific criticism is I suppose all right, though perhaps a trifle vapid. But rhetoric enables the historian of science to see the scientific criticism in detail. Why did Darwin persuade? Why do economists disagree? Why does paleoanthropology depend on a story of climbing down from trees? Why do experiments end? The tautology of "surviving criticism" cannot answer such questions.

As *The Rhetoric of the Human Sciences* shows, rhetoric can. The book shows in a couple of dozen case studies that rhetoric is and has been since Gorgias of Leontini and Protagoras of Abdera, not to speak of Aristotle of Stagirus, a rational study of all that persuades more and less reasonable people in science and elsewhere. To repeat: it is more not less rational to examine all the arguments.

Munz thinks of the new rhetoric as the study of irrationality. The equation of the new rhetoric with irrationality is mistaken on three counts.

In the first place, logically speaking and most controversially, what Munz reckons as evidence and logic themselves depend on rhetorical decisions (cf. McCawley 1981, 1990). The rhetorical decisions are not mere ornaments or trickery. They establish the constitution of rationality. Rules of argument, even something as fundamental as the law of the excluded middle (which is rationally set aside in some forms of logic and mathematics), are instituted by rhetorical agreement. That statement *A* must either be true or false and not both or neither is something we accept because it is agreed to be useful in certain classes of dispute between people. It wins arguments, unless the agreement is for some purpose set aside. It is not written in the stars. The law of the excluded middle is not God's own rhetoric. (And if it is one would like to know how we would get the news.)

So Munz's "logic" is not something timeless and independent of human rhetoric. It entails a rhetorical decision that we human beings make. It is perhaps unnecessary to argue the same point about Munz's "evidence." Historians and sociologists of science have long known that what counts as evidence depends on human decisions about what is persuasive (see again Fleck 1935 [1979] and the history and sociology and indeed philosophy of science that follows from it). Logically speaking, then, rhetoric grounds logic and evidence.

In the second place, rhetorically speaking, logic and evidence are forms of persuasion, part of human rhetoric. Munz cites with approval Horton's brisk assertion (which will come as a surprise to many anthropologists, such as Comaroff and Roberts 1981) that "primitive cultures do not share our standards of rationality and objectivity" because "they have been insufficiently exposed to debate." That seems unlikely. Ethnologists find orators in every society. And on evolutionary grounds one would expect several million years of hunting and gathering to result in a hardwired faculty for debate. A wandering band without a devotion to debate and persuasion – as Adam Smith puts it, "the natural inclination every one has to persuade" – would not last long. Rhetoric is the study of debates. A syllogism is an argument in a debate; so is an R^2 statistic; so is an analogy; so is an appeal to authority, such as any science must use daily. Rhetorically speaking, rhetoric includes logic and evidence.

In the third place, historically and sociologically speaking, arguments beyond logic and evidence narrowly defined have in fact played a large role in all inquiry, including science and scientific philosophy. It would be a poor rationality that left them out.

Having made the initial and apparently incorrigible error of identifying rhetoric with irrationality, Munz cannot see how one could mount a rhetorical criticism. "Criticism" in his lexicon is the same as evaluation, the giving of stars in the manner of movie critics. He has read Northrop Frye (it says in his footnotes) but on this point does not appear to have understood him. Munz asserts that if one cannot go "behind language" (Wittgenstein), "criticism of rhetorical figures is impossible." "The employment of rhetoric, in other words, escapes criticism." But *The Rhetoric of the Human Sciences* was about the criticism of rhetorics.

Munz's most unrestrained rhetoric against rhetoric is concentrated on "relativism." As usual in such circles, he identifies the authors of *The Rhetoric of the Human Sciences* with people who do not believe "in the real world or . . . what went on in the mind of . . . authors" and above all with people who are committed to "relativism." On the loosest rendering of "relativism" the identification is contradicted by the text (in his frequent remarks about relativism the text recedes into the background). And as is usual in such viewing with alarm, Munz connects epistemic with cultural relativism: "Where those values and ways differ, we have to conclude that all values and ways are relative." The argument is a commonplace, but it is a *non sequitur*, as Clifford Geertz notes in "Anti-anti-relativism" (Geertz 1984 [1989]). Why the Elongot's code of honor in the Philippines would alter the epistemological status of moral values in New Jersey is not clear. Munz identifies *The Rhetoric of the Human Sciences* with Humpty Dumpty and the view that "there is no question of using rhetoric to get people to support a standpoint . . . One simply hopes that people will like the rhetoric well enough to join in, endlessly and aimlessly, world without end." This is a strange remark, though as we have seen in the cases of Blaug and will see in the case of one H.-H. Hoppe it seems to flow spontaneously from the pens of Methodological conservatives who have not done their homework. On the contrary, in twenty different fields the book investigates precisely "using rhetoric to support a standpoint."

The Popperian philosophers who think they are enemies of rhetoric have a small set of arguments, commonplaces which they handle and rehandle like rosary beads, without attention to the history of philosophy since 1955. Most of the arguments are taken unexamined from Plato, or from the commonplaces of a culture vaguely remembering Plato, such as Munz's remark that rhetoric flourishes "in societies . . . in which propositions are counted as true because they are current in a given community"; for which see Plato, *Gorgias* (e.g. 471E, 474B, 475E, 487E; cf. 502E, 516E). A few arguments are taken from propositions current nowadays in the conservative community, especially the demonology of "relativism," and most especially the notion that there are serious people (as distinct from Valley girls and feature writers) who believe that, as Munz puts it, "all positions are considered to be equally valid." One wishes the epistemological conservatives from Munz to the writers for *The New York Times* would abandon the rhetorical device of waving a list of unnamed lunatics, lunatics holding opinions for which no textual evidence is offered, as though it were a list of communists in the State Department.

No relativist of repute says that all positions are equally valid; none says anything that could be reasonably construed as saying so. The conservatives must get this point straight if they wish to stop ranting and start conversing. The philosopher Richard Bernstein has defined a responsible relativism as the "claim that there can be no higher appeal than to a given conceptual scheme, language game, set of social practices, or historical epoch" (R.J. Bernstein 1983, p. 11). The claim is quite ordinary. A court of law, for example, is a set of social practices (Carlin Romano 1989 argues persuasively for a "World Court of Philosophy," in other words, for a legal rather than a military metaphor as a model for intellectual conflict in philosophy itself). That in a court there is no timeless rule, "an a priori universal and necessary structure of human knowledge," as Bernstein describes the "objectivist bias" (p. 10), does not mean that doing what comes naturally, as a matter of practice, thereby dissolves into arguments equally valid no matter what. Stanley Fish puts it well: there is no "standard or set of standards that operates independently of the institutional circumstances . . . *which is not the same thing as saying there is no standard*" (Fish 1989, p. 164).

Munz associates the writers of *The Rhetoric of the Human Sciences* with Nazis and other totalitarians. I have discussed the long and disreputable history of this turn repeatedly, because it comes up repeatedly in conservative rhetoric against "relativism." Again I ask my conservative friends to recognize and amend their rhetoric. As Piero Mini points out, "paradoxically, rational thinking shows itself to be a prey to passions exactly when true reason and fairness are most called for, i.e., in scholarly debates" (Mini 1974, p. 142). Recall Toulmin's definition of "rationality" in science, and one would hope in philosophy, as "preparedness to respond to novel situations with open minds" (1972, p. vii). Toulmin notes later that "Taking human history as a whole, heresy-hunting or intellectual conformism has been the rule, tolerance of free conceptual innovation the exception"

(1972, p. 220). Yes: Munz, and before him Popper, have contradicted their theme by repeatedly attempting to close their open society. *Sic transit ratio.*

Munz has garbled the book in his hurry to attack a political position that he does not like, a position largely unrepresented in the book and certainly unrelated to mine. I am reminded of a case some time ago in which an elderly economic historian attacked for its leftist leanings a book he was reviewing, which leanings were in fact those of a quite different author of a quite different book who happened to have the same last name.

Munz's intellectual as distinct from his political purpose is to clear a space for a Popperian, evolutionary epistemology. No fault in that. But he does not realize that the rhetoric of inquiry has points in common with such an epistemology. An epistemology which "characterises scientific knowledge as the set of hypotheses which are left over when all criticisms are temporarily exhausted" sounds reasonable to me, though it must be noted that the standards for exhaustion are rhetorical. When Munz praises Jean-Pierre Vernant for arguing that "social necessity" in the Greek city states required the evolution of rational discussion, I can only agree. Such is the traditional history of Sicilian sophists after the fall of the tyrants, a history replayed now in Eastern Europe. According to the tradition the sophists catalogued the rules of argument because they suddenly had to have rules in free courts of law.

Evolutionary epistemology, in other words, sounds like a fuzzy form of the rhetoric of inquiry. Munz inadvertently concedes the point when he claims that evolutionary epistemology makes rhetoric "redundant." If *EE* makes *R* redundant, then *EE* can function for *R*; which is to say that evolutionary epistemology has much in common with rhetoric. Still, it is a strange sort of history of ideas that sneers at a tradition of 2,500 years ramified throughout the culture, and then claims that a novelty favored by Karl Popper and Peter Munz, which "has barely managed to make itself heard at the end of our century," now makes the tradition "redundant."

Viewed from the rhetoric of inquiry, though, evolutionary epistemology has a defect. The defect is: it lacks arguments. Munz does not notice that his epistemology itself depends on a metaphor of evolution (Darwin or his modern students, by the way, would not recognize Munz's version of evolution). The evolutionary epistemologists want to claim the grounding of evolutionary Science itself (set aside that Popper himself was for decades scornful of Darwinism as a science). But the "evaluation," "criticism," and "refutation of mistakes" on which a Popperian wants to stand must themselves involve rhetorical standards, as I've noted. Refutation entails a *refutatio*. In Munz's treatment the standards by which "mistakes" in the evolution of science would be "criticized" are left as exercises to the reader. We can be more rigorous than this, by noting the rhetoric in science (Stephen Toulmin, who casts his arguments also in evolutionary terms, has done exactly this, from Toulmin 1950 through Toulmin 1958, down to Jonsen and Toulmin 1988; so the trick is not impossible, with sufficient scholarly care). Evolutionary epistemology in the hands of Munz is not rigorous about the matter it claims as its most rigorous concern: criticism. But becoming rigorous about criticism will entail learning some.

Munz's piece contains a good deal of mistaken history, too. The new rhetoric did not rise out of "linguistic imperialism" or, still less likely, "relativism," but out of a social fact: we live in an age of intellectual diversity. That is why so many serious people have turned to rhetoric. Kenneth Burke says somewhere that "Rhetoric is concerned with the state of Babel after the Fall." Rhetoric flourishes where disagreement flourishes, which is why rhetoric has a special connection with free and open societies.

In the intellectual world the diversity shows even in the realm of science, as I can attest as an economic and historical scientist and as others have attested as physical or biological scientists. The new rhetoric responds to the new diversity. Consequently it is wider than rhetoric as defined by Aristotle, as something distinguished from dialectic (this incidentally is another reason for a broad definition of rhetoric). The new rhetoric, in the old age of the idea, finds uncertainty even within the certainties of dialectic. We all have long agreed that the square root of 2 is irrational, new though the agreement once seemed. But on the frontiers even of mathematics the rhetorical rules must be argued and reargued – witness the recent controversy over the computer-assisted proof of the four-color theorem, and the doubts concerning the number theorists calculating pi to billions of places. In other words, a serious account of criticism and progress in science requires rhetoric. Munz and the other Popperians come to the borders of criticism and then stop. They stop on the verge of a rhetoric of inquiry because they are more interested in the project of demarcating Science from other thinking than in giving an account of science in its diversity. It is the same mistake that Rosenberg and Hutchison make: they tell us more about the thoughts of Karl Popper than about the science.

The point of *The Rhetoric of the Human Sciences,* and the present book, can be put briefly, so: the only way to evaluate an argument as a whole is by the standards of the whole art of argument. The whole art is not first-order predicate logic alone or falsification alone, or for that matter *verstehen* or narrative alone. It is the art of the good person speaking skillfully, the scientist inventing and arranging his arguments. In a word, it is rhetoric. The rhetoric of science cannot be practiced from the philosopher's armchair. It requires a trip, as recent philosophers have understood, to the library or to the laboratory.

chapter 18

Reactionary modernism: the Rosenberg

Alexander Rosenberg's reaction to the new criticism of science, then, is merely one example of how the Popperian philosophers of science react to being disturbed in their armchairs. Rosenberg wrote a very long review of *The Rhetoric of Economics*, reprinting it with additions in his recent book (1992, pp. 31-55). Plato's dialogues were given by editors a title that mentioned the chief character, usually the one sparring with Socrates. In referring to them the custom is to speak of the Crito, the Phaedrus, or, the shortest of the dialogues, an early one in which Socrates converses with a reciter of Homer who believes himself to have all wisdom, the Ion:

Socrates: Welcome, Ion! And whence come you to pay a visit? From your home in California?

Ion: No, Socrates, I come from Chicago and the festival of philosophers of science there.

Socrates: What! Do the citizens of Chicago, in honoring the field, have a contest between philosophers of science, too? And did you compete?

Ion: Yes. I carried off the second prize in Reactionary Declamation.

Socrates: Well done! I envy you philosophers of science, who must be conversant with so many fine scientists. And you have to understand their thought, not merely learn their lines. All that, of course, will excite one's envy.

Ion: What you say is true, Socrates. We are in the van producing "a body of knowledge about human behavior . . . that will enable us to improve the human condition."

Socrates: Bravo! You really are a splendid fellow, with your greathearted concern for the human condition. I suppose then you look into the empirical work of the scientists, in the manner of the sociologists or historians or rhetoricians of science, and help the scientists understand how they have arrived at this or that piece of knowledge. I mean those pieces of knowledge that will enable us to improve the human condition.

Ion: Well, no, not exactly. We tell them whether or not what they do is a science. And we warn them against "trendy" "new names, like 'de-construction.'" McCloskey's book puts me in mind of these trends, which I do not understand and cannot spell.

Socrates: And does this McCloskey refer to them in *The Rhetoric of Economics*, ever?

Ion: No.

Socrates: I see. And these new trends: they oppose factual inquiry?

Ion: No. But "the philosophical confidence of empirical social science seems everywhere in retreat. And empiricist social scientists can console themselves" only with philosophy.

Socrates: I see. The consolations of philosophy of science. Tell me, Ion, what do you mean by "empirical"?

Ion: It means, of course, "caring about the facts in one's science."

Socrates: And "empiric*ist*"? Is it the same?

Ion: No. It refers to a particular doctrine of certain British philosophers, these three centuries past.

Socrates: Then a scientist could be empiric*al*, that is, devoted to studying the world and its ways, yet not be an empiric*ist*, that is, devoted to a particular account of the relation between sense data and thought?

Ion: Yes, I suppose so.

Socrates: And such a one might be, say, a British economic historian, much devoted to factual inquiry, devoted more even than some philosophers of science, yet still think on empirical grounds that British empiricist philosophy has recently been an encouragement to intolerance and closemindedness in science, for example in economics?

Ion: What you say is true, Socrates. But it makes my Methodological arguments simpler when the two words are conflated. In any case, one who does not admire empiricist philosophy will doubtless indulge in a "sophistic invitation to complacency about economics, and an attempted seduction of the discipline into irrelevancy." This McCloskey, a Corinthian, I think, does exactly this. "If McCloskey's doctrine is right, there is no hope for improvement in economic knowledge."

Socrates: My word, Ion, that is terrible. Who are these terrible sophists like McCloskey?

Ion: I know about them from Plato, their first and chiefest enemy. Thank the gods, I've never read any of them – except, of course, you yourself, brave Socrates, the leading sophist of them all.

Socrates: You are too kind. I have never pretended to the rank of *sophistēs*, which is to say, a "wisdomer," a master of his craft, a professor. You say you have read nothing of them. I suppose if Plato says they are bad, at astonishing length, that will have to do. But have you read anything of their intellectual descendants – Cicero, say, or Quintilian, or St. Augustine's rhetorical works, or any of the modern masters, such as Burke or Perelman or Booth?

Ion: By Zeus, no! We philosophers don't read what we know we will reject! That would be a waste of time! Knowing what we will reject without reading any of it is a special philosophical knack, *verstehen* of a wonderfully non-empirical sort. One can do philosophy of science without reading science studies by historians, sociologists, and rhetoricians, as my friends Hausman and Backhouse can. One can do philosophy then without reading, just sitting in an armchair.

Socrates: I see. That certainly is wonderful.

Ion: Yes, it is. Roger Backhouse, for example, has written that "The challenge posed by scepticism to epistemology is not quite the same as the challenge posed by constructivist arguments to economic methodology, but parallels are sufficiently close that we can respond in a similar way" (Backhouse 1992b, p. 74). Do you see how easy it is? You don't need to actually read McCloskey and find places where he says this or that. You simply pound at an Aunt Sally called "skepticism." Then you can launch remarks like this: "Whilst it is certainly the case that knowledge is constructed . . . it is going too far to argue that there is no such thing as empirical evidence" (same place).

Socrates: My word. McCloskey says there is no such thing as empirical evidence?

Ion: Well, not exactly.

Socrates: Well, then, approximately? Close enough to justify saying he does?

Ion: Uh, no.

Socrates: I sometimes wonder, my dear Ion, if you and your friends know what "empirical evidence" is: the empirical evidence of textual citation, for example. But tell me, Ion, what exactly do you yourself find so objectionable about this wretched McCloskey's work?

Ion: Many, many things. Chiefly that "if he is right, economists will have to consign their subject to the status of a *genre*, a stylistic tradition in literature."

Socrates: But Ion, is philosophy a genre, that is, a *kind* of writing?

Ion: To be sure.

Socrates: And so also, I suppose, are history and mathematics? Are these not also written by human authors with intent? Or are they automatic writings, which appear without authorship and intention?

Ion: No. They are genres, it would seem.

Socrates: And economics? Is it not then a genre?

Ion: O Socrates, your elenctic style of argument is so very tiresome! Yes, I suppose it follows, but I cannot accept the conclusion. The *status* of economics would be lowered if we started to talk about it in literary ways. McCloskey views economics as "just a vast game, like literary criticism" (Rosenberg 1987, p. 217). He "is part of an attempt to drag all other intellectual activity down to the level of literary criticism, down to the level of deconstruction" (1987, p. 216).

Socrates: "Literary criticism"? What do you know about it?

Ion: Why, very little. It's just a vast game.

Socrates: I see: Aristotle, Johnson, Arnold, and then Trilling, Eliot, Empson, Leavis, Richards, Frye, Winters, Wellek, Todorov: just a vast game. And "deconstruction"?

Ion: About it I of course know nothing at all.

Socrates: Yet you know that both are on a lower "level" than what goes on in the Department of Philosophy.

Ion: Yes, of course: I read about them in *The New York Times*. That's where Clark Glymour and I get our views of the goddamn English professors. Wonderfully accurate, *The Times*. Everything you need to stay current with the herd of independent minds, right there, daily.

Socrates: Your devotion to logic and evidence has limits, Ion. What Macaulay said of Robert Southey might be said of you: "It has never occurred to him, that a man ought to be able to give some better account of the way in which he has arrived at his opinions than merely that it is his will and pleasure to hold them" (1830 [1881], vol. I, ii, p. 135). Or, to use a turn popular in modern analytic philosophy, I have never found an actual *argument* in your opinions (the italics are part of the turn). Tell me, would economics, if treated as a type of writing, be lowered in status below that of mathematics? One can talk of mathematics in these same ways.

Ion: Yes.

Socrates: You seem much concerned with status. Is a seeker after truth concerned with status?

Ion: Oh, that's all right for you to say, I am sure. But it is *frightfully* important for me that economics retain status as a science. After all, I am a philosopher of Science, not of that other rubbish. It is very, very important that my friends and I be able to sneer at library *science* or food *science* (about which, of course, we know nothing at all, except how awfully vulgar their practitioners must be, were we to meet them; nor, you can bet, will we undertake to learn anything about such matters; and this for a very good reason: *Because they are not Sciences*; thus Rosenberg 1992, p. 49). Demarcating science from non-science is the main activity of we reactionary philosophers of science, and I can tell you it is a very, very important thing to do. Very.

Socrates: I see. Would it matter to the conduct of physics whether it was called a science?

Ion: No.

Socrates: And would it matter in the laboratory or library if the word "science" lost its peculiarly English meaning?

Ion: No, I suppose not. But what would philosophy of science be about if science were just careful and honest thought and observation? After all, you can't expect to have academic societies for the study of such an ordinary thing, mere "inquiry," as other languages use the word. Nor would one have journals. Or academic positions. Really, you don't seem to understand how important it is that science be special, separate from the rest of culture. My word, if it weren't separate I would have to *learn* something about the rest of the culture!

Socrates: A powerful point. What else, then, of this beast McCloskey?

Ion: He "makes [his] claims about prediction the linchpin of his argument against 'modernism'". "[T]hat prediction is both unnecessary and absent in many sciences is central to the whole edifice of McCloskey's 'post-modernism'."

Socrates: Where does he say these things? I read the book last night and do not recall much on prediction and its absence in other sciences. In his later book, *If You're So Smart*, he talks about allegedly *profitable* prediction, and in a recent paper (McCloskey 1992a) he compares econometric forecasting in detail with Roman practices of augury. But in *The Rhetoric of Economics* he merely mentions prediction in a couple of places, in the midst of other arguments on which he seems to place greater weight. Nor, come to think of it, does he mention postmodernism.

Ion: There are plenty of places where McCloskey emphasizes prediction, I assure you, and I intend to devote a great deal of time to talking about them, whole numbered sections, and large slices of my book published many years after his reply to me challenging me to give the citations, because I know – I have *verstehen*, in fact – that they are there, concealed somewhere, implicit, immanent. Let me see. He says for example that "A modernist methodology consistently applied . . . would probably stop advances in economics." That's about prediction.

Socrates: I do not think so. Where is prediction mentioned or implied?

Ion: Uh . . . well, not in so many words. But I'll find those many, many places where McCloskey's strictures on positivism hinge on prediction, I assure you. McCloskey "recurs repeatedly to comparisons between [evolution] and the whole discipline of economics." It's somewhere here, repeatedly. Let me see . . . Anyway, I know as much about biology as I do about economics, and you can hardly blame me for using my stuff.

Socrates: In these passages that you cannot at present find, what does he say?

Ion: He wishes to waive "prediction as a reasonable demand on scientific theories."

Socrates: Really? That does seem extraordinary. I take it you have textual evidence that he says something of this sort.

Ion: Of course not: haven't you grasped my Methodology by now, Socrates? I don't need to have evidence to attribute opinions to people. Nor do Daniel Hausman or Terence Hutchison or Roger Backhouse or Mark Blaug: and for the very good reason that we are philosophers of *Science*.

Socrates: Suppose McCloskey does somewhere say that he "waives prediction." Do you mean that he would not care if a theory were predictive, if it could be?

Ion: No.

Socrates: Doesn't he say merely, in one or two places, among other arguments, that prediction is an unreasonable *requirement* for taking a field of study seriously, such as geology or evolutionary biology, neither of which is predictive?

Ion: Yes, I suppose he does. But I want prediction to be a "demand" on economic theory (Rosenberg 1992, p. 45). If not, not. And it is outrageous for him to compare economics with evolution, which is a theory with grave problems.

Socrates: I am again humbled before your wisdom. I, fool that I am, thought that evolution by natural selection was one of the half-dozen or so great ideas of the nineteenth century. Yet you can see grave problems in it from your easy chair.

Ion: You are right to think me wise. For instance, I can make astronomy lie down on a hypothetico-deductive bed, too, though astronomers do not think this way. And I am also an expert on the philosophy of history, of which all that anyone would wish to know is contained in a conveniently brief article by Carl Hempel in 1942. As Hempel said, if you cut the head and feet from the historical sciences they fit naïve positivism beautifully. All this is highly relevant to "McCloskey's mistakes about biology, astronomy, and geology."

Socrates: You seem angry at McCloskey.

Ion: As well I might be. He is a great danger. He is part of a conservative conspiracy to retain "the *status quo* in economic theory" (that, you see, is why his work is popular among Marxists and other revolutionaries, as a trick to lull the rest of us into complacency).

Socrates: Your friend Hausman accuses him of the opposite error, of overturning the status quo, "tempted by a skeptical relativism that denies that there are any rules of scientific practice" (Hausman 1992, p. 318).

Ion: Hausman is correct. We reactionaries can have it both ways: McCloskey, Feyerabend, Rorty, Kuhn, Polanyi, and all the other disturbing people are *both* lefties and righties, both wild men and fascists. Bertrand Russell taught us how to run such arguments, which he used with great success against John Dewey.

Socrates: But does McCloskey "deny that there are any rules of scientific practice"? Doesn't he use low brow rules of technique, "methodology" small m as the actual scientists use the word, in his own scientific work?

Ion: I suppose so, although I have not read his scientific work.

Socrates: Strange. You are a philosopher of *economics*, aren't you, and McCloskey writes economics, doesn't he?

Ion: Yes, but remember: my Method means I don't need to *read* economics to philosophize about it.

Socrates: Ah, yes: as you said before. What then of this "denial of rules"? Doesn't McCloskey advocate, and use, highbrow rules of *Sprachethik* for scientific practice?

Ion: You mean that blather about the morality of science, what my ally Terence Hutchison calls sneeringly "Boy Scout virtues" (Hutchison 1992, p. 59)?

Socrates: Yes, the blather and the Boy-Scout – one might say bourgeois – virtues that animate scientific journals and govern the libraries and laboratories: such as, Do Not Lie About One's Data; Do Not Indulge in Actionable Calumny of Other Scientists; and the like. Is McCloskey a "skeptical relativist" in the sense that Hausman appears to mean, adhering to the sort of paralyzing skepticism that is "cold comfort when one needs to decide what to do about unemployment" (Hausman 1992, p. 318)? Does McCloskey's philosophy require one to withhold judgment on practical issues of science?

Ion: No, I suppose not. I want you to notice, though, that we philosophers of Science, though you might at first think that we are mere ivory-tower types, are in fact very concerned about economic policies such as deciding about unemployment. Very, very, though of course we have not troubled to learn anything about the making of policy or the factual studies that go into it, this in sharp contrast to other students of science and technology recently.

Socrates: Congratulations: further testimony to the power of your Method.

Ion: Now you're catching on.

Socrates: Isn't McCloskey's philosophy merely that there is no God-given foundation for knowledge, a position consistent with modern epistemology and with carefully negotiated judgments for practical purposes?

Ion: Yes.

Socrates: Am I correct that Hausman is merely engaging in the McCarthyism of the middle when he uses such alarming-sounding terms to describe McCloskey – or whatever person he has in mind in the passage quoted, which as usual in such conservative rants, like McCarthy waving his list of communists in the State Department, is left unspecified?

Ion: What do you mean, "McCarthyism of the middle"?

Socrates: Senator McCarthy of Wisconsin accused without evidence, exploiting an ignorant terror of Communism in his audience. You (and Hausman, Blaug, and a few others) accuse McCloskey and the rest of the rhetoricians of holding various terrifying doctrines without troubling to offer textual evidence that they in fact hold them; and, crucially, you expect the audience to be horrified by the mere unsupported charge of – what? – Irrationalism, Deconstructionism, Fashionability, Things From Paris. What else would you call it?

Ion: Well, all right. But would you deny us our main rhetorical device, that of claiming that the mild relativism that rejects foundationalism is the same thing as Valley-Girl anything goes? I say that McCloskey "downgrade[s] the importance of empirical testing . . . Doing this requires repudiating Positivism. This is a motivation for surrendering the empiricism that economics shares with all the other social sciences."

Socrates: Does McCloskey ever propose to limit the facts that an observer in the social sciences should take into account?

Ion: No, I suppose not.

Socrates: Then he is not abandoning empirical work but empiri*cism*. Aren't you perhaps again mixing up empiri*cism* the doctrine and empiri*cal* work the scientific practice?

Ion: O Socrates, you are such a pedant! One must watch every little suffix when you're around. Yes, I suppose I am "mixing them up," as you put it. But what of it?

Socrates: I am not clear, Ion, what your empiricism has to do with better empirical testing. Enlighten me.

Ion: What do you mean? Isn't it obvious that empiri*cism* leads to the empiri*cal*?

Socrates: Does empiricism as a British philosophical doctrine, emerging as "logical empiricism" (positivism) when combined with the Continental a priori at the end of the nineteenth century, broaden or narrow the facts that an observer takes into account?

Ion: It radically narrows them to the facts observable by another.

Socrates: And when an economist infected by logical empiricism, this positivism, about which he in fact has read nothing but the introductions of economics books, scorns non-quantitative evidence, does his empiricism broaden or narrow the evidence?

Ion: Well, I guess it narrows it, to the quantitative.

Socrates: Which approach to science, then, is the most empirical, a positivism that radically narrows the evidence or an antipositivism that looks at it all?

Ion: I can't understand your words.

Socrates: Consider this, as Roy D'Andrade put it in the book you are holding there, and which I think you have glanced at, *Metatheory in Social Science* (D'Andrade 1986, p. 33): "[T]here is the potential of an enormous increase in fidelity of interpretation through taking account of wider rather than narrower ranges of relevant material."

Ion: Because of remarks like that I did not read much in the book.

Socrates: As is your habit.

Ion: But you don't understand. This narrowing positivism is *good*. It was expressly "designed to combat fanaticism and intolerance," especially from the Nazis and the Stalinists. Surely it is *good* to be narrow. "Marxism-Leninism and Racist science turn out to be simultaneously cognitively empty and morally dangerous." "[H]istoricist economics . . . [is] mere chronicle or taxonomy, and Veblen's work . . . [is] entertaining fiction."

Socrates: You sweep by several points of logic here, as is the custom of the philosophers most passionately devoted to logic, especially when they are speaking of their passion. For example, that positivism was "designed" to combat fanaticism does not I suppose guarantee that it will do so?

Ion: Why not? It is designed to do it. Like a law designed by legislators to place the burden of the gasoline tax on suppliers, what people intend is decisive evidence.

Socrates: I see that your study of the social sciences has not taken you far. What of the unintended consequence, what those English professors you spurn call the Intentional Fallacy?

Ion: You know what I think of English professors, whose activities rank well below those of philosophers of *Science*.

Socrates: Relax your sneer for a moment and try to learn something. Positivists have asserted from time to time that positivism was *designed* to have moral effect by prohibiting this or that form of argument, but like many legal prohibitions (a prediction of economics, this) its result diverged from its design.

Ion: You talk nonsense. Design equals outcome. Rational reconstruction is history. We learn that in philosophy.

Socrates: I see: I admire again your learning. But on another matter: I do not understand your sneering at the absurd and cognitively empty Karl Marx. Your confidence that a set of ideas that has engaged most of the social thinkers in the West for a century is "empty" is astonishing. Your tolerance, Ion, for other visions of economics, such as Marxism and the horrid taxonomy and fiction of Veblenesque institutionalism, is admirable.

Ion: Thank you. I have always prided myself on my tolerance. It comes from my devotion to narrowing the empirical evidence. I am persuaded, for example, that my auto mechanic uses positivism when he fixes my car.

Socrates: This is wonderful, Ion! An auto mechanic who is a philosopher.

Ion: I did not say he was a philosopher, merely that he behaves *as if* he were a philosopher. One can rationally reconstruct his behavior as following rules, which then allows one to sneer at the tacit knowledge and practical wisdom by which he actually fixes the car.

Socrates: Ah, I see. Well, that is certainly a powerful way of putting it, on which we can erect all manner of social policy, such as courses in philosophy for auto mechanics. Crash courses, perhaps, in mechanical philosophizing.

Ion: Yes, I intend to do so, and thereby "improve the human condition." And meanwhile I will cast out the skills of practical reasoning and public discourse that those wicked sophists first drew theoretical attention to and that despite all the attempts of we philosophers, and especially we philosophers of science, have survived in law schools, legislative assemblies, and departments of literature, not to speak of the fallacy-filled talk of the man and woman in the street. "[R]hetoric . . . cannot hope to foster any improvements in the cognitive merits of economics. It can only improve the marketing skills and public relations of economists."

Socrates: Ah, I see you are also a deep student of the rhetorical half of our civilization. Pray, what do you mean by "rhetoric"?

Ion: Sneaky talk.

Socrates: Is this the definition McCloskey gives?

Ion: No, but do you think I can listen all day to such stuff? His literary talk gives me a headache.

Socrates: You have read deeply in ancient and modern literary criticism?

Ion: Of course not! What do you take me for? I am an *analytic philosopher*, and, further, a *philosopher of Science*, school of Popper, a lover of blackboard wisdom and the easy chair, a disdainer of libraries, and therefore know instinctively, without reading, the "real meaning of the rhetorical approach." My recent book does not cite any representatives of the half of our culture that I disdain, except the demon McCloskey, and one of Wayne Booth's books, which I have not read, although I know from glancing hastily at the quotations from it in McCloskey's book that Booth, who has long served on the board of McCloskey's Project on Rhetoric of Inquiry and has written many books attacking positivism, must be in fact a supporter of positivism (Rosenberg 1992, p. 38). I just know it, by *verstehen*. A very distinguished fellow philosopher once told me that of course he had never read a page of Hegel, and proposed never to do so, whether or not scores of first-rate minds attest that there was much to be learned from those pages. He has the same preliterate *verstehen* of which I speak. I have it in extraordinary measure.

Socrates: I take it you are well acquainted with rhetoric, and have mastered at least one of its classic texts, on the level of an elementary book in first-order predicate logic. Otherwise you would not be so confident in your sneering.

Ion: By the gods, Socrates, you are dense! Haven't I already told you that we philosophers can deliver judgments on Hegel without reading Hegel, on science without doing science, on epistemology without keeping current with epistemology, on knowledge without telling how to achieve it? Do you think it would be much of a trick to have opinions about rhetoric without reading a few dead Greeks and their followers? Come, come, my good man: don't be a dunce. I pride myself for having never read anything by any rhetorician (except again a few pages of McCloskey, curse him). My knowledge of what a "sophist" is, as I said, comes from a recollection of the one or two of Plato's dialogues I read in English translation early in graduate school without critical apparatus or secondary literature. And considering I didn't read Aristotle, Cicero, and Kenneth Burke, it follows (logically, you see) that I would not read McCloskey with the attention due a serious argument. Mostly I just "yawn and say, 'so what?'"

Socrates: But surely this McCloskey isn't saying that unwarranted arguments are good?

Ion: He certainly is. Why, it's all over the book. I'll find the pages soon, I assure you. I predict it, in fact: you see, philosophy is a science. "McCloskey thinks he can persuade us that what makes a bit of science good is the artfulness of its presentation, instead of the warrant of its argument." "The rhetorical approach proceeds on the assumption that there are no such things as good or bad arguments, only persuasive and unpersuasive discourse" (Rosenberg 1992, p. 31).

Socrates: And where does he scorn warrants, these warrants that are arguments for an argument and help judge it good or bad? And where does he say there is no such thing as good and bad arguments, in economic history for example, or econometrics or other parts of economics?

Ion: Well, again I can't find him saying it in so many words. In fact he treats the goodness and badness of particular economic arguments at tedious length in all his works. But that's what he means, I know. My *verstehen* in such matters is astoundingly accurate. I have no need for the merely human device of close reading and textual evidence.

Socrates: Ah, *verstehen*. You have mentioned that several times. I thought you were hostile to mere "interpretation" and *verstehen* in science.

Ion: In science, yes. But philosophy is different.

Socrates: I see. I wonder then what becomes of the modern ambition, which you just referred to, for a "scientific" philosophy or the still more modern ambition for philosophy of science as an "empirical methodological inquiry." Let me ask you, though, about this wild McCloskey's advocacy of mere "artful presentation" in science. What do you mean by "presentation"?

Ion: The style, the ornaments. In a word, rhetoric.

Socrates: And this style is easily distinguished from the substance?

Ion: Of course: don't you know about the distinction between style and substance? My sophomores know it very well, and frequently speak to me about it. I have learned much from the intellectual distinctions current among my sophomores, a wise crowd, I assure you. Style vs. substance; subjective vs. objective; opinion vs. science. The sophomores are amazingly good metaphysicians.

Socrates: Tell me, Ion: does skiing have a style?

Ion: Of course. American or European, good or bad.

Socrates: And is bad skiing still skiing?

Ion: Certainly.

Socrates: At what point does bad style lose the *substance* of skiing?

Ion: I do not understand.

Socrates: Well, if I have no experience in skiing – have never seen it, say – and skis are strapped to my feet and I am ordered downhill, will I do a stylish bit of skiing?

Ion: Certainly not! You will fall every couple of yards. The very thought of Socrates on skis!

Socrates: When I finally reach the bottom, have I skied down the hill or not?

Ion: In a manner of speaking.

Socrates: And if I rolled down hill, skis still attached?

Ion: I suppose so.

Socrates: So style and substance are not separated by virtue of some essence of substance and style, but as a matter of speaking?

Ion: It would seem so.

Socrates: So the "artfulness of the presentation" in science is after all not so easy to distinguish from the "warrant of its argument," the style from the substance?

Ion: *Panu ge Sôkrates.*

Socrates: And, to consider the other side, McCloskey does not reduce his argument to mere style, in the sense of advertising, does he?

Ion: Oh yes he does.

Socrates: Wait. He examines at length the warrants for significance testing, for instance, and speaks at the same time about the style (or what is indistinguishable, the substance) of using them?

Ion: Yes. I rather skimmed that part of the book.

Socrates: Very well: you and I have moved together from the sophomore to the junior class in aesthetics, concerning style and substance.

Ion: Ugh! Aesthetics! Another one of those meaningless subjects. I am glad to say that I am as ignorant of it as of rhetoric or of literary criticism. Anyway, "McCloskey has abdicated the right to identify some reasons as cognitively good and others as bad."

Socrates: What does "cognitively" mean here?

Ion: It is a magic word among us philosophers. It means whatever species of argument my logic teacher in graduate school told me was non-fallacious.

Socrates: Does it include induction?

Ion: Certainly not! Why, it is scandalous how filled with fallacy are the practices of induction.

Socrates: Or Peirce's "abduction"?

Ion: A plain fallacy!

Socrates: And the storytelling of Darwin?

Ion: Madness!

Socrates: And the metaphors, called models, of physics?

Ion: Now you're talking about Science, the portions of physics that we philosophers of science spend all our time discussing, though I don't know why you use the word "metaphors," which is just literary.

Socrates: I often wonder if the philosophical prestige of storytelling would have been higher than model-making if a Darwin had published *The Origin of Species* in 1687 and a Newton had published *Principia* in 1859. Metaphors and models might then have been relegated to a poetic and unScientific realm.

Ion: I can't understand this literary talk of yours.

Socrates: Evidently. By your definition, then, most "cognitive" matters seem to have little to do with scientific practice. I recommend to you a paper by Rappaport, which deals with "evidential" arguments the same way.

Ion: Also "epistemic." That is another of our magic words.

Socrates: Ah, epistemology. I take it then that you are well acquainted with modern epistemology.

Ion: No, of course not: haven't you understood that we philosophers of *science* don't need to read anything, including philosophy. I stopped reading that stuff in graduate school. Still, I throw around the word "epistemic." It has a nice sound, don't you think?

Socrates: Yes, Ion, it is a lovely word. So let me understand your position. Scientists use induction, metaphors, stories, and appeals to authority daily, but your way of philosophizing about their activities will define all these as "non-cognitive" (or we might say "non-evidential" or "non-epistemic"), imprisoned forever back in the Fallacies section of the elementary logic books.

Ion: Dammit, that's where they belong! The actual reasonings and arguments of scientists are so *thick*! It is extremely difficult to fit them into this neat, simple bed we philosophers have prepared. I think we do better in philosophy of science if we *define away*, as "non-cognitive" or "non-epistemic," 95 percent of the problem of scientific reasoning. Then we can search for the keys over here, in the light of the lamppost.

Socrates: That's nice work, Ion, if you can get it. Does McCloskey offer arguments about good and bad arguments?

Ion: Yes. Besides repeated reference to good and bad practices of argument throughout (and his scientific work in economic history, which needless to say I have not read but would find, I am sure, filled with the usual fallacies I detect in most science), he has as I just said two long chapters on quantification and statistical significance towards the end of the book, a sustained treatment of the good and bad rhetoric of a major argument in economics. In *If You're So Smart* he discusses in detail the good and bad stories used in economics. Then in this book, chapters 9 through 13, he does a similar analysis of formalism, though in less detail. As I say, though, my interest was in the first three chapters of *The Rhetoric of Economics*, where he talks like a philosopher. To tell you the truth, I relied mainly on my memory of his first article on the subject, in 1983. For most of the book he talks like a literary critic or an economist or an historian, with episodes of statistician. I just couldn't bear his detailed talk about the goodness or badness of economic and statistical arguments. So I didn't read them. It is so much easier to be a philosopher if you read only about what you think you already know.

Socrates: So McCloskey writes much about good and bad arguments. I seem to recall that he said that being a good person, for instance, had to do with the sorts of arguments one produces; he says it again in chapter 8 here and elsewhere. Yet I thought you said McCloskey had "abdicated the right" to have such opinions.

Ion: Well, I didn't mean that he didn't assert his right and, damn him, exercise it. I mean that anyone who doesn't think all important arguments in science are "cognitive" as defined by a coterie of anglophone academic philosophers active in the 1940s and 1950s (excepting Wittgenstein and his students and since the 1950s most of the philosophers interested in epistemology) has no intellectual rights at all, and certainly no rights to courtesy or to close reading. McCloskey will be lucky if we do not get together and run him out of our Popperian Open Society. It's too *complicated* to assess arguments unless you use my 3" × 5"-card philosophy of science. The card is really neat: in about five minutes you can learn the philosophy of science without reading anything, and you will never again have to consider argument in science. If we don't get rid of these metaphors (Mary Hesse calls them models) or stories (Larry Laudan calls them research traditions), our lives as philosophers are going to get awfully complicated.

Socrates: So it would seem. But if McCloskey does offer a way to "criticize" economics in every sense, what is his crime?

Ion: He would make economics a non-policy science.

Socrates: Does he say that?

Ion: No. You really haven't been listening! McCloskey doesn't need to actually *say* something for my *verstehen* to detect it.

Socrates: I thought that McCloskey wrote on economic policy, past and present. I suppose, though, that your *verstehen* is again on target. Do you have an argument *for* economics as a policy science?

Ion: No. Economics is filled with predictive problems, just like that rubbish by Darwin. Understand, and this time try to pay attention: a certain branch of seventeenth-century physics, as interpreted by the nonphysicists of a century ago, supplemented by those parts of quantum mechanics that philosophers can grasp, is the only model for true science. Have you got that?

Socrates: Your friend Alan Randall disagrees, making the point that it is strange to freeze science in the imagined pose of the seventeenth century (Randall 1990, p. 263).

Ion: Well, he is obviously reading too many historians of science. I don't, and am the better for it. Economics doesn't qualify for my timeless tag of Science, nor does biology, history, geology, and numerous others. For instance, the "advances" in economics that McCloskey values are laughable.

Socrates: Why is that? As Philip Mirowski asked recently, "The question [in conventional Methodology] that was never asked was: why must economics be like physics, or like what Lakatos said science was?" (Mirowski 1991b, p. 292).

Ion: Aren't you listening? The so-called "advances" do not make economics more *predictive*. You really do need an ear examination. These "advances" – hah! – are mere applications, mere storytelling.

Socrates: I see. Science is defined as being what is predictive, in the pattern of amateur understandings of physics, contrary to how physics actually operates. So when science proves to be non-predictive or in some other way deviant from this conveniently simple model, expressible on a 3″ × 5″ card, it is the scientist not the philosopher of science that is wrong.

Ion: Certainly. At last you are hearing the point.

Socrates: In other words: you can second-guess the artists and scientists of the world, as one could of course if science were a matter of 3″ × 5″ cards and folk history of science. You can improve economic science, the better to "improve the human condition" and provide intellectual "comfort when one needs to decide what to do about unemployment" by *not* reading most economics, philosophy, history, rhetoric, and the rest of the library. As Feyerabend puts it, you are confident that "humanity . . . can be saved by groups of people shooting the breeze in well heated offices" (Feyerabend 1987, p. 17). That is truly wonderful.

Ion: Yes, so it is.

Socrates: I admire your wisdom more than I can say. Yet there is one respect in which I blame you: in our conversation you have quite unjustly neglected to reveal the Method of achieving this profitable wisdom in simple second-guessing to me. If it is so easy to acquire from the chair one would think you would give it to us your friends. We too could learn the 3" × 5" card for Science and proceed to collect the Nobel prize, or at least that prize in Reactionary Declamation that you won in Chicago. Such neglect is unjust. On the other hand, if it is not easy to acquire, and you are divinely possessed in having it, I cannot blame you. I conclude, Ion, that you are either a man unjust or a man divine. Which it is to be?

Ion: It is far lovelier to be deemed divine.

Socrates: Then this lovelier title, Ion, shall be yours, to be in our minds divine, and not scientific, in philosophizing about Science.

chapter 19

Methodologists of economics, big M and small

It has been hard for some philosophers of economics, then, to understand the rhetorical turn. Likewise the philosophically influenced economist-Methodologists, such as Mark Blaug, A. W. Coats, or Roger Backhouse, have had a difficult time reading. Like the philosophers they evince a lack of curiosity about the revolution in science studies, which may explain their difficulties. An article by Backhouse entitled "The Constructivist Critique of Economic Methodology" (1992b, chiefly a review of work by Roy Weintraub and myself) does not mention among fifty-five citations any sociologist or historian of science, aside from the lone and usual apotropaic reference to the Kuhn of *The Structure of Scientific Revolution*. So Backhouse and the other economist-philosophers are of course puzzled by the metamodern claim that science is a matter of communities.

Backhouse's puzzled response to my work is a good instance of how some philosophers and their students claim to speak for all time, yet make like the rest of us a rhetorical use of a time-bound community of speech. Backhouse uses the *tu quoque* popular among philosophers in the here and now yearning for the Last Judgment: "It is not possible to take such communities as 'given,' obviously recognizable, for this goes against the premise that there are no uninterpretable givens" (Backhouse 1992b, p. 73). Gotcha. But as usual the philosophical argument hinges on an equivocation, here between "givens" meaning "historically given," which we can examine and discuss, and "Givens" meaning "timeless Truths," which we shall never know. For example, the distinction in the late twentieth century between the department of philosophy and the department of English is an historical contingency, an instance of what is meant by saying that communities are "given." Backhouse's rhetoric shows how little he has understood the argument. There is nothing "obviously recognizable" about the distinction, if "obviously" means "for all time." Nor is it an "uninterpretable given," if "uninterpretable" means "outside of history." As recent epistemologists have recognized, nothing is obvious or uninterpretable forever and ever, outside of history. Trial by jury and the conventions of the dessert fork are given for the nonce, the way that the French and English meanings of "mouton" and "mutton" are. The Methodologists cleave to a search for timeless Truths, have not heard of the recent trouble with Truth (N. Goodman 1978, pp. 17-19), have not read the sociologists and historians of science, and are unaware of their own contingent history as mortal offspring of the immortal Popper. Therefore they are as I say puzzled by descriptions of science that are merely timefully, contingently true.

In other words, the economist-philosophers such as Backhouse are satisfied to ask, with an air of posing an unanswerable question, "How are we to determine who belongs to a speech community?" They are unaware of the hundreds of books and essays over the past decades that have shown in sociological, historical, and rhetorical detail how it's done (Backhouse cites his colleague at Birmingham the economist Willie Henderson, the professor of English Charles Bazerman, and other pioneers of the rhetoric of science, but does not appear to have understood the conversation in which they are speaking). The unanswerable question the Popperian philosophers want to go on posing is how we can demarcate good from bad argument forever and ever. The answerable question, on the other hand, answered by science studies over the past quarter century, is how we demarcate one from the other in the present condition of, say, British economic history (McCloskey 1990a, ch. 3) or in the seventeeth-century condition of experiments on air pressure (Shapin and Schaffer 1985). Economic Methodologists like Backhouse and Popperian philosophers of science like Peter Munz cannot grasp the point that demarcations, determinations, decisions *for all time* are not on offer. They prefer unanswerable metaphysical questions to answerable sociological or historical or rhetorical ones.

Backhouse defends evaluative Methodology by saying that in a constructivist view of knowledge the "knowledge would depend on power . . . This may be a fact of life, but there seems no place for such a concept in an evaluative methodology" (p. 73). He does not notice that he is begging the question. Evaluative Methodology, he begins, is good *because* it has no place for non-evaluative methodology, which examines how the science actually works. Giving grades to research programs, he therefore concludes, is good, *because* the effort of grading leaves no time for examining how the science actually works. The circle closes with a snap.

It is vexing, this inability of trained readers of economics to read what I and others have said in plain English. For example, Backhouse gets the point of *If You're So Smart* (1990a), summarized above in chapter 6, precisely upside down. In a footnote (Backhouse 1992b, note 14 on p. 79) he says of my argument that it "neglects competition and entry." What? I have often been accused of overusing competition and entry in argument, but never yet of neglecting them. What Chicago economist do you know who "neglects competition and entry"? Then with an air of correcting my careless oversight he then provides some arguments from competition and entry – the same arguments I use in the book. Backhouse thinks that the economics in the footnote undermines the proposition that profitable prediction is impossible. On the contrary, his and my economics supports it. I am astonished that another economist would think I "neglect competition and entry," in the book or anywhere else. He's not doing very well at his reading.

Nor is Larry Boland, who is usually sharper, when he reads my argument as a proposal that "we study literature rather than mathematics or logic" (Boland 1987, p. 211). What would be the point of that? Economists persuade in words, in mathematics, and in logic. A study of their rhetoric is going to require a study of all their devices of persuasion.

Nor is Bill Gerrard (1990), reading *The Rhetoric of Economics* and the book edited with Klamer, Solow, and McCloskey (1988). The rhetorical approach is foreign to the ears of conventional Methodologists and they therefore miss it, understandably and innocently, the way non-native speakers of English miss the difference between the phonemes "w" and "v" ("I vant to be alone . . . I yust vant to be alone"). Gerrard, for example, misses the definition of "modernism." He defines it as "authoritarianism" (Gerrard 1990, pp. 201, 209) and "dogma." On the contrary, modernism is the theory of the twentieth-century avant-garde, 1900-1968; it is not authoritarian in essence, only in accident. Some modernists indeed exhibit the accident of authoritarianism and dogmatism. But so do some non-modernists, or some a-modernists; and some do not. Authoritarianism in method is not the meaning of modernism, or else the pop versions of Derridean deconstruction and Thomist scholasticism (which have similarities, among which is their authoritarianism) would be called "modernist."

Gerrard then speaks (p. 201) as though I reject the 3″ × 5″-card version of modernist Method, falsificationism, *tout court*, rejecting it even as one argument among many a scientist might make. That would be a strange thing for me to do, since I have used falsifications in my historical work on British iron and steel and medieval open fields. I do not reject falsification as one among many arguments, sometimes a very good argument, sometimes not so good. I reject it merely as a 3″ × 5″-card demarcation of Science from the rest of argument. Gerrard caps his own argument by posing the alternative: either one signs up for falsificationism (alone, it would seem, without a description of how scientists in fact do their work) or one slips into Anything Goes. He sums up: "More empirical testing of economic theories is necessary. If this seems authoritarian to McCloskey, so be it. It is surely a less dangerous and debilitating prescription than the alternative of 'anything goes'" (p. 201). He later sees (without exhibiting a textual knowledge of Feyerabend) "links that the rhetorical approach has with Feyerabend's 'anything goes' philosophy" (p. 210).

Gerrard does not say where in my writings or elsewhere in the rhetorical literature he finds something other than the practice or commendation of "more empirical testing" or where I call empirical testing "authoritarian" or where I or Klamer or Weintraub advocate "anything goes." When conservatives are on a rant, as we have seen, they are excused from empirical testing, falsification, or precision of meaning. They get their results from uncriticized definitions – such as identifying modernism with authoritarianism in McCloskey's mind, or falsification with all empirical testing in Gerrard's mind – not from observations. In the enjoyment of his primitive Popperianism, Gerrard, with Garbo, yust vants to be alone.

Let me try again. The clash of views may make my own views clearer. The *Eastern Economic Journal* in 1987 contained another symposium on *The Rhetoric of Economics* (Coats, Pressman, Butos). The debate replayed the points made in other forums, with variations.

Steven Pressman, for example, argued that economic rhetoric needs to be reconsidered but claimed that McCloskey does not go far enough. His claim is that "McCloskey . . . does not provide guidelines for improving our rhetoric."

In the restricted sense in which Pressman understands "rhetoric," namely, as "clearly communicating," the glass through which we see the World As It Is, I have presumed to give guidelines at some length in *The Writing of Economics* (1986b). In a somewhat broader sense, as "guidelines for improving our arguments," chapters 8 and 9 among others of *The Rhetoric of Economics* do so, on the subject of quantitative arguments in economics. And like any economist I am filled with advice on how arguments in particular fields should be carried on – how we ought to think about late Victorian economic failure, for instance (see *If You're So Smart*, chapters 3 and 4), or about English open fields. That is the point. Scientific thinking consists of rhetoric; which is to say, of attempts to influence other scientists to take this or that argument seriously.

For example, the use of mathematics in economics of which Pressman disapproves (and of which I do not, so long as people admit candidly what it is) is in part an "ethical" appeal, as the rhetoricians say (from the Greek *ethos*, or character), an appeal to the character of a Proper Scientist (see chapter 6 in *The Rhetoric of Economics*, "The Rhetoric of Scientism: How John Muth Persuades"; and chapters 9 through 13 above). There's nothing wrong with ethical appeals. After all, it's good to be a Proper Scientist. So long as we admit that part of the force of mathematical arguments comes from this direction, no harm is done. That is one guideline for "improving our rhetoric."

In the same issue of the *Review* William Butos, writing from the viewpoint of the Austrian school of economics, agrees that science needs no "ratiomania of prescriptivism" (a sweet phrase, that) because science is a spontaneous order à la Hayek. Butos seems to think I disagree. But I say the same thing. I say, for example, that it is a social event that Muth's arguments came to be credible (p. 100, *The Rhetoric of Economics*; I omit marks around quotations from the book). The Keynesian revolution in economics would not have happened under the modernist legislation for science (McCloskey 1985a, p. 17). Only when enough economists believe will there be a demand for tests (p. 19, summarizing Ronald Coase's econo-sociology of science). Most explicitly among many other places (summarizing a point made in detail by Michael Polanyi):

> The notion of a conversation gives an answer to the demand for standards of persuasiveness . . . The conversations overlap enough to make one [somewhat] sure about [the standards of] neighboring fields . . . The overlapping conversations provide the standards. It is a market argument. There is no need for philosophical lawmaking

or methodological regulation to keep the economy of intellect running just fine.

McCloskey 1985a, pp. 27-28

Butos says that it's not right that "anything goes" in science, and in economic science, because "rules of conduct" (not rules of Method) are necessary to maintain the spontaneous order. McCloskey likewise says: far above method with a small m, at the peak of the scholarly enterprise, stand the conversational norms of civilization . . .*Sprache-thik* (McCloskey 1985a, p. 24). Were economists to give up their quaint modernism and open themselves officially to a wider range of discourse, they would not need to abandon data or mathematics or precision. They would merely agree to examine their language in action, and converse more politely with others in the conversation of mankind (p. 35). The classical solution was to insist that the orator be good as well as clever: Cato defined him as *vir bonus dicendi peritus*, the good man skilled at speaking (p. 37). It is people, not intellectual devices, that are good or bad. Good science demands good scientists – that is to say, moral, honest, hard-working scientists (p. 37). The best one can do, then, is recommend what is good for science now, and leave the future to the gods. What is good for science now . . . is good scientists, in most meanings of "good" (p. 53).

Butos says that rhetoric is epistemic, that "all knowing (and hence science) is rhetorical." But along with Cicero, Dewey, Wittgenstein Mark II, parts of Quine, all of late Richard Rorty, Nelson Goodman, Robert Scott, and many others since Protagoras of Abdera, McCloskey agrees: the language used [by science] is a social object, and using language is a social act. It requires . . . attention to the other minds present when one speaks. The paying of attention . . . is called "rhetoric" (McCloskey 1985a, p. xvii). The literary, epistemological, and methodological strands have not yet combined into one cord. They belong together, in a study of how scholars speak, a rhetoric of inquiry (McCloskey 1985a, p. 30). Other sciences, even the mathematical sciences, are rhetorical (p. 32). During crises in mathematics [t]he rhetoric of proof is in question (p. 33). As Frank Knight said, "We surely 'know' these propositions [in economics] better, more confidently and certainly, than we know the truth of any statement" (quoted McCloskey 1985a, p. 46). Literary forms are scientific (McCloskey 1985a, p. 55). Even the science of the counting house and the railroad station, cold-spirited as it is, draws on the gilded rhetoric of poets and mathematicians (p. 137). Science is social (*passim*).

The reader will see why I am puzzled that Butos thinks we disagree. The character "McCloskey" enters his piece as someone opposing or at best neglecting these fine ideas. They're not "mine" exactly (I stole them fair and square from Rorty, Toulmin, Feyerabend, Booth, Kuhn, and Kenneth Burke); but at least I deserve some credit for stealing them.

To go through the three points again without citations of chapter and verse, Butos believes that I ignore the idea of spontaneous order. Yet ignoring the spontaneous order in science or life would be hard for an economist who knew his or her trade beyond the mathematics of engineering. For that matter it would be hard for any social scientist after Locke or Mandeville or Smith. Enough said, for Butos has said it at length.

Butos believes that I adopt "anything goes," although he cannot find a place in the text where I do. Alexander Rosenberg, A. W. Coats, and certain other normally rational people allege this about me, too, against the evidence of what I say and what I do. Apparently Butos has picked it up from them. See again above: I believe in rules for serious games, and carry them out, but rules either at the level of technique or at the level of morality, not at the level of shortcut formulas for thinking ("Regress Y on X and publish"; "Never ever use questionnaires"; "Consider the observable implications only").

The phrase "anything goes" is Paul Feyerabend's, a persuasive philosopher of science. I mentioned in chapter 14 the places where Feyerabend explains what this alarming phrase means (Feyerabend 1978, pp. 39-40 and Feyerabend 1987, p. 283; Feyerabend likes alarming phrases: one of his titles is *Farewell to Reason* (1987); you can imagine the panic this creates in people who read the titles but do not read the books). He does not mean that one should say any old stupid thing (he leaves that office to rationalists), although he does mean that science and society should not be disciplined to say over and over again the same thing.

Although I think I agree with Feyerabend largely, here perhaps he falls for the modernist dichotomy between "ratiomania" and "irratiomania." Either you're a supporter of the Freedom Fighters in Nicaragua, says Colonel North, or you must be some kind of Communist (recall Senator Inouye at the hearings replying heatedly to North: "Colonel North, I am not a Communist"). Admirably, Feyerabend replies to the McCarthyites of positivism, to hell with you, then: in that case I *am* a Communist. If you dopes can't imagine more categories for thinking than following every dogma of the philosophers of science around 1955 on the one hand or an incoherent "irrationalism" on the other, then I'm for the irrationalism, and proud of it. So says our Paul, startling the bourgeoisie of science by catching them making up lies about, say, astrology. (And our Imre would not disagree, in some moods: Lakatos, though he used the word "irrationalist" to describe such a paragon of good sense as Michael Polanyi, apparently did not want the word to mean what it means to his less critical followers, such as Mark Blaug; see Lakatos 1978, p. 130 n3.)

By contrast I affirm, with Senator Inouye, that I am not (now) a Communist; nor (ever) an irrationalist, a nihilist, a deconstructionist, or any of the other nasty things that modernists call people who will not stand up smartly and salute their flag. I'm a conformist. I do not believe that Anything Goes (though neither does, I say again, anyone I have read, from Feyerabend to Derrida, if the word means a burbling irrationalism; and I've seen more *practice* of Anything Goes from the Republican National Committee and the conventional Methodologists of economics than from the people who are said to be advocating it). Butos agrees with me on this, but has gotten muddled about which side of the committee room he is on.

Butos believes that I am "reluctant" to use the "rhetorical theory literature." That sounds like the preacher blaming the Sunday congregation for the people who didn't show up. I have collaborated since coming to Iowa with Iowa's fine department of communication studies (since 1900 a largely Midwestern field, as old as Political Science: Iowa, Wisconsin, and Northwestern are acknowledged as the best departments; coasties doubt that the field is proper Science). In fact, I have taught a graduate course in the Department. I go to the Alta Conference in Utah, where the beleaguered clan restores itself biennially. I read books on rhetorical theory. The Project on Rhetoric of Inquiry is an outcome. The bibliography of *The Rhetoric of Economics*, taking only the "rhetorical theory literature" strictly defined to exclude other literary criticism, cites Aristotle, Cicero, Quintilian, Booth, Burke, Lanham, the Mechlings, Nelson, Perelman and Olbrechts-Tyteca, Robinson, Scott, and Wenzel. Later I became more immersed in the rhetorical theory literature, especially after encountering the ignorant coastie disdain for the field among deans and other service people. Feyerabend conspicuously defends astrology from the witch-hunters; a step down in boldness and impact, I quietly defend the department of communication studies. William Butos is barking up the wrong tree.

Another sympathetic approach to the argument that partly misfires is Uskali Mäki's recent writings, after reading books in rhetoric –

following the Rappaport example of learning something about what he criticizes. Or rather what he commends, because Mäki is helpfully developing what he calls a "realist" version of Klamer, Weintraub, and me. But like Butos, Mäki's is what soldiers call "friendly fire," that is, shots aimed at the enemy that fall on one's own troops.

In a paper in the Backhouse, Dudley-Evans, and Henderson volume (Mäki 1993a) and an overlapping paper delivered to the Network on Economic Method in January 1993, he explicates my arguments in the style of the analytic philosophy of around 1955. I know he is sincerely trying to illuminate the arguments. That I find the results murky is probably a result of my prejudice that the method of analytic philosophy around 1955 has, like the method of economics around 1975, stopped shedding much light. As Putnam puts it, "at the very point when analytic philosophy is recognized as the 'dominant movement' in world philosophy, it has come to the end of its own project – the dead end, not the completion" (Putnam 1990, p. 51).

Mäki takes the approach of analytic philosophy around 1955 particularly in supposing that "contradictions" are easy to prove and are decisive. Recall the "two-line *tu quoque*" and James' reply that it is like planting a stick in the middle of a river. "Analysis" means in Greek "break apart," and that is Mäki's technique. He takes an idea discussed in my writings, such as Rhetoric or Truth or truth, and breaks it apart into [i1], [i2], [i3], [i4], and so forth. The mere listing of many [i]'s will suggest that the author under analysis is guilty of contradictions and incoherence. The Philosopher then steps helpfully in to reestablish coherence. (Note that Mäki has for philosophical purposes a coherence theory of truth. Gotcha.)

He says for example that "nowhere does McCloskey give a concise definition of the concept of rhetoric." That is not correct. But in any case rhetoric is a word like democracy or freedom, a complicated matter not easily put onto a 3" × 5" card. The definition of our persuasive devices in science and politics is an essentially contested concept. By contrast, the rhetoric of analytic philosophy around 1955 depended on the belief that the world is simple – that sense data are simple to perceive, that language is reducible to simple statements such as "The cat is on the mat" or "Lo, the rabbit!" and therefore that simple definitions will suffice. The analytic philosophers were astonished that non-philosophers were so stupid as not to see the simplicity.

"Rhetoric" or "Truth" or any moderately complicated object is like an elephant. An elephant has large size, floppy ears, a tough skin, four thick legs, gray color, tusks, a trunk, and a tail. To fully describe an elephant in simple statements you are going to have to mention all these partial definitions, and more of them if you are talking to someone who is especially ignorant about elephants, your two-year-old son, say. (The better strategy, the sort that I and other people interested in economic rhetoric mainly pursue, as in chapters 4 through 9 of *The Rhetoric of Economics* or in Klamer's *Conversations with Economists*, or chapters 1 through 13 here, is an "ostensive" definition, that is, taking your son to the zoo and showing him an elephant. But an analytic philosophy that wants to reduce the world to "statements" does not go to the zoo, and does not care to look at the examples of economic rhetoric in the flesh.)

A blind man holding onto the tail is going to say, "An elephant is a tail." Another blind man will say, "No, you fool, a trunk!" Their dispute is preposterous. The trunk does not "contradict" the tail, as Mäki claims it does. Mäki's various definitions are parts of the elephant. "It is clear," says he (he uses "it is clear" when he wishes to sidestep saying why it is clear), "that [*t*4] contradicts [*t*1]."

One problem with seeing each simple and partial definition of "rhetoric" as a complete definition is that the partial definitions have connotations of their own. It is easy to use the connotations to make the argument look somehow defective. Thus Mäki's first attempt at defining rhetoric in Mäki 1993b, *R*1, mentions "conversation" ("adopted," he adds erroneously, "from the philosopher Richard Rorty"), and then is able to draw on the connotations of "conversation," such as the mere chitchat of a cocktail party, to second Solow's worry early in the new work that it was "too permissive." In the same way, A. W. Coats complained once about the metaphor of conversation that after all people write rather than speak to each other, and so literal conversation does not take place. (When Mäki complains surprisingly in his 1993 about my use of the word "God" to mean the nostalgia for the transcendental of theism he is making the same error in reading.) Later and likewise Mäki uses a partial definition of "Truth" to imply that I advocate majority voting on scientific questions. He quotes the passage in which I explicitly reject such a view, but not before he has discussed its weaknesses for a couple of pages. The discussion therefore insinuates that I in fact advocate chitchat and mere voting in science, contrary to the evidence of what I say and what I do.

But the main problem of seeing each part of the elephant as a definition of the whole is that each is thrown into a false dialectic with every other, making the parts the enemy of the whole. Tails against trunks. Color against size. You can see that something is wrong with Mäki's procedure by noting that it could be applied to any word that he himself uses (I employ here the figure cacosistaton), such as the word "economics" or "goals" or for that matter the definite article "the." One could write down partial definitions of "economics" in Mäki's own paper, or definitions of "the," and show that the parts are not all the same. Sometimes "economics" means [*e*1], "the reasoning in a particular piece of argument about prices"; sometimes it means [*e*2], "the profession self-consciously calling itself by the name"; sometimes [*e*3], "neoclassical economics"; and so forth. Sometimes "the" means [*t*1], "just mentioned"; sometimes "the" means [*t*2], "an abstraction of"; sometimes [*t*3], "a case in point of, not yet mentioned." Philosophy does not become deep merely by generating many numbered definitions and then declaring that they contradict one another.

The demand to give definitions carries with it a rhetoric of sturdy common sense. After all, isn't it sensible to know what we are talking about? But the demand is less sensible in practice than it sounds. And at the level of theory it can be proven rigorously to be impossible, though of course advisable in moderation. The average analytic philosopher around 1955 was not always moderate on this score, since he had mastered the ploy of making one partial definition the enemy of another. Give me now a complete definition of an elephant, he said, complete down to every part of that impressive beast, or I will start claiming you are contradicting yourself. And never mind showing me elephants, either.

That is what is wrong with Mäki's method in general. As one might expect from such a method, his particular conclusions are sometimes correct, sometimes mistaken. As an economist himself he says many wise and useful things about the project of looking at how economists argue. On the other side of the ledger, his most important mistake is a philosophical one, namely, his assertion that a coherence theory of truth/Truth "contradicts" a correspondence theory. He again takes his cue from analytic philosophy around 1955, assuming without argument that "the two [are] rival accounts of the concept of truth" (1993a, p. 37).

But we of course need not choose between the alleged rivals. We use both correspondence and coherence theories of truth in scientific argument daily. In particular, I do, and so does Mäki. The assertion that I as an alleged non-realist am "inclined to think that correspondence truth does not exist" is mistaken. It reminds me of the man asked whether he believed in infant baptism: "Believe it? I've *seen* it." Do I believe that the statement "The cat is on the mat" corresponds to Tilly my cat on the mat? Believe it? I've seen it.

The trouble with correspondence is that without coherence it applies only to simple cases, such as Tilly the cat at age thirteen on the worn kitchen mat at 320 Melrose Avenue on a winter's day at 10.36 a.m. We see the cat on the mat, and the reality corresponds in a simple way to the statement. But someone says "France is hexagonal" and we pause. We must have a set of coherences (a French capacity for self-involved abstraction, perhaps) in order to believe. That is what is wrong with the naïve idea that history, say, can be written by "just going to the archives." We had better go to the archives of course and we had better get our footnotes right. Yet no sensible historian would claim that correspondence without coherence makes good history.

But likewise coherence without correspondence is not much. It's just chitchat, or mathematics. So we need in science and in life both coherence and correspondence. If my definitions of truth/Truth include both, so what? What exactly is the problem? To say that we must choose is like saying we must choose whether demand or supply causes the price of soybeans. It's like nets and fish: one must have both to get broiled cod.

Notice that using only two words, coherence and correspondence, makes for a shallow description of knowledge. The rhetoricians – one half of Western culture since the Greeks – have complained about it, but the philosophers carry on. The philosophers are forced to proliferate definitional notation of the $[i1]$, $[i2]$, $[i3]$, $[i4]$ sort in order to make the simplest points, because they have denied themselves use of the natural language. But who says that we have to get along on a two-term rhetoric in discussing the Law of Demand or the prospects of the Bears next season? No one would agree to such shallow rules of rhetoric who wanted to talk about the real economic world, or even about academic life. A "realist" in Mäki's definition is someone who believes (*only*) a correspondence theory of truth. But as Putnam remarks, "realism is an impossible attempt to view the world from Nowhere" (Putnam 1990, p. 28). Mäki does not acknowledge that there are people calling themselves realists, such as Putnam or Rom Harré (1986) or me, who would not accede to such a definition. We want it both ways, and can get it.

The opportunity cost of abandoning Realism is not great, as the epistemologist Keith Lehrer argues:

> We need not mourn the passing of knowledge [that is, Knowledge] as a great loss. The assumption of dogmatists that some beliefs are

completely justified and that they are true, is not a great asset in scientific inquiry where all contentions should be subject to question and must be defended on demand . . . Indeed, economists and philosophers have suggested that an analysis of rational choice requires only subjective probabilities.

Lehrer 1971 (1993), p. 55

The amateur epistemologists in economics have not learned that economics and statistics can ground a justified belief. They want Truth, too.

Mäki is correct to conclude that I define the scholarly community ethically. Compare Putnam: "to claim of any statement that it is true . . . is, roughly, to claim that it would be justified were epistemic conditions good enough" (Putnam 1990, p. vii, italics omitted). He elaborates elsewhere:

> In my fantasy of myself as a metaphysical super-hero, all "facts" would dissolve into "values." That there is a chair in this room would be analyzed . . . into a set of obligations to think that there is a chair in this room if epistemic conditions are (were) "good" enough . . . I am not, alas! so daring as this. But the reverse tendency – the tendency to eliminate or reduce everything to description – seems to me simply perverse. What I do think, even outside my fantasies, is that fact and obligations are thoroughly interdependent . . . To say that a belief is justified is to say that it is what we ought to believe; justification is a normative notion on the face of it.

Putnam 1990, p. 115

Such a definition of knowing has nothing to do with "privilege" (Mäki 1993a, p. 33); it has to do with moral value. Like William James, Rom Harré, and many others I believe that in science as in life the check on cheating is moral, not mechanical. Mäki says, correctly in part (trunks and elephant ears again), that my definition of scientific truth is morally constrained coherence. (Note that he is mistaken in saying that I do not believe in correspondence, unless it is correspondence without coherence; he is also mistaken in saying that "McCloskey does not believe in prediction"; what I do not believe in is merely the simple formula by which an economist alleges to be able to make *profitable* prediction.)

But then Mäki asserts, without saying why, that the moral constraint is "unattainable." If by "unattainable" he means "not fully attainable, perfectly, by God's own standards," then of course he is right. So much we can prove on the blackboard, trivially. But what sense would there be in insisting that science meet such perfection? Nothing is attainable that way. We must get along on partial attainment, as on partial definitions. The partialness of argument in science – Aristotle called them "enthymemes" – makes it harder to locate "contradictions" in serious arguments, I understand, but that cannot be remedied. Strictly logical error is seldom the crux of the matter in science, or in philosophy.

Mäki is mistaken to claim that I must show "that the moral constraint in fact holds, that the intellectual market place is an ethically pure arena." In an imperfect world the showing would be impossible, and I reject the claim that I must show the world to be ethically pure in showing that ethics matters to scientists. The rhetorical ploy Mäki is using is the one used against Chicago assertions of "perfect" competition, namely, the ploy of blackboard proofs that things can't be perfect . . . if they are imperfect. Absolute perfection is not the scientific issue, and the degree of approximation to perfection cannot be ascertained on a blackboard. Does science work as though scientists were a speech community trying to hold each other to ethical standards? That is the positive question. Most modern students of science think the answer is, yes; and if no, they nonetheless admire it as a normative principle, consistent with the serious conversation of a republic. But most philosophers of economics have not gotten the news.

Mäki then says (in 1993) that I do not "provide detailed empirical studies on the social organization and functioning of the economics profession." He is again mistaken. I have provided large amounts of evidence, some of it autobiographical, a little statistical, together with a good deal of seat-of-the-pants sociological analysis. I don't always signal I'm doing it, as one has to with some readers. But my work is thick with detailed empirical remarks, which if collected and bound up with a Methodological preface might even count as a "study."

Mäki sneers, to take a tiny but revealing example, at a phrase of mine commending the West as "an open, plural, and pragmatic society" (1993a, p. 45). He apparently does not think the West is such a society. But he neglects to mention – perhaps he didn't notice – that the phrase occurred in a discussion of the social organization and functioning of the economics profession in the Eastern Europe of old. (When the context of the phrase is revealed I suppose it is uncontroversial that the West looks better.) I was telling of my encounters with two eminent economists in Eastern Europe who survived the lack of openness during the 1950s and 1960s: here is a tiny bit of a "detailed empirical study."

Others have provided the empirical studies in bulk, Arjo Klamer and David Colander, for example (Klamer and Colander 1990; Colander and Brenner 1992). The unempirical shoe is on the other foot. The "realists" like Mäki call for detailed empirical studies. But they neither do them nor read them. The detailed studies in the history, rhetoric, and sociology of science are done and read by "non-realists" in Mäki's definition, from Bruno Latour to Donald McCloskey. In his latest articles Mäki sneers, for example, at the professor of English Alan Gross; but Gross has actually done such detailed empirical studies of science (1990a).

What is wrong in Mäki's view with Latour, Harré, Gross, McCloskey, and the rest is not in truth that they have neglected the actualities of science. It is that they do not adhere to a particular philosophical doctrine. Adhering to the doctrine is what matters to Mäki. But adhering to it by the standard Mäki proposes would make it impossible to do science, or indeed to get out of bed.

Mäki is wholly sincere in wanting to help economists and Methodologists understand what Arjo Klamer, Roy Weintraub, William Milberg, Jane Rossetti, Willie Henderson, Tony Dudley-Evans, and others have been up to recently. I am suggesting that his method of analysis, [*i*1], [*i*2], [*i*3], [*i*4], does not help very much. Putnam noted about the "definitions" of analytic philosophy, "if what a term refers to depends on other people and on the way the entire society is embedded in its environment, then it is natural to look with scepticism at the claim that armchair 'conceptual analysis' can reveal anything of great significance about the nature of things" (Putnam 1990, p. 110). "Analysis" in the hands of analytic philosophers around 1955 was more than merely cognate with "paralysis."

The Rhetoric of Economics, its author has slowly realized, is a hard book to read. He worked hard sentence-by-sentence to make it clear. But the book has been constructed by its philosophically inclined readers differently from the way the author thought he wrote it. They see Anything Goes where he wrote *Sprachethik*, authoritarianism where he wrote modernism. But after all that's the point: writing in economics and about economics is not a glass window through which we read the world as it is. We need a way of reading our human, all too human, texts.

chapter 20

Getting "rhetoric": Mark Blaug and the Eleatic Stranger

Mark Blaug, the chief Popperian among economists, reviewed *The Rhetoric of Economics* in 1987 and showed like Backhouse and Pressman and Butos and Mäki that the argument must be elusive, since he didn't get it. I am puzzled. Over the 1980s he and several other economic methodologists (Coats, Caldwell, de Marchi, Backhouse, Hausman, McPherson) participated in conversations literal and epistolary about the rhetorical turn. You would think they would have come to understand it by the ordinary process of courteous conversation, which they all engaged in to the limits of their patience. If they understood the rhetorical turn I think they would agree with it, since it merely retails a liberal intellectuality that they themselves practice (that is, when they are not indulging in a McCarthyism of the center). The idea that economics might be "criticized" in the sense of literary criticism or of speech communications is implicit in much of their own work. As I've noted, Blaug subtitled his *The Methodology of Economics*, a Popperian survey of economic Method down to 1980, *How Economists Explain*.

Yet they do not understand. Perhaps enough examples have been given to show that they misread the text. Then they get abusive about what they think it says. We scholars and scientists have no reasonable theory of misreading. When we misread someone else's text we say that the text is badly written and when someone else misreads our own text we are quick to say that the readers are stupid or malicious or lazy.

For the most part I do not believe that it is stupidity or trade-union bloody-mindedness that drives them to fury. I know many of the conventional Methodologists personally, and know them in other matters to be honorable and intelligent. Probably it is this: unlike people who do not care about economic Methodology the Methodologists are hardwired in the part of their brain that might otherwise deal with rhetoric. Therefore they find the idea of rhetoric exceptionally difficult to understand (this is apparent in the comments of Hausman and McPherson, for example). Therefore they rant. It is not that the conventional Methodologists understand what they are reading and then disagree with it. One can show pretty easily that, unlike the non-Methodologists, they do not understand it at all. The existing pattern in their thinking obstructs their reception of rhetoric.

One is left, as I have said, with the Kantian filter, the Marxist ideology, the pragmatic context (for the filter, see Bicchieri 1988). Blaug and company come to the argument with a theory of science drawn from philosophy, if a trifle antique. So quite naturally they force my words to fit the philosophy, lopping off the excess, as they do when deciding that a piece of economics is Lakatosian. No blame attaches (although the thought does occur to me that Mark Blaug or Roger Backhouse, as historians of thought, may be similarly misunderstanding the dead economists they interpret for the rest of us as completely as they misunderstand my writings; I must get back to reading for myself the lesser works of Ricardo and see). Their response illustrates a major theme in the work, that argument is culturally bound, bound in this case by the culture of modernism. As Schopenhauer said, "It is quite natural that we should adopt a defensive and negative attitude towards every new opinion concerning something on which we have already an opinion of our own. For it forces its way as an enemy into the previously closed system of our own convictions, shatters the calm of mind we have attained through this system, demands renewed efforts of us and declares our former efforts to have been in vain" (Schopenhauer 1851 (1970), no. 19, p. 124).

For instance, as I have noted before, Blaug in his review and the other Methodologists in theirs focus on the first three chapters of *The Rhetoric of Economics*, which argue that Methodology as conventionally practiced is unhelpful to economics (a conclusion, by the way, that many of their own books come to, as in the self-immolation of the Lakatosian model in de Marchi and Blaug 1991). The non-Methodologists by contrast focus on the last seven chapters, which offer detailed examples of literary criticism, that is to say, an inquiry into what economic scientists do in their actual work. A literary criticism of economics will seem strange only to a scholar who has invested a lot in the other, philosophical criticism. Philip Mirowski, with Pamela Cook, has thoroughly explored the use of the physics metaphor in economics. In a comment on their work Nancy Wulwick notes that the metaphorical character of physics – say, the Rutherford-Bohr model of the atom as a solar system – has long been known: "The study of metaphors by economic methodologists [small m] no longer appears to be the outlandish endeavour some members of the economic profession have made it out to be. Clearly, the role of metaphors in scientific discovery has been a standard concern of philosophers of science" (Wulwick 1990, pp. 222-223; that is, of non-Popperian philosophers of science). The economic Methodologists, Popperians to a man, have not yet gotten the news.

Again, the Methodologists complain that I attack Methodology while adopting a Methodology. Gotcha. Blaug makes this point at length in his review, and Michael McPherson, Daniel Hausman, Martin Hollis, and others use the same topos of argument. They are missing the sense of "methodology" that I use throughout. Hausman, for example, believes that because I do not think economists can advise businesspeople about profitable futures (as in chapter 6 above) I must think that advice on Method is equally useless (Hausman 1992, p. 263n). He has misunderstood the economics: advice can make people wise and it can make them competent; it cannot make them smart, or else the teacher would be rich. Advice from philosophers might make economic scientists more wise about the morality of their field; and occasionally a philosopher might spot a piece of widespread incompetence at the level of technique, such as the overuse of statistical significance. Wisdom and competence can be obtained by advice. But advice on the third, middle term, scientific smartness, is another matter.

I think advice on middle-brow Methodology is worse than useless, but do not depend on a theoretical doubt. My empirical observation, like Hausman's as editor of *Economics and Philosophy* (see chapter 14 above), is that those who give advice on such smartness are angry, dishonest, uncharitable, and dogmatic. The rhetoric makes them so. Advice on competence and wisdom has no problem. Advice on the middle terms, smartness, does. I and other economists have seen empirically the unhappy results of Simple Simon's rules of Method: "No surveys, please: we're economists" or "Always reduce macro to micro" or "Science is math" or "Never give a Chicago [or Yale or New York University] economist an even break."

Blaug's filter does not let through this argument that useful method is a matter either of low technicalities (for example, Do not use significance tests, most of the time) or of high moralities (for example, Do not pretend you think significance tests are swell if you know their statistical theory is bankrupt). He does not have an answer to the observation that middle-level and philosophical Methodology has made our scientific culture narrow and intolerant, a fact his experience of life must confirm. As someone who has throughout his life fought narrowness and intolerance in economics, parts of it caused by middle-brow Methodological convictions, Blaug will I am sure come eventually to see the point. In economics the adoption of the middle-level rules that Blaug so ill-advisedly advocates has made economists technically incompetent to deal with inference and morally incompetent to deal with public policy.

Something is awry in Blaug's understanding of method. Look at the reasoning in his assault on the pluralism of Bruce Caldwell (Blaug's style is always an assault, scholarship as cavalry charge; but after the charge has spent its force and he is back in the regimental mess, drink in hand, he is quite a nice chap, really, and so we forgive him):

> How does [Caldwell] explain the repeated appeal to empirical evidence in the Keynesianism-versus-monetarism controversy? . . . [S]urely what is remarkable is the insistence of all participants in these debates that they must be resolved by *truly discriminating tests* of the respective predictions of each school of thought, *which so far have simply not been forthcoming*. If this is not the methodology of falsificationism *in action*, what is it?
>
> Blaug 1984, p. 35, my italics

Methodology *in action*? For twenty years a large part of the economics profession wrangled with each other on Keynesianism versus monetarism, strictly following falsificationism, yet on Blaug's admission (he attributes the point to Caldwell; Roger Backhouse and Tony Dudley-Evans give a brilliant rhetorical reading of the affair, from soup to nuts, in Backhouse 1993b and Dudley-Evans 1993) did not manage in all that time to come forth with a single falsification or even one truly discriminating test of a prediction. If this is the Methodology of falsification "in action," no wonder that no one believes it or acts on it. Blaug seems to understand "method" as "official rhetoric of argument, regardless of whether long tests in action of the official rhetoric yield a single instance of actually following it." By this standard the alleged Christians engaging in the pogroms of 1881 against Russian Jews were exhibiting in action their faith in the Lamb of God. What is remarkable, Blaug would say, what shows Christianity in action, is that the Russians shouted Christian slogans as they burned Jews alive in their houses. That is a strange and philosophical view of how to discover someone's method or someone's religion in action.

The linguist Geoffrey Pullam attacks in linguistics as I do in economics the "methodological moaners," who "while handing you their linguistic hypotheses . . . take the opportunity to stuff a few tracts on the philosophically correct view of falsifiability into your pocket" (1990, p. 125). Pullam's book is a rhetoric of linguistics, discussing for example the rhetoric of book titles (ten called simply *Semantics*) and the reasons people think falsely that Eskimos have a lot of words for snow. "Unsympathetic critics will no doubt charge that by doing so I instantiate the very kind of behavior I am railing against [namely, Methodology]. This is not so" (p. 125). Watching how linguists or economists make their arguments is not the same thing as importing ready-made formulas for Science, conveniently summarized in this pamphlet I am now stuffing into your pocket.

Finally the Methodologists like Blaug assert that I oppose empirical tests. Blaug uses some vehement rhetoric at the end of his 1987 piece to make the claim, though of course he does not give textual evidence that it is so. The notion is that admitting our rhetoric will reduce our interest in facts.

You can see how little the Methodologists have understood. They have believed for so long that modernism gives a complete account of how the world should affect one's opinions that they cannot understand other accounts, and therefore simply reduce them to nuttiness and proceed (cf. Gerrard 1990). Either you buy into modernism or you must be some kind of nut – a Communist, or Anything Goes. Nuts propose to abandon empirical tests. Therefore McCloskey, who must be a nut because he rejects modernism, must propose somewhere (I'll find the place in a minute) the abandonment of empirical tests. The syllogism exhibits the sort of care in critical thinking that we have come to expect from the line of Plato, Descartes, and Russell.

Let me certify that besides not being a Communist or a nut I am also not against empirical tests. My main complaint about modern economics is that unlike some of its branches (labor economics, economic history) it is more interested in theoretical and econometric entertainments than in serious empirical tests. Nothing I have written in economics, history, or methodology suggests the contrary. *Of course* the "past retrodictions" of monetarism, to take one of Blaug's indignant examples, are arguments that we should take seriously. (By the way, again, a criterion of retrodiction would erase the demarcation between science and non-science, since astrology easily passes the test; for me this is no problem, since I do not see any use for the demarcation except to close the society. But those like Blaug who are interested in demarcation may wish to take note and do further work on their criterion.) *Of course* "empirical data" are relevant. Someone who has earned his living by writing economic history could hardly speak otherwise.

The point of *The Rhetoric of Economics*, which Blaug's filter has prevented him from seeing, is that modernism narrows the meaning of "retrodiction" and "data" down to a nub of meaninglessness. Retrodiction, after all, is the telling of stories, a matter of economic rhetoric discussed at length in *If You're So Smart*. And the "data" include our self-awareness. The Methodology that Blaug advocates would leave us unable to think about storytelling or introspection. The literary criticism that I advocate would allow us to consider these, and tests of significance, too. As Putnam puts it, what distinguishes broadchurch reasoning from positivism is that the broadchurch reasoner refuses "to *limit in advance* what means of verification may become available to human beings. There is no restriction . . . to mathematical deduction plus scientific experimentation" (Putnam 1990, p. ix, his italics).

Arjo Klamer has an analysis deeper than my notion of the "Kantian filter" to explain why some of the conventional Methodologists have a hard time getting the point. The analysis shows at the same time what is peculiar about modern economics (Klamer 1990c, pp. 25-27). Klamer draws a square to stand for the rigid, axiomatic Method that dominates the rhetoric of most journals in the field. The square, he points out, is the ideal shape of modernist painting and architecture, of Mondrian and Mies van der Rohe. Squares are about facts and logic. Show me the theorem. The square contains the analytic philosophers of science. Then he draws a circle some distance from the square, or perhaps a half dozen of them scattered here and there. Circles are about metaphor and story. Circle reasoning is the other half of the culture. Tell me your story. Since the seventeenth century, and especially during the mid-twentieth century, the square and the circle have stood in non-overlapping spheres, sneering at each other.

Klamer then draws an amoeba shape encompassing the square and the circles, which is the realm of discourse, including both square and circle and much in between. The whole – the amoeba with square and circles encompassed – is the world presented for consideration by rhetoric, pragmatism, hermeneutics, discourse analysis, literary criticism, and sociology of knowledge. The purposes of

Table 3. *A Barnes table: the hermeneutics of the rhetorical program*

What rhetoricians, sociologists of science, hermeneuts, *et al.* mean, looking at the amoeba and its contents	What is heard by denizens of the square (conventional philosophers of science, newspaper reporters, and the like)
"The rhetoricians are attempting to . . ."	
Identify causes of belief in what is true or rational	Show that what seems true or rational isn't really so
Show that there are rationally defensible alternatives to accepted knowledge or science or mathematics	Debunk our accepted knowledge of science or mathematics
Show that the making and using of science cannot be pinned down to a narrow meaning of "rational"	Portray scientists and engineers as illogical and irrational
Show that much of science is accepted on authority	Claim that authority in science always overrides reason and fact
Show that science uses metaphors, stories, and other human devices	Demean science by claiming that it is mere art
Show how science actually works, in the journals and laboratories	Expose science as a matter of force and fraud
Bring science back to a reasonable relation to society as a whole	Undermine the status of scientists, taking away its dignity and funding
Deconstruct the words of science, giving us back a reasonable science	Demolish science, leaving us sunk in the Abyss Without Reason

Source: Klamer 1990c, p. 26, with amendments.

such a presentation are regularly misunderstood by denizens of the square, among them Blaug, Backhouse, McPherson, Hausman, Rappaport. The rhetoricians and the squareniks have a hermeneutical problem, as the sociologist Barry Barnes put it in a paper in 1987 for the Iowa conference on the rhetoric of science. What is understood as the message by the rhetoricians is heard quite differently by the squareniks (which of course illustrates the point made elsewhere by Barnes, Klamer, McCloskey, Collins, and the like that "communication" is not to be described by the Roto-Rooter theory; see table 3). The squareniks, Klamer points out, "interpret the denial of privilege to the formal [square] strategy *necessarily* as the awarding of privilege to the domain of the will (or the subjective, the emotional, the normative [in short, the circles in Klamer's diagram] . . . Enthymemes are squeezed into syllogistic form, abductive reasoning becomes deductive and what does not fit is speculative, ruled by will" (Klamer 1990c, pp. 26-27).

For these reasons I believe Blaug when he says that he was "unable to understand" my reply to Caldwell and Coats (Caldwell and Coats 1984; McCloskey 1984). It is difficult to understand Greek if one does not really believe it is different from English. I hope we can avoid the reaction of the old-style British tourist when confronted with a Greek: shout louder, in English.

The basic problem all these people have understanding the rhetorical turn is the very word, plain Greek "rhetoric." If they could grasp the reasons for giving it the broad definition that Klamer and I and others in the rhetoric of inquiry give it perhaps they would catch on.

Recall the observation in chapter 4 above that Plato defined rhetoric as mere ornament and Aristotle defined it as the available means of nonviolent persuasion. I have defined the word to include all means to unforced agreement, from mathematical induction to appeals to sympathy. But surely, someone will reply, the broad definition Goes Too Far. Always at this point someone, the Eleatic Stranger perhaps, will use the figure of argument *si omnia, nulla*, that is, "If rhetoric is everything, then it is nothing, since it is not distinct from anything." (The argument, by the way, is a piece of folk philosophy, mistaken even in its own terms: all matter, for example, is made up of atoms, which does not imply that atoms are nothing; non-rhetorical speech is never observed, which does not imply it is nothing.)

Surely, the Stranger will argue with some irritation (epistemological conservatives get angry very fast), we should acknowledge that usually people mean mere ornament when they use the word, and always have. The Stranger says, using the figure of argument from consequences, "If we do not use the word narrowly, what is to keep Science, with its well-known Scientific Method, involving numbers and lab-coats and so forth, separate from the rest of the culture? What is to prevent the sophists and advertisers from invading the laboratories? To speak of a 'rhetoric of science' is surely oxymoronic, or maybe just moronic."

The Stranger's reply, you see, is often accompanied by ornamental indignation. Usually it is accompanied, too, with some harsh words about advertising and Madison Avenue, especially if the Stranger is an American intellectual. American intellectuals are unhappy with the form of speech called advertising (cf. T.G. Palmer 1990, p. 308). Madison Avenue doesn't influence us, of course; but mere *hoi polloi*, we have observed, are its slaves. You know how stupid the common people are. Something should be done about it by we intellectuals shooting the breeze in warm offices. When Vance Packard wrote his book *The Hidden Persuaders* long ago he thought he was going to lose his friends on Madison Avenue. Quite the contrary: after the book appeared their business was better than ever. Packard had convinced businesspeople that advertising worked, something the advertisers themselves had experienced limited success in doing. Part of the myth of advertising effectiveness is an exaggeration of its economic power. Advertising is said to be all around us, an essential support of capitalism and therefore a threat to our non-profit sector of intellectuality. Most American intellectuals would be surprised to know that advertising takes up about one half of one percent of national product (Bureau of the Census, 1990, series 1381, SIC code 731; and series 691; the data are for 1988, the latest year for which figures are available; the share of advertising in national income, by the way, has been falling for decades). The nostalgia for a day without advertising is, as Lanham points out, "purest pastoralism," a vision of the simple shepherd and his maid, before speech with intentions.

The Stranger's love of word-free certitude cannot be satisfied, as adults will realize. A childish yearning for it has corrupted discourse. Narrowing persuasion down to a nub of philomathematical "proof" leaves what persuades reasonable people, including philosophers, unexamined. Philosophers have since Plato been the enemies of rhetoric (Edward Schiappa makes a persuasive case that Plato coined the very word "rhetoric" in order to differentiate his own art of words from that of his competitors [Schiappa 1991, pp. 40-49; cf. Cole 1991]).

But since Aristotle some of the philosophers have also been among its defenders. The arrogance of "proof" has been under attack by them for some time. Arnold Levison remarked in 1964 that "The most general characterization of a proof . . . is that it is a form of social practice directed at a certain kind of purpose, namely that of achieving agreement as to the acceptability of statements . . . Such criteria are as objective as any criteria of deductive proof, which also depend in the end on forms of social practice" (Levison 1964, pp. 559-560). The category "proof" is here seen as rhetorical. A subcategory of proof, Logic, has been similarly characterized recently by philosophers. John Passmore notes in *Recent Philosophers* that to the observation that "there are large classes of valid arguments which are not recognised as valid in formal systems . . . mathematical logicians have replied that such a logic could never be anything more than a miscellaneous hotch-potch *and that the critics were confusing logic and rhetoric*" (Passmore 1985, p. 7, my italics). Precisely. Passmore continues: "In the 1970s, however, quite a few logicians, if still very much a minority, came to be dissatisfied with this defense. They were unhappy with the suggestion that a logic could be regarded as adequate which could give no account, in a large class of cases, of the difference between acceptable and unacceptable reasoning" (p. 8). The realm of certitude, logic, and epistemology covers by philosophical convention a tiny portion of the wide realm of reasoning.

That is one reason to reject the narrow, Platonic, and modern philosophical definition of "rhetoric." We need a word for that "wordcraft" mentioned earlier, the art of felicitous speech acts, because there are a great many of them. Since about the time of Socrates or Plato the word has been "rhetoric." A reason to have a broad definition is to keep in view the variety of reasons that people in fact use. "Logic" could be the word for it, if it were freed from its narrow definition, or "argument." "Rhetoric" fits the history better.

But there is another reason for the broad definition. The second reason, beyond empirical accuracy, is consequence. We need a word that does not have room for a distinction between mere persuasion and actual, timeless, godlike demonstration. We do not get it if we waste "rhetoric" on the already crowded territory in English of ornament, garnish, decoration, bauble, embellishment, polish, chartjunk, adornment, imposture, cosmetics, ornateness, varnish, flamboyance, flourish, floridity, frill, grandiloquence, ostentation, pose, make-believe, dissimilation, affectation, mannerism, put-on, pretension, posturing, airs, hot air, blather, bombast, claptrap, codswallop, hokum, malarkey, insincerity, runaround, disingenuousness, front, disguise, duplicity, masquerade, evasion, shiftiness, overstatement, exaggeration, advertising, public relations, promotion, hoopla, hype, salesmanship, ballyhoo, manipulation, weasel-words, humbug, bluff, fourflushing, balderdash, put-on, poppycock, blarney, bunk, drivel, fiddlesticks, schlock, trivia, bilge, tripe, bosh, rubbish, rot, baloney, moonshine, gammon, hypocrisy, cant, mummery, smoothness, slickness, sham, subterfuge, bamboozlement, trickery, double-dealing, deception, fabrication, pretense, deceit, dishonesty, hoax, chicanery, skulduggery, cozenage, dodge, fraud, fakery, feigning, flimflam, counterfeiting, con, cheating, perjury, fib, yarn, falsehood, untruthfulness, mendacity, confabulation, prevarication, and plain lying. (Is there a language richer in words of contempt for the misuses of persuasion?)

The reason it is desirable to have a word that includes the most elevated form of mathematical proof and the lowest form of character assassination is this: if we do not have a word for all of wordcraft, then someone will try to claim the higher ground, and falsely. *His* argument, he will claim, is demonstrative, by contrast with the "mere" rhetoric of his opponents. He is thereby freed from having to give an account of why.

Of course, some arguments are better than others. Anything does not go. Recognizing that nonetheless they are all arguments does not entail slipping into a hot tub of "relativism" as defined by conservative philosophers of science. One does not give up the ability to distinguish between the Ajax Kitchen Cleanser jingle and Gödel's Proof by noting that both are designed with an audience in mind, with a perlocutionary force, with patterns of repetition, with a style suited to the occasion, with an implied author, with metaphor, synecdoche, and all the rest.

The trick of claiming certitude on no good grounds as a way of avoiding serious persuasion might be called Plato's Trope. He claimed a certitude like mathematics – not the mere opinions they trade in the courts of law – that kings should be philosophers and philosophers kings. "Don't you know that first-order predicate logic is enough to build a world upon?" the Platonist would say in 1920. Or, to give an example from economic rhetoric, "Don't you know that market capitalism is optimal, according to this blackboard proof?" Or, "Don't you know that capitalism labors under contradictions?" Such sneers have been presented as demonstrative, but in each case the so-called demonstration has been chiefly an excuse not to argue on all the grounds that persuade reasonable people.

To this the Eleatic Stranger will say, what else is scientific and philosophical argument of the demonstrative sort but such an account of its own argument?

He is again mistaken. One cost of the contempt for rhetoric among philosophers since Plato has been a naïveté about how they as philosophers argue, their rhetoric at home. (Plato was obsessed with the arguments of the rhetoricians, refuting them by his own lights at length. It does not occur to Plato's philosophical readers that arguments so troubling to the Master might warrant more than a moment of thought.) Some philosophers have tried to become self-conscious about philosophical rhetoric, but not many. As I have pointed out, the later Wittgenstein is an important example to the contrary, but his lead was not much followed (see, however, Warner 1989; Romano 1989; Lang 1990). The genre does not appear to have high status in philosophy, being associated with meta-philosophy rather than Doing Philosophy. The same American philosopher who told me that he did not read Hegel or much else in the history of the discipline explained: "I had to choose between reading *about* it or *doing* it." Economists have a similar attitude towards methodology and the history of thought (as the intellectual history of economics is called). They don't know much about rhetoric but they know what they like.

The Stranger will say in vexation: but this Rhetoric speaks of mere form, not the substance of the arguments.

A literary criticism whose only categories are Form and Substance is a poor thing, as we have seen. Humans convey substance, short of mental telepathy, through the details of form. They have no choice but to use language to make their arguments. In using language with intent to alter another human's thought they are "using rhetoric."

The most abstract argument uses rhetoric for working purposes, as when Euclid called the proposition that parallel lines do not meet a "definition" (*horos*) instead of a "postulate" (*aitêma*) expressing with the usual Greek deftness a shadow of a doubt (Bronowski 1978, p. 71; Euclid, pp. 440, 442). The plainest of styles is itself a rhetoric of plain speaking. The historian Allan Nevins asserted that Lincoln "was the *least rhetorical of speakers*, caring nothing for mere art, and everything for simplicity, directness, lucidity and honesty" (Nevins 1940, p. xxiii, my italics). Yet in supporting such a naïve assertion he had necessarily to contradict it, since there is no such thing as a non-rhetorical style. In Lincoln's writing, said Nevins, "the vocabulary and phrasing he had drawn from Shakespeare, the Bible and Blackstone were sufficient clothing for his honest thoughts." But the level of a writer's style is a rhetorical choice, which changes how readers think of the writer and his thoughts. "A few lines of homely diction" from a speech analyzing slavery in 1845 were "as lucid as a Euclidian demonstration" (p. xxiii). But again a choice of "homely diction" by a backwoods poet-lawyer is no accident; and the ancient rhetorical device of claiming to demonstrate a truth of the world from a truth of definition is no less rhetorical than Lincoln's frequent use of proverbs and metaphors. Most of all, said Nevins, Lincoln "thought always of the minds of his auditors and readers" (p. xxiii). But the master question of rhetoric is this very question of the audience intended. Lincoln was a master rhetorician. A later historian of the poet president has examined "How Lincoln Won the

War with Metaphors." During Lincoln's New England tour in the late winter of 1860 "a professor of rhetoric at Yale was so taken with Lincoln's speech that he followed him to another town to hear him speak again and then gave a lecture on Lincoln's techniques to his class" (McPherson 1985 [1991], p. 103).

But how, says the Stranger, can we protect ourselves from merely plausible arguments, not True? It is the oldest objection that, as the Muses boasted to Hesiod, "we know how to speak many false things as though they were true."

One answer, a weak one but not to be spurned, is suggested by the parallel question: how can we protect ourselves against evil philosophy or, for that matter, evil uses of the multiplication table? Racial philosophy is a case in point. I have argued that there does not appear to be a demarcation criterion convenient for a 3″ × 5″ card that would separate as though by machine the bad philosophy that leads to death camps from the good philosophy that leads to Trinity College. There is no demarcation *within arithmetic* which tells the uses of the multiplication table that are bad or good.

Aristotle speaks to the point in his *Rhetoric*: "And if it is argued that great harm can be done by unjustly using such power of words, this objection applies to all good things except for virtue [*kata panton tôn agathôn plên aretês*], and most of all to the most useful things" (*Rhet*. I. I. 13, Kennedy translation). Aristotle then himself supplies the ethical standards in the *Nicomachean Ethics*, not summarizable on the Methodologist's 3″ × 5″ card.

We can protect ourselves by raising up those *good* people skilled in speaking. The protection from evil in science and other human affairs is not theory, whether philosophical or rhetorical, but education and ethics, matters of practice (cf. Fish 1989). Method-talk is the jurisprudence of science, establishing punishments and rewards. But as Warren Hagstrom observed, "whenever strong commitment to values are expected [in the scientist], the rational calculation of punishments and rewards is regarded as an improper basis for making decisions" (Hagstrom 1965 [1982], p. 30; cf. McCloskey 1992c). The skilled physicist can lie about the experiment if he is a bad man, no matter what Method he claims, and it can be advantageous in a rational calculation. But he must not, if he is a good man.

In the uproar about cold fusion, as I have noted, the bad young men of physics were willing to use any device of rhetoric to punish Pons and Fleischman. Replication was the least of the physicists' weapons. Admittedly, the principals had made it difficult, though difficulty of replication is more usual at the scientific frontier than the critics averred. A regional bias, for instance, showed through in the rhetoric of the critics, coasties all. One physicist from the California Institute of Technology said cleverly for the TV cameras that he would believe the replications when they came from a university without a good football team. Another young physicist, from Yale, and himself given ready access to the columns of *The New York Times*, complained bitterly about the University of Utah's unscientific access to the media. Eugene Mallove, a science writer in Massachusetts Institute of Technology's news office, wrote a book in 1991 critical of the treatment of cold fusion researchers (he divides his acknowledgments at "the East Coast of the United States," p. xvii). According to a report in *The Chronicle of Higher Education*, Mallove was then made the object of censorship on the MIT campus. *Viri mali dicendi periti.*

The literary theorist and teacher of writing Richard Lanham, however, has called the good-man-skilled-at-speaking the "Weak Defense" of rhetoric, and has proposed another and stronger one. He uses the notion of a "toggle," that is, a switch in a canned program that allows one to move from, say, looking at a stripped-down version of a text on a screen to looking at a fully formatted version. The age of rhetoric before 1620 and the age of key-boarding after 1980, Lanham argues, both elevate toggling to the master art. In an earlier book he had spoken of Castiglione's glorification in *The Book of the Courtier* (*Il Cortegiano* 1528) of *sprezzatura*, the art of the gentleman, "the art of concealing art, of unaffected affectation" (Lanham 1976, p. 150). He quotes the American pragmatist George Herbert Mead on the multiple roles played by graceful living in the world: "It is the social process itself that is responsible for the appearance of the self; it is not there as a self apart from this type of experience. A multiple personality is in a certain sense normal" (Mead 1934, quoted in Lanham 1976, p. 152). In being a self, being a gentleperson, being a citizen, argues Lanham, "the same technique is required – holding opposite worlds in the mind at once" (1976, p. 154), and an attitude that "oscillates from realism to idealism and back again" (Lanham 1974, p. 39). You must know that the President's inaugural address is merely a speech, and note its figures, at the same time that you grasp its values, for what they are worth. To be unable to toggle between the two knowings is to be either a cynic or a fool.

In his recent work Lanham contrasts the rhetorical looking *at* the words with the philosophical looking *through*. The *sprezzaturatore*, the person skilled at speaking, can toggle between the two, and that is what a rhetorical education offers:

> The rhetorical paideia did not resolve the struggle [between form and substance], or simply teach the rhetorical side of it, but built the debate into Western education as its central operating principle. . . . Rhetorical man was a dramatic game-player but he was always claiming that the ground he presently stood upon was more than a stage. Rhetoric's central decorum enshrined just this bistable oscill-ation [i.e. toggling] . . . It thus represents not a nihilistic repudiation of the Western intellectual tradition but a self-conscious return to it.
>
> Lanham 1992, p. 47

In a comment on my work, Lanham explains how the Strong Defense arises out of all of this:

> [McCloskey's] stated defense is the weak one: "Rhetoric is merely a tool, no bad thing in itself." . . . But what he succeeds in doing, with his . . .close readings of the rhetoric of economics in action, is to suggest the Strong Defense we began to see emerging with [the Chicago Aristotelian Richard] McKeon. To read economics as McCloskey suggests is always to be toggling between looking at the prose and through it, reading it "rhetorically" and reading it "philosophically," and this toggling attitude toward utterance is what the rhetorical paideia was after all along. Train someone in it and, according to Quintilian's way of thinking, you have trained that person to be virtuous.
>
> Lanham, forthcoming, ch. 7, p. 22

Lanham argues persuasively that someone educated without the toggle, so to speak, is not only not automatically a good person (though skilled at speaking) but is likely to be bad. Being educated in rhetoric, acquiring the skill in speaking, is usually to acquire the toggle. The traditional case for traveling abroad or meeting many sorts of people or learning a second language fluently is that it throws light on life at home. You can see two sides. You are tolerant, without by any means abandoning the responsibility to choose.

The argument can be made more precise, and has been, economi-cally speaking. Two views allow one to toggle. Toggling allows one to see that one's view is a view. Monists are likely at this point to scream "relativism" and call for the guards. But being able to toggle from view to view does not imply indifference between the views. It is like the index-number problem in economics, which is that you can evaluate the standard of living in America and India using either the point of view of American prices (cheap cars, expensive servants) or of Indian prices (expensive cars, cheap servants). Knowing that there are two sets of prices at which one might evaluate the difference does not paralyze thought or lead to nihilism. On the contrary, it is necessary for wisdom. It is *sprezzatura*. Pick one view, know what you're doing, and from time to time, for the hell of it, toggle.

It can also be made more precise, and has been, psychologically speaking. The American psychologist James J. Gibson showed by pressing cookie cutters onto the hands of subjects and asking them what shape they felt that perception depends on movement, contrast, toggling, *sprezzatura*, index numbers, the ability to try out different perspectives. Rom Harré summarizes the experiments: "A subject held in a rigid frame, and so in a completely passive state, not only did not perceive the world as a world of things, but after a short time stopped perceiving anything at all" (Harré 1981 [1983], p. 135). Gibson's experiments influenced E. H. Gombrich's *Art and Illusion: A Study in the Psychology of Pictorial Representation* (1960 [1971]) – who pointed out that the notion is in fact ancient, as in Pliny: "the mind is the real instrument of sight and observation" (quoted in Gombrich 1960 [1971], p. 15). "A white hankerchief in the shade" of a painting, Gombrich notes, "may be objectively darker than a lump of coal in the sunshine. We rarely confuse the one with the other because the coal will on the whole be the blackest patch in our field of vision, the hankerchief the whitest" (Gombrich 1960 [1971], p. 52). "It is the 'more' or 'less' that counts, the relationship between the expected and the unexpected" (p. 60), discernible only by toggling.

Lanham's Strong Defense of rhetoric is then, to borrow some terms from political philosophy, that rhetoric provides procedural rather than end-state justice. Rhetoric, as against epistemology, does not provide conclusions; it provides methods or, better, stagings, lights, makeup, gestures to be used in a drama, in the courtroom or the classroom or the assembly. The best defense we have is the ability to see through the staging of the Nuremberg Rally or the doctoring of spin. Rhetorical self-consciousness – the ability to toggle between looking at and looking through a text, as Lanham puts it – is the best defense we have yet devised for what we value. It's a shabby thing by the standard of the Platonic forms or natural right, I admit, with their lovely if blinding uniformity of light. But it's all we've got. Like democracy, which it defends, rhetoric is the worst form of wisdom, except those others that have been tried from time to time.

In other words, if we break argument into rhetoric and dialectic (here even solider Aristotle erred), the dialectic takes immediately a falsely superior position. The toggle is always Off. The move is assured by the long and lunatic fascination with certitude since the Pythagoreans showed by force of reason that not all numbers are rational. The actual human argument of law courts is downgraded to mere persuasion or politics or advertising or teaching or something else without the dignity of Truth Saying. The actual human argument of scientific laboratories and blackboards is elevated to Scientific Method, beyond rhetorical scrutiny. (It is one reason for the Law of Academic Status: the most useful teaching, such as freshman English or education, has the lowest status.) Philosophers and scientists, believing themselves in possession of certitude, never requiring a toggle, are encouraged to sneer; planners and politicians, believing themselves in sight of utopia, are encouraged to ordain. It is not an encouragement they need.

chapter 21

Anti-post-pre-metamodernism: the Coats/McPherson/Friedman

A. W. Coats, an eminent student of economic thought, has properly complained that *The Rhetoric of Economics* did not deal adequately with economic methodologists now writing (his objections on this count and others were expressed in the *Eastern Economic Journal* symposium [1987], in a short comment with Bruce Caldwell [1984], and in his paper in the volume edited by Klamer and others in 1988). I have no excuse but exhaustion, from trying to avoid error in too many fields at once. Writing the book required breadth I do not possess, and something had to go; the opportunity cost of other reading was a close study of work by recent economic methodologists, including his own work. It is a failure of energy that I have since had reason to regret, for I could have learned much from the conventional Methodologists, and the oversight has angered them deeply. No scholar is forgiven for not citing another, and I have tried to make amends in this book by responding to every interlocutor, and reading every book. But of course I have failed again.

Coats would agree, however, that economic method in practice does not follow what the most enlightened economic methodologists are presently thinking. My reading of the economic methodologists since finishing the book suggests that they are natural allies of a rhetorical approach. (That some of them have at first been unfriendly to rhetoric can be attributed to my failure to treat the existing methodological literature with proper respect and to their failure to distinguish between what is good for philosophy and what is good for economics. I believe they will start understanding soon; some have already.)

Coats alludes to the same sociologists of science I discussed in chapter 8 above, where I noted Coats' suggestion that we economists take them more seriously. The sociologists have begun to agree that a rhetoric of science overlaps with a sociology of science. A conference on the matter was held at Iowa in 1987, under the auspices of the Russell Sage foundation, bringing Harry Collins, Trevor Pinch, Barry Barnes, Malcolm Ashmore, and others across from Britain. In 1991 another conference was held, this time in Blacksburg, Virginia, with more expressions of mutual esteem. So Coats and I are closer than he thinks.

Coats calls the Methodology preached by non-philosophical economists "the crude misuse . . . of 'modernist' claims," and says that it is "largely a dead horse." True, but as I have said it has been remade into a zombie horse, which can still deliver vicious kicks. How else would one explain the fetish for econometric evidence in the debate over rational expectations? Or the papers with results "consistent with" otherwise ridiculous hypotheses? Or the employment prospects of economists who do not follow the Methodological party line? Get rid of the zombie. Everyone says so. Robert Solow and Wassily Leontief and Charles Kindleberger and the late Harry Johnson and a lengthening list of our elders agree with Coats and me that the zombie must somehow be disposed of.

But Coats and I do not agree on everything. In particular, Coats still thinks that Science is to be demarcated. Against this view, as Alan Randall writes, is the empirical fact: we have found "no real demarcation between science and other forms of directed and scholarly inquiry . . . A meaningful new methodology must (among other things) explain, within a common framework, the empirical sciences, the humanities and the learned professions. Economics is at once an exemplar of all three and, hence, perhaps an ideal focus for exploratory initiatives to develop a new methodology" (Randall 1990, p. 267). Those like Coats who have strongly and self-consciously identified with the program of demarcating science from the rest of life have a hard time understanding what the rhetorical turn is about.

Coats then is a conservative; I am a postmodernist, or as I prefer, metamodernist. His views seem to be similar to those of Michael McPherson, already mentioned in connection with his piece with Hausman, who also cannot see why a broad definition of rhetoric and of science is necessary, and so McPherson will be included as the Platonic character Menexenus to Coats' Ctesippus in the following dialogue. At the conference on the rhetoric of economics at Wellesley College in 1986 Ctesippus gave a paper, published in the conference volume just mentioned (Klamer, Solow, and McCloskey 1988), from which some of his lines are taken. A version of the dialogue was circulated at the conference. (Ctesippus' nickname is "Bob.")

> *I was walking straight from the Academy to the Lyceum, by the road which skirts the outside of the walls, and had reached the little gate that leads to the spring of Hermes the All-Seeing, when I chanced there upon Ctesippus and Menexenus walking together. Ctesippus looked displeased.*

Ctesippus: Greetings, oh chief propagandist for economic rhetoric.

McCloskey: Hello, Menexenus. Hi, Bob.

Ctesippus: Hurrumph.

McCloskey: Bob, you appear to be in a foul mood this morning.

Ctesippus: The seemingly contradictory characterizations that abound in your recent writings have that effect on me. It is by no means clear to me whether they represent merely rhetorical flourishes or are meant to have substantive significance.

McCloskey: But isn't the main point that the ancient word "rhetoric" doesn't mean just "ornament"? And hasn't the distinction between "rhetoric" and "substance" been under attack for quite some time, by among many others Austin (J. L.; and by Austen, Jane, and your teacher of writing, for that matter)?

Ctesippus: There you go again, with that practice of blurring the distinction between familiar and useful categories.

McCloskey: I agree that the categories "style" and "substance" are familiar. But the point at issue was their usefulness. One would not want to prejudge the point before talking about it, would one?

Ctesippus: Humphh. Still, there are some shocking things in your writings. You say, "The worst academic sin is not to be illogical or badly informed." You believe that illogicality and ignorance are subordinate matters. I urge you to read T. W. Hutchison, who has many fine passages attacking ignorance.

McCloskey: My word, you *are* in a nasty mood today. Let's see: academic sins; and ignorance. Ah, I see the page you are quoting. Oh, look: you left off the ending of the sentence. Doesn't it seem less shocking if you add " . . . but to exhibit a cynical disregard for the norms of scholarly conversation"? The misquoted sentence suggests that I am advocating illogicality and ignorance, a strange position for a teacher of the young to take. But in truth I'm merely placing ignorance and illogicality, which can be reasonably easily fixed by teaching, in a category of sin less serious than moral badness, which I imagine you would agree is harder to fix. Indeed, your quoting the first half of the sentence without the second, which changes its meaning for bad rhetorical purposes, illustrates the point the sentence makes.

Ctesippus: Harrumph! Gak! Another one of your flippant and dismissive responses!

McCloskey: Isn't the flippancy on the other foot? Isn't it dismissively flippant to criticize a tradition without attempting to understand it, a tradition represented nowadays and for 2,500 years in large chunks of the culture? You philosophers of science and fellow travelers sometimes seem to me professionally ignorant. None of you have read any of the rhetorical studies you scorn, even in English – such as George A. Kennedy, *New Testament Interpretation through Rhetorical Criticism* (1984). Philosopher, cure thy ignorance.

Ctesippus: I can't follow you. Such works are demarcated to be outside of Science. It is a matter for debate how far the techniques of literary criticism, which come from the non-Scientific half of the culture, are appropriate to a Scientific subject.

McCloskey: Yes, it is a matter for debate, the one we're having. Calling it a "matter for debate" doesn't end a debate, does it? You like to end debates before they are begun, a common rhetorical device among modernists. That economic morality, for example, is "debatable" is supposed in modernist circles to end moral debate in economics. That's why we've spent fifty years in welfare economics chasing uncontroversial moral doctrines to no end instead of overcoming our ignorance about ethical thinking.

Ctesippus: Be that as it may, the debate about literature and Science is ended. Bazerman has demonstrated the inappropriateness of literary critical methods and techniques to the social and natural Scientists' objectives.

McCloskey: That is a bizarre reading of Charles Bazerman. You can't have spent much time with his writings. Bazerman is an English-professor friend of mine whose purpose is to read the scientific paper from the seventeenth century to the present as a literary text, with exactly those literary critical methods. See for example his two books published in the series I co-edit with the University of Wisconsin Press,

Shaping Written Knowledge: The Genre and Activity of the Experimental Article in Science (1988) and the book edited by him, *Textual Dynamics of the Professions,* with articles, among others, on Spencer, Huxley, and Dewey by J. P. Zappen, molecular biology by Greg Myers, sociology by Robert Schwegler and Linda Shamoon, and Priestley's chemistry by Bazerman himself.

Ctesippus: Hummph. That's a matter for debate. Another disconcerting feature of your approach is the focus on "conversation" and "talk" among economists and other inquirers, rather than the public record. Taken literally, this would eliminate the bulk of the evidence on which philosophers, historians, and sociologists of science have hitherto based their researches.

McCloskey: That is a bizarre reading of McCloskey, a history professor whose purpose is to read economic papers as literary texts. Isn't it clear that Arjo Klamer and I use "conversation" to mean more than literal conversation? Do invisible colleges have football teams and heating plants? I am put in mind of Bentham, who said that he could tell poetry from prose only by the ragged margins.

Ctesippus: Well, this rhetorical stuff touches on a less rich repertoire of issues than does recent sociology of science.

McCloskey: Maybe it does: I don't see much basis for disagreement between a rhetorical approach and the Strong Program in the sociology of science, for which see chapter 8 above. If there's a distinction it's pretty fine. Both demystify the notion of Science as a uniquely blest and superhuman activity. The one brings the intellectual traditions of sociology to the task; the other brings the intellectual traditions of the humanities since the Greeks.

Ctesippus: There you go again, blurring traditional distinctions.

McCloskey: Traditionalist, learn thy tradition. The sociologists agree with me. Your position seems to contain a nervous self-contradiction: you argue when attacking rhetoric that Science is a special way of producing Knowledge (I want you to notice the Rortian capitals here); but you affirm when advocating sociology of knowledge that science on the ground is a system of human discourse similar to other social systems. That seems to be what the fellow Whitley you cite is arguing (although more in a Mertonian, structural-functionalist way than would fit smoothly with the rhetorical work of

Bloor, Collins, Mulkay, Ashmore, and Pinch; though Robert Merton in fact told me recently that even he is a social constructionist). Protagoras of Abdera and a long line of students of discourse after him argued in the same way. That's not to devalue the British work, merely to welcome it into a longer and wider conversation. Wouldn't most of your blasts against rhetoric do damage to the strong program, too, a program you claim to support?

Ctesippus: Well, I suppose so. I don't know. I merely advocate institutional studies of economics.

McCloskey: Sure: that's fine. But I take it that you would want to agree with the British sociologists (and now Robert Merton) that institutions are themselves a collection of conversations.

Ctesippus: Not at all!

McCloskey: Then you *don't* agree with the strong program, which says precisely that?

Ctesippus: Gak! [*He turns angrily away.*]

Menexenus: Let me try, Bob. Obviously, there are specific universal criteria for identifying scientific practice.

McCloskey: I don't know why you should think there were. Mary Hesse doesn't think there are. Thomas Kuhn doesn't think there are. Mary Douglas doesn't think there are.

Menexenus: Plato thought so, and many philosophers since then.

McCloskey: True: it is the assumption of the project of epistemology since Plato. When you say that you have a "universal" formula for assessing the specific scientific practices of economics you mean "assess with respect to Truth."

Menexenus: Of course.

McCloskey: I say that philosophers, who are by definition assessors outside the special sciences, have not come up with anything decisive to say about Truth in 2,500 years of trying. And I say that truth, small t, is mainly the business of scientists themselves. The morality of the discourse is another matter, of course.

Menexenus: Morality? Morality is just a matter of opinion.

McCloskey: No. Since we are all practiced in morality, we can evaluate psychologists who tell fibs about their IQ data on identical twins or economists who slide by the distributional consequences of their policy recommendations. But we cannot evaluate much of the other small-t truths of their discourse.

Menexenus: Your problem is that you believe in Anything Goes. Butos says so. Blaug says so. I say so.

McCloskey: To repeat, McCloskey says: I didn't say so.

Menexenus: But you are in favor of whatever gains the assent of the profession.

McCloskey: No, of course not. What made you think that? There's a difference between insisting on serious talk about a point of economic argument on the one hand and taking an undiscussed majority vote on the other. You and Mark Blaug share a theory of politics as my blood against thine, shoot it out or vote it out, silently. I believe on the contrary that actual and scientific politics is a matter of how we talk. *Of course* there is a "further standard to appeal to" – the one you and I use daily: "Has this person brought forward all the arguments pro and con, thoughtfully, honestly, intelligently? All the stories that bear on the point? All the math? All the proffered metaphors? All the authorities, cited and justified? All the appeals to my understanding? In the terminology of the Irangate hearings, have we gotten 'the whole story'? If so, *now* what do I think?"

Menexenus: But how do you know if an argument is good?

McCloskey: I've told you; and what is more, you already know, in fields in which you are accustomed to seriously arguing. You and the others are claiming that positivism or some other 3" × 5" card offers "standards" of argument. I realize that it is annoying for me to keep insisting that people do at least a little reading in literary criticism. But on this very point read Stanley Fish, "Demonstration vs. Persuasion: Two Models of Critical Activity," pp. 322-328 in *Is There a Text in This Class?* (1980) or Fish's later restatement in *Doing What Comes Naturally* (1989), *passim*, for example, on the claim that there is "a standard or set of standards that operates independently of the institutional circumstances . . . My thesis is, first of all, that there is no such standard (which is not the same as saying their is no standard) and, second, that while we may, as a point of piety, invoke it as an ideal, in fact we violate it all the time by practices that are at once routine and obligatory" (Fish 1989, p. 164); or "I am not saying that 'anything goes,' that interpreters of the Eighth Amendment (or Virgil's *Eclogues*) are presented with a 'blank check' . . . ; only that insofar as the filling in of the check is constrained (and it always will be) . . . the constraints will inhere not in the language of the text (statute or poem) or in the context (unproblematically conceived ... as a 'higher' and self-declaring text) ... but by the cultural assumptions within which both texts and contexts take shape for situated agents" (Fish 1989, p. 300). I agree. To have *no* standards would obviously be self-contradictory, an impossibility, as you say.

Menexenus: Just as I said in my review of your 1985 book (McPherson 1987).

McCloskey: But the book is a disquisition precisely on what the standards should be. The standards are not some majority vote, another position the review attributes to me. They are the outcome of a way of scholarly life ("the cultural assumptions within which both texts and contexts take shape for situated agents"), which I call obeying the *Sprachethik*: that is to say, merely, Sit Down and Reason Together.

Menexenus: But in your chapters attacking statistical significance you contradict yourself, offering standards, explicitly rejecting the standard advanced elsewhere. That other standard is merely Anything Goes, or Majority Rule, whichever comes first.

McCloskey: Try to listen to what I am saying. The standard is open, reasonable, fair, patient, *sprachethiklich* conversation, as I say. Early in the book such a standard is contrasted with judgments *ex cathedra* from a metaphysics. When the conversation is not free, when an unexamined rhetoric makes it a poor conversation, when compulsory metaphysics substitutes for reasoned discourse, I have no scruples about pointing it out. Statistical significance, for example, is unargued. I am for persuasive arguments.

Menexenus: I am unpersuaded.

McCloskey: That statistical significance is grossly misused in economics?

Menexenus: No, you have persuaded me and quite a few economists of that. I am unpersuaded that you are free of contradiction of practicing Methodology when arguing against Methodology.

McCloskey: You have not noticed the big-M, little-m distinction. Try the following experiment. In the next econometrics-using seminar you attend try to make my criticism of statistical significance, which you and anyone else who has allowed the argument to pass through their frontal lobes agree with, and notice what reaction you get. Go ahead.

Notice what happens to blood pressures. Notice especially that the economists will not answer it, though I've never known a statistician to disagree with it: in fact they've been saying it for seventy years.

Menexenus:　But then you believe in a Methodology.

McCloskey:　No, not in your sense: that's the point of the experiment. No Methodology tells us about statistical significance. Only the conversation of statisticians and empirical workers does, small-m methodology. But the nasty reaction you will get from the thoughtless comes from Methodology. Calling for *some* argument, as I do, is not the same thing as calling for argument based on this or that Metaphysics. As Fish put it, saying that there is no standard independent of the institutions is not the same as saying there is no standard. Mine (and Fish's and Rorty's and Polanyi's and Wittgenstein Mark II's and Dewey's and Cicero's and Aristotle's and Protagoras') is a *procedural* methodology, not a substantive one. It is what Karl Popper would have advocated if he could have fully escaped from Vienna (he could not because his main ideas reacted to the Vienna Circle, and so retained the fond notion of leaping to a higher realm of Truth). It is what Socrates did advocate, so far as one can see him through the eyes of his brightest student, a student in favor of substantive Methodology. By "substantive Methodology" I mean those middle-level precepts, philosophically inspired, on which I heap such scorn in *The Rhetoric of Economics*: "Only math gives certitude" or "History is dialectic." I went too far in heaping scorn (one usually does). The metaphysical propositions of substantive Methodology are not literally meaningless: this would be to fall into positivist ranting. They are arguments, too. What I meant to convey, and said in those chapters, is that there's no very good reason to accord them *special* weight in assessing science. As the social psychologist Donald Campbell, a most insightful man, puts it, "the ideology and norms of science are not clearly distinguished from 'scientific method.' Scientific method is also to be seen as a product of cultural-evolutionary processes on the part of a bounded belief-transmitting subsociety of many generations . . . It is convenient to regard the ideology and practice of cooperative truth seeking as coming first and method [coming second]

as a rationalized summary of successful usage in the community" (D.T. Campbell 1986, p. 120).

Menexenus: I'm beginning to doubt that my point that you do
Methodology while attacking Methodology is right.

McCloskey: As well you might. Since Methodology is usually
thought of as what I'm calling here "substantive," it's
wrong to say I'm doing it. It's no middle-level Methodology
that inspires my assaults on statistical significance. It's
low-brow recognition that the way it is used does not match
the urn-drawing theory on which it claims to be based,
combined with a high-level annoyance that people who
know this are such peasants in their *Sprachethik* that they
will not say it out loud. The leaders of econometrics have
behaved badly, with a handful of honorable exceptions
(Arthur S. Goldberger 1991, for example; or see Arrow
[1959], Tullock [1959], Ohta and Griliches [1976], Feige
[1975], Leamer [1978 1983], Lovell [1983], Mayer [1975],
Denton [1988]). There's no central planning of science, no
claim – the claim characteristic of Methodology – that I
know from some abstract principle that this or that research
strategy would be progressive. I just say "Do you really
mean to use statistical significance this way? Do you think
your argument holds up?" Or at the higher level, "Do you
have some explanation why you as an econometrician can
know perfectly well that statistical significance is not the
same as scientific significance, and yet can go on letting
your students do the wrong thing?" So I think you've not
grasped the point of the book. The normative point of the
book is that economics needs to regain a scholarly life,
which I believe can be improved by rhetorical self-
consciousness. And the positive point is the scholarly life,
too: namely, that a rhetorical life in scholarship is inevit-
able, and can be detected in the most anti-rhetorical
economics.

Menexenus: Well, you were not very clear.

McCloskey: Authors always think they are perfectly clear – that's
why complaints about how other people read one's arguments so often take the form of "For God's sake, what a
stupid way to take my words!" As I've said in an earlier
chapter, we don't have sensible maps of misreading in
economics, and in consequence become vicious in disagreement (the phenomenon makes my main point: that

until we understand our rhetoric, our *Sprachethik* is going to be mixed up and unhelpful).

Menexenus: Come to the point.

McCloskey: I *know* I was unclear. How? Because you, Mark Blaug, Bruce Caldwell, Neil de Marchi, Bob Coats, Paul Roth, Kevin Hoover, Roger Backhouse, Riccardo Bellofiore, and Daniel Hausman miss the point, sometimes by miles and miles. If only one of you did, I could plausibly argue that it was a personal failing of that person. But you all miss it, *in exactly the same way*. So it's a failure of mine, not yours.

Menexenus: Precisely my point.

McCloskey: Wait a minute. As I've also said, *No non-Methodologist has misread the book*. The non-Methodologists all see that the point is the literary criticism of science, as a way of reading economics. No Methodologist can grasp the point. That's odd. Something's up.

Menexenus: What do you have in mind?

McCloskey: The economistic explanation would be that the Methodologists are worried about their jobs, "trade-union bloody-mindedness" as I called it in the last chapter. I can't take such a proposition seriously, though economists like to make jokes of this sort about self interest. Anyway, it would be silly to regard a new way of reading economic texts as a *threat* to the study of economic thinking. On the contrary, the more techniques the better.

Menexenus: I agree. What, then?

McCloskey: A more believable but still cynical explanation is that you all speak to each other, and have arrived at a common reading of McCloskey. Fair enough. I suppose that's possible, but not very powerful. The thinkers involved are too independent-minded to make mere cliquishness the explanation.

Menexenus: Naturally.

McCloskey: So here's the remaining explanation: The education in the conventional conversation of a narrow band of philosophers makes it extremely difficult for philosophically interested economists to see the literary character of economics. The Methodologists are so deep in modernism that they see "literary" as some sort of put-down. They cannot see a new idea because the old ones get in the way.

Menexenus: As Schopenhauer said a while ago.

McCloskey: You are catching on. I have mixed feelings about the experience of being so strangely misread by the economic philosophers. I'm hardened to being attacked for positions I *do* hold ("Dammit, you're so bloody *neoclassical*"; or "Gosh, why in your economic history are you so *quantitative?*"). But it's a new and irritating experience to be attacked for positions I would never hold and have worked against for decades ("Ah, I see: you're against empirical work"; or "Ah, I see: you are in favor of whatever succeeds in getting published in economics, regardless of whether it has been subject to an open and serious conversation").

Ctesippus [who has long been silent]:   It's your own fault for saying such strange things, which do not appear anywhere in the works of the two philosophers of science and the one sociologist of science I agree with. Not anywhere.

McCloskey: Yes, that's true, my dear Ctesippus. On the other hand, the misunderstanding has a curious advantage, namely, that I can make a simple point, which even I can hold in my head, and yet acquire a spurious reputation for profundity: briefly, "Economists in fact argue on wider grounds than certain philosophies would permit."

Ctesippus: Your literary talk is an invitation to the abyss. It is all most unScientific.

McCloskey: No, not in the non-English meaning of "scientific."

Ctesippus: You confuse me.

McCloskey: That is not my intent. I wish merely to understand by conversing.

Ctesippus: I don't know what to say.

McCloskey: I do not mean to drive you to silence, but to the truth. We are all ignorant together, in Plato's Cave.

Ctesippus: Aaach! Your imitation of Socrates is driving me mad. Or maybe it's an imitation of Feyerabend and the other postmodern nut cases. [*Turns to go.*] Whatever it is I have business in Durham.

McCloskey: Remember that Socrates was a great sophist (see Kerferd 1981, e.g. 55-57), or even a postmodern nut case. We must discuss this further, as it is a serious matter: *Ouden gar oimai tosouton kakon eivai anthrôpô, hoson doxa pseudês peri ôn tungchanei nun hémin ho logos ôn* (*Gorgias* 458B).

Ctesippus: [*As he strides away*] For Lord's sake!

McCloskey: [*Shouting at the receding figure of Ctesippus*] That is, "For I consider that a man cannot suffer any evil so great as a false opinion on the subjects of our actual argument."

What appears to be frightening the conventional Methodologists is postmodernism, about which they have read most terrifyingly in the pages of *The New York Times*. In the introduction to a recent issue of the *Critical Review* to which I contributed, its editor, Jeffrey Friedman, makes the terror plain and rails against it (Friedman 1991).

Yet whatever you think you have learned about it from *The Times*, postmodernism is mainly not from France. It is mainly not leftwing. It is mainly not deconstruction. It is mainly not about the Crisis of Reason or the Exhaustion of the Enlightenment Project or other Franco-German anxieties. On the contrary, it is what its name says: a suggestion that we go beyond the formulas of rigid modernism. Perhaps "metamodernism" would better convey what people like Richard Rorty or Stanley Fish, or Gary Madison, Calvin Schrag, and me in that issue of the *Critical Review*, are talking about.

Jeffrey Friedman is unwise to try to hitch his political program, of which I approve (I serve on the editorial board of the *Critical Review*), to the rigidities of architectural modernism in the style of the Vienna Circle, the modernist movement in architecture, and anglophone analytic philosophy around 1955. His and my minimal statism rests easier, I would suggest, with Gary Madison's "small-t truth" or "intersubjectivity," Calvin Schrag's "transversal rationality," and my "conjectivity." They all mean what we know together, and replace the three-century run of objective-subjective. They are metamodern attempts to get away from the $3'' \times 5''$-card epistemology that has dominated the intellectual world since 1920. They are not rejections of reason. On the contrary, they ask that after learning what we can from modernism we now go back to examining all the reasons.

Friedman asks: "without the discipline imposed by a putatively objective, non-metaphorical reality, is not each interpretive community licensed to convert its instincts into sacred cows on the ground that there is no higher standard of truth than whatever is arbitrarily self-imposed?" (J. Friedman 1991).

Briefly, no: to admit that our only standard is our interpretive community is not to surrender to *arbitrary* standards, but to standards. There are no timeless standards outside those of an interpretive community. As Aristotle put the point, "Since the persuasive is persuasive to someone . . . rhetoric theorize[s] . . . about what seems true to people of a certain sort, as is also true with dialectic" (*Rhet.*, I II. 11; 1356b).

In my article in *Critical Review* (McCloskey 1991c, a discussion of three books on law and literature) I mentioned the attack on Critical Legal Studies by Stanley Fish in *Doing What Comes Naturally* (1989).

Fish is well known for his relativism and postmodernism and trendy leftism. Why then does he not thrill to the late-1960s tactics of Critical Legal Studies? Because the Crits do not reach the standards of the interpretive community. Fish, the notorious constructivist, complains that for the Crits, "all of a sudden 'constructed' means 'fabricated' or 'made up'" (Fish 1989, p. 227). Fish is consistent and Fish is correct. "Rational debate," he says, "is always possible; not, however, because it is anchored in a reality outside it, but because it occurs in a history" (Fish 1989, p. 196). Yes. In Donald Campbell's words quoted just now, it is "cultural-evolutionary processes on the part of a bounded belief-transmitting subsociety of many generations" (Campbell 1986, p. 120). That a speech community must be addressed is a tighter, not a looser, constraint on what arguments are sustainable than the formula of modernism. Fish and Campbell and I believe that modernism, whether rationalist or irrationalist, has some screws loose. Metamodernists propose to tighten them up. The conservatives want to carry screwily on.

The other empirical problem with Friedman's modernism is that the "discipline" he mentions of "non-metaphoric reality" is phony. For one thing, since Mary Hesse's *Models and Analogies in Science* (1963), or for that matter Immanuel Kant, it has been hard to claim that scientists get along without metaphors. The philosopher Max Black wrote of metaphor "since philosophers . . . have so neglected the subject, I must get what help I can from the literary critics. They, at least, do not accept the commandment, 'Thou shalt not commit metaphor,' or assume that metaphor is incompatible with serious thought" (1962, p. 25).

For another, the "discipline" doesn't bite in practice. Modernists talk a lot about "discipline" and "rigor" and "compelling proof," in a vocabulary approaching the sado-masochistic, but when it gets down to the whips and chains they don't carry through. Any practitioner of a subject like economics under the sway of modernism knows in her heart that this is so, and can offer examples in practice. We can have a real discipline based on a serious relativism, a discipline admitting that we cannot achieve Truth but affirming that we can agree on truth. We cannot have an absolutist discipline, since we cannot ground it as it demands. The grounding is fake. So the discipline is fake, too. Unlike the real discipline of relativism, which demands we persuade each other, the fake discipline escapes in the end all demands.

Friedman asserts that interpretive communities must in practice act as though their standards were "transcendent." There's the "discipline." But only children and Platonists need transcendence. The children in *The Lord of the Flies* must worship absolutely the pig's, and Piggy's, head. Communities of adults, by contrast, have in practice no difficulty recognizing that their standards are not God's own, not transcendent and not ahistorical, while affirming that the standards are nonetheless worth enforcing.

Putnam says rightly "the time has come for a moratorium on the kind of ontological speculation that seeks to describe the Furniture of the Universe and to tell us what is Really There and what is Only a Human Projection, and for a moratorium on the kind of epistemological speculation that seeks to tell us the One Method by which all our beliefs can be appraised" (Putnam 1990, p. 118).

It is not the case empirically, as philosophical and political conservatives have always feared, that adults will descend into a war of all against all if they lose their faith in God or the divine right of kings or the synthetic a priori or some other principle of transcendence. The engineering standard for the height of road crowns is nowhere inscribed by the finger of God, and yet a contractor who fails to abide by it will accept that he needs to rebuild the road. The standard of replicability in biological experiment is not absolute, and cannot in principle be so. Yet the community of biologists can recognize conjectively, well enough for scientific purposes, when an experiment on oxidative phosphorylation has gone wrong (Mulkay 1985).

Friedman thinks that without a belief in transcendence we "would have no criteria of what counts as persuasive." Huh? Come again? Why exactly is that? He does not say. The argument he sketches is philosophical rather than empirical. But his assertion is self-contradictory even as philosophical argument. You can see it is by noting that it damages his own position as much as the position he is attacking. His words can be turned against himself: "by trying to achieve non-conjective Truth in God's eyes one tends to overlook one's own unarticulated, relative truths. To try to do away with theory is a recipe for bad theory." The anti-rhetoric of philosophy is, as I say, no more knock-down than the anti-philosophy of rhetoric. *Tu quoque.*

Gary Madison is quoted by Friedman as saying that modernism subscribes to a "Promethean illusion that by means of theory we can manipulate and control human affairs however we desire." Friedman calls this a "dubious reading of modern history," but again does not pause to say why. Yet Madison's description would satisfy empirically most members of a speech community who have lived through communism and anti-communism, Vietnam and the expansion of the modern state. Someone accurately described the illusion of modernism as the notion that we can in fact accomplish everything we rationally propose to do. With such a rationalism who needs *irrationalism*? And what else would you call such lunacy but a "Promethean illusion"? "All their doings were indeed without intelligent calculation until I showed them the rising of the stars, and the settings, hard to observe. And further I discovered to them numbering, pre-eminent among subtle devices . . . It was I who arranged all the ways of seercraft, and I first adjudged what things come verily true from dreams" (Aeschylus, *Prometheus Bound*, lines 452–461, 478). Prometheus might as well have been justifying a forecast from the social engineers of next year's interest rate. It is the Promethean, and modernist, illusion. It's why we must get on with the post-, or meta-, modern project, and must bring along with us somehow the terrified conservatives, mumbling their rosaries of "standards," "transcendence," and "discipline," those familiar and useful categories of modernist thought.

chapter 22

Splenetic rationalism, Austrian style

The Rhetoric of Economics has been reviewed by followers of the Austrian school four times to my knowledge, by Tom G. Palmer (1986-1987), by Peter J. Boettke (1988), by William Butos (1987, discussed above), and at much the greatest length by the philosopher Hans-Hermann Hoppe in the *Review of Austrian Economics* (1989). *If You're So Smart* (1990) was reviewed from an Austrian perspective by David Gordon (1991). The reviews by Palmer, Boettke, Butos, and Gordon were not as favorable as my mother would have written. But they engaged the work seriously, the most an author in these days of the paper blizzard can expect.

Among other things, they said that "rhetoric" was a characterization of economics favoring Austrian over conventional neoclassicism. I am beginning to think they are right, as can be seen in chapter 25 here, "The Economy as a Conversation." The neo-Austrian Don Lavoie has inaugurated a major alliance between economics and hermeneutics (the audience's side of rhetoric; Lavoie 1990a), and the authors in his book give impressive testimony to how an Austrian approach to rhetoric can reinvigorate economics.

To be sure, economists who attack the mainstream, such as these Austrians, tend to overlook the sweet currents of Real Keynesianism or Good Old Chicago, and take as being the whole of neoclassical economics the twiddling reported in the latest "theoretical" piece. A candid rhetoric would favor neoclassicals like Axel Leijonhufvud, Theodore Schultz, Robert Solow, James Buchanan, and the like over neo-neo-classicals who think that economics consists of Max Exp $U(X,Y)$ s.t. $k = k(X,Y)$. But the Austrians are right that a candid rhetoric would favor the more open kinds of Austrianism, too. Even

Gordon, who represents a more closed Austrianism and has difficulty understanding books outside his circle (he thinks for example that I adhere to the positivist criterion of meaning), understands very well that the main point is to read science in a literary way.

Hans-Hermann Hoppe's long piece, however, failed to engage the book, and in fact advocates a backward step. The Austrianism of Palmer, Boettke, or Butos (or of Kirzner, Lavoie, High, Rizzo, White, or Vaughn, to mention a few I am acquainted with), it seems to me as a sympathetic outsider, is different from Hoppe's. Hoppe's seems to deny at the outset the high valuation of discovery that is so central to Austrian thinking. Facts of the world beyond cloistered intuition or philosophies of science beyond Immanuel Kant do not seem to be available to Hoppe. Neither cloisters nor Kant are to be disdained, Lord knows. But discoveries from numerous entrepreneurs of intellect have taught us more, and perhaps it should be put to use. Even Max Exp $U(X,Y)$ has a thing or two worth using.

Hoppe's piece left I am sure a strange impression of the *The Rhetoric of Economics* in the minds of readers of *The Review of Austrian Economics* (a journal edited by Murray Rothbard since 1987; despite its inclusive title *The Review* is known in Austrian circles as carefully excluding all but Rothbard's views; Hoppe, for instance, is an academic colleague of Rothbard's). Like the other Methodologists, Hoppe has seized on the early and conventionally philosophical chapters, especially chapter 1. But he does not join the argument. His interest in the book flags after a few pages out of the first of the ten chapters.

Since chapter 1 with a couple of other slices was the bulk of an article published in 1983, I guess that Hoppe did once in 1983 cast his eye over the original article, with damage to his spleen, but has not found the time to read the book. This is my fault entirely: an author who cannot keep the reader's attention beyond the first half of the first chapter has no one to blame but himself. The book is qualitatively different from the article, being largely an empirical rather than a methodological study. I had the chance as the author to get this point across to Hoppe. By putting the "philosophy" first, I muffed it.

The length of Hoppe's review of portions of chapter 1 does not come from a complexity of argument; it comes from the repetitions of four simple points, a fugue with four themes, each repeated ten or a dozen times:

1. McCloskey shares "relativism" with some other misled people, none of whom, amazingly, see that "relativism" is self-refuting (section I of Hoppe's piece and elsewhere throughout).

2. McCloskey attacks empiricism, for which he is to be commended,

but does so in a way irritating to someone who prefers the *a priori* (section II and elsewhere).

3. McCloskey does not consider methodological dualism (Section III).

4. McCloskey attacks the possibility of profitable prediction, and even quotes Ludwig von Mises, but he should have pushed further into the a priori (Section IV).

A point of context will be helpful: Hoppe's piece is repetitious because he is on a big game hunt. The little McCloskey-Beast could not inspire such an expedition. Right from the beginning it is plain that his targets are Feyerabend, Rorty, Gadamer, and Derrida. I am flattered to be put in such company. Although, shamefully, I have not read more than a page or two of Gadamer or Derrida, I have read many pages of Feyerabend and Rorty, with pleasure and profit; and I count Rorty a friend. I would rather not be saddled, though, with every imagined disability of these eminent men. My poor argument has enough real disabilities, worthy of criticism and quite unrelated to what some philosopher has said, that a critic does not need to turn to imaginary ones. Much of Hoppe's argument, to put it another way, is irrelevant to the book I actually, clumsily wrote. Much of his argument derives from his hasty and ignorant reading of Richard Rorty or of Paul Feyerabend, not from his hasty and ignorant reading of Donald McCloskey.

Hoppe has a fine passion for ideas. But his passion has led to certain extraordinary misreadings, on which his argument turns.

First, I am not a "relativist," nor is the book "relativistic," if relativism is taken to mean what Hoppe wants it to mean. Hoppe wants relativism to mean the philosophy of a Southern California Valley Girl: anything goes, arguments are all equal, scholarship does not advance, we have no way of reaching common ground. Richard Rorty remarks that "If there *were* any relativists [in the conservative sense], they would, of course, be easy to refute" (Rorty 1982, p. 167).

I believe on the contrary that good scholarship must force its arguments over many difficult hurdles, that good and bad arguments are often easily distinguished, that scholarship does and will advance, and that scholars have numerous ways of reaching common ground, if they will stop yelling at each other and take them.

In one of Hoppe's numerous returns to this first theme he says, "such relativism would once more literally be impossible to adopt, because it is incompatible with our nature as acting talkers and knowers." Gotcha. I entirely agree, and say so to the Valley Girls in my classes. Chapters 2 through 10 of *The Rhetoric of Economics* and my later writings argue that our nature as acting talkers and knowers is crucial to economic science. Non-rhetorical approaches to science ignore our nature as acting talkers and knowers. Popper's refined positivism or Hoppe's splenetic rationalism or various other versions of science simpler and meaner than life itself, since they too would be incompatible with our nature, would be impossible to adopt (for a lucid and devastating attack on philosophical rationalism see Madison 1982).

Nor, second, am I a skeptic, as could be affirmed by people who know me or have read my books, including the book in question. Politically, if you care, I am a libertarian, but am very far from being a nihilist. In politics and in science I have a standard of truth. It is the same one that Hoppe advocates. He uses many times the metaphor of a "common ground as the basis for objective truth." That's fine with me. The book says it – though not in the chapter Hoppe studied – quoting for instance the mathematician Armand Borel: "something becomes objective . . . as soon as we are convinced that it exists in the minds of others in the same form that it does in ours, and that we can think about it and discuss it together" (quoted in McCloskey 1985a, p. 152).

As I have said before, chapters 8 and 9 of the earlier book are about "truth based on common, objective grounds," namely, truth in statistics, and tells how such truth depends on the common ground for comparison that we as acting speakers and knowers have occupied. Compare chapters 3 and 4 in *If You're So Smart* and chapters 9 through 13 above. Hoppe and I agree that science and scholarship do not provide "mere entertainment" but rather the common ground for action. His notion of "the common ground of terms being used and applied cooperatively in the course of a practical affair, an inter-action" says it well. He goes on to note that "Talk, whether fact or fiction, is inevitably a form of cooperation." Exactly. As Palmer put it, the "elevation of conversation to the ethical standard by which rationality is to be judged" leans McCloskey toward classical liberalism, "for the market economy is a kind of a grand conversation, a forum for persuasion" (T.G. Palmer 1986-1987, p. 13). We all agree, we Austrians and fellow travelers. It's in the book.

Nor, third, do I wish to "keep the conversation of economists going without ever claiming to say anything true." Hoppe says that McCloskey "wants to replace this permissiveness [of bad positivism] with an even greater one. He wants us to engage in talk, endless and unconstrained by any intellectual discipline whatsoever." On the contrary, I have no wish for conversations to go on forever, aimlessly, and I have never raised such a strange ideal. (Hoppe of course gives no textual evidence for his charge; we have seen this conservative trope of argument before.) I wish conversations to end when they should. I wish only that they would end rationally, as too often they do not. But by "rationally" I do not mean by prearranged formula, the business done as though by machinery, and I would suppose that an Austrian would take the same view. My rationality (and Richard Rorty's) offers space for creativity of an Austrian sort; to repeat, "the word [rationality] means something like 'sane' or 'reasonable' rather than 'methodical.' It names a set of moral virtues: tolerance, . . . , reliance on persuasion . . ." (Rorty 1987, p. 40).

Many conversations in economics are of course truncated by bad arguments, such as the conversation between some Austrian economists and the rest of the economics profession. Hoppe reads my opposition to bad arguments as advocating never-ending conversation. In particular he misreads my remarks about "conversation stoppers." I never would say that there do not exist proper conversation-stoppers, for some arguments. It would be silly to say so. (As I have already noted, people who have studied a lot of philosophy have a weakness for the rhetorical ploy of rewriting what someone has said in a new, silly form, thus simplifying their job of refutation.) There are plenty of conversation stoppers, such as the rhetorical *tu quoque* discussed in chapter 15, if "conversation" means a part of the larger conversation of humankind.

I suppose if Hoppe thought about it he would want to withdraw the suggestion that I or any other rational person would deny that conversations do end: "You don't think it's raining? Well, look outside" or "You think arithmetic is complete? Well, look at Gödel's proof." When I refer to "conversation stoppers" in economics it is not in aid of endless conversation. It is in aid of getting the stopping optimal. Maybe even Hoppe would agree that it is not correct to stop a conversation among economists by shouting "But Mises says you are wrong!" If Hoppe would read chapters 8 and 9 in *The Rhetoric of Economics* he would see this, because there I examine significance testing as the silliest of modern conversation stoppers in economics, one that Hoppe too would find silly.

Nor, fourth, do I wish intellectual constraints to be loosened. It is harder, not easier, to take into account all arguments in their rich entirety. That is what the book and the later writing advocates, all the arguments, up and down. Scientific life is easier, not harder, if by contrast we are satisfied merely with observable implications or synthetic *a priori* or any of the other 3" × 5"-card versions of how human beings argue with each other over serious matters. The 1985 book, and especially chapter 1, criticizes 3" × 5"-card philosophies of science. The wonder is that philosophers have been able to peddle them.

What gets in the way of Hoppe's understanding of the bit of chapter 1 he read is his adherence to what might be called Hoppe's Lemma (the honor of the name could be shared, with Mark Blaug, for example, since it is the commonest argument against pragmatists and rhetoricians). Hoppe's Lemma is: if you are not a rationalist you are an irrationalist. Irrationalists are mere feelers and jokers. According to the Lemma, a non-rationalist indulges in mere rhetoric, and has no standards of truth. You must either do what we philosophers claim to be doing – never mind what we actually do – or we will declare that you are interested merely in *entertainment* (to use Hoppe's indignant italics). There are two modes of mental activity, according to Hoppe: on the one hand science following rationalist postulates and on the other hand entertainment, emotion, mere opinion, chatter.

I am surprised that Hoppe thinks that novels and poetry are "entertainment" in such a sneer-provoking sense that *War and Peace* would rank with "Wheel of Fortune." I cannot believe that he thinks in such a crude way (Alexander Rosenberg speaks in the same way about how much he despises "poetry, metaphysics, astrology, and psychoanalysis" [Rosenberg 1992, p. 111]; it is a disease of modernist philosophers, this contempt for their culture). The word "entertainment" must be a mistake, and cannot summarize his real beliefs about literature and philosophy. According to his crude dichotomy of science and entertainment, either we engage in first-order predicate logic combined with a priori knowledge about human behavior or else we are engaging in mere gab. There is much in between.

War and Peace would be one candidate, philosophical argument another. To use a favorite rhetorical turn in philosophy, saying that "entertainment" covered such a broad area would leave philosophy with no account of its own activities. It would put philosophy into the category of [mere] entertainment. The argument is a variant of the reply to Hume's peroration about casting metaphysics into the flames: Hume's book would be the first to go. But that cannot be right. Something is wrong. Philosophy is serious, not flameworthy, and *Inquiry Concerning Human Understanding* deserves a leading place in the libraries. The point is that most modern philosophy of science does not fit into its own account of knowledge (modern epistemologists – Putnam, Davidson, and others – fit better, but have not entered the consciousness of the Methodologists yelling about Epistemology). Philosophical argument does, however, fit a rhetorical account of knowledge. So, as above: this being the case, philosophy and H.-H. Hoppe should perhaps relax the 2,500-year old sneer at rhetoric.

Hoppe believes his Lemma that anti-rationalism equals irra-tionalism because he has convinced himself, as many philosophers and their students have, that philosophy is a bulwark in defense of Truth. As I have argued, the fuzziness of the philosophical rhetoric shows in the way it overlooks the distinction between truth and Truth.

Small-t truth, as I've said several times here and said in the book Hoppe owns, is what we use every day to get across the street or to detect another subatomic particle. By contrast big-T Truth is a philosopher's construct, justified true belief. When I say, as I do in chapter 1 of *The Rhetoric of Economics*, that the philosopher's con-struct of big-T Truth is of no use to economic science, and that it in fact infects economics with the sneering rhetoric of modern philos-ophy of science, school of Pittsburgh, the philosophers and Hoppe turn to the audience and say, "You see: McCloskey is against truth [McC: small t]. He can't hold such a position and still make it across the street." They commit the usual fallacy of equivocation.

There's a lot of evidence in Hoppe's piece that he doesn't grasp the distinction between truth and Truth and therefore is not aware of his own rhetorical move. He would have been made aware of it if he had gotten as far as chapter 3 of *The Rhetoric*. When he quotes me advocating as rule of conversation, "Don't Lie," he adds *sotto voce*, "How could we, if there were no such thing as objective truth?" Well, there is such a thing as objective truth, the agreement we all make for purposes of navigating the world and society. We know when we are lying about the air temperature outside or the rational choice inside. The problem is that there doesn't seem to be any way of knowing whether we have hold of Objective Truth, big O, big T. Its presence or absence would seem to be knowable only to God. (Notice the pattern that the critics are falling into; it is a modern trope, apparent from the philosophy seminar to *The Times*, fiercely demanding Truth with a big T the better to assault someone else's truth with a small t, making the ideal the enemy of the good.) To repeat, no one from Plato down to the present has been able to say how we mortals would know an ideal, big-T Truth when we saw it.

I've said that I agree with Hoppe's pragmatic criterion of truth (he will be angry that I call it "pragmatic," because any deviation from his way of talking makes Hoppe angry; the anger, though, may at last send him to the texts he has not read in American pragmatism). But he wants to build a bridge from this pragmatic and sensible position to his favored ontology, Reality. "This is Reality with the big R, reality that makes the timeless claim, reality to which defeat can't happen" (James 1907 [1949], p. 262). Understand: James and I, like you, live squarely in a world of reality, small r, a world in which Iowa is hillier than Eastern Massachusetts and in which the Internal Revenue Service and now the Drug Enforcement Agency have unconstitutional powers. What is at issue here is the philosopher's construct, Reality, a thing deeper than what is necessary for daily life. The Real may or may not exist, like Truth. I don't know, though I reckon God does. In contrast to Hoppe, I claim only to know about the small-letter reality and truth that we humans might know.

But I do know from the history of philosophy that, unfortunately, there does not seem to be any way of getting from Truth in epistemology to Reality in ontology. We all wish there were, and many thinkers since Plato have contributed to floating logs and tossing bricks into the river to build a bridge between the two. But empirically speaking the bridge looks like a hopeless job. If you try to walk across the few finished pieces, you fall right in. The construction time has exceeded that of a new defense system, two-and-a-half millennia and counting. As an empirical scientist I have to conclude that further investment in the bridge should be given a low priority.

The philosophers claim that their notions of Truth and Reality and a Brooklyn Bridge between the two are necessary to prevent "permissiveness" and, as they invariably put it, "anything goes" (I note again and wearily that I never said such a thing as "anything goes," and never would). The philosophers should reflect on their worries (chapter 3 of the original book again may be therapeutic here). They will see that their fears about "permissiveness" and lack of discipline are neurotic and authoritarian, an appeal for a central planning of the intellectual marketplace. As James observed, "The rationalist mind, radically taken, is of a doctrinaire and authoritative complexion: the phrase 'must be' is ever on its lips" (James 1907 [1949], p. 259). I sometimes wonder if philosophers realize how much they sound like a Monty Python skit on sadomasochism when they talk about "discipline" and "permissiveness" and how thing "must be." John Cleese as The Philosopher.

And scrutiny of how people actually argue will persuade the philosophers that their constructs do not play a foundational role in mathematics or science or married life or common law or other species of practical reasoning. The philosophical definitions of Truth and Reality play "merely" rhetorical roles. It is crucial for the aggrieved husband to claim that his view of the marriage is Reality.

No biologist is going to claim anything less than Truth for her version of cell chemistry. But when it gets down to deciding who is going to take out the garbage or what the next experiment on crab glands is going to be, the lower-case, garden-variety reality and truth do the job just fine, thanks.

So Hoppe is quite wrong when he summarizes my argument as "Economics, too, is merely rhetoric . . . [The conversation of humanity] exists not for the sake of inquiring about what is true, but for its own sake; not in order to convince anyone of anything based on objective standards, but in the absence of any such standards, simply in order to be persuasive and persuade for persuasion's sake." His "merely" in "merely rhetoric" is the problem, and shows how little he grasps the point of the book. Repeatedly he uses the metaphor of the rhetorical approach ending up "in mid-air." "If statements are merely and exclusively verbal expressions hanging in mid-air, what reason could there be for any one statement to ever give way to another?!" (The punctuation is a good instance of his table pounding.)

He then broadens the attack to Kuhn and Feyerabend, wandering off the subject of the book and leaving him free to attribute his erroneous readings of Kuhn and Feyerabend to McCloskey. The device is usual among the conservative *enragés*. The threat to philosophy *circa* 1955, they feel, justifies any liberty with the enemy's texts. Hoppe, Blaug, and others have properly identified me as a reader of Paul Feyerabend. This infuriates them, which tempts me to goad them further, since they have misread Feyerabend, when they have read him at all. In truth I admit to an influence and a sympathy. Yet that does not warrant abandoning the task of finding the many errors in my text and launching instead an overheated and inaccurate assault on an imaginary character called "Feyerabend," remote from Paul Feyerabend the philosopher and living on another planet from Donald McCloskey the economist. The mention of certain other authors – Derrida, Fish, Rorty – provokes the same conservative rant. In commenting on my work Roger Backhouse, for example, sandwiches a summary of my views between large slices of Rorty and Fish (Backhouse 1992b, pp. 66-68), neither of whom he understands. He does the same later with Weintraub, treating him as a minnow among the Fish. Rorty was an influence on my work, as Fish was on Weintraub's, but so were Toulmin, Booth, Polanyi, and Burke, to mention a few – and Weintraub and I even have one or two ideas of our own, stated plainly in the books under review.

Hoppe proceeds by reducing McCloskey, Feyerabend, Rorty, *et al.*, to the transparently silly assertion that science is "merely and exclusively verbal expressions hanging in mid-air." Having made the reduction the remaining task is easy for a philosopher: just sneer. Of course one need not bother to give reasons why such a silly statement about science should be replaced by another, non-silly, Hoppean statement. To quote Macaulay on Robert Southey again (1830, [1881] p. 132), Hoppe "brings to the task two faculties which were never, we believe, vouchsafed in measure so copious to any human being, the faculty of believing without a reason, and the faculty of hating without a provocation."

It comes down, as I have noted before, to the rhetorical naïveté of philosophers. The philosopher Simon Blackburn (editor of *Mind*) gave a speech at the University of Iowa in the late 1980s on the necessity of philosophy. He used the ancient topos, familiar from Plato, that one was committed anyway to philosophizing, whether one knew it or not. It's the usual and sound argument for a philosophical education. In the question period he was asked to recognize that the same topos applied to his own talk; in other words, we are committed to rhetorizing, whether we know it or not, since we all argue. He was asked to recognize, therefore, that rhetoric was as inclusive a discipline as philosophy, since both were necessary for each other. Blackburn could not understand this rhetorical *tu quoque*, and could only repeat the usual Platonic insults against law courts and advertising and other democratic institutions. It is a rare philosopher, I have determined by scientific sampling, who has read as much as Aristotle's Rhetoric on the subject; the philosophers take their knowledge of rhetoric from Plato neat. Hoppe does.

Philosophical and scientific argument, in other words, has a rhetoric, too, as they argue things in the law courts and among the poets, but unexamined and therefore unchallenged. Plato, though inventing a realm without rhetoric, provides the first and best examples, as for instance in the leaps to mythmaking-as-argument in the *Phaedrus*. To expose the rhetoric in science and philosophy, capable of mischief, we need to recognize that arguing, after all, is what is going on.

I do not say that philosophical work cannot be done about lower-case truth and reality. It can, and has been. But to get the whole story the philosophers are going to have to examine all the arguments, not merely the ones that suit Hoppe's crystalline realm of Truth and Reality.

An Austrian approach to economics can be fully consistent with a rhetoric of inquiry, as is shown by Ludwig Lachmann's and Don

Lavoie's explorations of hermeneutic economics. What is not consistent with it is old-style rationalism of the sort Hoppe espouses. That is rational*ism*, mind you, not rational*ity*: the two, as Hoppe's unrestrained rhetoric illustrates, are not often found in the same company.

chapter 23

The economists of ideology: Heilbroner, Rossetti, and Mirowski

Economics, praise the Lord, is starting to look at itself with a richer theory of discourse than the received view in the philosophy of science. Economists believe they follow the received view, but of course they do not. No one does. As the psychologist David Bakan remarked early on, "The common rhetorical form 'science is this' and 'science is that' is hardly ever backed up with empirical observations on the scientific enterprise itself" (Bakan 1967, p. 140). Two books by Philip Mirowski (1989, 1991c), and a paper by Jane Rossetti (1990) in a book edited by Warren Samuels, and papers by Rossetti (1992) and Mirowski (1992) in a book edited by Neil de Marchi, identify fresh places from which to take empirical observations on the scientific enterprise in economics. They join in this Robert Heilbroner, who has been practising rhetorical analysis unaware since 1953 (and, more aware, Heilbroner 1986 [1988] and 1990). Heilbroner, Rossetti, and Mirowski, in a nutshell, advocate a soft form of the leftish (Veblenesque Marxoid) program in the history of economic thought, which sees economics as imbued with ideology.

Although I do not have much sympathy for their politics, I have only minor disagreements with their rhetorical programs. We agree that paying attention to words differs from claiming that economics is not scientific. To suppose that being literary about economics is a denial of the scientific character of economics is to fall into the dichotomy of modernism, that you are either a Dr. Strangelove Scientist or a burbling irrationalist. We cannot avoid ideology – "utterances in which the speaker deeply believes," as Heilbroner puts it (1990, p. 102), and continues: "statements to which the 'interests' themselves repair in search of enlightenment." He instances an ideological remark by Robert Lucas, which posits an "individual" receiving "income" from others, and notes that such a rhetoric "reveals a social framework to be a necessary prior posit to the individual-centered analysis" (p. 105). (He might have instanced his own writings, including the pieces in question. It has always been a puzzle in the tradition of Marx how the Marxists – many of them with bourgeois pocketbooks and mill-owning fathers – escape false consciousness. Gotcha.)

Heilbroner believes that the hardihood of ideologies fits a materialist story: "this intellectual rigidity suggests the need to impute to the belief systems of economics a sociopolitical base capable of explaining their resistance to, or insulation from, conceptual challenge" (Heilbroner 1990, p. 105). He quotes Marx with approval: "Economic categories are only the theoretical expression, the abstraction, and the social relations of production" (Heilbroner 1990, p. 107). The cash value of Marx's argument, though, depends on a detailed showing that relations of production matter in writing science. The operative word is "detailed." A rhetorical analysis shows in detail how a piece of scientific writing works. If the details can be related to the pocketbooks of the scientists or to the occupations of their fathers, I will not be displeased. As a recovering Marxist myself, however, I expect that more commonly the details will relate to the literary education of the writer. They will depend on the metaphors that his fellows find persuasive and the stories that they love. But in any case the first step is to get the detailed data.

My main disagreement with Jane Rossetti's gathering of some of the detailed data is unfair. She and I agree that the job in literary criticism is to read texts; the job in economics is to read the economy and to read the texts of economists about the economy. The jobs are similar, we say, and therefore economists can learn from literary critics. But if someone looked at Rossetti's papers alone, and had not dipped into the other literary criticism of economics by Arjo Klamer or Roy Weintraub or a few others, he might come away with the impression that literary criticism consists of (gasp!) deconstruction and the theories of (horrors!) the French philosopher Jacques Derrida.

In the 1950s an older man who had studied economics at college in his youth asked his friend Robert Solow to recommend him a book to freshen his knowledge. Solow told him that a good elementary book, which any lay person could handle, was "Samuelson," by which he meant *Economics* (1st edn. 1948), Samuelson's best-selling undergraduate text (which, incidentally, came just in time to support a set of triplets in the Samuelson family). A month later the man bumped into Solow again and said, "My word, economics has become mathematical! I couldn't make head nor tail of that book by Samuelson you recommended." It developed that the fellow had got hold of *Foundations of Economic Analysis* (1947), Samuelson's Ph.D. thesis and as we have seen the opening shot in the formalization of economics, instead of *Economics*. No wonder he found it hard going. I worry that Rossetti's emphasis on deconstruction, which is the *Foundations* of literary criticism though not its foundation, will have the same effect.

What is unfair about my disagreement with Rossetti is that at least she has made a start, and a most scholarly and insightful one at that. It is unfair of me to complain about an attempt to collect rhetorical data. Rossetti, after all, is serious about the use of literary theory in reading economics. She has taken the unusual step – spurned so far by Methodologists of the old school – of learning something about literary criticism, in her case especially about the deconstructive branch of literary theory.

Anyone who is serious, pro or con, ought to know something about deconstruction, even with its leftward slant. True, deconstruction is merely a piece of rhetorical thinking, learned by its French inventors during Greek class at their *lyceés*. J. Hillis Miller, the chief American deconstructionist, says flatly that "'Deconstruction', at least in one meaning for that multivalenced word, is a contemporary version of rhetoric . . . Rhetorical reading should be the center of literary study" (Miller 1993, p. 297). The rhetorician Richard Lanham complains that "the 'theory' world is forever taking bits of classical rhetoric and tarting them up in new French frocks" (Lanham forthcoming, ch. 10, p. 12). He notes too that the American Kenneth Burke invented deconstruction forty years before Derrida. Only wilful ignorance keeps the Parisians and their epigones from recognizing it.

Only wilful ignorance of another sort, however, keeps the highbrow conservatives snarling at deconstruction. But – this again is my disagreement with Rossetti – to recommend it as necessary for a literary reading of economics would be like recommending Tom Sargent's latest book as necessary for a non-literary reading of macroeconomics. Both French deconstruction and fresh-water macroeconomics, which have more than a few similarities, are good to know about and are sometimes useful. Yet anyone who viewed them as the whole of literary criticism or the whole of economic science would be making a big mistake. You could frighten someone away from modern economics by telling them that a branch of mathproud economics c. 1978 was its essence. Likewise you could frighten someone away from modern criticism by telling them that a branch of French criticism c. 1978 was its essence. I worry that focusing on something so terrifying as deconstruction will give economists and others a cheap excuse to go on bracketing the other half of their intellectual culture.

Deconstruction, for all the calls to arms against it from intellectually conservative magazines (and proud of it), constitutes a tiny part of criticism. It is not even the most recent fashion in literary theory. Feminism and the new historicism are, with the new economic criticism on the horizon. It is one of a score of overlapping ways to do literary criticism. A partial list of critical approaches in historical order from 400 BC to last month would include rhetorical, Talmudic, philological, Aristotelian, Thomist, neoclassical, romantic, Arnoldian, hermeneutic, belletristic, historical, textual, practical, new critical, Marxist, psychoanalytic, neo-Aristotelian, mythological, neo-rhetorical, structuralist, neo-Marxist, reader-response, affective, subjective, transitive, semiotic, phenomenological, deconstructive, linguistic, Lacanian, feminist, Foucauldian, neo-hermeneutic, new historicist, cultural-critical, and economic. In the same way you could divide economics into Good Old Chicago School, old institutionalist, new institutionalist, eclectic econometric macro, nouvelle Chicago, Old Marxist, highbrow general equilibrium, empirical Marxoid, policy-oriented micro, and so forth.

People have a way of seeing a novelty such as literary approaches to economics through the strangest version with which they imagine they are familiar. Thus outsiders to economics think they can reject a modest version of supply-side economics by attacking what they imagine to be the opinions of Arthur Laffer. Richard Posner in his egregious book *Law and Literature: A Misunderstood Relation* (1988) has used this rhetorical strategy to dismiss all literary criticism as applied to law. When explaining to his conservative readers among lawyers Everything You Need to Know About Literary Studies But Were Terrified to Ask you can imagine the sub-field he starts with: chapter five, section 1, "Deconstruction and Other Schools of Literary Criticism." One hopes that his decisions as a federal judge are not so rigged.

The reason people play such games is that they are conservative, intellectually speaking, and would rather avoid investing in a new set of thinking tools if they can get away with it. Thinking gives one headache. You cannot blame people outside of the thinking racket for taking evasive action when presented with a new idea. The critic and novelist David Lodge remarks that "one would have to go back to the eighteenth century to find a time at which writers and literary journalists were as united in their fear and loathing of academic criticism as they are now" (Lodge 1981 [1991], p. viii). But you can blame the professors. Contrary to what one might suppose, professors are especially inflexible about new ideas, as Schopenhauer and I have observed, because they are paid large sums to know things already. Harry Truman said, "An expert is someone who doesn't want to learn anything new, because then he wouldn't be an expert." The professors reckon they know a thing or two about literary criticism if they had a college English course as freshmen; or about economics if they took a course with Samuelson's *Economics* twenty years ago.

Rossetti tries to explain deconstruction to the economist (1990, pp. 226-231), but is not optimistic that the economist will get it: "Reader, do not lose heart," she writes, "The difficult aspects of deconstruction are now behind us" (p. 229). This is the rhetoric of arcania, much practiced by deconstructionists.

Deconstruction is not, I think, so very difficult. Rossetti is lucid on it, though she does make a mistake in one detail. The mistake arises from a confusion in her mind between "structuralism" and "foundationalism": "Deconstruction . . . is a critical technique of the . . . anti-foundationalist schools of literary theory. Whereas the structuralist critics of the 1950s and 1960s [believed so-and-so] . . . post-structuralists deny the possibility of finding an objective . . . foundation . . . Thus their label, anti-foundationalist" (Rossetti 1990, p. 226).

In fact structuralism is the rejection of foundationalism. Foundationalism in language thinks of the word "sheep" as naming a singular thing. In the dialogue called the Cratylus, Socrates expresses foundationalism in its most extreme form: "Cratylus is right in saying that things have names by nature, and that not every man is an artificer of names, but he only who looks to the name which each thing by nature has, and is able to express the true form of things in letters and syllables" (390, d-e). (Plato as usual identifies a social definition as arbitrary, whimsical, self-indulgent.) But as Socrates in his ironic way then goes on to demonstrate, the Cratylan hypothesis is impossible to sustain. As Rossetti notes, "if you could (which you emphatically cannot) read 'rock' outside any social context, it would tell you nothing" (Rossetti 1990, p. 228). A few words are onomatopoeic or in some other way suggestive of what each thing by nature has (the standard example is: which would you choose, "pong" as the word for "kitten" and "ping" as the word for "elephant," or the other way round?). But for the rest, as the linguist Ferdinand de Saussure reemphasized early in the twentieth century, words are conventions. (Rossetti describes Saussure as attacking what she calls structuralism; in fact he founded it, though he was not the artificer of its name; by the way, the economist John Davis [1990b], in a comment on Rossetti, gets the history right.) Saussure pointed out, as Rossetti explains, that any word, such as "sheep," depends on the system of oppositions happening to obtain in any particular language (sheep vs. lambs; sheep vs. wethers, ewes, rams; sheep vs. mutton in English, not reproduced in French; sheep vs. goats in the proverb; sheep vs. pigs in Deuteronomy; and so forth). That is all.

In short, an analogy with language makes for a structuralism. One can be structural in this sense about anything. The system of oppositions in the "language" of, say, British working-class meals may well have a structure, such as the anthropologist Mary Douglas discerned: hot and fluid starters to cold and rigid desserts. One can be structural about poetic language, noting the opposition of academic and common language in Auden, for example. This is old stuff – as old as Hermogenes in the Cratylus, and Protagoras before him; as old as medieval nominalists, and Aristotle before them; and in the twentieth century as old as the structuralism of the 1950s and 1960s, and Saussure before it. Much of Rossetti's "Derrida" is structuralism redux.

In a way I am being, again, unfair to Rossetti. Part of her attempt to distinguish deconstruction (and rhetoric and speech-act theory and much else that could be added) from the older form of structuralism is correct. As Sandy Petrey explains lucidly, the structuralists attempted to isolate language from the practical uses of language – Saussure's isolation of *langue* from *parole*, the Language from the particular clumsy exercises of it by its speakers. The trouble is that "to understand how to do things with words, we cannot take the words away from the social environment in which the things get done" (Petrey 1990, p. 49). It is the conclusion dawning on game theorists in economics. In a version that nonetheless tends, in a French way, to keep trying to get back to "pure," mechanical structuralism, it is deconstruction.

I myself have two tentative objections to deconstruction, which can only be taken seriously when I get down to work and do the homework I have not yet done. The first, from what I can gather from friends who are deconstructionists, is that, as *The New York Times* has discerned on similarly learned grounds, deconstruction combines politics with literature. I don't like the combination any better than does *The Times*. No one could deny that the two are connected, but the deconstructionists (and, by the way, Philip Mirowski) seem to think they are the same, and that the sameness can justify being abusive about literary and scientific and indeed political matters. They want to make every literary question into a political question and then start shouting.

The literary critic Gerald Graff argues against such a move. He wishes to "get beyond the whole dubious project of attaching specific political implications to [literary] theories independent of the way they operate in concrete social practice. A theory such as interpretive objectivism doesn't 'imply' any single politics . . . Making political judgments and classifications of theories requires an analysis of social practices. Is there any reason to think current literary critics possess such an analysis?" (Graff 1983, pp. 604f). When the poet (and businessman) Wallace Stevens regretted in the 1940s "that we have not experimented a little more extensively in public ownership of utilities" he had the sense to add that it was "rather a ridiculous thing for me to be talking about" (quoted in Longenbach 1991, p. 145). One wishes such diffidence were more widely shared by literary folk, most of whom are ignorant of economics and content to remain so.

My second and still more tentative objection is that deconstruction seems stuck on a problem that I do not regard as a problem. Jacques Derrida's problem, as I understand it from afar, is that he is vexed with his inability to found his beliefs on bedrock. Unlike American pragmatists, he cares. After all, he and the other deconstructionists are French people, schooled from childhood in Cartesian foundationalism (and in classical rhetoric, of which as I say deconstruction is a reinscribing). French people find American pragmatism or British eclecticism irritatingly casual about foundations. Deconstruction *à la français* freezes itself in the anguished moment of aporia, repeating over and over the mantra of lost illusions – "Seek not foundations for language." The American pragmatist admits it is so, gives a sympathetic smile, and gets back to her work. She knows with Protagoras that people are the measures of all things, and she does not regard such an ancient proposition as peculiar to modernity.

And yet the deconstructionists can help in literary work applied to economics, as Rossetti argues. One insight that I think Derrida and company are to be credited with (although I am aware of speaking from a profound ignorance) is the notion of verbal "hierarchy," as for example the ancient and damaging hierarchy of knowledge-belief, or the modern one, Science-Art. As Rossetti explains most lucidly in her 1990 paper, Derrida acquires his edge, and sets the teeth of conservatives on edge, by pointing out that the oppositions (sheep vs. pigs, say) are often ranked. Economists could use some help in "deprivileging," as the professors of literature put it, the superior term in pairs like "microfoundations-macroeconomics" or "general-partial" or "rigorous-informal."

In her 1990 paper Rossetti offers a deconstructive reading of Robert Lucas' papers of 1981 on "Unemployment Policy" and "Rules, Discretion and the Role of the Economic Advisor." Lucas himself deconstructs the Keynesian term "involuntary unemployment," although as Edward Puro notes in a comment on Rossetti, Lucas seems to mean simply that voluntary-involuntary "ought to be dropped from the language" (Puro 1990, p. 254). Rossetti notes that in Lucas' reconstruction "of unemployment as the outcome of choice" he sets up ranked oppositions between "economic theory" (high) and "policy" (low), "economist" (high) and "public" (low).

Rossetti does not offer a deconstructionist account of the work of the main economist she discusses in her other paper recommending deconstruction for economists, Wesley Clair Mitchell (Rossetti 1992). Mitchell was a pioneer between the First and Second World Wars of quantitative studies of business cycles and an enthusiast for making social science into social engineering.

The deconstruction of Mitchell, though, is not hard (it is easier to deconstruct writings from an earlier time than from one's own). Take the brief passage from Mitchell that Rossetti quotes: "it must never be forgotten that the development of the social sciences (including economics) is still a social process. Recognition of that view . . . leads one to study these sciences . . . [as] the product not merely of sober thinking but also subconscious wishing."

The passage contains at least these half-spoken hierarchies ready for liberating deconstruction (reading back to front, the terms in square brackets being those implied but not mentioned): sober-subconscious; thought-wishing; product-[mere ephemera]; sciences-[mere humanities]; study-[beach reading]; one-[you personally]; leads-[compels]; view-[grounded conviction]; sciences-[mere] processes; development-[mere chaotic change]; must-[can]. The first term of each is the privileged one – except that in the pairs leads-[compels] and view-[grounded conviction] they are in fact polite self-deprecation, with ironic force: Mitchell is on the contrary claiming the commanding heights of compelling and grounded conviction, not the soft valleys of mere gently leading "views."

That's quite a haul for two sentences, and suggests that Derrida might be onto something of use to the economic reader (for an English professor's interesting attempt to deconstruct Thatcherian economic rhetoric, see Selden 1991). To put it in the vernacular, the economist Mitchell is playing all kinds of mind games on us readers and we'd better watch out. Mitchell, of course, is not special in this.

Rossetti does well to remind us of Mitchell. American economists need to know about this influential man, as influential in shaping American economics as was Paul Samuelson a generation later. His rhetoric helped create the American enthusiasm for social engineering. He wrote for example in 1924 that "In economics as in other sciences we desire knowledge mainly as an instrument of control. Control means the alluring possibility of shaping the evolution of economic life to fit the developing purposes of the race" (quoted in Adelstein 1991, p. 168). The erotic fascism of such ambitions for a social science, which could use some modern deconstruction, was ravishing in the 1920s and 1930s. Despite its failures in practice, we have not gotten over it.

The social construction of knowledge, I am saying, is no invention of the deconstructionists. It has been a commonplace, I say again, from Protagoras to the present. When Mitchell himself speaks of sciences as "the product not merely of sober thinking but also of subconscious wishing" he is doing nothing more avant-garde than reinscribing Francis Bacon's idols (with a Freudian fillip). And when Rossetti discusses Mitchell she is doing nothing more avant-garde than reinscribing Protagoras. But whether the point is novel or not, Rossetti and I agree on it.

John Davis points out in a sophisticated comment on Rossetti's 1990 paper that deconstruction *per se*, as against Protagoras reinscribed or as against literary criticism more generally, is radically skeptical. In the usual way, Davis uses a *tu quoque* argument to attack the skepticism (Davis 1990a, p. 247). Unusually, however, his *tu quoque* works, since its target is the hidden and self-contradictory absolutism of Derrida and company. "To preserve the indeterminacy of meaning that texts reveal," he writes, "is to assume the multiplicity of perspectives that distinct readers bring to the text" (p. 247). Deconstruction ends up by affirming inadvertently the sort of speech community that rhetoricians, pragmatists, and sociologists of science celebrate. The solipsistic

Frenchmen from Descartes to Derrida are doomed, it seems, to providing social-constructivist arguments for anglophone pragmatists.

With Philip Mirowski I have more disagreement. Rossetti may be a little stuck on deconstruction. But Mirowski, judging from his books and articles, has not yet read literary criticism, deconstructive or rhetorical or reader response or new critical or whatever. Until he does some homework on literary criticism beyond an occasional look into the retrograde pages of *The New York Review of Books* – this applies to Heilbroner, too – it is going to be hard to take his literary criticism seriously. Mirowski, as I have remarked, believes in an ersatz sociology of knowledge that claims that there is an intimate connection between philosophies and practices. It is like saying that free verse and free love go together. Such a view written out in the final exam is what would come from not turning in one's homework.

This is my main problem with Mirowski and with some other, less sympathetic critics of a rhetorical approach. In brief, they do not know what they are talking about and seem to be pleased that they do not. His paper with Pamela Cook (1990) asserts impertinently that McCloskey has "not taken the lessons of literary criticism sufficiently to heart" and then defends its very self for not taking them to heart "as demonstration of how older or repudiated forms of writing [by which he means an older approach to the history of thought, which is of course satisfactory for many purposes] may indeed alter our perceptions of the actual subject matter" (Mirowski and Cook 1990, p. 190; Cook, surprisingly, is a professor of French, a colleague at Yale of Tom Greene, my teacher in 1988 at the Dartmouth Summer School of Criticism and Theory; she cannot have put much into the paper). In other words, we shall ignore what has been learned about reading texts in the past 2,500 years and pretend that we are doing so out of conviction rather than sloth. It's the sort of nerviness one associates with a bright undergraduate whose selfconfidence is high and whose time for reading is low.

But let me admit that even though Mirowski has not done his homework on literary criticism, he is so bright that he gets a pretty good grade in the exam anyway. Mirowski and I agree that the scientific paper is a literary device. If Mirowski must come to this realization through a sketchy reading of recent philosophy and sociology – I must say his reading there is shallow, too – I guess I should not object. At least he gets the point. True, it is vexing when he does not understand that the point is a commonplace of criticism, and has been since the Greeks. But anyway he comes to the same conclusion, which we agree is crucial for a reformed economics.

In a paper for the Lavoie volume (1990a) on *Economics and Hermeneutics*, for example, Mirowski ticks off the features of a pragmatic philosophy of science in the tradition of Peirce, James, Dewey (and, he argues, Veblen). They are just what I would recommend:

> 1 Science is primarily a process of inquiry by a self-identified community . . . Science has conformed to no set of ahistorical decision rules . . .
> 2 . . . Abduction [metaphor] is the explicit source of novelty, whereas induction [fact] and deduction [logic] provide checks and balances.
> 3 There is no single logic . . .
> 5 Without a strict mind-body duality, science has an irreducible anthropomorphic character . . . Hermeneutic techniques [stories, *récits*] are a necessary component of scientific inquiry
>
> Mirowski 1990, p. 94

And the substantive stories Mirowski tells are excellent. He tells the story of economic physics-worship in his book (1989) and in the paper with Cook, exposing the embarrassing ignorance of physics in physics-worshiping economists. And he tells in his paper of 1992 the story of Larry Summers, the crown prince of modern economics (the nephew of two Nobel laureates in the field), who had the temerity to complain at the annual conference of the macroeconomic barons at the National Bureau of Economic Research some years ago about the insincere rhetoric of modern macroeconomics. Summers' paper was quashed; and, contrary to what is usual, the paper was not published in the book that contained the others at the conference.

The chief disagreement between Mirowski and me is over the word "neoclassical." Like a lot of people, as I have noted before, he makes possible his scorn for the mainstream, neoclassical economics that innocents like me practice by characterizing it in its silliest possible terms. The problem is the same as in highlighting deconstruction. In like fashion the enemies of institutionalist or Marxist or Austrian economics make their lives simpler by characterizing the other side as so idiotic as to be self-refuting (recall H.-H. Hoppe). It is the usual rhetoric of intellectual war.

Mirowski has in mind the formalism that identifies economic science with certain routines of constrained maximization. Historically he is speaking of the triumph of Samuelsonian economics. As Don Lavoie put it, speaking of the Machlup-Lester debate of 1946 and its unintended consequences, "By the 1940s a process of atrophy had just begun that has led to our producing fewer and fewer economists with the kinds of interpretive skills Machlup exemplifies.

In other words the 'neoclassicism' that Machlup defended is not the same thing as the one that dominates the profession today" (Lavoie 1990d, p. 178). It would be hard to deny that today there exists a fair number of Monty Python "neoclassical" economists, outliers even from Samuelson's program, and often people with little experience of life. "The neoclassicals," says Mirowski, "have never been able to avail themselves of the full panoply of the 'experimental form of life', and worse, espouse a theory which presumes a form of radical methodological individualism" (Mirowski 1992).

But his characterization does not fit most neoclassicals historically, and does not fit many of those active today. Marshall was a neoclassical economist who wandered around factories; Keynes was a neoclassical economist who wandered around bourses and central banks. Sheila Dow, commenting on Lavoie's call for an anthropological economics, notes that "Keynes' great strength was the breadth of his experience in business and government life. His personal understanding of speculative behavior, for example, allowed him to understand the processes of speculative activity and its interaction with the rest of the economy" (Dow 1990, p. 186). Theodore Schultz is a neoclassical economist who has wandered around farms, Robert Solow is a neoclassical economist who has wandered around government offices, Ronald Coase is a neoclassical economist who has wandered around courts; and, to descend quite a few notches, I am a neoclassical economist, who at least keeps his eyes open for economics when he goes to the grocery store.

So it is wrong, to give an instance, for Mirowski to claim that neoclassical economics "has no explanation for how equilibrium is achieved" (Mirowski 1992). In partial equilibrium terms the story is simple and convincing. It is no less an explanation than institutionalist explanations for how institutions are achieved or Marxist explanations for how class dominance is achieved. Maybe general equilibrium with continuous traders in Banach space and other Monty Python versions of economic science have "no explanation" for what they see before them, but the same is not true of most neoclassical economics, working in the here and now.

Mirowski's basic argument against the rhetorical program is that there is something inconsistent between using neoclassical economics, as I do in economic history, and yet being self-conscious about rhetoric, as I claim to be. To "renounce the scientism of economic discourse while maintaining the scientistic explanatory structure was inherently self-contradictory" (Mirowski 1992). He is repeating a claim he made at some length a few years ago (Mirowski 1987 [1988]) in his fluent but ignorant reaction to *The Rhetoric of Economics*. He has repeated the notion since on many occasions, and seems satisfied to stop thinking there.

I admit that I still don't get it. Mirowski is trying to use what is known as "circumstantial *ad hominem*," namely, criticizing my argument as inconsistent with my other behavior, as though I were puffing away at a cigarette while an attorney for the American Cancer Society. It would be a good piece of reasoning if he had worked out the details, getting my argument right and representing my other behavior accurately, and bringing both under a valid enthymeme, informed by reading in the rhetorical tradition. But he doesn't: he hasn't worked out the details of the argument. Mirowski's argument sounds deep, and has fooled a few people (Sebberson 1990; Waller and Robertson 1990; Hands 1993, p. 194n37). But it does not come up to the standards of reasonable argument. His argument is an *ignoratio elenchi*, that is, an argument that claims to refute without in fact doing so, the first of Aristotle's Ten Fallacious Topics (Aristotle, *Rhetoric*, 1401a; p. 205 of Kennedy translation).

It is not made clear, for example, to speak of the governing enthymeme, why "the theory of social order in Rhetoric [is not] congruent with the notions of social order in neoclassical theory." Nor is it made clear why it matters if it is not. In any event, my kind of neoclassicism takes the order of the economy to be the same as the order of the speech: Mirowski has mistaken the argument I made and the personal circumstances in which I made it, and so his circumstantial *ad hominem* is ill made. My kind of neoclassicism is Keynes' kind and Coase's kind and Buchanan's kind and the kind of many other neoclassicals. My kind reverses the metaphor: the market itself is a conversation, to be negotiated, driven by rules of talk (as I have argued in chapter 6 and will continue arguing in chapter 25). No neoclassical economist who thinks with something other than his engineering math book, and not even all of them, would deny such notions.

William James contrasted a rationalist with a pragmatic approach in words that would fit the contrast between a formalist and a genuine neoclassical approach to economics: "The attitude of looking away from first things, principles, 'categories,' supposed necessities; and of looking towards last things, fruits, consequences, facts" (James 1907 [1949], p. 55). It is the rhetorical approach, too. There's nothing inconsistent with economics in a rhetorical approach. Notoriously, and to his regret, James used an economistic metaphor to explain what it meant to follow a pragmatic method: "You must bring out of each word its practical cash-value, set it at work within the stream of your experience" (James 1907 [1949], p. 53). The pragmatic principle, first enunciated by Peirce, quite unlike the essentialist, labor-theory notions of the philosophers, is an opportunity cost notion of meaning: "What difference would it practically make to any one if this notion rather than that notion were true?" What is the opportunity cost, in other words, of adopting this or that notion? It is genuine neoclassical thinking. Don't show me essences and ideal forms; show me practical consequences, argued out in the agora or the assembly.

Pragmatism itself, in other words, and rhetoric, can be brought under a broad-church neoclassicism in economics. Some institutionalists have agreed with Mirowski that there is something conservative about rhetoric (as I said, Sebberson 1990; Waller and Robertson 1990; Warren Samuels thought so in 1984 [p. 209] but I believe has altered his opinion). They do not like a Chicago-School economist doing literary criticism, and suspect that my sort of criticism must somehow be intrinsically conservative. They are mistaken, as may be seen by the radical uses to which rhetoric can be put, far from my own economic or political convictions (for example by Arrington, Milberg, Pietrykowski, Lind, Amariglio, Czarníawska-Joerges, Folbre, Hartmann, Wolff, and Resnick). The mistake comes from the desire to see lives as consistent in some simple, 3″ × 5″-card way. We want it to be true that someone who does something we regard as distasteful, such as neoclassical economics, will never, ever do something we regard as our own, such as a literary as against (as though it were "against") a mathematical reading of economics.

The neoclassical economists who have grasped the literary approach have mainly agreed with it: I would instance Robert Lucas and Theodore Schultz, Robert Solow and Frank Hahn. They are not agreeing to anything very shocking. Mirowski himself joins me in noting that even the formalism depends on, as Nietzsche put it, "a movable host of metaphors, metonymies, and anthropomorphisms: in short, a sum of human relations which have been poetically and rhetorically intensified, transferred, and embellished, and which, after long usage, seem to a people to be fixed, canonical, and binding" (Nietzsche 1870 [1979], p. 84).

Note that the analysis of a language game – deconstruction, among other possibilities, if you wish – is not the same as advocating its destruction. The deconstructionists themselves often commit this punning error, being often of a nihilist and radical hue, so it is not surprising that deconstruction has come to be associated with radicalism (root-and-branch). But as Stanley Fish is fond of saying when he is trying to make the same point, nothing is implied by analysis (Fish 1988). In particular, realizing that a language game is being played, with certain elaborate rules, does not imply that one wants to stop the game or even change its direction.

One realizes in baseball that there is an implicit rule that a player can "cheat" in certain ways (for example, hide the ball as a first baseman in an attempt to catch the runner off base) and that a player "cheating" in this way is not held up for opprobrium. Realizing that such rules are in force does not imply a criticism of baseball, in the non-academic sense of "criticism." It does not imply that one disapproves of the sanctioned "cheating," because in the game as played there are quotation marks around the word.

A lack of understanding of the rules is conservative, because it leads to an uncritical following of whatever rules happen to be in force at the moment: "That's the way we do it; don't ask me why, or even very closely what." The corresponding attitude in literary criticism is a seat-of-the-pants belletrism, such as most educated people evince, fiercely but uncritically devoted to a traditional canon of great works which they have not read. (I am not denying that a belletristic attitude can be argued seriously. It was by critics before *Scrutiny* and the New Critics. I am merely saying that it is seldom so argued by editorial writers who think they believe it.) Much of the non-professional reaction to modern literary criticism takes this character.

The opposite, however, does not follow. It does not follow that an understanding of the rules is necessarily radical. My radical friends, such as Mirowski, cannot get this straight. That conservatives do X does not mean that radicals necessarily do not-X. I admit that the sense of identity that motivates so much political and academic dispute tends to drive people into such absurdities as "Conservatives are polite in controversy and loyal to their benefactors [supposing for the sake of argument that they are; in my experience, actually, they are not]; therefore to be a proper radical I must be abusive in controversy and disloyal to my benefactors." Mirowski has tarnished much of his astonishing work in the history of economics by adopting this conversational anti-maxim. It reminds me of a remark of E. A. G. Robinson, in an obituary on Keynes, about "that nonsense syllogism that has so much bemused economics in recent years: I want to be a great man; Lord Keynes is a great man; Lord Keynes always says something that appears to be paradoxical nonsense; therefore I must discover something that is paradoxical nonsense and say it. Truth is too delicate a fabric to be best produced as a by-product of intellectual vanity" (Robinson 1947, p. 26).

In other words, it does not follow, *contra* Mirowski and others, that because I have noted some of the rules of economic discourse that I must be committed to overthrowing them. One can admire the economist's game, as I do, and yet look into its rules, even with a notion of improving them. Rhetoric is not intrinsically revolutionary or intrinsically conservative. It is not intrinsically anything. It opposes intrinsicality, the foundationalism that makes people think they can lever the world from the blackboard or the lecture podium. To notice the rules is to make possible the *sprezzatura* of which Lanham speaks, a double, toggling sensibility.

Klamer, Weintraub, Lind, Milberg, and, as you can see, Rossetti have in fact gone on to more detailed analyses in a literary vein. It is no longer just a proposal, to be rejected on speculative grounds. The conversation of conventional methodology in economics, which seems frozen around 1965, has not so much been rejected as supplemented by literary approaches to economics. If someone wants to go on ruminating on Milton Friedman's article of 1953, like a neurotic washing her hands fifty times a day, I suppose nothing can be done. But people who want a pointed and, yes, even a radical criticism of economics will look for something else.

chapter 24

Rhetoric as morally radical

The Review of Radical Political Economy, the main journal of the small group of Marxist economists in the United States, held a forum on *The Rhetoric of Economics* in 1987. Of the radical readers many – represented in the forum by the comments of Arjo Klamer and much of those by Hamish Stewart – approve of the book and the later works. They see them as weapons for overturning the more sterile version of neoclassical economics, mathematically speaking, Max $U(x,y,z)$ *s.t.* $y = x + Pz$. As a neoclassical I find Max U a more charming fellow than they do, but the work might well be used this way.

Even from a neoclassical point of view the rhetorical overturning might be useful. That mad Max, for all his charming simplicity, is by now getting on people's nerves. The graduate textbooks in economics are littered with his cigarette butts and half-empty cups of coffee. He has reprogrammed the heads of economists for fourth-rate applied mathematics, and too often has erased the first-rate economics. By now it's time to clean up the rubbish and wipe the blackboards, retaining the useful bits from Max's lesson but refixing our attention on the wide world outside.

Hamish Stewart, though, was alarmed by the claim that morality matters in science, calling it a "scary aspect of McCloskey's book." ("Scary," by the way, is a placeholder in leftwing thought for "I don't fully understanding this argument but I certainly do not like what I conceive to be its politics.") It shows how far we have come, that morality has dropped out of the intellectual discourse in the West. American intellectuals seem still to associate morality with the Baltimore Catechism and the nuns to enforce it. It does not occur to them that a civil discussion depends on *Sprachethik* or that moral questions of honesty and other matters are met and answered every few minutes in a scientific laboratory.

Stewart thinks I am "far too optimistic" that mere words would accomplish an improvement of speech morality. His argument against advocating tolerance in the academy comes down to the observation that tolerance does not already exist. He thinks it is all governed by something more fundamental (compare here Robert Heilbroner's views on ideology; or the vulgar Marxism in some versions of sociology of science). The professoriate, which cannot contemplate the issue of morality in science or art without acute embarrassment, believes that if words seem at first to have an effect one must think again. The supposed effect of words, whether in politics or in science, must be explained by something more basic – to wit, power, which is to say, money. Auden said in 1940, as the clever hopes expired of a low, dishonest decade, "Now Ireland has her madness and her weather still, / For poetry makes nothing happen." I've noted that Stanley Fish likes to say that rhetoric, which he supports enthusiastically in the study of everything from Milton to money, implies nothing. He means what he says: it, logically, necessarily, implies nothing. But of course rhetoric and poetry and philosophy do make things happen, if not logically and by strict implication, electing certain American presidents and supporting certain procedures in science.

The professors who do not get the point believe contrary to Fish and me and others that the discussion of mere words is not serious. It is merely literary. Even many professors of literature think this way, and stride about Being Political, although without pausing to learn much about the polity or the economy or the society. The left has a way of ending every argument by remarking ruefully, "But after all it is merely a matter of Political Power." The recognition of power in science – which the Methodologists, incidentally, should realize has more sociological and historical support by now than the one book by Kuhn – does not undermine science, even as presently constituted. We've done pretty well with science, slimy as its power politics often is. The mere words of philosophers, on the other hand, have done nothing to make the power less slimy, and have often made it worse, by convincing the scientists that they are witnesses to God's Truth. The words have power, too.

Economists like the late George Stigler, a vulgar Marxist though conservative, make the same mistake of attributing too little power to mere words. I once heard Stigler arguing with Milton Friedman about the matter in the Social Science tea room at the University of

Chicago, Stigler kidding Friedman for being such a "preacher." Friedman retorted that people were misled, and needed to be persuaded. To which Stigler said in effect, "They are not misled. They are following their pocketbooks, and have no use for your words." The vulgar Marxist views words as epiphenomenal. The real causes are "deeper," namely, power, money, sex. The hard right and the hard left agree on this. It is the source of their hardness.

But a vulgar Marxism that rejects the independent power of words is mistaken, as Marx in fact argued explicitly and showed in his rhetoric. Words have power: "bra burning," "gutter religion," "nigger," "Juden raus," "realism in foreign policy," "politically correct," "a front-page article in *The New York Times*," "that's not Scientific," "that's not Economics," "free enterprise," "all men are created equal," "Workers of the world, unite," and of course, "This note is legal tender for all debts public and private." It not enough to merely assert that power dominates words. Stewart asserts that "non-neoclassical economists would remain on the margin of the economic conversation until the society around them changes." Maybe, but one would like to see the evidence.

Jack Amariglio is another Marxist economist who has criticized me, although with more grasp of what he is criticizing. In masterful essays he has established himself as the interpreter of postmodernism to economics and of economics to postmodernism (Amariglio 1988; Amariglio, Resnick, and Wolff 1900; Amariglio 1990b). With Heilbroner 1986 (1988) he says that McCloskey "stresses only the form of argumentation and leaves completely untouched the 'content' of economic theory" (Amariglio 1990b, p. 25). I am glad he put nervous quotation marks around "content," for he knows that form and content are mixed. In fact I have sometimes objected to neoclassical economics, in the way that Amariglio, Stephen Resnick, and Richard Wolff (Resnick and Wolff 1987) have objected to their own Marxist economics, and I have done more of it lately. Chapters 9 through 13 above object to mathematical shortsightedness; *If You're So Smart* questions in some detail the assumptions of social engineering; and parts of the *The Rhetoric of Economics* complained about the naïve way that neoclassical economists measure the extent of the market.

But these will not satisfy Amariglio, since they are objections that many neoclassicals already make about their colleagues' work. As I say, there are good neoclassicals; but there are bad ones, too, the ones who think that economics belongs in the math department. But if Amariglio's radical suggestion to me is that I turn in my Chicago

School card and abandon supply and demand, no way. I say it's spinach and I say to hell with it.

Radicalism in methodology, or against Methodology, does not necessarily go with radicalism in politics. Nor does it go with a rejection of a good scientific tradition, such as that of Marshall, Keynes, and the other modern masters of neoclassical economics. The mindless pursuit of the avant-garde, so evident in modernist economics, irritates both Amariglio and me. It is he who is inconsistent, though, not I, in claiming that an avant-garde rhetoric must result in an avant-garde approach to economics. Neoclassicism, when it sees itself rightly, works well in economics, in the way that traditional pitched roofs, hidden structures, and the classical orders of architecture work well in buildings. Just because flat roofs, the exposure of structure, and the absence of decoration has notoriously not worked in modernist architecture is no reason to become still more scornful of the past than was the Bauhaus. Bring back pre-war architecture and pre-war economics, I say, refreshed and enlightened by its experiments with plate glass and set theory. We will have cities that look like the Empire State Building and an economics that looks like Ronald Coase.

My main leftist critic is my main collaborator, Arjo Klamer. In another journal in 1989, *Rethinking Marxism*, Klamer and I talked about the relation of rhetoric to radical thought. He and I disagree about many things. I believe that competition runs the economy and that people are driven by self-interest. Klamer believes that power runs it and that people are driven by more than self-interest. We disagree also on what is to be done politically: I am a libertarian; Klamer is a social democrat. And we disagree on how much economists disagree. I take an American – even Midwestern – view that underneath it all our shared values can bring us together for barn raisings and economic analysis. Klamer takes a European – even Dutch – view that emphasizes diversity and conflict as social facts.

Our one point of agreement is disagreement with the mechanical, scientistic notion of what economists do. Rhetoric points to a moral gap in the practice of economics. If the logic and fact of the simplest sort do not suffice by themselves to produce good economics – and if God does not put in an appearance to settle the matter – by what standards can economists be guided? We agree at the outset on the Maxim of Presumed Seriousness: that as serious scholars we must presume, until sound evidence contradicts it, that others are serious, too. The official rhetoric of scholarship presupposes the Maxim. In linguistic terms the Maxim is a "conversational implicature," which is to say, a rule of behavior necessary for making sense of what another scholar says to you.

The Maxim has a consequence, the Principle of Intellectual Trade, argued in chapter 6 above. The Maxim and the Principle are moral entry points into a conversation to which intellectuals and academics have already committed themselves. Just as differences in tastes or endowments are grounds for trade, disagreements about economics are grounds for serious conversation. Mutual respect prevents the conversation from degenerating into war. As Raymond Aron said, "Politics is dialectic when it unfolds between men who mutually acknowledge each other. It is war when it brings into opposition men who . . .wish to remain strangers to one another" (quoted in Alker 1988, p. 805). Klamer and I believe that the only alternative to dialogue in economic science is theologue.

McCloskey: You know, Arjo, disagreement in economics is exaggerated. We economists are all children of the blessed Adam.

Klamer: So you claim. But I can't entirely agree. For many purposes I see distinctive tribes within the community of economists (Klamer 1987b). The intellectual trade among the tribes is limited.

McCloskey: I know what you mean – the tribes of Veblen and Thoreau, Kropotkin and Chayanov, Marx and Menger and Marshall hold themselves apart. But they share much: entry and exit; the accounting of general equilibrium; and at the very least a concern with how people earn their daily bread.

Klamer: You betray, Donald, the neoclassical's lack of interest in cultural and ideological differences. The neoclassicals undervalue the experience of people excluded from their discourse, those for example with a low marginal product in the economy.

McCloskey: Wait a minute. We neoclassicals have no objection to other ways of thinking, such as the anthropological. But let the anthropologists do it.

Klamer: And then don't trade? Neoclassicals don't follow their own principle of intellectual trade.

McCloskey: Well, yes: so I have said.

Klamer: Neoclassical thinking is hegemonic in American economics, but even within the neoclassical camp there is massive miscommunication. James Tobin and Robert Lucas taken alone are reasonable men, but they cannot talk reasonably with each other (cf. Klamer 1983b, Chs. 2 and 5). Just try talking first with Harvard graduate students and then with Chicago graduate students.

McCloskey: I have, at some length.

Klamer: Well, so have I. You know then that it is like moving from one intellectual universe to another (Klamer and Colander 1990). Such differences are not trivial.

McCloskey: I agree. (Though literally, you know, they *are* "trivial" – that is, concerned with the medieval *trivium* on which education is based: grammar, logic, and above all rhetoric.) The best way for a professor to raise a laugh at Harvard in the 1960s was to mention the name of Milton Friedman. The teacher didn't have to say anything about Milton; he just had to mention him. But it turned out that the best way to raise a laugh at Chicago in the 1960s and 1970s was to mention J. K. Galbraith, or Joan Robinson; just mention.

Klamer: Of course: it's still the case now, as I've seen. Gossip, laughter, and sneering fills the halls and classrooms, despite the rhetoric of respect on the printed page. As Michael Polanyi wrote, "Suppose scientists were in the habit of regarding most of their fellows as cranks or charlatans. Fruitful discussion between them would become impossible . . . Thus their mutual collaboration on which scientific progress depends would be cut off" (Polanyi 1946 [1964], p. 52). Does that remind you of some field you know?

McCloskey: So I have slowly come to realize. It's a shame. But surely there is some basis for conversation among the tribes – genetic if nothing else: we *are* all progeny of Smith, and could on that basis refrain from thinking of each other as cranks or charlatans.

Klamer: I wish there were a basis. But I don't see it. We are not witnessing a communitarian, barnraising project in economics right now.

McCloskey: Well, all right, economics has a problem of communication.

Klamer: That sounds too easy.

McCloskey: Listen to what I'm saying. By "communication" I don't mean the drain-pipe image that most people carry around in their heads.

Klamer: Sure, we agree on that. The old image posits a drain-pipe between two minds through which communication takes place. The image makes conversation seem easy: *mere* communication, *just* semantics, *simply* a matter of style. Under such a theory we would all agree, or agree to disagree, if we "defined our terms."

McCloskey: That's right. Keep the pipes cleaned out and all is well: the Roto-Rooter theory of communication.

Klamer: A small part of communication is taken for the whole, ignoring such crucial matters as the standing of the speakers.

McCloskey: Yes. The theory of communication that you and I share is "rhetorical," which is to say that it recognizes that ideas change in the transmission. As Paul Goodman says, "Meaning is not *conveyed* by speech or *pointed to* by speech; it is speaker and hearer making sense to one another in a situation" (P.Goodman 1971 [1972], p. 34). Communication is something that happens in a society between people, like the ideas forming in the minds of you and me as we speak. Or indeed like the creation of economic value in the agora, the marketplace.

Klamer: In fact there are deep similarities between speech and commerce, as we are discovering and as Adam Smith already knew. The old theories ignore the social character of communication even as they exercise it. Plato wrote in his dialogues – masterpieces of social drama – that mathematical theorems were remembered within an isolated soul from its previous life. Descartes talked in his masterfully persuasive confessions of all sure knowledge as coming from an individual's excoriating doubt, "shut up in a room heated by an enclosed stove where I had complete leisure to meditate on my own thoughts."

McCloskey: Though practicing a social rhetoric, Plato and Descartes advocated a Robinson-Crusoe theory of knowledge, a theory of the lone person preparing packages in isolation for transmission to other isolated people. I just read a remark of William James that's pertinent to this: "The knower is not simply a mirror . . . passively reflecting an order that he comes upon and finds simply existing. The knower is an actor . . . He registers the truth which he helps to create. Mental interests . . . help make the truth which they declare" (quoted in Myers 1986, p. 8).

Klamer: Yes. The master myth of modernism is the myth of the Object perceived by the Subject. Somehow we as individual Subjects are able to grasp the Objective – yet no one has been able to explain how.

McCloskey: The Objective/Subjective figure of speech has burrowed deep into our culture, and keeps intruding on conversations about rhetoric. The Objective is supposed to be what's really there; the Subjective is supposed to be what's in our minds. Unhappily, both are unknowable or, what amounts to the same thing for practical purposes, untellable. What we can know is what one might call the *Conjective*, which is to say, what we know together, by virtue of social discourse, scientific argument, shared language; even, if you wish, by virtue of the social relations of production.

Klamer: I do wish. But I like "conjective." It calls up a realm beyond what I have called the square and the circle (Klamer 1990c; and see above chapter 20). The square is the realm of logic narrowly defined, of strict, first-order predicate deduction; the circle is the realm of will and feelings, the subjective. Your "conjective" is the (social) soup in which the square and the circle float. "Conjective" also reminds one of "conversation," which we both like. And Don Lavoie's "hermeneutics" in economics is the same notion: interpretive economics "does not entail some kind of mysterious access to the private contents of minds but takes place through the public medium of language . . . : meaning is social and public, shared through participation in the life world" (Lavoie 1990d, p. 177 and Gerrard 1993).

McCloskey: Good. The battle of square and circle, so characteristic of our recent culture, is seen to be lacking in point. William James wrote in 1909: "For humanism . . . has sincerely to renounce rectilinear arguments and ancient ideals of rigor and finality" (James 1907 [1949], p. 374, written for a book of 1909, *The Meaning of Truth*). Until the sixteenth century the very word "conscience," which the men of the terrible seventeenth made into the touchstone of isolation, was its Latin meaning, *con-scire*, knowing together. Listen to William Barrett drawing the moral from Wittgenstein's move from logic to language. He uses your spatial image: "neither dualism nor behaviorism really permit us to talk as we do in life. A conversation does not take place inside each other's heads alternately, nor at the surface of our bodies in their overt behavior; it is really in the region between the speakers that the conversation takes place" (Barrett 1979, p. 184).

Klamer: On so much we agree. But I suspect your motives. Why do you bring up the social, cooperative, conjective character of scholarship? It reminds me of the rhetorical and social contexts in which economists speak. You need only recognize that there are many contexts and you will be driven to admit that diversity, opposition, and conflict are the salient facts. I suspect you of favoring the terms "conjective" and "conversation" because they evoke bourgeois civility. Like Habermas you project the image of an ideal speech community; but unlike Habermas you seem to suggest we already live in it, or at least close by.

McCloskey: You insist on this European pessimism.

Klamer: And you on your American optimism. You see: we have found another cultural difference.

McCloskey: Touché. And yet I approve of "bourgeois civility." I am going to write a book some day called *Bourgeois Virtue* in defense of the good of the middle class. Intellectuals, themselves usually bourgeois, have recommended the morality of the peasants or of the nobility but never that of the bourgeoisie who make the society run.

Klamer: Good idea, and very Dutch. But back to method. You must grant me that the *conversation* among economists sometimes becomes warlike. I have even seen you yourself get upset about some economic conversations. What do you think goes wrong?

McCloskey: Among economists as among others the conversation goes wrong in sneering (an aristocratic vice, incidentally, not bourgeois). Habermas complains somewhere about the "strategy of mutually shrugging one's shoulders." Economists do a lot of shoulder shrugging; they have all been perpetrators and victims. Once during a conference I asked an economist whom I imagined to be a friend, an arrogant man in an arrogant profession, to check one of two boxes: either offer a reasoned reply to an argument I had just made, which he had sneered at, or go on sneering; with a smirk characteristic of the man he chose the box "go on sneering," much to the amusement of another false friend nearby who was courting his favor. Ha, ha. Very funny. But damaging to our joint purposes.

Klamer: We all have such stories, about what William James called "the smoking of cigarettes and the living on small sarcasms." He called it "the Harvard indifference."

McCloskey: Yes, though I know people even at Harvard who choose not to sneer, and have the bourgeois virtues. Sneering is the obstacle to conversation in economics. The Chicagoans sneer at the Marxists, the Marxists sneer at the Neoclassicals, the Neoclassicals sneer at the Austrians, and the Austrians sneer at the Chicagoans. $C > M > N > A > C$.

Klamer: So much for academic conversation as a mechanism of rational choice.

McCloskey: You are too pessimistic. But I admit some grounds for pessimism. The main purpose of sneering is to protect the sneerer from having to learn anything new. Economists are proudly ignorant these days. If one can simply sneer at neoclassical economics (or Marxist economics or institutional economics or whatever), then one does not have to follow the Maxim of Attributed Seriousness. In her book *Ordinary Vices* the political theorist Judith Shklar talked at length about snobbery, "the habit of making inequality hurt." The sneer is an assertion of rank. The economist sneers loftily at the sociologist, asserting rank and a fully finished education.

Klamer: Note the hierarchy that springs from the rhetoric.

McCloskey: Yes. The topmost are the worst; or rather the second to topmost, not the dukes but the minor barons.

Klamer: As you reported earlier, I know a leading macroeconomist who has never read Keynes and will never do so. But he doesn't smile when he says it: his shallow philosophy of science, not laziness or malice, tells him that reading old books is beside the point. Anyway, what would happen if the sneering stopped?

McCloskey: The economists would do better, by forming a community with others interested in economic matters.

Klamer: Your newfound socialism of the intellect seems to me utopian. Sneering is more than an uncivil and unbecoming speech act, correctable through mere exchange. The sneering betrays deeper problems of knowledge and discourse.

McCloskey: Deeper in one sense. The deeper problems are philosophical. The sneering, I like to say, is supported by $3'' \times 5''$-card philosophies – "Go forth and Falsify," for example, or "Measure regardless" or "Depend on the A Priori." Without them, and without the accompanying passion, the disagreements would fade.

Klamer: The $3'' \times 5''$-card philosophies are vicious, I agree. They make people insist that they can settle their disputes by attending to the card. Others fail to use the same one. Then the failure unleashes anger. Positivism for example makes the positivist believe that the only alternative to narrowly defined logic and fact is whim.

McCloskey: Yes: moral choices are *mere* matters of opinion, says Mark Blaug and other positivists, like one's taste for chocolate ice cream.

Klamer: That's right. Scientific conversation is supposed to forbid such expressions of taste, since they are "mere," and supposedly undiscussable. Allegedly, to introduce them is to declare war. You and I would wish such people would recognize a realm beyond and including autistic logic – the conjective as you say, the social and rhetorical grounds for what we believe, between my square and the circle. But I doubt that such recognition would eliminate the sneering.

McCloskey: Sure it would. And does. How do you think schools form in economics? A group talks intensively to each other, *respectfully*, regardless of whether all are geniuses warranting deep respect merely on the basis of their IQs. They allow each to influence the other. They stop sneering and start listening. They build something in the space between the circle and the square. I've seen it happen, in the bar of the Quad Club at Chicago, say, or at Iowa in the Project on Rhetoric of Inquiry. Such a community of scholars comes to have few disagreements, if the talking goes on long enough.

Klamer: There you are admiring "community" again. I share your admiration. I do occasionally come across people setting aside their harsh feelings and discussing economics openly. I have even seen you talk at length with Marxists.

McCloskey: Don't tell anyone, will you? They'll take away my Chicago card.

Klamer: Exchanges between radically opposed points of view are not common. Ideology affects the exchange even among well-intentioned people.

McCloskey: What do you mean?

Klamer: Rhetoric can uncover the way ideology operates in discourse. Given the limits of strictly deductive reasoning, economists must always argue by means of metaphors, analogies, exemplars, authorities, and stories. You've made this clear yourself, and Timothy Leonard and I explore the metaphorical part (Klamer and Leonard 1993).

McCloskey: The rhetorical tetrad: fact, logic, metaphor, and story. What of it?

Klamer: Ideology itself is couched in the metaphors and stories that economists use.

McCloskey: That's true enough. The Marxists see struggle everywhere, a story of *Sturm und Drang*.

Klamer: Yes. And you, like other neoclassical economists, think of human behavior in terms of individual calculation. Your basic metaphor is that of a Robinson Crusoe allocating scarce resources according to an optimizing algorithm.

McCloskey: You mean the Samuelson program in modern economics?

Klamer: Yes. Samuelson's master metaphor is that people come to their adult lives equipped with utility functions (which they know) and constraints (which they realize), then solve an engineering problem.

McCloskey: Yes: maximize under constraints. First-order conditions. Comparative statics. Methodological individualism. Sweet stuff.

Klamer: Or "neat," another adjective that your comrades like, borrowed from the mathematicians. My point is that the choice of your metaphor and your story is ideological: it privileges one way of thinking about the world while excluding others. Thinking in terms of individualistic calculation can therefore be obnoxious. In many situations it can also be paralyzing.

McCloskey: I don't see why. In some times and places the talk of individualism has been radically liberating.

Klamer: True enough, but this is not 1776 or 1789. Take one of our current projects, the writing of an elementary textbook. I grant you that each of us has his own reasons for collaborating. Call it self-interest if you wish. But our collaboration would break down if we were to specify equivalents in our exchanges too closely, calculating the optimum strategy to the third digit. Such behavior would be obnoxious, and would make the collaboration impossible.

McCloskey: I agree. In fact, a quarter of every economics department behaves in just such a way, excessively loyal to their model. It is neither aristocratic or bourgeois; more like the peasantry, maximizing under routinely-known constraints. That's what makes administering an economics department so difficult, this loyalty to the selfish model of humanity, the peasant's rationality.

Klamer: Sure. Real collaboration depends on trust and on negotiations more cultural than a game. You would say – I have my doubts – that it is "bourgeois." It takes us back into the realm of the conjective. Or think of a worker who gets fired because the foreman does not like her color or sex. Your neoclassical metaphor and story will leave the worker without a language to legitimize outrage and to mobilize for political action. After all, the black woman is paid "what she's worth," that is, to the white male employer, zilch.

McCloskey: Wait a minute . . .

Klamer: Accordingly, in spheres of both friendship and hostility the neoclassical rhetoric represents a dangerous or repressive ideology. In these cases people run up against the ideological walls of neoclassical discourse. Robert Heilbroner made a similar point about your book (Heilbroner 1986 [1988]).

McCloskey: I don't agree. The language of markets and rational behavior would be a powerful weapon in the hands of the angry worker. Where businesses stick to profit maximization the market forces will eliminate discrimination.

Klamer: That is a highly problematic argument.

McCloskey: It may or may not be now; in the past it has often worked. But here's another argument against giving up the neoclassical model of a labor market. The alternative rhetorics of outrage and mobilization have their own down side, too. They lend power to the state, with its clubs and jails and staged rallies.

Klamer: I doubt it has to. But apart from that, would you have advised Bishop Tutu in 1985 to preach the virtues of markets and self-interest?

McCloskey: It would not have been bad advice. Look at Japan, Korea, Hong Kong, and latterly Eastern Europe and China. Workers of all countries unite: demand capitalism.

Klamer: Even if you were right and a free market system would punish those who discriminate, I don't think that neoclassical thinking provides much insight into what was happening in South Africa under the race laws.

McCloskey: I'm not so sure. Look at *The Applied Theory of Price*, second edition, p. 496, problem 5.

Klamer: The major problem with neoclassical economics is its methodological individualism. Amitai Etzioni has a nice image here (Etzioni 1988.) He says that methodological individualism is like studying the behavior of a school of fish by taking one fish out of the school and watching what he does in a fish bowl by himself. It's the Robinson Crusoe story, a powerful one in economic literature. You take the businessman out of the culture to study him, as indeed Defoe did, but you can't take the culture out of the businessman (Crusoe was as bourgeois as they come, a regular Babbitt of his time). Likewise, you are not likely to take the racist culture out of white South Africans by unleashing market forces. We need to grasp the cultural and political context in which South Africans make their choices.

McCloskey: Your example puts me in mind again of the conjective *versus* the objective/subjective. But I still think methodological individualism is a sweet method of analysis, and gets us a long way. May I remind you that even some Marxists believe so, John Roemer and Jon Elster for example.

Klamer: Hmm. Their work complicates my argument. I agree that methodological individualism does not have a one-to-one relationship with a particular ideology. I have some problems with the Roemer-Elster approach – and so by the way do other contributors to *Rethinking Marxism* (see Amariglio, Resnick, and Wolff 1990). But let me confine the case to the mechanistic metaphor that neoclassical language uses to think about the individual.

McCloskey: Go ahead. What's the problem?

Klamer: It's the second problem. The problem is the unexamined rhetoricity of "self-interest." In fact one's personal interest has to be argued, with oneself and others. Anyone Christmas shopping or looking for a new job or doing anything that is not habitual knows this.

McCloskey: I can agree with that. We are each of us a committee.

Klamer: And "the firm's" interest has to be negotiated, too. A friend of ours in commercial publishing was contemplating moving to a job at a university press. His problem was that "bottom-line publishing" as he called it was in his eyes tougher, braver, more in the fight than university-press publishing. He hesitated long. It was not the calculation of advantage that was the hard problem; it was the arguing out of advantage, the social/cultural debate that raged within his utility function.

McCloskey: Well, sure. There's nothing in the neoclassical economics of Marshall that would deny such a line of argument. The rhetoric of negotiation in a Marshallian argument might be rather simple-minded (Leijonhufvud compares the Marshallian industry to a bunch of wind-up mice), but it could be accommodated.

Klamer: Can the vagueness of our knowledge of the future be accommodated in the metaphor of a calculating machine? That's the third disability, after the rigid individualism and the unreflective character of the individual. The individual deals in huge, cloudy symbols, not in budget lines.

McCloskey: I agree neoclassical economics can't easily handle constraints that only reveal themselves in the future, though we're trying. The point is in fact an old Austrian one, which has been rediscovered in the new classical macroeconomics. The problem in economic life is not calculating what to do *after* knowing all that you need to know. The problem is coming to know. The Austrians see the economy with a metaphor of fog, the fog in which we maximize what the neoclassicals so confidently describe as "objective functions." But this is peasant economics. The peasant maximizes, as I said, under known constraints (the aristocrat would never deign to indulge in something so vulgar as "maximizing"; his motives are to Be Himself). The real problem in a progressing economy is to discover the constraints in the first place (see Buchanan 1964). What *are* the investment opportunities? What *is* the next $20 bill to be picked up? "Search" or "information" theory à la Stigler doesn't make it: it is an attempt to do a bourgeois act (investment, foretelling, entrepreneurship) with peasant methods (routine maximizing). What the bourgeois actually does is to converse, with himself or with others. Gossip, shoptalk, schmoozing, committees, reasoning, hallway conferences: these are the guts of capitalism (Vaughn 1988). The next investment opportunity is constructed by words (it had better obey the laws of physics, too, but that does not make the behavior less social).

Klamer: I'm surprised you agree. Or are you just reporting on the Austrians?

McCloskey: No, I'm agreeing, as I think many neoclassical economists are beginning to agree with the Austrians, especially the neoAustrians who argue in ways other than "Mises-says-it's-so." Most of us wander in a fog of indecision, because decisions are of course about a future, which no man knows. The bright sunlight in which the rational man strides forward is hard to credit. Routine maximization is peasant economics, not bourgeois economics. I can't see how an academic could argue otherwise. After all, he or she is employed to help others organize the fog.

Klamer: Partial equilibrium analysis ignores the problem entirely. Game theory makes what it realizes are simpleminded assumptions about the knowledge of players. Neoclassical analysis reduces the problem of knowledge to one of information. But having data is one thing, knowing what they mean quite another.

McCloskey: Search models have attempted to model learning – though I admit that they don't go far in recognizing the depths of ignorance. But one can defend the notion that for large and unsubtle choices people make decisions that are rational as an approximation. I have argued so in economic history.

Klamer: Surely the general equilibrium and game-theoretical analysis is a lot of formal effort for little gain of social insight?

McCloskey: Maybe. I can give you another, non-mathematical example, just to show that it's not the mathematics that's the problem. Since Hobbes, as chapter 11 above pointed out, we have been transfixed by the following abstract question: can a collection of violently selfish and unsocialized people form spontaneously a true community? I'd maintain that this is an existence theorem we can do without, as economists. Whether or not hypothetical sociopaths from Mars, lacking human culture, would form a community is of little interest if the actual problem facing us is forming communities out of Frenchmen or Americans. As the philosopher Alan Nelson has shown, it is unlikely in any case that such a rational morality would qualify as a morality (A. Nelson 1988). But in any case we need theorems about what happens when already socialized people face temptations to cheat or to kill.

Klamer: I'm surprised you go along with all this. Have you given up the Chicago School?

McCloskey: Certainly not: I've been a Chicago economist since the third year of graduate school at Harvard, having deconverted by stages from sophomore socialism. Surely you can see this in my economic history or my microeconomics textbook.

Klamer: Yes, I can. You talk about rational choice and the magic of markets. It's very neoclassical, very Chicago.

McCloskey: Only in a sense. By "neoclassical" you mean the Mainstream Model of Samuelson and his students. That's one tribe of neoclassicals, and I admit the mainstream is how our students are trained. They are trained to think that economics is a matter of engineering math – though not in my textbook.

Klamer: But surely that's your own tribe, the Chicago School.

McCloskey: No. You stress differences but then overlook important differences within the neoclassical nation. I admit there has sprung up a *nouvelle* Chicago, the computer-generated and time-series nourished Max Expected *U*, a younger brother to Samuelson's Max *U*. But my Chicago is Good Old Chicago. Theodore Schultz is an example, an empirical economist who uses maximization lightly, as a mild presumption that people try to do what's good for them, mostly. Robert Fogel is another (a future recipient of the Nobel Prize in Economic Science if the Committee is serious about science), pursuing behavior through two centuries of primary sources. James Buchanan is another instance, a philosopher-economist, a student of Frank Knight's, criticizing the metaphor that "the individual responds to a set of externally determined, exogenous variables"; "its flaw lies in its conversion of individual choice behavior from a social-institutional context to a physical-computational one" (Buchanan 1964 [1979], p. 29).

Klamer: How about Friedman's Methodology paper? That provided the standard justification for Max *U*.

McCloskey: Yes, it did. And you can find plenty of people in the Chicago tradition who fell for the line. But Friedman himself doesn't actually follow his Methodology. He has a lot of Frank Knight in him.

Klamer: Yes. Frank Knight is a bit of a revelation to one who thinks of Chicago in 1980s terms. He took the problem of knowledge seriously. And in his writings you will look in vain for formal presentations of peasants, mechanical calculators.

McCloskey: Right: notice how reluctant Friedman has always been to write down the maximizing model for his monetarism. I can assure you it's not because he didn't know the math: a test in mathematical statistics that he invented in 1937 is still in use. And there is the old-style NBER connection in the careers of Fogel (a prize student of Kuznets), in Friedman himself, and in other patient workers in the observatories. The Good Old Chicago School was skeptical of formalization and was devoted to collecting facts. Marshall himself exhibited these tendencies. And look at Friedman's books with Anna Schwartz on the money supply. One could mention Ronald Coase, the inventor of law and economics, or A. C. Harberger, the inventor of modern cost/benefit analysis, or Merton Miller, the inventor of modern finance, or Gordon

Tullock, the inventor of political economy, or Earl Hamilton, the inventor of cliometrics, or Margaret Reid, the inventor of household economics, or Greg Lewis, the inventor of analytic labor economics, or Leland Yeager, the inventor of modern international finance. They are conservatives (in a manner of speaking), but not such easy targets for sneering as are the devotees of Max Expected *U*.

Klamer: I must say you are right about Coase. Maybe I'd better have a look at some of the others.

McCloskey: Yes. The Good Old Chicago School is alive and well and living in economic history, law and economics, and other fields that do not view economics as a blackboard subject.

Klamer: I've done you an injustice by associating you with the neoclassical camp of Samuelson and Lucas.

McCloskey: Wait a minute. I admire Samuelson's contribution to economics, and Lucas', too. It's their students and then their students and now their students to the third and fourth degree who have wandered away from the Good Old truths. After all, Samuelson (from Gary, Indiana) was as I've noted an undergraduate at Chicago long ago, and Lucas shifted (at David Landes' urging) from graduate work in the History Department at Berkeley to get his Ph.D. in economics from Chicago, under the old dispensation.

Klamer: Still, there's a sharp rhetorical difference between the Samuelson tradition and the one with which you associate yourself. While Samuelson *et al.* pursued a highly abstract theory of economic exchange, your brand of economics is more historical and calls for case studies. Their favorite metaphor is that of a mechanism while yours is organic. Samuelsonian economics values completeness and consistency whereas yours allows for the inadequacy of theory in recognition of human imperfections.

McCloskey: Maybe. I view the exact models as rough little instruments for measuring those "organic" beasts on the fly. I don't want to cut up the conversation so. Max *U* is a silly fellow sometimes, but sometimes he's just what we need for a problem. About Max Expected *U* I'm less sure, but even he must have a thing or two to say to us: the Principle of Intellectual Trade applies even to the work of those who would spurn the Principle. The "historical" and "case-study" approach of the Good Old Chicago School should not be seen as a rejection of economic theory: it's not back to the

German Historical School, with its naïveté about the relation between fact and theory.

Klamer: The difference in rhetoric, which you are acknowledging exists, is not merely a matter of preferring one metaphor over another. Even if we ignore its ideology, the Samuelsonian metaphor has consequences. It makes the formalistic style of reasoning seem natural; it makes it seem More Scientific. This also explains the common failure of your Let's-forget-about-the-formalities-and-just-talk scenario. The rational expectations types sneer at such conversation, as "not serious." They consider the "informal" analysis as undeserving of the label Science. Conversation is pushed right outside the realm of the negotiable.

McCloskey: That's a little harsh, although I admit that their conversation does seem to revolve around the news from certain parts of applied math, lagged a number of decades.

Klamer: I would argue that changing the discourse is not a matter of individual choice. Formalist discourse in economics is embedded in a larger, more comprehensive discourse. Its values and aspirations correspond to a modernism that has dominated music, physics, philosophy, visual arts, architecture, and mathematics since 1900 (Klamer 1991). Modernism is responsible for the formalism, axiomatization, avant-garde-ism, and professionalism in all these fields. Samuelson and Lucas owe their persuasiveness to a modernist environment. The Good Old Chicago School has been put in the shade because its organic way of reasoning did not suit the mood of the last thirty years.

McCloskey: I suppose so. The same could be said of most Marxists as well. They too are modernists.

Klamer: I agree, though there are Good Old Marxists, too. Wolff and Resnick (1988) and Amariglio (1987, 1988, 1990) argue this way. Marxists, they say, have bought into the modernist ideals of universal truth and scientific laws. Have you read their stuff?

McCloskey: Yes, a little, at conferences. Mainly I depend on vague memories of a Marxist youth. I pay professional attention to the historical studies of people like Bill Lazonick, Bernie Elbaum, Steve Marglin, and associates. What *are* the Rethinkers doing?

Klamer: They do stuff similar to our rhetorical work. They break open the rigid discourse of Marxism. They attack the essentialism and foundationalism in Marxist intellectual practice.

You see how similar it is? We're attacking foundationalism, too.

McCloskey: Yes, I do. Do they also get accused of being insanely "relativistic," and wanting to bring to earth a régime of "anything goes"?

Klamer: Sure, of course: just the way the American pragmatists were attacked, and indeed the way the political anarchists you say you admire were attacked.

McCloskey: Ah, yes: Prince Kropotkin, my hero at age 14! Rosa Luxemburg! The romance of it all!

Klamer: Calm down. The Rethinkers have some useful terms. For example, the concept of "overdetermination": any particular event is caused by many things.

McCloskey: You mean the world is not economical in its chains of causation?

Klamer: Indeed. And they use the notion of an "entry point" to a discourse. They use class as an entry point, the way neoclassicals use rational individuals. The entry point of course contributes to the determination – indeed, the overdetermination – of the science.

McCloskey: Hmm. You mean there is an "entry point" to neoclassical rhetoric, too?

Klamer: Yes. Rhetorically one could identify it with the commonplaces assumed at the beginning of a speech.

McCloskey: Let me reduce it to neoclassical terms. I'd say that the entry point is like the choice of a set of prices with which to value national income, the index number. It picks a point of view.

Klamer: The Rethinkers would not like such reductionism.

McCloskey: I suppose so, but they should try it out. I do admire what I've seen. What I most admire is the Rethinkers' openness to conversation. It never ceases to astonish me how few people in academic life are actually interested in testing their arguments in conversation. That's why people favor the false rhetoric that frees them from having to persuade doubters, which they call "testing." My test is your fallacy, but in any case we don't have to meet each other on common ground. It's the rhetoric that has been called "the empiricist monologue" (Mulkay 1985, p. 3).

Klamer: There's another rhetorical issue, with sociological consequences. The conversation of economics is defined to exclude people like the Rethinkers.

McCloskey: I know what you mean. The cry "that's not economics" means "I don't know what in hell you are talking about
and am not going to find out."

Klamer: Yes: and "I propose not to hire you, either."

McCloskey: A disgrace. Economists are willing to play hardball in
the job market without remorse. They think again that it's
made morally right by their model of the market. Anyway,
we agree – we rhetoricians and Rethinkers, neo-pragmatists,
social students of knowledge, social epistemologists – on
what does not work: the Platonic and Cartesian programs of
abstraction. Modernism is impractical, whether in flat-roofed
boxes of buildings that leak and drop their window panes on
passersby or in an economics designed on similarly modernist principles.

Klamer: Right you are, as I have said of modern art, so of modern
economics. The English poet Philip Larkin, who was also a
jazz critic and librarian, spoke of modernism as the curse of
The Three Ps: Pound, Picasso, and Charlie (Bird) Parker.

McCloskey: It doesn't work because the "human sciences" (in the
useful French expression) cannot be *profitably* predictive.
The ambition to construct an economic science modeled on
electrical engineering, say, runs up against its own discovery: that people anticipate the future, and trump whatever cards the others play. In economics if we were so smart
as to be able to predict the future of interest rates, for
example, we would be rich. Economics contradicts its own
ambitions. So too in linguistics, as economists can understand in terms of game theory or rational expectations. Recall
from chapter 6 above, in the third way of using economics to
criticize itself, the quotation from the linguist to the effect
that "there will also therewith arise the possibility of the
non-conventional *exploitation*" of any linguistic rule.

Klamer: That's a great quotation.

McCloskey: Yes, I thought so too. It undercuts the modernist
ambition to write down complete systems. Gödel and Turing
and Church showed that it doesn't work even for math. But
what's beyond modernism in economics?

Klamer: And beyond modernism in art and architecture.

McCloskey: Well, what? My neoclassical principles do not permit
me to claim to see into the future.

Klamer: The alternative is not *post*modernism, which seems to me
merely jokey and nihilistic, merely the last act in the decay of

modernism. The alternative is "interpretive" economics, an economics (or art) that attempts to grasp the meanings of economic life. As Don Lavoie puts it, "The systematic under-valuation of what I would call the interpretive dimension of economics has led to a gradual loss of relevance of what we consider our most 'advanced' and 'sophisticated' research and has caused a loss of crucial skills our profession had once developed" (Lavoie 1990d, p. 168).

McCloskey: I agree on the rejection of postmodernism as usually understood. We don't help ourselves much by handing over our lives to Parisian intellectuals. Anyway, they sneer at our attempts at French. "Metamodern," as I say, might better describe the uneasiness about modernism. And I agree with the call that you and Don Lavoie make for an interpretive economics. It's what most economists do anyway, I'd argue. Certainly Marshall and Keynes did it.

Klamer: We need an economics for human beings, not for godlike mathematicians. Gods see the Truth; humans interpret. When Ronald Coase wanders around in law books looking for a way to understand externalities that makes sense, when Michael Buroway participates on the shop floor looking for a way to see the struggle for control, when Bill Lazonick gets down to the old records of capitalism on the ground, when Bob Solow strains for a reasonable interpretation among the econometric models and journalistic rumors of the day – they're all doing *interpretive* economics, with a variety of purpose-built methods.

McCloskey: It's American.

Klamer: There you go again with your American chauvinism. Levi-Strauss called it "bricolage," handymanship, making do with the tools one has and getting on with the job. It's opposite is the pursuit of universal laws and perfectly general systems, which would be useless if we found them, except to make us slaves.

McCloskey: I entirely agree. The modernists have Plato and Descartes and Russell to admire. We have our own ancestors: Protagoras, Aristotle, Cicero, Quintilian, and then a stream of modern critics and maverick philosophers from James and Dewey to Burke, Polanyi, Toulmin, MacIntyre, and Rorty. Recall the discussion in chapter 2 above of John Ruskin's notion of the "Gothic" in *The Stones of Venice*.

Klamer: I should read that book. Anyhow you surprise me. By endorsing the interpretive approach, you've moved away from Good Old Chicago.

McCloskey: I think not. You need to get more acquainted with the traditions of applied economics in the United States. Agricultural economists, for example, have long practiced Gothic and interpretive economics.

Klamer: I suspect that interpretive economics will take us to places that are different from the ones your favorites like to inhabit. For instance, it will call attention to the rhetorical dimensions of economic life itself. It will encourage us to explore the social/ cultural/political contexts in which people make decisions. Consequently, interpretive economics may displace the individual decision maker as the central character. The work of Mary Douglas may be an indication, and of Albert Hirschman.

McCloskey: And other social scientists with a larger agenda than imitating what they imagine physicists do. But that's for another day. We must quit: onward and upward.

Klamer: Yes. Time's up. Notice, though, that you've come round to arguing for a difference – between Max *U* and Good Old Chicago.

McCloskey: Well, there *are* some differences, naturally.

Klamer: And you've also argued for the soft-hearted values of community.

McCloskey: I tell you, you're definitely going to get my Chicago card taken away from me.

Klamer: If you subscribe to "interpretive" economics they will do more than that. Consorting with anthropologists is a serious offense in the Social Science Building.

McCloskey: Not among the Good Old Chicago School.

Klamer: Yes. That's one major insight I've gotten from our dialogue – that all "neoclassical" economics is not *The Foundations of Economic Analysis* writ small.

McCloskey: Most American economists would recognize themselves to be "interpretive" if they tried it out. Anyway, I've also learned a thing or two from our conversation. Yes, there are intellectual differences, some of them bitter and unresolvable by this generation. I already knew there were differences in society. Mainly, though, I've learned that interpretive economics is a way of exploring the conjective, beyond the square or the circle.

Klamer: Peace and tolerance. The Principle of Intellectual Exchange works once again.

McCloskey: But wait. Before you go, look here over at the blackboard. I've got a sweet diagram of an Edgeworth box that shows the mutual benefit from intellectual exchange. Now suppose to start with we make the assumption that both parties are self-interested . . .

part VI

Peroration

peroration – Conclusion; Epilogue. The last part of the six-part classical oration . . . often an impassioned summary.

Lanham, *A Handlist of Rhetorical Terms* (1991), p. 114

chapter 25

The economy as a conversation

By now perhaps the metaphor of a conversation in economic science is persuasive. The study of science in the past twenty-five years has shown repeatedly that scientists are people arguing in the marketplace of ideas. But the economic actor, too, is a scientist (the Swiss psychologist Jean Piaget was fond of this metaphor). That is, the economy, like economics itself, is a conversation. Such a metaphor is no more strange on its face than the metaphor of the economy as, say, a system of equations in N-space. The test of both comes in the using.

The connection between the economy and the language occurred a century ago to the founder of modern linguistics, Ferdinand de Saussure, a professor at Geneva when Léon Walras was holding forth up the lake at Lausanne. In economic terms, Saussure distinguished between time series and crossection, thus: "Economics . . . is a science which is forced to recognize this duality . . .Recent work in [economics] emphasizes this distinction. It is a necessity entirely analogous to that which obliges us to divide linguistics into two parts, each based on principles of its own" (Saussure 1916 (1983), p. 79). Saussure may have had in mind the notorious *Methodenstreit* between the German historical school (time series) and the neoclassicals (crossection). Or perhaps he was reflecting Walras' talk of the "passage from the static to the dynamic point of view" (Walras 1874/1900 [1954] pp. 307; cf. 117, 318, 380; on p. 81 Saussure speaks of "static linguistics," the sort he was inventing, in the same style as neoclassical economics). He sounds like a general-equilibrium theorist when declaring that a small linguistic change is like a chess move: "the move has a repercussion upon the whole system. It is impossible for the player to foresee exactly where its consequences will end. The changes in values which result may be, in any particular circumstance, negligible, or very serious . . ." (p. 88).

Saussurean language is economistic throughout, eerily similar to Walrasian language. In a chapter called "Linguistic Value" Saussure arrives at a view of the "value" of a word similar to opportunity cost (a notion becoming clear to economists at about the same time): "These two features are necessary for the existence of any value. To determine the value of a five-franc coin, for instance, what must be known is: (1) that the coin can be exchanged for a certain quantity of something different, e.g. bread, and (2) that its value can be compared with another value in the same system, e.g. that of a one-franc coin, or of another coin belonging to another system (e.g. a dollar). Similarly, a word can be substituted for something dissimilar: an idea. At the same time, it can be compared to something of like nature: another word. Its value is therefore not determined merely by that concept or meaning for which it is a token. It must also be assessed against comparable values, by contrast with other words" (pp. 113-114). The notion of relative value must have permeated the Swiss atmosphere of the late nineteenth century.

Such highbrow analogies between transactions in the marketplace and on the tongues of men are worth exploring, though they will not be explored here. A more pedestrian analogy is the "marketplace for ideas," an idea with a big role in liberal theory since Mill (the phrase itself seems a late flower, perhaps from Holmes' dissent in Abrams v. United States [US 616, 630 (1919)]: "the test of truth is the power of thought to get itself accepted in the competition of the market"). Among economists Fritz Machlup most prominently has examined the sense in which the production of ideas is similar to the production of hamburgers. Prices-as-information merely, again, returns the theoretical favor, exploiting the other half of the analogy. A price is a remark in an on-going conversation. Why else would we speak of "*offer* curves" and "*contract* curves"?

The notion that prices carry "information" is one familiar sense in which the economy is a conversation. Friedrich Hayek was only the most insistent economist on the point, which appears also in the writings of Kenneth Arrow and Leonid Hurwicz. In a large economy the information must somehow be passed from person to person. Commands or exhortations or other speech acts can pass the information, sometimes clumsily, sometimes skillfully. The comparative advantage of speech and action, *peitho* and *bia*, depend on circumstances (thus Ronald Coase in his famous article of 1937 explaining the comparative advantage of direct orders within the firm and market pressures outside the firm). Prices, we economists argue, pass it better.

Notice that in some cases the speech and the action are one. An offer to buy hamburger at $3.00 a pound is a "speech act" in the sense linguists and philosophers use the phrase, namely in that it produces results in the very act of speaking (see Austin 1955, Searle 1969; Petrey 1990). Saying "I thee wed" is a mere form of words, which children can use in make-believe, but in the right circumstances the form of words does a deed. So does saying "I offer $3.00," when followed by the reply, "Sold." An unusually high price for beef "says" that more cattle should be raised. The eaters of beef converse with ranchers, telling them of their great hunger for steaks and hamburgers, backed by willingness to pay. The ranchers reply, "We shall be glad to give you more, but you must understand that we have expenses, too." It is a passing of information.

But there is more to speech acts than passing information. An economist can understand a conversation as a game, in the technical sense. In Austin's vocabulary, one must distinguish in such a game between the mere locution ("Let's make a deal," viewed merely linguistically) and the accompanying "illocution," which is to say, the skillful social act that intends to persuade, say, a bunch of oligopolists to form a monopoly. Illocutions are about intended persuasion. That is, they intend to change other people's behavior or speech. An incompetent rhetor will say "I thee wed" on his first date or "Let's make a deal" in the presence of lawyers from the Antitrust Division of the Department of Justice. Game-theoretically speaking the illocutions are the moves of Mr. Column. The moves of Mr. Row are those of the audience for the illocutions. What the audience then does in response is called by Austin a "perlocution" (accent on the "per"). A linguist would want to go back to the locutions; an economist would want to rush on to the perlocutions. But, as Sandy Petrey explains, the key to bringing language and the economy together is to stick with the middle term, the illocutions, those skillful or clumsy, felicitous or infelicitous acts of persuasion that take up one quarter of national income (Petrey 1990, p. 7).

Consider for example the vexed theory of the entrepreneur. As Metin Cosgel and Arjo Klamer have argued recently (1990), the entrepreneur is above all a persuader, a rhetor exercising the characteristic faculty of human nature for pay. For instance: the egregious Donald Trump. Trump offends. But for all the jealous anger he has provoked he is not a thief. He did not get his billions from aristocratic cattle raids, acclaimed in bardic glory. He did not use a broadsword or a tommy gun to get people to agree. He made, as he puts it, deals, described from his point of view in his book, *Trump: The Art of the Deal*. He bought the Commodore Hotel in New York low and sold it high. Penn Central, Hyatt Hotels, and the New York Board of Estimates valued the old hotel low; the customers valued the new place, suitably trumped up, high. Trump earned his entrepreneurial profit by noticing that a hotel in a low-valued use could be moved into a high-valued use. An omniscient central planner would have ordered the same move.

Crucially, Trump had the power of persuasion to close the deals, the art of felicitous speech acts. As he puts it, "you have to convince the other guy it's in his interest to make the deal" (Trump 1987, p. 53). Persuasion was the main way he transformed the Commodore Hotel into the Grand Hotel: "First, I had to keep [the owners of the hotel] believing [such and such] . . . At the same time, I had to convince an experienced hotel operator to [do so and so] . . . I also had to persuade city officials [thus and such] . . . That [persuasion] . . . would make it far easier to prove to the banks that [so and such]" (Trump 1987, p. 122).

Though featured on the front page of the business section daily, the point is ancient. A Sanskrit poet complained of the skilled persuader, as people do: "I have no skill to place my lips / upon another's ear / nor can deceive a master's heart / by inventing false adventures. / Too stupid am I to have learned / to speak words false but sweet; / what have I then to recommend me / to be a rich man's friend?" (Ingalls 1965, Number 1470).

The Austrian economist Israel Kirzner has argued that entrepreneurial profits are a reward for what he calls "alertness." Sheer – or as we say "dumb" – luck is one extreme. Hard work is the other. Trumpian alertness falls in between, being neither luck nor routine work. Alertness notices the opportunity to buy the Commodore low and to sell it high. Pure profit, says Kirzner, earned by pure entrepreneurs, is justified by alertness (Kirzner 1989). Neoclassical models are often models of routine work, that is to say, the calculated action that leads to an output. Calculative rationality, however, cannot make much of entrepreneurs (cf. Madison 1990, p. 56 n25; Mäki 1990).

Technological change can be viewed from this perspective. The systematic search for inventions can be expected in the end to earn only as much as its cost. It is hard work, merely. The routine inventor is an honest workman, but is worthy therefore only of his hire. The costs of routine improvements in the steam engine of 1800 ate up the profit. They had better, or else the improvements were not routine. Routine improvements are not free lunches. As the economic historian Joel Mokyr put it, "The cold and calculating minds of Research-and-Development engineers in white lab coats worn over three-piece suits" (Preface, 1990) created some of the improvements. But only some.

Nor, on the other hand, is it reasonable to hand technological history over to mere chance, the other end of Kirzner's spectrum. Mokyr shows this from the records of invention. What was required was something between dull effort and heedless luck, namely, a bird-like alertness, ready to get the worm. The alertness explains why entrepreneurs are worthy of their hire.

But the Trump story suggests that something is missing in the metaphor of "alertness," needed to complete the theory. From an economic point of view, alertness by itself is academic, in both the good and the bad sense. It is both intellectual and ineffectual, the occupation of the spectator, as Addison put it, who is "very well versed in the theory of a husband or a father, and can discern the errors of the economy, business, and diversion of others better than those engaged in them."

If his observation is to be effectual, however, the spectator has to persuade a banker. Even if he is himself the banker he has to persuade himself, in the councils of his own mind. What is missing, then, from the Austrian theory of entrepreneurship and technological change is persuasion. Between the conception and the creation, between the invention and the innovation, falls the shadow. Power runs between the two, and power is evoked with persuasive words. An idea without the persuasive words is just an idea. "A man may know the remedy, / but if he has not money, what's the use? / He is like one sitting without a goad / on the head of a must [lust intoxicated] elephant" (Ingalls 1965, Number 1681). The anonymous Yorkshireman who built the new idea of a windmill around 1185 was putting his money where his mouth was, or else putting someone else's money there, "to be a rich man's friend." In either case he had to persuade. In order for an invention to become an innovation the inventor must persuade someone with a bankroll.

This is as true of literary or scientific opportunity as it is of technological invention. Until he won the Goncourt prize in 1919, Proust was not much considered. The prize persuaded the French public to take him seriously. Until Saul Bellow put an imprimatur on his books, William Kennedy (*Ironweed* and other Albany novels) worked unknown as a reporter on the local newspaper. Intellectual bankers need to be persuaded as much as financial ones. The same is true of science. Scientists pursue certification as much as they pursue knowledge, because knowledge without persuasion of an audience is useless, the curse of Cassandra, to know all but to be able to persuade nobody.

What makes alertness work, and gets it power, then, is persuasion. At the root of technological progress is a rhetorical environment that makes it possible for inventors to be heard. Or as Lawrence Berger has argued, the "attention" of the entrepreneurs may be alerted (Berger 1990). The environment of persuasion or attention affected technological change, especially the great technological changes. The Industrial Revolution, one might venture as a hypothesis to be examined, was rhetorical. The places where speech was free to a fault were the first to grow rich: Holland, Scotland, England, Belgium, and the United States.

The division of labor, in short, is limited by the extent of the talk. The more specialized is the economy, the more divided is the airplane into special makers or the distribution of meat into special merchants, the more talk is necessary to establish trust among the cooperators. Trust is part of an economics of talk. The persuasive talk that establishes trust is of course necessary for doing much business. This is why co-religionists or co-ethnics deal so profitably with each other. Avner Greif has explored the business dealings of Mediterranean Jews in the Middle Ages, accumulating evidence for a reputational conversation: in 1055 one Abun ben Zedaka of Jerusalem, for example, "was accused (though not charged in court) of embezzling the money of a Maghribi [North African] trader. When word of this accusation reached other Maghribi traders, merchants as far away as Sicily canceled their agency relations with him" (Greif 1989, pp. 868-869). A letter from Palermo to an Alexandrian merchant who had disappointed the writer said, "Had I listened to what people say, I never would have entered into a partnership with you . . ." (p. 871). Reputational gossip, Greif notes, was cheap, "a by-product of the commercial activity [itself] and passed along with other commercial correspondence" (p. 880). With such information, cheating was profitless within the community.

Old Believers in Russia during the eighteenth and nineteenth centuries held a similar position. The Old Believers refused to adopt the late seventeenth-century reforms in the Russian church, and were in other ways far from progressive. Yet because of their peculiarity they were able to establish a speech community within the larger society. Old Believers on the northern River Vyg, for example, were able in the early eighteenth century to become major grain merchants to the new St. Petersburg "by utilizing their connections with the other Old Believers' communities in the southern parts of the country" (Gerschenkron 1970, p. 19). Gerschenkron quotes Sir William Petty observing that "trade is not fixed to any species of religion as such, but rather to the heterodox part of the whole" (p. 45). Any distinction will suffice. Thus Quakers were great merchants in eighteenth-century England. The overseas Chinese, segregated from the rest of the population (and therefore able to talk inexpensively with each other about breaches of contract among their own), are more successful in trade than their cousins at home.

The observation that small communities talk to each other more easily than do large communities is of course a sociological cliché. Knowledge of a bad deal will fill a small town but is lost in the din of a metropolis. Plato said in the *Laws* (V, 737e) that the optimal city state had 5,040 citizens, on the strange grounds that this number is evenly divisible by every number up to 10, the better to form exactly equal-sized groups for political or military purposes. Aristotle on characteristically more sensible grounds said that "the citizens of a state must know one another's characters" (*Politics* VII. iv. 13). The extreme case of a small town is a two-person society, in which Robinson Crusoe knows every defection by Friday, and vice versa. Furthermore, in this case Crusoe and Friday do all their business with each other. In a world of strangers, by contrast, a new sucker arrives every minute. It is good business to establish friendships with your suppliers and customers and even with your competitors (who may be employing you next year). The dealings of strangers are subject to defection from social norms. In a world of Hobbesian asocial monads the next stranger you meet would just as soon shoot you as shake your hand. That is why the airlines are crowded with business travelers, on their way to making friends.

The economic point of friendship and other supergames is to establish rules of interpretation that cannot be broken cheaply. The literary critic Wayne Booth speaks of "stable irony," which is to say irony in such a context that it can be reliably interpreted. A similar point was made by the philosopher H. P. Grice, noting "conversational implicatures," the rules by which a conversation lives. One "maxim of conversation," we have seen, is "the maxim of Quality," that is, to state only what you believe to be true. A conversation of liars would end in paradox.

What is economically suggestive about the linguistic idea is that such maxims are implicated by the very act of conversing. Grice argues that they are not conventional, in the sense that different cultures could have different maxims, but implied by the setting of any talk. In other words, they are dominant strategies of talk. False, perverse, prolix, laconic, irrelevant, disordered, obscure talk does not serve the purposes of straight talk. As soon as it is recognized as aberrant it will be broken off, or else reinterpreted as crooked talk to some purpose. If a banker says falsely "Business is fine" in circumstances – such as a bank examiner's visit – in which he is expected to be candid he will continue the conversation in jail. On the other hand, the examiner, seeing the books are $1,000,000 short, and knowing that the banker knows he knows, may take the remark as proper irony about the malfeasance of a former vice president, now a resident of Brazil.

And it is obvious, to give another example of the saliency of talk, that cooperation inside the firm depends on speech. Persuasion through speech is necessary for teamwork, from a coxswain pounding out the strokes per minute to Colonel Joshua L. Chamberlain (a professor of rhetoric in civilian life) persuading the 20th Maine to make a bayonet charge down Little Round Top at the Battle of Gettysburg. David Lodge's novel, *Nice Work*, shows an English professor, Robyn Penrose, seeing that the businessman she was assigned to watch was a persuader:

> [I]t did strike [her] that Vic Wilcox stood to his subordinates in the relation of teacher to pupils . . . [S]he could see that he was trying to teach the other men, to coax and persuade them to look at the factory's operations in a new way. He would have been surprised to be told it, but he used the Socratic method: he prompted the other directors and middle managers and even the foremen to identify the problems themselves and to reach by their own reasoning the solutions he had himself already determined upon. It was so deftly done that she had sometimes to temper her admiration by reminding herself that it was all directed by the profit-motive.
>
> Lodge 1988, p. 219

The point is this: the search for a selfish model of efficiency wages, agency costs, insider–outsider deals, and the like will be half successful. Motivating people by deals will work only if the deals convey to them the right story of their own lives. The earning of profit, for example, can be justified on moral and on utilitarian grounds. But it can also be justified as something we bourgeois Westerners (or Easterners) do, a practice of ours, a habit that makes us what we are.

The score-keeping in business is otherwise hard to understand. People rich beyond the dreams of avarice, Ross Perots and Donald Trumps, continue to play a game of entrepreneurship.

The most obvious form of economic talk is of course advertising. Advertising can be explained in part as information. The more naïve critics of advertising understate how much is transmitted by commercial public address. After all, there are new people born every minute who do not yet know that Coke is the Real Thing. The technical definition of the amount of information is its ability to surprise. Not everyone knows that the next exit has a Holiday Inn, and so the sign announcing it that can be noticed even on a rainy winter night by a driver yelling at disorderly children in the back seat is economically justified. The cacophony of "information" on highway billboards is much scorned: "I think that I shall never see / A billboard lovely as a tree. / In fact, unless the billboards fall, / I'll never see a tree at all." Yet on Highway 401 in Canada, where billboards are strictly forbidden, travelers are puzzled about where to relieve their hunger or tiredness.

Simple information, to be sure, could be conveyed in classified advertisements or characterless lists of addresses. But an assessment of the character of the information depends on the surrounding hoopla, or on its tasteful absence. Advertisements convey judgment, which is what we chiefly need in evaluating a new drug for our medical practice or a new book for our professional library. Knowledge is not mere information. As Michael Oakeshott put it, "what we may be said to know will be found to be conjunctions of what is called 'information' and what I shall call 'judgement'" (Oakeshott 1965 [1989], p. 51). Information is conveyed to the receiver; but the receiver makes a judgment, which the sender tries to influence by design. The judgment is properly or improperly influenced by the implied audience, the implied author, the story, the metaphor, the style, by the whole of rhetoric (cf. Cosgel 1990 on fashion).

The chatter in the stock market – that model of economic behavior – is still another example of talk in the economy. Portfolio managers talk full time to decide on buying or selling. Stockbrokers talk to clients and to each other. Technical elves spend their days researching the thoughts the brokers ought to have. Journalists spend their careers reporting the talk on Wall Street, elvish or human. Their reports feed, in turn, the talk among stockbrokers, between stockbrokers and their clients and among the clients themselves. Wall Street buzzes with chatter and is littered with paper reporting the chatter.

The buzzing and littering look odd in the neoclassical account of the stock market. The New York Stock Exchange, after all, is a market with numerous buyers and sellers and low transaction costs, as near to efficiency as can be hoped for. Efficient markets convey through prices all the information that a trader would want. No need to talk. Any informational advantage is reflected in price changes. Such efficiency would provide few rewards to talking if the talkless model were the whole story. The best a loquacious trader could hope for would be the quick exploitation of minor information advantages, or a turn of luck. Efficiency gives no account of the chatter. The conventional story conjures up a silent film of people throwing darts or staring at computer screens, and typing (silently) their orders. Under neoclassical and most other economic principles the processing of the information that prices convey does not require talk.

Robert Shiller has examined the matter closely (Shiller 1989). He starts from the observed price fluctuations in the stock market, arguing that they cannot be attributed to the flow of mere information. He suggests that traders exercise judgment on their information, producing Oakeshott's "knowing":

> News stories or commonly noted events that remind people of the stock may make it more likely that individuals will talk about the stock . . . The rate of spread of interest in one stock is likely to be inhibited by the spread of interest in another stock, since people can talk seriously about a limited number of stocks at a given time. Thus, for example, a big earnings announcement in a different firm may cause conversations that displace conversations about the stock. The lumpiness of media attention is also a factor inducing randomness in the behavior of diffusion traders. Opportunities to talk seriously about a given stock with others may be influenced by patterns of social interaction that may vary irregularly over time.
>
> Shiller 1989, p. 56.

Shiller does not examine the significance and consequences of selective talk directly. But he questioned participants in the market immediately after the collapses of October 1987 and 1989. His surveys (an epistemologically unsound technique, remember) suggest that the participants reacted to no particular news story. Instead, "[a]lmost all of the responses reported . . . advice of brokers and friends, or predictions others made about the future course of the market" (Shiller 1989, p. 387). Shiller found that in his 1987 sample the average institutional investor talked to 7.4 other people on the day of the crash and the average individual investor to 19.7 other people (Shiller 1989, p. 388). The talk is probably meant to reduce cognitive dissonance, as the psychologists say, getting us all to believe in the current madness by sharing it promiscuously with others. Shiller found a significant "contagion of fear," of a sort familiar in other contexts (such as the Great Fear during the French Revolution).

The last example is expectations. Since that master rhetorician, J. M. Keynes, spoke out loud and bold the academic economists have been trying to accommodate expectations into economic theory (cf. Dow 1990; Amariglio 1990). The problem goes beyond Keynes' sweetly expressed warning to Harrod against mechanical models of man: "It is as though the fall of the apple to the ground depended on the apple's motives, on whether it was worthwhile falling to the ground, on whether the ground wanted the apple to fall, and on mistaken calculations on the part of the apple as to how far it was from the center of the earth" (quoted in Lachmann 1990, p. 144). The problem is also that the apples are talking to each other about whether it is worthwhile falling to the ground. For a long time economists thought they could get along without mentioning that expectations are formed through talk. But in the past two decades they have found it increasingly difficult to think about expectations without thinking about the role of public talk. The government announces a new monetary policy. The sweetness of the government's talk determines much of its impact, since a rational public will listen critically, not like gullible fools.

All right. So what? Talk is important in the economy, and seems even to be economically important. What of it?

If the economy depends on the faculty of speech, then the economy will require verbal interpretation (cf. Cosgel 1990; Ebeling 1990; Rector 1990). Economists already give the economy a systemic interpretation, and so the next step does not seem like a large one. Economists already say, "The market in hogs can be interpreted as a diagram of supply and demand." But if the market for hogs depends on how people talk in the market and about the market, then economic institutions will look to some degree like religious ceremonies or social gatherings. They will need to be read in terms of human intentions and beliefs. An economy that depends on speech is one that can be listened to and read, like a text. As Paul Goodman says, "It makes a difference whether people don't speak or speak" (1971 [1972], p. 3).

The conclusion is that of Austrian and hermeneutical economists, most prominently in the collection edited by Don Lavoie (1990a). The neoclassical division of subjective and objective, preference and constraints, should give way to the conjective. A conjective economics would acknowledge, when it matters for explaining what is going on, that expectations of inflation or optimism about entrepreneurial prospects or the conditions of persuasion affect the economy and are themselves a result of human talk. "If economics is indeed a social science," says Gary Madison, "it ought to avoid overprivileging the individual (the 'subjective'); its object is not so much subjective meaning and intention as it is intersubjective patterns of action" (and, one would add, of belief and conversation; Madison 1990, p. 43). As Madison argues, one result would be a more narrative economics (pp. 48-49). Or as Judith Mehta has put it, with a Derridean twist, in modern game theory, with its apparently limitless number of solutions, "we require a methodology which permits us to think pluralistically, appealing to the differences between narratives instead of seeking to apply our own privileged narrative to contexts and contents for which it is ill-suited" (Mehta 1993, p. 95).

The average economist is going to view such a conclusion with alarm. He has been raised to believe that his tools are epistemologically superior to those of the departments of English or anthropology. But the belief is false, even ignorant, even silly. The economists who can get beyond it will have a new set of scientific tools at their disposal, those of interpretation. The conclusion is not that the present tools are worthless and should be discarded. They are worth a lot and should be retained. But if the economy needs sometimes to be measured rather than hammered, or planed rather than sawn, one had better have a tape measure and a plane. An economics that says "Only hammering and sawing done here" is limiting its craft.

chapter 26

The consequences of rhetoric

The Last Word suggests a rhetoric of bringing the conversation to a conclusion. A Conclusion for all time, the sort favored by modernism, would be too ambitious. After all, apart from the trickle of anticipations by Veblen, Machlup (Machlup 1967; and see Langlois 1985, p. 232), Robert Clower (1972 [1988]), Albert Hirschman (1970, 1981, 1984, 1991), Mark Perlman (1978), Shackle (1983, p. 116) and a few others, economists have only thought about words like rhetoric, humanism, conversation, and the social structure of scientific discourse for a few years. We are just beginning an economic criticism, as in "literary criticism," giving new readings of economics and maybe of the economy, too. A handful of people have tried to write economic criticism; many more are thinking about it, drafting and corresponding and reading. But the arbitrage between economics and the rest of the culture has only just begun. So wait and see. At present it would be premature for advocates of the rhetorical approach to erect Conclusions for all time.

Likewise, it would be premature for those who now consider themselves its opponents – we live in hope they will realize soon that they are its natural allies – to throttle the infant in its cradle. For reasons I do not understand I have acquired from my writings on rhetoric a group of a dozen or so opponents willing to go to bizarre lengths of malice, including infanticide. It suggests either that the writings are truths hitting a properly sore nerve or that they are outrageous rubbish that should be suppressed. I haven't made up my mind.

The conservative rhetoric has been "Show me now sixty-seven full and finished pieces of literary criticism of economics, or I won't take it seriously." We can show them twenty or thirty, and daily produce more. Each day another economist sees that economics deserves a richer technique of reading than a 3" × 5"-card philosophy of science. It dawns on her that those people in English and linguistics and communication studies cannot all be idiots unworthy of attention. The ex-idiots' subject is reading and writing, in mathematics or in prose, of a sort that economists and watchers of economists do on the job habitually if unselfconsciously. She begins to grasp what a literary criticism of economics could mean. But it's early days yet, as I say. For the real test, the proof of the pudding, you'll have to wait.

Instead I want here to try to respond to the best of all questions one can ask about any argument: "So What?" An economist conversing with other economists can well ask why he should listen to different talkers, such as ancient rhetoricians and modern literary critics. Economic mathematics in its infancy had the same problem: why should I listen to this stuff? So What?

Note that I am only trying to "respond to" the question, not answer it once and for all. Let us have a conversation, under the Maxim of Presumed Seriousness. Question and response; you may be right; I see what you mean. But note that "So What?" is a question about what is significant to economists, what it means to human beings, what matters to us. It matters to us – not to God or Nature or Analytic Statements. As the rhetoric of inquiry in other fields has pointed out recently, the question of what matters in scholarship can be answered only by attending to the conversation of the scholars who decide. Recall Aristotle's observation that "the persuasive is persuasive *to someone* [tini] . . . *to people of a certain sort* [toioisde] (*Rhetoric*, I. ii. 11; 1356b). The question of what is persuasive, then, is not answered in God's rules of Method or a table of Student's-*t*. It is answered in the conversation of the people of the certain sort to be persuaded.

The So What comes from two sides. On the one side, some economists are puzzled by claims that economics is rhetorical or that economists tell stories. Since they are not much acquainted with the humanities, or even sorry that they aren't, they do not see how such literary claims are freighted. The word "metaphor" calls to their minds fancy writing, not models. The word "story" calls to mind fairy tales, not equilibrium. The word "authority" calls to mind the army, not scientific tradition. Dozens of economists have asked me in honest puzzlement, "But 'rhetoric' means 'fancy talk,' doesn't it?" They do not see how the words of the humanities could fit a science like economics.

Some of the humanists themselves, such as Stanley Fish, do not see how it could matter if the words did apply. (The title "humanists," by the way, makes them uncomfortable, because it seems pretentiously parallel with "scientists" in the religion of our culture, and is equivocal with a party name inside literary studies, as Democrat is with democrat. But let it stand.) The humanists have heard all this before. So what else is new? They do not appreciate how unsettling it is for someone educated in modernist science to realize suddenly that argument is more than syllogism. The humanists thought everyone knew that, and cannot believe that what they teach at low wages to sophomores is here useful. They cannot believe that the argumentativeness and literariness and figurativeness of economics has not been discounted already. They are like the bankers in a *New Yorker* cartoon gazing out on a War-of-the-Worlds scene: "I suppose," says one with a look of resignation, "that the market has discounted *this*, too."

At the highest and noblest level a scientist is a teller of truth (small t), so it cannot be irrelevant to say truly that economic science uses metaphors and stories and other devices of rhetoric. The first answer to the question why it matters, in other words, is that economics, dammit, *is* rhetorical.

Unfortunately, the answer is not very helpful unless one is already prepared to see the devices of rhetoric as significant. After all, economics uses the roman alphabet, too, but no one says that economics would be a lot different if it were written in the arabic alphabet (now, if it were written *in Arabic* that would be another story). The alphabet is not significant: changing to another alphabet would not matter, at least to us. Similarly, someone who is outside the word-culture, or who anyway believes fondly that he is, resists the idea that words matter. Rhetoric is just a surface ornament, right?

The problem with responding to such resistance to the significance of words is that you need to be raised up to take things as significant. The attribution of significance is a human habit, limited by nature but not forced by it. Someone unacquainted with the culture of baseball will see episodes of meaningless rushing about in a context of meaningless standing around. Someone acquainted with it, who takes the meaning and knows the story of the game so far, sees an infield shift for a pull hitter, a hard grounder to deep shortstop, and a sweetly turned double play, Tinker to Evers to Chance.

Therefore the most general argument from truth-telling is not persuasive to the audience addressed. It is rhetorically ineffective, the central teaching of rhetoric being that speech is addressed to an audience. The "simple truth" (as I and a slowly growing set of economists see it) that economics is rhetorical may be accepted as "true" in some weak sense, but not in the strong sense of "true and, by God, significant."

Klamer and I discovered this at the conference on the rhetoric of economics in 1986. The conference contained mostly people working in another tradition than the humanistic. (Although it must be admitted that Klamer and I have come to our humanistic learning a trifle late, in my own case after forty and after Iowa. Our lack of believable claims to expertise in such stuff is another complication in our rhetorical task.) It was hard for the audience at the conference to agree to our changing the subject. Changing the subject is always hard, because the audience must accept that the new subject is significant. And that is a matter of intellectual culture.

To come down a turret or two from the heights of plain truth, then, one can argue alternatively yet equally grandly that a literary approach to economics will bring economics back into the conversation of mankind. As Oakeshott put it, "the final measure of intellectual achievement is in terms of its contribution to the conversation in which all universes of discourse meet" (Oakeshott 1959 [1991], p. 491). By showing that economics works in ways that poems and novels work, one shows economics to be humanistic as well as scientific (to stick with the modernist dichotomy). Economics is part of the rest of the conversation, as it should be to measure up. We economists cannot go on and on with our autistic game, either for ourselves or for others. Oakeshott observes that "each voice is prone to *superbia* [pride], that is, an exclusive concern with its own utterance, which may result in its identifying the conversation with itself and its speaking as if it were speaking only to itself. And when this happens, barbarism may be observed to have supervened" (p. 492).

But you see the rhetorical problem. The argument is again unpersuasive to many in the audience, the many who sneer at the very word "humanistic" and could care less if some Oxford don thinks they are "barbarians." Surely, they say as their lips curl in contempt, the purpose of all this wearisome mathematics is precisely to get away from the imprecise, touchie-feelie, value-laden, and, yes, let it be said, feminine world of words and to get over into the solid, precise, masculine world of Science. If such a proud world speaks only to itself, so much the better. The *superbia* yields good pay for talking to ourselves, in the style of pure mathematics.

All right. Let's be harshly practical. A lowbrow answer to the So

What question is this: a literary, humanistic, rhetorical approach to economics provides the economist, as I have argued, with a place where she can stand outside the field. She needs it, and thinks so, as she demonstrates in her frequent appeals to fancied rules of epistemology or scientific Method. ("All macroeconomics must be grounded in microeconomics" [against which see A. Nelson 1984]; "Survey research cannot yield truthful results"; "Economics will only become scientific when it becomes experimental.") We economists cannot see what we are doing from inside economics itself.

"Well," the modernist will reply, "in finding places from which to look at economics, why not stick at least with the old familiar lookouts in epistemology and philosophy of science?" I have answered that question at some length. Recall the argument of chapter 8, illustrated elsewhere: the humanistic half of our conversation, a theory of reading and writing now two-and-a-half millenia from its beginnings, is thicker in description than the thin little philosophies of epistemology and scientific Method permitted to a modernist. It gives us more true things to say about economic science, more analogies to draw on, more insights into why we agree or disagree. An uncriticized science is not worth having. As a place from which to articulate an economic criticism, humanism works better than modernism.

To put the point another way, a rhetorical approach to economics fits better with being human. This is not to say that the Method of Science is inhuman. The problem is that it is only one tiny part of being human.

The defenders of modernism at this stage leap up and shout, "Aha! Yes: it is the *Scientific* part of being human." They exhibit again their strange parochialism about a border between Science and other things. When asked why the border is desirable they will start talking politics. Their political arguments, we have seen, are not very good. Democratic values would seem to be defended best by open-minded pragmatism and good rhetoric. "The proposal," writes Arjo Klamer, "is to honor truth without claiming it [viz., Truth]. It's pragmatism" (Klamer 1987a, p. 212). Democratic values are not well defended by chanting some philosopher's Credo of Scientific Method while turning the spoonbenders and psychoanalysts over to the secret police. In any case the philosophical border patrol, jack-booted and bureaucratized, has not succeeded. The philosophical distinction between scientific and other thinking, as chapters 2, 5, and others have argued, has proven to be imaginary, self-contradictory, and lacking in point. I say it again: sociologists and historians of science have found nothing corresponding to the distinction in the lives of actual scientists.

Rhetoric fits a life in science better. It seems so in my own life. A rhetorical view of economics, for instance, fits the human love of stories. The stories in Robert Heilbroner's book *The Worldly Philosophers* (1953 and subsequent editions) entranced many a sophomore like me, because it solved sweetly the problem of an economics without a past, an economics inaccessible to outsiders and unpersuasive to insiders. Even high theory speaks with such stories, an intellectual adventure story in which D. Ricardo's and A. Smith's verbal insights are rendered wonderfully exact and portentous by P. Sraffa or F. Hahn.

Rhetoric, again, gives a way to understand the persuasive power of diagrams in economics, their metaphors and symmetries, which like so many other economic majors I came to love in my second year. For the same aesthetic reasons I came in my third and fourth years to love the mathematics. Its beauty is its truth, or had better be. A thin little philosophy of predictions – although it, too, as I have said, had its attractions to a graduate student – cannot account for our scientific passions.

Rhetoric provides a place to stand from which to admire and criticize radically different metaphors of economic life, such as the Marxist metaphor of class struggle, which I clung to as an undergraduate, or the institutionalist metaphor of human geography, which I fell into naturally as an early graduate student, or, at length discovering the truth in my third year at Harvard graduate school, the Chicago-school metaphor of plebeian little monads rushing about in search of rents. Rhetoric therefore allows human politics to matter, in an open and self-critical spirit. At present we allow it only secretly, a secrecy that poisons the economic conversation. Here is an answer to Heilbroner's argument, made in a genial review of *The Rhetoric of Economics* (Heilbroner 1986 [1988]), that after all rhetoric is just about style, not political substance. As I have said, Wolff and Resnick, Amariglio and Klamer, Folbre and Hartmann find rhetoric useful for a politics which is not mine (Wolff and Resnick 1988, Folbre and Hartman 1988). And the style in economics conceals the politics: better understand the style.

The anti-rhetorical split of fact from value in the modernism I espoused as a graduate student had the advantage of allowing specialized work on one metaphor. The specialization allowed many an economist-in-training to believe that his values did not figure in his science. It allowed at least one economist to make the traverse from socialist to libertarian without noticing the role that the learning of economics itself had played in the traverse. At some stage, though – perhaps after age thirty – self-knowledge is more productive.

Rhetoric also makes for understanding between different styles of thought, such as economics and history, the one metaphorical, the other storytelling. I experienced this, too, as an economist speaking after age thirty to historians and later as a nineteenth-century liberal speaking to twentieth-century liberals. The tolerance in rhetoric is not, to repeat, the thoughtless pluralism forced on the modernist by his lack of a way of debating values – "Heh, man: you have your opinion; I have mine. Let's leave it at that." It is not a public opinion poll, voting for the worst rock lyric in history by sending postcards to Dave Barry at the Miami *Herald.* To the contrary, it is a principled pluralism insisting that people defend their values openly (thus in economics Caldwell 1988; and in literature Booth 1979). It is not apolitical. Rhetoric is a theory of democratic pluralism and of general education in a free society. Rhetoric was known as the handmaiden of freedom in the Greek assemblies, in the Roman law courts, and latterly in the parliaments of Europe. It was the education of the West, the rhetorical *paideia,* from Socrates to Francis Bacon.

The good of having economists educated to see their field from the outside, to be able as Lanham puts it to toggle between looking at and looking through the words, will be certain improvements in the practice of economic argument. To the sneer that learning rhetoric "isn't economics" one can only point out that most of what economists do is reading and writing and argumentative arithmetic. It would be like saying that learning mathematics "isn't economics," and then expecting the economist denied mathematical sophistication to read and write well in a subject often requiring it. Economists at present misread. The humanities constitute a theory of reading and a way of improving the readings.

Economists cannot be honest about their arguments if they cannot see what they are. "Lying to oneself about oneself, deceiving yourself about the pretense in your own state of will, must have a harmful influence on style." Economists write badly because their audience is not their colleagues in labor economics or trade theory across the hall – unlike, for example, most historians, the economists barely read their colleagues' work in other fields even for cases of promotion, and depend instead on the candidate's reputation among his fellow specialists, established around the bar at the meetings of the American Economic Association. This makes for quick and voluminous but shallow and fashion-ridden science. Rhetorical self-awareness is a useful substitute for critical reading by colleagues in different fields.

A metaphor of human capital dominates the graduate programs. People are supposed to get "trained" and to be supplied with "tools," which they use until age forty, when they go into administration. It is a poor model of graduate work. The psychologist Lee Cronbach complains that "the apprentice is positively discouraged from wide-eyed unstructured observation, and many investigators seem never to throw away the crutches supplied in the first year of graduate school" (Cronbach 1986, p. 101). The better metaphor than human capital is education, literally "leading out," the making of wide-eyed and serious people, ready to read all the days of their lives.

Humanistic criticism in other fields, such as literature and painting, does not so much change the practice of the artists as create an audience of sophisticated readers and viewers. Economists who could see that Becker's theory of the family depends on the aptness of certain metaphors or that Keynes' theory of the business cycle depends on the reader filling in certain blanks with his own stories would be better scientists and more cautious advocates. A better reader of Jane Austen, or of Joan Robinson, has critical understanding (again: Booth 1979).

An audience of better readers of economics would demand that the writers be better, too. The derived demand for courses on writing would at last force the graduate schools to do their job of teaching people to write. Attractive prospects open: of economic writing without table-of-contents paragraphs ("The organization of this paper is as follows") or without pointless acronyms ("The coefficient on DMWITSCI is significant at the .05 level and the coefficient on FAKESCHL at the .01 level").

But more than literary style is at stake. The substance of economic scholarship depends on how well we argue with each other. "Aha," says the modernist, "He's finally gotten to the Substance, after all the maundering about Style." To which comes the reply: get serious. The distinction between Style and Substance has burrowed like a worm deep into our culture, and even people who recognize its sophomoric character can barely keep it out of their speech. Yet it has few merits. As Socrates showed to Rosenberg/Ion, it is all style and no substance. God dwells in the details. Style is not a frosting added to a Substantial cake. The cake itself has Style, as when whipped egg whites produce angel food. The "substance" of a cake is not the list of basic ingredients. The substance is the style in which they are combined. Talking about the style of modern economics, therefore, does not forsake the substance.

All right, all right: get to it, then. If economists pay more attention to their style, and recognize their rhetoric, how will economics change?

The question should make an economist uncomfortable. To answer it is to claim prescience – pre-science, as I have said, knowing before one knows. The Methodologies do this. They say that they know what will make for good economics, an economics of this or that sort; and they say they know it before it is known. Wait a minute, an economist should say.

Still, one or two predictions may be ventured. I offer some examples from fields of economics where I have done a little work and have scientific opinions not entirely ungrounded, but the predictions are merely illustrative. If they turn out better than the predictions of interest rates or of the Dow Jones average I'll be surprised, and for the same economic reasons.

The chief way that a rhetorical economics would differ from the present economics, to repeat, is that it would face the arguments. An economics that does not recognize its own rhetoric can avoid facing the arguments of opponents indefinitely. That is how things have gone so far, one "paradigm" (Thomas Kuhn cringes) ignoring another. George Stigler described John Stuart Mill as "perhaps the fairest economist who ever lived: He treated other people's theories at least as respectfully as his own, a mistake no other economist has repeated" (Stigler 1987, p. 99). Unrhetorical economics claims to "test" its "hypotheses" by confronting "the facts" and scrutinizing "the theory." This is not a persuasive description of economic discourse, as may be inferred from one decisive observation: economists go on disagreeing violently about the degree of competition in American markets, the degree of dependence on international markets, the closeness of fit of rational models to ordinary people, and fifty other things. If economic discourse were as simple-minded as economists claim in their official Methodology, then it would be astonishing that economists would disagree on anything at all.

As I said at the beginning, the question of what arguments should count in settling the economic disagreements, a variant of the question "So What?", is about what is significant to economists, what matters to them. It matters to *us*, not to God. We economists have no way to get outside our own human conversations and get into the mind of God in order to tell whether such and such an argument is True. We have only ourselves to argue with, displaying to each other whatever numbers and symmetries and metaphors we think should matter. In the absence of rhetorical self-consciousness – note that the rough-and-tumble of seminars or the conversations of co-authors can often produce such self-consciousness without explicit education – we have low argumentative standards. (Take note again: the "lack of standards" so often attributed to an anti-epistemological approach is on the other foot. Epistemology does not provide standards of argument; rhetoric does.) The ignorance of rhetoric leaves economists unable to confront doubts. Run another regression that no one else believes in. Deduce another consequence that no one else is persuaded by. Adduce another institutional fact that no one else sees as relevant.

For instance, it would be hard for a rhetorically sophisticated economist to go on speaking of macroeconomics in a closed economy. A rhetorical approach would show most of macroeconomics to be misled, as should have been clear since the monetary approach to the balance of payments, introduced in the 1970s. Rhetoric notes that economic theory is a way of speaking, convenient to human purposes, not a report on the mind of God. We speak about the openness of, say, Iowa to the prices and interest rates of the rest of the world, and would not think of building a closed model of the Iowa economy. The price of soybeans and the wage of well-motivated and well-educated workers is determined in the world economy, not in Iowa. Iowa is open. But by the same standards of speaking we would not think of the American economy as closed.

Even the best minds confuse the point with the small-country assumption, which is testimony to the rhetorical muddle. Edmond Malinvaud, for example, says that one should model an economy as open or closed "depending on how small and open the economy is" (1989, p. 313). Open, yes; small, no. (I have correspondence from Charles Kindleberger that makes persistently the same mistake; James Tobin made it, I am told; Robert Lucas made to it me in conversation; Milton Friedman makes it in his histories; Harry Johnson and Robert Mundell did not.) On the contrary, whether America bulks large or small in the world is theoretically irrelevant. What is relevant is whether the American price for wheat is connected with that of India. Paris is not small in France, but it is open, and so prices and interest rates in Paris are not determined in Paris itself; they are influenced by Parisian events, of course, but Paris is not the world.

A rhetorically alert economist can see that there is no standard for the openness or closedness of an economy beyond what definitions we choose to give the words. God will not tell us what She has in mind for a standard of openness. We human economists have to decide. And when we decide for one economy (Iowa's, say), we have implicitly decided for economies as open as our standard.

It suddenly became a commonplace in the late 1980s to talk about one world economy. About time. Since the eighteenth century the American economy has been as open in some respects as Iowa is today. By what may be called the Gulliver Effect we are tied to the world economy by a thousand tiny threads. We have been in the world economy for some centuries now, as economic historians informed the rest of the profession decades ago, though to deaf ears. To say that we are now in a single world economy is behindtimes. (The real theory of international trade, invented around 1817, assumed without comment that prices are arbitraged internationally; the financial theory, asymmetrically, did not.) The United States is located between the Atlantic and Pacific oceans, not on Mars (see McCloskey and Zecher 1976, 1984).

Why should it matter? Again: So what? Well, to put it sharply but I am sorry to say without exaggeration, the models of the money supply or the aggregate demand or the rational expectations that have depended on an economy being closed have been mistaken, all this time. I know this is hard to believe. That such smart people as the macroeconomic theorists could get their main business so wrong seems incredible. But keep an open mind for a moment, and see how it follows from the fact of openness. Open economies do not have exogenous money supplies or solely American interest rates or domestically determined expectations, as open-economy macroeconomics has recognized. All the earlier models depend on such assumptions, and they are still being used for research, policy, and teaching. So the models have to be fitted again, because they do not acknowledge the openness of the economy. The econometrics on which macroeconomists claim to have based their beliefs is mistaken. Variables that were specified as endogenous were in fact to some large degree exogenous. The fitted coefficients are biased and even inconsistent. Throw away all the previous work. Because we were not paying attention to our rhetorical standards, we economists blew it. Amazingly, entirely. Modern macroeconomics is erroneous. (Don't get mad: think about it.) The theorizing is misinformed and therefore irrelevant to an economy in a world. The empiricism is wrong.

The models of Friedman, Tobin, Lucas, Barro, or the other admirable closed-economy thinkers may or may not work for the world considered as one. That remains to be seen, and is the relevant question. But the theories would hold for the American economy in isolation only if it were reasonable to locate America outside the world. Only in that case would American prices and interest rates be determined by largely American phenomena, which is the mistaken premise of our teaching in Introductory Economics 1 and Macroeconomics 105.

The journalists and politicians naturally echo the economists. American monetary policy, they say, determines American interest rates. The Federal deficit changes American interest rates relative to foreign. The price level of the United States is determined, for a given exchange rate, by American monetary policy. But, unfortunately, Not. By ignoring the rhetorical character of science and the human persuasion on which it turns, leaving the argument to Proofs and Tests, godlike but unpersuasive, the economists have wasted their time and misled their public. The costs in policies unrealistically imposed has probably amounted to tens if not hundreds of billions of dollars, all from a merely rhetorical mistake.

The former chairman of the Federal Reserve Board, Paul Volcker, tells a story about the closed-economy attitude of some economists (Volcker and Gyohten 1992, pp. 96-97). In 1973 George Shultz was Secretary of the Treasury, Volcker his Undersecretary for Monetary Affairs, and Arthur Burns the Chairman of the Fed. Shultz and Burns faced a news conference in Paris after one of the many crises of the Bretton Woods system during its slow collapse, this one finally and officially allowing the dollar itself to float against gold itself. A reporter asked Shultz what the floating dollar meant for American monetary policy. As Volcker recounts it, "Burns, always conscious of the prerogatives of an independent Federal Reserve Chairman, reached over and took the microphone from Shultz and pronounced in his most authoritarian tone, 'American monetary policy is not made in Paris; it is made in Washington.'" No, Mr. Chairman, it is not. Under fixed exchange rates it is made in the markets of the world.

The rhetorical point is a general one, applying to many of the differences that separate economists. Take perfect competition. The Chicago School believes that perfect competition, near enough, characterizes the American economy (I do, for example: cf. McCloskey 1985b, chs. 14, 18). Everyone else says perfect competition is "unrealistic" (see Baran and Sweezy 1966, for example). Neither side has any effect on the arguments of the other. Economists spend careers on one side or the other, uninterested in new arguments.

Yet both sides agree that the decision whether or not perfect competition best characterizes the economy is foundational. If perfect competition does not reign, to give an instance, free trade may not be the best policy. If on the other hand the Chicagoans are correct then antitrust may worsen the performance of an industry. If the Marxists are correct then politics may be hopelessly corrupted by monopoly capital. If the school of Veblen–Berle–Galbraith is correct then advertising may run the show. Whole empires of economic argument depend on whether or not competition is perfect.

Perhaps what Milton Friedman was groping for in his famous dismissal of talk about realism in 1953 was a rhetorical standard. What mattered, he was saying in a pragmatic way, was how a proposition was used, its human use in argument, not God's Truth. This is surely right about perfect competition. We can't go on hurling insults at each other about the "realism" of our opponent's assumptions. We should come to agree on some particular, human, rhetorical standard by which the quarrel can yield progress. The ability to predict might be one such standard, though we have found that a lot hinges on what "ability to predict" means. For all the dominance of it as a rhetorical standard since the 1950s it has not ended many arguments in economics. That is one correct point amongst a good deal of Error in Blaug's book of 1980 on Methodology: Blaug was certainly correct to nail economists for not actually using prediction with the thoroughness they so smarmily claim to achieve.

Friedman's rhetorical suggestion, however, got mixed up in positivism, with its supposition that "good prediction," like "empirical observation" or "economic theory," is a simple thing that any child can detect. Does perfect competition yield good predictions? That is all ye need to know. But positivism, as we have seen, begs the main scientific issue. The main issue is the adequacy of the "prediction" from a hypothesis like perfect competition (more likely in economics a postdiction, or more precisely, to use a technical word from literary criticism, a story). The adequacy of course can only be determined by standards of human speech.

A prediction from a theory of perfect competition or international arbitrage is not good or bad all by itself, without the intrusion of human standards of good or bad. An R-squared of 0.90 is adequately "good" for some human purposes, rotten for others. It would probably be good enough as a correlation between national incomes for the purpose of justifying the notion of an international business cycle; but it would probably be too low in a correlation of exchange rates for the purpose of making money on the exchanges. Scientific explanation is a human purpose, not that glimpse into the mind of God which philosophers since Plato have been promising us. We humans decide the purposes of the phrase "perfect competition." R-squares are important but they are not enough. We need to join the argument. "What do you mean by 'perfect competition'? What standard would you accept as showing it to be usefully true? All right: let's go together and settle the matter" (McCloskey 1973, ch. 2). If economists would recognize this, and stop thinking that irrelevant t-statistics or fatuous "predictions" will answer their questions free of human intervention, they would come to grips with each others' arguments.

A trial at law requires a pragmatic decision. The trial cannot go on forever, or just stop without decision when the lawyers get tenure. The two sides must agree to a standard of evidence that puts a strain on them, enough strain to separate the winner from the loser. The positivist philosopher will claim reflexively, without argument, that using such a rhetorical and forensic approach to science would not have standards (see, for example, Kevin Hoover's remarks in 1991, p. 123, which he concedes may be "not completely well informed"). But the positivist is mistaken. On the contrary: the standards of "consistent theory" or "good prediction" presently in use are low to the point of scientific fraud (again Blaug said it well in 1980). They are six-inch hurdles over which the economist leaps with a show of athletic effort. A non-rhetorical economics has low argumentative standards.

The standard of a rhetorical economics would be higher, fully forty inches of hurdle: the standard, namely, of persuading readers, honestly. As Feyerabend says, "an absence of 'objective' standards [in a non-social definition of Objective] does not mean less work; it means that scientists have to check all ingredients of their trade and not only those which philosophers and establishment scientists regard as characteristically scientific" (Feyerabend 1987, p. 284, his italics).

Consider this. Is it more difficult for a Chicago economist (McCloskey forthcoming) to produce still another regression "consistent with the hypothesis" of, say, the rationality of peasant cultivators in medieval England; or, on the other hand, to produce a set of arguments, drawn from all the evidence he can find and his audience thinks relevant, that can actually persuade an economist from Yale?

The claim that rhetoric has "no standards" is supported by an equivocation between "empirical" and "empiricism," as I have said earlier. No one in their right mind opposes "empirical work," so long as the phrase is understood as consulting the phenomena. It really would be anti-scientific madness suddenly to begin advocating the closing down of libraries and laboratories and computer centers. Not just mad, but evil. Let it be said, then, that no one who wishes economists to become more self-conscious about their arguments is against empirical work – especially genuine empirical work, going beyond fitting still another hyperplane to data culled from the appendix to the *Economic Report of the President.*

Yet a rhetorical approach to economics does oppose the narrowing of science associated especially with British "empiric*ist*" philosophy since Hume. I have explained this, though Ion and the other conventional Methodologists did not get it: empiricism in the form in which it has affected the philosophical thinking of scientists would reduce all argument to first-order predicate logic and all observation to controlled experiment. In this form it has had a rotten effect on many sciences. Take a look at psychology some day; or much of economics. In a search for godlike certainty the evidence has been narrowed to a rump unpersuasive to anyone. The result is a lowering of standards, the six-inch hurdles just mentioned. So: it does not justify the narrowness of empiric*ism* to appeal to the undoubted virtues of the broadly empiric*al.* Empirical work would be better, not worse, in a rhetorically self-conscious economics. The work is already better in fields like urban economics or economic history that take seriously their responsibility to persuade an audience with facts and relevant simulations.

A rhetorical economics would be tougher and more cumulative. This sounds paradoxical, but only because the Method of Science is accustomed to sneering at human argument. Arguments are not arbitrary. They get settled if they get joined, like cases at law. The examples of closed-economy macroeconomics and of perfect competition show that most arguments in economics have not been joined, at least by the standard met daily in the law courts, or even in most domestic squabbles. Economics since the war has been mostly noncumulative. What do we know about international trade that we did not know in 1965? Oh, yeah? What large issue in economics since 1940 has been settled by an econometric finding? I said "large." Why has economic history, where arguments are open and broad-based, mainly because its practitioners are forced to speak to both economists and historians, made cumulative progress since 1960, and labor economics, similarly catholic in its arguments, since 1970? What argument about the economic world has general equilibrium theory advanced since 1950? I said "about the economic world."

A rhetorically sophisticated economics would get down to work. Economics would begin to look more like evolutionary biology, the identical twin to economics raised separately, but embarrassingly more serious about scientific persuasion and more self-conscious about its rhetoric (see Gould 1993). Economics would be better if it took the arguments more seriously, by getting them out in the open. We need a scientific economics. Oddly, to get one and to defend it against the monists who would make it into dogma we need rhetorical sophistication.

And a rhetorical economics would better suit the institutions of a democratic society. As Lanham puts it,

> The Strong Defense [of rhetorical education] argues that, since truth comes to humankind in so many diverse and disagreeing forms, we cannot base a polity on it. We must, instead, devise some system by which we can agree on a series of contingent operating premises. The system which rhetoric devised . . . was built upon an oscillation very like Castiglione's *sprezzatura*. The most familiar example . . . is the Anglo-Saxon system of jurisprudence . . . The magic moment of transmutation, what drives the system, is the need to reach a decision.
>
> Lanham, forthcoming, ch. 7, p. 48

And so too for political and scientific decisions.

On the other hand, some alleged consequences of rhetoric do not seem plausible. The openness of rhetoric gives voice to minority opinions. To this extent rhetoric is hostile to the mainstream, if the mainstream can hold its dominance only by erecting big dams to stop the flow of alternative arguments. That's good. But rhetoric is not intrinsically hostile to the mainstream. Rhetorical alertness can be used to force the dominant groups to face up to institutionalism or Marxism or feminism or Austrianism, as they should. But nothing inside the rhetoric itself implies one or the other view.

In particular the attacks from various quarters on mainstream "neoclassical" economics, as I have argued, seem to depend on a misapprehension of its core. A notion that important social forces arise out of self-interested behavior and that these forces are hedged about by entry and competition is plausible on its face and perfectly healthy as a scientific program in economics. Along with some parallel and very different programs in economics, it has been going strong since the eighteenth century. It helps to explain many of the social facts we wish to explain, from the rise of real wages since 1840 to the difficulties of big bankers in the 1980s. Rhetorical self-awareness is consistent with the genuinely neoclassical. Rhetoric is consistent with any number of beliefs about the economy, between which one can toggle.

The rhetoricians of economics are accused sometimes by conservatives of being "trendy" (the conservatives Rosenberg and Blaug, for example, are free with such attributions, their excuse for not doing the homework). If the charge is meant to suggest that we came to our ideas by looking around in Paris for What's New, it is biographically false and rhetorically unfair. Arjo Klamer's experience in journalism and the history of thought, for example, or E. Roy Weintraub's in mathematics and intellectual history, or mine in the Chicago School and economic history led us naturally to wonder about speech communities. Being shouted at across disciplinary boundaries, as many economists could testify, is a practical education in rhetoric.

If the charge of being "trendy" means merely that we have noticed lots of other people thinking about rhetoric in their fields, and wonder dimly whether we should join, then it is true. Every week or so I find another part of the intellectual community that has discovered the rhetorical character of human speech, military history one week (Keegan 1976), mathematical logic the next (McCawley 1981), psychiatry in the third (Frank and Frank 1961 [1991]), statistical theory in the fourth (MacKenzie 1981; Porter 1986), and management in the fifth (Czarníawska-Joerges 1992, 1993). Month by month the list of rhetorics of inquiry grows. The (incomplete and recent) computer catalogue at the Library of the University of Iowa contains 2,524 book titles concerning rhetoric, 340 beginning literally with the word "rhetoric" or "rhetorical." To speak only of those I am familiar with, setting aside studies of literature and communications themselves and mentioning only works not discussed earlier, I have seen rhetorical analysis also in studies of mathematics (Polya 1954; Steiner 1975; Solow 1982; Livingstone 1986), design (Margolin 1989; Tufte 1983, 1990; R. Buchanan 1989), political theory (Barry 1965; Nelson 1983; Seery 1990); fashion (Lurie 1981), early New England housing (Deetz 1977, pp. 108–109), political economy (Keohane 1988; Galbraith 1988; Hirschman 1991; Mechling and Mechling 1983; Gusfield 1981), feminism (Elshtain 1988), anthropology (Rosaldo 1987; Clifford and Marcus 1986; Shweder 1991), paleoanthropology (Landau 1987), paleontology (Gould 1987, 1989), population biology (Kingsland 1985), psychology (Bruner 1986), law (James Boyd White 1985b), linguistics (Lakoff and Johnson 1980; Lakoff and Turner 1989); history (Hayden White 1973, 1981; Carrard 1992), American political history (Jamieson 1988; Cmiel 1990; McPherson 1985 [1991]), intellectual history (LaCapra 1983; Megill 1985), talmudic studies (Jacobs 1984), biblical exegesis (G.A. Kennedy 1984; Hartman and Budick 1986; Kinneavy 1987), ethics (Toulmin 1950 [1986]; Jonsen and Toulmin 1988), philosophy (Ortony 1979; Johnson 1981, 1987). They do not all use the word "rhetoric," and will not all be recognized immediately as rhetorical. But they see the breadth of human argument, the limits to formulas for thinking, the way that words matter to the conclusions drawn, the conversations in politics and the politics in conversations. They have learned that speech has designs on us, and that we had better know the designs outright. They are self-conscious about wordcraft.

Rhetorically self-conscious argument, when all is said, is something like growing up. Perhaps the time has come, after a useful childhood spent in positivism, for economics to grow up, too.

works cited

When citations in the text mention two years, as in "Arnold 1885 (1949)," the first is the original date of publication and the second the date of the reprint for page reference.

Adelstein, Richard P. 1991. "'The Nation as an Economic Unit.' Keynes, Roosevelt and the Managerial Idea." *Journal of American History* 78 (June): 160–187.

Aeschylus. *Prometheus Bound.* Trans. David Greene, in David Greene and Richard Lattimore, eds., *Greek Tragedies*, vol. I, Chicago: University of Chicago Press, 1942 (1960).

Akerlof, George A., and W. T. Dickens. 1982. "The Economic Consequences of Cognitive Dissonance." *American Economic Review* 72 (June): 307–319.

Alchian, Armen. 1950. "Uncertainty, Evolution, and Economic Theory." *Journal of Political Economy* 58 (June): 211–221.

Aldridge, John W. 1990. "The New American Assembly-Line Fiction: An Empty Blue Center." *The American Scholar* 59 (Winter): 17–38.

Alker, Jr., Hayward R. 1988. "The Dialectical Logic of Thucydides' Melian Dialogue." *American Political Science Review* 82 (September): 805–820.

Allais, Maurice. 1989. "My Life Philosophy." *The American Economist* 33 (2, Fall): 3–17.

Amariglio, Jack. 1984. "Epistemology, Literary Theory, and Neoclassical Economics." Unpublished paper, Department of Economics, Merrimack College, Andover, Mass.

——— 1987. "Marxism Against Economic Science: Althusser's Legacy." *Research in Political Economics.* Volume X. Greenwich, Conn. JAI press.

——— 1988. "The Body, Economic Discourse, and Power: An Economist's Introduction to Foucault." *History of Political Economy* 20: 583–613.

——— 1990a. "Poster's Foucault, Marxism and History and Barnes' About Science: Review Essay." *Research in the History of Thought and Methodology* 7: 227–238.

——— 1990b. "Economics as a Post-modern Discourse." Pp. 14–46 in Samuels, *Economics as Discourse.*

Amariglio, Jack, Stephen Resnick, and Richard Wolff. 1990. "Division and Difference in the 'Discipline' of Economics." *Critical Inquiry* 17 (Autumn): 108–137.

Andvig, Jens-Christoph. 1991. "Verbalism and Definitions in Interwar Theoretical Macroeconomics." *History of Political Economy* 23 (Fall): 431–455.

Aristotle. *Politics*. Trans. E. Barker. Oxford: Clarendon Press, 1946.

Rhetoric. Trans. George A. Kennedy. New York: Oxford University Press, 1991.

Arnold, Matthew. 1885 (1949). "Literature and Science." Pp. 405–429 in L. Trilling, ed., *The Portable Matthew Arnold*. New York: Viking Press.

Arrington, C. Edward. 1990. "Comment on Benton." Pp. 90–100 in Samuels, ed., *Economics as Discourse*.

Arrow, Kenneth. 1959. "Decision Theory and the Choice of a Level of Significance for the t-Test." In Ingram Olkin J., and others, eds., *Contributions to Probability and Statistics: Essays in Honor of Harold Hotelling*. Stanford: Stanford University Press.

1986. "History: The View from Economics." Pp. 13–20 in W. N. Parker, ed., *Economic History and the Economist*. Oxford: Basil Blackwell.

Ashmore, Malcolm, Michael Mulkay, and Trevor Pinch. 1989. *Health and Efficiency: A Sociology of Health Economics*. Milton Keynes and Philadelphia: Open University Press.

Austen, Jane. 1818 (1965). *Persuasion*. New York: Houghton Mifflin.

Austin, J. L. 1955 (1965, 1977). *How to Do Things with Words*. Second edn. Ed. J. O. Urmson and M. Sbisà. Cambridge, Mass.: Harvard University Press.

1962 (1975). *How to Do Things with Words*. Cambridge, Mass.: Harvard University Press.

Ayer, A. J., ed. 1959. *Logical Positivism*. New York: Free Press.

Backhouse, Roger E. 1985. *A History of Modern Economic Analysis*. New York: Basil Blackwell.

1988. *Economists and the Economy: The Evolution of Economic Ideas, 1600 to the Present Day*. Oxford and New York: Basil Blackwell.

1991. "The Neo-Walrasian Research Program in Macroeconomics." Pp. 403–426 in de Marchi and Blaug, eds., *Appraising Economic Theories*.

1992a. "Fact, Fiction or Moral Tale: How Should We Approach the History of Economic Thought?" *Journal of the History of Economic Thought* 14 (Spring): 18–35.

1992b. "The Constructivist Critique of Economic Methodology." *Methodus* 4 (June): 65–82.

1993a. "Rhetoric and Methodology." R. F. Hébert, ed., *Perspectives in the History of Economic Thought*. Aldershot: Edward Elgar.

1993b. "The Debate Over Milton Friedman's Theoretical Framework: An Economist's View." Pp. 103–131 in Backhouse, Dudley-Evans, and Henderson, eds., *Economics and Language*.

Backhouse, Roger, Tony Dudley-Evans, and Willie Henderson, eds. 1993a. *Economics and Language*. London: Routledge.

1993b. "Exploring the Language and Rhetoric of Economics." Pp. 1–20 in Backhouse, Dudley-Evans, and Henderson, eds., *Economics and Language.*

Bacon, Francis. 1620 (1965). "The New Organon and The Great Instauration [Instauratio Magna]." In S. Warhaft, ed., *Francis Bacon: A Selection of His Works.* Indianapolis: Bobbs-Merrill.

Bakan, David. 1967. *On Method: Toward a Reconstruction of Psychological Investigation.* San Francisco: Jossey-Bass.

Ball, Milner S. 1985. *Lying Down Together: Law, Metaphor, and Theology.* Rhetoric of the Human Science. Madison: University of Wisconsin Press.

Baran, Paul A. and Paul M. Sweezy. 1966. *Monopoly Capital: An Essay on the American Economic and Social Order.* New York: Monthly Review Press.

Barnes, Barry and David Edge, eds. 1982. *Science in Context: Readings in the Sociology of Science.* Cambridge, Mass.: MIT Press.

Barrett, William. 1979. *The Illusion of Technique: A Search for Meaning in a Technological Civilization.* Garden City, N.Y.: Anchor.

Barry, Brian. 1965. *Political Argument.* London: Routledge Kegan Paul.

1970 (1978) *Sociologists, Economists and Democracy.* Chicago: University of Chicago Press (London: Collier-Macmillan, 1970).

Bartley, William W., III. 1962 (1984). *The Retreat to Commitment.* Second edn. La Salle, Ill.: Open Court.

Bazerman, Charles. 1987. "Codifying the Social Scientific Style: The APA *Publication Manual* as a Behaviorist Rhetoric." Pp. 125–144 in Nelson, Megill, and McCloskey, eds., *Rhetoric of the Human Sciences.*

1988. *Shaping Written Knowledge: The Genre and Activity of the Experimental Article in Science.* Rhetoric of the Human Sciences. Madison: University of Wisconsin Press.

1993. "Money Talks: The Rhetorical Project of *The Wealth of Nations.*" Pp. 173–199 in Backhouse, Dudley-Evans, and Henderson, eds., *Economics and Language.*

Bazerman, Charles and James Paradis, eds. 1991. *The Textual Dynamics of the Professions.* Rhetoric of the Human Sciences. Madison: University of Wisconsin Press.

Beardsley, Monroe C. 1956. *Thinking Straight: Principles of Reasoning for Readers and Writers.* 2nd edn. Englewood Cliffs, N.J.: Prentice Hall.

Becker, Gary S. 1964. *Human Capital: A Theoretical and Empirical Analysis, with Special Reference to Education.* National Bureau for Economic Research. New York: Columbia University Press.

1965. "A Theory of the Allocation of Time." *Economic Journal* 75 (September): 493–517.

Becker, Gary S. and George J. Stigler. 1977. "De Gustibus Non Est Disputandum." *American Economic Review* 67 (March): 76–90.

Benton, Raymond, Jr. 1990. "A Hermeneutic Approach to Economics: If Economics is Not Science, and If It is Not Merely Mathematics, Then What Could It Be?" Pp. 65–89 in Samuels, ed., *Economics as Discourse.*

Berger, John. 1985. *The Sense of Sight: Writings by John Berger.* Ed. L. Spencer. New York: Pantheon.

Berger, Lawrence A. 1990. "Self-Interpretation, Attention, and Language: Implications for Economics of Charles Taylor's Hermeneutics." Pp. 262–284 in Lavoie, ed., *Economics and Hermeneutics.*

Berlin, Isaiah. 1969. *Four Essays on Liberty.* Oxford: Oxford University Press.

Bernstein, Jeremy. 1989. "Michele Angelo Besso." *New Yorker,* February 27.

Bernstein, Richard J. 1983. *Beyond Objectivism and Relativism: Science, Hermeneutics, and Praxis.* Philadelphia: University of Pennsylvania Press.

Bianchi, Marina and Hervé Moulin. 1991. "Strategic Interactions in Economics: The Game Theoretic Alternative." Pp. 179–196 in de Marchi and Blaug, eds., *Appraising Economic Theories.*

Bicchieri, Cristina. 1988. "Should a Scientist Abstain from Metaphor?" Pp. 100–114 in Klamer, Solow, and McCloskey, eds., *Consequences.*

Billig, Michael. 1987. *Arguing and Thinking: A Rhetorical Approach to Social Psychology.* Cambridge: Cambridge University Press.

Billington, David P. 1983 (1985). *The Tower and the Bridge: The New Art of Structural Engineering.* Princeton: Princeton University Press.

Black, Fischer. 1986. "Review of The Rhetoric of Economics." *Journal of Finance* 41 (December): 1183–1185.

Black, Max. 1962. *Models and Metaphors.* Ithaca: Cornell University Press.

Blaug, Mark. 1980. *The Methodology of Economics: Or, How Economists Explain.* Cambridge: Cambridge University Press.

   1984. "Comment 2" (on T. Hutchison, "Our Methodological Crisis"), pp. 30–36 in Peter Wiles and Guy Routh, eds., *Economics in Disarray.* Oxford: Basil Blackwell.

   1987. "Methodology with a Small m." *Critical Review* 1 (Spring): 1–5.

   1991. "Afterword." Pp. 499–512 in de Marchi and Blaug, eds., *Appraising Economic Theories.*

Bloor, David. 1983. *Wittgenstein: A Social Theory of Knowledge.* London: Macmillan.

Bloor, Meriel and Thomas Bloor. 1993. "How Economists Modify Propositions." Pp. 153–169 in Backhouse, Dudley-Evans, and Henderson, eds., *Economics and Language.*

Blundell, William E. 1988. *The Art and Craft of Feature Writing.* New York: New American Library.

Boettke, Peter J. 1988. "Storytelling and the Human Sciences." *Market Process* 6 (Fall): 4–7.

Boland, Larry. 1987. "Contribution to Session on 'Methodological Diversity in Economics.'" *Research in the History of Thought and Methodology* 5: 207–239.

Boland, Lawrence A. 1982. *The Foundations of Economic Method.* London: Allen and Unwin.

Bonello, Frank J. 1987. "Review of The Rhetoric of Economics." *Social Science Quarterly* 68 (March): 209–210.

Booth, Wayne, C. 1974. *Modern Dogma and the Rhetoric of Assent.* Chicago: University of Chicago Press.

   1979. *Critical Understanding: The Powers and Limits of Pluralism.* Chicago: University of Chicago Press.

1988. *The Company We Keep: An Ethics of Fiction.* Berkeley and Los Angeles: University of California Press.

Bordo, Susan. 1987. *The Flight to Objectivity: Essays on Cartesianism and Culture.* Albany: State University of New York Press.

Borenstein, Nathaniel S. 1992. "Colleges Need to Fix the Bugs in Computer-Science Courses." *Chronicle of Higher Education* 38 (45, July 15): B3–4.

Borges, Jorge Luis. 1952 (1964). "The Analytical Language of John Wilkes." Pp. 101–105 in his *Other Inquisitions.* New York: Simon and Schuster.

Boring, Edwin G. 1919. "Mathematical versus Scientific Significance." *Psychological Bulletin* 16 (October): 335–338.

Bornemann, Alfred H. 1987. "Review of The Rhetoric of Economics." *Kyklos* 40 (1): 128–29.

Boulding, Kenneth. 1979. *Ecodynamics: A New Theory of Societal Evolution.* Beverly Hills: Sage Publications.

Bowles, Samuel and Herbert Gintis. 1990. "Contested Exchange: New Microfoundations of the Political Economy of Capitalism." *Politics and Society* 18: 165–222.

Boynton, Robert. 1989. "The Senate Agriculture Committee Produces a Homeostat." *Policy Sciences* 22: 51–80.

1990. "Ideas in Action: A Cognitive Model of the Senate Agriculture Committee." *Political Behavior* 12(2): 181–213.

Braithwaite, Richard B. 1953. *Scientific Explanation.* Cambridge: Cambridge University Press.

Brennan, Timothy J. 1984. "Is Economic Methodology Special?" *Research in the History of Thought and Methodology* 2: 127–149.

Broad, William, and Nicholas Wade. 1982. *Betrayers of the Truth: Fraud and Deceit in the Halls of Science.* New York: Simon and Schuster.

Brock, William A. 1988. "Introduction to Chaos and Other Aspects of Nonlinearity." In W. A. Brock and A. G. Malliaris, eds., *Differential Equations, Stability, and Chaos in Dynamic Economics.* New York: North Holland (October 30, 1987 draft, Department of Economics, University of Wisconsin).

1989. "Chaos and Complexity in Economic and Financial Science." Pp. 421–447 in George M. Furstenberg, ed., *Acting Under Uncertainty: Multidisciplinary Conceptions.* Boston: Kluwer Academic.

Bronowski, Jacob. 1951 (1960). *The Common Sense of Science.* Harmondsworth: Pelican Books.

1977. *A Sense of the Future.* Cambridge, Mass.: MIT Press.

1978. *The Origins of Knowledge and Imagination.* New Haven: Yale University Press.

Brown, Richard Harvey. 1977. *A Poetic for Sociology: Toward a Logic of Discovery for the Human Sciences.* Cambridge: Cambridge University Press.

1987. *Society as Text: Essays on Rhetoric, Reason, and Reality.* Chicago: University of Chicago Press.

1989. *Social Science as Civic Discourse: Essays on the Invention, Legitimation, and Uses of Social Theory.* Chicago: University of Chicago Press.

Brown, Vivienne. 1993. "Decanonizing Discourses: Textual Analysis and the

History of Economic Thought." Pp. 64–84 in Backhouse, Dudley-Evans, and Henderson, eds., *Economics and Language*.

Bruner, Jerome. 1983. *In Search of Mind: Essays in Autobiography*. New York: Harper and Row.

1986. *Actual Minds, Possible Worlds*. Cambridge, Mass.: Harvard University Press.

Brunner, José. 1992. "'Every Path Will End in Darkness,' Or, Why Psychoanalysis Needs Metapsychology." Unpublished paper for "Narrative Patterns in Scientific Disciplines," April 27–30, 1992, Cohn Institute, Tel Aviv University; Edelstein Center, Hebrew University; and the Van Leer Jerusalem Institute.

Bruns, Gerald L. 1984. "The Problem of Figuration in Antiquity". Pp. 147–164 in G. Shaprio and A. Sica, eds., *Hermeneutics: Questions and Prospects*. Amherst: University of Massachusetts Press.

Brush, Stephen G. 1989. "Prediction and Theory Evaluation: The Case of Light Bending." *Science* 246 (December 1): 1124–1129.

Buchanan, James. 1964 (1979). "What Should Economists Do?" Pp. 17–38 in his *What Should Economists Do?* Indianapolis: Liberty Press.

Buchanan, Richard. 1989. "Declaration by Design: Rhetoric, Argument, and Demonstration in Design Practice." Pp. 145–156 in Victor Margolin, ed., *Design Discourse: History, Theory, Criticism*. Chicago: University of Chicago Press.

Burke, Kenneth. 1950 (1969). *A Rhetoric of Motives*. Berkeley: University of California Press.

Butchvarov, Panayot. 1989. *Scepticism in Ethics*. Bloomington: Indiana University Press.

Butos, William. 1987. "Rhetoric and Rationality: A Review Essay of McCloskey's The Rhetoric of Economics." *Eastern Economic Journal* 13 (July–September): 295–304.

Bye, Raymond T. 1924. "Some Recent Developments of Economic Theory." Pp. 271–300 in R. G. Tugwell, ed., *The Trend of Economics*. New York: Knopf.

Cairncross, Alec. 1992. "From Theory to Policy-Making: Economics as a Profession." *Banco Nazionale del Lavoro Quarterly Review* 180 (March): 3–20.

Caldwell, Bruce J. 1982. *Beyond Positivism: Economic Methodology in the Twentieth Century*. London and Boston: Allen and Unwin.

ed. 1984. *Appraisal and Criticism in Economics: A Book of Readings*. Boston: Allen and Unwin.

1988. "The Case for Pluralism." Pp. 231–244 in de Marchi, ed., *The Popperian Legacy*.

ed. 1987. "Methodological Diversity in Economics." (A debate among Larry Boland, Arjo Klamer, and Alexander Rosenberg.) *Research in the History of Economic Thought and Methodology*, ed. Warren Samuels, Greenwich, Conn. JAI Press.

1991. "Comment on Lavoie." Pp. 487–491 in de Marchi and Blaug, eds., *Appraising Economic Theories*.

Caldwell, Bruce J. and A. W. Coats. 1984. "The Rhetoric of Economists: A Comment on McCloskey." *Journal of Economic Literature* 22 (June): 575–578.

Campbell, Donald T. 1986. "Science's Social System of Validity-Enhancing Belief Change and the Problem of the Social Sciences." Pp. 108–135 in Fiske and Shweder, eds., *Metatheory in Social Science*.

Campbell, John Angus. 1987. "Charles Darwin: Rhetorician of Science." Pp. 69–86 in Nelson, Megill, and McCloskey, eds., *Rhetoric of the Human Sciences*.

1990. "Scientific Discovery and Rhetorical Invention: The Path to Darwin's Origin." Pp. 58–90 in Simons, ed., *The Rhetorical Turn*.

Carlston, Donal E. 1987. "Turning Psychology on Itself: The Rhetoric of Psychology and the Psychology of Rhetoric." Pp. 145–162 in Nelson, Megill, and McCloskey, eds., *Rhetoric of the Human Sciences*.

Carrard, Phillipe. 1992. *Poetics of the New History: French Historical Discourse from Braudel to Chartier*. Baltimore: The Johns Hopkins University Press.

Case, K. E. and R. J. Shiller. 1989. "The Efficiency of the Market for Single-Family Homes." *American Economic Review*, March.

Chandrasekhar, S. 1987. *Truth and Beauty: Aesthetics and Motivations in Science*. Chicago: University of Chicago Press.

Cheung, Steven N. S. 1969. *The Theory of Share Tenancy: With Special Reference to Asian Agriculture and the First Phase of Taiwan Land Reform*. Chicago: University of Chicago Press.

Cicero, Marcus Tullius. c. 55BC. *De Oratore*. Vol. I. Trans. E. W. Sutton. Cambridge, Mass.: Harvard University Press, 1942.

Clifford, James and George E. Marcus, eds. 1986. *Writing Culture: The Poetics and Politics of Ethnography*. Berkeley and Los Angeles: University of California Press.

Clower, Robert. 1972 (1988). "The Ideas of Economists." Pp. 64–84 in Klamer, Solow, and McCloskey, eds., *Consequences*.

Cmiel, Kenneth. 1990. *Democratic Eloquence: The Fight Over Popular Speech in Nineteenth-Century America*. New York: W. Murrow.

Coase, Ronald H. 1937. "The Nature of the Firm." *Economica*, n.s. 4 (November): 386–405.

1960. "The Problem of Social Cost." *Journal of Law and Economics* 1: 1–44.

1988. *The Firm, the Market and the Law*. Chicago: University of Chicago Press.

1992. "The Institutional Structure of Production." *American Economic Review* 82 (September): 713–719.

Coates, John. 1986. "Review of The Rhetoric of Economics." *Times Literary Supplement*, August 1.

Coats, A. W. 1984. "The Sociology of Knowledge and the History of Economics." In W. Samuels, ed., *Research in the History of Economic Thought and Methodology*, vol. II. Greenwich, Conn.: JAI Press.

1987. "Comment on McCloskey." *Eastern Economic Journal* 13 (July–September): 305–307.

1988. "Economic Rhetoric: The Social and Historical Context." Pp. 64–84 in Klamer, Solow, and McCloskey, eds., *Consequences*.

Colander, David and Reuven Brenner. 1992. *Educating Economists*. Ann Arbor: University of Michigan Press.

Colander, David C. and Arjo Klamer. 1987. "The Making of an Economist." *Journal of Economic Perspectives* 1: 95–112.

Cole, Thomas. 1991. *The Origins of Rhetoric in Ancient Greece*. Baltimore and London: The Johns Hopkins University Press.

Collins, H. M. 1985. *Changing Order: Replication and Induction in Scientific Practice*. London and Beverly Hills: Sage.

1990. *Artificial Experts: Social Knowledge and Intelligent Machines*. Cambridge, Mass.: MIT Press.

1991a. "History and Sociology of Science and History and Methodology of Economics." Pp. 492–498 in de Marchi and Blaug, eds., *Appraising Economic Theories*.

1991b. "Comment on Smith, McCabe, and Rassenti." Pp. 227–231 in de Marchi and Blaug, eds., *Appraising Economic Theories*.

Collins, H. M. and Trevor J. Pinch. 1982. *Frames of Meaning: The Social Construction of Extraordinary Science*. London: Routledge Kegan Paul.

Collins, Randall. 1982. *Sociological Insight: An Introduction to Non-Obvious Sociology*. New York: Oxford University Press.

Comaroff, John L. and Simon Roberts. 1981. *Rules and Processes: The Cultural Logic of Dispute in an African Context*. Chicago: University of Chicago Press.

Conrad, Alfred H. and John R. Meyer. 1964. *The Economics of Slavery and Other Studies in Econometric History*. Chicago: Aldine.

Cooley, T. F. and S. F. LeRoy. 1981. "Identification and Estimation of Money Demand." *American Economic Review* 71 (December): 825–844.

Copi, Irving. 1978. *Introduction to Logic*, 5th edn. New York: Macmillan.

Cosgel, Metin. 1990. "Rhetoric in the Economy: Consumption and Audience." Unpublished manuscript. Department of Economics, University of Connecticut.

Cosgel, Metin and Arjo Klamer. 1990. "Entrepreneurship as Discourse." Unpublished Manuscript. Departments of Economics, University of Connecticut/George Washington University.

Courant, Richard. 1937. *Differential and Integral Calculus*. Trans. E. J. McShane. Vol. I. Second edn. New York: Interscience.

Cowen, Tyler. 1990. "What a Non-Paretian Welfare Economics Would Have to Look Like." Pp. 285–298 in Lavoie, ed., *Economics and Hermeneutics*.

Cronbach, Lee J. 1986. "Social Inquiry by and for Earthlings." Pp. 83–107 in Fiske and Shweder, eds., *Metatheory in Social Science*.

Cross, Rodney. 1982. "The Duhem–Quine Thesis, Lakatos and the Appraisal of Theories in Macroeconomics." *Economic Journal* 92 (June): 320–340, reprinted in Caldwell, *Appraisal and Criticism in Economics*.

1991. "Alternative Accounts of Equilibrium Unemployment." Pp. 294–323 in de Marchi and Blaug, eds., *Appraising Economic Theories*.

Czarniawska-Joerges, Barbara. 1992. *Exploring Complex Organizations: A Cultural Perspective*. Newbury Park: Sage.

1993. *The Three-Dimensional Organization: A constructivist view*. Lund: Studentlitteratur.

D'Andrade, Roy. 1986. "Three Scientific World Views and the Covering Law Model." Pp. 19–41 in Fiske and Shweder, eds., *Metatheory in Social Science*.

Darwin, Charles. 1859 (1968). *The Origin of Species*. Harmondsworth: Penguin Books.

David, Paul A. and Albert Fishlow. 1961. "Optimal Resources Allocation in an Imperfect Market Setting." *Journal of Political Economy* 69 (December): 529–546.

Davis, John B. 1990a. "Rorty's Contribution to McCloskey's Understanding of Conversation as the Methodology of Economics." *Research in the History of Thought and Methodology* 7: 73–85.

1990b. "Comment on Rossetti's 'Deconstructing Robert Lucas.'" Pp. 244–250 in Samuels, ed., *Economics as Discourse.*

1990c. "Comments on the Rhetoric Project in Methodology." *Methodus* 2 (June): 38–39.

Davis, Philip J. and Reuben Hersh. 1981. *The Mathematical Experience.* Boston: Houghton Mifflin.

1987. "Rhetoric and Mathematics." Pp. 53–68 in Nelson, eds. Megill, and McCloskey, eds., *Rhetoric of the Human Sciences.*

Debreu, Gerard. 1984. "Economic Theory in the Mathematical Mode." *American Economic Review* 74 (June): 267–278.

1991. "The Mathematization of Economic Theory." *American Economic Review* 81 (March): 1–7.

Deetz, James. 1977. *In Small Things Forgotten: The Archaeology of Early American Life.* Garden City, New York: Anchor/Doubleday.

de Felice, Emidio, and Aldo Duro. 1985. *Dizionario della Lingua e della Civiltà Italiana Contemporanea.* Palermo: Palumbo.

de Marchi, Neil, ed. 1988. *The Popperian Legacy in Economics.* Cambridge: Cambridge University Press.

1991. "Introduction: Rethinking Lakatos." Pp. 1–30 in de Marchi and Blaug, eds., *Appraising Economic Theories.*

ed. 1992a. *The Post-Popperian Methodology of Economics: Recovering Practice.* Boston and Dordrecht: Kluwer and Neijhoff.

1992b. "Introduction." Pp. 1–16 in de Marchi, ed., *Post-Popperian Methodology.*

de Marchi, Neil and Mark Blaug, eds. 1991. *Appraising Economic Theories: Studies in the Methodology of Research Programs.* Aldershot, England: Elgar.

Denton, Frank. 1985. "Data Mining as an Industry." *Review of Economics and Statistics* 67 (February): 124–127.

1988. "The Significance of Significance: Rhetorical Aspects of Statistical Hypothesis Testing in Economics." Pp. 163–183 in Klamer, Solow, and McCloskey, eds., *Consequences.*

Dewald, William G., Jerry G. Thursby, and Richard G. Anderson. 1986. "Replication in Empirical Economics: The JMCB Project." *American Economic Review* 76 (September): 587–603.

Dewey, John. 1929 (1960). *The Quest for Certainty: A Study of the Relation of Knowledge and Action.* New York: G. P. Putnam's Sons.

Diamond, Arthur M., Jr. 1984. "An Economic Model of the Life-Cycle Research Productivity of Scientists." *Scientometrics* 6 (Winter): 30–36.

1987. "The Determinants of a Scientist's Choice of Research Projects." Working Paper, Department of Economics, University of Nebraska - Omaha.

1988. "The Empirical Progressiveness of the General Equilibrium Research Program." *History of Political Economy* 20 (Spring): 119–135.

Divine, T. J. and Nicholas M. Kiefer. 1991. *Empirical Labor Economics.* Oxford: Oxford University Press.

Dow, Sheila. 1990. "Comment on Lavoie's 'Hermeneutics, Subjectivity.'" Pp. 185–188 in Samuels, ed., *Economics as Discourse.*

1993. "Postmodernism and Economics." In J. Doherty, E. Graham, and M. Malek, eds., *Postmodernism in the Social Sciences.* London: Macmillan.

Dudley-Evans, Tony. 1993. "The Debate Over Milton Friedman's Theoretical Framework: An Applied Linguist's View." Pp. 132–152 in Backhouse, Dudley-Evans, and Henderson, eds., *Economics and Language.*

Dudley-Evans, Tony and Willie Henderson. 1987. "Changes in the Economics Article." Unpublished manuscript. Department of Extramural Studies, University of Birmingham.

eds. 1990. *The Language of Economics: The Analysis of Economic Discourse.* ELT, Doc. no. 134. Oxford Modern English Publications, in association with the British Council.

Dyer, Alan W. 1988. "Economic Theory as an Art Form (Rhetoric vs. Semiotics)." *Journal of Economic Issues* 22 (March): 157–166.

Ebeling, Richard M. 1990. "What is a Price: Explanation and Understanding (With Apologies to Paul Ricoeur)." Pp. 177–194 in Lavoie, ed., *Economics and Hermeneutics.*

Eco, Umberto. 1985. *Reflections on the Name of the Rose.* Trans. W. Weaver. London: Secker and Warburg.

Eemeren, Frans H. van and Rob Grootendorst. 1983. *Speech Acts in Argumentative Discussions.* Dordrecht; Cinnaminson, N. J.: Foris Publications.

Eldredge, Niles. 1985 (1989). *Time Frames: The Evolution of Punctuated Equilibrium.* Princeton: Princeton University Press, 1989.

Elshtain, Jean Bethke. 1988. "Feminist Political Rhetoric and Women's Studies." Pp. 319–340 in Nelson, Megill, and McCloskey, eds., *Rhetoric of the Human Sciences.*

Emmett, Ross B. 1992. "Review of Tully's Meaning and Context: Quentin Skinner and His Critics." *History of Political Economy* 24 (1): 257–260.

Etzioni, Amitai. 1988. *The Moral Dimension: Toward a New Economics.* New York: Free Press.

Euclid. Selections from *The Elements,* pp. 437ff in Ivor Thomas, ed. and trans., *Selections Illustrating the History of Greek Mathematics.* Vol. I. Cambridge, Mass.: Harvard University Press, 1939.

Evensky, Jerry. 1992. "Ethics and the Classical Liberal Tradition in Economics." *History of Political Economy* 24 (Spring): 61–77.

Farley, John and Gerald L. Geison. 1974. "Science, Politics and Spontaneous Generation in Nineteenth-century France: The Pasteur–Pouchet Debate." *Bulletin of the History of Medicine* 48: 161–198.

Farmer, Mary K. 1992. "Ever since Adam Smith: The Mythical History of Individual Rationality in Economic Analysis." *Research in the History of Thought and Methodology* 9: 105–127.

Farrell, Joseph. 1988. "Meaning and Credibility in Cheap-Talk Games." Department of Economics, Berkeley. First version 1983. Forthcoming in

M. Dempster, ed., *Mathematical Models in Economics*. New York: Oxford University Press.

Feige, Edgar. 1975. "The Consequences of Journal Editorial Policies and a Suggestion for Revision." *Journal of Political Economy* 83 (December): 1291–96.

Feiwel, George R. 1987. *Arrow and the Ascent of Modern Economics*. Basingstoke: Macmillan.

Feldhay, Revka. 1992. "Narrative Constraints on Historical Writing: The Case of the Scientific Revolution." Unpublished manuscript for "Narrative Patterns in Scientific Disciplines," April 27–30, 1992, Cohn Institute, Tel Aviv University; Edlestein Center, Hebrew University; and the Van Leer Jerusalem Institute.

Feyerabend, Paul. 1975 (1978). *Against Method: Outline of an Anarchistic Theory of Knowledge*. London: Verso.

1978. *Science in a Free Society*. London: New Left Books.

1987. *Farewell to Reason*. New York: Verso.

1991. *Three Dialogues on Knowledge*. Oxford: Basil Blackwell.

Feynman, Richard. 1963. *The Feynman Lectures on Physics*. Vol. I. Reading, Mass.: Addison-Wesley.

1985. *"Surely You're Joking, Mr. Feynman!" Adventures of a Curious Character*. As told to R. Leighton, edited by E. Hutchings. New York: W. W. Norton.

Finocchiaro, Maurice. 1980. *Galileo and the Art of Reasoning: Rhetorical Foundations of Logic and Scientific Method*. Boston Studies in the Philosophy of Science. Dordrecht and Boston: Reidel.

Fish, Stanley. 1980. *Is There a Text in This Class? The Authority of Interpretive Communities*. Cambridge, Mass.: Harvard University Press.

1988. "Comments from Outside Economics." Pp. 21–30 in Klamer, Solow and McCloskey, eds., *Consequences*.

1989. *Doing What Comes Naturally: Change, Rhetoric, and the Practice of Theory in Literary and Legal Studies*. Durham, N.C.: Duke University Press.

Fisher, Franklin M. 1989. "Games Economists Play: A Noncooperative View." *RAND Journal of Economics* 20 (Spring): 113–124.

Fisher, Walter and Robert Goodman, eds., forthcoming. *Knowledge, Value, and Praxis*.

Fiske, Donald and Richard A. Shweder, eds. 1986. *Metatheory in Social Science: Pluralisms and Subjectivities*. Chicago: University of Chicago Press.

Fleck, Ludwik. 1935 (1979). *Genesis and Development of a Scientific Fact*. Chicago: University of Chicago Press.

Floud, Roderick, Kenneth V. Wachter, and Annabel Gregory. 1989. *Height, Health and History: Nutritional Status in the United Kingdom, 1750–1980*. Cambridge and New York: Cambridge University Press.

Fogel, Robert W. 1964. *Railroads and American Economic Growth: Essays in Econometric History*. Baltimore: The Johns Hopkins University Press.

Folbre, Nancy, and Hartmann, Heidi. 1988. "The Rhetoric of Self-Interest: Ideology and Gender in Economic Theory." Pp. 184–203 in Klamer, Solow, and McCloskey, eds., *Consequences*.

France, Peter. 1972. *Rhetoric and Truth in France, Descartes to Diderot*. Oxford: Clarendon Press.

Frank, Jerome D. and Julia B. Frank. 1961 (1991). *Persuasion and Healing: A*

Comparative Study of Psychotherapy. Third edn. Baltimore: The Johns Hopkins University Press.

Frankel, Henry. 1987. "The Continental Drift Debate." Pp. 203–248 in H. T. Engelhardt Jr. and A. L. Caplan, eds., *Scientific Controversies: Case Studies in the Resolution and Closure of Disputes in Science and Technology.* Cambridge: Cambridge University Press.

Freedman, David. 1990. "Common Sense and the Computer." *Discover* 11 (August): 64–71.

Freedman, David H., Robert Pisani, and Roger Purves. 1978. *Statistics.* New York: W. W. Norton.

Friedman, Jeffrey. 1991. "Postmodernism vs. Postlibertarianism." *Critical Review* 5, no. 2 (Spring 1991): 145–158.

Friedman, Milton. 1953. "The Methodology of Positive Economics." Pp. 3–43 in his *Essays in Positive Economics.* Chicago: University of Chicago Press. January 10, 1983. Letter to Donald McCloskey.

Friedman, Milton and Anna J. Schwartz. 1963. *A Monetary History of the United States, 1867–1960.* Princeton: Princeton University Press.

Frye, Northrop. 1957. *An Anatomy of Criticism.* New York: Atheneum.

1964. *The Educated Imagination.* Bloomington: Indiana University Press.

Fuller, Steve. 1988. *Social Epistemology.* Bloomington: Indiana University Press.

1989. *Philosophy of Science and Its Discontents.* Boulder: Westview Press.

Gal, Ofer. 1992. "Tropes and Tropics in Scientific Discourse: Galileo's De Motu." Unpublished manuscript for "Narrative Patterns in Scientific Disciplines," April 27–30, 1992, Cohn Institute, Tel Aviv University; Edelstein Center, Hebrew University; and the Van Leer Jerusalem Institute.

Galbraith, James. 1988. "The Grammar of Political Economy." Pp. 221–239 in Klamer, Solow, and McCloskey, eds., *Consequences.*

Galbraith, John Kenneth. 1990. *A Tenured Professor: A Novel.* Boston: Houghton Mifflin.

Galison, Peter. 1987. *How Experiments End.* Chicago: University of Chicago.

Gay, David E. R. 1987. "Review of The Rhetoric of Economics." *Social Science Journal* 24 (4): 466–468.

Geertz, Clifford. 1984 (1989). "Anti-anti-relativism." *American Anthropologist* 86 (June 1984: 263–278, reprinted as pp. 12–34 in Michael Krausz, ed., *Relativism: Interpretation and Confrontation.* Notre Dame: University of Notre Dame Press.

1988. *Works and Lives: The Anthropologist as Author.* Stanford: Stanford University Press.

George, David. 1990. "The Rhetoric of Economics Texts." *Journal of Economic Issues* 24 (September): 861–878.

Gergen, Kenneth J. 1986. "Correspondence versus Autonomy in the Language of Understanding Human Action." Pp. 136–162 in Fiske and Shweder, eds., *Metatheory in Social Science.*

Gergen, Kenneth J. and Mary M. Gergen. 1980. "Causal Attribution in the Context of Social Explanation." In D. Gorlitz, ed., *Perspectives on Attribution Research and Theory: The Bielefeld Symposium.* Cambridge: Ballinger.

Gerrard. Bill. 1990. "On Matters Methodological in Economics." *Journal of Economic Surveys* 4 (2): 197–219.

1993. "The Significance of Interpretation in Economics." Pp. 51–63 in Backhouse, Dudley-Evans, and Henderson, eds., *Economics and Language*.

Gerschenkron, Alexander. 1962a. *Economic Backwardness in Historical Perspective: A Book of Essays*. Cambridge, Mass.: Harvard University Press.

1962b. "The Approach to European Industrialization: A Postscript." Pp. 353–364 in his *Economic Backwardness in Historical Perspective: A Book of Essays*. Cambridge, Mass.: Harvard University Press.

1970. *Europe in the Russian Mirror*. Cambridge: Cambridge University Press.

Gettier, Edmund L. 1963. "Is Justified True Belief Knowledge?" *Analysis* 23: 121–123. Reprinted as pp. 134–136 in Pojman, ed., *The Theory of Knowledge*.

Gibbard, Allan and Hal R. Varian. 1979. "Economic Models." *Journal of Philosophy* 75: 664–677.

Gilbert, Christopher L. 1991. "Do Economists Test Theories? – Demand Analysis and Consumption Analysis as tests of Theories of Economic Methodology." Pp. 137–168 in de Marchi and Blaug, eds., *Appraising Economic Theories*.

Gilbert, G. Nigel and Michael Mulkay. 1984. *Opening Pandora's Box*. Cambridge: Cambridge University Press.

Gilligan, Carol. 1982. *In a Different Voice: Psychological Theory and Women's Development*. Cambridge, Mass.: Harvard University Press.

Glymour, Clark. 1980. *Theory and Evidence*. Princeton: Princeton University Press.

Goldberger, Arthur S. 1991. *A Course in Econometrics*. Cambridge, Mass.: Harvard University Press.

Goldratt, Eliyahu M. and Jeff Cox. 1986. *The Goal: A Process of Ongoing Improvement*. Revised edition. Croton-on-Hudson, N.Y.: North River Press.

Gombrich, E. H. 1960 (1971). *Art and Illusion: A Study in the Psychology of Pictorial Representation*. Princeton: Princeton University Press.

Goodman, Nelson. 1955. *Fact, Fiction and Forecast*. Indianapolis: Bobbs-Merrill.

1978. *Ways of Worldmaking*. Indianapolis: Hackett.

Goodman, Paul. 1971 (1972). *Speaking and Language: Defense of Poetry*. New York: Vintage.

Goodstein, David. 1991. "Scientific Fraud." *The American Scholar* 60 (Autumn): 505–515.

Goodwin, Craufurd. 1988. "The Heterogeneity of the Economists' Discourse: Philosopher, Priest and Hired Gun." Pp. 207–220 in Klamer, Solow, and McCloskey, eds., *Consequences*.

Gordon, David. 1991. "Review of McCloskey's If You're So Smart." *Review of Austrian Economics* 5 (2): 123–127.

Gordon, J. E. 1976. *The New Science of Strong Materials: or Why You Don't Fall Through the Floor*. Second edn. Princeton: Princeton University Press.

Gould, Stephen Jay. 1981. *The Mismeasure of Man*. New York: W. W. Norton.

1984. *Hen's Teeth and Horse's Toes: Further Reflections in Natural History*. New York: W. W. Norton.

1987. *Time's Arrow, Time's Cycle: Myth and Metaphor in the Discovery of Geological Time*. Cambridge, Mass.: Harvard University Press.

1989. *Wonderful Life: The Burgess Shale and the Nature of History*. New York: Norton.

1993. "The Composition and Reception of 'The Spandrels of San Marco.'" In John L. Selzer, ed., *Understanding Scientific Prose*. Madison: University of Wisconsin Press.

Graff, Gerald. 1983. "The Pseudo-Politics of Interpretation." *Critical Inquiry* 9 (March): 597–610.

Graves, Robert and Alan Hodge. 1943 (1961). *The Reader Over Your Shoulder*. New York: Macmillan.

Graziano, Loretta. 1987. "Review of The Rhetoric of Economics." *Et Cetera* 44 (Winter): 417–420.

Greif, Avner. 1989. "Reputation and Coalitions in Medieval Trade: Evidence on the Maghribi Traders. *Journal of Economic History* 49 (December): 857–882.

Gross, Alan G. 1990a. "The Origin of Species: Evolutionary Taxonomy as an Example of the Rhetoric of Science." Pp. 91–115 in Simons, ed., *The Rhetorical Turn*.

1990b. *The Rhetoric of Science*. Cambridge: Harvard University Press.

Grubel, Herbert G. and Lawrence A. Boland. 1986. "On the Efficient Use of Mathematics in Economics." *Kyklos* 39: 419–442.

Gusfield, Joseph R. 1981. *The Culture of Public Problems: Drinking-Driving and the Symbolic Order*. Chicago: University of Chicago Press.

Guthrie, W. K. C. 1971. *The Sophists*. London: Cambridge University Press.

Habermas, Jurgen. 1975. *Legitimation Crisis*. Trans. T. McCarthy. Boston: Beacon Press.

Hagstrom, Warren O. 1965 (1982). "Gift Giving as an Organizing Principle in Science." Pp. 21–34 in Barry Barnes and Bruno Latour, eds. *Science in Context: Readings in the Sociology of Science*. Cambridge, Mass.: MIT Press.

Hahn, Frank. 1973. *On the Notion of Equilibrium in Economics: An Inaugural Lecture*. Cambridge: Cambridge University Press.

Sept 13, 1983. Letter to Donald McCloskey.

1984. *Equilibrium and Macroeconomics*. Oxford: Basil Blackwell.

1986. "Review of the Collected Works of Kenneth Arrow." *Times Literary Supplement* (August 1): 833–834.

1987. "Review of The Rhetoric of Economics." *Journal of Economic Literature* 25 (March): 110–111.

Halmos, Paul R. 1985. *I Want to be a Mathematician: An Automathography*. New York: Springer-Verlag.

Hamminga, Bert. 1983. *Neoclassical Theory Structure and Theory Development*. New York: Springer-Verlag.

Hammond, J. Daniel. 1990. "McCloskey's Modernism and Friedman's Methodology: A Case Study with New Evidence." *Review of Social Economy* 48 (Summer): 158–171.

1991. "Frank Knight's Antipositivism." *History of Political Economy* 23 (Fall): 359–381.

Hands, D. Wade. 1985. "Second Thoughts on Lakatos." *History of Political Economy* 17 (Spring): 1–16.

1987. "Contribution to Session on 'Methodological Diversity in Economics.'" *Research in the History of Thought and Methodology* 5: 207–239.

1988. "Ad Hocness in Economics and the Popperian Tradition." Pp. 121–137 in de Marchi, ed., *The Popperian Legacy*.

1990. "Second Thoughts on 'Second Thoughts': Reconsidering the Lakatosian Progress of The General Theory." *Review of Political Economy* 2 (1): 69–81.

1991a. "Review of The Consequences of Economic Rhetoric." *Journal of Economic Literature* 29 (March): 85–87.

1991b. "The Problem of Excess Content: Economics, Novelty and a Long Popperian Tale." Pp. 58–75 in de Marchi and Blaug, eds., *Appraising Economic Theories*.

1991c. "Reply to Hamminga and Mäki." Pp. 91–102 in de Marchi and Blaug, eds., *Appraising Economic Theories*.

1992. "Falsification, Situational Analysis and Scientific Research Programs: The Popperian Tradition in Economic Methodology." Pp. 19–53 in de Marchi, ed., *Post-Popperian Methodology*.

1993. *Testing, Rationality, and Progress: Essays on the Popperian Tradition in Economic Methodology*. Lanham, Md.: Rowman and Littlefield.

Harman, Gilbert. 1986. *Change in View: Principles of Reasoning*. Cambridge, Mass.: MIT Press.

Harré, Rom. 1981 (1983). *Great Scientific Experiments*. Oxford: Oxford University Press.

1986. *Varieties of Realism: A Rationale for the Natural Sciences*. Oxford: Basil Blackwell.

1990. "Some Narrative Conventions of Scientific Discourse." Pp. 81–101 in Christopher Nash, eds., *Narrative in Culture*. London and New York: Routledge.

Hartman, Geoffrey H. and Sanford Budick. 1986. *Midrash and Literature*. New Haven: Yale University Press.

Hausman, Daniel M. 1981. *Capital, Profits and Prices: An Essay in the Philosophy of Economics*. New York: Colombia University Press.

ed. 1984. *The Philosophy of Economics: An Anthology*. New York: Cambridge University Press.

1988. "An Appraisal of Popperian Methodology." Pp. 65–86 in de Marchi, ed., *The Popperian Legacy*.

1992. *The Inexact and Separate Science of Economics*. Cambridge. Cambridge University Press.

Hausman, Daniel M. and Michael S. McPherson. 1987. "Standard." *Economics and Philosophy* 4 (June): 1–7.

Hayek, Friedrich A. 1945. "The Use of Knowledge in Society." *American Economic Review* 35 (September): 519–530.

Hayles, N. Katherine. 1984. *The Cosmic Web: Scientific Models and Literary Strategies in the 20th Century*. Ithaca: Cornell.

1990. *Chaos Bound: Orderly Disorder in Contemporary Literature and Science*. Ithaca: Cornell.

ed. 1991. *Chaos and Order: Complex Dynamics in Literature and Science*. Chicago: University of Chicago Press.

Heckman, J. J., and B.S. Payner. 1989. "Determining the Impact of Antidiscrimination Policy on the Economic Status of Blacks: A Study of South Carolina." *American Economic Review* 79 (March): 138–177.

Heilbroner, Robert L. 1986 (1988). "The Murky Economists." *New York Review of Books* April 24. Reprinted with revisions as pp. 38–43 in Klamer, Solow, and McCloskey, eds., *Consequences*.

1990. "Economics as Ideology." Pp. 101–116 in Samuels, ed., *Economics as Discourse*.

Heinzelman, Kurt. 1980. *The Economics of the Imagination*. Amherst: University of Massachusetts Press.

Hempel, Carl G. 1942 (1959). "The Function of General Laws in History." Reprinted in P. Gardiner, ed., *Theories of History*. New York: Free Press.

Henderson, Willie. 1982. "Metaphor in Economics." *Economics* (Winter): 147–153.

1993. "The Problem of Edgeworth's Style." Pp. 200–222 in Backhouse, Dudley-Evans, and Henderson, eds., *Economics and Language*.

Henderson, Willie and A. Hewings. 1987. *Reading Economics: How Text Helps or Hinders*. British National Bibliography Research Fund Report, Number 28, British Library Publications Sales Unit, Boston Spa, West Yorkshire.

1988. "Entering the Hypothetical World: Assume, Suppose, Consider, and Take as Signals in Economics Text." Department of Extramural Studies, University of Birmingham, Birmingham B15 2TT, England.

Hesse, Mary. 1963. *Models and Analogies in Science*. Notre Dame: University of Notre Dame Press.

1980. *Revolutions and Reconstructions in the Philosophy of Science*. Bloomington: Indiana University Press.

Hewings, Ann and Willie Henderson. 1987. "A Link Between Genre and Schemata: A Case Study of Economics Text." *English Language Research Journal* 1 (1987): 156–175.

Hexter, J. H. 1986. "The Problem of Historical Knowledge." Unpublished manuscript. Washington University, St. Louis.

Hibbeler, R. C. 1989. *Engineering Mechanics: Statics and Dynamics*. 5th edn. New York: Macmillan.

Hirsch, Abraham, and Neil de Marchi. 1990. *Milton Friedman: Economics in Theory and Practice*. Ann Arbor: University of Michigan Press.

Hirschman, Albert O. 1970. *Exit, Voice and Loyalty*. Cambridge, Mass.: Belknap Press of Harvard University Press.

1981. *Essays in Trespassing: Economics to Politics and Beyond*. Cambridge: Cambridge University Press.

1984. "Against Parsimony: Three Easy Ways of Complicating Some Categories of Economic Discourse." *American Economic Review* 74 (May): 89–96.

1991. *The Rhetoric of Reaction: Perversity, Futility, Jeopardy*. Cambridge, Mass.: Harvard University Press.

Hodges, Andrew. 1983. *Alan Turing: The Enigma*. New York: Simon and Schuster.

Hoffer, Eric. 1951 (1963). *The True Believer: Thoughts on the Nature of Mass Movements*. New York: Time, Inc.

1952 (1964). *The Ordeal of Change*. New York: Harper and Row.

1979. *Before the Sabbath*. New York: Harper and Row.

Hollis, Martin. 1985. "The Emperor's Newest Clothes." *Economics and Philosophy* 1: 128–33.

Hollis, Martin and Steven Lukes. 1982. "Introduction." In Hollis and Lukes, eds., *Rationality and Relativism*. Cambridge, Mass.: MIT Press.

Homer. *The Iliad*. Trans. R. Lattimore. Chicago: University of Chicago Press, 1951.

Hoover, Kevin D. 1991. "Scientific Research Program or Tribe? A Joint Appraisal of Lakatos and the New Classical Macroeconomics." Pp. 364–394 in de Marchi and Blaug, eds., *Appraising Economic Theories*.

Hoover, Kevin D. and Young Bak Choi. 1991. "An Interview with Kevin Hoover." *Methodus* 3: 118–127.

Hoppe, Hans-Hermann. 1989. "In Defense of Extreme Rationalism: Thoughts on Donald McCloskey's The Rhetoric of Economics." *Review of Austrian Economics* 3: 179–214.

Howitt, Peter and Hans-Werner Sinn. 1989. "Gradual Reform of Capital Income Taxation." *American Economic Review* 79 (March): 106–124.

Humphreys, Sally. 1992. "Serious Stories: Modifications of Narrative in Early Greek Prose." Unpublished manuscript for "Narrative Patterns in Scientific Disciplines," April 27–30, 1992, Cohn Institute, Tel Aviv University; Edelstein Center, Hebrew University; and the Van Leer Jerusalem Institute.

Hunter, Albert, ed. 1990. *The Rhetoric of Social Research: Understood and Believed*. New Brunswick: Rutgers University Press.

Hutchison, Terence. 1938 (1960). *The Significance and Basic Postulates of Economic Theory*, 2nd edn. New York: Kelley.

1992. *Changing Aims in Economics*. Oxford: Basil Blackwell.

Ingalls, D. H. H., ed. 1965. *An Anthology of Sanskrit Court Poetry*. Cambridge, Mass.: Harvard University Press.

Jacobs, Louis. 1984. *Talmudic Argument: A Study in Talmudic Reasoning and Methodology*. Cambridge: Cambridge University Press.

Jaeger, Werner. 1933 (1965). *Paideia: The Ideals of Greek Culture*. Vol. I. *Archaic Greece. The Mind of Athens*. Trans. G. Highet. New York: Oxford University Press.

Jakobson, Roman and Morris Halle. 1956 (1988). "The Metaphoric and Metonymic Poles" (a selection from "Two Aspects of Language and Two Types of Aphasic Disturbances," in *Fundamentals of Language*). Pp. 57–61 in David Lodge, ed., *Modern Criticism and Theory*. London and New York: Longmans.

James, William. 1907 (1949). *Pragmatism: A New Name for Some Old Ways of Thinking, together with Four Essays from The Meaning of Truth (1909)*. Reprinted (with original pagination of the 1907 edition). New York: Longmans, Green.

Jamieson, Kathleen Hall. 1988. *Eloquence in an Electronic Age: The Transformation of Political Speechmaking.* New York and Oxford: Oxford University Press.

Johnson, Mark, ed. 1981. *Philosophical Perspectives on Metaphor.* Minneapolis: University of Minnesota Press.

1987. *The Body in the Mind: The Bodily Basis of Meaning, Imagination, and Reason.* Chicago: University of Chicago Press.

Johnson, Samuel. 1775 (1984). *A Journey to the Western Islands of Scotland.* Harmondsworth: Penguin.

Jones, Eric L. 1981. *The European Miracle.* Cambridge: Cambridge University Press.

1988. *Growth Recurring: Economic Change in World History.* Oxford: Clarendon Press.

Jonsen, Albert R. and Stephen Toulmin. 1988. *The Abuse of Casuistry: A History of Moral Reasoning.* Berkeley and Los Angeles: University of California Press.

Just, Richard E. and Gordon C. Rausser. 1989. "An Assessment of the Agricultural Economics Profession." *American Journal of Agricultural Economics* 71 (December): 1177–1190.

Kaufer, David S. 1986. "Review of The Rhetoric of Economics." *Clio* 15 (Spring): 330–333.

Keegan, John. 1976 (1978). *The Face of Battle: A Study of Agincourt, Waterloo and the Somme.* Harmondsworth: Penguin Books.

Keller, Evelyn Fox. 1985. *Reflections on Gender and Science.* New Haven: Yale University Press.

Kelsey, Timothy W. 1990. "The Rhetoric of 'Government Intervention': A Suggestion." *Research in the History of Thought and Methodology* 7: 63–71.

Kelvin, William Thompson, Lord. 1883 (1888–1889). "Electrical Units of Measurement." In his *Popular Lectures and Addresses.* Vol. I. London.

Kennedy, George A. 1984. *New Testament Interpretation through Rhetorical Criticism.* Chapel Hill: University of North Carolina Press.

Kennedy, William P. 1987. *Industrial Structure, Capital Markets and the Origins of British Economic Decline.* Cambridge: Cambridge University Press.

Kenner, Hugh. 1984 (1989). "The Making of the Modernist Canon." Pp. 28–42 in Kenner, *Mazes: Essays.* San Francisco: North Point.

Keohane, Robert. 1988. "The Rhetoric of Economics as Viewed by a Student of Politics." Pp. 240–246 in Klamer, Solow, and McCloskey, eds., *Consequences.*

Kerferd, G. B. 1981. *The Sophistic Movement.* Cambridge: Cambridge University Press.

Keynes, John Neville. 1891, 1917 (1984). *The Scope and Method of Political Economy.* Pp. 70–98 in Hausman, *The Philosophy of Economics*, excerpts.

Khalil, Elias L. 1992. "Fox, Hedgehog, and Owl: Three Temperaments in Economic Discourse." *Methodus* 4 (1): 101–109.

Kim, Jinbang. 1991. "Testing in Modern Economics: The Case of Job Search Theory." Pp. 105–131 in de Marchi and Blaug, eds., *Appraising Economic Theories.*

Kingsland, Sharon E. 1985. *Modeling Nature: Episodes in the History of Population Ecology*. Chicago: University of Chicago Press.

Kinneavy, James L. 1987. *Greek Rhetorical Origins of Christian Faith: An Inquiry*. New York and Oxford: Oxford University press.

Kirby, John T. 1990. "The 'Great Triangle' in Early Greek Rhetoric and Poetics." *Rhetorica* 8: 213–228.

Kirzner, Israel. 1989. *Discovery, Capitalism, and Distributive Justice*. Oxford: Basil Blackwell.

Klamer, Arjo. 1983a. "Empirical Arguments in New Classical Economics." *Economie Appliquée* 36: 229–254.

1983b. *Conversations with Economists: New Classical Economists and Opponents Speak out on the Current Controversy in Macroeconomics*. Totawa, N. J.: Rowman and Allanheld.

1984. "Levels of Discourse in New Classical Economics." *History of Political Economy* 16 (Summer): 263–290.

1986a. "La Nouvelle Economie Classique." In André Grjebine, ed. *Theories de la Crise et Politiques Economiques*. Paris: Editions de Seuil.

1986b. "Self-Portrait of a Discipline: Economics Through Its Textbooks." Unpublished manuscript. Department of Economics, George Washington University.

1986c. "Review of The Rhetoric of Economics." *Quarterly Journal of Speech* 72 (November): 469–472.

1987a. "Contribution to Session on 'Methodological Diversity in Economics.'" *Research in the History of Thought and Methodology* 5: 207–239.

1987b. "As If Economists and Their Subjects were Rational . . ." Pp. 163–183 in Nelson, Megill, and McCloskey, eds., *Rhetoric of the Human Sciences*.

1988a. "Economics as Discourse." Pp. 259–278 in de Marchi, ed., *The Popperian Legacy*.

1988b. "Negotiating a New Conversation about Economics." Pp. 265–279 in Klamer, Solow, and McCloskey, eds., *Consequences*.

1990a. "White's When Words Lose Their Meaning: Review Essay." *Research in the History of Thought and Methodology* 7: 239–249.

1990b. "The Textbook Presentation of Economic Discourse." Pp. 129–154 in Samuels, ed., *Economics as Discourse*.

1990c. "Towards the Native's Point of View: The Difficulty of Changing the Conversation." Pp. 19–33 in Lavoie, ed., *Economics and Hermeneutics*.

1991. "The Advent of Modernism in Economics." Unpublished manuscript. Department of Economics, George Washington University, Washington, D.C.

Klamer, Arjo and David C. Colander. 1990. *The Making of Economists*. Boulder: Westview.

Klamer, Arjo and Thomas C. Leonard. 1993. "So What's a Metaphor?" In Philip Mirowski, ed., *Natural Images in Economics*. Cambridge: Cambridge University Press.

Klamer, Arjo and D. N. McCloskey. 1988. "Economics in the Human Conversation." Pp. 3–20 in Klamer, Solow, and McCloskey, eds., *Consequences*.

1989. "The Rhetoric of Disagreement." *Rethinking Marxism* 2 (Fall).

1992. "Accounting as the Master Metaphor of Economics." *The European Accounting Review* 1 (May): 145–160.

Klamer, Arjo, Robert M. Solow, and D. N. McCloskey, eds. 1988. *The Consequences of Economic Rhetoric.* New York: Cambridge University Press.

Klant, J. J. 1984. *The Rules of the Game.* Cambridge: Cambridge University Press.

Klemm, David. 1987. "The Rhetoric of Theological Argument." Pp. 276–297 in Nelson, Megill, and McCloskey, eds., *Rhetoric of the Human Sciences.*

Kline, Morris. 1980. *Mathematics: The Loss of Certainty.* New York: Oxford University Press.

Knight, Frank. 1929 (1947). "Freedom as Fact and Criterion." Pp. 1–18 in *Freedom and Reform: Essays in Economics and Social Philosophy.* New York: Harper and Brothers (reissued 1969 Port Washington, New York: Kennikat Press).

1940. "'What is Truth' in Economics?" [review of Hutchison's *The Significance and Basic Postulates of Economic Theory*]. *Journal of Political Economy* 48 (February): 1–32. Reprinted in his *On the History and Method of Economics: Selected Essays.* Chicago: University of Chicago Press, 1963.

Knorr-Cetina, Karin. 1981. *The Manufacture of Knowledge: An Essay on the Constructivist and Contextual Nature of Science.* Oxford: Pergamon Press.

Koopmans, Tjalling. 1957. *Three Essays on the State of Economic Science.* New York: McGraw Hill.

Kregel, J. A. 1987. "Review of The Rhetoric of Economics." *Economic Journal* 97 (March): 278–280.

Kretzenbacher, Heinz L. 1992. "'Just Give Us the Facts': The Connection Between the Narrative Taboo, the Ego Taboo and the Metaphor Taboo in Scientific Style." Unpublished manuscript for "Narrative Patterns in Scientific Disciplines," April 27–30, 1992, Cohn Institute, Tel Aviv University; Edelstein Center, Hebrew University; and the Van Leer Jerusalem Institute.

Krips, Henry. 1992. "Ideology, Rhetoric and Boyle's New Experiments." Unpublished manuscript for "Narrative Patterns in Scientific Disciplines," April 27–30, 1992, Cohn Institute, Tel Aviv University; Edelstein Center, Hebrew University; and the Van Leer Jerusalem Institute.

Kroszner, Randall. 1990. "On the Microfoundations of Money: Walrasian and Mengerian Approaches Considered in the Light of Richard Rorty's Critique of Foundationalism." Pp. 239–261 in Lavoie, ed., *Economics and Hermeneutics.*

Kruskal, William H. 1978. "Significance Tests." Article in *International Encyclopedia of Statistics.* New York: Free Press.

Kuhn, Thomas. 1957. *The Copernican Revolution.* Chicago: University of Chicago Press.

1962 (1970). *The Structure of Scientific Revolutions.* Second edn. 1970. Chicago: University of Chicago Press.

1977. *The Essential Tension: Selected Studies in Scientific Tradition and Change.* Chicago: University of Chicago Press.

Kuttner, Robert. 1985. "The Poverty of Economics." *Atlantic* 255: 74–80 and reply by McCloskey in Letters of the next edition.

LaCapra, Dominick. 1983. *Rethinking Intellectual History: Texts, Contexts, Language*. Ithaca: Cornell University Press.

Lachmann, Ludwig M. 1990. "Austrian Economics: A Hermeneutic Approach." Pp. 134–146 in Lavoie, ed., *Economics and Hermeneutics*.

Lakatos, Imre. 1976. *Proofs and Refutations: The Logic of Mathematical Discovery*. Ed. J. Worrall and E. Zahar. Cambridge: Cambridge University Press.

1978. *The Methodology of Scientific Research Programmes. Philosophical Papers*. Vol. I. J. Ed. Worrall and G. Currie. Cambridge: Cambridge University Press.

Lakoff, George and Mark Johnson. 1980. *Metaphors We Live By*. Chicago: University of Chicago Press.

Lakoff, George and Mark Turner. 1989. *More than Cool Reason: A Field Guide to Poetic Metaphor*. Chicago: University of Chicago Press.

Landau, Misia. 1987. "Paradise Lost: The Theme of Terrestriality in Human Evolution." Pp. 111–124 in Nelson, Megill, and McCloskey, eds., *Rhetoric of the Human Sciences*.

Lang, Berel. 1990. *The Anatomy of Philosophical Style: Literary Philosophy and the Philosophy of Literature*. Oxford: Basil Blackwell.

Langlois, Richard. 1985. "From the Knowledge of Economics to the Economics of Knowledge: Fritz Machlup on Methodology and the 'Knowledge Society'." *Reviews in the History of Economic Thought and Methodology*, 3: 225–235.

Lanham, Richard A. 1974. *Style: An Anti-Textbook*. New Haven: Yale University Press.

1976. *The Motives of Eloquence: Literary Rhetoric in the Renaissance*. New Haven: Yale University Press.

1991. *A Handlist of Rhetorical Terms*. Second edn. Berkeley and Los Angeles: University of California Press.

1992. "The Extraordinary Convergence: Democracy, Technology, Theory, and the University Curriculum." Pp. 33–56 in Darryl J. Gless and Barbara Herrnstein Smith, eds., *The Politics of Liberal Education*. Durham N.C.: Duke University Press.

forthcoming. *The Electronic Word: Democracy, Technology, and the Arts*. Chicago: University of Chicago Press.

Latour, Bruno. 1988. *The Pasteurization of France*. Trans. A. Sheridan and J. Law. Cambridge, Mass. and London: Harvard University Press.

Latour, Bruno, and Steve Woollgar. 1979. *Laboratory Life: The Social Construction of Scientific Facts*. Beverly Hills: Sage Publications.

Laudan, Larry. 1977. *Progress and Its Problems: Towards a Theory of Scientific Growth*. Berkeley and Los Angeles: University of California Press.

Lavoie, Don C., ed. 1990a. *Economics and Hermeneutics*. London and New York: Routledge & Kegan Paul.

1990b. "Introduction." Pp. 1–18 in Lavoie, ed., *Economics and Hermeneutics*.

1990c. "The Discovery and Interpretation of Profit Opportunities: Culture and the Kirznerian Entrepreneur." Unpublished manuscript. Department of Economics, George Mason University, Fairfax, Virginia.

1990d. "Hermeneutics, Subjectivity, and the Lester/Machlup Debate: Toward a More Anthropological Approach to Empirical Economics." Pp. 167–184 in Samuels, ed., *Economics as Discourse.*

1991. "The Progress of Subjectivism." Pp. 470–486 in de Marchi and Blaug, eds., *Appraising Economic Theories.*

Leamer, Edward. 1978. *Specification Searches: Ad Hoc Inferences with Nonexperimental Data.* New York: Wiley.

1983. "Let's Take the Con Out of Econometrics." *American Economic Review* 73 (March): 31–43.

Lehrer, Keith. 1971 (1933). "Why Not Skepticism?" *The Philosophical Forum* 2: 283–298. Reprinted as pp. 48–55 (footnotes edited) in Pojman, ed., *The Theory of Knowledge.*

Lehrer, Keith and Carl Wagner. 1981. *Rational Consensus in Science and Society.* Dordrecht and Boston: Reidel.

Leijonhufvud, Axel. 1985. "Ideology and Analysis in Macroeconomics." Pp. 182–207 in P. Koslowski, ed., *Economics and Philosophy.* Tübingen: J. C. B. Mohr.

1991. "Introduction." *Economic Notes* 20 (1): 1–5.

Leontief, Wassily. 1971. "Theoretical Assumptions and Non-observable Facts." *American Economic Review* 61 (March): 107.

1982. "Letter: Academic Economics." *Science* 217: 104, 107.

Leopardi, Giacomo. 1845 (1984). *Pensieri.* Trans. W. S. Di Piero. New York: Oxford University Press, 1984.

Levi, Primo, and Tullio Regge. 1992. *Conversations.* Trans. R. Rosenthal. Harmondsworth: Penguin Books.

Levins, Richard and Richard Lewontin. 1985. *The Dialectical Biologist.* Cambridge, Mass.: Harvard University Press.

Levinson, Stephen C. 1983. *Pragmatics.* Cambridge: Cambridge University Press.

Levison, Arnold. 1964. "The Concept of Proof." *The Monist* 48 (October): 547–566.

Levy, David M. 1992. *The Economic Ideas of Ordinary People.* London and New York: Routledge & Kegan Paul.

Lewis, C.S. 1967. "The Poison of Subjectivism." Pp. 72–81 in his *Christian Reflections.* Grand Rapids, Mich.

Lewis, T. and D. E. M. Sappington. 1989. "Inflexible Rules in Incentive Problems." *American Economic Review* 79 (March): 69–84.

Lind, Hans. 1992. "A Case Study of Normal Research in Theoretical Economics." *Economics and Philosophy* 8 (April): 83–102.

Livingstone, Eric. 1986. *The Ethnomethodological Foundation of Mathematics.* London and Boston: Routledge & Kegan Paul.

Loasby, Brian. 1971. "Hypothesis and Paradigm in the Theory of the Firm." *Economic Journal* 81 (December): 863–885.

Lodge, David. 1981 (1991). *Working with Structuralism: Essays and Reviews on Nineteenth and Twentieth-century Literature.* London: Routledge & Kegan Paul.

1988. *Nice Work.* Harmondsworth: Penguin Books.

1990. *After Bakhtin: Essays on Fiction and Criticism.* London and New York: Routledge & Kegan Paul.

Longenbach, James. 1991. *Wallace Stevens: The Plain Sense of Things.* New York: Oxford University Press.

Lönnroth, Lars. 1976. *Njáls Saga: A Critical Introduction.* Berkeley and Los Angeles: University of California.

Lovell, Michael C. 1983. "Data Mining." *Review of Economics and Statistics* 65 (February): 1012.

Lucas, Robert E., Jr. 1973. "Some International Evidence on Output-Inflation Tradeoffs." *American Economic Review* 63 (June): 326–334.

Lucas, Robert E., Jr. and Thomas J. Sargent, eds. 1981. *Rational Expectations and Econometric Practice.* Vol. I. Minneapolis: University of Minnesota Press.

Lurie, Alison. 1981. *The Language of Clothes.* New York: Vintage Books.

Lyne, John. 1990. "Bio-Rhetorics: Moralizing the Life Sciences." Pp. 35–57 in Simons, ed., *The Rhetorical Turn.*

Lyne, John and Michael McGee. 1987. "What Are Nice Folks Like You Doing in a Place Like this? Some Entailments of Treating Knowledge Claims Rhetorically." Pp. 381–406 in Nelson, Megill, and McCloskey, eds., *Rhetoric of the Human Sciences.*

Macaulay, Thomas Babington. 1828 (1881). "History." [*Edinburgh Review*]. Pp. 376–432 in his *Critical, Historical and Miscellaneous Essays.* Boston: Houghton Mifflin. Six vols. in three. Vol. I, part 1.

   1830 (1881). "Southey's Colloquies." [*Edinburgh Review*]. Pp. 132–187 in his *Critical, Historical and Miscellaneous Essays.* Boston: Houghton Mifflin. Six vols. in three. Vol. I. part 1.

McCawley, James D. 1981. *Everything that Linguists have Always Wanted to Know About Logic (but were Ashamed to Ask).* Chicago: University of Chicago Press.

   1990. "The Dark Side of Reason [Review of Feyerabend's Farewell to Reason.]" *Critical Review* 4 (3, Summer): 377–385.

McCloskey, D. N. 1973. *Economic Maturity and Entrepreneurial Decline: British Iron and Steel, 1870–1913.* Cambridge, Mass.: Harvard University Press.

   1976. "Does the Past Have Useful Economics?" *Journal of Economic Literature* 14 (June): 434–61.

   1983. "The Rhetoric of Economics." *Journal of Economic Literature* 21 (June): 482–517.

   1984. "The Literary Character of Economics." *Daedalus* (Summer): 97–119.

   1985a. *The Rhetoric of Economics.* Madison: University of Wisconsin Press.

   1985b. *The Applied Theory of Price.* Second edn. New York: Macmillan.

   1985c. "The Loss Function Has Been Mislaid: The Rhetoric of Significance Tests." *American Economic Review* 75 (May): 201–205.

   1985d. "A Dialogue on the Two Methodological Systems." *Eastern Economic Journal* 11 (October–December 1985): 293–296.

   1986a. "A Post–Modern Rhetoric of Sociology: D. W. Fiske and R. A. Shweder's Metatheory in Social Science." *Contemporary Sociology* 15 (November): 812–815.

   1986b. *The Writing of Economics.* New York: Macmillan.

   1987. "The Rhetoric of Economic Development." *Cato Journal* 7 (Spring/ Summer): 249–254.

1988a. "The Limits of Expertise: If You're So Smart, Why Ain't You Rich?" *The American Scholar* 57 (Summer 1988): 393–406.

1988b. "The Rhetoric of Law and Economics." *Michigan Law Review* 86 (February): 752–767.

1990a. *If You're So Smart: The Narrative of Economic Expertise.* Chicago University of Chicago Press.

1990b. "Storytelling in Economics." Pp. 61–75 in Lavoie, ed., *Economics and Hermeneutics.*

1990c. "Their Blackboard Right or Wrong: A Comment on Contested Exchange." *Politics and Society* 18: 223–232.

1991a. "Economic Science: A Search Through the Hyperspace of Assumptions?" *Methodus* 3 (June): 6–16.

1991b. "Voodoo Economics: Some Scarcities of Magic." *Poetics Today* 12 (Winter): 287–300.

1991c. "The Essential Rhetoric of Law, Literature, and Liberty" [Review of Posner's Law as Literature, Fish's Doing What Comes Naturally and White's Justice as Translation]." *Critical Review* 5 (Spring): 203–223.

1992a. "The Art of Forecasting, Ancient to Modern Times." *Cato Journal* 11 (Winter):.

1992b. "In Defense of Rhetoric: The Rhetorical Tradition in the West." *Common Knowledge* 1 (3).

1992c. "Writing as a Responsibility of Science: A Reply to Laband and Taylor." *Economic Inquiry.*

ed. 1993. *Second Thoughts: Myths and Morals of U. S. Economic History.* New York: Oxford.

Forthcoming, *The Prudent Peasant: English Open Fields and Enclosure.* Princeton: Princeton University Press.

McCloskey, D. N. and George Hersh, Jr., eds. 1991. *A Bibliography of Historical Economics to 1980.* Cambridge: Cambridge University Press.

McCloskey, D.N. and John Nelson. 1990. "The Rhetoric of Political Economy." Pp. 155–174 in J. H. Nichols, Jr. and C. Wright, eds., *Political Economy to Economics – And Back?* San Francisco: Institute for Contemporary Studies Press.

eds. 1994. *A Handbook on Rhetoric of Inquiry.* London: Basil Blackwell.

McCloskey, D. N. and J. Richard Zecher. 1976. "How the Gold Standard Worked, 1880–1913." Pp. 357–385 in Jacob A. Frenkel and Harry G. Johnson, eds., *The Monetary Approach to the Balance of Payments.* London: Allen and Unwin.

1984. "The Success of Purchasing Power Parity: Historical Evidence and Its Implications for Macroeconomics." Pp. 121–150 in Michael Bordo and Anna J. Schwartz, eds., *A Retrospective on the Classical Gold Standard 1821–1931.* Chicago: University of Chicago Press for the National Bureau of Economic Research.

McGrath, Francis C. 1985. "How Metaphor Works: What Boyle's Law and Shakespeare's 73rd Sonnet Have in Common." Department of English, University of Southern Maine, Portland, Maine.

1986. *The Sensible Spirit: Walter Pater and the Modernist Paradigm.* Tampa: University of South Florida Press.

MacIntyre, Alasdair. 1981. *After Virtue: A Study in Moral Theory.* Notre Dame Ind.: University of Notre Dame Press.

1988. *Whose Justice? Which Rationality?* London: Duckworth.

MacKenzie, Donald A. 1981. *Statistics in Britain, 1865–1930: The Social Construction of Scientific Knowledge.* Edinburgh: Edinburgh University Press.

McKeon, Richard. 1942–1973 (1987). *Rhetoric: Essays in Invention and Discovery.* [From essays published 1942–1973.] Woodbridge, Conn.: The Ox Bow Press.

McPherson, James M. 1985 (1991). "How Lincoln Won the War with Metaphors." Preprinted pp. 93–112 in his *Abraham Lincoln and the Second American Revolution.* New York: Oxford University Press.

McPherson, Michael. 1987. "Review of The Rhetoric of Economics." *Journal of Economic History* 47 (June): 596–598.

Machlup, Fritz. 1967. *Essays in Economic Semantics.* Ed. M. M. Miller. New York: Norton.

Maddock, Rodney. 1991. "The Development of New Classical Macroeconomics: Lessons for Lakatos." Pp. 335–359 in de Marchi and Blaug, eds. *Appraising Economic Theories.*

Madison, Gary B. 1982. *Understanding: A Phenomenological-Pragmatic Analysis.* Westport, Conn.: Greenwood.

1990. "Getting Beyond Objectivism: The Philosophical Hermeneutics of Gadamer and Ricoeur." Pp. 34–658 in Lavoie, ed., *Economics and Hermeneutics.*

Mahoney, Michael J. 1976. *Scientist as Subject: The Psychological Imperative.* Cambridge, Mass: Ballinger.

Mäki, Uskali. 1986. "Rhetoric at the Expense of Coherence: A Reinterpretation of Milton Friedman's Methodology." *Research in the History of Thought and Methodology* 4: 127–144.

1987. "Contribution to Session on 'Methodological Diversity in Economics.'" *Research in the History of Thought and Methodology* 5: 207–239.

1988a. "How to Combine Rhetoric and Realism in the Methodology of Economics." *Economics and Philosophy* 4 (April): 89–109.

1988b. "Realism, Economics, and Rhetoric: A Rejoinder to McCloskey." *Economics and Philosophy* 4 (April): 167–169.

1990. "Practical Syllogism, Entrepreneurship, and the Invisible Hand: A Critique of the Analytic Hermeneutics of G. H. von Wright." Pp. 149–175 in Lavoie, ed., *Economics and Hermeneutics.*

1991. "Comment on Hands." Pp. 85–90 in de Marchi and Blaug, eds., *Appraising Economic Theories.*

1992. "Social Conditioning of Economics." Pp. 65–104 in de Marchi, ed., *Post-Popperian Methodology.*

1993a. "Two Philosophies of the Rhetoric of Economics." Pp. 23–50 in Backhouse, Dudley-Evans, and Henderson, eds., *Economics and Language.*

1993b. "Diagnosing McCloskey." Unpublished paper presented to the Network on Economic Method, at the January 1993 meetings of the American Economic Association, Anaheim, California.

Malinvaud, Edmond. 1989. "The Challenge of Macroeconomic Under-standing." Pp. 297–316 in J. A. Kregel, ed., *Recollections of Eminent Economists*. New York: New York University Press.

Mallove, Eugene F. 1991. *Fire from Ice: Searching for the Truth Behind the Cold Fusion Furor*. New York: Wiley.

Marcus, Solomon. 1974. "Fifty-two Oppositions between Scientific and Poetic Communication." Pp. 83–96 in C. Cherry, ed., *Pragmatic Aspects of Human Communication*. Dordrecht, Holland: Reidel.

Marglin, Stephen A. 1984. *Growth, Distribution, and Prices*. Cambridge, Mass.: Harvard University Press.

Margolin, Victor. 1989. *Design Discourse: History, Theory, Criticism*. Chicago: University of Chicago Press.

Marshall, Alfred. 1895 (1961). *Principles of Economics*. 3rd ed. from Ninth (Variorum) edition. London: Macmillan.

1920. *Principles of Economics*. London: Macmillan.

Martin, Wallace. 1986. *Recent Theories of Narrative*. Ithaca: Cornell University Press.

Mayer, Thomas. 1975. "Selecting Economic Hypotheses by Goodness of Fit." *Economic Journal* 85 (December): 887–83.

1980. "Economics as a Hard Science: Realistic Goal or Wishful Thinking?" *Economic Inquiry* 18 (April): 165–178.

1992. *Truth Versus Precision*. London: Edward Elgar.

1993. *Truth Versus Precision in Economics*. Aldershot, England and Brookfield, Vt.: Edward Elgar.

Mead, R. and W. Henderson. 1983. "Conditional Form and Meaning in Economics Text." *English for Specific Purposes* 2: 139–160.

Mechling, Elizabeth Walker and Jay Mechling. 1983. "Sweet Talk: The Moral Rhetoric Against Sugar." *Central States Speech Journal* 34 (Spring): 19–32.

Medawar, Peter. 1964. "Is the Scientific Paper Fraudulent?" *Saturday Review* August 1: 42–43.

Megill, Allan. 1985. *Prophets of Extremity: Nietzsche, Heidegger, Foucault, Derrida*. Berkeley: University of California Press.

Megill, Allan and D. N. McCloskey. 1987. "The Rhetoric of History." Pp. 221–238 in Nelson, Megill, and McCloskey, eds., *Rhetoric of the Human Sciences*.

Megill, Allan, John Nelson, and D. N. McCloskey. 1987. "Rhetoric of Inquiry." Pp. 3–18 in Nelson, Megill, and McCloskey, eds., *Rhetoric of the Human Sciences*.

Mehta, Judith. 1993. "Meaning in the Context of Bargaining Games – Narratives in Opposition." Pp. 85–99 in Backhouse, Dudley-Evans, and Henderson, eds., *Economics and Language*.

Mendelsohn, Everett. 1987. "The Political Anatomy of Controversy in the Sciences." Pp. 93–124 in H. T. Engelhardt Jr. and A. L. Caplan, eds., *Scientific Controversy: Case Studies in the Resolution and Closure of Disputes in Science and Technology*. Cambridge: Cambridge University Press.

Milberg, William. 1988. "The Language of Economics: Deconstructing the Neoclassical Texts." *Social Concepts* 4 (2): 33–57.

1991. "Marxism, Post–Structuralism, and the Discourse of Economics." *Rethinking Marxism* 4 (2): 93–104.

1992. "The Rhetoric of Policy Relevance in International Economics." Unpublished manuscript. Department of Economics, New School for Social Research.

Milberg, William and Bruce A. Pietrykowski. 1990. "Realism, Relativism and the Importance of Rhetoric for Marxist Economics." Unpublished manuscript. Department of Economics, New School for Social Research.

Mill, John Stuart. 1836 (1844, 1877). "On the Definition of Political Economy and the Method of Investigation Proper to It." Pp. 52–69 in Hausman, ed., *The Philosophy of Economics.*

Miller, Carolyn R. 1990. "The Rhetoric of Decision Science, or Herbert A. Simon Says." Pp. 162–184 in Simons, ed., *The Rhetorical Turn.*

Miller, Jonathan. 1983. *States of Mind.* New York: Pantheon.

Miller, J. Hillis. 1993. "Thinking Like Other People." Pp. 289–306 in M. Edmundson, ed., *Wild Orchids and Trotsky: Messages from American Universities.* New York: Penguin Books.

Millis, Harry A. 1935. "The Union in Industry: Some Observations on the Theory of Collective Bargaining." *American Economic Review* 25 (March): 1–13.

Mills, C. Wright. 1959. "On Intellectual Craftsmanship." In his *The Sociological Imagination.* New York: Grove.

Mini, Piero. 1974. *Philosophy and Economics: The Origins and Development of Economic Theory.* Gainesville: The University Presses of Florida.

Mirowski, Philip. 1987 (1988). "Shall I Compare Thee to a Minkowski-Ricardo-Leontief-Metzler Matrix?" *Economics and Philosophy* 3 (April): 67–96. Reprinted pp. 117–145 in Klamer, Solow, and McCloskey, eds., *Consequences.*

1989. *More Heat than Light: Economics as Social Physics, Physics as Nature's Economics.* New York: Cambridge University Press.

1990. "The Philosophical Bases of Institutional Economics." Pp. 76–112 in Lavoie, ed., *Economics and Hermeneutics.*

1991a. "Comment on Weintraub." Pp. 291–293 in de Marchi and Blaug, eds., *Appraising Economic Theories.*

1991b. "The When, the How, and the Why of Mathematical Expression in the History of Economic Analysis." *Journal of Economic Perspectives* 5 (Winter): 145–158.

1991c. *Against Mechanism: Protecting Economics from Science.* Totowa, N.J.: Rowman and Littlefield.

1992. "Three Vignettes in the State of Economic Rhetoric." Pp. 235–259 in de Marchi, ed., *Post-Popperian Methodology.*

Mirowski, Philip and Pamela Cook. 1990. "Walras' 'Economics and Mechanics': Translation, Commentary, Context." Pp. 189–215 in Samuels, ed., *Economics as Discourse.*

Mokyr, Joel. 1990. *The Lever of Riches.* New York: Oxford University Press.

Monk, Ray. 1990 (1991). *Ludwig Wittgenstein: The Duty of Genius.* London: Jonathan Cape (Vintage edn. 1991).

Montague, F. C. 1900. Morality. In R. H. Palgrave, ed., *Dictionary of Political Economy.* London: Macmillan.

Moore, Ruth. 1966 (1985). *Niels Bohr: The Man, His Science, and the World They Changed.* Cambridge, Mass. and London: MIT Press.

Morgan, Mary. 1991. "The Stamping Out of Process Analysis in Econometrics." Pp. 237–265 in de Marchi and Blaug, eds., *Appraising Economic Theories.*

Morishima, Michio. 1984. "The Good and Bad Uses of Mathematics." Pp. 51–73 in P. Wiles and G. Routh, eds., *Economics in Disarray.* Oxford: Basil Blackwell.

Morison, Denton E. and Ramon E. Henkel, eds. 1977. *The Significance Test Controversy: A Reader.* Chicago: Aldine.

Mulkay, Michael. 1979. *Science and the Sociology of Knowledge.* London: Allen and Unwin.

1985. *The Word and the World: Explorations in the Form of Sociological Analysis.* Winchester, Mass.: Allen and Unwin.

Munz, Peter. 1990. "The Rhetoric of Rhetoric." *Journal of the History of Ideas* 51 (January/March): 121–142.

Myers, Gerald P. 1986. *William James: His Life and Thought.* New Haven: Yale University Press.

1990. *Writing Biology: Text in the Social Construction of Scientific Knowledge.* Series in the Rhetoric of the Human Sciences. Madison: University of Wisconsin Press.

Nash, Christopher and Martin Warner, eds. 1989. *Narrative in Culture.* London: Routledge & Kegan Paul.

Nelson, Alan. 1984. "Some Issues Surrounding the Reduction of Macroeconomics to Microeconomics." *Philosophy of Science* 51: 573–594.

1988. "Economic Rationality and Morality." *Philosophy and Public Affairs* 17 (Spring): 149–166.

Nelson, John. 1983. "Models, Statistics, and Other Tropes of Politics: Or, Whatever Happened to Argument in Political Science?" In Zarefsky, D., Sillars, M. O., and Rhodes, J., eds, *Argument in Transition: Proceedings of the Third Summer Conference on Argumentation.* Annandale, Virginia: Speech Communication Association.

1987. "Seven Rhetorics of Inquiry: A Provocation." Pp. 407–436 in Nelson, Megill, and McCloskey, eds., *The Rhetoric of the Human Sciences.*

Nelson, John, Allan Megill, and D. N. McCloskey, eds. 1987. *The Rhetoric of the Human Sciences: Language and Argument in Scholarship and Public Affairs.* Rhetoric of the Human Sciences. Madison: University of Wisconsin Press.

Nelson, Robert H. 1991. *Reaching for Heaven on Earth: The Theological Meaning of Economics.* Savage, Md.: Rowman and Littlefield.

Nevins, Allan. 1940. "Lincoln in His Writings." Pp. xvii–xxvi in Philip van Doren Stern, ed., *The Life and Writings of Abraham Lincoln.* New York: Modern Library.

Neyman, Jerzy and E. S. Pearson. 1933. "On the Problem of the Most Efficient Tests of Statistical Hypotheses." *Philosophical Transactions of the Royal Society* A 231 (1933): 289–337.

Nicholas, Stephen. 1982. "Total Factor Productivity Growth and the Revision of Post-1870 British Economic History." *Economic History Review* 2nd ser. 25 (February): 83–98.

Nietzsche, Friedrich W. 1870 (1979). *Philosophy and Truth: Selections from Nietzsche's Notebooks of the Early 1870's.* Atlantic Highlands, N.J.: Humanities Press.

Niggle, Christopher. 1988. "Review of The Rhetoric of Economics." *Social Science Journal* 25 (1): 111–113.

North, Douglass C. and Roger L. Miller. 1983. *The Economics of Public Issues,* 6th edn. New York: Harper Collins.

Novick, Peter. 1988. *That Noble Dream: The "Objectivity Question" and the American Historical Profession.* New York: Cambridge University Press.

Oakeshott, Michael. 1959 (1991). "The Voice of Poetry in the Conversation of Mankind." Pp. 488–541 in Oakeshott, *Rationalism in Politics and Other Essays.* Indianapolis: Liberty Classics.

   1965 (1989). "Learning and Teaching." Pp. 43–62 in Timothy Fuller, ed., *The Voice of Liberal Learning: Michael Oakeshott on Education.* New Haven and London: Yale University Press.

O'Brien, Denis P. 1976. "The Longevity of Adam Smith's Vision: Paradigms, Research Programmes and Falsifiability in the History of Economic Thought." *Scottish Journal of Political Economy* 23 (June): 133–151.

Ohta, Nakota and Zvi Griliches. 1976. "Automobile Prices Revisited: Extensions of the Hedonic Hypothesis." Pp. 325–398 in N. E. Terleckyj, ed., *Household Production and Consumption, Studies in Income and Wealth.* Vol. XL. New York: National Bureau of Economic Research.

Ortony, Andrew, ed. 1979. *Metaphor and Thought.* Cambridge: Cambridge University Press.

Oswald, Andrew J. 1991. "Progress and Micro-economic Data." *Economic Journal* 101 (January): 75–80.

Oxford University Press. 1933. *The Oxford English Dictionary,* vol. IX, S – Soldo. Oxford: Clarendon Press.

   1982. *A Supplement to the Oxford English Dictionary,* vol. III, O – Scz. Oxford: Clarendon Press.

   1989. *The Oxford English Dictionary.* 2nd edn. Vol. XIV, Rob–Sequyle. Oxford: Clarendon Press.

Palmer, Richard. 1988. "Statistical Mechanics Approaches to Complex Optimization Problems." Pp. 177–193 in P. W. Anderson, K. J. Arrow, and D. Pines, eds., *The Economy as an Evolving Complex System.* Santa Fe Institute Studies in the Sciences of Complexity. Reading, Mass.: Addison-Wesley.

Palmer, Tom G. 1986–1987. "An Economist Looks at His Science." *Humane Studies Review* 4 (Winter): 1, 12–13.

   1990. "The Hermeneutical View of Freedom: Implications of Gadamerian Understanding for Economic Policy." Pp. 299–318 in Lavoie, ed., *Economics and Hermeneutics.*

Pareto, Vilfredo. 1927 (1971). *Manual of Political Economy.* Trans. Ann Schwier. New York: A. M. Kelley.

Passmore, John. 1961. *Philosophical Reasoning.* 2nd edn. 1970. London: Duckworth.

   1967. "Logical Positivism." Article in P. Edwards, ed., *The Encyclopedia of Philosophy.* New York and London: Macmillan and Collier Macmillan.

1985. *Recent Philosophers*. La Salle, Ill.: Open Court.

Pearson, Karl. 1990. *The Grammar of Science*. 2nd edn. London: Black.

Pen, Jan. 1984. *Among Economists*. Trans. T. Preston. Amsterdam: North Holland.

Pera, Marcello and William R. Shea. 1991. *Persuading Science: The Art of Scientific Rhetoric*. Canton, Mass.: Science History Publications.

Perelman, Chaim. 1982. *The Realm of Rhetoric*. Notre Dame, Ind.: University of Notre Dame Press.

Perelman, Chaim and L. Olbrechts-Tyteca. 1958 (1969). *The New Rhetoric: A Treatise on Argumentation*. Trans. J. Wilkinson and P. Weaver. Notre Dame Ind.: University of Notre Dame Press.

Perlman, Mark. 1978. "Review of Hutchison's Knowledge and Ignorance in Economics. *Journal of Economic Literature* 16 (June): 582–585.

Petrey, Sandy. 1990. *Speech Acts and Literary Theory*. New York and London: Routledge & Kegan Paul.

Pickering, Andrew. 1984. *Constructing Quarks: A Sociological History of Particle Physics*. Edinburgh: University of Edinburgh Press.

1992. "From Science as Knowledge to Science as Practice." Pp. 1–26 in Pickering, ed., *Science as Practice and Culture*. Chicago: University of Chicago Press.

Pinch, Trevor J. 1986. *Confronting Nature*. Holland: Reidel.

Plato. *Euthyphro*. Trans. H. N. Fowler. Cambridge, Mass.: Harvard University Press, 1914.

Georgias. Trans. W. R. M. Lamb. Cambridge, Mass.: Harvard University Press, 1925.

The Laws. Trans. A. E. Taylor. In E. Hamilton, ed., *The Collected Dialogues of Plato*. Princeton: Princeton University Press.

Phaedrus. Trans. H. N. Fowler. Cambridge, Mass.: Harvard University Press, 1914.

Sophist. in Plato VII: *Theaetetus, Sophist*. Trans. H. N. Fowler, Cambridge: Harvard University Press, 1921.

Pojman, Louis J. 1993. *The Theory of Knowledge: Classical and Contemporary Readings*. Belmont, Calif.: Wadsworth.

Polanyi, Michael. 1946 (1964). *Science, Faith and Society*. Chicago: University of Chicago Press.

1958 (1962). *Personal Knowledge: Towards a Post–critical Philosophy*. Chicago: University of Chicago Press.

1966. *The Tacit Dimension*. Garden City, N.J.: Doubleday.

Polya, George. 1954. *Induction and Analogy in Mathematics*, being vol. I of *Mathematics and Plausible Reasoning*. Princeton: Princeton University Press.

Pool, Robert. 1989. "Strange Bedfellows." *Science* 245 (18 August): 700–703.

Popper, Karl R. 1934 (1959). *The Logic of Scientific Discovery*. New York: Harper and Row.

1974 (1976). *Unended Quest: An Intellectual Autobiography*. London, Fontana.

Porter, Theodore M. 1986. *The Rise of Statistical Thinking, 1820–1900*. Princeton: Princeton University Press.

Posner, Richard. 1988. *Law and Literature: A Misunderstood Relation.* Cambridge, Mass.: Harvard University Press.

Prelli, Lawrence J. 1989. *A Rhetoric of Science. Inventing Scientific Discourse.* Columbia: University of South Carolina Press.

Pressman, Steven. 1987. "Comment on McCloskey." *Eastern Economic Journal* 13 (July–September), 305–307.

Pullam, Geoffrey K. 1990. *The Great Eskimo Vocabulary Hoax and Other Irreverent Essays on the Study of Language.* Chicago: University of Chicago Press.

Puro, Edward. 1990. "Comment on Rossetti's 'Deconstructing Robert Lucas.'" Pp. 251–256 in Samuels, ed., *Economics as Discourse.*

Putnam, Hilary. 1990. *Realism with a Human Face.* Ed. James Conant. Cambridge, Mass.: Harvard University Press.

Quine, W. V. 1948 (1953). "On What There Is." Pp. 1–19 in his *From a Logical Point of View.* Cambridge, Mass.: Harvard University Press.

    1987. *Quiddities: An Intermittently Philosophical Dictionary.* Cambridge, Mass.: Harvard University Press.

Quintilian, Marcus F. *Institutio Oratoria.* Trans. H. E. Butler. Cambridge, Mass.: Harvard University Press, 1920.

Randall, Alan. 1990. "Review Essay on Johnson's Research Methodology for Economists." *Research in the History of Thought and Methodology* 7: 263–268.

Rappaport, Steven. 1988a. "Economic Methodology: Rhetoric or Epistemology?" *Economics and Philosophy* 4 (April): 110–128.

    1988b. "Arguments, Truth, and Economic Methodology: A Rejoinder to McCloskey." *Economics and Philosophy* 4 (April): 170–172.

Rector, Ralph A. 1990. "The Economics of Rationality and the Rationality of Economics." Pp. 195–235 in Lavoie, ed., *Economics and Hermeneutics.*

Redman, Deborah A. 1991. *Economics and the Philosophy of Science.* New York and Melbourne: Oxford University Press.

Reid, Joseph D., Jr. 1973. "Sharecropping as an Understandable Market Response – The Post-Bellum South." *Journal of Economic History* 33: 106–130.

Resnick, Stephen and Richard Wolff. 1987. *Knowledge and Class: A Critique of Political Economy.* Chicago: University of Chicago Press.

Resnick, Stephen and Richard Wolff. 1988. "Marxian Theory and the Rhetoric of Economics. Pp. 47–63 in Klamer et al. *Consequences.*

Rhoads, Steven E. 1987. "Review of The Rhetoric of Economics." *American Political Science Review* 81 (March): 338–39.

Richards, I. A. 1925. *Principles of Literary Criticism.* New York: Harcourt Brace Jovanovich.

    1936. *The Philosophy of Rhetoric.* New York: Oxford University Press.

Robbins, Lionel. 1932. *The Nature and Significance of Economic Science.* London: Macmillan.

Robinson, E. A. G. 1947. "John Maynard Keynes 1883–1946." *Economic Journal* 57 (March): 1–68.

Romano, Carlin. 1987 "Review of The Rhetoric of Economics." *Philadelphia Inquirer* March 22, p. S2.

1989. "The Illegality of Philosophy." Pp. 199–216 in Avner Cohen and Marcelo Dascal, eds., *The Institution of Philosophy: A Discipline In Crisis?* Lasalle, Ill.: Open Court.

Rorty, Amélie Oksenberg. 1983. "Experiments in Philosophic Genre: Descartes' Meditations." *Critical Inquiry* 9 (March): 545–565.

Rorty, Richard. 1979. *Philosophy and the Mirror of Nature.* Princeton: Princeton University Press.

1982. *Consequences of Pragmatism.* Minneapolis: University of Minnesota Press.

1987. "Science as Solidarity." Pp. 38–52 in Nelson, Megill, and McCloskey, eds., *Rhetoric of the Human Sciences.*

1989. *Contingency, Irony, and Solidarity.* Cambridge: Cambridge University Press.

Rosaldo, Renato. 1987. "Where Objectivity Lies: The Rhetoric of Anthropology." Pp. 87–110 in Nelson, Megill, and McCloskey, eds., *Rhetoric of the Human Sciences.*

Rosen, Stanley. 1980. *The Limits of Analysis.* New York: Basic Books.

1987. *Hermeneutics as Politics.* New York: Oxford University Press.

Rosenberg, Alexander. 1976. *Microeconomic Laws: A Philosophical Analysis.* Pittsburgh: University of Pittsburgh Press.

1983. "If Economics Isn't a Science, What Is It?" *Philosophical Forum* 14: 296–314.

1986a. "Lakatosian Consolations for Economists." *Economics and Philosophy* 2: 127–140.

1986b. "Philosophy of Science and the Potentials for Knowledge in the Social Sciences." Pp. 339–346 in Fiske and Shweder, eds., *Metatheory in Social Science.*

1987. "Contribution to Session on 'Methodological Diversity in Economics.'" *Research in the History of Thought and Methodology* 5: 207–239.

1988a. "Economics is Too Important to Be Left to the Rhetoricians." *Economics and Philosophy* 4 (April): 129–149.

1988b. "Rhetoric is Not Important Enough for Economists to Bother About." *Economics and Philosophy* 4 (April): 173–175.

1992. *Economics – Mathematical Politics or Science of Diminishing Returns?* Chicago: University of Chicago Press.

Rosenberg, Nathan and L. E. Birdzell. 1986. *How the West Grew Rich: The Economic Transformation of the Industrial World.* New York; Basic Books.

Rosenblatt, Louise M. 1978. *The Reader, the Text, the Poem: The Transactional Theory of the Literary Work.* Carbondale: Southern Illinois University Press.

Rossetti, Jane. 1990. "Deconstructing Robert Lucas." Pp. 225–243 in Samuels, ed., *Economics as Discourse.*

1992. "Deconstruction, Rhetoric, and Economics." Pp. 211–234 in de Marchi, ed., *Post-Popperian Methodology.*

Rozeboom, William W. 1967 (1993). "Why I Know So Much More Than You Do." *American Philosophical Quarterly* 4: 281–290. Reprinted as pp. 175–185 in Pojman, ed., *The Theory of Knowledge.*

Ruccio, David F. 1987. "Review of The Rhetoric of Economics." *American Journal of Sociology* 93 (Nov): 723–725.

Runyon, Damon. 1958 (1933). "Money From Home." Pp. 18–32 in *A Treasury of Damon Runyon*. New York: Modern Library.

Ruskin, John. 1851–53 [1890]. *The Stones of Venice*. Three vols. New York: Peter Fenelon Collier.

Ruttan, Vernon. 1970. "Agricultural Economics." Pp. 144–51 in Nancy Ruggles, ed., *Economics*. Englewood Cliffs, N.J.: Prentice-Hall.

Ryan, Richard. 1991. "Facts, Phenomena, and Fantasies." *National Review* March 18: 56–58.

Samuels, Warren J. 1984. "Comments on McCloskey on Methodology and Rhetoric." *Research in the History of Thought and Methodology* 2: 207–210.

1990a. "Introduction." Pp. 1–14 in Samuels, ed., *Economics as Discourse*.

ed. 1990b. *Economics as Discourse: An Analysis of the Language of Economists*. Boston, Dordrecht and London: Kluwer Academic.

Samuelson, Paul A. 1947. *Foundations of Economic Analysis*. Cambridge, Mass.: Harvard University Press.

1948. *Economics*. New York: McGraw-Hill.

Sanders, Robert E. 1990. "Discursive Constraints on the Acceptance and Rejection of Knowledge Claims: The Conversation about Conversation." Pp. 145–161 in Simons, ed., *The Rhetorical Turn*.

Santayana, George. 1947 (1987). *Persons and Places: Fragments of Autobiography*. ed. W. G. Holzberger and H. J. Saatkamp, Jr. Cambridge, Mass.: MIT Press.

Sassower, Raphael. 1985. *Philosophy of Economics: A Critique of Demarcation*. Lantham, Md.: University Press of America.

Saussure, Ferdinand de. 1916 (1983). *Course in General Linguistics*. Trans. Roy Harris. London: Duckworth.

Schiappa, Edward. 1991. *Protagoras and Logos: A Study In Greek Philosophy and Rhetoric*. Columbia: University of South Carolina Press.

Schmidt, Christian. 1985. *La Sémantique economique en question: recherche sur les fondements de l'economique théorique*. Paris: Calmann-Lévy.

Schön, David A. 1983. *The Reflective Practitioner: How Professionals Think in Action*. New York: Basic Books.

Schopenhauer, Arthur. 1851 (1970). *Essays and Aphorisms*. Trans. R. J. Hollingdale. Harmondsworth: Penguin Books.

Schumpeter, Joseph A. 1954. *History of Economic Analysis*. New York: Oxford University Press.

Scitovsky, Tibor. 1976. *The Joyless Economy*. New York: Oxford University Press.

Scott, Robert. 1967. "On Viewing Rhetoric as Epistemic." *Central States Speech Journal* 18 (February): 9–17.

Searle, John R. 1969. *Speech Acts: An Essay in the Philosophy of Language*. Cambridge: Cambridge University Press.

Sebberson, David. 1990. "The Rhetoric of Inquiry or the Sophistry of the Status Quo? Exploring the Common Ground Between Critical Rhetoric and Institutional Economics." *Journal of Economic Issues* 24 (December): 1017–1026.

Seery, John Evan. 1990. *Political Returns: Irony in Politics and Theory from Plato to the Antinuclear Movement.* Boulder: Westview Press.

Seiz, Janet A. 1990. "Comment on Klamer's 'The Textbook Presentation of Economic Discourse.'" Pp. 155–166 in Samuels, ed., *Economics as Discourse.*

1992. "Gender and Economic Research." Pp. 273–319 in de Marchi, ed., *Post-Popperian Methodology.*

Selden, Raman, 1991. "The Rhetoric of Enterprise." Pp. 58–71 in R. Keat and N. Abercrombie, eds., *Enterprise Culture.* London: Routledge & Kegan Paul.

Shackle, George L. S. 1983. "A Student's Pilgrimage." *Banco Nazionale del Lavoro Quarterly Review* 145: 110–116.

Shapin, Steven and Simon Schaffer. 1985. *Leviathan and the Air-Pump: Hobbes, Boyle and the Experimental Life.* Princeton: Princeton University Press.

Shearmur, Jeremy. 1991. "Popper, Lakatos and Theoretical Progress in Economics." Pp. 35–52 in de Marchi and Blaug, eds., *Appraising Economic Theories.*

Shiller, Robert J. 1989. *Market Volatility.* Cambridge, Mass.: MIT Press.

Shweder, Richard A. 1986. "Divergent Rationalities." Pp. 163–196 in Fiske and Shweder, eds., *Metatheory in Social Science.*

1991. *Thinking Through Cultures: Expeditions in Cultural Psychology.* Cambridge, Mass.: Harvard University Press.

Simons, Herbert W., ed. 1989. *Rhetoric in the Human Sciences.* London: Sage.

ed. 1990. *The Rhetorical Turn: Invention and Persuasion in the Conduct of Inquiry.* Chicago: University of Chicago Press.

Smith, Adam. 1762–1763 (1982). *Lectures on Jurisprudence.* Glasgow Edition of 1978. Ed. R. L. Meek, D. D. Raphael, and P. G. Stein. Indianapolis: Liberty Classics.

1776 (1981). *An Inquiry into the Nature and Causes of the Wealth of Nations.* Glasgow Edition of 1976. Ed. Campbell, Skinner, and Todd. 2 vols. Indianapolis: Liberty Classics.

1790 (1982). *The Theory of Moral Sentiments.* Glasgow Edition of 1976. Ed. D. D. Raphael and A. L. Macfie. Indianapolis: Liberty Classics.

Smith, Vernon L., Kevin A. McCabe, and Stephen J. Rassenti. 1991. "Lakatos and Experimental Economics." Pp. 197–226 in de Marchi and Blaug, eds., *Appraising Economic Theories.*

Solow, Daniel. 1982. *How to Read and Do Proofs: An Introduction to Mathematical Thought Processes.* New York: Wiley.

Solow, Robert. 1957. "Technical Change and the Aggregate Production Function." *Review of Economics and Statistics* 39 (August): 312–320.

1981. "Does Economics Make Progress?" *Bulletin of the American Academy of Arts and Sciences* 26 (December): 11–31.

Spitzer, Alan B. 1990. "John Dewey, the 'Trial' of Leon Trotsky and the Search for Historical Truth." *History and Theory* 29 (1): 16–37.

Stebbing, L. Susan. 1939. *Thinking to Some Purpose.* Harmondsworth: Pelican Books.

1943. *A Modern Elementary Logic.* 5th edn. 1965 (revised by C. W. K. Mundle). London: Methuen.

Steedman, Ian. 1991. "Negative and Positive Contributions: Appraising Sraffa and Lakatos." Pp. 435–450 in de Marchi and Blaug, eds., *Appraising Economic Theories*.

Stein, Herbert. 1986. *Washington Bedtime Stories: The Politics of Money and Jobs*. New York: Free Press.

Steiner, George. 1967 (1982). *Language and Silence: Essays on Language, Literature, and the Inhuman*. New York: Atheneum.

Steiner, Mark. 1975. *Mathematical Knowledge*. Ithaca: Cornell University Press.

Stevens, Wallace. 1972. *The Palm at the End of the Mind: Selected Poems and a Play*. Ed. Holly Stevens. New York: Vintage.

Stigler, George. 1966. *The Theory of Price*. Third edn. New York: Macmillan.

1976. "The Scientific Uses of Scientific Biography, with Special Reference to J. S. Mill." In J. M. Robson and M. Lane, eds., *James and John Stuart Mill: Papers of the Centenary Conference*. Toronto: University of Toronto Press.

1987. *The Theory of Price*. Fourth edn. New York: Macmillan.

Stove, David. 1982. *Popper and After: Four Modern Irrationalists*. Oxford: Pergamon Press.

Summers, Lawrence. 1991. "The Scientific Illusion in Empirical Economics." *Scandinavian Journal of Economics* 93 (2): 27–39.

Sutch, Richard. 1991. "All Things Reconsidered: The Life–Cycle Perspective and the Third Task of Economic History." *Journal of Economic History* 51 (June): 271–288.

Swales, John M. 1993. "The Paradox of Value: Six Treatments in Search of the Reader." Pp. 223–239 in Backhouse, Dudley-Evans, and Henderson, eds., *Economics and Language*.

Sweezy, Paul M. 1938. *Monopoly and Competition in the English Coal Trade, 1550–1850*. Cambridge, Mass.: Harvard University Press.

Tacitus. *Dialogus of Tacitus in Five Volumes*. Vol. I. Trans. Peterson and Winterbottom. Cambridge, Mass.: Harvard University Press, 1914.

Throgmorton, James. 1993. "Analytical Tools as Rhetorical Tropes: Survey Research as Part of Electrical Power Planning Arguments in Chicago." In John Forester and Frank Fischer, eds., *The Argumentative Turn in Policy and Planning*. Durham N.C.: Duke University Press.

Thucydides. *History of the Peloponnesian War*. Trans. R. Warner. Harmondsworth: Penguin Books, 1972.

Thurow, Lester. 1985. *The Zero-Sum Solution: Building a World-Class American Economy*. New York: Simon and Schuster.

Toulmin, Stephen. 1950 (1986). *The Place of Reason in Ethics*. Chicago: University of Chicago Press.

1958. *The Uses of Argument*. Cambridge: Cambridge University Press.

1972. *Human Understanding: The Collective Use and Evolution of Concepts*. Princeton: Princeton University Press.

Traweek, Sharon. 1988. *Beamtimes and Lifetimes: The World of High Energy Physics*. Cambridge, Mass.: Harvard University Press.

Tribe, Keith. 1978. *Land, Labour and Economic Discourse*. London: Routledge & Kegan Paul.

1986. "Review of The Rhetoric of Economics." *Manchester School of Economic and Social Studies* 54 (December): 447–448.

Trump, Donald, with Tony Schwartz. 1987. *Trump: The Art of the Deal.* New York: Warner Books.

Tufte, Edward R. 1983. *The Visual Display of Quantitative Information.* Cheshire, Conn.: Graphics Press.

1990. *Envisioning Information.* Cheshire, Conn.: Graphics Press.

Tukey, John W. 1986. "Sunset Salvo." *The American Statistician* 40 (February): 72–76.

Tullock, Gordon. 1959. "Publication Decisions and Tests of Significance: A Comment." *Journal of the American Statistical Association* 54: 593 only.

US Bureau of the Census. 1982. *Statistical Abstract of the United States* (103rd edn.). Washington, D.C.: Government Printing Office.

1990. *Statistical Abstract of the United States* (110th edn.). Washington, D.C.: Government Printing Office.

Ulam, Stanislaw M. 1976. *Adventures of a Mathematician.* New York: Scribners.

Vaihinger, Hans. 1924. *The Philosophy of As-If.* Trans. from 8th German edition by C. K. Ogden.

Vaubel, Roland. 1988. "Review of The Rhetoric of Economics." *Economic History Review* 41 (May): 340–342.

Vaughn, Karen I. 1988. "Austrian Economics/Feminine Economics." Paper presented to the session organized by the Committee on the Status of Women in the Economics Profession, Southern Economic Association, San Antonio, November 20. Unpublished paper: George Mason University.

Vickers, Brian. 1970 (1989). *Classical Rhetoric in English Poetry.* Carbondale, Ill.: Southern Illinois University Press.

1988. *In Defense of Rhetoric.* Oxford: Oxford University Press.

Viner, Jacob. 1950 (1991). "A Modest Proposal for Some Stress on Scholarship in Graduate Training." Pp. 385–395 in Jacob Viner, *Essays on the Intellectual History of Economics.* Ed. Douglas A. Irwin. Princeton: Princeton University Press.

Vlastos, Gregory. 1991. *Socrates: Ironist and Moral Philosopher.* Ithaca: Cornell University Press.

Volcker, Paul and Toyoo Gyohten. 1992. *Changing Fortunes: The World's Money and the Threat to American Leadership.* New York: Times Books.

von Neumann, John and Oskar Morgenstern. 1947. *The Theory of Games and Economic Behavior.* Second edn. Princeton: Princeton University Press.

Wald, Abraham. 1939. "Contributions to the Theory of Statistical Estimation and Testing Hypotheses." *Annals of Mathematical Statistics* 10 (December): 299–326.

Waller, William T., Jr., and Linda R. Robertson. 1990. "Why Johnny (Ph.D. Economics) Can't Read: A Rhetorical Analysis of Thorstein Veblen and a Response to Donald McCloskey." *Journal of Economic Issues* 24 (Dec): 1027–1044.

Wallis, John Joseph, and Douglass North. 1986. "Measuring the Transaction Sector in the American Economy, 1870–1970." Pp. 95–161 in S. L.

Engerman and R. E. Gallman, eds., *Long-Term Factors in American Economic Growth*. Chicago: University of Chicago Press for the National Bureau of Economic Research.

Walras, Léon. 1874/1900 (1954). *Elements of Pure Economics*. Trans. William Jaffé. Homewood, Ill.: Richard D. Irwin.

Walton, Douglas N. 1985. *Arguer's Position: A Pragmatic Study of "Ad Hominem" Attack, Criticism, Refutation, and Fallacy*. Westport, Conn.: Greenwood Press.

Ward, Benjamin. 1972. *What's Wrong with Economics?* New York: Basic Books.

Warner, Martin. 1989. *Philosophical Finesse: Studies in the Art of Rational Persuasion*. Oxford: Oxford University Press.

Warsh, David. 1988. "'Yellow Rain' and 'Supply-side Economics': Some Rhetoric That Failed." Pp. 247–262 in Klamer, Solow, and McCloskey, eds., *Consequences*.

———. 1993. "Trust-Buster in the Idea Business." In his *Economic Principals*. New York: Free Press.

Webly, Simon. 1987. "Review of The Rhetoric of Economics." *International Affairs* 63 (Summer): 489–490.

Weinberg, Steven. 1983. "Beautiful Theories." Department of Physics, University of Texas, Austin. Revision of the Second Annual Gordon Mills Lecture on Science and the Humanities, University of Texas, April 5.

Weintraub, E. Roy. 1985. *General Equilibrium Analysis: Studies in Appraisal*. Cambridge: Cambridge University Press.

———. 1988a. "On the Brittleness of the Orange Equilibrium." Pp. 146–162 in Klamer, Solow, and McCloskey, eds., *Consequences*.

———. 1988b. "The NeoWalrasian Program is Empirically Progressive." Pp. 213–230 in de Marchi, ed., *The Popperian Legacy*.

———. 1990. "Comment on Heilbroner's 'Economics as Ideology.'" Pp. 117–128 in Samuels, ed., *Economics as Discourse*.

———. 1991a. "Stabilizing Dynamics." Pp. 273–290 in de Marchi and Blaug, eds., *Appraising Economic Theories*.

———. 1991b. *Stabilizing Dynamics: Constructing Economic Knowledge*. Cambridge: Cambridge University Press.

———. 1992. "Review of Redman's Economics and Philosophy of Science." *Journal of Economic Literature* 30 (March 1992): 183–184.

Wendt, Paul. 1990. "Comment on Amariglio's 'Economics as a Postmodern Discourse'." Pp. 47–64 in Samuels, ed., *Economics as Discourse*.

Whately, Richard. 1834. "Letter to J. H. Newman, November 3, 1834." Pp. 283–284 in John Henry Cardinal Newman, *Apologia Pro Vita Sua*. Ed. D. J. DeLaura. New York: W. W. Norton, 1968.

White, J. Hayden. 1973. *Metahistory: The Historical Imagination in Nineteenth-Century Europe*. Baltimore: The Johns Hopkins University Press.

———. 1981. "The Value of Narrativity in the Representation of Reality." Pp. 1–24 in W. J. T. Mitchell, ed., *On Narrative*. Chicago: University of Chicago Press.

White, James Boyd. 1984. *When Words Lose Their Meaning: Constitutions and Reconstitutions of Language, Character, and Community*. Chicago: University of Chicago Press.

1985a. *Heracles' Bow: Essays on the Rhetoric and Poetry of Law*. Rhetoric of the Human Sciences. Madison: University of Wisconsin Press.

1985b. *The Legal Imagination*. Abridged edn. Chicago: University of Chicago Press.

Wible, James R. 1990. "Implicit Contracts, Rational Expectations, and Theories of Knowledge." *Research in the History of Thought and Methodology 7*: 141–170.

Wilamowitz-Moellendorff, Ulrich von. 1927 (1982). *History of Classical Scholarship*. Trans. H. Lloyd-Jones. London: Duckworth.

1928 (1930) *My Recollections*. Trans. G. C. Richards. London: Chatto & Windus.

Wilson, Edmund. 1965. *The Bit Between My Teeth: A Literary Chronicle of 1950–1965*. New York: Farrar, Straus and Giroux.

Winch, Peter. 1958 (1990). *The Idea of a Social Science*. Atlantic Highlands, N.J.: Humanities Press.

Winston, Gordon C. 1988. "Introduction." Pp. 1–12 in G. C. Winston and R. F. Teichgraeber III, eds., *The Boundaries of Economics*. Cambridge: Cambridge University Press.

Wisman, Jon D. 1990. "The Scope and Goals of Economic Science: A Habermasian Perspective." Pp. 113–133 in Lavoie, ed., *Economics and Hermeneutics*.

Wittgenstein, Ludwig. 1932–1934 (1974). *Philosophical Grammar*. Ed. R. Rhees. Trans. A. Kenny. Berkeley and Los Angeles: University of California Press.

1945 (1958). *Philosophical Investigations: The English Text of the Third Edition*. Trans. G. E. M. Anscombe. New York: Macmillan.

Woo, Henry K. H. 1986. *What's Wrong with Formalization in Economics? An Epistemological Critique*. Newark, California: Victoria Press.

Woolf, Virginia. 1923 (1980). *The Diary of Virginia Woolf*. Vol. II: 1920–1924. Ed. A. O. Bell. New York: Harcourt Brace Jovanovich.

1924 (1967). *Collected Essays*, vol. I. New York: Harcourt, Brace, World.

1925 (1953). *The Common Reader*. First Series. New York and London: Harcourt Brace Jovanovich.

Wu, Shih-Yen. 1989. *Production, Entrepreneurship, and Profits*. Oxford and New York: Basil Blackwell.

Wulwick, Nancy. 1990. "Comment on Mirowski and Cook." Pp. 216–224 in Samuels, ed., *Economics as Discourse*.

Yonay, Yuval T. 1991. "When Black Boxes Clash: The Struggle Over the Soul of Economics, 1918–1945." Unpublished Ph.D. dissertation, Department of Sociology, Northwestern University.

index

3″ × 5″ card, 9, 16, 22, 23, 66, 107, 182, 193, 217, 234, 262, 263, 264, 268, 273, 292, 303, 309, 317–318, 337, 349, 380; *see also* Method

A-prime, C-prime theorem, the, 138–139, 140, 142–143, 150, 153, 154, 175–176, 223
   in Marxist economics, 155, 168, 170, 172–173
accounting, 5, 112, 113, 114, 198, 225, 233, 344
Adelstein, Richard P., 332
advertising, 39, 40, 51, 288, 375
Aeschylus, 312
agricultural economics, 22, 112–113, 131, 226, 362
Akerlof, George, 49
Alchian, Armen, 23, 159, 160, 218
Aldridge, John, 174, 175
Alker, Hayward R., Jr., 344
Allais, Maurice, 171
Amariglio, Jack, 71–72, 104, 337, 342–343, 353, 358, 377, 384
analytic philosophy, 23, 188, 193, 205–206, 209, 210, 251, 257, 273–275, 279, 285, 309
Anderson, Philip, 131
Anderson, Richard G., 29
Andvig, Jens-Christoph, 113, 146, 198
anthropology, 13, 18, 28, 36, 58, 59, 65, 75, 80, 239, 240, 241, 329, 335, 344, 362, 378, 395
anything goes, 138, 186, 255, 268–272, 279, 284, 303–304, 315, 320, 359
aporia of the Enlightenment, the, 71–72, 330

architectural modernism, xii, xv, 21–22, 24, 64, 174, 285, 309, 343, 358, 360; *see also* Gothic economics
Arendt, Hannah, 17
Aristotle, 35, 40, 148, 240, 245, 250, 258, 278, 287–288, 292, 295, 305, 309, 322, 329, 336, 361, 373, 380
Arnold, Matthew, 57, 61
arrangement, 123–124
Arrington, Edward, 337
Arrow, Kenneth, 22, 39, 131, 135, 146, 147, 148, 151, 152, 153, 172, 225, 306, 368
Ashmore, Malcolm, 104, 228, 298, 302
astrology, 98, 217, 272, 285, 318
Augustine, St., 118, 119, 249
Austen, Jane, 122, 183, 197, 299, 386
Austin, J. L., 188, 196, 203, 208, 213, 240, 269, 299
Austrian school of economics, 28, 42, 49, 63, 88, 171, 178, 186, 197, 198, 269, 313–323, 317, 334, 349, 370–373, 377, 394
avant garde of art, xii, 8, 18, 64, 267, 343, 358
Axiom of Modest Greed, 72
Ayer, A. J., 5, 22

Backhouse, Roger, 4, 88, 89, 100, 103, 111, 181, 202, 249, 252, 265–267, 269, 273, 280, 281, 286, 307, 321
Bacon, Francis, 8, 11, 33, 38, 68, 75, 89, 92, 93, 147, 200, 231, 332, 385
Bakan, David, 20, 64, 76, 324
Bakhtin, Mikhail, 123
Ball, Milners, 36
Baran, Paul, 155, 390
Barnes, 60, 228, 286, 298

Barrett, William, 6, 184, 205, 347
Barry, Brian, 14, 39
Bartley, William W., III, 202
Bauhaus, 24, 174, 343; *see also*
    architectural modernism, Gothic
    economics
Bazerman, 36, 111, 229, 266, 300, 301
Beardsley, Monroe, 149
Becker, Gary S., xi, 14, 15, 31, 45, 159, 162,
    172, 220
behaviorism, 17, 75–76, 347
Bellofiore, Riccardo, 307
Benchley, Robert, 70
Bentham, Jeremy, 301
Benton, Thomas Hart, 18
Berger, John, 41
Berger, Lawrence, 372
Bergmann, Gustav, 17, 21
Berkeley, Bishop, 135
Bernstein, Richard J., 243
Besso, Michele Angelo, 11
Bianchi, Marina, 88
Bicchieri, Cristina, 45, 281
Billig, Michael, 36
Billington, David P., xiii, 224
biology
    as standard, 56, 65, 107, 122, 124, 125,
        127, 150, 172, 223–225, 227, 230, 231,
        252, 253, 263, 394, 395
    colonization by physics, 59, 127, 129
Birdzell, L. E., 7
Black, Fischer, 181
Black, Max, 239, 310
blackboard economics, 66, 133, 136, 138,
    140–141, 145–148, 150, 153–154, 225–
    226, 277–278, 290, 339–340, 357, 363
    in Marxism, 155, 157, 161–162, 166, 169
Blackburn, Simon, 322
Blau, Francine, 11
Blaug, Mark, 27, 92, 94, 95, 96, 103, 169,
    197, 215, 217, 219, 221, 222, 228, 239,
    242, 252, 255, 265, 272, 280–287, 303,
    307, 318, 321, 350, 391, 392, 395; *see
    also* conservatives, emotivism,
    Popper, Lakatos
    and *tu quoque*, 202
    emotivism of, 97, 195, 303, 350
Bloor, David, 60, 228, 302
Bloor, Thomas and Meriel, 120
Blundell, William, 46, 66
Boettke, Peter J., 313
Bohr, Niels, 41, 193
Boland, Lawrence, 88, 127, 128, 172, 173,
    176, 223, 267
Bonello, Frank J., 181
Booth, Wayne, 15, 36, 64, 106, 199, 249,
    257, 258, 271, 321, 373, 385
Bordo, Susan, 11

Borel, Armand, 316
Borenstein, Nathaniel S., 140
Borges, Jorge Luis, 193
Bornemann, Alfred H., 181
Bourbaki, Nicholas, 28, 128–131
Bowles, Samuel, 155–163
Bowman, Mary Jean, 160
Boynton, Robert, 36
Braithwaite, R. B., 6
Brennan, Timothy J., 181
Brenner, Reuven, 173
Bridgeman, Percy, 89, 92
Broad, William, 67
Brock, William, 132, 164
Bronowski, Jacob, 69, 93, 291
Brown, Ford Maddox, 34
Brown, Richard Harvey, 36
Brown, Vivienne, 102, 123
Bruner, Jerome, 76, 395
Brunner, José, 58
Bruns, Gerald, 118, 119
Brush, Stephen G., 72
Buchanan, James, xi, 147, 159, 160, 218,
    313, 336, 354, 356
Buchanan, Richard, 395
Budick, Sanford, 396
Burke, Kenneth, 36, 44, 245, 249, 258, 271,
    272, 321, 326, 361
Burns, Arthur, 114, 390
Buroway, Michael, 361
Burt, Cyril, 67
Butchvarov, Payanot, 190
Butos, William, 269, 270, 271, 272, 313
Bye, Raymond, 166

Cairncross, Sir Alec, 50
Caldwell, Bruce, 4, 89, 98, 101, 182, 280,
    283, 287, 297, 307, 385
Campbell, Donald T., 104, 305, 306, 310
Campbell, John Angus, 68
Carrard, Phillipe, 395
Case, K. E., 116
Cato the Elder, 270
Chandrasekhar, S., xiii
chemistry
    as standard, 29, 43, 74, 91, 112, 124, 131,
        133, 144, 171, 173, 220, 224, 225, 233,
        301
    cold fusion, 292, 293
    in hierarchy of science, 65, 76
Cheung, Steven N. S., 160
Chicago school, 13–15, 28, 186, 220, 267,
    278, 327, 337, 342, 345, 348, 350, 355,
    384, 390–391, 392, 395; *see also* Good
    Old Chicago School
Cicero, 10, 200, 249, 258, 270
Clark, Norman, 224
Clifford, James, 36, 395

Clower, Robert, 379
Cmiel, Kenneth, 396
Coase, Ronald H., xi, 13, 15, 120, 160, 269, 335, 336, 343, 356, 357, 361, 368
Coates, John, 181
Coats, A. W., 103, 228, 265, 271, 274, 280, 287, 297, 298, 307
Colander, David, 123, 173, 279, 345
Cole, Thomas, 288
Collins, Harry M., 21, 60, 89, 104, 105, 228, 286, 298, 302
Collins, Randall, 55
Comaroff, John L., 241
communication, Roto rooter theory of, 33–35, 286, 345–346
communication studies, 17, 272, 380
Comte, Auguste, 9
conjective, 203, 311, 347–348, 350, 352, 353, 362, 378
Conrad, Alfred, 7
conservatives, methodological, rhetoric, 20, 68, 95, 96, 202, 204, 208, 214, 242–243, 253, 254, 268, 287, 290, 310–312, 315, 317, 321, 327, 338–339, 379, 395
conversation
  market as, 76–83, 336, 367–377
  metaphor of economics as, 15, 17, 21, 27, 30, 34, 36–37, 42–50, 79, 85, 86, 89, 91, 98, 99–102, 105, 106, 107, 118, 123, 148, 155, 176, 182, 184, 186–190, 197, 203, 208, 216, 238, 239, 266, 269, 274, 278, 299, 301–302, 304, 308, 316–317, 319, 342–345, 346–350, 357, 358, 359, 367, 370–380, 384, 396
  of humankind, 34, 69, 71, 76, 92, 98, 99–102, 203, 270, 278, 321, 379, 382, 383, 387
Cook, Pamela, 151, 282, 333
Cooley, T. F., 32
Copi, Irving, 149
Cosgel, Metin, 22, 369, 375, 377
Courant, Richard, 144
Cox, Jeffrey, xiii
Cronbach, Lee, 386
Cross, Rodney, 88, 105
Czarníawska-Joerges, 36, 337, 395

D'Andrade, Roy, 76, 233, 234
Dante Alighieri, 115
Darwin, Charles, 68, 260, 261, 263
David, Joseph Ben, 104
David, Paul A., 128
Davidson, Donald, 237, 240
Davies, G. R., 123
da Vinci, Leonardo, 61
Davis, John B., 35, 184, 194, 329, 332
Davis, Phillip J., xv, 36, 135

Debreu, Gerard, 127, 131, 135, 137, 152, 166, 168, 175, 176
deconstruction, 83, 119, 248, 250, 255, 267, 272, 309, 325–332, 334, 337, 387
Deetz, James, 395
Defoe, Daniel, 353
de Man, Paul, 20
demarcation, 7, 17, 30, 43–44, 58, 60, 69, 98, 193–194, 209, 215, 234, 245, 251, 266, 268, 285, 292, 298, 300, 383
de Marchi, Neil, 4, 27, 86, 87, 88, 182, 217, 219, 221, 222, 228, 239, 280, 307
democracy and rhetoric, 17, 39, 51, 96, 98, 188, 295, 322, 383, 385, 394
Demsetz, Harold, 23, 159, 160
Dennett, Daniel, 238
Denton, Frank, 29, 306
Derrida, Jacques, 315, 321, 325, 329, 330, 331
Descartes, 11, 22, 33, 36, 93, 203, 346
Dewald, William, 29
Dewey, John, xiii, 18, 97, 270
Diamond, Arthur M., Jr., 91, 103, 176
disagreements among economists, 27, 28, 29; *see also* schools: Austrian, Good Old Chicago, institional economics, Marxism, neoclassical economics
Divine, T. J., 226
Donne, John, 44
Douglas, Mary, 302, 329, 362
Dow, Sheila, 335, 377
dress designing, rhetoric of, in economics, 32, 176; *see also* Gerard Debreu
Dudley-Evans, Tony, 111, 116, 117, 123, 183, 279, 283
Dummett, Michael, 237

Ebeling, Richard M., 377
Eco, Umberto, 64
Edge, David, 60, 228
Edgeworth, F. Y., 106, 151, 152
education in economics, 172–175, 384–385, 386
Eemeren, Frans H. van, 206, 209
Einstein, Albert, 11, 176
Elbaum, Bernard, 358
Eldredge, Niles, 61
Elshtain, Jean Bethke, 395
Emmett, Ross B., 106
emotivism, moral theory based on, 96–98, 195, 219, 303, 350
empiricism vs. empirical, 3, 20, 38, 101, 123, 210, 221, 232, 248, 255, 314, 392, 393
engineering, as standard, 65, 80, 129, 131, 135, 139–140, 142, 144, 175, 224, 311, 360; *see also* social engineering

enthymeme, 278, 287, 336
entrepreneur, Austrian theory of, 88, 370–372
epistemology, chapters 14–22 *passim*, 58, 84, 96, 101, esp. 182, 189, 192–193, 195, 203, 210, 236–238, 244, 261, 276, 302, 378, 383, 388
    social, xiii
Erlich, Isaac, 15
Etzioni, Amitai, 352
Euclid, 291
Evensky, Jerry, 101, 187
existence theorems, 30, 127
expectations, 377

fact/value split, 4, 6, 23, 98, 384; *see also* emotivism
faculty of speech, 83
falsification, 6, 33, 85–86, 88, 90, 94–95, 101, 232, 240, 246, 268, 283–284
Farley, Hohn, 7
Farmer, Mary K., 111
Farrell, Joseph, 82, 120–121
Feige, Edgar, 306
Feldhay, Revka, 36
feminism, in economics, 10–11, 99
Feyerabend, Paul, 15, 29, 86, 94, 130, 165, 167, 186, 193, 207, 227, 228, 235, 264, 271–272, 315, 321, 392
Feynman, Richard, 129–130, 139, 143
Finocchario, Maurice, 36, 60, 64, 125, 149, 206
Fish, Stanley, 36, 197, 243, 303, 309, 310, 321, 338, 341, 381
Fisher, Franklin, 81, 138
Fisher, R. A., 113
Fishlow, Albert, 128
Fleck, Ludwik, 60, 227, 228, 241
Floud, Roderick, 59
Fogel, Robert, xi, 14, 22, 23, 143, 356
Folbre, Nancy, 337, 384
France, Peter, 200
Frank, Jerome and Julia, 395
Frankel, Henry, 184–185
Freud, Sigmund, 58
Friedman, Jeffrey, 309–312
Friedman, Milton, xi, 4, 5, 14, 23, 46, 97, 114, 159, 160, 183, 190, 191, 218, 220, 339, 341, 345, 356, 388, 391
Frye, Northrop, 102, 164, 242, 250
Fuller, Steve, xiii, 60

Gadamer, Hans-Georg, 315
Gal, Ofer, 36, 125
Galbraith, James, 395
Galbraith, John Kenneth, xi, 46, 118, 345, 391
Galileo Galilei, 61, 125

Galison, Peter, 105, 228
game theory, 77, 81, 82, 119, 135, 141, 169, 174, 224, 226, 329, 355, 369
Gay, David E. R., 181
Geertz, Clifford, 36, 50, 242
Geison, Gerald, 7, 228
general equilibrium theory, 379–396
geology, as standard, 56, 65, 67, 125, 131, 150, 184, 223, 227, 253, 263
Gergen, Kenneth and Mary M., xiii, 36, 42
German Historical School, 358, 367; *see also* institutional economics
Gerrard, Bill, 267, 268, 284
Gerschenkron, Alexander, 8, 373
Gettier example, 212
Gibbard, Allan, 141, 142
Gibson, James J., 295
Gilbert, Christopher L., 222–223, 229
Gilligan, Carol, 99
Gintis, Herbert, 155–163
Glymour, Clark, 23, 99
Goethe, W., 61
Goldberger, Arthur A., 113, 306
Goldin, Claudia, 11
Goldratt, Eliyahu M., 34
Gombrich, E. H., 295
Good Old Chicago School, 13, 107, 156, 157, 159, 160, 163, 313, 327, 349, 356–358, 362
Goodfield, June, 67
Goodman, Nelson, 203, 212, 237, 238, 239, 240, 266, 270
Goodman, Paul, 102, 346, 377
Goodstein, David, 67
Goodwin, Craufurd, 182
Gordon, David, 42, 313
Gordon, J. E., 224
Gorgias of Leontini, 240
Gothic economics, 362
Gould, Stephen Jay, 19, 125, 230, 394, 395
Graff, Gerald, 330
Graves, Robert, 125
Graziano, Loretta, 182
Greene, Thomas, 333
Greenwald, John, 46
Gregory, Annabel, 59
Greif, Avner, 372
Grice, H. P., 81, 206, 373
Griliches, Zvi, 29, 306
Grootendorst, Rob, 206
Gross, Alan, 229, 279
growth theory, 140–141, 174, 225
Grubel, Herbert, 127, 128, 172, 173, 176
Gusfield, Joseph R., 395
Gyohten, Toyoo, 390

Habermas, Jürgen, 99, 348; *see also* *Sprachethik*

Hagstrom, Warren O., 292
Hahn, Frank, 138, 146, 147, 148, 149, 151,
    152, 153, 177, 178, 181, 337, 384
Halmos, Paul R., 153
Hammond, J. Daniel, 4, 208
Hands, D. Wade, 87, 88, 92, 93, 182, 201, 336
Harberger, A. C., 45, 46, 159, 356
Harman, Gilbert, 204
Harré, Rom, 34, 95, 96, 204, 276, 277, 279,
    295
Hartman, Geoffrey H., 396
Hartmann, Heidi, 337, 384
Hasuman, Daniel M., 4, 5, 75, 85, 182, 183,
    184, 185, 191, 192, 195, 196, 201, 211,
    215, 217, 219, 220, 221, 223, 227, 228,
    229, 236, 238, 239, 252, 254, 280, 281,
    286, 307
Hayek, Friedrich A., 368
Hayles, N. Katherine, 229
Heckman, James J., 115
Heilbroner, Robert L., xi, 181, 324, 325,
    333, 341, 352, 384
Heisenberg, W., 41
Hempel, Carl G., 6, 238, 253
Henderson, Willie, 106, 111, 116–117, 121,
    183, 266, 279
hermeneutics, 29, 33, 49, 194, 205, 286,
    313, 323, 347, 377
Hersh, Reuben, xv, 36, 135
Hesse, Mary, 63, 217, 237, 240, 310
Hewings, Ann, 106, 111, 121, 183
High, Jack, 314
Hirsch, Abraham, 4
Hirschman, Albert, xi, 71, 80, 157, 362,
    379, 395
Hobbes, Thomas, 11, 147, 355, 373
Hodge, Alan, 125
Hodges, Andrew, 165
Hoffer, Eric, 8
Hollis, Martin, 181, 210, 211, 212, 282
Holmes, Oliver Wendell, Jr., 368
Homer, 41, 183
Hoover, Kevin, 89, 228, 242, 307
Hoppe, Hans-Hermann, 242, 313–323, 334
Housman, A. E., 37, 129
Houthakker, Hendrick, 5
Howitt, Peter, 115
Hume, David, 69, 318, 393
Humphreys, Sally, 75
Hunter, Albert, 36
Hurwicz, Leonid, 368
Hutchison, Terence, 5, 18, 97, 140, 232,
    245, 252, 254
Huxley, Thomas, 57
hyperspace searching, mathematical
    theory as, 137, 141–143, 168, 172, 173
hypothetico-deductive model of science,
    xiii, 4, 6, 9

ignoratio elenchi, 336
implied author, 115, 122–123, 156
implied reader, 116–117, 120, 124, 156
institutional economics, 42, 83, 107, 133,
    163, 178, 256, 334, 335, 337, 349, 384,
    394
international trade theory, 100, 136, 140,
    389, 393
interpretive economics, 22–23, 71, 310,
    334, 347, 361–362
invention, 124

Jacobs, Louis, 396
Jaeger, Werner, 38
Jakobson, Roman, 63
James, William, 8, 70, 156, 202, 210, 211,
    212, 213, 215, 235, 273, 277, 320, 336,
    346, 347, 348
Jamieson, Kathleen Hall, 396
Jevons, William Stanley, 49
Johnson, Gale, 160
Johnson, Harry, 14, 298, 388
Johnson, Mark, 395, 396
Johnson, Samuel, 57
Jones, Eric L., 59
Jonsen, Albert R., 396

Keegan, John, xiii, 395
Keller, Evelyn Fox, 11
Kelvin, William Thompson, Lord, 57, 67,
    68
Kennedy, George A., 300, 396
Kennedy, William P., 153, 154
Kenner, Hugh, xii
Keohane, Robert, 395
Kerferd, G. B., 308
Keynes, J. M., 118, 119, 125, 198, 335, 336,
    338, 377
Keynes, John Neville, 197
Khalil, Elias L., 129
Kiefer, Nicholas M., 226
Kim, Jinbang, 88
Kindleberger, Charles P., 298, 388
Kingsland, Sharon E., 395
Kinneavy, James L., 396
Kirby, John T., 40
Kirzner, Israel, xi, 88, 370–371
Kissinger, Henry, 41
Klamer, Arjo, xi, xv, xviii, 6, 22, 35, 42, 49,
    101, 106, 113, 121, 123, 173, 181, 183,
    196, 197, 218, 273, 274, 279, 285, 286,
    287, 297, 301, 314, 325, 339, 340, 343–
    365, 369, 382, 383, 384, 395
    in dialogue, 344–362
Klant, J. J., 27, 85, 88
Klein, Lawrence, 22
Klemm, David, 36
Kline, Morris, 167

Knight, Frank, 13, 15, 208, 270, 356
Knorr-Cetina, Karin, 228
Koopmans, Tjalling, 137–138
Kregel, J. A., 181
Kretzenbacher, Heinz, 122
Krips, Henry, 200
Kropotkin, Prince Peter, 344, 359
Kroszner, Randall, 152
Krugman, Paul, 48
Kuhn, Thomas, 7, 15, 29, 43, 60, 194, 223, 227, 228, 265, 271, 302, 321
Kuttner, Robert, 47, 182
Kuznets, Simon, 10

labor economics, 112, 142, 226, 284, 393
LaCapra, Dominick, 396
Lachmann, Ludwig, 322, 377
Laffer, Arthur, 327
Lakatos, Imre, xv, 11, 29, 85–92, 102, 189, 235, 237, 272, 281
Lakoff, George, 120, 395
Landau, Misia, 395
Landes, William, 162
Lang, Berel, 291
Langlois, Richard, 379
Lanham, Richard, 36, 38, 40, 43, 75, 119, 122, 126, 137, 239, 288, 293–295, 326, 385, 394
Larkin, Philip, 360
Latour, Bruno, 7, 106, 228, 279
Laudan, Larry, 7, 262
Lavoie, Don, 22, 79, 88, 89, 228, 229, 313, 314, 323, 334, 347, 361, 377
Lazonick, William, 161, 358, 361
Leamer, Edward, 22, 306
Leary, Timothy, 70
Lehrer, Keith, 196, 276, 277
Leijonhufvud, Axel, 106, 126, 313, 353
Leonard, Thomas C., 35, 42, 350
Leontief, Wassily, 112, 131, 170, 172, 220, 298
Leopardi, Giacomo, 24
LeRoy, S. F., 32
Lever, Janet, 99
Levi, Primo, 43
Levins, Richard, xiii
Levinson, Stephen, 81
Levison, Arnold, 207, 288
Levy, David, 103
Lewis, C. S., xi
Lewis, H. Gregg, 357
Lewis, T., 115
Lewontin, Richard, 230
liberal values in economics, 99, 101, 280, 316, 368, 385
Liddy, Gordon, 70
Lincoln, Abraham, as rhetorician, 291
Lind, Hans, 136, 337, 339

linguistics, 24, 27, 38, 191, 206, 284, 343, 360, 367–368, 369, 373, 380, 395
literary criticism of economics, xiii, xv, 45, 88, 102, 106–107, 111, 114–126, 183, 197, 250, 257, 280–282, 285, 291, 300, 303, 307, 325–327, 332–333, 338, 379–380; see also arrangement, deconstruction, implied author, invention, linguistics, point of view, story, style vs. substance
Livingstone, Eric, 395
Loasby, Brian, 106
Lodge, David, xii, 107, 328, 374
logic, not all of inquiry, 35–37, 41, 42, 44, 50, 61–64, 105, 149, 165, 206, 214, 241, 246, 255, 260, 289, 290, 318, 343, 347, 350, 393, 395
logical empiricism, 255
Longenbach, James, 197
Lovell, Michael C., 306
Lucas, Robert E., Jr., 31, 72, 125, 325, 331, 337, 344, 357, 388; see also rational expectations
Lurie, Alison, 395
Lyell, Charles, 125
Lyne, John, 36

Macaulay, Thomas Babington, 57, 250, 322
McCawley, James D., 41, 50, 167, 207, 241, 395
McClintock, Barbara, 10, 11
McGee, Michael, 36
McGrath, Francis C., 42
Mach, Ernst, 9, 11, 89
Machlup, Fritz, 334, 335, 368
MacIntyre, Alasdair, xv, 34, 204
Mackenzie, Donald A., 20, 395
McKeon, Richard, 86, 209, 294
McPherson, in dialogue, 302–307
McPherson, James M., 292, 396
McPherson, Michael, 182–185, 195–196, 280, 281, 282, 286, 298
Maddock, Rodney, 89
Madison, Gary B., 36, 60, 137, 196, 309, 311, 316, 370, 378
Mahoney, Michael J., xiii, 202
Mäki, Uskali, 103, 182, 199, 200, 202, 203, 204, 205, 228, 272, 273, 274, 275, 276, 277, 278, 279, 280
Mallove, Eugene, 21, 68, 293
Mandeville, Bernard, 147
Marcus, George E., 36, 395
Marcus, Solomon, 43, 45
Marglin, Stephen A., 155, 156, 358
Margolin, Victor, xiii, 395
Marshall, Alfred, 19, 57, 132, 335, 353
Martin, Wallace, 122

Marx and Marxian economics, 21, 28, 34,
42, 49, 95, 99, 103, 106, 133, 147, 155,
186, 193, 253, 255, 281, 324, 325, 334,
335, 340–343, 344, 349, 350–351, 353,
358, 359, 384, 391, 394
Marxism, vulgar, 103, 341–342
mathematics
rhetoric of, xiv, 16, 34, 36, 37, 38, 51, 86,
189, 245, 250, 270, 290, 320, 337, 360,
395
rhetorical force in economics, xv, 27,
28, 32, 34–35, 36, 50, 58, 98, 102, 107,
111, 114, 115, 119, 125, 127–154, 156,
162–163, 165–178, 187, 225, 226, 267,
269, 351, 382, 384, 385
use enforcing hierarchy, 7, 59, 65, 76,
198, 219, 251, 290
values contrasted with science, 129–
134, 137, 138, 139, 148, 150–151, 166,
169, 176–177, 223, 224, 235, 276, 342,
355
see also Arrow, Debreu, Hahn, Paul
Samuelson
Maxim of Intellectual Exchange, 83
Maxim of Presumed Seriousness, 343
Mayer, Thomas, 167, 221
Mead, George Herbert, 293
Mechling, Elizabeth Walker and Jay, 395
Megill, Allan, 36, 396
Mehta, Judith, 378
Mendelsohn, Everett, 105
Menger, Carl, 344
Merton, Robert, 104, 302
metamodernism, 265, 298, 309–310, 361
metaphor
compared with fact, logic, and story,
19, 23, 41, 61–63, 129, 261, 285, 350,
381, 385
in other sciences, 42, 61, 93, 167, 240,
260–261, 282, 334, 337
in philosophical argument, 33–35, 101,
208–210, 243, 244, 309–310, 316, 321,
336
not mere ornament, 60, 183, 196, 291,
380
see also conversation, metaphor of
economics as; rhetorical tetrad;
literary criticism
Method and methodology, 9, 10, 23, 24,
49, 282, 283, 287, 296, 305, 349, 383,
393
Meyer, John R., 5, 7
Milberg, Willliam, 136, 183, 279, 337, 339
Mill, John Stuart, 27, 57, 92, 223, 387
Miller, J. Hillis, 326
Miller, Merton, 356
Miller, Roger L., 55
Millis, Harry A., 127

Mini, Piero, 174, 203, 238, 243
Mirowski, Philip, 102, 127, 134, 151, 223,
238, 263, 282, 324, 333, 334, 335, 336,
338
Mitchell, Wesley Clair, 107, 331, 332
modernism
defined, xii–xiii, 267, 279
dichotomies of, 24, 58, 69–70, 271, 318,
324, 382
influence on economics, 15, 204, 268,
309, 383
influence on other intellectual life, 24,
64, 65, 69–71, 195, 281, 284–285, 307,
310–311, 324, 343, 346, 358, 360
moral theory of, 96–98, 195, 219, 303,
350
Truce of, xii, 97
Mokyr, Joel, 7, 59, 371
Monk, Ray, 112, 137, 167
Montaigne, Michel, 40
morality
and economics, 101; *see also* Blaug
chocolate-ice-cream theory of, 96, 97;
see also emotivism
Morgan, Mary, 88
Morgenstern, Oskar, 169
Morishima, Mischio, 146, 170, 175
Moulin, Hervé, 88
Mulkay, Michael, 7, 60, 105, 111, 121, 228,
302, 311, 359
Mundell, Robert, 388
Munz, Peter, 35, 239, 240, 241, 243, 244,
245, 266
Muth, John, 90, 125, 269
Myers, Greg, 111, 168, 301

National Science Foundation, 21, 59
Nelson, Alan, 355, 383
Nelson, John, xii, 16, 36, 39, 239, 395
Nelson, Robert H., 65, 69
neoclassical economics
character of, 28, 48, 49, 88, 91, 334, 340,
342, 344, 351–352, 355, 359, 367, 370,
376, 378
defense of, 117–118, 133, 159, 308, 336–
337
defined, 42, 48, 151, 223, 225, 313, 334–
335, 356, 394
wars with other schools, 28, 71, 88, 107,
155, 349
Neurath, Otto, 5
Nevins, Allan, 291
Newton, Isaac, 123, 261
Nicholas, Stephen, 117
Nietzsche, Friedrich, 18, 20, 95, 337
Niggle, Christopher, 182
North, Douglass, 55, 76, 77
Novick, Peter, 18

Nozick, Robert, 147

O'Brien, Denis P., 231
Oakeshott, Michael, 16, 27, 45–46, 375, 376, 382
Ohta, Nakota, 306
Olbrechts-Tyteca, L., 36
Olson, Maneur, xi
Ortony, Andrew, 396
Oswald, A. J., 143

Packard, Vance, 288
Palmer, Richard, 65, 144
Palmer, Tom G., 181, 313, 316
Pareto, Vilfredo, 49
Parker, Charlie Bird, 360
Passell, Peter, 46
Passmore, John, 3, 190, 191, 237, 288, 289
Pauli, Wolfgang, 93
Pauling, Linus, 90, 133
Payner, 115
Pearson, Karl, 18–19
Peirce, C. S., 18, 208, 260, 334, 337
Pen, Jan, 181
Pera, Marcello, 36
Perelman, Chaim, 36, 249
Perlman, Mark, 379
Petrey, Sandy, 40, 196, 213, 329, 369
Philospher's *tu quoque*, 200, 265, 332
physics, as standard of comparison, 4, 27, 31, 41, 59, 65, 72, 93, 107, 111, 112, 122, 124, 129–132, 134–135, 137, 142, 144, 150–151, 166, 169, 171, 216, 220, 227, 231–233
Piaget, Jean, 99, 367
Pickering, Andrew, 60, 227, 228
Pietrykowski, 337
Pinch, Trevor, 21, 60, 104, 228, 298, 304
Plato, 33, 36, 39–40, 92, 93, 126, 148, 187, 188, 189, 191, 192, 200, 207, 210–211, 216, 235, 242, 243, 247, 249, 258, 284, 287–288, 290, 302, 311, 319–320, 322, 328, 346, 361, 373, 392
pluralism, 283, 385; *see also* Caldwell, Richard Rorty, Booth
point of view, literary, 121–122
Pojman, Louis P., 238
Polanyi, Michael, xiii, 15, 60, 90, 95, 177, 227, 228, 269, 272, 321, 345
political science, 5, 14, 28, 64
Polya, George, 395
Pool, Robert, 65, 130, 131
Popper, Karl R., 3, 7, 15, 29, 69, 85, 88, 89, 91, 94, 217, 228, 229, 230, 235, 236, 237, 239, 240, 242, 244, 262, 266, 268
Porter, Theodore M., 395
positivism
    defined, xii, xv, 17, 29, 34, 64, 98, 116, 316, 349

effects on economics, xii, 4–24, 137, 183, 201, 205, 219, 255–258, 392, 396
history in philosophy, 116
not Chicago economics, 4, 15, 391
see also 3" × 5" card, Method
Posner, Richard, 147, 197, 327
Post-Keynesians, 187
postmodernism, 29, 71, 137, 202, 251–252, 308–310, 342, 360–361
pragmatics, 32, 38, 206–210
pragmatism, 11, 39, 49, 91, 190, 195, 202, 211–212, 235, 278, 293, 318–319, 334, 336–337, 383
    and Friedman, 4, 97, 391
    American origins, 18, 20, 70, 83, 97, 195, 208, 293, 330, 332, 359
prediction, 4, 17, 72, 73, 91, 94, 201, 231, 232, 233, 234, 251, 252, 283, 315, 354, 360, 384, 387, 391, 392
Pressman, Steven, 268–269
Principle of Intellectual Exchange, the, 362
Project on Rhetoric of Inquiry, xvii, 16, 122, 258, 272, 350
Protagoras of Abdera, 36, 93, 233, 240, 270, 302, 332
Pullam, Geoffrey, 284
Puro, Edward, 331
Putnam, Hilary, 3, 23, 191–192, 200, 212, 234, 235, 237, 240, 273, 276, 277, 279, 285, 311

questionnaires and surveys, 23, 49, 101, 282, 371, 376, 383
Quine, W. V., 3, 39, 238, 270
Quintilian, Marcus F., 36, 249, 294, 361

Ramus, Peter, 40, 75
Randall, Alan, 226, 263, 298
Rappaport, Steven, 182, 199, 205, 206, 208, 209, 210, 211, 212, 214, 217, 286
rational expectations, 31, 72, 83, 125, 138, 140, 169, 186, 224, 229, 231, 298, 358, 360, 389
rationalism vs. rationality, 38, 69–70; *and see* Hoppe
Rector, Ralph, 377
Redman, Deborah A., 96, 99
Reid, Joseph D., Jr., 160
Reid, Margaret, 11, 13
Reiter, Stanley, 154
relativism, 195, 200–202, 204, 207, 211, 212, 242–243, 253–255, 290, 294, 310, 314–315, 359
Resnick, Stephen, 337, 342, 353, 358, 384
rhetoric
    definition of, xiii, xiv, 29, 39, 51, 257, 273, 274, 287–288, 289

of inquiry, 16, 36, 39, 105, 239, 244–245, 270, 287, 322, 380; *see also* Project on Rhetoric of Inquiry
of journalism, 30–31, 39, 46–52, 66–68
rhetorical paideia, 38, 294, 385
rhetorical tetrad (fact, logic, metaphor, and story), 19, 23–24, 41, 61–63, 128–129, 285, 350, 381, 385
Rhetorician's *tu quoque*, 200–204, 212, 265, 273, 311, 317, 322, 332
Rhoads, Steven E., 182
Ricardo, David, 146
Richards, I. A., 36
Rizzo, Mario, 314
Robbins, Lionel, 97
Roberts, Simon, 241
Robertson, Linda, 336, 337
Robinson, E. A. G., 338
Robinson, Joan, 118, 140, 345
Romano, Carlin, 182, 196, 243, 291
Rorty, Amélie Oksenberg, 36, 100, 200
Rorty, Richard, xv, 29, 33, 50, 60, 84, 86, 96, 97, 99, 194, 200, 211–212, 237, 238, 240, 270, 271, 274, 309, 315
Rosaldo, Renato, 36, 395
Rosen, Stanley, xv, 23, 36, 71, 209
Rosenberg, Alexander, 18, 152, 186, 201, 210, 211, 214, 215, 217, 218, 219, 220, 221, 222, 225, 226, 227, 228, 229, 230, 231, 232, 233, 234, 235, 238, 239, 245, 247–264, 271, 318;
as Ion in dialogue, 247–264
Rosenberg, Nathan, 7
Rosenblatt, Louise, 45
Rossetti, Jane, 183, 279, 324, 325, 326, 327, 328, 330, 331, 332, 339
Roth, Paul, 307
Rothbard, Murray, 76, 314
Rozeboom, William, 192
Ruccio, David F., 181
Rukeyser, Louis, 46, 47
Runyon, Damon, 73
Ruskin, John, 21, 22, 72, 57, 361
Russell, Bertrand, 6, 64, 253
Ryan, Richard, 182

Samuels, Warren J., 181, 211, 215, 324, 337
Samuelson, Paul, xi, xii, 22, 23, 46, 82, 86, 92, 107, 141–142, 155, 172, 176, 326, 332, 334, 357
Samuelson, Robert, 46
Samuelsonian economics, 107, 142, 334, 351, 357–358
Santa Fe Institute, 130, 144
Santayana, George, 64
Sargent, Thomas, 125
Sarker, Husain, 101
Saussure, Ferdinand de, 329, 367, 368

Schaffer, Simon, 7, 194, 208, 228
Schelling, Thomas, xi
Schiappa, Edward, 288
Schön, David A., xiii
schools of economics, 27, 33, 100, 107, 177–178, 182, 186, 32, 350; *see also* Austrian, Good Old Chicago, institutional, Marxist, neoclassical, Post-Keynesians
Schopenhauer, Arthur, 281
Schrag, Calvin, 309
Schultz, Theodore W., 13, 14, 15, 22, 23, 313, 335, 336, 357
Schumpeter, Joseph A., 97, 103, 146
Schwartz, Anna Jacobson, 11, 190, 356
Schwegler, Robert, 301
science, English definition of, 7, 10, 56–60, 61, 64, 69, 114, 219, 221, 226, 227, 251, 308
science, morality in, 96–97, 177, 270, 277–278, 341
Scott, Robert, 36
Searle, John R., 196, 369
Sebberson, David, 336, 337
Seery, John Evan, 395
Seiz, Janet, 196
Selden, Raman, 332
Sen, Amartya, 49
Shackle, George, 69, 379
Shamoon, Linda, 301
Shapin, Steven, 7, 194, 208, 228
Shea, William R., 36
Shearmur, Jeremy, 87, 238, 239
Shiller, Robert J., 22, 116, 376, 377
Shklar, Judith, 349
Shultz, George, 390
Shweder, Richard, 65, 395
Silk, Leonard, 46
Simons, Herbert W., xiii, 239
simulation, as core of science, 30, 113, 128, 130, 133, 134, 137, 144, 224, 393
skepticism, 189, 190, 249, 254, 316, 332
Smith, Adam, 43, 49, 55, 70, 74, 95, 133–136, 150, 151, 159, 187, 191, 345
on persuasion, 77, 80, 82, 83, 241, 346
Smith, Vernon, 89
social constructionism, xiii, 212, 302, 322, 333
social engineering, 3, 6, 30, 72, 73, 74, 84, 151, 218, 312, 331–332, 342
social epistemology, xiii
sociology, 13, 28, 55, 56, 59, 70, 76, 119, 373
as rhetoric, 103–106, 121, 238–239, 241, 248, 279, 286, 297, 301, 332, 359
in relation to economics, 80, 83, 129, 141, 148, 171, 178, 219, 349

of science, xiii, 7, 29, 30, 59, 69, 87, 89,
    90, 92, 103–106, 111, 121, 196, 198,
    201, 223, 224, 227–230, 265–266, 269,
    278, 308, 333, 341, 383
solipsism, 34, 190, 203, 332; *see also*
    Descartes
Solow, Daniel, 395
Solow, Robert, 31, 122, 172, 221, 247, 298,
    313, 325, 335, 337, 361
sophists, 93, 106, 244, 249, 257
Soule, George, 107
specialization, in academic life, 74–76,
    118, 173, 187, 384
speech act, 38, 40, 196, 204, 207, 289, 329,
    368–370
speech, in the economy, 50–52, 76–83,
    336, 367–377
Spinoza, Baruch, 11, 146
Spitzer, Alan B., 18
Sprachethik, 99–101, 184–187, 254, 270,
    279, 304, 306–307, 340
Sraffa, Peiro, 89
standards, 18, 30, 94, 96, 101, 167, 171, 176,
    182, 184, 186, 187, 190, 194, 197, 204,
    214, 243, 245, 318, 321, 388, 389, 391,
    392, 393
statistical significance, 32, 101, 113, 181,
    184, 261, 282, 304, 305, 306, 317, 392
Stebbing, Susan, 149
Steedman, Ian, 89
Stein, Herbert, 147, 218, 219
Steiner, George, 20
Steiner, Mark, 395
Stevens, Wallace, 197, 213, 330
Stewart, Hamish, 340, 341, 342
Stigler, George, 4, 14, 76, 86, 103, 220, 231,
    341, 342, 354, 387
stock market, 42, 44, 201, 375–377
story, 6, 9, 121, 233, 240, 260–261
    as part of rhetorical tetrad, 24, 41,
        62–63, 128, 285, 350
    in economics, 46–47, 50–52, 73, 84, 157,
        285, 335, 351, 352, 371, 376, 391
Stove, David, 20
style vs. substance, 117–121, 126, 259, 299,
    384, 386
stylized facts, 115, 132, 226
Summers, Lawrence, 182, 334
Sutch, Richard, 131
Swales, John M., 106
Sweezy, Paul M., 155, 390

tacit knowledge, 9
Telser, Lester, 160
Thompson, William Lord Kelvin, 57, 67,
    68
Throgmorton, James, 36, 41
Thucydides, 36

Thurow, 46, 47, 48
Thursby, Jerry G., 29
Tobin, James, 123, 344, 388
Todorov, Tzvetan, 250
toggle, 172, 293, 294, 295, 296, 385
Tolley, George, 160
Toulmin, Stephen, xv, 15, 29, 36, 96, 243,
    245, 271, 321, 396
Traweek, Sharon, 130, 228
Tribe, Keith, 106, 181
Truman, Harry, 328
Trump, Donald, 369, 370, 375
truth, definition of, 101, 210–212, 275, 276,
    277, 319, 320; *see also* epistemology,
    Goodman, James, Plato, Putnam,
    standards
Tufte, Edward R., xii, xiv, 395
Tullock, Gordon, 29, 160, 306, 357
Turing, Alan, 165, 166
Turner, Mark, 395
Two Cultures, 60

Ulam, Stanislaw, 168

Vaihinger, Hans, 195
Varian, Hal, 141, 142
Vaubel, Roland, 215
Vaughn, Karen, 314
Veblen, 324, 344, 379, 391; *see also*
    institutional economics
Vernant, Jean-Pierre, 244
Vickers, Brian, 239
Vienna Circle, 17, 24, 97, 226, 305, 309
Viner, Jacob, 75
Vlastos, Gregory, 188, 189
Volcker, Paul, 390
von Neumann, John, 133, 169

Wachter, Kenneth V., 59
Wade, Nicholas, 67
Wagner, Carl, 196
Wald, Abraham, 133, 226
Waller, William T., 337
Wallis, John J., 76
Walras, Léon, 128, 151, 178, 367
Walton, Douglas N., 36, 196
Ward, Benjamin, 127, 142, 167
Warner, Martin, 196, 291
Warsh, David, 46, 66, 182
Webly, Simon, 182
Weinberg, Steven, 60
Weintraub, E. Roy, xv, 86, 88, 90, 91, 96,
    134, 218, 223, 228, 229, 238, 265, 273,
    279, 321, 325, 339, 395
Wendt, Paul, 71
Whately, Richard, 181
White, James Boyd, 36, 395

White, J. Hayden, 36, 122, 395
White, Lawrence, 314
Whitley, Richard, 103, 228
Wible, James R., 194
Wilamowitz-Moellendorff, Ulrich von, 10
Wilson, Edmund, 216
Winch, Peter, 194
Winston, Gordon C., 182
Wisman, Jon, 99
Wittgenstein, Ludwig, 41, 112, 126, 137, 165, 166, 167, 189, 240, 242, 270, 347
Wolff, Richard, 337, 342, 353, 358, 384

Woo, Henry, 167, 176
Wood, Grant, 18
Woolf, Virginia, xii, 118, 125
Woolgar, Steve, 7, 228
wordcraft, xiv, 51
Wu, Henry, 88
Wulwick, Nancy, 282

Yeager, Leland, 160, 357
Yonay, Yuval, 106, 107, 166

Zecher, J. R., 389